P9-AGN-473

Writing and Reading Across the Curriculum

THIRTEENTH EDITION

Writing and Reading Across the Curriculum

THIRTEENTH EDITION

Laurence Behrens
University of California Santa Barbara

Leonard J. Rosen
Bentley University

New!
2016
MLA
Updates

PEARSON

Boston   Columbus   Hoboken   Indianapolis   New York   San Francisco
Amsterdam   Cape Town   Dubai   London   Madrid   Milan   Munich   Paris   Montréal   Toronto
Delhi   Mexico City   São Paulo   Sydney   Hong Kong   Seoul   Singapore   Taipei   Tokyo

Senior Acquisitions Editor: Brad Potthoff
Program Manager: Anne Shure
Product Marketing Manager: Ali Arnold
Field Marketing Manager: Mark Robinson
Senior Media Producer: Stefanie Snajder
Content Specialist: Erin Reilly Jenkins
Project Manager: Shannon Kobran
Project Coordination, Text Design, and Electronic Page Makeup: Integra
Cover Designer: Barbara Atkinson
Cover Illustration: vanias/Shutterstock
Senior Manufacturing Buyer: Roy L. Pickering, Jr.
Printer/Binder: Edwards Brothers Malloy
Cover Printer: Lehigh-Phoenix Color–Hagerstown

Acknowledgments of third-party content appear on the appropriate page within text and on pages 611–617 which constitute an extension of this copyright page.

PEARSON, ALWAYS LEARNING, and MYWRITINGLAB are exclusive trademarks, in the United States and/or other countries, of Pearson Education, Inc., or its affiliates.

Unless otherwise indicated herein, any third-party trademarks that may appear in this work are the property of their respective owners and any references to third-party trademarks, logos, or other trade dress are for demonstrative or descriptive purposes only. Such references are not intended to imply any sponsorship, endorsement, authorization, or promotion of Pearson's products by the owners of such marks, or any relationship between the owner and Pearson Education, Inc., or its affiliates, authors, licensees, or distributors.

Library of Congress Cataloging-in-Publication Data

Behrens, Laurence, author.
  Writing and reading across the curriculum/Laurence Behrens; Leonard J. Rosen.—Thirteenth Edition.
    pages cm
  ISBN 978-0-13-399901-3—ISBN 0-13-399901-7
    1. College readers.   2. Interdisciplinary approach in education—Problems, exercises, etc.
  3. English language—Rhetoric—Problems, exercises, etc.   4. Academic writing—Problems,
  exercises, etc.   I. Rosen, Leonard J., author.   II. Title.
  PE1417.B396 2015
  808'.0427—dc23

                                                                    2014039841

Copyright © 2016, 2013, 2011 by Laurence Behrens and Leonard J. Rosen

All rights reserved. Printed in the United States of America. This publication is protected by copyright, and permission should be obtained from the publisher prior to any prohibited reproduction, storage in a retrieval system, or transmission in any form or by any means, electronic, mechanical, photocopying, recording, or otherwise. For information regarding permissions, request forms and the appropriate contacts within the Pearson Education Global Rights & Permissions Department, please visit www.pearsoned.com/permissions/.

3   17

Student Edition
ISBN-10:   0-13-458632-8
ISBN-13: 978-0-13-458632-8

À la Carte Edition
ISBN-10:   0-13-458260-8
ISBN-13: 978-0-13-458260-3

www.pearsonhighered.com

o the memory of Phil Rodkin (1968–2014)

Brief Contents

Detailed Contents

Chapter 2   Critical Reading and Critique   51

Chapter 3   Thesis, Introduction, and Conclusion   78

Chapter 4   Explanatory Synthesis   96

Chapter 5   Argument Synthesis   130

Part ▐▐ Brief Takes   239

MUSIC

Chapter 8 "Stormy Weather" and the Art of the Musical Cover   241

Whose version of "Please Don't Stop the Music" do you prefer? Rihanna's or Jamie Cullum's? Such questions are at the heart of this chapter on music—specifically, the art of the musical "cover," in which a musician or band puts a unique spin on a previously recorded song. Because music isn't a verbal art form, writing about it might seem challenging—but we offer a useful model example of how to go about it. We also provide a useful glossary of key musical terms, both in print and as a series of online videos. A review of a Paul McCartney album of cover songs makes some provocative claims about what makes for a successful cover and why so many cover albums disappoint. We conclude with Rolling Stone's *list of "greatest covers" for you to explore and debate.*

ETHICS

Chapter 9 Ethical Dilemmas in Everyday Life   264

Would you steal to save a life? Sacrifice one life to save five? In this chapter we provide a variety of sources on the ways that "thought experiments" in ethics—scenarios that ask you to decide on courses of right action (and to justify your decisions)—can serve as a guide for facing everyday ethical dilemmas. When there is no clear right and wrong choice, how do you decide? To what principles can you turn for guidance? Your task in the chapter will be to wrestle with ethical dilemmas and to argue for a clear course of action based on principles you make plain to your readers.

"Readers are like smart fish," suggests novelist K.M. Weiland: "They aren't about to surrender themselves to the lure of your story unless you've presented them with an irresistible hook."

ECONOMICS

Chapter 12 The Changing Landscape of Work in the Twenty-First Century   429

In this famous commencement address at Stanford University in 2005, a titan of the computer industry advises graduating seniors to follow their passion in the search for work. His advice provokes a furious debate.

This columnist believes that "[t]elling someone to follow their passion...has probably resulted in more failed businesses than all the recessions combined."

Perhaps more young people would be happier in their jobs, according to this writer and musician, if "love [was] a consequence of meaningful work instead of...the motivation for it."

An art historian brings a socialist critique to the "do what you love" debate, arguing that people who work for love of the job often achieve their goals by employing others who come to hate their jobs.

SOCIOLOGY

A famous Saturday Evening Post *cover tracks a fast-moving rumor as it wends its way to, from, and around the local townsfolk, who react with amusement, surprise, and dismay.*

Would you like fries with your genetically engineered chicken? How one fast food chain lost control of its secret recipe.

Won't the truth make us free? No, reports a Los Angeles Times *columnist: "we tend to reject theories and rumors—and facts and truths—that challenge our worldview and embrace those that affirm it."*

PHILOSOPHY

Chapter 14 Happiness and Its Discontents   523

PSYCHOLOGY

Chapter 15 Obedience to Authority   572

Preface for Instructors

When *Writing and Reading Across the Curriculum* was first published, the response was both immediate and enthusiastic. Instructors found the topics in *WRAC* both interesting and teachable, and students appreciated the links that such topics suggested to the courses they were taking concurrently in the humanities, the social sciences, and the sciences. Readers told us how practical they found our "summary, synthesis, and critique" approach to writing college-level papers, and in later editions welcomed the addition of "analysis" to our coverage in Part I.

In developing each successive edition of *WRAC*, we strive to retain the essential multidisciplinary character of the text while providing ample new topics and individual readings to keep it fresh and timely. Some topics have proven particularly enduring—our "Obedience" chapter has been a fixture. But we take care to make sure that at least half of the book is completely new every time, both by extensively revising existing chapters and by creating new ones. While we retain an emphasis on summary, critique, synthesis, and analysis, we continue to develop content on topics such as the process of writing and argumentation that address the issues and interests of today's classrooms.

WHAT'S NEW IN THIS EDITION?

- **Over 60 new readings** throughout the book span the disciplines, represent a range of perspectives, and encourage students to write critical responses, summaries, analyses, and syntheses.

- **A new research chapter, "Locating, Mining, and Citing Sources,"** details the latest developments in digital resources and search strategies; includes a new discussion of plagiarism, its causes, and strategies for fair and accurate source citation; and incorporates the latest MLA and APA citation formats (Ch. 7).

- **A new "Brief Takes" chapter on "'Stormy Weather' and the Art of the Musical Cover"** introduces students to writing about music. The chapter provides a model comparative analysis of three versions of "Stormy Weather," directs students to a series of music glossary videos that explain and demonstrate key musical concepts, and includes suggestions for exploring and evaluating covers of more recent works, such as Leonard Cohen's "Hallelujah" (Ch. 8).

- **A new "Brief Takes" chapter on "Ethical Dilemmas in Everyday Life"** invites readers to apply classic principles of ethics—like utilitarianism—to argue for one or another course of action within more than a dozen scenarios. A carefully sequenced set of assignments (summary, critique, synthesis, and analysis) guides students through the readings and offers principles for choosing among the competing demands of ethical dilemmas (Ch. 9).

- **A new anthology chapter, "First Impressions,"** provides three readings that discuss what elements should be at work in effective openings, then prompts students to consider opening scenes of eighteen films and seven classic novels. Students then apply a critical apparatus for understanding how storytellers engage their audiences (Ch. 11).

- **An almost entirely revised "The Changing Landscape of Work in the Twenty-First Century"** continues to emphasize the promise and perils of the new economy as well as to draw from a number of disciplines—including economics, sociology, public policy, business, and investigative journalism. The chapter features thirteen new selections that ensure currency and explore the changing nature of work, the role of technology in these changes, and the security of jobs (Ch. 12).

- **A new student model paper on the topic of bullying** explores characteristics of bullying; its extent and effects; and national, state, and local solutions to the problem. The model paper builds on articles in the chapter itself (and on other sources) to illustrate methods for bringing multiple voices into an argument in support of a writer's claim (Ch. 5).

- **A new reading selection and model summary** not only demonstrate summary skills but also offer a provocative view of empathy: one that argues against using our tendency to identify with the suffering of others as a guide to public policy (Ch. 1).

- **New examples model strategies** for effective introductions and conclusions (Ch. 3).

- **Online text and video sources** are referenced throughout with recommended search terms and strategies.

STRUCTURE AND SIGNATURE STRENGTHS

Structure

Writing and Reading Across the Curriculum is divided into a rhetoric and an anthology of readings. The anthology of readings is further subdivided into two parts, the first of these serving as a kind of bridge between the rhetoric and the anthology.

Part I takes students step-by-step through the process of writing papers based on source material, explaining and demonstrating how summaries, critiques, syntheses, and analyses can be generated from the kinds of readings students will encounter later in the book—and throughout their academic careers.

Part II, "Brief Takes," offers mini-chapters of five to seven readings that are accompanied by a set of sequential writing exercises. We see working on one or more of these brief takes as a kind of "warm-up" exercise for the more intensive intellectual activities involved in tackling the full-length chapters. "The Roar of the Tiger Mom" is carried over from the previous edition. Two new mini-chapters, "Ethical Dilemmas in Everyday Life" and "'Stormy Weather' and the Art of the Musical Cover," round out this section of the text.

Part III offers full-length anthology chapters of ten or so readings (approximately 75 pages) on compelling topics selected to stimulate student interest. Tackling a range of perspectives, voices, and writing and argument strategies, these units immerse students in the kinds of sustained reading and writing required for other college courses.

Signature Strengths

Continued focus on argument in Part I emphasizes the following:

- The Elements of Argument: Claim, Support, Assumption. This section adapts the Toulmin approach to the kinds of readings students will encounter in Parts II and III of the text.
- The Three Appeals of Logos, Ethos, Pathos. This discussion may be used to analyze arguments in the readings in Parts II and III of the book.
- Developing and Organizing the Support for Your Arguments. This section helps students mine source materials for facts, expert opinions, and examples that will support their arguments.
- Annotated Student Argument Paper. A sample student paper highlights and discusses argumentative strategies that a student writer uses in drafting and developing a paper.

RESOURCES FOR TEACHERS AND STUDENTS

Now Available for Composition   MyWritingLab™

Integrated solutions for writing. *MyWritingLab* is an online homework, tutorial, and assessment program that provides engaging experiences to today's instructors and students. New features designed specifically for composition instructors and their course needs include a new writing space for students, customizable rubrics for assessing and grading student writing, multimedia instruction on all aspects of composition, and advanced reporting to improve the ability to analyze class performance.

Adaptive learning. *MyWritingLab* offers pre-assessments and personalized remediation so students see improved results and instructors spend less time in class reviewing the basics. Visit www.mywritinglab.com for more information.

eTextbooks

Pearson eText. This electronic option gives students access to *Writing and Reading Across the Curriculum,* thirteenth edition, whenever and wherever they can access the Internet. The eText pages look exactly like the printed text, and include powerful interactive and customization functions. Users can create notes, highlight text in different colors, create bookmarks, zoom, click hyperlinked words and phrases to view definitions, and view as a single page or as two pages. Pearson eText also links students to associated media files, enabling them to view videos as they read the text, and offers a full-text search and the ability to save and export notes. The Pearson eText also includes embedded URLs in the chapter text with active links to the Internet.

The Pearson eText app is a great companion to Pearson's eText browser-based book reader. It allows existing subscribers who view their Pearson eText titles on a Mac or PC to additionally access their titles in a bookshelf on the iPad or an Android tablet either online or via download.

CourseSmart eTextbook. Students can subscribe to *Writing and Reading Across the Curriculum* at CourseSmart.com. The format of the eText allows students to search the text, bookmark passages, save their own notes, and print reading assignments that incorporate lecture notes.

Instructor's Manual

The *Instructor's Manual* for the thirteenth edition of *Writing and Reading Across the Curriculum* provides sample syllabi and course calendars, chapter summaries, classroom ideas for writing assignments, introductions to each set of readings, and answers to review questions.

ACKNOWLEDGMENTS

We have benefited over the years from the suggestions and insights of many teachers—and students—across the country. We would especially like to thank these reviewers of the thirteenth edition: Dr. Iona Joseph Abraham, Lorain County Community College; Dianne Donnelly, University of South Florida; William Donovan, Idaho State University; Derek G. Handley, Community College of Allegheny County; Deanna M. Jessup, Indiana University; Kim Karshner, Lorain County Community College; Eliot Parker, Mountwest Community and Technical College; Denise Paster, Coastal Carolina University; and Mary R. Seel, SUNY Broome Community College.

We would also like to thank the following reviewers for their help in the preparation of past editions: Angela Adams, Loyola University Chicago; James Allen, College of DuPage; Fabián Álvarez, Western Kentucky University; Chris Anson, North Carolina State University; Phillip Arrington, Eastern Michigan University; Anne Bailey, Southeastern Louisiana University; Carolyn Baker, San Antonio College; Joy Bashore, Central Virginia Community College; Nancy Blattner, Southeast Missouri State University; Mary Bly, University of California, Davis; Laurel Bollinger, University of Alabama in Huntsville; David Bordelon, Ocean County College; Bob Brannan, Johnson County Community College; Paul Buczkowski, Eastern Michigan University; Jennifer Bullis, Whatcom Community College; Paige Byam, Northern Kentucky University; Susan Callendar, Sinclair Community College; Anne Carr, Southeast Community College; Jeff Carroll, University of Hawaii; Joseph Rocky Colavito, Northwestern State University; Michael Colonneses, Methodist College; James A. Cornette, Christopher Newport University; Timothy Corrigan, Temple University; Kathryn J. Dawson, Ball

State University; Cathy Powers Dice, University of Memphis; Kathleen Dooley, Tidewater Community College; Judith Eastman, Orange Coast College; David Elias, Eastern Kentucky University; Susan Boyd English, Kirkwood Community College; Kathy Evertz, University of Wyoming; Kathy Ford, Lake Land College; University of Wyoming; Wanda Fries, Somerset Community College; Bill Gholson, Southern Oregon University; Karen Gordon, Elgin Community College; Deborah Gutschera, College of DuPage; Lila M. Harper, Central Washington University; M. Todd Harper, University of Louisville; Kip Harvigsen, Ricks College; Michael Hogan, Southeast Missouri State University; Sandra M. Jensen, Lane Community College; Anita Johnson, Whatcom Community College; Mark Jones, University of Florida; Daven M. Kari, Vanguard University; Jane Kaufman, University of Akron; Kerrie Kawasaki-Hull, Ohlone College; Rodney Keller, Ricks College; Walt Klarner, Johnson County Community College; Jeffery Klausman, Whatcom Community College; Alison Kuehner, Ohlone College; Michelle LaFrance, University of Massachusetts Dartmouth; William B. Lalicker, West Chester University; Dawn Leonard, Charleston Southern University; Lindsay Lewan, Arapahoe Community College; Clifford L. Lewis, U Mass Lowell; Signee Lynch, Whatcom Community College; Jolie Martin; San Francisco State University; Meg Matheny, Jefferson Community and Technical College, Southwest; Krista L. May, Texas A&M University; Kathy Mendt, Front Range Community College–Larimer Campus; RoseAnn Morgan, Middlesex County College; David Moton, Bakersfield College; Roark Mulligan, Christopher Newport University; Joan Mullin, University of Toledo; Stella Nesanovich, McNeese State University; Catherine Olson, Lone Star College-Tomall; Susie Paul, Auburn University at Montgomery; Thomas Pfau, Bellevue Community College; Jeff Pruchnic, Wayne State University; Aaron Race, Southern Illinois University–Carbondale; Nancy Redmond, Long Beach City College; Deborah Reese, University of Texas at Arlington; Alison Reynolds, University of Florida; Priscilla Riggle, Bowling Green State University; Jeanette Riley, University of New Mexico; Robert Rongner, Whatcom Community College; Sarah C. Ross, Southeastern Louisiana University; Deborah L. Ruth, Owensboro Community & Technical College; Amy Rybak, Bowling Green State University; Raul Sanchez, University of Utah; Mary R. Seel, Broome Community College; Rebecca Shapiro, Westminster College; Mary Sheldon, Washburn University; Horacio Sierra, University of Florida; Philip Sipiora, University of Southern Florida; Joyce Smoot, Virginia Tech; Ellen Sorg, Owens Community College; Bonnie A. Spears, Chaffey College; Bonnie Startt, Tidewater Community College; R. E. Stratton, University of Alaska–Fairbanks; Katherine M. Thomas, Southeast Community College; Scott Vander Ploeg, Madisonville Community College; Victor Villanueva, Washington State University; Deron Walker, California Baptist University; Jackie Wheeler, Arizona State University; Pat Stephens Williams, Southern Illinois University at Carbondale; and Kristin Woolever, Northeastern University.

The authors wish to thank Robert Krut, of the University of California, Santa Barbara Writing Program, for his contributions to the new "Rumor" chapter. We also acknowledge the work of Barbara Magalnick in contributing to the "Summary" and "Ethical Dilemmas" chapters. For their numerous comments and suggestions on developing the research chapter, "Locating, Mining, and Citing Sources," we thank Ayanna Gaines, associate librarian at Ventura College, and Richard Caldwell, head of library instruction at the University of California, Santa Barbara Library.

For his consultation on the model synthesis "Responding to Bullies" in Chapter 4, we gratefully acknowledge the assistance of Philip Rodkin, Professor of Psychology at the University of Illinois at Urbana-Champaign. Tragically, Phil died in May 2014, and he will be sorely missed by all who knew him.

We thank musician Greg Blair for his expertise in writing the model paper on "Stormy Weather" and for creating a series of entertaining and instructive videos to accompany his glossary of musical terms.

For this edition we were fortunate indeed to work with Michael Kardos, who codirects the creative writing program at Mississippi State University. Mike contributed in equal part to the new chapters on "'Stormy Weather' and the Art of the Musical Cover" and "First Impressions: The Art and Craft of Storytelling." Participating in the development and writing of these chapters, he was an inexhaustible fount of good ideas and good humor. His deep knowledge of literature, the art of storytelling, and the contemporary music scene were invaluable to us.

Finally, special thanks to Brad Potthoff, Anne Shure, Shannon Kobran, Joseph Croscup, and Margaret McConnell for helping shepherd the manuscript through the editorial and production process. And our continued gratitude to Joe Opiela, longtime friend and supporter.

LAURENCE BEHRENS
LEONARD J. ROSEN

Your sociology professor asks you to write a paper on attitudes toward the homeless population of an area near your campus. You are expected to consult online sources, articles, and books on the subject. You are also encouraged to conduct surveys and interviews.

Your professor is making a number of assumptions about your capabilities—among them, that you can:

- research and assess the value of relevant sources;
- comprehend college-level material, both print and digital;
- use theories and principles learned from one set of sources as tools to investigate other sources (or events, people, places, or things);
- synthesize separate but related sources;
- intelligently respond to such material.

In fact, these same assumptions underlie practically all college writing assignments. Your professors will expect you to demonstrate that you can read and understand not only textbooks, but also critical articles and books, primary sources, Internet sources, online academic databases, and other material related to a particular subject of study.

An example: For a paper on the changing nature of the workforce in the twenty-first century, you would probably look to articles and Internet sources for the latest information. Using an online database, you might find articles in such journals as the *Green Labor Journal*, the *Economic Journal*, and the *Journal of Labor Research*, as well as in leading newspapers and magazines. A Web search might lead you to the Occupational Employment Statistics homepage, published online by the Bureau of Labor Statistics. You'd be expected to assess the relevance of such sources to your topic and to draw from them the information and ideas you need. The final product of your research and reading might not be a conventional paper at all, but rather a Web site that alerts students to job categories experts think are expanding or disappearing.

You might, for a different class, be assigned a research paper on the films of director Wes Anderson. To get started, you might consult your film studies textbook, biographical sources on Anderson, and anthologies of criticism. Instructor and peer feedback on a first draft might lead you to articles in both popular magazines (such as *Time*) and scholarly journals (such as *Literature/Film Quarterly*); you might also consult relevant Web sites (such as the Internet Movie Database).

These two example assignments are very different, of course, but the skills you need to work on them are the same. You must be able to research relevant sources, read and comprehend these sources, perceive the relationships among several pieces of source material, and apply your own critical judgments to these materials.

Writing and Reading Across the Curriculum provides you with the opportunity to practice the essential college-level skills we have just outlined and the forms of writing associated with them, namely:

- the summary
- the critique
- the synthesis
- the analysis

Each chapter of Parts II and III of this text represents a subject from a particular area of the academic curriculum: Sociology, Economics, Psychology, Business, Public Policy, Music, Literary Studies, Ethics, Film Studies, and Philosophy. These chapters—dealing with such topics as rumor, the pursuit of happiness, obedience to authority, and ethical dilemmas—illustrate the types of material you might study in your other courses.

Questions following the readings will allow you to practice typical college writing assignments:

- "Review Questions" help you recall key points of content.
- "Discussion and Writing Suggestions" ask you for personal responses to readings.
- "Synthesis Activities" allow you to practice assignments of the type that are covered in detail in Part I of this book. For instance, you may be asked to summarize the Milgram experiment and the reactions to it, or to compare and contrast a controlled experiment with a real-life (or fictional) situation.
- "Research Activities" ask you to go beyond the readings in this text and to conduct your own independent research on these subjects.

In this book, you'll find articles and essays written by literary critics, sociologists, psychologists, musicians, attorneys, political scientists, journalists, and specialists from other fields. Our aim is that you become familiar with the various subjects and styles of academic writing and that you come to appreciate the interrelatedness of knowledge. Happiness can be studied by philosophers, psychologists, sociologists, economists, geographers, religious thinkers, and poets. Human activity and human behavior are classified into separate subjects only for convenience. The novel you read in your literature course may be able to shed some light upon an assigned article for your economics course—and vice versa.

We hope, therefore, that your writing course will serve as a kind of bridge to your other courses and that, as a result of this work, you will become more skillful at perceiving relationships among diverse topics. Because it involves such critical and widely applicable skills, your writing course may well turn out to be one of the most valuable—and one of the most interesting—of your academic career.

LAURENCE BEHRENS
LEONARD J. ROSEN

Writing and Reading Across the Curriculum

THIRTEENTH EDITION

Part

I

Structures and Strategies

Summary, Paraphrase, and Quotation

After completing this chapter, you will be able to:

1.1 Explain what a summary is.

1.2 Apply systematic strategies as you read in order to prepare a summary.

1.3 Write summaries of varying lengths.

1.4 Write summaries of visual presentations, including graphs, charts, and tables.

1.5 Write paraphrases to clarify difficult or confusing source material.

1.6 Use direct and indirect quotations, and integrate them into your writing.

1.7 Avoid plagiarism by citing sources and using your own words and sentence structure.

WHAT IS A SUMMARY?

1.1 Explain what a summary is.

The best way to demonstrate that you understand the information and the ideas in any piece of writing is to compose an accurate and clearly written summary of that piece. By a summary we mean a brief restatement, in your own words, of the content of a passage (a group of paragraphs, a chapter, an article, a book). This restatement should focus on the central idea of the passage. The briefest of summaries (one or two sentences) will do no more than this. A longer, more complete summary will indicate, in condensed form, the main points in the passage that support or explain the central idea. It will reflect the order in which these points are presented and the emphasis given to them. It may even include some important examples from the passage. But it will not include minor details. It will not repeat points simply for the purpose of emphasis. And it will not contain any of your own opinions or conclusions. A good summary, therefore, has three central qualities: brevity, completeness, and objectivity.

Can a Summary Be Objective?

Of course, the last quality mentioned, objectivity, might be difficult to achieve in a summary. By definition, writing a summary requires you to select some aspects of the original and leave out others. Since deciding what to select and what to leave out calls for your personal judgment, your summary really is a work of interpretation. And, certainly, your interpretation of a passage may differ from another person's.

One factor affecting the nature and quality of your interpretation is your prior knowledge of the subject. For example, if you're attempting to summarize an anthropological article and you're a novice in that field, then your summary of the article will likely differ from that of your professor, who has spent 20 years studying this particular area and whose judgment about what is more or less significant is undoubtedly more reliable than your own. By the same token, your personal or professional frame of reference may also affect your interpretation. A union representative and a management representative attempting to summarize the latest management offer would probably come up with two very different accounts. Still, we believe that in most cases it's possible to produce a reasonably objective summary of a passage if you make a conscious, good-faith effort to be unbiased and to prevent your own feelings on the subject from distorting your account of the text.

WHERE DO WE FIND WRITTEN SUMMARIES?

Here are just a few of the types of writing that involve summary:

Academic Writing

- **Critique papers.** Summarize material in order to critique it.
- **Synthesis papers.** Summarize to show relationships between sources.
- **Analysis papers.** Summarize theoretical perspectives before applying them.
- **Research papers.** Note-taking and reporting research require summary.
- **Literature reviews.** Overviews of work presented in brief summaries.
- **Argument papers.** Summarize evidence and opposing arguments.
- **Essay exams.** Demonstrate understanding of course materials through summary.

Workplace Writing

- **Policy briefs.** Condense complex public policy.
- **Business plans.** Summarize costs, relevant environmental impacts, and other important matters.
- **Memos, letters, and reports.** Summarize procedures, meetings, product assessments, expenditures, and more.
- **Medical charts.** Record patient data in summarized form.
- **Legal briefs.** Summarize relevant facts of cases.

Using The Summary

In some quarters, the summary has a bad reputation—and with reason. Summaries often are provided by writers as substitutes for analyses. As students, many of us have summarized books that we were supposed to review critically. All the same, the summary does have a place in respectable college work. First, writing a summary is an excellent way to understand what you read. This in itself is an important goal of academic study. If you don't understand your source material, chances are you won't be able to refer to it usefully in an essay or research paper. Summaries help you understand what you read because they force you to put the text into your own words. Practice with writing summaries also develops your general writing habits because a good summary, like any other piece of good writing, is clear, coherent, and accurate.

Second, summaries are useful to your readers. Let's say you're writing a paper about the McCarthy era in the United States, and in part of that paper you want to discuss Arthur Miller's *Crucible* as a dramatic treatment of the subject. A summary of the plot would be helpful to a reader who hasn't seen or read—or who doesn't remember—the play. Or perhaps you're writing a paper about the politics of recent American military interventions. If your reader isn't likely to be familiar with American actions in Kosovo and Afghanistan, it would be a good idea to summarize these events at some early point in the paper. In many cases (an exam, for instance), you can use a summary to demonstrate your knowledge of what your professor already knows; when writing a paper, you can use a summary to inform your professor about some relatively unfamiliar source.

Third, summaries are required frequently in college-level writing. For example, on a psychology midterm, you may be asked to explain Carl Jung's theory of the collective unconscious and to show how it differs from Sigmund Freud's theory of the personal unconscious. You may have read about this theory in your textbook or in a supplementary article, or your instructor may have outlined it in his or her lecture. You can best demonstrate your understanding of Jung's theory by summarizing it. Then you'll proceed to contrast it with Freud's theory—which, of course, you must also summarize.

THE READING PROCESS

1.2 Apply systematic strategies as you read in order to prepare a summary.

It may seem to you that being able to tell (or retell) in summary form exactly what a passage says is a skill that ought to be taken for granted in anyone who can read at high school level. Unfortunately, this is not so: For all kinds of reasons, people don't always read carefully. In fact, it's probably safe to say that usually they don't. Either they read so inattentively that they skip over words, phrases, or even whole sentences, or, if they do see the words in front of them, they see them without registering their significance.

When a reader fails to pick up the meaning and implications of a sentence or two, usually there's no real harm done. (An exception: You could lose credit on an exam or paper because you failed to read or to realize the significance of a crucial direction by your instructor.) But over longer stretches—the paragraph, the section, the article, or the chapter—inattentive or haphazard reading interferes with your goals as a reader: to perceive the shape of the argument, to grasp the central idea, to determine the main points that compose it, to relate the parts of the whole, and to note key examples. This kind of reading takes a lot more energy and determination than casual reading. But, in the long run, it's an energy-saving method because it enables you to retain the content of the material and to use that content as a basis for your own responses. In other words, it allows you to develop an accurate and coherent written discussion that goes beyond summary.

CRITICAL READING FOR SUMMARY

- *Examine the context.* Note the credentials, occupation, and publications of the author. Identify the source in which the piece originally appeared. This information helps illuminate the author's perspective on the topic he or she is addressing.
- *Note the title and subtitle.* Some titles are straightforward, whereas the meanings of others become clearer as you read. In either case, titles typically identify the topic being addressed and often reveal the author's attitude toward that topic.
- *Identify the main point.* Whether a piece of writing contains a thesis statement in the first few paragraphs or builds its main point without stating it up front, look at the entire piece to arrive at an understanding of the overall point being made.
- *Identify the subordinate points.* Notice the smaller subpoints that make up the main point, and make sure you understand how they relate to the main point. If a particular subpoint doesn't clearly relate to the main point you've identified, you may need to modify your understanding of the main point.
- *Break the reading into sections.* Notice which paragraphs make up a piece's introduction, body, and conclusion. Break up the body paragraphs into sections that address the writer's various subpoints.
- *Distinguish between points, examples, counterarguments.* Critical reading requires careful attention to what a writer is doing as well as what he or she is saying. When a writer quotes someone else or relays an example of something, ask yourself why this is being done. What point is the example supporting? Is another source being quoted as support for a point or as a counterargument that the writer sets out to address?
- *Watch for transitions within and between paragraphs.* In order to follow the logic of a piece of writing, as well as to distinguish between points, examples, and counterarguments, pay attention to the transitional words and phrases writers use. Transitions function like road signs, preparing the reader for what's next.

- *Read actively and recursively.* Don't treat reading as a passive, linear progression through a text. Instead, read as though you are engaged in a dialogue with the writer: Ask questions of the text as you read, make notes in the margin, underline key ideas in pencil, put question or exclamation marks next to passages that confuse or excite you. Go back to earlier points once you finish a reading, stop during your reading to recap what's come so far, and move back and forth through a text.

HOW TO WRITE SUMMARIES

1.3 Write summaries of varying lengths.

Every article you read will present a unique challenge as you work to summarize it. As you'll discover, saying in a few words what has taken someone else a great many can be difficult. But like any other skill, the ability to summarize improves with practice. Here are a few pointers to get you started. They represent possible stages, or steps, in the process of writing a summary. These pointers are not meant to be ironclad rules; rather, they are designed to encourage habits of thinking that will allow you to vary your technique as the situation demands.

GUIDELINES FOR WRITING SUMMARIES

- *Read the passage carefully.* Determine its structure. Identify the author's purpose in writing. (This will help you distinguish between more important and less important information.) Make a note in the margin when you get confused or when you think something is important; highlight or underline points sparingly, if at all.

- *Reread.* This time divide the passage into sections or stages of thought. The author's use of paragraphing will often be a useful guide. Label, on the passage itself, each section or stage of thought. Underline key ideas and terms. Write notes in the margin.

- *Write one-sentence summaries,* on a separate sheet of paper, of each stage of thought.

- *Write a thesis—a one- or two-sentence summary of the entire passage.* The thesis should express the central idea of the passage, as you have determined it from the preceding steps. You may find it useful to follow the approach of most newspaper stories—naming the what, who, why, where, when, and how of the matter. For persuasive passages, summarize in a sentence the author's conclusion. For descriptive passages, indicate the subject of the description and its key feature(s). Note: In some cases, a suitable thesis may already be in the original passage. If so, you may want to quote it directly in your summary.

(continued)

- *Write the first draft of your summary* by (1) combining the thesis with your list of one-sentence summaries or (2) combining the thesis with one-sentence summaries plus significant details from the passage. In either case, eliminate repetition and less important information. Disregard minor details or generalize them (e.g., George H. W. Bush and Bill Clinton might be generalized as "recent presidents"). Use as few words as possible to convey the main ideas.
- *Check your summary against the original passage* and make whatever adjustments are necessary for accuracy and completeness.
- *Revise your summary,* inserting transitional words and phrases where necessary to ensure coherence. Check for style. Avoid a series of short, choppy sentences. Combine sentences for a smooth, logical flow of ideas. Check for grammatical correctness, punctuation, and spelling.

DEMONSTRATION: SUMMARY

To demonstrate these points at work, let's go through the process of summarizing a passage of expository material—that is, writing that is meant to inform and/or persuade. The following essay, "The Baby in the Well," concerns the topic of empathy, that aspect of our human nature that permits us to identify with others, "to feel their pain," so to speak, and then to offer our help. The question of "Who deserves our help—and why?" is an interesting and difficult one. Someone who has suffered a terrible loss or someone in difficult circumstances (like the homeless person we pass on the street) may well prompt empathy and even strong feelings in us. Such feelings do us credit as individuals. But should our empathic impulses always serve as a guide for our personal actions? More broadly, should they serve as a guide for elected officials charged with designing and implementing public policies—for the homeless, for instance, or the chronically underemployed?

In "The Baby in the Well," Paul Bloom makes a provocative and counterintuitive argument about empathy. You may agree or disagree with his thesis. But before you take a position, you'll have to understand the point he's making and the support he offers for that point. "The Baby in the Well" is a challenging essay. Some of Bloom's terminology may be unfamiliar (for instance, "cognitive neuroscience"—the study of the brain and how we think; or "neural systems"—the physical pathways our minds take in forming a thought or feeling). So keep a dictionary nearby. (Or, if you're online, type "define [the unfamiliar term]" into the Google or Bing search box.)

More challenging than the vocabulary may be ideas that test the limits of your understanding. But dealing with difficult ideas will be a common experience in your college-level classes. Indeed, it's the whole point of studying topics you don't know. What is important is that you use a systematic approach to understanding challenging reading material. We offer one such approach here. You may be pleasantly surprised: With a systematic approach and some perseverance, you will grasp the challenging material—and you will feel good about that.

First, read Bloom's essay with care. Try to identify its component parts and understand how they work together to create a coherent argument.

THE BABY IN THE WELL: THE CASE AGAINST EMPATHY*

Paul Bloom

Paul Bloom, professor of psychology and cognitive science at Yale University, is also coeditor-in-chief of the scientific journal Behavioral and Brain Sciences. *He is the author of numerous articles and books, including* How Children Learn the Meaning of Words *(2000) and* How Pleasure Works: The New Science of How We Like What We Like *(2010). This article appeared in the* New Yorker *on May 20, 2013.*

In 2008, Karina Encarnacion, an eight-year-old girl from Missouri, wrote to President-elect Barack Obama with some advice about what kind of dog he should get for his daughters. She also suggested that he enforce recycling and ban unnecessary wars. Obama wrote to thank her, and offered some advice of his own: "If you don't already know what it means, I want you to look up the word 'empathy' in the dictionary. I believe we don't have enough empathy in our world today, and it is up to your generation to change that."

This wasn't the first time Obama had spoken up for empathy. Two years earlier, in a commencement address at Xavier University, he discussed the importance of being able "to see the world through the eyes of those who are different from us —the child who's hungry, the steelworker who's been laid off, the family who lost the entire life they built together when the storm came to town." He went on, "When you think like this—when you choose to broaden your ambit of concern and empathize with the plight of others, whether they are close friends or distant strangers—it becomes harder not to act, harder not to help."

The word "empathy"—a rendering of the German *Einfühlung*, "feeling into"—is only a century old, but people have been interested for a long time in the moral implications of feeling our way into the lives of others. In "The Theory of Moral Sentiments" (1759), Adam Smith observed that sensory experience alone could not spur us toward sympathetic engagement with others: "Though our brother is upon the rack, as long as we ourselves are at our ease, our senses will never inform us of what he suffers." For Smith, what made us moral beings was the imaginative capacity to "place ourselves in his situation...and become in some measure the same person with him, and thence form some idea of his sensations, and even feel something which, though weaker in degree, is not altogether unlike them."

In this sense, empathy is an instinctive mirroring of others' experience— James Bond gets his testicles mashed in "Casino Royale," and male moviegoers grimace and cross their legs. Smith talks of how "persons of delicate fibres" who notice a beggar's sores and ulcers "are apt to feel an itching or uneasy sensation

*Copyright © 2013 Conde Nast. From the *New Yorker*. All rights reserved. By Paul Bloom. Reprinted by permission.

in the correspondent part of their own bodies." There is now widespread support, in the social sciences, for what the psychologist C. Daniel Batson calls "the empathy-altruism hypothesis." Batson has found that simply instructing his subjects to take another's perspective made them more caring and more likely to help.

5   Empathy research is thriving these days, as cognitive neuroscience undergoes what some call an "affective revolution." There is increasing focus on the emotions, especially those involved in moral thought and action. We've learned, for instance, that some of the same neural systems that are active when we are in pain become engaged when we observe the suffering of others. Other researchers are exploring how empathy emerges in chimpanzee and other primates, how it flowers in young children, and the sort of circumstances that trigger it.

This interest isn't just theoretical. If we can figure out how empathy works, we might be able to produce more of it. Some individuals stanch their empathy through the deliberate endorsement of political or religious ideologies that promote cruelty toward their adversaries, while others are deficient because of bad genes, abusive parenting, brutal experience, or the usual unhappy goulash of all of the above. At an extreme lie the 1 percent or so of people who are clinically described as psychopaths. A standard checklist for the condition includes "callousness; lack of empathy"; many other distinguishing psychopathic traits, like lack of guilt and pathological lying, surely stem from this fundamental deficit. Some blame the empathy-deficient for much of the suffering in the world. In *The Science of Evil: On Empathy and the Origins of Cruelty* (Basic Books), Simon Baron-Cohen goes so far as to equate evil with "empathy erosion."

In a thoughtful new book on bullying, *Sticks and Stones* (Random House), Emily Bazelon writes, "The scariest aspect of bullying is the utter lack of empathy"—a diagnosis that she applies not only to the bullies but also to those who do nothing to help the victims. Few of those involved in bullying, she cautions, will turn into full-blown psychopaths. Rather, the empathy gap is situational: bullies have come to see their victims as worthless; they have chosen to shut down their empathetic responses. But most will outgrow—and perhaps regret—their terrible behavior. "The key is to remember that almost everyone has the capacity for empathy and decency—and to tend that seed as best as we possibly can," she maintains.

Two other recent books, *The Empathic Civilization* (Penguin), by Jeremy Rifkin and *Humanity on a Tightrope* (Rowman & Littlefield), by Paul R. Ehrlich and Robert E. Ornstein, make the powerful argument that empathy has been the main driver of human progress, and that we need more of it if our species is to survive. Ehrlich and Ornstein want us "to emotionally join a global family." Rifkin calls for us to make the leap to "global empathic consciousness." He sees this as the last best hope for saving the world from environmental destruction, and concludes with the plaintive question "Can we reach biosphere consciousness and global empathy in time to avoid planetary collapse?" These are sophisticated books, which provide extensive and accessible reviews of the scholarly literature on empathy. And, as befits the spirit of the times, they enthusiastically champion an increase in empathy as a cure for humanity's ills.

This enthusiasm may be misplaced, however. Empathy has some unfortunate features—it is parochial, narrow-minded, and innumerate.[1] We're often at our best when we're smart enough not to rely on it.

10   In 1949, Kathy Fiscus, a three-year-old girl, fell into a well in San Marino, California, and the entire nation was captivated by concern. Four decades later, America was transfixed by the plight of Jessica McClure—Baby Jessica—the eighteen-month-old who fell into a narrow well in Texas, in October 1987, triggering a fifty-eight-hour rescue operation. "Everybody in America became godmothers and godfathers of Jessica while this was going on," President Reagan remarked.

The immense power of empathy has been demonstrated again and again. It is why Americans were riveted by the fate of Natalee Holloway, the teen-ager who went missing in Aruba, in 2005. It's why, in the wake of widely reported tragedies and disasters—the tsunami of 2004, Hurricane Katrina the year after, or Sandy last year—people gave time, money, and even blood. It's why, last December [2012], when twenty children were murdered at Sandy Hook Elementary School, in Newtown, Connecticut, there was a widespread sense of grief, and an intense desire to help. Last month [April, 2013], of course, saw a similar outpouring of support for the victims of the Boston Marathon bombing.

Why do people respond to these misfortunes and not to others? The psychologist Paul Slovic points out that, when Holloway disappeared, the story of her plight took up far more television time than the concurrent genocide in Darfur. Each day, more than ten times the number of people who died in Hurricane Katrina die because of preventable diseases, and more than thirteen times as many perish from malnutrition.

There is, of course, the attention-getting power of new events. Just as we can come to ignore the hum of traffic, we become oblivious of problems that seem unrelenting, like the starvation of children in Africa—or homicide in the United States. In the past three decades, there were some sixty mass shootings, causing about five hundred deaths; that is, about one-tenth of 1 percent of the homicides in America. But mass murders get splashed onto television screens, newspaper headlines, and the Web; the biggest ones settle into our collective memory—Columbine, Virginia Tech, Aurora, Sandy Hook. The 99.9 percent of other homicides are, unless the victim is someone you've heard of, mere background noise.

The key to engaging empathy is what has been called "the identifiable victim effect." As the economist Thomas Schelling, writing forty-five years ago, mordantly observed, "Let a six-year-old girl with brown hair need thousands of dollars for an operation that will prolong her life until Christmas, and the post office will be swamped with nickels and dimes to save her. But let it be reported that without a sales tax the hospital facilities of Massachusetts will deteriorate

---

[1]By *innumerate* Bloom means unable to think quantitatively, especially in terms of conceiving or appreciating large numbers. Used in this context, *innumerate* means unable to conceive of the great numbers of people who are or will become victims of natural or human-made disasters.

and cause a barely perceptible increase in preventable deaths—not many will drop a tear or reach for their checkbooks."

15   You can see the effect in the lab. The psychologists Tehila Kogut and Ilana Ritov asked some subjects how much money they would give to help develop a drug that would save the life of one child, and asked others how much they would give to save eight children. The answers were about the same. But when Kogut and Ritov told a third group a child's name and age, and showed her picture, the donations shot up—now there were far more to the one than to the eight.

The number of victims hardly matters—there is little psychological difference between hearing about the suffering of five thousand and that of five hundred thousand. Imagine reading that two thousand people just died in an earthquake in a remote country, and then discovering that the actual number of deaths was twenty thousand. Do you now feel ten times worse? To the extent that we can recognize the numbers as significant, it's because of reason, not empathy.

In the broader context of humanitarianism, as critics like Linda Polman have pointed out, the empathetic reflex can lead us astray. When the perpetrators of violence profit from aid—as in the "taxes" that warlords often demand from international relief agencies—they are actually given an incentive to commit further atrocities. It is similar to the practice of some parents in India who mutilate their children at birth in order to make them more effective beggars. The children's debilities tug at our hearts, but a more dispassionate analysis of the situation is necessary if we are going to do anything meaningful to prevent them.

A "politics of empathy" doesn't provide much clarity in the public sphere, either. Typically, political disputes involve a disagreement over whom we should empathize *with*. Liberals argue for gun control, for example, by focusing on the victims of gun violence; conservatives point to the unarmed victims of crime, defenseless against the savagery of others. Liberals in favor of tightening federally enforced safety regulations invoke the employee struggling with work-related injuries; their conservative counterparts talk about the small businessman bankrupted by onerous requirements. So don't suppose that if your ideological opponents could only ramp up their empathy they would think just like you.

On many issues, empathy can pull us in the wrong direction. The outrage that comes from adopting the perspective of a victim can drive an appetite for retribution. (Think of those statutes named for dead children: Megan's Law, Jessica's Law, Caylee's Law.) But the appetite for retribution is typically indifferent to long-term consequences. In one study, conducted by Jonathan Baron and Ilana Ritov, people were asked how best to punish a company for producing a vaccine that caused the death of a child. Some were told that a higher fine would make the company work harder to manufacture a safer product; others were told that a higher fine would discourage the company from making the vaccine, and since there were no acceptable alternatives on the market the punishment would lead to more deaths. Most people didn't care; they wanted the company fined heavily, whatever the consequence.

20   This dynamic regularly plays out in the realm of criminal justice. In 1987, Willie Horton, a convicted murderer who had been released on furlough from the Northeastern Correctional Center, in Massachusetts, raped a woman after beating and tying up her fiancé. The furlough program came to be seen as a humiliating mistake on the part of Governor Michael Dukakis, and was used against him by his opponents during his run for President, the following year. Yet the program may have *reduced* the likelihood of such incidents. In fact, a 1987 report found that the recidivism rate in Massachusetts dropped in the eleven years after the program was introduced, and that convicts who were furloughed before being released were less likely to go on to commit a crime than those who were not. The trouble is that you can't point to individuals who *weren't* raped, assaulted, or killed as a result of the program, just as you can't point to a specific person whose life was spared because of vaccination.

There's a larger pattern here. Sensible policies often have benefits that are merely statistical, but victims have names and stories. Consider global warming—what Rifkin calls the "escalating entropy bill that now threatens catastrophic climate change and our very existence." As it happens, the limits of empathy are especially stark here. Opponents of restrictions on CO_2 emissions are flush with identifiable victims—all those who will be harmed by increased costs, by business closures. The millions of people who at some unspecified future date will suffer the consequences of our current inaction are, by contrast, pale statistical abstractions.

The government's failure to enact prudent long-term policies is often attributed to the incentive system of democratic politics (which favors short-term fixes), and to the powerful influence of money. But the politics of empathy is also to blame. Too often, our concern for specific individuals today means neglecting crises that will harm countless people in the future.

Moral judgment entails more than putting oneself in another's shoes. As the philosopher Jesse Prinz points out, some acts that we easily recognize as wrong, such as shoplifting or tax evasion, have no identifiable victim. And plenty of good deeds—disciplining a child for dangerous behavior, enforcing a fair and impartial procedure for determining who should get an organ transplant, despite the suffering of those low on the list—require us to put our empathy to one side. Eight deaths are worse than one, even if you know the name of the one; humanitarian aid can, if poorly targeted, be counterproductive; the threat posed by climate change warrants the sacrifices entailed by efforts to ameliorate it. "The decline of violence may owe something to an expansion of empathy," the psychologist Steven Pinker has written, "but it also owes much to harder-boiled faculties like prudence, reason, fairness, self-control, norms and taboos, and conceptions of human rights." A reasoned, even counter-empathetic analysis of moral obligation and likely consequences is a better guide to planning for the future than the gut wrench of empathy.

Rifkin and others have argued, plausibly, that moral progress involves expanding our concern from the family and the tribe to humanity as a whole.

Yet it is impossible to empathize with seven billion strangers, or to feel toward someone you've never met the degree of concern you feel for a child, a friend, or a lover. Our best hope for the future is not to get people to think of all humanity as family—that's impossible. It lies, instead, in an appreciation of the fact that, even if we don't empathize with distant strangers, their lives have the same value as the lives of those we love.

25   That's not a call for a world without empathy. A race of psychopaths might well be smart enough to invent the principles of solidarity and fairness. (Research suggests that criminal psychopaths are adept at making moral judgments.) The problem with those who are devoid of empathy is that, although they may recognize what's right, they have no motivation to act upon it. Some spark of fellow feeling is needed to convert intelligence into action.

But a spark may be all that's needed. Putting aside the extremes of psychopathy, there is no evidence to suggest that the less empathetic are morally worse than the rest of us. Simon Baron-Cohen observes that some people with autism and Asperger's syndrome, though typically empathy-deficient, are highly moral, owing to a strong desire to follow rules and insure that they are applied fairly.

Where empathy really does matter is in our personal relationships. Nobody wants to live like Thomas Gradgrind—Charles Dickens's caricature utilitarian, who treats all interactions, including those with his children, in explicitly economic terms. Empathy is what makes us human; it's what makes us both subjects and objects of moral concern. Empathy betrays us only when we take it as a moral guide.

Newtown, in the wake of the Sandy Hook massacre, was inundated with so much charity that it became a burden. More than eight hundred volunteers were recruited to deal with the gifts that were sent to the city—all of which kept arriving despite earnest pleas from Newtown officials that charity be directed elsewhere. A vast warehouse was crammed with plush toys the townspeople had no use for; millions of dollars rolled in to this relatively affluent community. We felt their pain; we wanted to help. Meanwhile—just to begin a very long list—almost twenty million American children go to bed hungry each night, and the federal food-stamp program is facing budget cuts of almost 20 percent. Many of the same kindly strangers who paid for Baby Jessica's medical needs support cuts to state Medicaid programs—cuts that will affect millions. Perhaps fifty million Americans will be stricken next year by foodborne illness, yet budget reductions mean that the FDA will be conducting two thousand fewer safety inspections. Even more invisibly, next year the average American will release about twenty metric tons of carbon dioxide into the atmosphere, and many in Congress seek to loosen restrictions on greenhouse gases even further.

Such are the paradoxes of empathy. The power of this faculty has something to do with its ability to bring our moral concern into a laser pointer of focused attention. If a planet of billions is to survive, however, we'll need to take into consideration the welfare of people not yet harmed—and, even more, of people not yet born. They have no names, faces, or stories to grip our conscience or stir our fellow feeling. Their prospects call, rather, for deliberation and calculation. Our hearts will always go out to the baby in the well; it's a measure of our humanity. But empathy will have to yield to reason if humanity is to have a future.

Read, Reread, Highlight

Let's consider our recommended pointers for writing a summary.

As you reread the passage, note in the margins of the article important points, transitions, and questions you may have. Consider the essay's significance as a whole and its stages of thought. What does it say? How is it organized? How does each part of the passage fit into the whole? What do all these points add up to? Here is how a few paragraphs (5–9) of Bloom's article might look after you mark the main ideas by highlighting and by adding marginal notations.

Empathy research has increasing focus on moral thought, emotion, and action.

Empathy research is thriving these days, as cognitive neuroscience undergoes what some call an "affective revolution." There is increasing focus on the emotions, especially those involved in moral thought and action. We've learned, for instance, that some of the same neural systems that are active when we are in pain become engaged when we observe the suffering of others. Other researchers are exploring how empathy emerges in chimpanzee and other primates, how it flowers in young children, and the sort of circumstances that trigger it.

This interest isn't just theoretical. If we can figure out how empathy works, we might be able to produce more of it. Some individuals stanch their empathy through the deliberate endorsement of political or religious ideologies that promote cruelty toward their adversaries, while others are deficient because of bad genes, abusive parenting, brutal experience, or the usual unhappy goulash of all of the above.

Psychopaths lack empathy — a cause of much suffering in the world.

At an extreme lie the one percent or so of people who are clinically described as psychopaths. A standard checklist for the condition includes "callousness; lack of empathy"; many other distinguishing psychopathic traits, like lack of guilt and pathological lying, surely stem from this fundamental deficit. Some blame the empathy-deficient for much of the suffering in the world.

Evil as "empathy erosion"

In *The Science of Evil: On Empathy and the Origins of Cruelty* (Basic), Simon Baron-Cohen goes so far as to equate evil with "empathy erosion."

Empathy absent in bullies — and those who witness bullying and stand by.

In a thoughtful new book on bullying, Sticks and Stones (Random House), Emily Bazelon writes, "The scariest aspect of bullying is the utter lack of empathy"—a diagnosis that she applies not only to the bullies but also to those who do nothing to help the victims. Few of those involved in bullying, she cautions, will turn into full-blown psychopaths. Rather, the empathy gap is situational: bullies have come to see their victims as worthless; they have chosen to shut down their empathetic responses. But most will outgrow—and perhaps regret—their terrible behavior. "The key is to remember that almost everyone has the capacity for empathy and decency—and to tend that seed as best as we possibly can," she maintains.

Recent authors argue that empathy is a force for progress and even necessary for human survival.

Two other recent books, *The Empathic Civilization* (Penguin), by Jeremy Rifkin, and *Humanity on a Tightrope* (Rowman & Littlefield), by Paul R. Ehrlich and Robert E. Ornstein, make the powerful argument that empathy has been the main driver of human progress, and that we need more of it if our species is to survive. Ehrlich and Ornstein want us "to emotionally join a global family." Rifkin calls for us to make the leap to "global empathic consciousness." He sees this as the last best hope for saving the world from environmental destruction, and concludes with the plaintive question "Can we reach biosphere consciousness and global empathy in time to avoid planetary collapse?" These are sophisticated books, which provide extensive and accessible reviews of the scholarly literature on empathy. And, as befits the spirit of the times, they enthusiastically champion an increase in empathy as a cure for humanity's ills.

Pivot point: Shifts focus from the benefits to the problems of empathy.

This enthusiasm may be misplaced, however. Empathy has some unfortunate features—it is parochial, narrow-minded, and innumerate. We're often at our best when we're smart enough not to rely on it.

Divide into Stages of Thought

When a selection doesn't contain section headings, as is the case with "The Baby in the Well," how do you determine where one section—stage of thought—ends and the next one begins? Assuming that what you have read is coherent and unified, this should not be difficult. (When a selection is unified, all of its parts pertain to the main subject; when a selection is coherent, the parts follow one another in logical order.) Look, particularly, for transitional sentences at the beginning of paragraphs. Such sentences generally work in one or both of the following ways: (1) they summarize what has come before; (2) they set the stage for what is to follow.

Look at the sentence that opens paragraph 9: "This enthusiasm may be misplaced, however." Notice how this sentence signals a sudden shift in focus. Bloom began by discussing the prevailing view of empathy and offered examples to demonstrate this discussion. He also pointed to recent books supporting this view. But now he tells us that empathy may be overrated and goes on to explain why. The second sentence of paragraph 9 amplifies the first: "Empathy has some unfortunate features—it is parochial, narrow-minded, and innumerate." He offers reasons for his initial statement, announcing in the process the focus of his remaining essay. Bloom is in total control of his subject, setting up his thesis mid-essay in a way that would be totally surprising if not for the subtitle of his article ("The Case Against Empathy"). Now he has our attention. We want to know more about what he means by "This enthusiasm may be misplaced." In the third and final sentence of that paragraph, he writes: "We're often at our best when we're smart enough not to rely on [empathy]." The setup is now ready to take us in another direction from that of the beginning of the article.

Each section of an article generally takes several paragraphs to develop. Between paragraphs, and almost certainly between sections of an article, you will usually find transitions that help you understand what you have just read and what you are about to read. For articles like Bloom's that have no sub- (that is, section) headings, try writing your own section headings in the margins as you take notes. Articles with such headings make your job easier. But note that *if* a selection is well written, you'll be able to identify how the writer develops an argument or explanation over distinct sections of thought.

Here we divide Bloom's article into eight sections. This division is not absolute. Some readers might identify seven sections, others six. The number is less important than the clarity with which you understand, and can reproduce in your summary, the author's step-by-step logic.

Section 1: *Definition and importance of empathy* (paragraphs 1–4).

Section 2: *Empathy necessary to human survival?* (paragraphs 5–8).

Section 3: *The problem with empathy: Its focus on "babies in wells"* (paragraphs 9–11).

Section 4: *How empathy operates* (paragraphs 12–16).

Section 5: *How empathy leads us astray* (paragraphs 17–22).

Section 6: *Empathy isn't enough* (paragraphs 23–24).

Section 7: *Concession: Where empathy does matter* (paragraphs 25–27).

Section 8: *Conclusion: Empathy should yield to reason* (paragraphs 28–29).

Write a Brief Summary of Each Stage of Thought

The purpose of this step is to wean you from the language of the original passage so that you are not tied to it when writing the summary. Here are brief summaries for each stage of thought in the sections of "The Baby in the Well."

Section 1: *Definition and importance of empathy* (paragraphs 1–4).

> Many believe that what makes us moral beings is empathy, the ability to see the world from others' points of view, to feel their pain and distress, and to feel the impulse to help them.

Section 2: *Empathy necessary to human survival?* (paragraphs 5–8).

> Empathy research focuses on how our moral impulses are affected when we see or sense others who are in pain. Some people feel no distress at the pain of others, but most are capable of empathy, a quality Bloom believes is necessary not only for human progress but also for the survival of our species.

Section 3: *The problem with empathy: its focus on "babies in wells"* (paragraphs 9–11).

> Empathy is "parochial, narrow-minded, and innumerate."[2] It tends to focus on individuals or relatively small groups of individuals who are in well-publicized distress.

Section 4: *How empathy operates* (paragraphs 12–16).

> Because of the "identifiable victim effect," people care about the effects of highly publicized tragedies on people whose faces they can see. But at the same time, they seem oblivious to large-scale catastrophes such as genocide, mass starvation, and deaths due to preventable illnesses as well as to routine homicides that occur in the thousands every year.

Section 5: *How empathy leads us astray* (paragraphs 17–22).

> So empathy "can lead us astray." Our empathetic impulses may overpower our "dispassionate analysis of a situation." Acting on impulses of empathy may help a relatively small number of identifiable individuals, but it may also hurt many other individuals of whom we are less aware, who don't have "names or stories," or with whose values we don't politically sympathize.

Section 6: *Empathy isn't enough* (paragraphs 23–24).

> Moral judgment often requires us to put empathy aside, to assume that all lives have the same value, and to use qualities like "prudence, reason, fairness [and] self-control" to plan for the well-being of humanity as a whole.

Section 7: *Concession: Where empathy does matter* (paragraphs 25–27).

> No one wants to live in a world without empathy, a quality that is so vital in maintaining our human relationships.

Section 8: *Conclusion: Empathy should yield to reason* (paragraphs 28–29).

> But as a moral guide, empathy should "yield to reason." Assistance to the few is often wasted because it is too much or it is unneeded. But "guided by deliberation and calculation," assistance to the many is essential for the future well-being of the billions of people who constitute humankind.

Write a Thesis: A Brief Summary of the Entire Passage

The thesis is the most general statement of a summary (or any other type of academic writing). It is the statement that announces the paper's subject and the claim that you or—in the case of a summary—another author will be making

---

[2]See definition of *innumerate*, p. 11.

about that subject. Every paragraph of a paper illuminates the thesis by providing supporting detail or explanation. The relationship of these paragraphs to the thesis is analogous to the relationship of the sentences within a paragraph to the topic sentence. Both the thesis and the topic sentences are general statements (the thesis being the more general) that are followed by systematically arranged details.

To ensure clarity for the reader, *the first sentence of your summary should begin with the author's thesis, regardless of where it appears in the article itself.* An author may locate her thesis at the beginning of her work, in which case the thesis operates as a general principle from which details of the presentation follow. This is called a *deductive* organization: thesis first, supporting details second. Alternatively, an author may locate his thesis at the end of the work, in which case he begins with specific details and builds toward a more general conclusion, or thesis. This is called an *inductive* organization. And, as you might expect, an author might locate the thesis anywhere between beginning and end, at whatever point it seems best positioned—which is what Bloom chooses to do.

A thesis consists of a subject and an assertion about that subject. How can we go about fashioning an adequate thesis for a summary of Bloom's article? Probably no two versions of Bloom's thesis statement would be worded identically. But it is fair to say that any reasonable thesis will indicate that Bloom's subject is the inadequacy of empathy for dealing with large-scale human suffering, an inadequacy resulting from what he calls the "identifiable victim effect"—our tendency to respond more favorably to individuals whose names and faces we know than to large numbers of present or future victims who remain anonymous to us.

Does Bloom make a statement anywhere in this passage that pulls all this together? Examine paragraph 9 and you will find his thesis—two sentences that sum up the problems with empathy: "Empathy has some unfortunate features—it is parochial, narrow-minded, and innumerate. We're often at our best when we're smart enough not to rely on it." You may have learned that a thesis statement must be expressed in a single sentence. We would offer a slight rewording of this generally sound advice and say that a thesis statement must be *expressible* in a single sentence. For reasons of emphasis or style, a writer might choose to distribute a thesis across two or more sentences. Certainly, the sense of Bloom's thesis can take the form of a single statement, one that explains why it's a good idea not to rely on empathy. For reasons largely of emphasis, he divides his thesis into two sentences.

Here is a one-sentence version of Bloom's two-sentence thesis, using his language: It's best not to rely on empathy because this emotion can be "parochial, narrow-minded, and innumerate." Notice that such a statement anticipates a summary of the *entire* article: both the discussion leading up to Bloom's thesis and his discussion after. To put this thesis in our own words and alert readers that the idea is Bloom's, not ours, we might recast it as follows:

> In "The Baby in the Well: The Case Against Empathy," Paul Bloom argues that while empathy is important in fostering positive human relationships, we should prefer reason as a guide to social policy because empathy's focus on the distress of one individual may blind us to the suffering of thousands whose names and faces we do not know.

The first sentence of a summary is crucially important, for it orients readers by letting them know what to expect in the coming paragraphs. In the example, the sentence refers directly to an article, its author, and the thesis for the upcoming summary. The author and title reference could also be indicated in the summary's title (if this were a freestanding summary), in which case their mention could be dropped from the thesis statement. And lest you become frustrated too quickly with how much effort it takes to come up with this crucial sentence, keep in mind that writing an acceptable thesis for a summary takes time. In this case, it took three drafts, roughly ten minutes, to compose a thesis and another few minutes of fine-tuning after a draft of the entire summary was completed. The thesis needed revision because the first draft was vague; the second draft was improved but too specific on a secondary point; the third draft was more complete but too general on a key point:

Draft 1: In "The Baby in the Well: The Case Against Empathy," Paul Bloom argues that we should not rely on empathy.

(Vague. It's not clear from this statement why Bloom thinks we should not rely on empathy.)

Draft 2: In "The Baby in the Well: The Case Against Empathy," Paul Bloom argues against empathy because of its focus on the distress of the individual rather than on the suffering of large numbers of people.

(Better, but the thesis should note that Bloom acknowledges the value of empathy and indicate what he sees as a preferable alternative to empathy.)

Draft 3: In "The Baby in the Well: The Case Against Empathy," Paul Bloom argues that while empathy has its place, we should prefer reason because empathy's focus on the distress of one individual may blind us to the suffering among thousands of individuals.

(Close — but a better thesis would formulate a more precise phrase than "has its place" and would introduce the crucial idea of the "identifiable victim affect" — one indicated in the final thesis in the phrase "whose names and faces we do not know.")

Final Draft: In "The Baby in the Well: The Case Against Empathy," Paul Bloom argues that while empathy is important in fostering positive human relationships, we should prefer reason as a guide to social policy because empathy's focus on the distress of one individual may blind us to the suffering of thousands whose names and faces we do not know.

Write the First Draft of the Summary

Let's consider two possible summaries of Bloom's article: (1) a short summary, combining a thesis with brief section summaries, and (2) a longer summary, combining thesis, brief section summaries, and some carefully chosen details. Again, keep in mind that you are reading final versions; each of the following summaries is the result of at least two full drafts. Highlighting indicates transitions added to smooth the flow of the summary. The thesis sentence is also highlighted.

Summary 1: Combine Thesis Sentence with Brief Section Summaries

In "The Baby in the Well: The Case Against Empathy," Paul Bloom argues that while empathy is important in fostering positive human relationships, we should prefer reason as a guide to social policy because empathy's focus on the distress of one individual may blind us to the suffering of thousands whose names and faces we do not know. Bloom begins with an uncontroversial point: Many believe that what makes us moral beings is empathy, the ability to see the world from others' points of view, to feel their pain and distress, and to feel the impulse to help them. Most people are capable of empathy, a quality Bloom believes is necessary not only for human progress but also for the survival of our species.

There is a downside to empathy, however: It is "parochial, narrow-minded, and innumerate." Empathy tends to focus on the distress of individuals or relatively small groups of individuals whose names and faces we know, a phenomenon known as the "identifiable victim effect." But the same people who feel empathetic toward individuals can be oblivious to large-scale catastrophes such as genocide, mass starvation, and deaths due to preventable illnesses as well as to routine homicides that occur in the thousands every year. Because our empathetic impulses may overpower our "dispassionate analysis of a situation," empathy can "lead us astray." When we act only on impulses of empathy, we may help a relatively small number of identifiable individuals, but we often ignore many other individuals who don't have "names or stories" or with whose political values we don't sympathize.

For this reason, good moral judgment often requires us to put empathy aside, to assume that all lives have the same value, and to use qualities like "prudence, reason, fairness [and] self-control" to plan for the well-being of humanity as a whole. Of course, no one wants to live in a world without empathy. As a moral guide, however, empathy should "yield to reason." Our generous assistance to the few is often wasted. But assistance to the many, "guided by deliberation and calculation," is essential for the future well-being of the billions of people who constitute humankind.

The Strategy of the Shorter Summary

This short summary consists essentially of a restatement of Bloom's thesis plus the section summaries, modified, expanded a little, and even slightly rearranged for stylistic purposes. You'll recall that Bloom locates his thesis midway through the article, in paragraph 9. But note that this model summary *begins* with a restatement of his thesis. Notice also the relative weight given to the section summaries within the model. Bloom's main argument, that empathy is "parochial, narrow-minded, and innumerate," is summarized in paragraph 2 of the model. The other paragraphs combine summaries of material leading up to the main argument and material explaining the implications of the argument—primarily, that reason is a better guide to both moral judgment and social policy than empathy. Paragraph 1 of the short summary combines material from the article's Sections 1 and 2 (paragraphs 1–8 of the article); paragraph 2 combines material from the article's Sections 3–5 (paragraphs 9–22); and paragraph 3 combines summaries of Sections 6, 7, and 8 (paragraphs 23–29).

Notice the insertion of several (highlighted) transitional phrases. The first, "Bloom begins with an uncontroversial assertion," bridges the thesis and the first section of the article itself in which Bloom focuses on the benefits and even the study of empathy. The second, "There is a downside, however," sets up the sentence that represents the main idea of the article focusing on problems associated with empathy. The third and fourth highlights, "For this reason" and "of course" in paragraph 3, serve respectively as a transition between paragraphs and as an introduction to a brief concession sentence. The concession, which Bloom makes in paragraphs 25–27, acknowledges the fact that no one wants to live in a world without empathy; it then reaffirms the main idea of the thesis: that the welfare of humankind's billions is better left to "deliberation and calculation" than to empathy.

Summary 2: Combine Thesis Sentence, Section Summaries, and Carefully Chosen Details

The thesis and brief section summaries could also be used as the outline for a more detailed summary. However, most of the details in the passage won't be necessary in a summary. It isn't necessary even in a longer summary of this passage to discuss all of Bloom's examples of the kind of situations that evoke (or fail to evoke) empathy. It would be appropriate, though, to mention *some* examples of such situations or to describe the lab experiment that demonstrates how the "identifiable victim effect" works.

Such details don't appear in the first summary, but in a longer summary, a few carefully selected examples might be desirable for clarity. How do you decide which examples to include? One hint may be their degree of prominence: The fact that Bloom opens with Barack Obama's comments on empathy and devotes the first four paragraphs of his article to detailing the comments of important individuals like Obama and Adam Smith is an indication that such references may be worth mentioning in a longer summary. And the fact that Bloom titles the article "The Baby in the Well" suggests the importance of explaining the significance of this striking image in illustrating Bloom's overall thesis. Otherwise, it may not make much difference which examples you cite. In the following longer summary, the writer discusses the case of Willie Horton, the convicted murderer who was furloughed and, while on release, subsequently committed a horrific crime. Other examples cited by Bloom, however, might work just as well in illustrating his point that reason is better than empathy as a guide to enlightened social policy.

You won't always know which details to include and which to exclude. Developing good judgment in comprehending and summarizing texts is largely a matter of reading skill and prior knowledge (see p. 4). Consider the analogy of the seasoned mechanic who can pinpoint an engine problem by simply listening to a characteristic sound that to a less experienced person is just noise. Or consider the chess player who can plot three separate winning strategies from a board position that to a novice looks like a hopeless jumble. In the same way, the more practiced a reader you are, the more knowledgeable you will become about the subject and the better able you will be to make critical distinctions between elements of greater and lesser importance. In the meantime, read as carefully as you can and use your own best judgment as to how to present your material.

Here's one version of a completed summary with carefully chosen details. Note that we have highlighted phrases and sentences added to the original, briefer summary.

In "The Baby in the Well: The Case Against Empathy" Paul Bloom argues that while empathy is important in fostering positive human relationships, we should prefer reason as a guide to social policy because empathy's focus on the distress of one individual may blind us to the suffering of thousands whose names and faces we do not know. Bloom begins by citing assertions of the importance of empathy from well-known figures like Barack Obama and Adam Smith. He points out that many believe that what makes us moral beings is empathy, the ability to see the world from others' points of view, to feel their pain and distress, and to feel the impulse to help them. Some people, either because of their own belief systems or because of abuse they have suffered at the hands of others, lack this essential human capacity. Bullies, for example, according to Emily Bazelon, show "an utter lack of empathy." Fortunately, most people are capable of this quality that Bloom believes is necessary not only for human progress but also for the survival of our species.

There is a downside to empathy, however: It is "parochial, narrow-minded, and innumerate." Empathy tends to focus on the distress of individuals or relatively small groups of individuals whose names and faces we know, a phenomenon known as the "identifiable victim effect." Bloom explains how America becomes transfixed by the plight of young children who fall into wells: In 1949 it was three-year-old Kathy Ficus; in 1987 it was 18-month-old Jessica McClure (Baby Jessica). Americans have also poured out their empathy to Natalee Holloway, who disappeared in Aruba in 2005, as well as to the victims of both natural disasters, like tsunamis and hurricanes, and mass killings like the Sandy Hook school shooting and the Boston Marathon bombing. But the same people who feel empathetic toward individuals and relatively small groups of individuals can be oblivious to large-scale catastrophes such as genocide, mass starvation, and deaths due to preventable illnesses as well as to routine homicides that occur in the thousands every year. A lab experiment has shown that people tend to be more generous in donating money for the development of a life-saving drug when they know the name and age—and can see the photo—of a particular child who needs the drug.

Because our empathetic impulses may overpower our "dispassionate analysis of a situation," empathy can "lead us astray." When we act only on impulses of empathy, we may help a relatively small number of identifiable individuals, but we often ignore many other individuals who don't have "names or stories" or with whose political values we don't sympathize. The nonidentifiable individuals include those who would be helped if we acted on the basis of reason rather than empathy. Bloom cites the case of those Massachusetts citizens who are safer as the result of a prison furlough program that was successful in reducing crime; however, the program was discredited because of a single notorious case in which a prisoner out on furlough committed a horrendous act that created understandable empathy toward the victim.

For this reason, good moral judgment often requires us to put empathy aside, to assume that all lives have the same value, and to use qualities like "prudence, reason, fairness [and] self-control" to plan for the well-being of humanity as a whole. Of course, no one wants to live in a world without empathy. Empathy is particularly important in our personal relationships, in ensuring that we treat one another with care. As a moral guide, however, empathy should "yield to reason." Our generous assistance to the few is often wasted. But assistance to the many, "guided by deliberation and calculation," is essential for the future well-being of the billions of people who constitute humankind.

The Strategy of the Longer Summary

Compared with the first, briefer summary, this effort (75 percent longer than the first) includes several specific examples that illustrate Bloom's thesis about the "parochial, narrow-minded, and innumerate" features of empathy. It begins by emphasizing the great value that we place on empathy; it more fully develops the way that empathetic thinking embodies the "identifiable victim effect," and it expands upon the reasons, in terms of social policy, for preferring reason to empathy as a moral guide.

The final two of our suggested steps for writing summaries are (1) to check your summary against the original passage, making sure that you have included all the important ideas, and (2) to revise so that the summary reads smoothly and coherently. The structure of this summary generally reflects the structure of the original article—with one significant departure, as noted earlier. Bloom uses a modified inductive approach, stating his thesis midway through the article. The summary, however, states the thesis immediately, then proceeds deductively to develop that thesis.

How Long Should a Summary Be?

The length of a summary depends both on the length of the original passage and on the use to which the summary will be put. If you are summarizing an entire article, a good rule of thumb is that your summary should be no longer than one-fourth the length of the original passage. Of course, if you were summarizing an entire chapter or even an entire book, it would have to be much shorter than that.

The longer summary is one-fifth the length of Paul Bloom's original. Although it shouldn't be very much longer, you have seen (p. 21) that it could be quite a bit shorter.

The length as well as the content of the summary also depend on the *purpose* to which it will be put. Let's suppose you decided to use Bloom's piece in a paper about bullying. In this case, you would pay particular attention to what Bloom writes in paragraphs 6 and 7 about people characterized by a partial or total lack of empathy and whose behavior exhibits itself as bullying. You would probably also draw upon Emily Bazelon's comment about "the scariest aspect of bullying [being] a lack of empathy." On the other hand, in a paper dealing with some aspect of social policy (for example, parole reform or reducing the urban homicide rate), you might draw upon Bloom's larger point that "reasoned…analysis of moral obligation and likely consequences is a better guide to planning for the future than the gut wrench of empathy." So, depending on your purpose, you would summarize one particular section of the article or another. We will see this process more fully demonstrated in the upcoming chapters on syntheses.

MyWritingLab™   Exercise 1.1 ◯

Individual and Collaborative Summary Practice

Turn to Chapter 15 and read Solomon A. Asch's article "Opinions and Social Pressures." Follow the steps for writing summaries outlined above—read, underline, and divide into stages of thought. Write a one- or two-sentence summary of each stage of thought in Asch's article. Then gather in groups of three or four classmates and compare your summary sentences. Discuss the differences in your sentences, coming to some consensus about the divisions in Asch's stages of thought—and the ways in which to best sum them up.

As a group, write a one- or two-sentence thesis statement summing up the entire passage. You could go even further, and, using your individual summary sentences—or the versions of them your group revised—put together a brief summary of Asch's essay. Model your work on the brief summary of Bloom's article, on pages 9–15.

SUMMARIZING GRAPHS, CHARTS, AND TABLES

1.4 Write summaries of visual presentations, including graphs, charts, and tables.

In your reading in the sciences and social sciences, you will often find data and concepts presented in nontext forms—as figures and tables. Such visual devices offer a snapshot, a pictorial overview of material that is more quickly and clearly communicated in graphic form than as a series of (often complicated) sentences. Note that in essence, graphs, charts, and tables are themselves summaries. The writer uses a graph, which in an article or book is often labeled as a numbered "figure," and presents the quantitative results of research as points on a line or a bar or as sections ("slices") of a pie. Pie charts show relative proportions, or percentages. Graphs, especially effective in showing patterns, relate one variable to another: for instance, income to years of education or sales figures of a product over a period of three years.

Writers regularly draw on graphs, charts, and tables to provide information or to offer evidence for points they are arguing. Consider the following passage from the prefatory "Discussion" to the study done for the Center for Immigration Studies (CIS), *Immigrants in the United States: A Profile of America's Foreign-Born Population*, by Steven A. Camarota:

> There are many reasons to examine the nation's immigrant population. First, immigrants and their minor children now represent one-sixth of the U.S. population. Moreover, understanding how immigrants are doing is the best way to evaluate the effects of immigration policy. Absent a change in policy, between 12 and 15 million new immigrants (legal and illegal) will likely settle in the United States in the next decade. And perhaps 30 million new immigrants will arrive in the next 20 years. Immigration policy determines the number allowed in, the selection criteria used, and the level of resources devoted to controlling illegal immigration. The future, of course, is not set and when formulating immigration policy, it is critically important to know the impact of recent immigration.
>
> It is difficult to understate the impact of immigration on the socio-demographics of the United States. New immigration plus births to immigrants added more than 22 million people to the U.S. population in the last decade, equal to 80 percent of total population growth. Immigrants and their young children (under 18) now account for more than one in five public school students, one-fourth of those in poverty, and nearly one-third of those without health insurance, creating very real challenges for the nation's schools, health care systems, and physical infrastructure. The large share of immigrants who arrive as adults with relatively few years of schooling is the primary reason so many live in poverty, use welfare programs, or lack health insurance, not their legal status or an unwillingness to work.
>
> Despite the fact that a large share of immigrants have few years of schooling, most immigrants do work. In fact, the share of immigrant men holding a job is higher than native-born men. Moreover, immigrants make significant progress the longer they reside in the United States. This is also true for the least educated. While many immigrants do very well in the United States, on average immigrants who have been in the country for 20 years lag well behind natives in most measures of economic well-being.

Camarota, who is the director of research at CIS, uses a good deal of data that likely came from graphs, charts, and tables. In the following pages, we present graphs, charts, and tables from a variety of sources, all focused on the subject of U.S. immigration.

Bar Graphs

Figure 1.1 is a *bar graph* indicating the countries that have sent the highest number of immigrants to the United States in the decades from 1901–1910 through 2001–2010. The horizontal—or x—axis indicates the decades from 1901 through 2010. The vertical—or y—axis on the left indicates the percent of immigrants represented by each country. Each vertical bar, for each decade, is subdivided into sections representing the countries that sent the most immigrants in that decade. Note that in the decade 1901 to 1910, the three top sending countries were Italy, Russia, and Austria-Hungary. A hundred years later, in the decade 2001 through 2010, the top sending countries were led by Mexico, the Philippines, and China. (Note that the decades from 1931 through 1950 and from 1961 through 1980 are not represented in the graph.)

Here is a summary of the information presented in Figure 1.1:

> Between 1900 and 2010, the flow of immigration to the United States has dramatically shifted from Europe to Asia and the Americas. In the decade from 1901 to 1910, three European countries—Italy, Russia, and

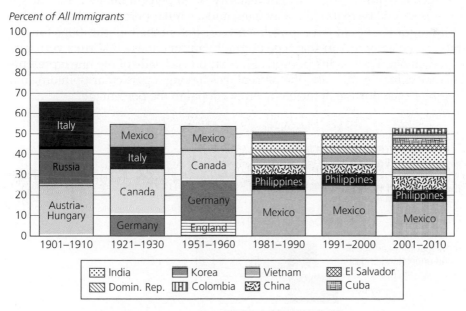

Figure 1.1   Top Sending Countries: Selected Periods[3]

[3]"Top Sending Countries (Comprising at Least Half of All L[egal] P[ermanent] R[esidents]): Selected Periods." Ruth Ellen Wasem [Specialist in Immigration Policy], "U.S. Immigration Policy: Chart Book of Key Trends, C[ongressional] R[esearch] S[ervice]: Report for Congress," Figure 2, p. 3. Source: CRS Analysis of Table 2, Statistical Yearbook of Immigration, U.S. Department of Homeland Security, Office of Immigration Statistics, FY2010. www.crs.gov, http://www.fas.org/sgp/crs/ho-mesec/R42988.pdf.

Austria-Hungary—accounted for most of the immigrant flow to this country. Starting in the next decade, however, two countries in the Americas—Mexico and Canada—became the top sources of immigrants to the United States. Mexico has remained a top sending country for most of the twentieth century and into the present century, currently accounting for more immigrants than any other nation. At the same time, immigration from Mexico dropped off slightly in the decade from 2001 to 2010. All of the other top sending countries during this decade are in Asia and South and Central America. The top sending Asian countries are Korea, India, Vietnam, China, and the Philippines; those from the Americas include—in addition to Mexico—Colombia, Cuba, El Salvador, and the Dominican Republic. Collectively, immigrants from the Asian and American countries represented on the chart in the 2001–2010 decade account for slightly more than 50 percent of all immigrants admitted.

Figure 1.2 is a horizontal bar graph summarizing the results of an opinion survey concerning the requirements that should be levied on illegal immigrants. The Pew survey shows that 76 percent of respondents believe that such immigrants should have to show that they can speak and understand English (23 percent oppose such a requirement). A slight majority of 56 percent believes that illegal immigrants should be required to pay fines, and a similar percentage believes that illegal immigrants should have to wait ten years before their applications for citizenship can be accepted. In this type of graph, an imaginary line runs vertically through each bar. The shaded portion of the bar on each side of the line represents a particular value (in this case, the percentages having a particular opinion), and the length of each portion of the bar is proportional to the percentage.

**Most Favor Requiring Those in U.S.
Illegally to Learn English**

*Legislation allowing undocumented immigrants to
stay legally should require them to ...*

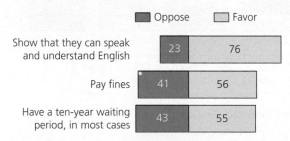

Pew Research Center/*USA Today* June 12–16, 2013. Q47.

Figure 1.2   Survey on Favored Requirements for Illegal Immigrants[4]

---

[4]Pew Research Center. "Immigration: Key Data Points from Pew Research," 26 June 2013. 3rd chart. http://www.pewresearch.org/key-data-points/immigration-tip-sheet-on-u-s-public-opinion/.

MyWritingLab™

Summarizing Graphs

Write a brief summary of the data in Figure 1.2. Use our summary of Figure 1.1 as a general model.

Line Graphs

Line graphs are useful for showing trends over a period of time. Usually, the horizontal axis indicates years, months, or shorter periods, and the vertical axis indicates a quantity: dollars, barrels, personnel, sales, anything that can be counted. The line running from left to right indicates the changing values, over a given period, of the object of measurement. Frequently, a line graph will feature multiple lines (perhaps in different colors, perhaps some solid, others dotted, etc.), each indicating a separate variable to be measured. Thus, a line graph could show the changing approval ratings of several presidential candidates over the course of a campaign season. Or it could indicate the number of iPads versus Android tablets sold in a given year.

Figure 1.3 is a line graph indicating the fluctuations in the number of nonimmigrant ("legal temporary") visas issued by the U.S. State Department from 1987

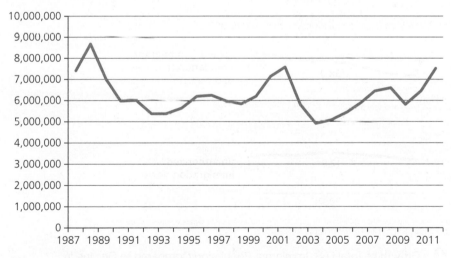

Figure 1.3   Nonimmigrant Visas Issued by the U.S. Department of State[5]

---

[5]"Nonimmigrant Visas Issued by the U.S. Department of State." Source: CRS presentation of data from Table XVIII of the annual reports of the U.S. Department of State Office of Visa Statistics. Ruth Ellen Wasem [Specialist in Immigration Policy], "U.S. Immigration Policy: Chart Book of Key Trends, C[ongressional] R[esearch] S[ervice]: Report for Congress, Figure 6, p. 7. www.crs.gov http://www .fas.org/sgp/crs/homesec/R42988.pdf.

through 2011. The number of such visas reached its highest level—nearly nine million—in 1988–1989. The lowest number of visas—fewer than five million—was issued in 2004. Following the line allows us to discern the pattern of nonimmigrant migration. By combining the information gleaned from this figure with other information gathered from other sources, you may be able to make certain conjectures or draw certain conclusions about the patterns of immigration.

In Figure 1.4, we have a double line graph, which allows us to view at the same time the changes in authorized immigration and the changes in unauthorized immigration. The horizontal axis lists only three years, and to the right of the vertical axis we see two types of immigrants categorized. With only three years being considered and with the key numbers printed right below each line, the reader can easily absorb a great deal of information in an efficient way. The two simple lines are dramatic evidence of the increase of the immigrant population in the years from 2000 to 2011.

MyWritingLab™   Exercise 1.3

Summarizing Line Graphs

Write a brief summary of the key data in Figure 1.4. Use our summary of Figure 1.1 (or your summary of Figure 1.2) as a model.

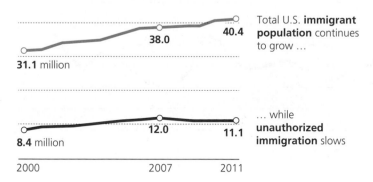

Since 2000, the immigrant population has increased by **30%**.

Total U.S. **immigrant population** continues to grow …

38.0   **40.4**

31.1 million

… while **unauthorized immigration** slows

12.0   **11.1**

8.4 million

2000   2007   2011

Immigrant population and unauthorized immigrant population estimates based on separate data sets. See Pew Research Hispanic Center, "A Nation of Immigrants," Jan. 29, 2013.

Figure 1.4   Growth of Total U.S. Immigrant Population Compared to Decline in Unauthorized Immigration[6]

---

[6]"Growth of Total U.S. Immigrant Population Compared to Decline in Unauthorized Immigration." Pew Research Hispanic Center tabulations of 2011 American Community Survey (1% IPUMS) Chart 5. http://www.pewhispanic.org/2013/02/15/u-s-immigration-trends/ph_13-01-23_ss_immigration_01_title/.

Pie Charts

Bar and line graphs are useful for visually comparing numerical quantities. *Pie charts*, on the other hand, are useful for visually comparing percentages of a whole. The pie represents the whole; the individual slices represent the relative sizes of the parts.

Figure 1.5 is an exploded pie chart, created by pulling out at least one individual slice of the pie to emphasize the data represented. The chart shows that among foreign-born adults age 25 and older, more than twice as many have a high school diploma or equivalent than those who don't. This simple chart, produced by the Pew Research Hispanic Center and based on the U.S. Census Bureau's 2011 American Community Survey, provides only one key fact about immigrants. There is no breakdown of sending countries or any other pertinent data.

Figure 1.6 is a more complex pie chart indicating the major categories of immigrants who were classified as legal permanent residents (LPRs) in fiscal year 2011. This chart shows that almost 65 percent of such immigrants entered the United States because of family ties to immigrants already in the country.

MyWritingLab™   Exercise 1.4

Summarizing Pie Charts

Write a brief summary of the data in Figure 1.6. Use our summary of Figure 1.1 (or your summary of Figure 1.2) as a model.

Most *immigrant adults are high school graduates …*

Percent of foreign-born adults ages 25 and older …

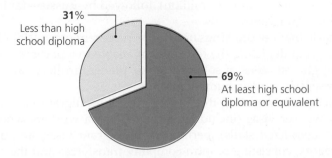

31%
Less than high
school diploma

69%
At least high school
diploma or equivalent

Pew Research Hispanic Center tabulations of 2011 American Community Survey (1% IPUMS)

Figure 1.5   Percentages of Immigrants with and Without High School Diplomas[7]

---

[7]"Percentages of Immigrant Adults with and Without High School Diplomas." Pew Research Hispanic Center tabulations of 2011 American Community Survey (1% IPUMS). http://www.pewhispanic.org/2013/02/15/u-s-immigration-trends/ph_13-01-23_ss_immigration_01_title/. Chart 14.

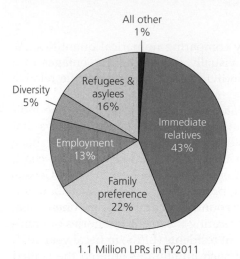

1.1 Million LPRs in FY2011

Figure 1.6   Breakdown of Legal Permanent Residents (LPRs) in Fiscal Year 2011[8]

Other Charts: Bubble Maps, Pictograms, and Interactive Charts

A *bubble map* is a type of chart characterized by discs of various sizes placed on a map of the world, a country, or a smaller region. The relative sizes of the discs represent various percentages or absolute numbers, making it easy to see at a glance which countries or regions have larger or smaller numbers of whatever variable is represented by the disc.

Figure 1.7 depicts a bubble map in which variously sized bubbles, placed over particular countries or regions, represent the total number of immigrants in a particular country. A quick look at the map reveals that the United States has by far the greatest number of immigrants (40.4 million), followed by Russia—far behind with only 12.3 million immigrants.

Pictograms are charts that use drawings or icons to represent persons or objects. For example, a pictogram depicting the resources available to a particular nation engaged in a war might use icons of soldiers, tanks, planes, artillery, and so on, with each icon representing a given number of units.

Figure 1.8 is a pictogram depicting three categories of immigrant visas issued in 2012: temporary worker visas (including those "H" visa workers who have high-level or other specialized skills), permanent immigrant visas, and a third (miscellaneous) category, consisting of intra-company transferees and their families, along with other temporary workers and their families.

In this particular figure, each icon of an individual represents approximately 10,000 immigrants. Each of the three major classes of immigrant visas is

[8]Ruth Ellen Wasem [Specialist in Immigration Policy], "U.S. Immigration Policy: Chart Book of Key Trends, C[ongressional] R[esearch] S[ervice]: Report for Congress, www.crs.gov, http://www.fas .org/sgp/crs/homesec/R42988.pdf, p. 5 (second chart—pie).

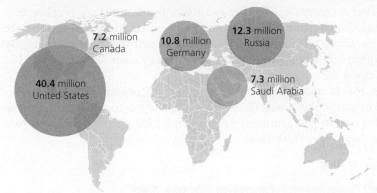

2011 American Community Survey (1% IPUMS) for U.S. and 2010 World Bank estimates for all others.

Figure 1.7   The United States Is World's Leader as Destination for Immigrants[9]

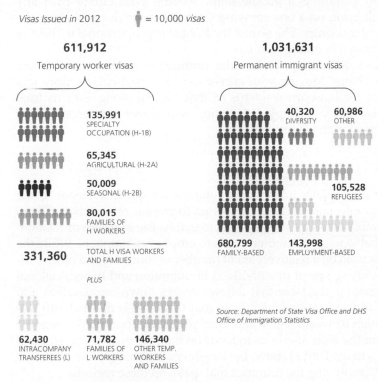

Figure 1.8   Visas Issued in 2012[10]

---

[9]Pew Research Hispanic Center. "The U.S. is the World's Leader as a Destination for Immigrants." Tabulations of 2011 American Community Survey (1% IPUMS), Chart 3. http://www.pewhispanic .org/2013/02/15/u-s-immigration-trends/ph_13-01-23_ss_immigration_01_title/.

[10]"Visas Issued in 2012." Jill H. Wilson, Brookings Institute, "Immigration Facts: Temporary Foreign Workers" 18 June 2013. Pictogram under paragraph 2. http://www.brookings.edu/research/ reports/2013/06/18-temporary-workers-wilson.

subdivided into several categories. So, for example, the temporary worker visa category is subdivided into those who have specialty occupations, those who are agricultural workers, those who are seasonal workers, and those who are family members of the workers. The other two main categories of visas are subdivided in other ways, based upon the makeup of those categories.

Interactive charts, found online, allow you to bring up concealed data by moving your cursor over particular areas. (If all the data were actually shown on the chart, it would overwhelm the graphic.) For example, locate the following two interactive maps from the *New York Times*.

Go to: Google or Bing

Search terms: "snapshot global migration new york times"

"immigration explorer new york times"

The global migration graphic is a bubble map. Moving your cursor over any particular bubble will bring up a box showing the increase or decrease in immigrants for that particular country. The size of the bubble is proportional to the size of the increase or decrease in immigration.

The immigration explorer map depicts the immigrant component of every county in the United States. Moving your cursor over any particular county will reveal the number of foreign-born residents of that county, along with its total population in the year 2000. A simple calculation will reveal the percentage of foreign-born residents in each county.

Tables

A table presents numerical data in rows and columns for quick reference. If the writer chooses, tabular information can be converted to graphic information. Charts and graphs are preferable when the writer wants to emphasize a pattern or relationship; tables are preferable when the writer wants to emphasize numbers. While the previous charts are focused on a relatively small number of countries and other variables (such as the declining rate of unauthorized immigration and the educational levels of legal immigrants), the table that follows breaks down immigration into numerous countries and several regions.[11] Note that this table is divided into two sets of data: immigration by world region and immigration by country. Whereas the regional component of the table allows us to focus on the "big picture," in terms of sources of immigrants to the United States, the longer country component allows us to draw finer distinctions among the countries that make up these regions.

A table may contain so much data that you would not want to summarize *all* of it for a particular paper. In this case, you would summarize the *part* of the table that you find useful. Here is a summary drawn from the information from Table 1.1

---

[11]Randall Monger and James Yankay, Table 3: "Legal Permanent Resident Flow by Region and Country of Birth: Fiscal Years 2010 to 2012." *U.S. Legal Permanent Residents 2012*, March 2013, p. 4. Department of Homeland Security, Office of Immigration Statistics Policy Directorate. http://www.dhs.gov/sites/default/files/publications/ois_lpr_fr_2012_2.pdf.

Table 1.1 Legal Permanent Resident Flow by Region and Country of Birth, Fiscal Years 2010 to 2012[12]

Region and Country of Birth	2012 Number	2012 Percent	2011 Number	2011 Percent	2010 Number	2010 Percent
REGION						
Total	1,031,631	100.0	1,062,040	100.0	1,042,625	100.0
Africa	107,241	10.4	100,374	9.5	101,355	9.7
Asia	429,599	41.6	451,593	42.5	422,063	40.5
Europe	81,671	7.9	83,850	7.9	88,801	8.5
North America	327,771	31.8	333,902	31.4	336,553	32.3
Caribbean	127,477	12.4	133,680	12.6	139,951	13.4
Central America	40,675	3.9	43,707	4.1	43,951	4.2
Other North America	159,619	15.5	156,515	14.7	152,651	14.6
Oceania	4,742	0.5	4,980	0.5	5,345	0.5
South America	79,401	7.7	86,096	8.1	87,178	8.4
Unknown	1,206	0.1	1,245	0.1	1,330	0.1
COUNTRY						
Total	1,031,631	100.0	1,062,040	100.0	1,042,625	100.0
Mexico	146,406	14.2	143,446	13.5	139,120	13.3
China, People's Republic	81,784	7.9	87,016	8.2	70,863	6.8
India	66,434	6.4	69,013	6.5	69,162	6.6
Philippines	57,327	5.6	57,011	5.4	58,173	5.6
Dominican Republic	41,566	4.0	46,109	4.3	53,870	5.2
Cuba	32,820	3.2	36,452	3.4	33,573	3.2
Vietnam	28,304	2.7	34,157	3.2	30,632	2.9
Haiti	22,818	2.2	22,111	2.1	22,582	2.2
Colombia	20,931	2.0	22,635	2.1	22,406	2.1
Korea South	20,846	2.0	22,824	2.1	22,227	2.1
Jamaica	20,705	2.0	19,662	1.9	19,825	1.9
Iraq	20,369	2.0	21,133	2.0	19,855	1.9
Burma	17,383	1.7	16,518	1.6	12,925	1.2
El Salvador	16,256	1.6	18,667	1.8	18,806	1.8
Pakistan	14,740	1.4	15,546	1.5	18,258	1.8
Bangladesh	14,705	1.4	16,707	1.6	14,819	1.4
Ethiopia	14,544	1.4	13,793	1.3	14,266	1.4
Nigeria	13,575	1.3	11,824	1.1	13,376	1.3
Canada	12,932	1.3	12,800	1.2	13,328	1.3
Iran	12,916	1.3	14,822	1.4	14,182	1.4
All other countries	354,270	34.3	359,794	33.9	360,377	34.6

(Countries ranked by 2012 LPR flow)

Source: U.S. Department of Homeland Security, Computer Linked Application Information Management System (CLAIMS), Legal Immigrant Data, Fiscal Years 2010 to 2012.

---

[12]"Legal Permanent Resident Flow by Region and Country of Birth, Fiscal Years 2010 to 2012." Source: U.S. Department of Homeland Security, Computer Linked Application Information Management System (CLAIMS), Legal Immigrant Data, Fiscal Years 2010 to 2012. Dept. of Homeland Security, "U.S. Legal Permanent Residents 2012," p. 4. http://www.dhs.gov/sites/default/files/publications/ois_lpr_fr_2012_2.pdf.

focusing primarily on those regions and countries that provide the largest numbers and the smallest numbers of immigrants, but also pointing out other interesting data points. Notice that the summary requires the writer to read closely and discern which information is significant. The table reports raw data and does not speak for itself. Toward the end of the summary, the writer—who draws upon data from other sources (such as the bar graph in Figure 1.1) and who also calculates percentages—speculates on the reason for the changing numbers of immigrants from Pakistan and then sums up her overall impression of the data in the table:

> During the years 2010 to 2012, by far the largest number of legal immigrants to the United States came from Asian countries, primarily the People's Republic of China, India, and the Philippines. After Asia, North America—chiefly Mexico, the Caribbean countries, and Central America—provided the greatest number of immigrants. Together, these two regions accounted for more than 73 percent of the more than 1,031,000 immigrants who entered the United States legally in 2012. By contrast, the region of Oceania—made up of Melanesia, Micronesia, and Polynesia, islands in the tropical Pacific—accounted during the same year for only half of 1 percent of total U.S. legal immigration. Europe in 2012 provided about 8 percent of the total—a far cry from a century ago when this region provided more than 60 percent of total U.S. immigrants.
>
> In terms of individual countries during the period 2010–2012, Mexico, by a huge margin, provided more immigrants to the United States than any other country, with the number rising at a small but steady rate in all three years. As indicated above, China was second after Mexico as the source country of the highest numbers of immigrants, though the pattern in these three years does not indicate a trend: There were 17,000 more Chinese immigrants in 2011 than there were in 2010, but in 2012 the number dropped by more than 5,000. On the other hand, immigration from the Dominican Republic shows a steady drop: from 53,780 in 2010 to 46,109 in 2011 to 42,566 in 2012. Pakistan also provided 20 percent fewer immigrants in 2012 than it did in 2010, a significant decline possibly related to the war against the Taliban and to American military strikes in that country. On the whole, however, during this three-year period there were no major shifts in total numbers of immigrants, with increases or decreases no greater than 3 percent.

MyWritingLab™   Exercise 1.5

Summarizing Tables

Focus on other data in Table 1.1 and write a brief summary of your own. Or use a search engine to locate another table on the general topic of immigration and summarize its data.

PARAPHRASE

1.5 Write paraphrases to clarify difficult or confusing source material.

In certain cases, you may want to *paraphrase* rather than summarize material. Writing a paraphrase is similar to writing a summary: It involves recasting a passage into your own words, so it requires your complete understanding of the material. The difference is that while a summary is a shortened version of the original, the paraphrase is approximately the same length as the original.

Why write a paraphrase when you can quote the original? You may decide to offer a paraphrase of material written in language that is dense, abstract, archaic, or possibly confusing.

Let's consider some examples. If you were investigating the ethical concerns relating to the practice of in vitro fertilization, you might conclude that you should read some medical literature. You might reasonably want to hear from the doctors who are themselves developing, performing, and questioning the procedures that you are researching. In professional journals and bulletins, physicians write to one another, not to the general public. They use specialized language. If you wanted to refer to the following technically complex selection, you might need to write a paraphrase.

> [I]t is not only an improvement in the success-rate that participating research scientists hope for but, rather, developments in new fields of research in in-vitro gene diagnosis and in certain circumstances gene therapy. In view of this, the French expert J. F. Mattei has asked the following question: "Are we forced to accept that in vitro fertilization will become one of the most compelling methods of genetic diagnosis?" Evidently, by the introduction of a new law in France and Sweden (1994), this acceptance (albeit with certain restrictions) has already occurred prior to the application of in vitro fertilization reaching a technically mature and clinically applicable phase. This may seem astonishing in view of the question placed by the above-quoted French expert: the idea of embryo production so as to withhold one or two embryos before implantation presupposes a definite "attitude towards eugenics." And to destroy an embryo merely because of its genetic characteristics could signify the reduction of a human life to the sum of its genes. Mattei asks: "In face of a molecular judgment on our lives, is there no possibility for appeal? Will the diagnosis of inherited monogenetic illnesses soon be extended to genetic predisposition for multi-factorial illnesses?"[13]

Like most literature intended for physicians, the language of this selection is somewhat forbidding to nonspecialists, who will have trouble with phrases such

---

[13]Dietmar Mieth, "In Vitro Fertilization: From Medical Reproduction to Genetic Diagnosis," *Biomedical Ethics: Newsletter of the European Network for Biomedical Ethics* 1.1 (1996): 45.

as "predisposition for multi-factorial illnesses." As a courtesy to your readers and in an effort to maintain a consistent tone and level in your essay, you could paraphrase this paragraph from a medical newsletter. First, of course, you must understand the meaning of the passage, perhaps no small task. But, having read the material carefully (and consulted a dictionary), you might prepare a paraphrase like this one:

> Writing in *Biomedical Ethics,* Dietmar Mieth reports that fertility specialists today want not only to improve the success rates of their procedures but also to diagnose and repair genetic problems before they implant fertilized eggs. Because the result of the in vitro process is often more fertilized eggs than can be used in a procedure, doctors may examine test-tube embryos for genetic defects and "withhold one or two" before implanting them. The practice of selectively implanting embryos raises concerns about eugenics and the rights of rejected embryos. On what genetic grounds will specialists distinguish flawed from healthy embryos and make a decision whether or not to implant? The appearance of single genes linked directly to specific, or "monogenetic," illnesses could be grounds for destroying an embryo. More complicated would be genes that predispose people to an illness but in no way guarantee the onset of that illness. Would these genes, which are only one factor in "multi-factorial illnesses," also be labeled undesirable and lead to embryo destruction? Advances in fertility science raise difficult questions. Already, even before techniques of genetic diagnosis are fully developed, legislatures are writing laws governing the practices of fertility clinics.

We begin our paraphrase with the same "not only/but also" logic of the original's first sentence, introducing the concepts of genetic diagnosis and therapy. The next four sentences in the original introduce concerns of a "French expert." Rather than quote Mieth quoting the expert and immediately mentioning new laws in France and Sweden, we decided (first) to explain that in vitro fertilization procedures can give rise to more embryos than needed. We reasoned that nonmedical readers would appreciate our making explicit the background knowledge that the author assumes other physicians possess. Then we quote Mieth briefly ("withhold one or two" embryos) to provide some flavor of the original. We maintain focus on the ethical questions and wait until the end of the paraphrase before mentioning the laws to which Mieth refers. Our paraphrase is roughly the same length as the original, and it conveys the author's concerns about eugenics. As you can see, the paraphrase requires a writer to make decisions about the presentation of material. In many, if not most, cases, you will need to do more than simply "translate" from the original, sentence by sentence, to write your paraphrase.

When you come across a passage that you don't understand, the temptation is to skip over it. Resist this temptation! Use a paraphrase as a tool for explaining to yourself the main ideas of a difficult passage. By translating another writer's language into your own, you clarify what you understand and pinpoint what you don't. The paraphrase therefore becomes a tool for learning the subject.

The following pointers will help you write paraphrases.

HOW TO WRITE PARAPHRASES

- Make sure that you understand the source passage.
- Substitute your own words for those of the source passage; look for synonyms that carry the same meaning as the original words.
- Rearrange your own sentences so that they read smoothly. Sentence structure, even sentence order, in the paraphrase need not be based on that of the original. A good paraphrase, like a good summary, should stand by itself.

Paraphrases are generally about the same length as (and sometimes shorter than) the passages on which they are based. But sometimes clarity requires that a paraphrase be longer than a tightly compacted source passage. For example, suppose you wanted to paraphrase this statement by Sigmund Freud:

> We have found out that the distortion in dreams which hinders our understanding of them is due to the activities of a censorship, directed against the unacceptable, unconscious wish-impulses.

If you were to paraphrase this statement (the first sentence in the Tenth Lecture of his *General Introduction to Psychoanalysis*), you might come up with something like this:

> It is difficult to understand dreams because they contain distortions. Freud believed that these distortions arise from our internal censor, which attempts to suppress unconscious and forbidden desires.

Essentially, this paraphrase does little more than break up one sentence into two and somewhat rearrange the sentence structure for clarity.

Like summaries, then, paraphrases are useful devices, both in helping you understand source material and in enabling you to convey the essence of source material to your readers. When would you choose to write a summary instead of a paraphrase (or vice versa)? The answer depends on your purpose in presenting the source material. As we've said, summaries are generally based on articles (or sections of articles) or books. Paraphrases are generally based on particularly difficult (or important) paragraphs or sentences. You would seldom paraphrase a long passage, or summarize a short one, unless there were particularly good reasons for doing so. (A lawyer might want to paraphrase several pages of legal language so that his or her client, who is not a lawyer, could understand it.) The purpose of a summary is generally to save your reader time by presenting him or her with a brief version of a lengthy source. The purpose of a paraphrase is generally to clarify a short passage that might otherwise be unclear. Whether you summarize or paraphrase may also depend on the importance of your source. A particularly important source—if it is not too long—may rate a paraphrase. If it is less important or peripheral to your central argument, you may write a summary instead. And, of course, you may choose to summarize only part of your source—the part that is most relevant to the point you are making.

MyWritingLab™ 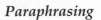   Exercise 1.6

Paraphrasing

Locate and photocopy three relatively complex, but brief, passages from readings currently assigned in your other courses. Paraphrase these passages, making the language more readable and understandable. Attach the photocopies to the paraphrases.

QUOTATIONS

1.6 Use direct and indirect quotations, and integrate them into your writing.

A *quotation* records the exact language used by someone in speech or writing. A *summary*, in contrast, is a brief restatement in your own words of what someone else has said or written. And a *paraphrase* is also a restatement, although one that is often as long as the original source. Any paper in which you draw upon sources will rely heavily on quotation, summary, and paraphrase. How do you choose among the three?

Remember that the papers you write should be your own—for the most part: your own language and certainly your own thesis, your own inferences, and your own conclusion. It follows that references to your source materials should be written primarily as summaries and paraphrases, both of which are built on restatement, not quotation. You will use summaries when you need a *brief* restatement; use paraphrases, which provide more explicit detail than summaries, when you need to follow the development of a source closely. When you quote too much, you risk losing ownership of your work: More easily than you might think, your voice can be drowned out by the voices of those you've quoted. So *use quotation sparingly,* as you would a pungent spice.

Nevertheless, quoting just the right source at the right time can significantly improve your papers. The trick is to know when and how to use quotations.

Quotations can be direct or indirect. A *direct* quotation is one in which you record precisely the language of another. An *indirect* quotation is one in which you report what someone has said without repeating the words exactly as spoken (or written):

Direct quotation: Franklin D. Roosevelt said, "The only thing we have to fear is fear itself."
Indirect quotation: Franklin D. Roosevelt said that we have nothing to fear but fear itself.

The language in a direct quotation, which is indicated by a pair of quotation marks (" "), must be faithful to the wording of the original passage. When using an indirect quotation, you have the liberty of changing words (although not changing meaning). For both direct and indirect quotations, *you must credit your sources*, naming them either in (or close to) the sentence that includes the quotation or in a parenthetical citation. (See Chapter 7, pp. 232–238, for specific rules on citing sources properly.)

Choosing Quotations

You'll find that using quotations can be particularly helpful in several situations.

Quoting Memorable Language

You should quote when the source material is worded so eloquently or powerfully that to summarize or paraphrase it would be to sacrifice much of the impact and significance of the meaning. Here, for example, is the historian John Keegan describing how France, Germany, Austria, and Russia slid inexorably in 1914 into the cataclysm of World War I:

> In the event, the states of Europe proceeded, as if in a dead march and a dialogue of the deaf, to the destruction of their continent and its civilization.

No paraphrase could do justice to the power of Keegan's words as they appear in his book *The First World War* (1998). You would certainly want to quote them in any paper dealing with the origins of this conflict.

WHEN TO QUOTE

- Use quotations when another writer's language is particularly memorable and will add interest and liveliness to your paper.
- Use quotations when another writer's language is so clear and economical that to make the same point in your own words would, by comparison, be ineffective.
- Use quotations when you want the solid reputation of a source to lend authority and credibility to your own writing.

Quoting Clear and Concise Language

You should quote a source when its language is particularly clear and economical—when your language, by contrast, would be wordy. Read this passage from a biology text by Patricia Curtis:

> The honeybee colony, which usually has a population of 30,000 to 40,000 workers, differs from that of the bumblebee and many other social bees or wasps in that it survives the winter. This means that the bees must stay warm despite the cold. Like other bees, the isolated honeybee cannot fly if the temperature falls below 10°C (50°F) and cannot walk if the temperature is below 7°C (45°F). Within the wintering hive, bees maintain

their temperature by clustering together in a dense ball; the lower the temperature, the denser the cluster. The clustered bees produce heat by constant muscular movements of their wings, legs, and abdomens. In very cold weather, the bees on the outside of the cluster keep moving toward the center, while those in the core of the cluster move to the colder outside periphery. The entire cluster moves slowly about on the combs, eating the stored honey from the combs as it moves.[14]

A summary of this paragraph might read:

Honeybees, unlike many other varieties of bee, are able to live through the winter by "clustering together in a dense ball" for warmth.

A paraphrase of the same passage would be considerably more detailed:

Honeybees, unlike many other varieties of bee (such as bumblebees), are able to live through the winter. The 30,000 to 40,000 bees within a honeybee hive could not, individually, move about in cold winter temperatures. But when "clustering together in a dense ball," the bees generate heat by constantly moving their body parts. The cluster also moves slowly about the hive, those on the periphery of the cluster moving into the center, those in the center moving to the periphery, and all eating honey stored in the combs. This nutrition, in addition to the heat generated by the cluster, enables the honeybee to survive the cold winter months.

In both the summary and the paraphrase, we've quoted Curtis's "clustering together in a dense ball," a phrase that lies at the heart of her description of wintering honeybees. For us to describe this clustering in any language other than Curtis's would be pointless when her description is admirably brief and precise.

Quoting Authoritative Language

You should use quotations that lend authority to your work. When quoting an expert or a prominent political, artistic, or historical figure, you elevate your own work by placing it in esteemed company. Quote respected figures to establish background information in a paper, and your readers will tend to perceive that information as reliable. Quote the opinions of respected figures to endorse a statement that you've made, and your statement becomes more credible to your readers. Here, in a discussion of space flight, the writer David Chandler refers to a physicist and a physicist-astronaut:

A few scientists—notably James Van Allen, discoverer of the Earth's radiation belts—have decried the expense of the manned space program and called for an almost exclusive concentration on unmanned scientific exploration instead, saying this would be far more cost-effective.

Other space scientists dispute that idea. Joseph Allen, physicist and former shuttle astronaut, says, "It seems to be argued that one takes away from the other. But before there was a manned space program, the funding on space science was zero. Now it's about $500 million a year."

---

[14]Patricia Curtis, "Winter Organization," *Biology*, 2nd ed. (New York: Worth, 1976): 822–23.

In the first paragraph, Chandler has either summarized or used an indirect quotation to incorporate remarks made by James Van Allen into the discussion on space flight. In the second paragraph, Chandler directly quotes Joseph Allen. Both quotations, indirect and direct, lend authority and legitimacy to the article, for both James Van Allen and Joseph Allen are experts on the subject of space flight. Note that Chandler provides brief but effective biographies of his sources, identifying each one so that their qualifications to speak on the subject are known to all:

James Van Allen, *discoverer of the Earth's radiation belts...*

Joseph Allen, *physicist and former shuttle astronaut...*

The phrases in italics are *appositives*. Their function is to rename the nouns they follow by providing explicit, identifying detail. Any information about a person that can be expressed in the following sentence pattern can be made into an appositive phrase:

James Van Allen is the *discoverer of the Earth's radiation belts.*

He has decried the expense of the manned space program.

Sentence with an appositive:

James Van Allen, discoverer of the Earth's radiation belts, has decried the expense of the manned space program.

Appositives (in the example above, "discoverer of the Earth's radiation belts") efficiently incorporate identifying information about the authors you quote, while adding variety to the structure of your sentences.

Incorporating Quotations into Your Sentences

Quoting Only the Part of a Sentence or Paragraph That You Need

We've said that a writer selects passages for quotation that are especially vivid, memorable, concise, or authoritative. Now put these principles into practice. Suppose that while conducting research on climate change, you've come across the following, written by a graduate student conducting his own research on the threats climate change poses to low-lying coastal areas:

> Already, the rise in sea levels is affecting Pacific Island nations like Tuvalu. If the Earth's climate continues to change, within a century we may find ourselves contemplating the unthinkable: abandoning great coastal cities like New York, Calcutta, and Tokyo for higher ground. If the potential human destruction isn't enough to force policy makers to relocate whole populations away from the coasts, in time the loss of money will. Insurance companies, the ones who pay out on billion-dollar losses from major storms, may simply stop insuring those who insist on living and working by the sea. When people can no longer insure themselves against heavy losses from

climate-related events, the inevitable course of action will be clear: to build on higher ground, further from danger. In two hundred years, the coastal maps of the world will look very different than they do today.[15]

Suppose that in this paragraph you find a sentence that will enliven your discussion:

> If the Earth's climate continues to change, within a century we may find ourselves contemplating the unthinkable: abandoning great coastal cities like New York, Calcutta, and Tokyo for higher ground.

Incorporating the Quotation into the Flow of Your Own Sentence

Once you've selected the passage you want to quote, you need to work the material into your paper in as natural and fluid a manner as possible. Here's one way to quote Hawkins:

> Allen Hawkins, graduate student in climate science at the University of Massachusetts, asserts that "within a century we may find ourselves contemplating the unthinkable: abandoning great coastal cities like New York, Calcutta, and Tokyo for higher ground."

Note that we've used an appositive to identify Hawkins. And we've used only the part of the paragraph that we thought memorable enough to quote directly.

Avoiding Freestanding Quotations

A quoted sentence should never stand by itself, as in the following example:

> We face a variety of risks that threaten large populations. "If the Earth's climate continues to change, within a century we may find ourselves contemplating the unthinkable: abandoning great coastal cities like New York, Calcutta, and Tokyo for higher ground." Unfortunately, predictions of future harm decades distant seldom mobilize present action.

Even if it were followed by a parenthetical citation, a freestanding quotation would be jarring to the reader. You need to introduce the quotation with a *signal phrase* that attributes the source, not in a parenthetical citation but in some other part of the sentence—beginning, middle, or end. Thus, you could write:

> As Allen Hawkins notes, "If the Earth's climate continues to change, within a century we may find ourselves contemplating the unthinkable: abandoning great coastal cities like New York, Calcutta, and Tokyo for higher ground."

Here's a variation with the signal phrase in the middle:

> "If the Earth's climate continues to change," asserts Allen Hawkins, "within a century we may find ourselves contemplating the unthinkable: abandoning great coastal cities like New York, Calcutta, and Tokyo for higher ground."

---

[15]Allen Hawkins, unpublished student paper.

Another alternative is to introduce a sentence-long quotation with a colon:

> But Allen Hawkins disagrees: "If the Earth's climate continues to change, within a century we may find ourselves contemplating the unthinkable: abandoning great coastal cities like New York, Calcutta, and Tokyo for higher ground."

Use colons also to introduce indented quotations (as when we introduce long quotations in this chapter).

When attributing sources in signal phrases, try to vary the standard *states, writes, says,* and so on. Stronger verbs you might consider are: *asserts, argues, maintains, insists, asks,* and even *wonders.*

MyWritingLab™   Exercise 1.7

Incorporating Quotations

Return to the article "The Baby in the Well" by Paul Bloom (pp. 9–15). Find sentences that you think make interesting points. Imagine you want to use these points in a paper you're writing on empathy. Write five different sentences that use a variety of the techniques discussed thus far to incorporate whole sentences as well as phrases from Bloom's article.

Using Ellipses

Using quotations becomes somewhat complicated when you want to quote the beginning and end of a passage but not its middle. Here's part of a paragraph from Thoreau's *Walden:*

> To read well, that is to read true books in a true spirit, is a noble exercise, and one that will task the reader more than any exercise which the customs of the day esteem. It requires a training such as the athletes underwent, the steady intention almost of the whole life to this object. Books must be read as deliberately and reservedly as they were written.[16]

And here is how we can use this material in a quotation:

> Reading well is hard work, writes Henry David Thoreau in *Walden,* "that will task the reader more than any exercise which the customs of the day esteem.... Books must be read as deliberately and reservedly as they were written."

Whenever you quote a sentence but delete words from it, as we have done above, indicate this deletion to the reader with three spaced periods—called an "ellipsis"—in the sentence at the point of deletion. The rationale for using an ellipsis mark is that a direct quotation must be reproduced *exactly* as it was written or spoken. When writers delete or change any part of the quoted material, readers must be alerted so they don't think the changes were part of the original. When deleting an entire sentence or

---

[16]Henry David Thoreau, *Walden* (New York: Signet Classic, 1960): 72.

sentences from a quoted paragraph, as in the preceding example, end the sentence you have quoted with a period, place the ellipsis, and continue the quotation.

If you are deleting the middle of a single sentence, use an ellipsis in place of the deleted words:

> "To read well...is a noble exercise, and one that will task the reader more than any exercise which the customs of the day esteem."

If you are deleting material from the end of one sentence through to the beginning of another sentence, add a sentence period before the ellipsis:

> "It requires a training such as the athletes underwent.... Books must be read as deliberately and reservedly as they were written."

If you begin your quotation of an author in the middle of his or her sentence, you need not indicate deleted words with an ellipsis. Be sure, however, that the syntax of the quotation fits smoothly with the syntax of your sentence:

> Reading "is a noble exercise," writes Henry David Thoreau.

Using Brackets to Add or Substitute Words

Use brackets whenever you need to add or substitute words in a quoted sentence. The brackets indicate to the reader a word or phrase that does not appear in the original passage but that you have inserted to prevent confusion. For example, when a pronoun's antecedent would be unclear to readers, delete the pronoun from the sentence and substitute an identifying word or phrase in brackets. When you make such a substitution, no ellipsis mark is needed. Assume that you wish to quote either of the underlined sentences in the following passage by Jane Yolen:

> Golden Press's *Walt Disney's Cinderella* set the new pattern for America's Cinderella. This book's text is coy and condescending. (Sample: "And her best friends of all were—guess who—the mice!") The illustrations are poor cartoons. And Cinderella herself is a disaster. She cowers as her sisters rip her homemade ball gown to shreds. (Not even homemade by Cinderella, but by the mice and birds.) <u>She answers her stepmother with whines and pleadings. She is a sorry excuse for a heroine, pitiable and useless</u>. She cannot perform even a simple action to save herself, though she is warned by her friends, the mice. She does not hear them because she is "off in a world of dreams." Cinderella begs, she whimpers, and at last has to be rescued by—guess who—the mice![17]

In quoting one of these sentences, you would need to identify to whom the pronoun *she* refers. You can do this inside the quotation by using brackets:

> Jane Yolen believes that "[Cinderella] is a sorry excuse for a heroine, pitiable and useless."

[17]Jane Yolen, "America's 'Cinderella,'" *Children's Literature in Education* 8 (1977): 22.

When the pronoun begins the sentence to be quoted, you can identify the pronoun outside the quotation and begin quoting your source one word later:

> Jane Yolen believes that in the Golden Press version, Cinderella "is a sorry excuse for a heroine, pitiable and useless."

WHEN TO SUMMARIZE, PARAPHRASE, AND QUOTE

Summarize:

- To present main points of a lengthy passage (article or book)
- To condense peripheral points necessary to discussion

Paraphrase:

- To clarify a short passage
- To emphasize main points

Quote:

- To capture another writer's particularly memorable language
- To capture another writer's clearly and economically stated language
- To lend authority and credibility to your own writing

Here's another example of a case where the pronoun needing identification occurs in the middle of the sentence to be quoted. Newspaper reporters must use brackets when quoting a source, who in an interview might say this:

> After the fire they did not return to the station house for three hours.

If the reporter wants to use this sentence in an article, he or she needs to identify the pronoun:

> An official from City Hall, speaking on the condition that he not be identified, said, "After the fire [the officers] did not return to the station house for three hours."

You will also need to add bracketed information to a quoted sentence when a reference essential to the sentence's meaning is implied but not stated directly. Read the following paragraph from Walter Isaacson's biography of Albert Einstein, *Einstein: His Life and Universe*:

> Newton had bequeathed to Einstein a universe in which time had an absolute existence that tick-tocked along independent of objects and observers, and in which space likewise had an absolute existence. Gravity was thought to be a force that masses exerted on one another rather mysteriously across empty space. Within this framework, objects obeyed mechanical laws that

had proved remarkably accurate—almost perfect—in explaining everything
from the orbits of the planets, to the diffusion of gases, to the jiggling of mol-
ecules, to the propagation of sound (though not light) waves.

If you wanted to quote only the underlined sentence above, you would need
to provide readers with a bracketed explanation; otherwise, the phrase "this
framework" would be unclear. Here is how you would manage the quotation:

> According to Walter Isaacson, Newton's universe was extremely regular
> and predictable:
>> Within this framework [that time and space exist independently of their
>> observation and that gravity results from masses exerting a remote attraction
>> on one another], objects obeyed mechanical laws that had proved remark-
>> ably accurate—almost perfect—in explaining everything from the orbits of
>> the planets, to the diffusion of gases, to the jiggling of molecules, to the
>> propagation of sound (though not light) waves. (223)

INCORPORATING QUOTATIONS INTO YOUR SENTENCES

- *Quote only the part of a sentence or paragraph that you need.* Use no more of the writer's language than necessary to make or reinforce your point.
- *Incorporate the quotation into the flow of your own sentence.* The quotation must fit, both syntactically and stylistically, into your surrounding language.
- *Avoid freestanding quotations.* A quoted sentence should never stand by itself. Use a *signal phrase*—at the beginning, the middle, or the end of the sentence—to attribute the source of the quotation.
- *Use ellipsis marks.* Indicate deleted language in the middle of a quoted sentence with ellipsis marks. Deleted language at the beginning or end of a sentence generally does not require ellipsis marks.
- *Use brackets to add or substitute words.* Use brackets to add or substitute words in a quoted sentence when the meaning of the quotation would otherwise be unclear—for example, when the antecedent of a quoted pronoun is ambiguous.

MyWritingLab™

Exercise 1.8

Using Brackets

Write your own sentences incorporating the following quotations. Use brackets
to clarify information that isn't clear outside its original context—and refer to the
original sources to remind yourself of this context.

From the David Chandler paragraph on James Van Allen (p. 42):

   a.   Other space scientists *dispute that idea.*
   b.   Now *it's about $500 million a year.*

From the Jane Yolen excerpt on Cinderella (p. 46):

  a. *This book's* text is coy and condescending.
  b. *She* cannot perform even a simple action to save herself, though she is warned by her friends, the mice.
  c. She does not hear *them* because she is "off in a world of dreams."

Remember that when you quote the work of another, you are obligated to credit—or cite—the author's work properly; otherwise, you may be guilty of plagiarism. See pages 232–238 for guidance on citing sources.

AVOIDING PLAGIARISM

1.7 Avoid plagiarism by citing sources and using your own words and sentence structure.

Plagiarism is generally defined as the attempt to pass off the work of another as one's own. Whether born out of calculation or desperation, plagiarism is the least tolerated offense in the academic world. The fact that most plagiarism is unintentional—arising from an ignorance of the conventions rather than deceitfulness—makes no difference to many professors.

The ease of cutting and pasting whole blocks of text from Web sources into one's own paper makes it tempting for some to take the easy way out and avoid doing their own research and writing. But, apart from the serious ethical issues involved, the same technology that makes such acts possible also makes it possible for instructors to detect them. Software marketed to instructors allows them to conduct Web searches using suspicious phrases as keywords. The results often provide irrefutable evidence of plagiarism.

Of course, plagiarism is not confined to students. Recent years have seen a number of high-profile cases—some of them reaching the front pages of newspapers—of well-known scholars who were shown to have copied passages from sources into their own book manuscripts without proper attribution. In some cases, the scholars maintained that these appropriations were simply a matter of carelessness, that in the press and volume of work, they had lost track of which words were theirs and which were the words of their sources. But such excuses sounded hollow: These careless acts inevitably embarrassed the scholars professionally, tarnished their otherwise fine work and reputations, and disappointed their many admirers.

You can avoid plagiarism and charges of plagiarism by following the basic rules provided on page 50.

Following is a passage from an article by Richard Rovere on Senator Joseph P. McCarthy, along with several student versions of the ideas represented.

> McCarthy never seemed to believe in himself or in anything he had said. He knew that Communists were not in charge of American foreign policy. He knew that they weren't running the United States Army. He knew that he had spent five years looking for Communists in the government and that—although some must certainly have been there, since Communists had turned up in practically every other major government in the world—he hadn't come up with even one.[18]

One student version of this passage reads:

> McCarthy never believed in himself or in anything he had said. He knew that
> Communists were not in charge of American foreign policy and weren't running the
> United States Army. He knew that he had spent five years looking for Communists
> in the government, and although there must certainly have been some there, since
> Communists were in practically every other major government in the world, he
> hadn't come up with even one.

Clearly, this is intentional plagiarism. The student has copied the original passage almost word for word.

Here is another version of the same passage:

> McCarthy knew that Communists were not running foreign policy or the army. He
> also knew that although there must have been some Communists in the government,
> he hadn't found a single one, even though he had spent five years looking.

This student has attempted to put the ideas into her own words, but both the wording and the sentence structure are so heavily dependent on the original passage that even if it *were* cited, most professors would consider it plagiarism.

In the following version, the student has sufficiently changed the wording and sentence structure, and she uses a *signal phrase* (a phrase used to introduce a quotation or paraphrase, signaling to the reader that the words to follow come from someone else) to properly credit the information to Rovere so that there is no question of plagiarism:

> According to Richard Rovere, McCarthy was fully aware that Communists were run-
> ning neither the government nor the army. He also knew that he hadn't found a
> single Communist in government, even after a lengthy search (192).

And although this is not a matter of plagiarism, as noted above, it's essential to quote accurately. You are not permitted to change any part of a quotation or to omit any part of it without using brackets or ellipses.

RULES FOR AVOIDING PLAGIARISM

- Cite *all* quoted material and *all* summarized and paraphrased material, unless the information is common knowledge (e.g., the Civil War was fought from 1861 to 1865).

- Make sure that both the *wording* and the *sentence structure* of your summaries and paraphrases are substantially your own.

MyWritingLab™   Visit Ch. 1 Summary, Paraphrase, and Quotation in MyWritingLab to test your understanding of the chapter objectives.

---

[18]Richard Rovere, "The Most Gifted and Successful Demagogue This Country Has Ever Known,"
New York Times Magazine, 30 Apr. 1967.

Critical Reading and Critique

After reading this chapter, you will be able to:

2.1 Read an article, editorial, or chapter critically.

2.2 Write a critique of an article, editorial, or chapter.

CRITICAL READING

2.1 Read an article, editorial, or chapter critically.

When writing papers in college, you are often called on to respond critically to source materials. Critical reading requires the abilities to both summarize and evaluate a presentation. As you have seen in Chapter 1, a *summary* is a brief restatement in your own words of the content of a passage. An *evaluation* is a more ambitious undertaking. In your college work, you read to gain and *use* new information. But because sources are not equally valid or equally useful, you must learn to distinguish critically among them by evaluating them.

There is no ready-made formula for determining validity. Critical reading and its written equivalent—the *critique*—require discernment, sensitivity, imagination, knowledge of the subject, and, above all, willingness to become involved in what you read. These skills are developed only through repeated practice. But you must begin somewhere, and so we recommend you start by posing two broad questions about passages, articles, and books that you read: (1) To what extent does the author succeed in his or her purpose? (2) To what extent do you agree with the author?

Question 1: To What Extent Does the Author Succeed in His or Her Purpose?

All critical reading *begins with an accurate summary.* Before attempting an evaluation, you must be able to locate an author's thesis and identify the selection's content and structure. You must understand the author's *purpose.* Authors write to inform, to persuade, and to entertain. A given piece may be primarily *informative* (a summary of the research on cloning), primarily *persuasive* (an argument on what the government should do to alleviate homelessness), or primarily *entertaining* (a play about the frustrations of young lovers). Or it may be all three (as in John Steinbeck's novel *The Grapes of Wrath,* about migrant workers during the Great Depression). Sometimes authors are not fully conscious of their purpose. Sometimes their purpose changes as they write. Also, multiple purposes can overlap: A piece of writing may need to inform the reader about an issue in order to make a persuasive point. But if the finished piece is coherent, it will have a primary reason for having been written, and it should be apparent that the author is attempting primarily to inform, persuade, or entertain a particular audience.

To identify this primary reason—this purpose—is your first job as a critical reader. Your next job is to determine how successful the author has been in achieving this objective.

WHERE DO WE FIND WRITTEN CRITIQUES?

Here are just a few of the types of writing that involve critique:

Academic Writing

- **Research papers** critique sources in order to establish their usefulness.
- **Position papers** stake out a position by critiquing other positions.
- **Book reviews** combine summary with critique.
- **Essay exams** demonstrate understanding of course material by critiquing it.

Workplace Writing

- **Legal briefs and legal arguments** critique previous arguments made or anticipated by opposing counsel.
- **Business plans and proposals** critique other less cost-effective, efficient, or reasonable approaches.
- **Policy briefs** communicate strengths and weaknesses of policies and legislation through critique.

As a critical reader, you bring various criteria, or standards of judgment, to bear when you read pieces intended to inform, persuade, or entertain.

Writing to Inform

A piece intended to inform will provide definitions, describe or report on a process, recount a story, give historical background, and/or provide facts and figures. An informational piece responds to questions such as:

What (or who) is _____?

How does _____ work?

What is the controversy or problem about?

What happened?

How and why did it happen?

What were the results?

What are the arguments for and against _____?

To the extent that an author answers these and related questions and that the answers are a matter of verifiable record (you could check for accuracy if you had the time and inclination), the selection is intended to inform. Having identified such an intention, you can organize your response by considering three other criteria: accuracy, significance, and fair interpretation of information.

Evaluating Informative Writing

Accuracy of Information If you are going to use any of the information presented, you must be satisfied that it is trustworthy. One of your responsibilities as a critical reader, then, is to find out if the information is accurate. This means you should check facts against other sources. Government publications are often good resources for verifying facts about political legislation, population data, crime statistics, and the like. You can also search key terms in library databases and on the Web. Since material on the Web is essentially self-published, however, you must be especially vigilant in assessing its legitimacy. A wealth of useful information is now available on the Internet—as are distorted "facts," unsupported opinion, and hidden agendas.

Significance of Information   One useful question that you can put to a reading is "So what?" In the case of selections that attempt to inform, you may reasonably wonder whether the information makes a difference. What can the reader gain from this information? How is knowledge advanced by the publication of this material? Is the information of importance to you or to others in a particular audience? Why or why not?

Fair Interpretation of Information At times you will read reports whose sole purpose is to relate raw data or information. In these cases, you will build your response on Question 1, introduced on page 52: To what extent does the author succeed in his or her purpose? More frequently, once an author has presented information, he or she will attempt to evaluate or interpret it—which is only reasonable, since information that has not been evaluated or interpreted is of little use. One of your tasks as a critical reader is to make a distinction between the author's presentation of facts and figures and his or her attempts to evaluate them. Watch for shifts from straightforward descriptions of factual information ("20 percent of the population") to assertions about what this information means ("a *mere* 20 percent of the population"), what its implications are, and so on. Pay attention to whether the logic with which the author connects interpretation with facts is sound. You may find that the information is valuable but the interpretation is not. Perhaps the author's conclusions are not justified. Could you offer a contrary explanation for the same facts? Does more information need to be gathered before firm conclusions can be drawn? Why?

Writing to Persuade

Writing is frequently intended to persuade—that is, to influence the reader's thinking. To make a persuasive case, the writer must begin with an assertion that is arguable, some statement about which reasonable people could disagree. Such an assertion, when it serves as the essential organizing principle of the article or book, is called a *thesis.* Here are two examples:

> Because they do not speak English, many children in this affluent land are being denied their fundamental right to equal educational opportunity.

> Bilingual education, which has been stridently promoted by a small group of activists with their own agenda, is detrimental to the very students it is supposed to serve.

Thesis statements such as these—and the subsequent assertions used to help support them—represent conclusions that authors have drawn as a result of researching and thinking about an issue. You go through the same process yourself when you write persuasive papers or critiques. And just as you are entitled to evaluate critically the assertions of authors you read, so your professors—and other students—are entitled to evaluate *your* assertions, whether they be written arguments or comments made in class discussion.

Keep in mind that writers organize arguments by arranging evidence to support one conclusion and to oppose (or dismiss) another. You can assess the validity of an argument and its conclusion by determining whether the author has (1) clearly defined key terms, (2) used information fairly, and (3) argued logically and not fallaciously (see pp. 59–62).

MyWritingLab™   Exercise 2.1

Informative and Persuasive Thesis Statements

With a partner from your class, identify at least one informative and one persuasive thesis statement from two passages of your own choosing. Photocopy these passages and highlight the statements you have selected.

As an alternative, and also working with a partner, write one informative and one persuasive thesis statement for *three* of the topics listed at the end of this exercise. For example, for the topic of prayer in schools, your informative thesis statement could read:

> Both advocates and opponents of school prayer frame their position as a matter of freedom.

Your persuasive thesis statement might be worded:

> As long as schools don't dictate what kinds of prayers students should say, then school prayer should be allowed and even encouraged.

Don't worry about taking a position that you agree with or feel you could support; this exercise doesn't require that you write an essay. The topics:

school prayer

gun control

immigration

stem cell research

grammar instruction in English class

violent lyrics in music

teaching computer skills in primary schools

curfews in college dormitories

course registration procedures

Evaluating Persuasive Writing

Read the argument that follows on the cancellation of the National Aeronautics and Space Administration's lunar program. We will illustrate our discussion on defining terms, using information fairly, and arguing logically by referring to Charles Krauthammer's argument, which appeared as an op-ed in the *Washington Post* on July 17, 2009. The model critique that follows these illustrations will be based on this same argument.

THE MOON WE LEFT BEHIND*

Charles Krauthammer

Michael Crichton once wrote that if you told a physicist in 1899 that within a hundred years humankind would, among other wonders (nukes, commercial airlines), "travel to the moon, and then lose interest...the physicist would almost certainly pronounce you mad." In 2000, I quoted these lines expressing

*From *The Washington Post*, July 17, 2009 © 2009 Washington Post Company. All rights reserved. Used by permission and protected by the Copyright Laws of the United States. The printing, copying, redistribution, or retransmission of this Content without express written permission is prohibited.

Crichton's incredulity at America's abandonment of the moon. It is now 2009 and the moon recedes ever further.

Next week marks the 40th anniversary of the first moon landing. We say we will return in 2020. But that promise was made by a previous president, and this president [Obama] has defined himself as the antimatter to George Bush. Moreover, for all of Barack Obama's Kennedyesque qualities, he has expressed none of Kennedy's enthusiasm for human space exploration.

So with the Apollo moon program long gone, and with Constellation,[1] its supposed successor, still little more than a hope, we remain in retreat from space. Astonishing. After countless millennia of gazing and dreaming, we finally got off the ground at Kitty Hawk in 1903. Within 66 years, a nanosecond in human history, we'd landed on the moon. Then five more landings, 10 more moonwalkers and, in the decades since, nothing.

To be more precise: almost 40 years spent in low Earth orbit studying, well, zero-G nausea and sundry cosmic mysteries. We've done it with the most beautiful, intricate, complicated—and ultimately, hopelessly impractical—machine ever built by man: the space shuttle. We turned this magnificent bird into a truck for hauling goods and people to a tinkertoy we call the international space station, itself created in a fit of post-Cold War internationalist absentmindedness as a place where people of differing nationality can sing "Kumbaya" while weightless.

5   The shuttle is now too dangerous, too fragile and too expensive. Seven more flights and then it is retired, going—like the Spruce Goose[2] and the Concorde[3]— into the Museum of Things Too Beautiful and Complicated to Survive.

America's manned space program is in shambles. Fourteen months from today, for the first time since 1962, the United States will be incapable not just of sending a man to the moon but of sending anyone into Earth orbit. We'll be totally grounded. We'll have to beg a ride from the Russians or perhaps even the Chinese.

So what, you say? Don't we have problems here on Earth? Oh, please. Poverty and disease and social ills will always be with us. If we'd waited for them to be rectified before venturing out, we'd still be living in caves.

Yes, we have a financial crisis. No one's asking for a crash Manhattan Project. All we need is sufficient funding from the hundreds of billions being showered

---

[1]Constellation was a NASA human spaceflight program designed to develop post–space shuttle vehicles capable of traveling to the moon and perhaps to Mars. Authorized in 2005, the program was canceled by President Obama in 2010.

[2]Spruce Goose was the informal name bestowed by critics on the H4 Hercules, a heavy transport aircraft designed and built during World War II by the Hughes Aircraft Company. Built almost entirely of birch (not spruce) because of wartime restrictions on war materials, the aircraft boasted the largest height and wingspan of any aircraft in history. Only one prototype was built, and the aircraft made only one flight, on November 2, 1947. It is currently housed at the Evergreen Aviation Museum in McMinnville, Oregon.

[3]Admired for its elegant design as well as its speed, the Concorde was a supersonic passenger airliner built by a British-French consortium. It was first flown in 1969, entered service in 1976 (with regular flights to and from London, Paris, Washington, and New York), and was retired in 2003, a casualty of economic pressures. Only twenty Concordes were built.

from Washington—"stimulus" monies that, unlike Eisenhower's interstate highway system or Kennedy's Apollo program, will leave behind not a trace on our country or our consciousness—to build Constellation and get us back to Earth orbit and the moon a half-century after the original landing.

Why do it? It's not for practicality. We didn't go to the moon to spin off cooling suits and freeze-dried fruit. Any technological return is a bonus, not a reason. We go for the wonder and glory of it. Or, to put it less grandly, for its immense possibilities. We choose to do such things, said JFK, "not because they are easy, but because they are hard." And when you do such magnificently hard things—send sailing a Ferdinand Magellan or a Neil Armstrong—you open new human possibility in ways utterly unpredictable.

10   The greatest example? Who could have predicted that the moon voyages would create the most potent impetus to—and symbol of—environmental consciousness here on Earth: Earthrise, the now iconic Blue Planet photograph brought back by Apollo 8?

Ironically, that new consciousness about the uniqueness and fragility of Earth focused contemporary imagination away from space and back to Earth. We are now deep into that hyper-terrestrial phase, the age of iPod and Facebook, of social networking and eco-consciousness.

But look up from your BlackBerry one night. That is the moon. On it are exactly 12 sets of human footprints—untouched, unchanged, abandoned. For the first time in history, the moon is not just a mystery and a muse, but a nightly rebuke. A vigorous young president once summoned us to this new frontier, calling the voyage "the most hazardous and dangerous and greatest adventure on which man has ever embarked." And so we did it. We came. We saw. Then we retreated.

How could we?

MyWritingLab™   Exercise 2.2

Critical Reading Practice

Look back at the Critical Reading for Summary box on pages 6–7 of Chapter 1. Use each of the guidelines listed there to examine the essay by Charles Krauthammer. Note in the margins of the selection, or on a separate sheet of paper, the essay's main point, subpoints, and use of examples.

Persuasive Strategies

Clearly Defined Terms   The validity of an argument depends to some degree on how carefully an author has defined key terms. Take the assertion, for example, that American society must be grounded in "family values." Just what do people who use this phrase mean by it? The validity of their argument depends on whether they and their readers agree on a definition of "family values"—as well as what it means to be "grounded in" family values. If an author writes that in the recent past, "America's elites accepted as a matter of course that a free society can sustain itself only through virtue and temperance in the people,"[4] readers need to know what exactly the author means by "elites" and by "virtue and temperance" before they can assess the validity of the argument. In such cases, the success of the argument—its ability to persuade—hinges on the definition of a term. So, in responding to an argument, be sure you (and the author) are clear on what exactly is being argued. Unless you are, no informed response is possible.

Note that in addition to their *denotative* meaning (their specific or literal meaning), many words carry a *connotative* meaning (their suggestive, associative, or emotional meaning). For example, the denotative meaning of "home" is simply the house or apartment where one lives. But the connotative meaning—with its associations of family, belongingness, refuge, safety, and familiarity—adds a significant emotional component to this literal meaning. (See more on connotation in "Emotionally Loaded Terms," p. 59.)

In the course of his argument, Krauthammer writes of "America's abandonment of the moon" and of the fact that we have "retreated" from lunar exploration. Consider the words "abandon" and "retreat." What do these words mean to you? Look them up in a dictionary for precise definitions (note all possible meanings provided). In what contexts are we most likely to see these words used? What emotional meaning and significance do they generally carry? For example, what do we usually think of people who abandon a marriage or military units that retreat? To what extent does it appear to you that Krauthammer is using these words in accordance with one or more of their dictionary definitions, their denotations? To what extent does the force of his argument also depend upon the power of these words' connotative meanings?

When writing a paper, you will need to decide, like Krauthammer, which terms to define and which you can assume the reader will define in the same way you do. As the writer of a critique, you should identify and discuss any undefined or ambiguous term that might give rise to confusion.

Fair Use of Information   Information is used as evidence in support of arguments. When you encounter such evidence, ask yourself two questions: (1) "Is the information accurate and up to date?" At least a portion of an argument becomes invalid when the information used to support it is wrong or stale. (2) "Has the author cited *representative* information?" The evidence used in an argument must be presented in a spirit of fair play. An author is less than ethical when he presents only the evidence favoring his own views even though he is well aware that contrary evidence exists. For instance, it would be dishonest to argue that an economic recession is imminent and to cite only indicators of economic downturn while ignoring and failing to cite contrary (positive) evidence.

"The Moon We Left Behind" is not an information-heavy essay. The success of the piece turns on the author's powers of persuasion, not on his use of facts and figures. Krauthammer does, however, offer some key facts relating

---

[4]Charles Murray, "The Coming White Underclass," *Wall Street Journal*, October 20, 1993.

to Project Apollo and the fact that President Obama was not inclined to back a NASA-operated lunar-landing program. And, in fact, Krauthammer's fears were confirmed in February 2010, about six months after he wrote "The Moon We Left Behind," when the president canceled NASA's plans for further manned space exploration flights in favor of government support for commercial space operations.

Logical Argumentation: Avoiding Logical Fallacies

At some point, you'll need to respond to the logic of the argument itself. To be convincing, an argument should be governed by principles of *logic*—clear and orderly thinking. This does *not* mean that an argument cannot be biased. A biased argument—that is, an argument weighted toward one point of view and against others, which is in fact the nature of argument—may be valid as long as it is logically sound.

Let's examine several types of faulty thinking and logical fallacies you will need to watch for.

Emotionally Loaded Terms   Writers sometimes attempt to sway readers by using emotionally charged words. Words with positive connotations (e.g., "family values") are intended to sway readers to the author's point of view; words with negative connotations (e.g., "paying the price") try to sway readers away from an opposing point of view. The fact that an author uses emotionally loaded terms does not necessarily invalidate an argument. Emotional appeals are perfectly legitimate and time-honored modes of persuasion. But in academic writing, which is grounded in logical argumentation, they should not be the *only* means of persuasion. You should be sensitive to *how* emotionally loaded terms are being used. In particular, are they being used deceptively or to hide the essential facts?

We've already noted Krauthammer's use of the emotionally loaded terms "abandonment" and "retreat" when referring to the end of the manned space program. Notice also his use of the term "Kumbaya" in the sentence declaring that the international space station was "created in a fit of post-Cold War internationalist absentmindedness as a place where people of differing nationality can sing 'Kumbaya' while weightless." "Kumbaya" is an African-American spiritual dating from the 1930s, often sung by scouts around campfires. The song uses the word "Kumbaya" to connote spiritual unity among peoples, but in more recent times, the term has been used sarcastically to poke fun at what is viewed as a rose-colored optimism about human nature. Is Krauthammer drawing upon the emotional power of the original meaning or upon the more recent significance of this term? How does his particular use of "Kumbaya" strengthen (or weaken) his argument? What appears to be the difference in his mind between the value of the international space station and the value of returning to the moon? As someone evaluating the essay, you should be alert to this appeal to your emotions and then judge whether the appeal is fair and convincing. Above all, you should not let an emotional appeal blind you to shortcomings of logic, ambiguously defined terms, or a misuse of facts.

***Ad Hominem* Argument**   In an *ad hominem* argument, the writer rejects opposing views by attacking the person who holds them. By calling opponents names, an author avoids the issue. Consider this excerpt from a political speech:

> I could more easily accept my opponent's plan to increase revenues by collecting on delinquent tax bills if he had paid more than a hundred dollars in state taxes in each of the past three years. But the fact is, he's a millionaire with a millionaire's tax shelters. This man hasn't paid a wooden nickel for the state services he and his family depend on. So I ask you: Is *he* the one to be talking about taxes to *us?*

It could well be that the opponent has paid virtually no state taxes for three years, but this fact has nothing to do with, and is used as a ploy to divert attention from, the merits of a specific proposal for increasing revenues. The proposal is lost in the attack against the man himself, an attack that violates principles of logic. Writers (and speakers) should make their points by citing evidence in support of their views and by challenging contrary evidence.

In "The Moon We Left Behind," Krauthammer's only individual target is President Obama. While he does, at several points, unfavorably compare Obama to Kennedy, he does not do so in an *ad hominem* way. That is, he attacks Obama less for his personal qualities than for his policy decision to close down NASA's manned space program. At most, he laments that Obama "has expressed none of Kennedy's enthusiasm for human space exploration."

Faulty Cause and Effect   The fact that one event precedes another in time does not mean that the first event has caused the second. An example: Fish begin dying by the thousands in a lake near your hometown. An environmental group immediately cites chemical dumping by several manufacturing plants as the cause. But other causes are possible: A disease might have affected the fish; the growth of algae might have contributed to the deaths; or acid rain might be a factor. The origins of an event are usually complex and are not always traceable to a single cause. So you must carefully examine cause-and-effect reasoning when you find a writer using it. In Latin, this fallacy is known as *post hoc, ergo propter hoc* ("after this, therefore because of this").

Toward the end of "The Moon We Left Behind," Krauthammer declares that having turned our "imagination away from space and back to Earth...[w]e are now deep into that hyper-terrestrial phase, the age of iPod and Facebook, of social networking and eco-consciousness." He appears here to be suggesting a pattern of cause and effect: that as a people, we are no longer looking outward but, rather, turning inward; and this shift in our attention and focus has resulted in—or at least is a significant cause of—the death of the manned space program. Questions for a critique might include the following: (1) To what extent do you agree with Krauthammer's premise that we live in an inward-looking, rather than an outward-looking, age and that it is fair to call our present historical period "the age of iPod and Facebook"? (2) To what extent do you agree that because we may live in such an age, the space program no longer enjoys broad public or political support?

TONE

"Tone" refers to the overall emotional effect produced by a writer's choice of language. Writers might use especially emphatic words to create a tone: A film reviewer might refer to a "magnificent performance," or a columnist might criticize "sleazeball politics."

These are extreme examples of tone; tone can also be more subtle, particularly if the writer makes a special effort *not* to inject emotion into the writing. As we indicated in the section on emotionally loaded terms, the fact that a writer's tone is highly emotional does not necessarily mean that the writer's argument is invalid. Conversely, a neutral tone does not ensure an argument's validity.

Many instructors discourage student writing that projects a highly emotional tone, considering it inappropriate for academic or preprofessional work. (One sure sign of emotion: the exclamation mark, which should be used sparingly.)

Either/Or Reasoning   Either/or reasoning also results from an unwillingness to recognize complexity. If in analyzing a problem an author artificially restricts the range of possible solutions by offering only two courses of action and then rejects the one that he opposes, he cannot logically argue that the remaining course of action, which he favors, is therefore the only one that makes sense. Usually, several other options (at least) are possible. For whatever reason, the author has chosen to overlook them. As an example, suppose you are reading a selection on genetic engineering in which the author builds an argument on the basis of the following:

> Research in gene splicing is at a crossroads: Either scientists will be carefully monitored by civil authorities and their efforts limited to acceptable applications, such as disease control; or, lacking regulatory guidelines, scientists will set their own ethical standards and begin programs in embryonic manipulation that, however well intended, exceed the proper limits of human knowledge.

Certainly, other possibilities for genetic engineering exist beyond the two mentioned here. But the author limits debate by establishing an either/or choice. Such a limitation is artificial and does not allow for complexity. As a critical reader, you need to be on the alert for reasoning based on restrictive, either/or alternatives.

Hasty Generalization   Writers are guilty of hasty generalization when they draw their conclusions from too little evidence or from unrepresentative evidence. To argue that scientists should not proceed with the Human Genome Project because a recent editorial urged that the project be abandoned is to make a hasty generalization. That lone editorial may be unrepresentative of the views of most individuals—both scientists and laypeople—who have studied and written about the matter. To argue that one should never obey authority because Stanley Milgram's Yale University experiments in the 1960s showed the dangers of obedience is to ignore the fact that Milgram's experiments were concerned primarily with obedience to *immoral* authority. The experimental situation was unrepresentative of most routine demands for obedience—for example, to obey a parental rule or to comply with a summons for jury duty—and a conclusion about the malevolence of all authority would be a hasty generalization.

False Analogy   Comparing one person, event, or issue to another may be illuminating, but it can also be confusing or misleading. Differences between the two may be more significant than their similarities, and conclusions drawn from one may not necessarily apply to the other. A candidate for governor or president who argues that her experience as CEO of a major business would make her effective in governing a state or the country is assuming an analogy between the business and the political/civic worlds that does not hold up to examination. Most businesses are hierarchical, or top down: when a CEO issues an order, he or she can expect it to be carried out without argument. But governors and presidents command only their own executive branches. They cannot issue orders to independent legislatures or courts (much less private citizens); they can only attempt to persuade. In this case the implied analogy fails to convince the thoughtful reader or listener.

Begging the Question   To beg the question is to assume as proven fact the very thesis being argued. To assert, for example, that America does not need a new health care delivery system because America currently has the best health care in the world does not prove anything: It merely repeats the claim in different—and equally unproven—words. This fallacy is also known as *circular reasoning*.

Non Sequitur   *Non sequitur* is Latin for "it does not follow"; the term is used to describe a conclusion that does not logically follow from the premise. "Since minorities have made such great strides in the past few decades," a writer may argue, "we no longer need affirmative action programs." Aside from the fact that the premise itself is arguable (*Have* minorities made such great strides?), it does not follow that because minorities *may* have made great strides there is no further need for affirmative action programs.

Oversimplification   Be alert for writers who offer easy solutions to complicated problems. "America's economy will be strong again if we all 'buy American,'" a politician may argue. But the problems of America's economy are complex and cannot be solved by a slogan or a simple change in buying habits. Likewise, a writer who argues that we should ban genetic engineering assumes that simple solutions ("just say no") will be sufficient to deal with the complex moral dilemmas raised by this new technology.

MyWritingLab™   Exercise 2.3

Understanding Logical Fallacies

Make a list of the nine logical fallacies discussed in the preceding section. Briefly define each one in your own words. Then, in a group of three or four classmates, review your definitions and the examples we've provided for each logical fallacy. Collaborate with your group to find or invent additional examples for each of the fallacies. Compare your examples with those generated by the other groups in your class.

Writing to Entertain

Authors write not only to inform and persuade but also to entertain. One response to entertainment is a hearty laugh, but it is possible to entertain without encouraging laughter: A good book or play or poem may prompt you to reflect, grow wistful, become elated, get angry. Laughter is only one of many possible reactions. Like a response to an informative piece or an argument, your response to an essay, poem, story, play, novel, or film should be precisely stated and carefully developed. Ask yourself some of the following questions (you won't have space to explore all of them, but try to consider the most important ones):

- Did I care for the portrayal of a certain character?
- Did that character (or a group of characters united by occupation, age, ethnicity, etc.) seem overly sentimental, for example, or heroic?
- Did his adversaries seem too villainous or stupid?
- Were the situations believable?
- Was the action interesting or merely formulaic?
- Was the theme developed subtly or powerfully, or did the work come across as preachy or unconvincing?
- Did the action at the end of the work follow plausibly from what had come before? Was the language fresh and incisive or stale and predictable?

Explain as specifically as possible what elements of the work seemed effective or ineffective and why. Offer an overall assessment, elaborating on your views.

Question 2: To What Extent Do You Agree with the Author?

A critical evaluation consists of two parts. The first part, just discussed, assesses the accuracy and effectiveness of an argument in terms of the author's logic and use of evidence. The second part, discussed here, responds to the argument—that is, agrees or disagrees with it.

Identify Points of Agreement and Disagreement

Be precise in identifying where you agree and disagree with an author. State as clearly as possible what *you* believe, in relation to what the author believes, as presented in the piece. Whether you agree enthusiastically, agree with reservations, or disagree, you can organize your reactions in two parts:

- Summarize the author's position.
- State your own position and explain why you believe as you do. The elaboration, in effect, becomes an argument itself, and this is true regardless of the position you take.

Any opinion that you express is effective to the extent you support it by supplying evidence from your reading (which should be properly cited), your observation, or your personal experience. Without such evidence, opinions cannot be authoritative. "I thought the article on inflation was lousy." Or: "It was terrific." Why? "I just thought so, that's all." Such opinions have no value because the criticism is imprecise: The critic has taken neither the time to read the article carefully nor the time to carefully explore his or her own reactions.

MyWritingLab™   Exercise 2.4

Exploring Your Viewpoints—in Three Paragraphs

Go to a Web site that presents short persuasive essays on current social issues, such as reason.com, opinion-pages.org, drudgereport.com, or Speakout.com. Or go to an Internet search engine like Google or Bing and type in a social issue together with the word "articles," "editorials," or "opinion," and see what you find. Locate a selection on a topic of interest that takes a clear, argumentative position. Print out the selection on which you choose to focus.

- Write one paragraph summarizing the author's key argument.
- Write two paragraphs articulating your agreement or disagreement with the author. (Devote each paragraph to a *single* point of agreement or disagreement.)

Be sure to explain why you think or feel the way you do and, wherever possible, cite relevant evidence—from your reading, experience, or observation.

Explore the Reasons for Agreement and Disagreement: Evaluate Assumptions

One way of elaborating your reactions to a reading is to explore the underlying *reasons* for agreement and disagreement. Your reactions are based largely on assumptions that you hold and how those assumptions compare with the author's. An *assumption* is a fundamental statement about the world and its operations that you take to be true. Often, a writer will express an assumption directly, as in this example:

> #1 One of government's most important functions is to raise and spend tax revenues on projects that improve the housing, medical, and nutritional needs of its citizens.

In this instance, the writer's claim is a direct expression of a fundamental belief about how the world, or some part of it, should work. The argumentative claim *is* the assumption. Just as often, an argument and its underlying assumption are not identical. In these cases, the assumption is some other statement that is implied by the argumentative claim—as in this example:

> #2 Human spaceflight is a waste of public money.

The logic of this second statement rests on an unstated assumption relating to the word *waste*. What, in this writer's view, is a *waste* of money? What is an effective or justified use? In order to agree or not with statement #2, a critical reader must know what assumption(s) it rests on. A good candidate for such an assumption would be statement #1. That is, a person who believes statement #1 about how governments ought to raise and spend money could well make statement #2. This may not be the only assumption underlying statement #2, but it could well be one of them.

Inferring and Implying Assumptions

Infer and *imply* are keywords relating to hidden, or unstated, assumptions; you should be clear on their meanings. A critical reader *infers* what is hidden in a statement and, through that inference, brings what is hidden into the open for examination. Thus, the critical reader infers from statement #2 on human space-flight the writer's assumption (statement #1) on how governments should spend money. At the same time, the writer of statement #2 *implies* (hints at but does not state directly) an assumption about how governments should spend money. There will be times when writers make statements and are unaware of their own assumptions.

Assumptions provide the foundation on which entire presentations are built. You may find an author's assumptions invalid—that is, not supported by fac- tual evidence. You may disagree with value-based assumptions underlying an author's position—for instance, what constitutes "good" or "correct" behavior. In both cases, you may well disagree with the conclusions that follow from these assumptions. Alternatively, when you find that your own assumptions are con- tradicted by actual experience, you may be forced to conclude that certain of your fundamental beliefs about the world and how it works were mistaken.

An Example of Hidden Assumptions from the World of Finance

An interesting example of an assumption fatally colliding with reality was revealed during a recent congressional investigation into the financial melt- down of late 2008 precipitated by the collapse of the home mortgage market— itself precipitated, many believed, by an insufficiently regulated banking and financial system run amuck. During his testimony before the House Oversight Committee in October of that year, former Federal Reserve chairman Alan Greenspan was grilled by committee chairman Henry Waxman (D-CA) about his "ideology"—essentially an assumption or set of assumptions that become a governing principle. (In the following transcript, you can substitute the word "assumption" for "ideology.")

Greenspan responded, "I do have an ideology. My judgment is that free, competitive markets are by far the unrivaled way to organize economies. We have tried regulation; none meaningfully worked." Greenspan defined an ideology as "a conceptual framework [for] the way people deal with reality. Everyone has one. You have to. To exist, you need an ideology." And he pointed out that the assumptions on which he and the Federal Reserve operated were supported by "the best banking lawyers in the business...and an outside counsel of expert professionals to advise on regulatory matters."

Greenspan then admitted that in light of the economic disaster engulfing the nation, he had found a "flaw" in his ideology—that actual experience had violated some of his fundamental beliefs. The testimony continues:

> Chairman Waxman: You found a flaw?
>
> Mr. Greenspan: I found a flaw in the model that I perceived is the critical functioning structure that defines how the world works, so to speak.
>
> Chairman Waxman: In other words, you found that your view of the world, your ideology, was not right, it was not working.
>
> Mr. Greenspan: Precisely. That's precisely the reason I was shocked, because I had been going for 40 years or more with very considerable evidence that it was working exceptionally well.[5]

The lesson? All the research, expertise, and logical argumentation in the world will fail if the premise (assumption, ideology) on which it is based turns out to be "flawed."

How do you determine the validity of assumptions once you have identified them? In the absence of more scientific criteria, you start by considering how well the author's assumptions stack up against your own experience, observations, reading, and values—while remaining honestly aware of the limits of your own personal knowledge.

Readers will want to examine the assumption at the heart of Krauthammer's essay: that continuing NASA's manned space program and, in particular, the program to return human beings to the moon is a worthwhile enterprise. The writer of the critique that follows questions this assumption. But you may not: You may instead fully support such a program. That's your decision, perhaps made even *before* you read Krauthammer's essay, perhaps as a *result* of having read it. What you must do as a critical reader is to recognize assumptions, whether they are stated or not. You should spell them out and then accept or reject them. Ultimately, your agreement or disagreement with an author will rest on your agreement or disagreement with that author's assumptions.

---

[5]United States. Cong. House Committee on Oversight and Government Reform. *The Financial Crisis and the Role of Federal Regulators.* 110th Cong., 2nd sess. Washington GPO, 2008.

CRITIQUE

2.2 Write a critique of an article, editorial, or chapter.

In Chapter 1 we focused on summary—the condensed presentation of ideas from another source. Summary is fundamental to much of academic writing because such writing relies so heavily on the works of others for the support of its claims. It's not going too far to say that summarizing is the critical thinking skill from which a majority of academic writing builds. However, most academic thinking and writing goes beyond summary. Generally, we use summary to restate our understanding of things we see or read. We then put that summary to use. In academic writing, one typical use of summary is as a prelude to critique.

A *critique* is a *formalized, critical reading of a passage.* It is also a personal response, but writing a critique is considerably more rigorous than saying that a movie is "great" or a book is "fascinating" or "I didn't like it." These are all responses, and, as such, they're a valid, even essential, part of your understanding of what you see and read. But such responses don't illuminate the subject—even for you—if you haven't explained how you arrived at your conclusions.

Your task in writing a critique is to turn your critical reading of a passage into a systematic evaluation in order to deepen your reader's (and your own) understanding of that passage. When you read a selection to critique, determine the following:

- What an author says
- How well the points are made
- What assumptions underlie the argument
- What issues are overlooked
- What implications can be drawn from such an analysis

When you write a critique, positive or negative, include the following:

- A fair and accurate summary of the passage
- Information and ideas from other sources (your reading or your personal experience and observations) if you think these are pertinent
- A statement of your agreement or disagreement with the author, backed by specific examples and clear logic
- A clear statement of your own assumptions

Remember that you bring to bear on any subject an entire set of assumptions about the world. Stated or not, these assumptions underlie every evaluative comment you make. You therefore have an obligation, both to the reader and to yourself, to clarify your standards by making your assumptions explicit. Not only do your readers stand to gain by your forthrightness, but you do as well. The process of writing a critical assessment forces you to examine your own knowledge, beliefs, and assumptions. Ultimately, the critique is a way of learning about yourself—yet another example of the ways in which writing is useful as a tool for critical thinking.

How to Write Critiques

You may find it useful to organize a critique into five sections: introduction, summary, assessment of the presentation (on its own terms), your response to the presentation, and conclusion.

The box on below offers guidelines for writing critiques. These guidelines do not constitute a rigid formula. Most professional authors write critiques that do not follow the structure outlined here. Until you are more confident and practiced in writing critiques, however, we suggest you follow these guidelines. They are meant not to restrict you, but rather to provide a workable sequence for writing critiques until a more fully developed set of experiences and authorial instincts are available to guide you.

GUIDELINES FOR WRITING CRITIQUES

- *Introduce.* Introduce both the passage under analysis and the author. State the author's main argument and the point(s) you intend to make about it.

    Provide background material to help your readers understand the relevance or appeal of the passage. This background material might include one or more of the following: an explanation of why the subject is of current interest; a reference to a possible controversy surrounding the subject of the passage or the passage itself; biographical information about the author; an account of the circumstances under which the passage was written; a reference to the intended audience of the passage.

- *Summarize.* Summarize the author's main points, making sure to state the author's purpose for writing.

- *Assess the presentation.* Evaluate the validity of the author's presentation, distinct from your points of agreement or disagreement. Comment on the author's success in achieving his or her purpose by reviewing three or four specific points. You might base your review on one or more of the following criteria:

    Is the information accurate?

    Is the information significant?

    Has the author defined terms clearly?

    Has the author used and interpreted information fairly?

    Has the author argued logically?

- *Respond to the presentation.* Now it is your turn to respond to the author's views. With which views do you agree? With which do you disagree? Discuss your reasons for agreement and disagreement, when possible tying these reasons to assumptions—both the author's and your own. Where necessary, draw on outside sources to support your ideas.

- *Conclude.* State your conclusions about the overall validity of the piece—your assessment of the author's success at achieving his or her aims and your reactions to the author's views. Remind the reader of the weaknesses and strengths of the passage.

Demonstration: Critique

The critique that follows is based on Charles Krauthammer's op-ed piece "The Moon We Left Behind" (pp. 55–57), which we have already begun to examine. In this formal critique, you will see that it is possible to agree with an author's main point, at least provisionally, yet disagree with other elements of the argument. Critiquing a different selection, you could just as easily accept the author's facts and figures but reject the conclusion he draws from them. As long as you carefully articulate the author's assumptions and your own, explaining in some detail your agreement and disagreement, the critique is yours to take in whatever direction you see fit.

Let's summarize the preceding sections by returning to the core questions that guide critical reading. You will see how, when applied to Krauthammer's argument, they help to set up a critique.

To What Extent Does the Author Succeed in His or Her Purpose?

To answer this question, you will need to know the author's purpose. Krauthammer wrote "The Moon We Left Behind" to persuade his audience that manned space flight must be supported. He makes his case in three ways: (1) he attacks the Obama administration's decision to "retreat" from the moon—i.e., to end NASA's manned space program; (2) he argues for the continuation of this program; and (3) he rebuts criticisms of the program. He aims to achieve this purpose by unfavorably comparing President Obama to President Kennedy, who challenged the nation to put a man on the moon within a decade; by arguing that we should return to the moon for "the wonder and glory of it"; and by challenging the claims that (a) we need first to fix the problems on earth and that (b) we can't afford such a program. One of the main tasks of the writer of a critique of Krauthammer is to explain the extent to which Krauthammer has achieved his purpose.

To What Extent Do You Agree with the Author? Evaluate Assumptions

Krauthammer's argument rests upon two assumptions: (1) it is an essential characteristic of humankind to explore—and going to the moon was a great and worthwhile example of exploration; and (2) inspiring deeds are worth our expense and sacrifice—and thus continuing NASA's manned program and returning to the moon is worth our time, effort, and money. One who critiques Krauthammer must determine the extent to which she or he shares these assumptions. The writer of the model critique does, in fact, share Krauthammer's first assumption while expressing doubt about the second.

One must also determine the persuasiveness of Krauthammer's arguments for returning to the moon, as well as the persuasiveness of his counterarguments to those who claim this program is too impractical and too expensive. The writer of the model critique believes that Krauthammer's arguments are generally persuasive, even (in the conclusion) judging them "compelling." On the other hand, the critique ends on a neutral note—taking into account the problems with Krauthammer's arguments.

Remember that you don't need to agree with an author to believe that he or she has succeeded in his or her purpose. You may well admire how cogently and forcefully an author has argued without necessarily accepting her position. Conversely, you may agree with a particular author while acknowledging that he has not made a very strong case—and perhaps has even made a flawed one—for his point of view. For example, you may heartily approve of the point Krauthammer is making—that the United States should return to the moon. At the same time, you may find problematic the substance of his arguments and/or his strategy for arguing, particularly the dismissive manner in which he refers to the U.S. efforts in space over the past forty years:

> To be more precise: almost 40 years spent in low Earth orbit studying, well, zero-G nausea and sundry cosmic mysteries. We've done it with the most beautiful, intricate, complicated—and ultimately, hopelessly impractical—machine ever built by man: the space shuttle. We turned this magnificent bird into a truck for hauling goods and people to a tinkertoy we call the international space station....

Perhaps you support Krauthammer's position but find his sarcasm distasteful. That said, these two major questions for critical analysis (whether the author has been successful in his purpose and the extent to which you agree with the author's assumptions and arguments) are related. You will typically conclude that an author whose arguments have failed to persuade you has not succeeded in her purpose.

The selections you are likely to critique will be those, like Krauthammer's, that argue a specific position. Indeed, every argument you read is an invitation to agree or disagree. It remains only for you to speak up and justify your own position.

MODEL CRITIQUE

Andrew Harlan

Professor Rose Humphreys

Writing 2

11 January 2014

A Critique of Charles Krauthammer's

"The Moon We Left Behind"

(1) In his 1961 State of the Union address, President John F. Kennedy issued a stirring challenge: "that this nation should commit itself to achieving the goal, before this decade is out, of landing a man on the Moon and returning him safely to the Earth."

Harlan 2

At the time, Kennedy's proposal seemed like science fiction. Even the scientists and engineers of the National Aeronautics and Space Administration (NASA) who were tasked with the job didn't know how to meet Kennedy's goal. Spurred, however, partly by a unified national purpose and partly by competition with the Soviet Union, which had beaten the United States into space with the first artificial satellite in 1957, the Apollo program to land men on the moon was launched. On July 20, 1969, Kennedy's challenge was met when Apollo 11 astronauts Neil Armstrong and Buzz Aldrin landed their lunar module on the Sea of Tranquility.

During the next few years, five more Apollo flights landed on the moon. In all, twelve Americans walked on the lunar surface; some even rode on a 4-wheeled "Rover," a kind of lunar dune buggy. But in December 1972 the Apollo program was cancelled. Since that time, some 40 years ago, humans have frequently returned to space, but none have returned to the moon. In February 2010 President Obama ended NASA's moon program, transferring responsibility for manned space exploration to private industry and re-focusing the government's resources on technological development and innovation. The administration had signaled its intentions earlier, in 2009. In July of that year, in an apparent attempt to rouse public opinion against the President's revised priorities for space exploration, Charles Krauthammer wrote "The Moon We Left Behind." It is these revised priorities that are the focus of his op-ed piece, a lament for the end of lunar exploration and a powerful, if flawed, critique of the administration's decision.

Trained as a doctor and a psychiatrist, Charles Krauthammer is a prominent conservative columnist who has won the Pulitzer Prize for his political commentary. Krauthammer begins and ends his op-ed with expressions of dismay and anger at "America's abandonment of the moon." He unfavorably compares the current president, Barack Obama, with the "vigorous young" John F. Kennedy, in terms of their support for manned space exploration. It is inconceivable to Krauthammer that a program that achieved such technical glories and fired the imaginations of millions in so short a span of time has fallen into such decline.

Krauthammer anticipates the objections to his plea to keep America competitive in manned space exploration and to return to the moon. We have problems enough on earth, critics will argue. His answer: "If we waited to solve these perennial problems before continuing human progress, we'd still be living in caves." Concerning the expense of continuing the space program, Krauthammer argues that a fraction of the funds being "showered" on the government's stimulus programs (some $1 trillion) would be sufficient to support a viable space program. And as for practicality, he dismisses the idea that we need a practical reason to return to the moon. "We go," he argues, "for the wonder and glory of it. Or, to put it less grandly, for its immense possibilities." Ultimately, Krauthammer urges us to turn away from our mundane preoccupations and look up at the moon where humans once walked. How could Americans have gone so far, he asks, only to retreat?

5   In this opinion piece, Charles Krauthammer offers a powerful, inspiring defense of the American manned space program; and it's hard not to agree with him that our voyages to the moon captured the imagination and admiration of the world and set a new standard for scientific and technical achievement. Ever since that historic day in July 1969, people have been asking, "If we can land a man on the moon, why can't we [fill in your favorite social or political challenge]?" In a way, the fact that going to the moon was not especially practical made the achievement even more admirable: we went not for gain but rather to explore the unknown, to show what human beings, working cooperatively and exercising their powers of reason and their genius in design and engineering, can accomplish when sufficiently challenged. "We go," Krauthammer reminds us, "for the wonder and glory of it...for its immense possibilities."

6   And what's wrong with that? For a relatively brief historical moment, Americans, and indeed the peoples of the world, came together in pride and anticipation as Apollo 11 sped toward the moon and, days later, as the lunar module descended to the surface. People collectively held their breaths after an oxygen tank explosion disabled Apollo 13 on the way to the moon and as the astronauts and Mission Control guided the spacecraft to a safe return. A renewed moon program might similarly help to reduce divisions among people—or at least among Americans—and highlight the reality that we are all residents of the same planet, with more common interests (such as protecting the environment) than is often apparent from our perennial conflicts. Krauthammer's praise of lunar exploration and its benefits is so stirring that many who do not accept his conclusions may share his disappointment and indignation at its demise.

7   "The Moon We Left Behind" may actually underestimate the practical aspects of moon travel. "Any technological return," Krauthammer writes, "is a bonus, not a reason."

But so many valuable bonuses have emerged from space flight and space exploration that the practical offshoots of lunar exploration may in fact be a valid reason to return to the moon. For instance, the technology developed from the special requirements of space travel has found application in health and medicine (breast cancer detection, laser angioplasty), industrial productivity and manufacturing technology, public safety (radiation hazard detectors, emergency rescue cutters), and transportation (studless winter tires, advanced lubricants, aids to school bus design) ("NASA Spinoffs"). A renewed moon program would also be practical in providing a huge employment stimulus to the economy. According to the NASA Langley Research Center, "At its peak, the Apollo program employed 400,000 people and required the support of over 20,000 industrial firms and universities" ("Apollo Program"). Returning to the moon would create comparable numbers of jobs in aerospace engineering, computer engineering, biology, general engineering, and meteorology, along with hosts of support jobs, from accounting to food service to office automation specialists ("NASA Jobs").

Krauthammer's emotional call may be stirring, but he dismisses too quickly some of the practical arguments against a renewed moon program. He appears to assume a degree of political will and public support for further lunar exploration that simply does not exist today. First, public support may be lacking—for legitimate reasons. It is not as if with a renewed lunar program we would be pushing boundaries and exploring the unknown: we would not be *going* to the moon; we would be *returning* to the moon. A significant percentage of the public, after considering the matter, may reasonably conclude: "Been there, done that." They may think, correctly or not, that we should set our sights elsewhere rather than collecting more moon rocks or taking additional stunning photographs from the lunar surface. Whatever practical benefits can be derived from going to the moon, many (if not all) have already been achieved. It would not be at all unreasonable for the public, even a public that supports NASA funding, to say, "Let's move on to other goals."

Second, Krauthammer's argument that poverty and disease and social ills will always be with us is politically flawed. This country faces financial pressures more serious than those at any other time since the Great Depression; and real, painful choices are being made by federal, state, and local officials about how to spend diminished tax dollars. The "vigorous young" JFK, launching the moon program during a time of expansion and prosperity, faced no such restrictions. Krauthammer's dismissal of ongoing

Harlan 5

poverty and other social ills is not likely to persuade elected representatives who are shuttering libraries, closing fire stations, ending unemployment benefits, and curtailing medical services. Nor will a public that is enduring these cuts be impressed by Krauthammer's call to "wonder and glory." Accurately or not, the public is likely to see the matter in terms of choices between a re-funded lunar program (nice, but optional) and renewed jobless benefits (essential). Not many politicians, in such distressed times, would be willing to go on record by voting for "nice" over "essential"—not if they wanted to keep their jobs.

(10)   Finally, it's surprising—and philosophically inconsistent—for a conservative like Krauthammer, who believes in a smaller, less free-spending government, to be complaining about the withdrawal of massive government support for a renewed moon program. After all, the government hasn't banned moon travel; it has simply turned over such projects to private industry. If lunar exploration and other space flights appear commercially viable, there's nothing to prevent private companies and corporations from pursuing their own programs.

(11)   In "The Moon We Left Behind," Charles Krauthammer stirs the emotions with his call for the United States to return to the moon; and, in terms of practical spinoffs, such a return could benefit this country in many ways. Krauthammer's argument is compelling, even if he too easily discounts the financial and political problems that will pose real obstacles to a renewed lunar program. Ultimately, what one thinks of Krauthammer's call to renew moon exploration depends on how one defines the human enterprise and the purpose of collective agreement and collective effort—what we call "government." To what extent should this purpose be to solve problems in the here and now? To what extent should it be to inquire and to push against the boundaries for the sake of discovery and exploration, to learn more about who we are and about the nature of our universe? There have always been competing demands on national budgets and more than enough problems to justify spending every tax dollar on problems of poverty, social justice, crime, education, national security, and the like. Krauthammer argues that if we are to remain true to our spirit of inquiry, we cannot ignore the investigation of space because scientific and technological progress is also a human responsibility. He argues that we can—indeed, we must—do both: look to our needs here at home and also dream and explore. But the public may not find his argument convincing.

Harlan 6

Works Cited

Harwood, William. "Obama Kills Moon Program, Endorses Commercial Space." *Spaceflight Now*, 1 Feb. 2010, spaceflightnow.com/news/n1002/01nasabudget/.

Kennedy, John F. "Rice University Speech." 12 Sept. 1962, *Public Papers of the United States*, vol. 1, 1962, pp. 669–70.

---. "Special Message to the Congress on Urgent National Needs." *John F. Kennedy Presidential Library and Museum*, 25 May 1961, www.jfklibrary.org/Asset-Viewer/Archives/JFKPOF-034-030.aspx.

Krauthammer, Charles. "The Moon We Left Behind." *The Washington Post*, 17 July 2009, p. A17.

"Langley NASA Research Program Contributions to the Apollo Program." *NASA*, National Aeronautics and Space Administration, 2 July 2009, www.nasa.gov/centers/langley/news/factsheets/Apollo.html.

"NASA Jobs." *Careers at NASA*, National Aeronautics and Space Administration, 28 July 2009, www.nasa.gov/about/career/index.html.

O'Rangers, Eleanor A., "NASA Spinoffs: Bringing Space Down to Earth." *Space.com*, 26 Jan. 2005, www.space.com/731-nasa-spin-offs-bringing-space-earth.html.

MyWritingLab™

Exercise 2.5

Informal Critique of the Model Critique

Before reading our analysis of this model critique, write your own informal response to it. What are its strengths and weaknesses? To what extent does the critique follow the general Guidelines for Writing Critiques that we outlined on page 68? To the extent that it varies from the guidelines, speculate on why. Jot down ideas for a critique that takes a different approach to Krauthammer's op-ed.

CRITICAL READING FOR CRITIQUE

- *Use the tips from Critical Reading for Summary on page 6.* Remember to examine the context; note the title and subtitle; identify the main point; identify the subpoints; break the reading into sections; distinguish between points, examples, and counterarguments; watch for transitions within and between paragraphs; and read actively.

(continued)

- *Establish the writer's primary purpose in writing.* Is the piece meant primarily to inform, persuade, or entertain?
- *Evaluate informative writing. Use these criteria (among others):*
    Accuracy of information
    Significance of information
    Fair interpretation of information
- *Evaluate persuasive writing. Use these criteria (among others):*
    Clear definition of terms
    Fair use and interpretation of information
    Logical reasoning
- *Evaluate writing that entertains. Use these criteria (among others):*
    Interesting characters
    Believable action, plot, and situations
    Communication of theme
    Use of language
- *Decide whether you agree or disagree with the writer's ideas, position, or message.* Once you have determined the extent to which an author has achieved his or her purpose, clarify your position in relation to the writer's.

The Strategy of the Critique

- Paragraphs 1 and 2 of the model critique introduce the topic. They provide a context by way of a historical review of America's lunar-exploration program from 1962 to 1972, leading up to the president's decision to scrub plans for a return to the moon. The two-paragraph introduction also provides a context for Krauthammer's—and the world's—admiration for the stunning achievement of the Apollo program. The second paragraph ends with the thesis of the critique, the writer's overall assessment of Krauthammer's essay.

- Paragraphs 3–4 introduce Krauthammer and summarize his arguments.
    - Paragraph 3 provides biographical information about Krauthammer and describes his disappointment and indignation at "America's abandonment of the moon."
    - Paragraph 4 treats Krauthammer's anticipated objections to the continuation of the manned space program and rebuttals to these objections.

- Paragraphs 5, 6, and 7 support Krauthammer's argument.
    - Paragraphs 5 and 6 begin the writer's evaluation, focusing on the reasons that Krauthammer finds so much to admire in the lunar-exploration program. Most notably: It was a stunning technological achievement that brought the people of the world together (if only briefly). The writer shares this admiration.

- Paragraph 7 indirectly supports Krauthammer by pointing out that even though he downplays the practical benefits of lunar exploration, the space program has yielded numerous practical technological spinoffs.
- Paragraphs 8–10 focus on the problems with Krauthammer's argument.
  - In paragraph 8, the writer points out that there is little public support for returning to the moon, a goal that many people will see as already accomplished and impractical for the immediate future.
  - Paragraph 9 argues that Krauthammer underestimates the degree to which an electorate worried about skyrocketing deficits and high unemployment would object to taxpayer dollars being used to finance huge government spending on a renewed lunar program.
  - Paragraph 10 points out how surprising it is that a conservative like Krauthammer would advocate a government-financed manned space program when the same goal could be accomplished by private enterprise.
- Paragraph 11 concludes the critique, summing up the chief strengths and weaknesses of Krauthammer's argument and pointing out that readers' positions will be determined by their views on the "human enterprise" and the purpose of government. How do we balance our "human responsibility" for the expansion of knowledge and technology with the competing claims of education, poverty, crime, and national security?

MyWritingLab™   Visit Ch. 2 Critical Reading and Critique in MyWritingLab to test your understanding of the chapter objectives.

3

Thesis, Introduction, and Conclusion

After completing this chapter, you will be able to:

3.1 Write a thesis that makes an assertion about your topic and provides a structure for your paper.

3.2 Write introductions that provide a context for your readers.

3.3 Write conclusions that move beyond a summary of your paper.

Three features of your paper deserve particular attention: your *thesis*, which presents the paper's underlying rationale; your *introduction*, which draws readers into the world of your subject matter; and your *conclusion*, which leaves readers thinking about your particular take on the subject matter. Here we take a closer look at each of these crucial components.

WRITING A THESIS

3.1 Write a thesis that makes an assertion about your topic and provides a structure for your paper.

A thesis is a one- or two-sentence summary of a paper's content. Whether explanatory, mildly argumentative, or strongly argumentative, the thesis is an assertion about that content—for instance, what the content is, how it works, what it means, if it is valuable, if action should be taken, and so on. A paper's thesis is similar to its conclusion, but it lacks the conclusion's concern for broad implications and significance. The thesis is the product of your thinking; it therefore represents *your* conclusion about the topic on which you're writing. So you have to have spent some time thinking about this conclusion (that is, during the invention stage) in order to arrive at the thesis that will govern your paper.

For a writer in the drafting stages, the thesis establishes a focus, a basis on which to include or exclude information. For the reader of a finished product, the thesis forecasts the author's discussion. A thesis, therefore, is an essential tool for both writers and readers of academic papers.

The Components of a Thesis

Like any other sentence, a thesis includes a subject and a predicate that together make an assertion about the subject. In the sentence "Lee and Grant were different kinds of generals," "Lee and Grant" is the subject and "were different kinds of generals" is the predicate. What distinguishes a thesis from any other sentence with a subject and a predicate is that *the thesis presents the controlling idea of the paper.* The subject of a thesis, and the assertion about it, must present the right balance between the general and the specific, to allow for a thorough discussion within the allotted length of the paper. The discussion might include definitions, details, comparisons, contrasts—whatever is needed to illuminate a subject and support the assertion. (If the sentence about Lee and Grant were a thesis, the reader would assume that the rest of the paper contained comparisons and contrasts between the two generals.)

Bear in mind when writing theses that the more general your subject and the more complex your assertion, the longer your discussion must be to cover the subject adequately. The broadest theses require book-length treatments, as in this case:

> Meaningful energy conservation requires a shrewd application of political, financial, and scientific will.

You couldn't write an effective ten-page paper based on this thesis. The topic alone would require pages just to define what you mean by "energy conservation" and "meaningful." Energy can be conserved in homes, vehicles, industries, appliances, and power plants, and each of these areas would need consideration. Having accomplished this first task of definition, you would then turn your attention to the claim, which entails a discussion of how politics, finance, and science individually and collectively influence energy conservation. Moreover, the thesis requires you to argue that "shrewd application" of politics, finance, and science is required. The thesis may very well be accurate and compelling, yet it promises entirely too much for a ten-page paper.

So to write an effective thesis and therefore a controlled, effective paper, you need to limit your subject and your claims about it. This narrowing process should help you arrive at a manageable topic for your paper. You will convert that topic to a thesis when you make an assertion about it—a *claim* that you will explain and support in the paper.

Making an Assertion

Thesis statements make an assertion or claim *about* your paper's topic. If you have spent enough time reading and gathering information and brainstorming ideas about the assignment, you'll be knowledgeable enough to have something to say based on a combination of your own thinking and the thinking of your sources.

If you have trouble coming up with such an assertion, devote more time to invention strategies: Try writing your subject at the top of a page and then listing everything you now know and feel about it. Often, from such a list you'll venture an assertion you can then use to fashion a working thesis. One good way to gauge the reasonableness of your claim is to see what other authors have asserted about the same topic. Keeping good notes on the views of others will provide you with a useful counterpoint to your own views as you write and think about your claim, and you may want to use those notes in your paper.

Next, make several assertions about your topic, in order of increasing complexity, as in the following:

1. Fuel-cell technology has emerged as a promising approach to developing energy-efficient vehicles.

2. To reduce our dependence on nonrenewable fossil fuel, the federal government should encourage the development of fuel-cell vehicles.

3. The federal government should subsidize the development of fuel-cell vehicles as well as the hydrogen infrastructure needed to support them; otherwise, the United States will be increasingly vulnerable to recession and other economic dislocations resulting from our dependence on the continued flow of foreign oil.

Keep in mind that these are *working theses.* Because you haven't begun a paper based on any of them, they remain *hypotheses* to be tested. You might choose one and use it to focus your initial draft. After completing a first draft, you would revise it by comparing the contents of the paper to the thesis and making adjustments as necessary for unity. The working thesis is an excellent tool for planning broad sections of the paper, but—again—don't let it prevent you from pursuing related discussions as they occur to you.

Starting with a Working Thesis

As a student, you are not yet an expert on the subjects of your papers and therefore don't usually have the luxury of beginning writing tasks with a definite thesis in mind. But let's assume that you *do* have an area of expertise, that you are in your own right a professional (albeit not in academic matters). We'll suppose that you understand some nonacademic subject—say, backpacking—and have been given a clear purpose for writing: to discuss the relative merits of backpack designs. Your job is to write a recommendation for the owner of a sporting-goods chain, suggesting which line of backpacks the chain should carry. Because you already know a good deal about backpacks, you may have some well-developed ideas on the subject before you start doing additional research.

Yet even as an expert in your field, you will find that crafting a thesis is challenging. After all, a thesis is a summary, and it is difficult to summarize a presentation yet to be written—especially if you plan to discover what you want to say during the process of writing. Even if you know your material well, the best you can do at first is to formulate a working thesis—a hypothesis of sorts, a well-informed hunch about your topic and the claim you intend to make about it. After completing a draft, you can evaluate the degree to which your working thesis accurately summarizes the content of your paper. If the match is a good one, the working thesis becomes the final thesis. But if sections of the paper drift from the focus of the working thesis, you'll need to revise the thesis and the paper itself to ensure that the presentation is unified. (You'll know that the match between content and thesis is good when every paragraph directly refers to and develops some element of the thesis.) Later in this chapter, we'll discuss useful revision techniques for establishing unity in your work.

This model works whether dealing with a subject in your area of expertise—backpacking, for example—or one that is more in your instructor's territory, such as government policy or medieval poetry. The difference is that when approaching subjects that are less familiar to you, you'll likely spend more time gathering data and brainstorming in order to make assertions about your subject.

Using the Thesis to Plan a Structure

A working thesis will help you sketch the structure of your paper, because an effective structure flows directly from the thesis. Consider, for example, the third thesis on fuel-cell technology (see p. 80):

> The federal government should subsidize the development of fuel-cell vehicles as well as the hydrogen infrastructure needed to support them; otherwise, the United States will be increasingly vulnerable to recession and other economic dislocations resulting from our dependence on the continued flow of foreign oil.

This thesis is *strongly argumentative*, or *persuasive*. The economic crises mentioned suggest urgency in the need for the solution recommended: the federal subsidy of a national hydrogen infrastructure to support fuel-cell vehicles. A well-developed paper based on this thesis would require you to commit yourself to explaining (1) why fuel-cell vehicles are a preferred alternative to gasoline-powered vehicles; (2) why fuel-cell vehicles require a hydrogen infrastructure (i.e., you must explain that fuel cells produce power by mixing hydrogen and oxygen, generating both electricity and water in the process); (3) why the government needs to subsidize industry in developing fuel-cell vehicles; and (4) how continued reliance on fossil fuel technology could make the country vulnerable to economic dislocations.

This thesis, then, helps you plan the paper, which should include a section on each of the four topics. Assuming that the argument follows the organizational plan we've proposed, the working thesis would become the final thesis. Based on this thesis, a reader could anticipate sections of the paper to come. A focused thesis therefore becomes an essential tool for guiding readers.

At this stage, however, your thesis is still provisional. It may turn out that as you do research or begin drafting, the paper to which this thesis commits you looks to be too long and complex. As a result, you may decide to drop the second clause of the thesis (concerning the country's vulnerability to economic dislocations) and focus instead on the need for the government to subsidize the development of fuel-cell vehicles and a hydrogen infrastructure, relegating the economic concerns to your conclusion (if used at all). With such a change, your final thesis might read: "The federal government should subsidize the development of fuel-cell vehicles as well as the hydrogen infrastructure needed to support them."

HOW AMBITIOUS SHOULD YOUR THESIS BE?

Writing tasks vary according to the nature of the thesis.

- The *explanatory thesis* is often developed in response to short-answer exam questions that call for information, not analysis (e.g., "How does James Barber categorize the main types of presidential personality?").
- The *mildly argumentative thesis* is appropriate for organizing reports (even lengthy ones), as well as for essay questions that call for some analysis (e.g., "Discuss the qualities of a good speech").
- The *strongly argumentative thesis* is used to organize papers and exam responses that call for information, analysis, *and* the writer's forcefully stated point of view (e.g., "Evaluate the proposed reforms of health maintenance organizations").

The strongly argumentative thesis, of course, is the riskiest of the three, because you must state your position forcefully and make it appear reasonable—which requires that you offer evidence and defend against logical objections. But such intellectual risks pay dividends; and if you become involved enough in your work to make challenging assertions, you will provoke challenging responses that enliven classroom discussions as well as your own learning.

This revised thesis makes an assertive commitment to the subject even though the assertion is not as complex as the original. Still, it is more argumentative than the second proposed thesis:

> To reduce our dependence on nonrenewable fossil fuel, the federal government should encourage the development of fuel-cell vehicles.

Here we have a *mildly argumentative* thesis that enables the writer to express an opinion. We infer from the use of the words "should encourage" that the writer endorses the idea of the government's promoting fuel-cell development. But a government that "encourages" development is making a lesser commitment than one that "subsidizes," which means that it allocates funds for a specific policy. So the writer who argues for mere encouragement takes a milder position than the one who argues for subsidies. Note also the contrast between the second thesis and the first one, in which the writer is committed to no involvement in the debate and suggests no government involvement whatsoever:

> Fuel-cell technology has emerged as a promising approach to developing energy-efficient vehicles.

This, the first of the three thesis statements, is *explanatory*, or *informative*. In developing a paper based on this thesis, the writer is committed only to explaining how fuel-cell technology works and why it is a promising approach to energy-efficient vehicles. Given this thesis, a reader would *not* expect to find the writer strongly recommending, for instance, that fuel-cell engines replace internal combustion engines in the near future. Neither does the thesis require the writer to defend a personal opinion; he or she need only justify the use of the relatively mild term "promising."

In sum, for any topic you might explore in a paper, you can make any number of assertions—some relatively simple, some complex. On the basis of these assertions, you set yourself an agenda for your writing—and readers set for themselves expectations for reading. The more ambitious the thesis, the more complex will be the paper and the greater the readers' expectations.

To review: A thesis (a one-sentence summary of your paper) helps you organize your discussion, and helps your reader anticipate it. Theses are distinguished by their carefully worded subjects and predicates, which should be just broad and complex enough to be developed within the length limitations of the assignment. Both novices and experts typically begin the initial draft of a paper with a working thesis—a statement that provides writers with sufficient structure to get started but latitude enough to discover what they want to say, as they write. Once you have completed a first draft, you test the "fit" of your thesis with what you have written. If the fit is good, every element of the thesis will be developed in the paper that follows. Discussions that drift from your thesis should be deleted, or the thesis revised to accommodate the new discussions. These revision concerns will be more fully addressed when we consider the revision stage of the writing process.

MyWritingLab™   Exercise 3.1

Drafting Thesis Statements

Working individually or in small groups, select a topic of current interest on your campus: perhaps the administration's dormitory visitor policy or the role of fraternities and sororities. Draft three theses on this topic: one explanatory, one mildly argumentative, and one strongly argumentative.

INTRODUCTIONS

3.2 Write introductions that provide a context for your readers.

Writing introductions and conclusions is usually difficult. How to start? What's the best way to approach your topic? With a serious tone, a light touch, an anecdote? And how to end? How to leave the reader feeling satisfied, intrigued, provoked?

Often, writers avoid such decisions by putting them off—and productively so. Bypassing careful planning for the introduction and conclusion, they begin writing the body of the piece. Only after they've finished the body do they go back to write the opening and closing paragraphs. There's a lot to be said for this approach: Because you've presumably spent more time thinking and writing about the topic itself than about how you're going to introduce or conclude it, you're in a better position to set out your ideas. Often it's not until you've actually seen the text on paper or on screen and read it over once or twice that a natural or effective way of introducing or concluding it occurs to you. Also, you're generally in better psychological shape to write both the introduction and the conclusion after the major task of writing is behind you and you've already set down the main body of your discussion or argument.

An effective introduction prepares the reader to enter the world of your paper. It makes the connection between the more familiar world inhabited by the reader and the less familiar world of the writer's topic; it places a discussion in a context that the reader can understand. If you find yourself getting stuck on an introduction at the beginning of a first draft, skip over it for the moment. State your working thesis directly and move on to the body of the paper.

Here are some of the most common strategies for opening a paper:

Quotation

Consider the two introductory paragraphs to an article titled "Blinded by the War on Terrorism," from journalist Sarah Chayes's article in the *Los Angeles Times*:

> "This is a great time to be a white-collar criminal."
> An assistant U.S. attorney I know startled me with this remark in 2002. The bulk of her FBI investigators, she explained, had been pulled off to work on terrorism, which left traditional crime investigations sorely understaffed.[1]

Chayes uses a provocative remark by a U.S. attorney to grab our attention. Our assumption, perhaps naïve, is that in a stable society governed by laws there should *never* be a good time to be a white-collar (or any other kind of) criminal. But we learn that this is apparently not the case, as Chayes pivots on the quotation to open her report on the stretched resources at the U.S. Department of Justice. Quoting the words of others offers many points of departure for your paper: You can agree with the quotation. You can agree and expand. You can sharply disagree. Or you can use the quotation to set a historical context or establish a tone.

Historical Review

Often the reader will be unprepared to follow the issue you discuss without some historical background. Consider this introduction to an article on second-term presidents:

> Second terms in the White House have, in many cases, ranged from the disappointing to the disastrous. Sick of the political infighting that intensified after his reelection, George Washington could hardly wait to retire to Mount

---

[1]Sarah Chayes. "Blinded by the War on Terrorism." *Los Angeles Times* 28 Jul. 2013.

Vernon. Ulysses S. Grant's second term was plagued by political scandal and economic panic. Woodrow Wilson left office a broken man, having suffered a massive stroke during his failed crusade to persuade America to join the League of Nations. Republican Dwight D. Eisenhower was routed in his last political battle, leaving Democrats in control of the presidency, the House, the Senate, and the Supreme Court for nearly the rest of his life. More recently, Richard Nixon resigned in disgrace; Ronald Reagan was tarred by the Iran-Contra scandal; Bill Clinton was impeached; and George W. Bush watched helplessly as his opponents surged into both houses of Congress and then the White House.

Hence the legendary "second-term curse." In the early days of the republic, second-termers were by tradition discouraged from seeking another term, and nowadays, presidents are legally barred from a third term, thanks to the Twenty-Second Amendment. Popular wisdom has it that second-termers are therefore lame ducks. Unable to run again, how can a term-limited president reward his allies or restrain his adversaries? If he is seen as a fading force, won't his allies hitch themselves to the next rising star? Won't his adversaries attack relentlessly?

Fortunately for Barack Obama, the situation is not that bleak.[2]

In this introduction, Akhil Reed Amar reviews how badly previous presidents have fared in their second terms to explain the "second-term curse." This review sets a context for his thesis, which begins his next paragraph: that Obama's experience may well be more positive than those of his predecessors. Setting a historical context requires familiarity with a topic, and for most student writers this will involve research. Readers will appreciate this research (they didn't have to do it, after all!). Note that the historical review lends itself to chronological development. Amar organizes his introduction as a sequence, from the presidency of George Washington to the presidency of George W. Bush.

Review of a Controversy

A particular type of historical review provides the background on a controversy or debate. Consider this introduction:

Is America a melting pot or a salad bowl? How people answer this question should indicate whether they support or oppose bilingual education programs. First established in 1968, such programs mandate that students who are non-native speakers of English be taught in their own language until they become proficient in English. Proponents of bilingual education believe that the programs provide a vital period of transition for ethnic, non-English speaking students who would otherwise fall behind in their academic work and eventually drop out of school in discouragement. Opponents argue that the sooner non-English speaking students "immerse" themselves in English, the sooner they will master their studies and integrate themselves into the American mainstream. Which side is right? The answer is clear-cut, depending on your political

[2]Akhil Reed Amar. "Second Chances." *The Atlantic* Jan/Feb 2013.

point of view—which is exactly the problem. The decades-old debate over bilingual education cannot be resolved until antagonists can find at least some area of agreement on the role and significance of ethnic cultures in the American life.[3]

The writer sets out a controversy by reviewing the main arguments for and against bilingual education. Instead of taking sides in the debate, however, the writer argues (in the thesis, the final sentence of the paragraph) that a *prior* issue—the role of ethnicity in America—must be addressed before taking on bilingual education.

From the General to the Specific

Another way of providing a transition from the reader's world to the less familiar world of the paper is to work from a general subject to a specific one. The following paper begins a critique that evaluates an argument about the ways in which the media has idealized body types in American culture.

> Most freshmen know how it feels to apply to a school and be rejected. Each year, college admissions officers mail out thousands of thin letters that begin: "Thank you for your application. The competition this year was unusually strong...." We know we will not get into every college on our list or pass every test or win every starring role after every audition, but we believe we deserve the chance to try. And we can tolerate rejection if we know that we compete on a level playing field. When that field seems to arbitrarily favor some candidates over others, however, we take offense. At least that's what happened when an ambitious mother took offense, bringing to court a suit that claimed her eight-year-old daughter, Fredrika Keefer, was denied admission to a prestigious San Francisco Ballet School because she had the wrong "body type."[4]

Anecdote and Illustration: From the Specific to the General

The following three paragraphs each offer an anecdote that moves the reader from a specific case to a more general subject:

> On April 13 of this year, a Wednesday, my wife got up later than usual and didn't check her e-mail until around 8:30 a.m. The previous night, she had put her computer to "sleep," rather than shutting it down. When she opened it that morning to the Gmail account that had been her main communications center for more than six years, it seemed to be responding very slowly and jerkily. She hadn't fully restarted the computer in several days, and thought that was the problem. So she closed all programs, rebooted the machine, and went off to make coffee and have some breakfast.

---

[3]Leslie Weingarten. Unpublished paper.
[4]Ron Labare. Unpublished paper.

When she came back to her desk, half an hour later, she couldn't log into Gmail at all. By that time, I was up and looking at e-mail, and we both quickly saw what the real problem was. In my inbox I found a message purporting to be from her, followed by a quickly proliferating stream of concerned responses from friends and acquaintances, all about the fact that she had been "mugged in Madrid." The account had seemed sluggish earlier that morning because my wife had tried to use it at just the moment a hacker was taking it over and changing its settings—including the password, so that she couldn't log in again....

It was at about this time that I started thinking about the ramifications of this problem beyond our own situation....[5]

The previous introduction about the need to design alternative forms of energy-efficient transportation moved from the general (the statement that humans are "selfish") to the specific (that the alternative forms of transportation we design must meet "our selfish interests"). This introduction moves from the specific (a particular instance of computer hacking) to the general (the ramifications of trusting critical electronic information to storage in the "cloud"). The anecdote is one of the most effective means at your disposal for capturing and holding your reader's attention. It's also one of the most commonly used types of introduction in popular articles. For decades, speakers have begun their remarks with a funny, touching, or otherwise appropriate story. (In fact, plenty of books are nothing but collections of such stories, arranged by subject.)

Question

Frequently you can provoke the reader's attention by posing a question or a series of questions:

At what point in the history of domestic service, I wonder, did lords and ladies start saying *Thank you* to their staff, instead of just kicking them into the fireplace? When did it begin, this treacherous acquisition of personhood by the dishwashing classes? Was there perhaps a single, pivotal moment, deep in some ancestral pile, when a purple-faced baronet looked upon his vassal and experienced—wildly, disconcertingly—the first fizzings of human-to-human recognition? Blame Saint Francis of Assisi. Blame Charles Dickens. By the early 20th century, at any rate, the whole master-servant thing was plainly in ruins. *Individuals* were everywhere. The housekeeper had opinions; the chauffeur had a private life; and the gentleman found himself obliged to take an interest, however slight, in the affairs of his gentleman's gentleman. "And what will you do with your weekend off, Bassett?"[6]

Opening your paper with a question invites readers to formulate a response and then to test that response against the one you will develop in your paper. At what

[5]James Fallows, "Hacked!" *The Atlantic* Nov. 2011.
[6]James Parker, "Brideshead Regurgitated: The Ludicrous Charms of *Downton Abbey*, TV's Reigning Aristo-soap." *The Atlantic* Jan./Feb. 2013, p. 36.

point did the British aristocracy begin treating servants as fellow humans? It's a question that hooks readers, who are likely to continue reading with interest.

Statement of Thesis

Perhaps the most direct method of introduction is to begin immediately with the thesis:

> Nuclear power was beginning to look like a panacea—a way to lessen our dependence on oil, make our energy supply more self-sufficient and significantly mitigate global warming, all at the same time. Now it looks more like a bargain with the devil.
> I wish this were not so....[7]

This selection begins with a two-sentence general assertion—that reliance on nuclear fission is inherently dangerous (as any "bargain with the devil" is bound to be). This is Eugene Robinson's thesis for an article titled "Japan's Nuclear Crisis Might Not Be the Last," in which he addresses what he thinks is a naïve enthusiasm for nuclear power as a route to energy independence. Beginning with a thesis statement (as opposed to a quotation, question, or anecdote) works well when, as in this case, a debate is well understood (there's no need to provide context for readers) and you want to settle immediately into making your argument. Opening with your thesis also works well when you want to develop an unexpected, or controversial, argument. If, for example, you open with the provocative assertion that "Reading is dead" in a paper examining the problem of declining literacy in the digital age, the reader is bound to sit up and take notice, perhaps even protest: "No, it's not—I read all the time!" This strategy "hooks" a reader, who is likely to want to find out how you will support such an emphatic thesis.

One final note about our model introductions: They may be longer than introductions you have been accustomed to writing. Many writers (and readers) prefer shorter, snappier introductions. The ideal length of an introduction depends on the length of the paper it introduces, and it may also be a matter of personal or corporate style. There is no rule concerning the correct length of an introduction. If you feel that a short introduction is appropriate, use one. Conversely, you may wish to break up what seems like a long introduction into two paragraphs.

MyWritingLab™   Exercise 3.2

Drafting Introductions

Imagine that you are writing a paper using the topic you selected in Exercise 3.1. Conduct some preliminary research on the topic, using an Internet search engine such as Google or Bing, or an article database available at your college. Choose one of the seven types of introductions we've discussed—preferably one you have never used before—and draft an introduction that would work to open a paper on your topic. Use our examples as models to help you draft your introduction.

---

[7]Eugene Robinson. "Japan's Nuclear Crisis Might Not Be the Last." *Washington Post* 14 Mar. 2011.

CONCLUSIONS

3.3 Write conclusions that move beyond a summary of your paper.

You might view your conclusion as an introduction in reverse: a bridge from the world of your paper back to the world of your reader. The simplest conclusion is a summary of the paper, but at this point you should go beyond mere summary. You might begin with a summary, for example, and then extend it with a discussion of the paper's significance or its implications for future study, for choices that individuals might make, for policy, and so on. You could urge readers to change an attitude or modify a behavior. Certainly, you're under no obligation to discuss the broader significance of your work (and a summary, alone, will satisfy the formal requirement that your paper have an ending); but the conclusions of effective papers often reveal that their authors are "thinking large" by placing their limited subject into a larger social, cultural, or historical context.

Two words of advice: First, no matter how clever or beautifully executed, a conclusion cannot salvage a poorly written paper. Second, by virtue of its placement, the conclusion carries rhetorical weight: It is the last statement a reader will encounter before turning from your work. Realizing this, writers who expand on the basic summary conclusion often wish to give their final words a dramatic flourish, a heightened level of diction. Soaring rhetoric and drama in a conclusion are fine as long as they do not unbalance the paper and call attention to themselves. Having labored long hours over your paper, you may be inclined at this point to wax eloquent. But keep a sense of proportion and timing. Make your points quickly and end crisply.

Summary (Plus)

Concluding paragraphs that summarize the article as a whole are useful if the article is lengthy or if the writer simply wants to reemphasize the main point. In his article "Wind Power Puffery," H. Sterling Burnett argues that the benefits of wind power have been considerably exaggerated and the drawbacks considerably downplayed. He explains why wind is an unreliable source of steady power and how conventional power plants must, at considerable expense, supplement the electrical energy derived from wind farms. Wind power also creates its own environmental problems, Barnett argues, and wind towers pose deadly hazards to birds and other flying creatures. He concludes with a summary of his main points—and an opinion that follows from these points:

> Wind power is expensive, doesn't deliver the environmental benefits it promises and has substantial environmental costs. In short, wind power is no bargain. Accordingly, it doesn't merit continued government promotion or funding.[8]

The final sentence goes beyond summary to articulate the main conclusion Barnett draws from the arguments he has made.

---

[8]H. Sterling Barnett, "Wind Power Puffery." *Washington Times* 4 Feb. 2004.

Statement of the Subject's Significance

One of the more effective ways to conclude a paper is to discuss the larger significance of your subject. Here you move from the specific concern of your paper to the broader concerns of the reader's world. A paper on the Wright brothers might end with a discussion of air travel as it affects economies, politics, or families; a paper on contraception might end with a discussion of its effect on sexual mores, population, or the church. But don't overwhelm your reader with the importance of your remarks. Keep your discussion focused.

In this paragraph, folklorist Maria Tatar concludes the introduction to her book *The Annotated Classic Fairy Tales* (2002):

> Disseminated across a wide variety of media, ranging from opera and drama to cinema and advertising, fairy tales have become a vital part of our cultural capital. What keeps them alive and pulsing with vitality and variety is exactly what keeps life pulsing: anxieties, fears, desires, romance, passion, and love. Like our ancestors, who listened to these stories at the fireside, in taverns, and in spinning rooms, we remained transfixed by stories about wicked stepmothers, bloodthirsty ogres, sibling rivals, and fairy godmothers. For us, too, the stories are irresistible, for they offer endless opportunities to talk, to negotiate, to deliberate, to charter, and to prattle on endlessly as did the old wives from whom the stories are thought to derive. And from the tangle of that talk and chitchat, we begin to define our own values, desires, appetites, and aspirations, creating identities that will allow us to produce happily-ever-after endings for ourselves and our children.[9]

After a lengthy discussion of what fairy tales are about and how they work, Tatar concludes with a theory about why these ancient stories are still important: They are "a vital part of our cultural capital." They deal with "what keeps life pulsing," and in the way that they encourage opportunities to talk about these classic motifs, they serve to connect our ancestors' "values, desires, appetites, and aspirations" with our own and our children's. Ending the paper with a statement of the subject's significance is another way of saying, "The conclusions of this paper matter." If you have taken the trouble to write a good paper, the conclusions *do* matter. Don't be bashful: State the larger significance of the point(s) you have made. (But avoid claiming too great a significance for your work, lest by overreaching you pop the balloon and your reader thinks, "No, the subject's not *that* important.")

Call for Further Research

Scientists and social scientists often end their papers with a review of what has been presented (as, for instance, in an experiment) and the ways in which the subject under consideration needs to be further explored. *A word of caution:* If you raise questions that you call on others to answer, make sure you know that the research you are calling for hasn't already been conducted.

---

[9]Maria Tatar, "An Introduction to Fairy Tales." *The Annotated Classic Fairy Tales* (2002), ed. and trans. by Maria Tatar. W. W. Norton & Company, Inc.

The following conclusion ends an article titled "Toward an AIDS Vaccine" by Bruce D. Walker and Dennis R. Burton:

> With few exceptions, even the most critical and skeptical of scientists, who have stressed the difficulties of developing an HIV vaccine, feel that this is no time to give up. However, far more selectivity than hereto in advancing immunogens to large-scale clinical trials is required. The mantra of "the only way we will know if it is likely to be effective is to try it in humans" is not appropriate given the current state of knowledge. Trust in science, making full use of the tool kit that is provided by modern molecular biology, immunology, virology, structural biology, chemistry, and genomics is crucial. There is a critical need to understand how other vaccines work with a level of detail that has never been necessary for pathogens less adapted to immune evasion. The way forward is without question very difficult and the possibility of failure high, but the global need is absolutely desperate, and this is an endeavor that must be pursued, now with greater passion than ever.[10]

Notice how this call for further research emphasizes both the difficulty of the task ahead and the critical nature of pursuing that task. The authors point to some of the pitfalls ahead and, in their plea to "[t]rust in science," point to a way forward.

Solution/Recommendation

The purpose of your paper might be to review a problem or controversy and to discuss contributing factors. In such a case, after summarizing your discussion, you could offer a solution based on the knowledge you've gained while conducting research, as in the following conclusion. Of course, if your solution is to be taken seriously, your knowledge must be amply demonstrated in the body of the paper. Here's the concluding paragraph from a student paper titled "Balancing Privacy and Safety in the Wake of Virginia Tech."

> What happened at Virginia Tech was a tragedy. Few of us can appreciate the grief of the parents of the shooting victims at Virginia Tech, parents who trusted that their children would be safe and who were devastated when that faith was betrayed. We cannot permit lone, deranged gunmen to exorcise their demons on campus. We should support changes that involve a more proactive approach to student mental health and improvements in communication between departments that can identify students at risk of becoming violent. But we must also guard against allowing a few isolated incidents, however tragic, to restrict the rights of millions of other, law-abiding students. Schools must not use Virginia Tech as a pretext to bring back the bad old days of resident assistants snooping into the personal lives of students and infringing on their privacy— all in the name of spotting the next campus killer. Both the federal courts and Congress have rejected that approach and for good reason have established the importance of privacy rights on campus. These rights must be preserved.[11]

---

[10]From "Toward an AIDS Vaccine" by Bruce D. Walker and Dennis R. Burton. *Science* 9 May 2008: 760-764. DOI: 10.1126/science.1152622. Reprinted with permission from AAAS. http://www.sciencemag.org/content/320/5877/760.abstract

[11]Alison Tucker. Unpublished paper.

In this conclusion, the author recommends dealing with violence on campus not by infringing on student privacy but by supporting improvements to mental health services and communication among departments to spot potentially troubled students. Her recommendation urges a balanced approach to addressing the problem of campus violence.

Anecdote

As we've seen in our discussion of introductions, an anecdote is a briefly told story or joke, the point of which is to shed light on your subject. The anecdote is more direct than an allusion. With an allusion, you merely refer to a story ("We would all love to go floating down the river like Huck..."); with the anecdote, you retell the story. The anecdote allows readers to discover for themselves the significance of a reference to another source—an effort most readers enjoy because they get to exercise their creativity.

The following anecdote concludes an article by Newton Minow, former chairman of the Federal Communications Commission, who, more than fifty years ago, gained instant celebrity by declaring that television was a "vast wasteland." In his article, "A Vaster Wasteland," Minow discusses "critical choices about the values we want to build into our 21st-century communications system—and the public policies to support them." He explains how we should commit to six major goals and concludes:

> As we think about the next 50 years, I remember a story President Kennedy told a week before he was killed. The story was about French Marshal Louis-Hubert-Gonzalve Lyautey, who walked one morning through his garden with his gardener. He stopped at a certain point and asked the gardener to plant a tree the next morning. The gardener said, "But the tree will not bloom for 100 years." The marshal replied, "In that case, you had better plant it this afternoon."[12]

Minow doesn't bother to explain the significance of the anecdote, which he assumes should be clear: The task ahead will not see fruit for a long time, but unless we get to work immediately, it will take even longer.

Quotation

A favorite concluding device is the quotation—the words of a famous person, an authority in the field on which you are writing, or simply someone in a position to know a great deal about the subject. By quoting another, you link your work to that person's, thereby gaining authority and credibility. The first criterion for selecting a quotation is its suitability to your thesis. But consider carefully what your choice of sources says about you. Suppose you are writing a paper on the American work ethic. If you could use a line either by the comedian Jon Stewart or by the current secretary of labor to make the final point of your conclusion, which would you choose and why? One source may not be inherently more effective than the other, but the choice would affect the tone of your paper.

---

[12]Newton S. Minow, "A Vaster Wasteland." *The Atlantic* Apr. 2011, p. 52.

The following paragraph concludes an article called "Tiger Mom vs. Tiger Mailroom." The author, Patrick Goldstein, who writes about the film industry for the *Los Angeles Times*, joined the "Tiger Mom" debate, sparked by Amy Chua. In an earlier article titled "Chinese Mothers Are Superior," Chau explained why she forbade her children to engage in normal childhood recreational and after-school activities (except for learning the piano or violin), insisting that they work as hard as possible to earn grades no lower than A. Goldstein argues that in most professions, drive and initiative are more important than grade point averages: "charm, hustle, and guile are the aces in the deck." He concludes:

> In Hollywood, whether you were a C student or a *summa cum laude*, it's a level playing field. "When you're working on a movie set, you've got 50 film professors to learn from, from the sound man to the cinematographer," says producer David Permut, who dropped out of UCLA to work for [independent filmmaker] Roger Corman. "I've never needed a resume in my whole career. All you need is a 110-page script that someone is dying to make and you're in business."[13]

Goldstein's quotation from Permut drives home his point that, in the real world, it's not grades but talent, connections, and old-fashioned "hustle" that are the crucial elements in professional success.

Question

Just as questions are useful for opening papers, they are useful for closing them. Opening and closing questions function in different ways, however. The introductory question promises to be addressed in the paper that follows. But the concluding question leaves issues unresolved, calling on the readers to assume an active role by offering their own answers. Consider the following two paragraphs, written to conclude an article on artificial intelligence, as represented by the IBM computer named Watson that in 2011 defeated a group of humans on the television game show *Jeopardy!*:

> As these computers make their way into law offices, pharmaceutical labs and hospitals, people who currently make a living by answering questions must adjust. They'll have to add value in ways that machines cannot. This raises questions not just for individuals but for entire societies. How do we educate students for a labor market in which machines answer a growing percentage of the questions? How do we create curricula for uniquely human skills, such as generating original ideas, cracking jokes, carrying on meaningful dialogue? How can such lessons be scored and standardized?
>
> These are the challenges before us. They're similar, in a sense, to what we've been facing with globalization. Again we will find ourselves grappling with a new colleague and competitor. This time around, it's a

---

[13]Patrick Goldstein, "Tiger Mom vs. Tiger Mailroom." *Los Angeles Times* 6 Feb. 2011.

machine. We should scrutinize that tool, focusing on the questions it fails to answer. Its struggles represent a road map for our own cognitive migration. We must go where computers like Watson cannot.[14]

The questions Stephen Baker raises in the penultimate paragraph of his article are meant to stimulate the reader to consider possible answers. In his final paragraph, Baker makes no attempt to provide his own answers to these questions, preferring to leave them hanging. Instead, he continues to ponder the nature of the problem.

Speculation

When you speculate, you consider what might happen as well as what has happened. Speculation involves a spinning out of possibilities. It stimulates readers by immersing them in your discussion of the unknown, implicitly challenging them to agree or disagree. The following paragraphs conclude a student paper on the effects of rising sea levels.

> The fate of low-lying coastal cities like Tacloban in the Philippines or Pacific island nations like Tuvalu can now be plotted, and the news is not good either for them or for coastal dwellers in more developed areas of the world. We have seen numerous examples of how rising sea levels have resulted in storm surges responsible for destroying dwellings and farms and for killing thousands. According to a recent United Nations report, sixty million people now live in low-lying coastal areas "within one meter of sea level," and by the end of the century that number is likely to double (United Nations Radio). We know enough to understand the risks of concentrating populations by the oceans. Yet even after devastating storms, governments continue to rebuild communities, indeed whole villages and towns, in the same vulnerable areas.
>
> Over time, Nature generally doesn't lose contests like these, and sooner or later we will find ourselves contemplating the unthinkable: abandoning great coastal cities like New York, Calcutta, and Tokyo for higher ground. If the potential human destruction isn't enough to force policy makers to relocate whole populations away from the coasts, in time the loss of money will. Insurance companies, the ones who pay out on billion-dollar losses from major storms, may simply stop insuring cities and businesses that insist on living and working by the sea. When people can no longer insure themselves against heavy losses from climate-related events, the inevitable course of action will be clear: to build on higher ground, further from danger. In two hundred years, the coastal maps of the world will look very different than they do today.[15]

The prospect of nations abandoning great coastal cities like New York and Tokyo might seem extreme, but it is the author's intent to suggest a scenario that challenges readers to agree or not. If you have provided the necessary information prior to your concluding speculation, you will send readers back into their lives

---

[14]Stephen Baker, "Watson Is Far From Elementary." *Wall Street Journal* 14 Mar. 2011.
[15]Allen Hawkins. Unpublished student paper.

(and away from your paper) with an implicit challenge: Do they regard the future as you do? Whether they do or not, you have set an agenda. You have got them thinking.

MyWritingLab™   Exercise 3.3

Drafting Conclusions

Choose one of the eight types of conclusions we've discussed—preferably one you have never used before—and draft a conclusion for the topic you chose in Exercises 3.1 and 3.2. Use our examples as models to help you draft your conclusion.

MyWritingLab™   Visit Ch. 3 Thesis, Introduction, and Conclusion in MyWritingLab to test your understanding of the chapter objectives.

4

Explanatory Synthesis

After completing this chapter, you will be able to:

4.1 Define synthesis as a purposeful discussion of inferred relationships among sources.

4.2 Distinguish between explanatory and argument syntheses.

4.3 Explain the process involved in writing a synthesis.

4.4 Write an explanatory synthesis.

WHAT IS A SYNTHESIS?

4.1 Define synthesis as a purposeful discussion of inferred relationships among sources.

A *synthesis* is a written discussion that draws on two or more sources. It follows that your ability to write syntheses depends on your ability to infer relationships among sources like these:

- Essays
- Fiction
- Interviews
- Articles
- Lectures
- Visual media

This process is nothing new for you because you infer relationships all the time—say, between something you've read in the newspaper and something you've seen for yourself, or between the teaching styles of your favorite and least favorite instructors. In fact, if you've written research papers, you've already written syntheses.

In a *synthesis,* you make explicit the relationships that you have inferred among separate sources.

Summary and Critique as a Basis for Synthesis

The skills you've already learned and practiced in the previous two chapters will be vital in writing syntheses. Before you're in a position to draw relationships between two or more sources, you must understand what those sources say; you must be able to *summarize* those sources. Readers will frequently benefit from at least partial summaries of sources in your synthesis essays. At the same time, you must go beyond summary to make judgments—judgments based on your *critical reading* of your sources: what conclusions you've drawn about the quality and validity of these sources, whether you agree or disagree with the points made in your sources, and why you agree or disagree.

Inference as a Basis for Synthesis: Moving Beyond Summary and Critique

In a synthesis, you go beyond the critique of individual sources to determine the relationships among them. Is the information in source B, for example, an extended illustration of the generalizations in source A? Would it be useful to compare and contrast source C with source B? Having read and considered sources A, B, and C, can you infer something else—in other words, D (not a source, but your own idea)?

Because a synthesis is based on two or more sources, you will need to be selective when choosing information from each. It would be neither possible nor desirable, for instance, to discuss in a ten-page paper on the American Civil War every point that the authors of two books make about their subject. What you as a writer must do is select from each source the ideas and information that best allow you to achieve your purpose.

Purpose

Your purpose in reading source materials and then drawing on them to write your own material is often reflected in the wording of an assignment. For instance, consider the following assignments on the Civil War:

American History: Evaluate the author's treatment of the origins of the Civil War.

Economics: Argue the following proposition, in light of your readings: "The Civil War was fought not for reasons of moral principle but for reasons of economic necessity."

Government: Prepare a report on the effects of the Civil War on Southern politics at the state level between 1870 and 1917. Focus on one state.

Mass Communications: Discuss how the use of photography during the Civil War may have affected the perceptions of the war by Northerners living in industrial cities.

Literature: Select two Southern writers of the twentieth century whose work you believe was influenced by the divisive effects of the Civil War. Discuss the ways this influence is apparent in a novel or a group of short stories written by each author. The works should not be *about* the Civil War.

Applied Technology: Compare and contrast the technology of warfare available in the 1860s with the technology available a century earlier.

Each of these assignments creates a particular purpose for writing. Having located sources relevant to your topic, you would select for possible use in a paper only the parts of those sources that helped you in fulfilling this purpose. And how you used those parts—how you related them to other material from other sources—would also depend on your purpose.

Example: Same Sources, Different Uses

If you were working on the government assignment, you might draw on the same source as a student working on the literature assignment by referring to Robert Penn Warren's novel *All the King's Men,* about Louisiana politics in the early part of the twentieth century. But because the purposes of the two assignments are

WHERE DO WE FIND WRITTEN SYNTHESES?

Here are just a few of the types of writing that involve synthesis:

Academic Writing

- **Analysis papers** synthesize and apply several related theoretical approaches.
- **Research papers** synthesize multiple sources.
- **Argument papers** synthesize different points into a coherent claim or position.
- **Essay exams** demonstrate understanding of course material through comparing and contrasting theories, viewpoints, or approaches in a particular field.

Workplace Writing

- **Newspaper and magazine articles** synthesize primary and secondary sources.
- **Position papers and policy briefs** compare and contrast solutions for solving problems.
- **Business plans** synthesize ideas and proposals into one coherent plan.
- **Memos and letters** synthesize multiple ideas, events, and proposals into concise form.
- **Web sites** synthesize information from various sources to present in Web pages and related links.

different, you and the other student would make different uses of this source. The parts or aspects of the novel that you find worthy of detailed analysis might be mentioned only in passing—or not at all—by the other student.

Using Your Sources

Your purpose determines not only what parts of your sources you will use but also how you will relate those parts to one another. Since the very essence of synthesis is the combining of information and ideas, you must have some basis on which to combine them. *Some relationships among the material in your sources must make them worth synthesizing.* It follows that the better able you are to discover such relationships, the better able you will be to use your sources in writing syntheses. Notice that the mass communications assignment requires you to draw a *cause-and-effect* relationship between photographs of the war and Northerners' perceptions of the war. The applied technology assignment requires you to *compare and contrast* state-of-the-art weapons technology in the eighteenth and nineteenth centuries. The economics assignment requires you to *argue* a proposition. In each case, *your purpose will determine how you relate your source materials to one another.*

Consider some other examples. You may be asked on an exam question or in the instructions for a paper to *describe* two or three approaches to prison reform during the past decade. You may be asked to *compare and contrast* one country's approach to imprisonment with another's. You may be asked to *develop an argument* of your own on this subject, based on your reading. Sometimes (when you are not given a specific assignment) you determine your own purpose: You are interested in exploring a particular subject; you are interested in making a case for one approach or another. In any event, your purpose shapes your essay. Your purpose determines which sources you research, which ones you use, which parts of them you use, at which points in your paper you use them, and in what manner you relate them to one another.

TYPES OF SYNTHESES: EXPLANATORY AND ARGUMENT

4.2 Distinguish between explanatory and argument syntheses.

In this and the next chapter we categorize syntheses into two main types: *explanatory* and *argument*. The easiest way to recognize the difference between the two types may be to consider the difference between a news article and an editorial on the same subject. For the most part, we'd say that the main purpose of the news article is to convey *information* and that the main purpose of the editorial is to convey *opinion* or *interpretation*. Of course, this distinction is much too simplified: News articles often convey opinion or bias, sometimes subtly, sometimes openly; and editorials often convey unbiased information along with opinion. But as a practical matter we can generally agree on the distinction between a news article that primarily conveys information and an editorial that primarily conveys opinion. Consider the balance of explanation and argumentation in the following two selections.

What Are Genetically Modified (GM) Foods?

GENETICALLY MODIFIED FOODS AND ORGANISMS

The United States Department of Energy
November 5, 2008

Combining genes from different organisms is known as recombinant DNA technology, and the resulting organism is said to be "genetically modified," "genetically engineered," or "transgenic." GM products (current or those in development) include medicines and vaccines, foods and food ingredients, feeds, and fibers.

Locating genes for important traits—such as those conferring insect resistance or desired nutrients—is one of the most limiting steps in the process. However, genome sequencing and discovery programs for hundreds of organisms are generating detailed maps along with data-analyzing technologies to understand and use them.

In 2006, 252 million acres of transgenic crops were planted in 22 countries by 10.3 million farmers. The majority of these crops were herbicide- and insect-resistant soybeans, corn, cotton, canola, and alfalfa. Other crops grown commercially or field-tested are a sweet potato resistant to a virus that could decimate most of the African harvest, rice with increased iron and vitamins that may alleviate chronic malnutrition in Asian countries, and a variety of plants able to survive weather extremes.

On the horizon are bananas that produce human vaccines against infectious diseases such as hepatitis B; fish that mature more quickly; cows that are resistant to bovine spongiform encephalopathy (mad cow disease); fruit and nut trees that yield years earlier, and plants that produce new plastics with unique properties.

WHY A GM FREEZE?

The GM Freeze Campaign
November 11, 2010

Genetic modification in food and farming raises many fundamental environmental, social, health and ethical concerns. There is increasing evidence of contamination of conventional crops and wild plants, and potential damage to wildlife. The effects on human health of eating these foods remain uncertain and some scientists are calling for much more rigorous safety testing. It is clear that further research into all these issues is vital. Furthermore the public has not been properly involved in decision making processes, despite strong public support for the precautionary approach to GM in the [United Kingdom] and the [European Union].

Much more time is needed to assess the need for and implications of using genetic modification in food and farming, in particular the increasing control of corporations who rely on patents to secure their future markets.

Both of these passages deal with the topic of genetically modified (GM) foods. The first is excerpted from a largely informational Web site published by the U.S. Department of Energy, which oversees the Human Genome Project, the government's ongoing effort to map gene sequences and apply that knowledge. We say the DOE account is "largely informational" because readers can find a great deal of information here about genetically modified foods. At the same time, however, the DOE explanation is subtly biased in favor of genetic modification: Note the absence of any language raising questions about the ethics or safety of GM foods; note also the use of terms like "desired nutrients" and "insect resistance"—with their positive connotations. The DOE examples show GM foods in a favorable light, and the passage as a whole assumes the value and importance of genetic manipulation.

As we see in the second passage, however, that assumption is not shared by all. Excerpted from a Web site advocating a freeze on genetically modified crops, the second passage primarily argues against the ethics and safety of such manipulation, calling for more study before modified crops are released widely into the environment. At the same time, the selection provides potentially important explanatory materials: (1) the claim that there is "increasing evidence of contamination of conventional crops and wild plants, and potential damage to wildlife"; (2) the claim that corporations control GM crops, and potentially the food supply, through patents. We can easily and quickly confirm these claims through research; if confirmed, the information—which is nested in a primarily argumentative piece—could prove useful in a paper on GM foods.

So while it is fair to say that most writing can be broadly categorized as explanatory or argumentative, understand that in practice, many of the materials you read will be a mix: *primarily* one or the other but not altogether one or the other. It will be your job as an alert, critical reader to determine when authors are explaining or arguing—sometimes in the same sentence.

For instance, you might read the following in a magazine article: "The use of goats to manufacture anti-clotting proteins for humans in their milk sets a dangerous precedent." Perhaps you did not know that scientists have genetically manipulated goats (by inserting human genes) to create medicines. That much of the statement is factual. It is explanatory. Whether or not this fact "sets a dangerous precedent" is an argument. You could agree or not with the argument, but your views would not change the fact about the genetic manipulation of farm animals. Even within a single sentence, then, you must be alert to distinguishing between explanation and argument.

HOW TO WRITE SYNTHESES

4.3 Explain the process involved in writing a synthesis.

Although writing syntheses can't be reduced to a lock-step method, it should help you follow the guidelines listed in the box below.

In this chapter, we'll focus on explanatory syntheses. In the next chapter, we'll discuss the argument synthesis.

GUIDELINES FOR WRITING SYNTHESES

- *Consider your purpose in writing.* What are you trying to accomplish in your paper? How will this purpose shape the way you approach your sources?
- *Select and carefully read your sources* according to your purpose. Then reread the passages, mentally summarizing each. Identify those aspects or parts of your sources that will help you fulfill your purpose. When rereading, *label* or *underline* the sources' main ideas, key terms, and any details you want to use in the synthesis.
- *Take notes on your reading.* In addition to labeling or underlining key points in the readings, you might write brief one- or two-sentence summaries of each source. This will help you in formulating your thesis statement and in choosing and organizing your sources later.
- *Formulate a thesis.* Your thesis is the main idea that you want to present in your synthesis. It should be expressed as a complete sentence. You might do some predrafting about the ideas discussed in the readings in order to help you work out a thesis. If you've written one-sentence summaries of the readings, looking over the summaries will help you brainstorm connections between readings and devise a thesis.

  When you write your synthesis drafts, you will need to consider where your thesis fits in your paper. Sometimes the thesis is the first sentence, but more often it is the final sentence of the first paragraph. If you are writing an inductively arranged synthesis (see p. 145), the thesis sentence may not appear until the final paragraphs.
- *Decide how you will use your source material.* How will the information and the ideas in the passages help you fulfill your purpose?
- *Develop an organizational plan,* according to your thesis. How will you arrange your material? It is not necessary to prepare a formal outline. But you should have some plan that will indicate the order in which you will present your material and the relationships among your sources.
- *Draft the topic sentences for the main sections.* This is an optional step, but you may find it a helpful transition from organizational plan to first draft.
- *Write the first draft* of your synthesis, following your organizational plan. Be flexible with your plan, however. Frequently, you will use an outline to get started. As you write, you may discover new ideas and make room for them by adjusting the outline. When this happens, reread your work frequently, making sure that your thesis still accounts for what follows and that what follows still logically supports your thesis.

- *Document your sources.* You must do this by crediting sources within the body of the synthesis—citing the author's last name and the page number from which the point was taken—and then providing full citation information in a list of "Works Cited" at the end. Don't open yourself to charges of plagiarism! (See pp. 49–50.)
- *Revise your synthesis,* inserting transitional words and phrases where necessary. Make sure that the synthesis reads smoothly, logically, and clearly from beginning to end. Check for grammatical correctness, punctuation, and spelling.

Note: The writing of syntheses is a recursive process, and you should accept a certain amount of backtracking and reformulating as inevitable. For instance, in developing an organizational plan (Step 6 of the procedure), you may discover a gap in your presentation that will send you scrambling for another source—back to Step 2. You may find that formulating a thesis and making inferences among sources occur simultaneously; indeed, inferences are often made before a thesis is formulated. Our recommendations for writing syntheses will give you a structure that will get you started. But be flexible in your approach; expect discontinuity and, if possible, be assured that through backtracking and reformulating, you will produce a coherent, well-crafted paper.

THE EXPLANATORY SYNTHESIS

4.4 Write an explanatory synthesis.

Many of the papers you write in college will be more or less explanatory in nature. An explanation helps readers understand a topic. Writers explain when they divide a subject into its component parts and present them to the reader in a clear and orderly fashion. Explanations may entail descriptions that re-create in words some object, place, emotion, event, sequence of events, or state of affairs.

- As a student reporter, you may need to explain an event—to relate when, where, and how it took place.
- In a science lab, you would observe the conditions and results of an experiment and record them for review by others.
- In a political science course, you might review research on a particular subject—say, the complexities underlying the debate over gay marriage—and then present the results of your research to your professor and the members of your class.

Your job in writing an explanatory paper—or in writing the explanatory portion of an argumentative paper—is not to argue a particular point, but rather *to present the facts in a reasonably objective manner.* Of course, explanatory papers, like other academic papers, should be based on a thesis (see pp. 111–112). But the purpose of a thesis in an explanatory paper is less to advance a particular opinion than to focus the various facts contained in the paper.

DEMONSTRATION: EXPLANATORY SYNTHESIS—GOING UP? AN ELEVATOR RIDE TO SPACE

To illustrate how the process of synthesis works, we'll begin with a number of short extracts from several articles on the same subject.

Suppose you were writing a paper on an intriguing idea you came across in a magazine: a space elevator—a machine that would lift objects into earth orbit, and beyond, not by blasting them free of earth's gravity using rockets but by lifting them in ways similar to (but also different from) the way elevators on earth lift people and material in tall buildings. Once considered a fancy of science fiction, the idea has received serious attention among scientists and even NASA. In fact, an elevator to space could be built relatively soon.

Fascinated by the possibility of an elevator to space being built in your lifetime, you decide to conduct some research with the goal of *explaining* what you discover to interested classmates.

MyWritingLab™   Exercise 4.1

Exploring the Topic

Read the selections that follow on the subject of space elevators. Before continuing with the discussion after the selections, write a page or two of responses. You might imagine the ways an elevator to space might change you and, more broadly, the economy, the military, and international relations. What do you imagine will concern some people about a space elevator? What do you think might be of interest to journalists, the military, politicians, businesspeople, entertainers, artists?

In the following pages we present excerpts from the kinds of source materials you might locate during the research process.

Note: To save space and for the purpose of demonstration, we offer excerpts from three sources only; a full list of sources appears in the "Works Cited" of the model synthesis on pages 127–128. In preparing your paper, of course, you would draw on the entire articles from which these extracts were taken. (The discussion of how these passages can form the basis of an explanatory synthesis resumes on p. 110.)

THE HISTORY OF THE SPACE ELEVATOR

P. K. Aravind

P. K. Aravind teaches in the Department of Physics at the Worcester Polytechnic Institute, Worcester, Massachusetts. The following is excerpted from "The Physics of the Space Elevator" in *The American Journal of Physics* (May 2007).

I. Introduction

A space elevator is a tall tower rising from a point on the Earth's equator to a height well above a geostationary orbit,* where it terminates in a counterweight (see Fig. 1a). Although the idea of such a structure is quite old, it is only within the last decade or so that it has attracted serious scientific attention. NASA commissioned some studies of the elevator in the 1990s that concluded that it would be feasible to build one and use it to transport payload cheaply into space and also to launch spacecraft on voyages to other planets.[1] Partly as a result of this study, a private organization called Liftport[2] was formed in 2003 with the goal of constructing a space elevator and enlisting the support of universities, research labs, and businesses that might have an interest in this venture. Liftport's website features a timer that counts down the seconds to the opening of its elevator on 12 April 2018. Whether that happens or not, the space elevator represents an application of classical mechanics to an engineering project on a gargantuan scale that would have an enormous impact on humanity if it is realized. As such, it is well worth studying and thinking about for all the possibilities it has to offer.

This article explains the basic mechanical principles underlying the construction of the space elevator and discusses some of its principal applications. It should be accessible to anyone who has had a course in undergraduate mechanics and could help give students in such a course a feeling for some of the contemporary applications of mechanics. Before discussing the physics of the space elevator, we recall some of the more interesting facts of its history. The earliest mention of anything like the elevator seems to have been in the book of Genesis, which talks of an attempt by an ancient civilization to build a tower to heaven—the "Tower of Babel"—that came to naught because of a breakdown of communication between the participants. In more recent times the concept of the space elevator was first proposed by the Russian physicist Konstantin Tsiolkovsky in 1895 and then again by the Leningrad engineer, Yuri Artsutanov, in 1960.[3] The concept was rediscovered by the American engineer, Jerome Pearson,[4] in 1975. In 1978 Arthur Clarke brought the idea to the attention of the general public through his novel *Fountains of Paradise*[5] and at about the same time Charles Sheffield, a physicist, wrote a novel[6] centered on the same concept. Despite this publicity,

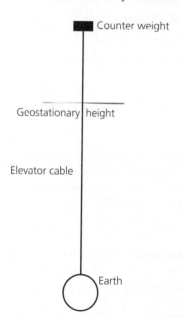

Fig. 1a

Reprinted with permission from "The Physics of the Space Elevator" by P. K. Aravind in *American Journal of Physics* 75.2 (2007): 125. Copyright © 2007 American Association of Physics Teachers.

*Geostationary orbit, also referred to as geostationary earth orbit (or GEO), marks the altitude above the earth's equator (22,236 miles) at which a satellite will rotate at the same speed as the earth itself and, thus, appear to remain motionless in the sky.

the idea of the elevator did not really catch on among scientists because an analysis of its structure showed that no known material was strong enough to build it.

This pessimism was largely neutralized by the discovery of carbon nanotubes in 1991.[7] Carbon nanotubes, which are essentially rolled up sheets of graphite, have a tensile strength greatly exceeding that of any other known material. Their high tensile strength, combined with their relatively low density, makes nanotubes an excellent construction material for a space elevator and led to a resurgence of interest in the concept.

Notes

[1] See the story "Audacious and outrageous: Space elevators" at http://science.nasa.gov/headlines/y2000/ast07sep_1.htm.

[2] Liftport, http://www.liftport.com/.

[3] K. E. Tsiolkowskii, *Dreams of Earth and Sky* 1895, reissue, Athena Books, Barcelona-Singapore, 2004. Y. Artsutanov, "V Kosmos na Elektrovoze" "To the cosmos by electric train" *Komsomolskaya Pravda*, 31 July 1960.

[4] J. Pearson, "The orbital tower: A spacecraft launcher using the Earth's rotational energy," *Acta Astronaut.* 2, 785–799 1975.

[5] Arthur C. Clarke, *Fountains of Paradise*. Harcourt Brace Jovanovich, New York, 1978.

[6] Charles Sheffield, *The Web Between the Worlds*. Baen, Simon and Schuster, Riverdale, NY, 2001.

[7] S. Iijima, "Helical microtubules of graphitic carbon," *Nature London* 354, 56–58 1991.

APPLICATIONS OF THE SPACE ELEVATOR

Bradley C. Edwards

Bradley Edwards, director of research for the Institute for Scientific Research (ISR), is the best-known advocate of the space elevator. Rejected as a young man from the astronaut corps due to health concerns, he earned an advanced degree in physics and worked at the Los Alamos National Laboratory on projects related to space technologies. The selection that follows is excerpted from a 2003 report *(The Space Elevator: National Institute for Advanced Concepts Phase II Report)* prepared on the completion of a grant from NASA.

Every development must have some value to be worth doing. In the case of the space elevator there are both short and long-term applications.... The immediate first use of the space elevator is deployment of Earth-orbiting satellites for telecommunications, military, Earth monitoring, etc....

The traditional markets the space elevator will address include:

- Telecommunications
- Remote sensing
- Department of Defense

The U.S. satellite launch market is expected to be at 110 launches per year when we enter the market.[1]

However, we plan to extend this traditional base and target smaller institutions who are interested in space activities—clients who, until now, have been unable to afford it. The new markets we will encourage and target include:

- Solar Energy Satellites (clean, limitless power from space)
- Space-System Test-Bed (universities, aerospace)
- Environmental Assessment (pollution, global change)
- Agricultural Assessment (crop analysis, forestry)
- Private Communications Systems (corporate)
- National Systems (developing countries)
- Medical Therapy (aging, physical handicaps, chronic pain)
- Entertainment/Advertising (sponsorships, remote video adventures)
- Space Manufacturing (biomedical, crystal, electronics)
- Asteroid Detection (global security)
- Basic Research (biomedical, commercial production, university programs)
- Private Tracking Systems (Earth transportation inventory, surveillance)
- Space Debris Removal (International environmental)
- Exploratory Mining Claims (robotic extraction)
- Tourism/Communities (hotels, vacations, medical convalescence)

We expect solar power satellites to be one of the major markets to develop when we become operational and have begun dialogs with [British Petroleum] Solar about launch requirements and interest. Solar power satellites consist of square miles of solar arrays that collect solar power and then beam the power back to Earth for terrestrial consumption. Megawatt systems will have masses of several thousand tons[2] and will provide power at competitive rates to fossil fuels, without pollution, if launch costs get below $500/lb....

5   Another market we expect to emerge is solar system exploration and development. Initially this would be unmanned but a manned segment, based on the Mars Direct (Zubrin) scenario, could emerge early after elevator operations begin. The exploration market would include:

- Exploratory and mining claims missions to asteroids, Mars, Moon, and Venus
- Science-based, university and private sponsored missions
- In-situ resource production on Mars and Moon
- Large mapping probes for Mars and the asteroids
- Near-Earth object catastrophic impact studies from space

The exploration market would be expected to consist of only a few lifts a year within two years of operations but each mission would be a larger one and produce substantial media attention. In the long-term, such practices will increase our revenue as manned activities in space grow.

Another market to consider in the coming decades is space tourism. We may encourage tourism early on with day-long joyrides to space and later possibly lease a ribbon for long-term, hotels in space. Such activities will produce positive public perception and broaden the long-term market. In a recent survey by Zogby International it was found that "7% of affluent (people) would pay $20 million for 2-week orbital flight; 19% would pay $100,000 for 15-minute sub-orbital flight." These numbers indicate a possible future market that could be tapped as well.

Notes

[1] Zogby International

[2] NASA and ESA studies

*GOING UP**

Brad Lemley

The following excerpt appeared in the July 2004 issue of *Discover* magazine.

Ocean-based platform for a space elevator

The key to conquering the solar system is inside a black plastic briefcase on Brad Edwards's desk. Without ceremony, he pops open the case to reveal it: a piece of black ribbon about a foot long and a half-inch wide, stretched across a steel frame.

Huh? No glowing infinite-energy orb, no antigravity disk, just a hunk of tape with black fibers. "This came off a five-kilometer-long spool," says Edwards, tapping it with his index finger. "The technology is moving along quickly."

The ribbon is a piece of carbon-nanotube composite. In as little as 15 years, Edwards says, a version that's three feet wide and thinner than the page you are reading could be anchored to a platform 1,200 miles off the coast of Ecuador and stretch upward 62,000 miles into deep space, kept

*From *Discover*, July 25, 2004 © 2004 Discover Media. All rights reserved. Used by permission and protected by the Copyright Laws of the United States. The printing, copying, redistribution, or re-transmission of this Content without express written permission is prohibited.

taut by the centripetal force provided by Earth's rotation. The expensive, dangerous business of rocketing people and cargo into space would become obsolete as elevators climb the ribbon and hoist occupants to any height they fancy: low, for space tourism; geosynchronous, for communications satellites; or high, where Earth's rotation would help fling spacecraft to the moon, Mars, or beyond. Edwards contends that a space elevator could drop payload costs to $100 a pound versus the space shuttle's $10,000. And it would cost as little as $6 billion to build—less than half what Boston spent on the Big Dig highway project.

Science fiction writers, beginning with Arthur C. Clarke in his 1979 novel, *The Fountains of Paradise*, and a few engineers have kicked around fantastic notions of a space elevator for years. But Edwards's proposal—laid out in a two-year $500,000 study funded by the NASA Institute for Advanced Concepts—strikes those familiar with it as surprisingly practical. "Brad really put the pieces together," says Patricia Russell, associate director of the institute. "Everyone is intrigued. He brought it into the realm of reality."

5   "It's the most detailed proposal I have seen so far. I was delighted with the simplicity of it," says David Smitherman, technical manager of the advanced projects office at NASA's Marshall Space Flight Center. "A lot of us feel that it's worth pursuing."

Still, there's many a slip between speculative space proposals and the messy real world. The space shuttle, to name one example, was originally projected to cost $5.5 million per launch; the actual cost is more than 70 times as much. The International Space Station's cost may turn out to be 10 times its original $8 billion estimate. While NASA takes the space elevator seriously, the idea is officially just one of dozens of advanced concepts jostling for tight funding, and it was conspicuously absent from President Bush's January 14 [2004] address, in which he laid out plans for returning to the moon by 2020, followed by a manned mission to Mars.

So the United States does not appear to be in a mad rush to build an elevator to heaven anytime soon. On the other hand, for reasons Edwards makes abundantly clear, the United States cannot afford to dither around for decades with his proposal. "The first entity to build a space elevator will own space," he says. And after several hours spent listening to Edwards explain just how and why that is so, one comes away persuaded that he is probably right.

Climber

Ascent vehicles will vary in size, configuration, and power, depending on function. All will climb via tractorlike treads that pinch the ribbon like the wringers of an old-fashioned washing machine. Power for the motors will come from photovoltaic cells on the climbers' undersides that are energized by a laser beamed up from the anchor station. At least two additional lasers will be located elsewhere in case clouds block the anchor station's beam.

Counterweight

A deployment booster, carried aloft in pieces by a vehicle such as the space shuttle and assembled in low Earth orbit, will unfurl two thin strips of ribbon stretching

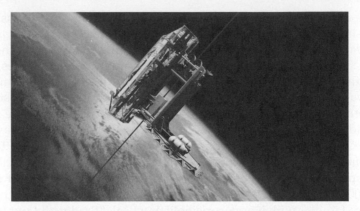

Space elevator in earth orbit showing tether and laser
power beam

from Earth to deep space. Once the strips are anchored to a site on Earth, 230
unmanned climbers will "zip" together and widen the strips. Those climbers will
then remain permanently at the far end of the ribbon, just below the deployment
booster, to serve as a counterweight.

Consider Your Purpose

We asked a student, Sheldon Kearney, to read these three selections and to use
them (and others) as sources in an explanatory paper on the space elevator. (We
also asked him to write additional comments describing the process of developing his ideas into a draft.) His paper (the final version begins on p. 122) drew on
eighteen selections on space elevator technology. How did he—how would you—
go about synthesizing the sources?

First, remember that before considering the *how*, you must consider the *why*.
In other words, what is your *purpose* in synthesizing these sources? You might
use them for a paper dealing with a broader issue: the commercialization of
space, for instance. If this were your purpose, any sources on the space elevator would likely be used in only one section devoted to cost-effective options
for lifting materials from earth into zero gravity. Because such a broader paper
would consider topics other than the space elevator (for instance, a discussion of
business opportunities in earth orbit or of possible legal problems among companies operating in space), it would need to draw on sources unrelated to space
elevators.

For a business or finance course, you might search for sources that would help
you present options for private and government funding of space elevators. The
sources gathered by Sheldon Kearney could help explain the technology, but,
again, you would need to find other sources to investigate the advantages and

disadvantages of public versus private funding or types of private funding. Your overall intention would still be explanatory, yet your focus and your selection of sources would need to broaden from what a space elevator is (the focus of his present paper) to a consideration of the ways in which different classes of investors could pay for actual construction. *Your purpose in writing, then, governs your choice of sources.*

Assume that your goal is to write an explanation of space elevators: a *synthesis* that will explain what the elevator is, how it works, its pros and cons, and why advocates believe it should be built. As part of a larger paper, this explanation would be relatively brief. But if your intention is to explain in greater detail, for an audience of nonspecialists, the basics of space elevator technology and the challenges we can expect with its development, then you will write a paper much like the one Kearney has, the development of which you'll follow in the coming pages. The goal: to present information but not advance a particular opinion or slant on the subject.

MyWritingLab™   Exercise 4.2

Critical Reading for Synthesis

Review the three readings on space elevators and list the ways they explain the technology, address potential advantages and disadvantages, and identify obstacles to construction. Make your list as specific and detailed as you can. Assign a source to each item on the list.

Formulate a Thesis

The difference between a purpose and a thesis is primarily a difference of focus. Your purpose provides direction to your research and gives a focus to your paper. Your thesis sharpens this focus by narrowing it and formulating it in the words of a single declarative statement. (Chapter 6 has more on formulating thesis statements.)

Since Kearney's purpose in this case was to synthesize source material with little or no comment, his thesis would be the most obvious statement he could make about the relationship among the source readings. By "obvious" we mean a statement that is broad enough to encompass the main points of all the readings. Taken as a whole, what do they *mean*? Here Kearney describes the process he followed in coming up with a thesis for his explanatory synthesis:

> I began my writing process by looking over all the readings and noting the main point of each reading in a sentence on a piece of paper.
>
> Then I reviewed all of these points and identified the patterns in the readings. These I recorded underneath my list of main points: All the readings focus on the space elevator: definition, construction, technical obstacles, uses, potential problems. The readings explain a technology that has significant business, military, and environmental implications.

Looking over these points, I drafted what I thought was a preliminary thesis. This thesis summed up for me the information I found in my sources:

> Building a space elevator has garnered the attention of NASA, the U.S. Air Force, foreign nations, private industry, and scientists alike as a feasible and cost effective means of reaching into space.

This was a true statement, the basis of my first draft. What ended up happening, though (I realized this even before my instructor read the draft and commented), was that my supposed thesis wasn't a thesis at all. Instead, I had written a statement that allowed me to write a series of summaries and bullet points and call that a paper. So this first effort was not successful, although one good thing happened: in my conclusion, when I forced myself to sum up, I wrote a sentence that looked more like an organizing thesis statement:

> The development of the space elevator will undoubtedly become a microcosm of the human spirit, for better and for worse.

This statement seemed more promising, and my instructor suggested I use this as my thesis. But the more I thought about "microcosm of the human spirit," the more nervous I got about explaining what the "human spirit" is. That seemed to me too large a project. I figured that might be a trap, so I used a different thesis for my second draft:

> Building the space elevator could lead to innovation and exploration; but there could be problems—caused both by technology and by people—that could derail the project.

This version of the thesis allowed me to write more of a synthesis, to get a conversation going with the sources. After I wrote a second draft, I revised the thesis again. This time, I wanted to hint more directly at the types of problems we could expect. I introduced "earth-bound conflicts" to suggest that the familiar battles we fight down here could easily follow us into space:

> If built, the space elevator would likely promote a new era of innovation and exploration. But one can just as easily imagine progress being compromised by familiar, earth-bound conflicts.

I added "if built" to plant a question that would prepare readers for a discussion of obstacles to constructing the elevator. Originally this thesis was one sentence, but it was long and I split it into two.

Decide How You Will Use Your Source Material

To begin, you will need to summarize your sources—or, at least, be *able* to summarize them. That is, the first step to any synthesis is understanding what your sources say. But because you are synthesizing *ideas* rather than sources, you will have to be more selective than if you were writing a simple summary. In your synthesis, you will not use *all* the ideas and information in every source, only the ones related to your thesis. Some sources might be summarized in their entirety; others, only in part. Look over your earlier notes or sentences discussing the topics covered in the readings, and refer back to the readings themselves. Focusing on the more subtle elements of the issues addressed by the authors, expand your earlier summary sentences. Write brief phrases in the margin of the sources, underline key phrases or sentences, or take notes on a separate sheet of paper or in a word processing file or electronic data-filing program. Decide how your sources can help you achieve your purpose and support your thesis.

For example, how might you use a diagram to explain the basic physics of the space elevator? How would you present a discussion of possible obstacles to the elevator's construction or likely advantages to the country, or business, that builds the first elevators? How much would you discuss political or military challenges?

Develop an Organizational Plan

An organizational plan is your map for presenting material to the reader. What material will you present? To find out, examine your thesis. Do the content and structure of the thesis (that is, the number and order of assertions) suggest an organizational plan for the paper? For example, consider Kearney's revised thesis:

> If built, the space elevator would likely promote a new era of innovation and exploration. But one can just as easily imagine progress being compromised by familiar, earth-bound conflicts.

Without knowing anything about space elevators, a reader of this thesis could reasonably expect the following:

- Definition of the space elevator: What is it? How does it work?
- "If built"—what are the obstacles to building a space elevator?
- What innovations?
- What explorations?
- What problems ("conflicts") on earth would jeopardize construction and use of a space elevator?

Study your thesis, and let it help suggest an organization. Expect to devote at least one paragraph of your paper to developing each section that your thesis promises. Having examined the thesis closely and identified likely sections, think through the possibilities of arrangement. Ask yourself: What information does the reader need to understand first? How do I build on this first section— what block of information will follow? Think of each section in relation to others until you have placed them all and have worked your way through to a plan for the whole paper.

Bear in mind that any one paper can be written—successfully—according to a variety of plans. Your job before beginning your first draft is to explore possibilities. Sketch a series of rough outlines:

- Arrange and rearrange your paper's likely sections until you develop a plan that both enhances the reader's understanding and achieves your objectives as a writer.
- Think carefully about the logical order of your points: Does one idea or point lead to the next?
- If not, can you find a more logical place for the point, or are you just not clearly articulating the connections between the ideas?

Your final paper may well deviate from your final sketch; in the act of writing you may discover the need to explore new material, to omit planned material, or to refocus or reorder your entire presentation. Just the same, a well-conceived organizational plan will encourage you to begin writing a draft.

Summary Statements

In notes describing the process of organizing his material, Kearney refers to all the sources he used, including the three excerpted in this chapter.

> In reviewing my sources and writing summary statements, I detected four main groupings of information:
> - The technology for building a space elevator is almost here. Only one major obstacle remains: building a strong enough tether.
> - Several sources explained what the space elevator is and how it could change our world.
> - Another grouping of articles discussed the advantages of the elevator and why we need it.
> - A slightly different combination of articles presented technical challenges and also problems that might arise among nations, such as competition.
>
> I tried to group some of these topics into categories that would have a logical order. What I first wanted to communicate was the sense that the technical obstacles to building a space elevator have been (or soon will be) solved or, in theory, at least, are solvable.
> Early in the paper, likely in the paragraph after the introduction, I figured I should explain exactly what a space elevator is.
> I would then need to explain the technical challenges—mainly centered on the tether and, possibly, power issues. After covering the technical challenges, I could follow with the challenges that people could pose (based largely on competition and security needs).
> I also wanted to give a sense that there's considerable reason for optimism about the space elevator. It's a great idea, but, typically, people could get in the way of their own best interests and defeat the project before it ever got off the ground.

I returned to my thesis and began to think about a structure for the paper. Building the space elevator could lead to innovation and exploration, but there could be problems—caused both by technology and by people—that could derail the project.

Based on his thesis, Kearney developed an outline for an eight-paragraph paper, including introduction and conclusion:

1. Introduction: The space elevator <u>can</u> be built a lot sooner than we think.
2. The basic physics of a space elevator is not that difficult to understand.
3. The key to the elevator's success is making a strong tether. Scientists believe they have found a suitable material in carbon nanotubes.
4. Weather and space junk pose threats to the elevator, but these potential problems are solvable with strategic placement of the elevator and sophisticated monitoring systems.
5. Powering the elevator will be a challenge, but one likely source is electricity collected by solar panels and beamed to the climber.
6. Space elevators promise important potential benefits: cost of transporting materials to space will be drastically reduced; industries, including tourism, would take advantage of a zero-gravity environment; and more.
7. Among the potential human-based (as opposed to technology-based) problems to building a space elevator: a new space race; wars to prevent one country from gaining strategic advantage over others, ownership, and access.
8. A space elevator could be inspiring and could usher in a new era of exploration.

Write the Topic Sentences

Writing draft versions of topic sentences (an optional step) will get you started on each main idea of your synthesis and will help give you the sense of direction you need to proceed. Here are Kearney's draft topic sentences for sections, based on the thesis and organizational plan he developed. Note that when read in sequence following the thesis, these sentences give an idea of the logical progression of the essay as a whole.

- A space elevator is exactly what it sounds like.
- A space elevator is not a standard elevator, but a rope—or tether—with a counterweight at the far end kept in place by centrifugal force and extending 60,000 miles into space.
- There already exists a single material strong enough to act as a tether for the space elevator, carbon nanotubes.

- Because the space elevator would reach from earth through our atmosphere and into space, it would face a variety of threats to the integrity of its tether.
- Delivering power to the climbers is also a major point of consideration.
- The ability of a space elevator to lift extremely heavy loads from earth into space is beneficial for a number of reasons.
- Ownership, as any homeowner can tell you, comes with immense responsibility; and ownership of a technology that could change the world economy would almost certainly create huge challenges.
- The ambition to build a tower so high it would scrape the heavens is an idea stretching back as far as the story of the Tower of Babel.

ORGANIZE A SYNTHESIS BY IDEA, NOT BY SOURCE

A synthesis is a blending of sources organized by *ideas*. The following rough sketches suggest how to organize and how *not* to organize a synthesis. The sketches assume you have read seven sources on a topic, sources A–G.

Incorrect: Organizing by Source + Summary

Thesis

Summary of source A in support of the thesis.

Summary of source B in support of the thesis.

Summary of source C in support of the thesis.

(etc.)

Conclusion

This is *not* a synthesis because it does not blend sources. Each source stands alone as an independent summary. No dialogue among sources is possible.

Correct: Organizing by Idea

Thesis

First idea: Refer to and discuss *parts* of sources (perhaps A, C, F) in support of the thesis.

Second idea: Refer to and discuss *parts* of sources (perhaps B, D) in support of the thesis.

Third idea: Refer to and discuss *parts* of sources (perhaps A, E, G) in support of the thesis.

(etc.)

Conclusion

This *is* a synthesis because the writer blends and creates a dialogue among sources in support of an idea. Each organizing idea, which can be a paragraph or group of related paragraphs, in turn supports the thesis.

Write Your Synthesis

Here is the first draft of Kearney's explanatory synthesis. Thesis and topic sentences are highlighted. Modern Language Association (MLA) documentation style, explained in Chapter 7, is followed throughout.

Alongside this first draft we have included comments and suggestions for revision from Kearney's instructor. For purposes of demonstration, these comments are likely to be more comprehensive than the selective comments provided by most instructors.

EXPLANATORY SYNTHESIS: FIRST DRAFT

Kearney 1

Sheldon Kearney

Professor Leslie Davis

Technology and Culture

October 1, 2014

The Space Elevator

A space elevator is exactly what it sounds like: an elevator reaching into space. And though some thirty years ago the notion of a such an elevator was little more than science fiction, today, building a space elevator has garnered the attention of NASA, the U.S. Air Force, foreign nations, private industry, and scientists alike as a feasible and cost-effective means of reaching into space.

A space elevator is not a standard elevator, but a rope—or tether—with a counterweight at the far end kept in place by centrifugal force and extending 60,000 miles into space (citation needed). The *rotation of the earth combined with the* weight and size of the tether would keep the line taught. As __ notes, imagine a rope hanging down from the earth rather than extending up (citation needed). Rather than having a counterweight moving cargo up and down the tether, as in a conventional elevator, a space elevator would make use of mechanical climbers to move cargo into and down from space. (Image needed for this?)

There already is a material strong enough to act as a tether for the space elevator, carbon nanotubes. Discovered in 1991 by Sumio Iijima,

Title and Paragraph ①
Your title could be more interesting and imaginative. Your first paragraph has no organizing statement, no thesis. Devise a statement—or find one in the draft (see your last paragraph—"microcosm of the human spirit")—that can create a map for your readers. Finally, expand the first paragraph and make it an interesting (fascinating?) transition into the world of space elevators.

Paragraph ②
Consider using an image to help readers understand what a space elevator is and how it works. Also consider using an analogy—what is the space elevator like that readers would understand?

Paragraph ③
The tether is a crucial component of the space elevator. Any obstacles to building? Expand this part of the explanation.

Kearney 2

carbon nanotubes have been tested in labs to be X times stronger and X times lighter than steel (get stats). In theory the production of a carbon nanotube ribbon only a meter wide and millimeters thick would be strong enough to act as the space elevator's tether. "Small quantities of some nanotubes have been made that are sufficiently strong enough to be used in a space elevator," though the scale of production would need to be drastically increased to build the tether needed for the space elevator (Olson interview).

(4)   Threats. Because the space elevator would reach from Earth through our atmosphere and into space, there are threats it will face to the integrity of its tether. Weather conditions such as hurricanes and lightning pose a threat to the space elevator, as do impacts from Earth-bound objects, i.e. planes, as well as low earth orbit objects such as satellites and meteors and orbital debris. These types of threats have possible solutions. Locating the space elevator off of the Galapagos Islands in open water, if possible, minimizes the likelihood of lightning, wind, and hurricanes damaging the elevator. In this sight, the occurrence of such events are extremely rare (footnote needed, as well as image provided by Edwards). Furthermore, by attaching the space elevator to a large ocean vessel, such as a deep water oil platform, it would be possible to move the tether in the case of severe weather conditions. The ability to move the space elevator is important: NASA estimates that there are some 500,000 objects within the Earth's orbit that could catastrophically damage the space elevator (NASA sight and Edwards).

(5)   Delivering power to the climbers is also a major point of consideration. Bringing along the fuel would be prohibitively heavy due to the length of the trip, as would dragging a long power cord. Powering the elevator with laser beams of electricity generated by solar cells on the ground has been proposed by advocates of the space elevator. Lasers powerful enough to be used to fuel the climbers are already commercially available (Olsen interview).

(6)   The ability of a space elevator to lift extremely heavy loads from Earth into space is beneficial for a number of reasons. Chemical rockets are only able to carry approximately 6% of their total weight into space as cargo, with the remaining 94% used for fuel to escape the Earth's gravity and

Paragraphs ④ and ⑤

Reverse the order of paragraphs 4 and 5. "Power" is a core element of the elevator's success. A discussion of "threats" assumes the space elevator is already functional. Logically, "power" should come first.

Kearney 3

launch vehicles (Swan 2006 2.2). For a space elevator, however, the immense strength of the tether would allow for mechanical climbers to lift extremely heavy loads. There are several obvious advantages to a space elevator:

- As the tether's strength builds over time, there is virtually no limit to the strength and payload capacity of the elevator.
- Inexpensive access to space would quickly permit the development of entirely new space-based industries like tourism and manufacturing.
- The increased ability to place satellites into space would increase the security and amount of digital information needed in the global economy.
- The development of a space elevator could also further act as a launching point for future interplanetary exploration.

Dr. Edwards notes that "the first entity to build a space elevator will own space" (Edwards 2000 needed). In this he is certainly correct. But ownership, as any homeowner can tell you, comes with immense responsibility; and ownership of a technology that could change the world economy would almost certainly create huge challenges (Eric Westling Interview). Key questions to consider:

- Will the creation of one space elevator create a new space race between nations?
- Will one nation's desire to prevent its construction lead to war?
- Who will own the elevator?
- Who will have access to space via the elevator?

The ambition to build a tower so high it would scrape the heavens is an idea stretching back as far as the story of the Tower of Babel. For these ancient builders their ambition was too great and they were punished. The development of the space elevator will undoubtedly become a microcosm of the human spirit, for better and for worse. A space elevator will inspire untold technological developments and usher in a yet unknown expansion of the human condition as we begin in earnest to explore beyond the confines and limitations of the Earth. Yet, the development of a space elevator will almost certainly act as a lightning rod for international conflict.

Paragraph ⑥
This paragraph, currently in both sentence and bullet format, needs to be split up and expanded. The cost analysis is an important piece of justifying the space elevator. Expand this discussion and explain the expected savings. Also, as part of justifying a new thesis re: "the human spirit," expand your bulleted list of benefits. Possibly develop a full paragraph for each bullet.

Paragraph ⑦
Similar to the comment re: paragraph 6: split the current paragraph and expand bulleted points. If your paper is to account "for better and for worse" elements of the human spirit (see par. 8), then you need a full discussion of problems associated with the elevator. Presently, only these abbreviated bullets suggest possible problems. Expand—possibly a paragraph for each bullet.

Paragraph ⑧
You have found your thesis in this paragraph: "The developments…for better and for worse." Consider moving this sentence to the head of the paper and building out the conclusion to discuss the space elevator and "the human spirit."

Revise Your Synthesis: Global, Local, and Surface Revisions

Many writers find it helpful to plan for three types of revision: global, local, and surface.

Global revisions affect the entire paper: the thesis, the type and pattern of evidence employed, and the overall organization. A global revision may also emerge from a change in purpose—say, when a writer realizes that a paper works better as an argument than as an explanation. In this case, Kearney decided to revise globally based on his instructor's suggestion to use a statement from the conclusion as a thesis in the second draft. The immediate consequence of this decision: Kearney realized he needed to expand substantially the discussion of the benefits of the space elevator and also its potential problems. Such an expansion would make good on the promise of his new thesis for the second draft (a reformulation of his "human spirit" statement at the end of the first draft): "Building the space elevator could lead to innovation and exploration, but there could be problems—caused both by technology and by people—that could derail the project."

Local revisions affect paragraphs: topic and transitional sentences; the type of evidence presented within a paragraph; evidence added, modified, or dropped within a paragraph; logical connections from one sentence or set of sentences within a paragraph to another.

Surface revisions deal with sentence style and construction, word choice, and errors of grammar, mechanics, spelling, and citation form.

Revising the First Draft: Highlights

Global

- At present, the paper has no organizing thesis. Consider moving the sentence underlined in the final paragraph to the first paragraph and letting it serve as your thesis for the revision. "Microcosm of the human spirit" is promising because our reach into space does speak to the human spirit.

- Be careful in your conclusion not to move your explanatory synthesis into the territory of argument. The paragraph as written shifts away from your sources to your personal point of view concerning what might happen post-development of a space elevator.

- Expand the bullet points on the benefits and key challenges facing development of the space elevator (paragraphs 6–7). Expanded, each bullet point could become a paragraph. Considered together, these discussions of benefits and challenges could justify your explanatory claim about "microcosm."

- In paragraph 6, explain in more detail the cost advantages of the space elevator. Relatively inexpensive access to space is one of the key benefits.

Local

- Your introduction needs work. Create more of a context for your topic that moves readers to your (new) thesis. The topic is fascinating. Show your fascination to readers! Work as well on your concluding paragraph; assuming you move the underlined statement in that paragraph to your introduction (where it would serve as a thesis), the remaining conclusion will be weak.

- Expand your discussion of power requirements for the elevator (paragraph 5) and move that before your discussion of threats (currently paragraph 4). Logic: A discussion of threats assumes an operational space elevator, one of the requirements of which is a dependable power supply.

- Expand your discussion of the tether in paragraph 3—a key component of the elevator. We need to know more, including obstacles to making the tether.

- Graphic images could be very helpful to your explanation of the space elevator. You consider using them in paragraphs 2 and 4.

- Assuming you expand the paper and justify your explanatory claim about the development of the elevator providing a "microcosm of the human spirit," you could expand your conclusion. What do you mean, exactly, by "human spirit"—and, also, by "for better and for worse"?

Surface

- Avoid weak verbs (see the first sentence of paragraph 5). Revise passive constructions such as "has been proposed by" in paragraph 5 and "were punished" in paragraph 8.

- Avoid constructions like "there is" and "there are" in paragraphs 3 and 4.

- Watch for errors like "taught" vs. "taut" in paragraph 2 and "sight" vs. "site" in paragraph 4.

- Fix grammatical errors—for instance, subject-verb agreement in paragraph 4: "the occurrence of such events "are" or "is"?

MyWritingLab™

Exercise 4.3

Revising the Explanatory Synthesis

Try your hand at creating a final draft of the paper on pages 122–128 by following the revision suggestions above and using your own best judgment about how to improve the first draft. Make global, local, and surface changes. After writing your own version of the paper, compare it with the revised version of our student paper below.

MODEL EXPLANATORY SYNTHESIS

Sheldon Kearney

Professor Leslie Davis

Technology and Culture

October 12, 2014

Going Up? An Elevator Ride to Space

(1)   In his 1979 science fiction novel *The Fountains of Paradise,* Arthur C. Clarke introduced his readers to space elevators. While Clarke's idea of a platform that would ride a tether into space (eliminating the need for rockets) was not new, his novel helped focus scientific imaginations on the possibilities. A space elevator is exactly what it sounds like: a platform rising from the ground, not to the top floor of a building but into the weightlessness of earth orbit. It's a real-life Tower of Babel, built to "reach unto heaven" (Gen. 11.4). For thirty years, the elevator has been little more than science fiction hinting at future space tourism, manufacturing in zero gravity, mining of asteroids, abundant solar power beamed to anywhere on earth, and dramatically less expensive inter-planetary travel. Today, however, NASA, the U.S. Air Force, and private industry regard the technology as both feasible and cost-effective. If built, the space elevator would likely promote a new era of innovation and exploration. But one can just as easily imagine progress being compromised by familiar, earth-bound conflicts.

(2)   The physics of a space elevator should be familiar to any child who has spun a rope with a rock attached to one end: as the arm spins, the rope remains extended to its full length in the air, apparently defying gravity. The rope and the rock stay up because centrifugal force acts to push the weight outward, while the rope keeps the rock from flying off. In the case of a space elevator, instead of the child spinning the weight, it is the earth that's spinning. And instead of a rope perhaps three feet in length extending taut from the child's hand out to the rock, the far end of a space tether would be attached to a weight extending 62,000 miles from earth (Aravind 125–26; Kent 3). Movement up and down the tether would not involve the use of a counterweight and pulley system, as with terrestrial elevators, but rather a mechanical climber to ferry cargo to and from space.

(3)   When the space elevator was first envisioned, no known material was strong enough to serve as a tether. Then in 1991, Sumio Iijima, a Japanese physicist and materials scientist at Meijo University in Nagoya, discovered the carbon nanotube: "a material that is theoretically one hundred or more times stronger and ten times lighter than steel" (Kent iii). In principle,

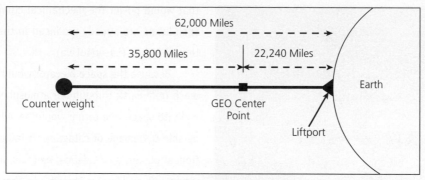

Space Elevator Basic Layout

Fig. 1. "The space elevator...is a 1-meter wide tether stretching from the surface of the earth out to a point some 62,000 miles in orbit. The base of the ribbon is attached to a platform on the surface (floating at sea) while the space end of the tether extends past geosynchronous orbit to a counter weight. Lifters...would clamp onto the tether and, using a series of rollers powered by lasers, ascend and descend in order to carry people, material, and cargo to and from orbit." (Kent 3)

the production of a carbon nanotube ribbon only a meter wide and millimeters thick would be strong enough to act as the tether for a space elevator. According to Brad Edwards, a former NASA scientist and leading proponent of space elevators, a nanotube strong enough to serve as a tether will soon be available (Interview, NOVA), though the scale of production would have to increase dramatically to achieve the required 62,000 mile length. Because scaling to that extent could create an "unavoidable presence of defects" (Pugno), materials investigation continues. But Edwards is confident enough to predict an operational space elevator by 2031 (Liftport). Production of nanotubes aside, the major obstacles to construction are not technical but rather financial (funds must be found to build the elevator); legal (the 62,000 mile tether cannot interfere with existing satellites); and political (interests representing the chemical rocket industry will object to and likely attempt to thwart the elevator) (Edwards, *Phase II* 40).

    NASA has been sufficiently intrigued by the concept to join with the Spaceward Foundation in creating "The Space Elevator Games," which awards cash prizes to promising elevator technologies (Shelef). Key modifications to terrestrial elevators have already been designed. For instance, because carrying the fuel necessary to power the elevator platform would render the project as expensive as chemical rockets (which also carry their own fuel), engineers believe that ground-based lasers, powered by the sun, could aim energy beams

⑤

that would power the mechanical climber. Such lasers are already produced in the United States (LaserMotive).

Because the space elevator would reach from Earth through our atmosphere and into space, the tether would be vulnerable to damage or catastrophic failure from airplanes, space debris, meteors, and violent storms. Impact threats like these also have likely solutions, one being to locate the space elevator in a weather-stable climate—for example, off the Galapagos Islands—in open water, which would minimize the likelihood of damage from lightning or wind (SpaceRef). Attaching the earth-end of the elevator to a large ocean vessel, such as a deep water oil platform, would permit moving a tether threatened by impending collisions with space debris or meteors, which would be tracked by an array of telescopes (Edwards, *Phase I* 5.8; *Phase II* 23).

Fig. 2.   Ocean-based platform for a space elevator

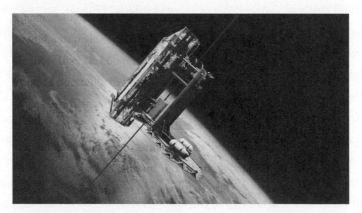

Fig. 3.   Space elevator in earth orbit showing tether and laser power beam
Source: Images created by Brad Edwards and used with permission.

At present, NASA and other space agencies around the globe are limited to ferrying ⑥ relatively small quantities of cargo into space, with dozens of launches needed to build (for example) the international space station. Today, at a per-kilogram cost of $11,000, chemical rockets are able to carry only 6% of their total weight into space as cargo, with the remaining 94% used for fuel to escape the Earth's gravity and to launch vehicles (Swan 2.2). For a space elevator, however, the immense strength of the tether would allow mechanical climbers to lift extremely heavy loads for roughly $100 per kilogram. Edwards estimates that within as few as two years of operation, the elevator could be "capable of supporting a 22 ton (20,000 kg) climber with a 14 ton (13,000 kg) payload" (*Phase I* 1.4). He and others estimate the cost of building a space elevator within the next ten to twenty years to be a tiny fraction of the cost of a trip to Mars (*Phase 1* 1.8; Lemley).

The construction of a space elevator could usher in a new era of exploration and devel- ⑦ opment akin to the reach of the railroad across the continental United States. In this case, however, not only would the economy of a nation be transformed but also, possibly, the global economy. With the low-cost lifting of materials into orbit commonplace, the dreams of science fiction writers could come true, including "mining the asteroid belt, building zero-G hotels, sailing the solar winds to the moon or Mars, [and] disposing of our radioactive waste by shooting it into the sun" (Taylor). Inexpensive access to space would quickly permit the development of entirely new space-based industries. Proposals already exist to use a space elevator to develop orbiting solar arrays capable of providing cheap, abundant, and clean electrical power to almost anywhere in the world (Edwards, *Phase I* 1.7). Such a clean and economically viable energy source made available to much of the world could decrease dependence on fossil fuels and the nations that export them (Swan 2.3.1.), which in turn could potentially transform the political and economic landscape here on earth.

The comparatively inexpensive satellite launches made possible by a space elevator ⑧ would secure global data transfer, including communications. A recent study conducted by the University of California, San Diego, concluded that "the average American consumes about 34 gigabytes of data and information each day" (Bilton). The invention of the iPhone and other Web- and video-capable mobile devices as well as the global proliferation of high-speed Internet in recent years have only increased the need for secure, fast data transfer. Satellites, along with cell towers and fiber-optic cables, form the pillars of this transfer. With regular, relatively inexpensive access to earth orbit provided by a space elevator, military and commercial

Kearney 5

interests could have replacement satellites ready for deployment in the event of malfunctions (or attack). Sufficient redundancy could be built into these systems to secure the communications and data exchange on which the global economy will increasingly depend.

(9)   A space elevator could also prove crucial to the success of future interplanetary exploration, since cheap access to space would make manned missions economically feasible. In January 2010 President Obama's proposed federal budget eliminated NASA's Constellation program, which planned for manned missions to the moon within ten years. A working space elevator would significantly reduce the cost of such programs and could make them more attractive in the future. Space agencies would be able to build vehicles on earth, where they are more easily and cheaply assembled, and lift large pieces into space for final assembly.

(10)   But no one should imagine that the construction of a space elevator will bring only good news or that every predicted benefit will be achieved. The prospect of building a space elevator (like the prospect of building an anti-ballistic missile system) carries with it the potential for fatal misunderstandings and conflicts. For example, a platform in space could provide the builder with enormous military and economic advantages that other nations might find intolerable. We don't need to look much further than the last century to know that nations will launch wars to block rivals from seizing territory that would confer real or perceived advantages. It is not difficult to imagine a scenario in which Russia or China would vigorously protest America's building an elevator capable of creating a military advantage. Even if the United States explained its peaceful intentions, other nations might remain skeptical and, acting out of self-preservation, rush to build their own elevators.

(11)   And just as nations with nuclear bomb-making capacity strongly discourage other nations from joining that club, one can easily imagine the United States discouraging Iran, for instance, from building a space elevator. Already doubtful of that country's claims for peaceful nuclear development, the United States might also doubt Iran's stated peaceful intentions for a space elevator and move to block its development. The resulting political struggle might look very much like the current effort to keep Iran from becoming a nuclear state. An alternate scenario: other nations, incapable of building the elevator but not willing to see the United States have one, could launch attacks to disable it. Edwards has already considered the implications of a bomb exploding a mechanical climber and severing the nanotube tether (*Phase II* 38).

(12)   Economic gains, real or perceived, of the nation that builds an elevator could also create problems. Not every nation could afford to build its own elevator. Who, then, would

Kearney 6

control access? Would poor(er) nations be welcomed to share in the expected bounty? Would the elevator become one more resource that separates nations into haves and have-nots? One can imagine the country that builds and operates the elevator saying to others: "You don't cooperate with us here on earth, so we won't grant you cheap access to space." In this scenario, the elevator could become a political and economic weapon.

Ninety-eight countries, including the United States and Russia, have signed the Outer Space Treaty, which prohibits the placing of nuclear weapons and other weapons of mass destruction into space and establishes the principle that no country can claim sovereignty of space or celestial bodies beyond earth. The spirit of the agreement is hopeful in being "[i]nspired by the great prospects opening up before mankind as a result of man's entry into outer space" (3); but the agreement is somber as well in recognizing implicitly that nations act in their own interests: "The exploration and use of outer space, including the Moon and other celestial bodies, shall be carried out for the benefit and in the interests of all countries, irrespective of their degree of economic or scientific development, and shall be the province of all mankind" (4). Proponents hope that the nations that build space elevators will adhere to these principles and not seek to make earth orbit the ultimate high ground for economic and military advantage. ⑬

The construction of an elevator to space should excite our collective imaginations; but, human nature being what it is, no one should be surprised if conflicts, along with our hopes, follow the platform into orbit. This is no reason not to pursue research and construction: the elevator and what it makes possible could bring great benefits, including pharmaceuticals and exotic materials manufactured in zero gravity, space tourism, endless supplies of renewable energy, secure communications, and a cost-effective platform from which to explore the solar system and beyond. But the space elevator will likely also act as a lightning rod for international competition. In this way, it could well become just another stage on which to play out our quarrels on earth. ⑭

Kearney 7

Works Cited

Aravind, P. K. "The Physics of the Space Elevator." *American Journal of Physics*, vol. 75, no. 2, 2007, pp. 125–30.

The Bible. Authorized King James Version. Oxford UP, 1998.

Kearney 8

Bilton, Nick. "Part of the Daily American Diet, 34 Gigabytes of Data." *The New York Times*,
9 Dec. 2009, www.nytimes.com/2009/12/10/technology/10data.html?_r=0.

Clarke, Arthur C. *Fountains of Paradise*. V. Gollancz, 1979.

Edwards, Bradley C. Interview. NOVA: *Science Now, Ask the Expert*. PBS, 16 Jan. 2007,
www.pbs.org/wgbh/nova/space/edwards-elevator.html.

---. Interview by Sander Olson. *Nextbigfuture.com*. Lifeboat Foundation, 1 Dec. 2009,
nextbigfuture.com/2016/03/sander-olson-interviewed-dr-stephen.html.

---. *The Space Elevator*. National Institute for Advanced Concepts Phase I Report, 2000,
www.niac.usra.edu/studies/472Edwards.html.

---. *The Space Elevator*. National Institute for Advanced Concepts Phase II Report, 2003,
www.niac.usra.edu/files/studies/final_report/521Edwards.pdf.

Kent, Jason R. "Getting to Space on a Thread: Space Elevator as Alternative Access to
Space." Center for Strategy and Technology/Air War College, April 2007, www.au.af.
mil/au/awc/awcgate/cst/bh_kent.pdf.

Lasermotive. 2007–present.www.lasermotive.com.

Lemley, Brad. "Going Up." *Discover*, Kalmbach Publishing, 25 July 2004.
discovermagazine.com/2004/jul/cover.

"LiftPort Announces Support of the Space Elevator Concept by the National Space
Society." *SpaceRef*, SpaceRef Interactive, 25 June 2003, www.spaceref.com/news/
viewpr.html?pid=11935.

LiftPort Group, 2003–present. www.liftport.com.

Pugno, Nicola M. "On the Strength of the Carbon Nanotube-based Space Elevator Cable:
From Nanomechanics to Megamechanics." *Journal of Physics*: *Condensed Matter*,
vol. 18, 2006, pp. 1971–90.

Shelef, Ben. "Did You Just Say 'A Space Elevator'?!" *Spaceward.org*, 2008, Spaceward
Foundation, www.spaceward.org/elevator.

Swan, Cathy W., and Peter A. Swan. "Why We Need a Space Elevator." *Space Policy*,
vol. 22, no. 2, 2006, pp. 86–91. *ResearchGate*, doi: 10.1016/j.spacepol.2006.02.008.

Taylor, Chris. "Space Elevator Entrepreneurs Shoot for the Stars." *CNN Money*, 8 Dec. 2009,
money.cnn.com/2009/12/07/smallbusiness/space_elevator.fsb/.

United Nations. "Treaty on Principles Governing the Activities of States in the Exploration
and Use of Outer Space, Including the Moon and Other Celestial Bodies." *Treaties
and Principles on Outer Space*, United Nations, 2002, pp. 3–8.

CRITICAL READING FOR SYNTHESIS

- *Use the tips from Critical Reading for Summary on page 6.* Remember to examine the context; note the title and subtitle; identify the main point; identify the subpoints; break the reading into sections; distinguish between points, examples, and counterarguments; watch for transitions within and between paragraphs; and read actively and recursively.

- *Establish the writer's primary purpose.* Use some of the guidelines discussed in Chapter 2. Is the piece primarily informative, persuasive, or entertaining? Assess whether the piece achieves its purpose.

- *Read to identify a key idea.* If you begin reading your source materials with a key idea or topic already in mind, read to identify what your sources have to say about the idea.

- *Read to discover a key idea.* If you begin the reading process without a key idea in mind, read to discover a key idea that your sources address.

- *Read for relationships.* Regardless of whether you already have a key idea or you are attempting to discover one, your emphasis in reading should be on noting the ways in which the readings relate to each other, to a key idea, and to your purpose in writing the synthesis.

MyWritingLab™   Visit Ch. 4 Explanatory Synthesis in MyWritingLab to test your understanding of the chapter objectives.

Argument Synthesis

After completing this chapter, you will be able to:

5.1 Apply the elements of argument to the writing of argument syntheses.

5.2 Write an argument synthesis.

5.3 Use various strategies to develop and support your arguments.

5.4 Use comparison-and-contrast, where appropriate, to develop your argument synthesis.

WHAT IS AN ARGUMENT SYNTHESIS?

5.1 Apply the elements of argument to the writing of argument syntheses.

An argument is an attempt to persuade a reader or listener that a particular and debatable claim is true. Writers argue in order to establish facts, to make statements of value, and to recommend policies. For instance, answering the question *Why do soldiers sometimes commit atrocities in wartime?* would involve making an argument. To develop this argument, researchers might conduct experiments, interview experts, collect historical evidence, and examine and interpret data. The researchers might then present their findings at professional conferences and in journals and books. The extent to which readers (or listeners) accept these findings will depend on the quality of the supporting evidence and the care with which the researchers have argued their case. What we are calling an argument *synthesis* draws upon evidence from a variety of sources in an attempt to persuade others of the truth or validity of a debatable claim.

By contrast, the explanatory synthesis, as we have seen, is fairly modest in purpose. It emphasizes the sources themselves, not the writer's use of sources to persuade others. The writer of an explanatory synthesis aims to inform, not persuade. Here, for example, is a thesis devised for an explanatory synthesis on the ubiquity of cell phones in contemporary life:

> Cell phones make it possible for us to be always within reach, though many people would prefer *not* to be always within reach.

This thesis summarizes two viewpoints about the impact of cell phones on contemporary life, arguing neither for nor against either viewpoint.

An argument thesis, however, is *persuasive* in purpose. A writer working with the same source material might conceive and support an opposing thesis:

> Cell phones have ruined our ability to be isolated, to be willfully *out of touch* with the rest of the world.

So the thesis for an argument synthesis is a claim about which reasonable people could disagree. It is a claim with which—given the right arguments—your audience might be persuaded to agree. The strategy of your argument synthesis is therefore to find and use convincing *support* for your *claim.*

The Elements of Argument: Claim, Support, and Assumption

One way of looking at an argument is to see it as an interplay of three essential elements: claim, support, and assumption. A *claim* is a proposition or conclusion that you are trying to prove. You prove this claim by using *support* in the form of fact, statistics, or expert opinion. Linking your supporting evidence to your claim is your *assumption* about the subject. This assumption, also called a *warrant*, is an underlying belief or principle about some aspect of the world and how it operates (see our discussion of assumptions in Chapter 2, pp. 64–67). By their nature, assumptions (which are often unstated) tend to be more general than either claims or supporting evidence.

Here are the essential elements of an argument advocating parental restriction of television viewing for high school students:

Claim

> High school students should be restricted to no more than two hours of TV viewing per day.

Support

> An important new study and the testimony of educational specialists reveal that students who watch more than two hours of TV a night have, on average, lower grades than those who watch less TV.

Assumption

> Excessive TV viewing adversely affects academic performance.

As another example, here's an argumentative claim on the topic of computer-mediated communication (CMC)—a term sociologists use to describe online contacts among friends and family:

> CMC threatens to undermine human intimacy, connection, and ultimately community.

Here are the other elements of this argument:

Support

- People are spending increasing amounts of time in cyberspace: In 1998, the average Internet user spent more than four hours per week online, a figure that has quadrupled in the past fifteen years.
- College health officials report that excessive Internet use threatens many college students' academic and psychological well-being.
- New kinds of relationships fostered on the Internet often pose challenges to preexisting relationships.

Assumptions

- The communication skills used and the connections formed during Internet contact fundamentally differ from those used and formed during face-to-face contact.
- "Real" connection and a sense of community are sustained by face-to-face contact, not by Internet interactions.

For the most part, arguments should be constructed logically so that assumptions link evidence (supporting facts, statistics, and expert opinions) to claims. As we'll see, however, logic is only one component of effective arguments.

MyWritingLab™   **Exercise 5.1**

Practicing Claim, Support, and Assumption

Devise two sets of claims, support, and assumptions. First, in response to the example above on computer-mediated communication and relationships, write a one-sentence claim addressing the positive impact (or potentially positive impact) of CMC on relationships—whether you personally agree with the claim or not. Then list the supporting statements on which such a claim might rest and the assumption that underlies them. Second, write a claim that states your own position on any debatable topic you choose. Again, devise statements of support and relevant assumptions.

The Three Appeals of Argument: *Logos, Ethos, Pathos*

Speakers and writers have never relied on logic alone in advancing and supporting their claims. More than 2000 years ago, the Athenian philosopher and rhetorician Aristotle explained how speakers attempting to persuade others to their point of view could achieve their purpose by relying on one or more *appeals*, which he called *logos, ethos,* and *pathos.*

Since we frequently find these three appeals employed in political argument, we'll use political examples in the following discussion. All three appeals are also used extensively in advertising, legal cases, business documents, and many other types of argument. Bear in mind that in academic writing, the appeal to logic (*logos*) is by far the most commonly used appeal.

Logos

Logos is the rational appeal, the appeal to reason. Academic presentations, including the papers you will write across the curriculum, build almost exclusively on appeals to logic and evidence. If writers and speakers expect to persuade their audiences, they must argue logically and must supply appropriate evidence to support their case. Logical arguments are commonly of two types (often combined): deductive and inductive.

Deductive Reasoning   The *deductive* argument begins with a generalization, then cites a specific case related to that generalization from which follows a conclusion. An example of a deductive argument may be seen in President John F. Kennedy's address to the nation in June 1963 on the need for sweeping civil rights legislation. Kennedy begins with the generalizations that it "ought to be possible...for American students of any color to attend any public institution they select without having to be backed up by troops" and that "it ought to be possible for American citizens of any color to register and vote in a free election without interference or fear of reprisal." Kennedy then provides several specific examples (primarily recent events in Birmingham, Alabama) and statistics to show that this was not the case. He concludes:

> We face, therefore, a moral crisis as a country and a people. It cannot be met by repressive police action. It cannot be left to increased demonstrations in the streets. It cannot be quieted by token moves or talk. It is time to act in the Congress, in your state and local legislative body, and, above all, in all of our daily lives.

Underlying Kennedy's argument is this reasoning:

All Americans should enjoy certain rights. (*assumption*)

Some Americans do not enjoy these rights. (*support*)

We must take action to ensure that all Americans enjoy these rights. (*claim*)

Inductive Reasoning   Another form of logical argumentation is *inductive* reasoning. A speaker or writer who argues inductively begins not with a generalization, but with several pieces of specific evidence. The speaker then draws a conclusion from this evidence. For example, in a debate on gun control, former senator Robert C. Byrd cited specific examples of rampant crime involving guns: "I read of young men being viciously murdered for a pair of sneakers, a leather jacket, or $20." He also offered statistical evidence of the increasing crime rate: "In 1951, there were 3.2 policemen for every felony committed in the United States; this year nearly 3.2 felonies will be committed per every police officer." He concluded, "Something has to change. We have to stop the crimes that are distorting and disrupting the way of life for so many innocent, law-respecting Americans. The bill that we are debating today attempts to do just that."

Former senator Edward M. Kennedy also used statistical evidence in arguing for passage of the Racial Justice Act of 1990, which was designed to ensure that minorities are not disproportionately singled out for the death penalty. Kennedy pointed out that between 1973 and 1980, seventeen defendants in Fulton County, Georgia, were charged with killing police officers, but that the only defendant who received the death sentence was a black man. Kennedy also cited statistics to show that "those who killed whites were 4.3 times more likely to receive the death penalty than were killers of blacks" and that "in Georgia, blacks who killed whites received the death penalty 16.7 percent of the time, while whites who killed blacks received the death penalty only 4.2 percent of the time."

Maintaining a Critical Perspective   Of course, the mere piling up of evidence does not in itself make the speaker's case. As Donna Cross explains in "Politics: The Art of Bamboozling,"[1] politicians are very adept at "card-stacking"—lining up evidence in favor of a conclusion without bothering to mention (or barely mentioning) contrary evidence. And statistics can be selected and manipulated to prove anything, as demonstrated in Darrell Huff's landmark book *How to Lie with Statistics* (1954). Moreover, what appears to be a logical argument may in fact be fundamentally flawed. (See Chapter 2 for a discussion of logical fallacies and faulty reasoning strategies.)

On the other hand, the fact that evidence can be distorted, statistics misused, and logic fractured does not mean that these tools of reason should be dismissed. It means only that audiences have to listen and read critically and to question the use of statistics and other evidence.

MyWritingLab™   Exercise 5.2

Using Deductive and Inductive Logic

Choose an issue currently being debated at your school or a college-related issue about which you are concerned. Write a claim about this issue. Then write two paragraphs addressing your claim—one in which you organize your points deductively (beginning with your claim and following with support) and one in which you organize them inductively (presenting supporting evidence and following with a claim). Possible issues might include college admissions policies, classroom crowding, or grade inflation. Alternatively, you could base your paragraphs on a claim generated in Exercise 5.1.

Ethos

Ethos, or the ethical appeal, is based not on the ethics relating to the subject under discussion, but rather on the ethical status of the person making the argument. A person making an argument must have a certain degree of credibility: That

---

[1]Donna Cross, *Word Abuse: How the Words We Use Use Us* (New York: Coward, 1979).

person must be of good character, have sound sense, and be qualified to argue based either on expert experience with the subject matter or on carefully conducted research. Students writing in academic settings establish their appeal to *ethos* by developing presentations that are well organized, carefully reasoned, and thoroughly referenced with source citations. These are the hallmarks of writers and speakers who care deeply about their work. If you care, your audience will care and consider your argument seriously.

Appeals to *ethos* are usually most explicit in political contests. For example, Elizabeth Cervantes Barrón, running for senator as the Peace and Freedom candidate, establishes her credibility this way: "I was born and raised in central Los Angeles. I grew up in a multiethnic, multicultural environment where I learned to respect those who were different from me.... I am a teacher and am aware of how cutbacks in education have affected our children and our communities." On the other end of the political spectrum, the American Independent gubernatorial candidate Jerry McCready also begins with an ethical appeal: "As a self-employed businessman, I have learned firsthand what it is like to try to make ends meet in an unstable economy being manipulated by out-of-touch politicians." Both candidates are making an appeal to *ethos*, an appeal based on the strength of their personal qualities for the office they seek. Both argue, in effect, "Trust me. My experience makes me a credible, knowledgeable candidate."

L. A. Kauffman is not running for office but writing an article arguing against socialism as an ideology around which to build societies.[2] To establish his credibility as someone who understands socialism well enough to criticize it meaningfully, Kauffman begins with an appeal to *ethos:* "Until recently, I was executive editor of the journal *Socialist Review*. Before that I worked for the Marxist magazine, *Monthly Review*. My bookshelves are filled with books of Marxist theory, and I even have a picture of Karl Marx up on my wall." Thus, Kauffman establishes his credentials to argue knowledgeably about Marxism.

MyWritingLab™

Exercise 5.3 ◯

Using Ethos

Return to the claim you used for Exercise 5.2, and write a paragraph in which you use an appeal to *ethos* to make a case for that claim.

Pathos

Finally, speakers and writers appeal to their audiences by using *pathos*, an appeal to the emotions. Writers in academic settings rely heavily on the force of logic and evidence and rarely make appeals to *pathos*. Beyond academic settings, however, appeals to the emotions are commonplace. Nothing is inherently wrong with using an emotional appeal. Indeed, because emotions often move people far more

---

[2]L. A. Kauffman, "Socialism: No," *Progressive*, 1 Apr. 1993.

successfully than reason alone, speakers and writers would be foolish not to use emotion. And it would be a drab, humorless world if human beings were not subject to the sway of feeling as well as reason. The emotional appeal becomes problematic only when it is the *sole* or *primary* basis of the argument.

President Ronald Reagan was a master of emotional appeal. He closed his first inaugural address with a reference to the view from the Capitol to Arlington National Cemetery, where lie thousands of markers of "heroes":

> Under one such marker lies a young man, Martin Treptow, who left his job in a small-town barbershop in 1917 to go to France with the famed Rainbow Division. There, on the western front, he was killed trying to carry a message between battalions under heavy artillery fire. We're told that on his body was found a diary. On the flyleaf under the heading, "My Pledge," he had written these words: "America must win this war. Therefore, I will work, I will save, I will sacrifice, I will endure, I will fight cheerfully and do my utmost, as if the issue of the whole struggle depended on me alone." The crisis we are facing today does not require of us the kind of sacrifice that Martin Treptow and so many thousands of others were called upon to make. It does require, however, our best effort and our willingness to believe in ourselves and to believe in our capacity to perform great deeds, to believe that together with God's help we can and will resolve the problems which now confront us.

Surely, Reagan implies, if Martin Treptow can act so courageously and so selflessly, we can do the same. His logic is somewhat unclear because the connection between Martin Treptow and ordinary Americans of 1981 is rather tenuous (as Reagan concedes), but the emotional power of the heroism of Martin Treptow, whom reporters were sent scurrying to research, carries the argument.

A more recent president, Bill Clinton, also used *pathos*. Addressing an audience of the nation's governors about his welfare plan, Clinton closed his remarks by referring to a conversation he had had with a welfare mother who had gone through the kind of training program Clinton was advocating. Asked by Clinton whether she thought that such training programs should be mandatory, the mother said, "I sure do." Clinton in his remarks explained what she said when he asked her why:

> "Well, because if it wasn't, there would be a lot of people like me home watching the soaps because we don't believe we can make anything of ourselves anymore. So you've got to make it mandatory." And I said, "What's the best thing about having a job?" She said, "When my boy goes to school, and they say, 'What does your mama do for a living?' he can give an answer."

Clinton counts on the emotional power in that anecdote to set up his conclusion: "We must end poverty for Americans who want to work. And we must do it on terms that dignify all of the rest of us, as well as help our country to work better. I need your help, and I think we can do it."

MyWritingLab™

Exercise 5.4

Using **Pathos**

Return to the claim you used for Exercises 5.2 and 5.3, and write a paragraph in which you use an appeal to *pathos* to argue for that claim.

The Limits of Argument

Our discussion of *ethos* and *pathos* indicates a potentially troubling but undeniable reality: Arguments are not won on the basis of logic and evidence alone. In the real world, arguments don't operate like academic debates. If the purpose of argument is to get people to change their minds or to agree that the writer's or speaker's position on a particular topic is the best available, then the person making the argument must be aware that factors other than evidence and good reasoning come into play when readers or listeners are considering the matter.

These factors involve deep-seated cultural, religious, ethnic, racial, and gender identities, moral preferences, and the effects of personal experiences (either pleasant or unpleasant) that are generally resistant to logic and evidence, however well framed. You could try—using the best available arguments—to convince someone who is pro-life to agree with the pro-choice position (or vice versa). Or you could try to persuade someone who opposes capital punishment to believe that state-endorsed executions are necessary for deterrence (or for any other reason). You might even marshal your evidence and logic to try to persuade someone whose family members have had run-ins with the law that police efforts are directed at protecting the law-abiding.

However, on such emotionally loaded topics, it is extremely difficult, if not impossible, to get people to change their minds because they are so personally invested in their beliefs. As Susan Jacoby, author of *The Age of American Unreason,* notes, "Whether watching television news, consulting political blogs, or (more rarely) reading books, Americans today have become a people in search of validation for opinions that they already hold."[3] Put Jacoby's claim to the test: On any given evening, watch a half-hour of Fox News and MSNBC News. The news coverage of at least a few stories will likely overlap. Can you detect a slant, or bias, in this coverage? Which program would a political conservative be inclined to watch? A liberal? Why?

Fruitful Topics for Argument

The tenacity with which people hold onto longtime beliefs does not mean, however, that they cannot change their minds or that subjects like abortion, capital punishment, and gun control should be off-limits to reasoned debate. The past twenty years has seen some contentious issues, like gay marriage, resolved both in the courts and through elections; and reasoned argument—as well as appeals

---

[3]Susan Jacoby, "Talking to Ourselves: Americans Are Increasingly Close-Minded and Unwilling to Listen to Opposing Views," *Los Angeles Times* 20 Apr. 2008: M10.

to *pathos* and *ethos*—has played a significant role. Still, you should be aware of the limits of argument. The most fruitful topics for argument in a freshman composition setting tend to be those on which most people are persuadable, either because they know relatively little about the topic or because deep-rooted cultural, religious, or moral beliefs are not involved. At least initially in your career as a writer of academic papers, it's probably best to avoid "hot-button" topics that are the focus of broader cultural debates and to focus instead on topics in which *pathos* plays less of a part.

For example, most people are not emotionally invested in plug-in hybrid or hydrogen-powered vehicles, so an argument on behalf of the more promising technology for the coming decades will not be complicated by deep-seated beliefs. Similarly, most people don't know enough about the mechanics of sleep to have strong opinions on how to deal with sleep deprivation. Your arguments on such topics, therefore, will provide opportunities both to inform your readers or listeners and to persuade them that your arguments, if well reasoned and supported by sound evidence, are at least plausible, if not entirely convincing.

DEMONSTRATION: DEVELOPING AN ARGUMENT SYNTHESIS—RESPONDING TO BULLIES

To demonstrate how to plan and draft an argument synthesis, let's suppose that your composition instructor has assigned a research paper and that in pondering possible topics you find yourself considering what can be done to discourage widespread bullying in American schools. Perhaps you have a personal motivation to write on this topic: You were bullied as a child or recall watching others being bullied but did nothing to intervene. So you do some preliminary reading and discover that the problem of bullying is widespread and that forty-nine states have adopted anti-bullying legislation. Still, however, the problem persists. What can be done to solve it?

You have a topic, and you have a guiding question for a paper.

Suppose, in preparing to write a paper in which you will argue for a workable solution to the problem of bullying, you locate (among others) the following sources:

- *Bullying Statistics* (a Web site)
- *The 2011 National School Climate Survey: The Experiences of Lesbian, Gay, Bisexual and Transgender Youth in Our Nation's Schools* (a report)
- *Olweus Bullying Prevention Program: Scope and Sequence* (a publisher's catalogue description of a widely adopted anti-bullying program)
- "Bullying—And the Power of Peers" (a scholarly article also delivered as a paper at a White House conference on bullying)

Carefully read these sources (which follow), noting the kinds of evidence—facts, expert opinions, and statistics—you could draw on to develop an *argument synthesis.* These passages are excerpts only; in preparing your paper, you would draw on the entire articles, reports, and Web sites from which these passages were taken. And you would draw on more sources than these in your search for supporting materials (as the writer of the model synthesis has done; see pp. 148–157). But these four sources provide a good introduction to the subject. Our discussion of how these passages can form the basis of an argument synthesis resumes on page 144.

BULLYING STATISTICS

Pacer.org

- **Nearly one-third of all school-aged children are bullied each year— upwards of 13 million students.**
  - Nationwide, 20 percent of students in grades 9–12 experienced bullying. Source: The 2011 Youth Risk Behavior Surveillance System (Centers for Disease Control and Prevention).
  - Nationwide, 28 percent of students in grades 6–12 experienced bullying. Source: The 2008–2009 School Crime Supplement (National Center for Education Statistics and Bureau of Justice Statistics).
- **64 percent of children who were bullied did not report it; only 36 percent reported the bullying.** (Petrosino 2010) Petrosino, Anthony J. *What Characteristics of Bullying, Bullying Victims, and Schools Are Associated with Increased Reporting of Bullying to School Officials?* Washington, DC: National Center for Education Evaluation and Regional Assistance, 2010.
- More than half of bullying situations (57 percent) stop when a peer intervenes on behalf of the student being bullied. Wendy M.Craig, Lynn D. Hawkins, Debra J. Pepler. *Naturalistic Observations of Peer Interventions in Bullying.* Social Development, Volume 10, Issue 4, pages 512–527, November 2001.

Statistics about bullying of students with disabilities

- Only 10 U.S. studies have been conducted on the connection between bullying and developmental disabilities, but all of these studies found that **children with disabilities were two to three times more likely** to be bullied than their nondisabled peers. ("Disabilities: Insights from Across Fields and Around the World," 2009).
- Researchers discovered that students with disabilities were more worried about school safety and being injured or harassed by other peers compared to students without a disability (Saylor & Leach, 2009).
- The National Autistic Society reports that 40 percent of children with autism and 60 percent of children with Asperger's syndrome have experienced bullying.

The 2011 National School Climate Survey: The Experiences of Lesbian, Gay, Bisexual and Transgender Youth in Our Nation's Schools

Joseph Kosciw,
Emily Greytak,
Mark Bartkiewicz,
Madelyn Boesen, and
Neal Palmer

In 1999, the Gay, Lesbian and Straight Education Network (GLSEN) identified the need for national data on the experiences of lesbian, gay, bisexual, and transgender (LGBT) students and launched the first National School Climate Survey (NSCS). At the time, the school experiences of LGBT youth were under-documented and nearly absent from national studies of adolescents. For more than a decade, the biennial NSCS has documented the unique challenges LGBT students face and identified interventions that can improve school climate. The survey explores the prevalence of anti-LGBT language and victimization, the effect that these experiences have on LGBT students' achievement and well-being, and the utility of interventions in lessening the negative effects of a hostile school climate and promoting a positive educational experience. The survey also examines demographic and community-level differences in LGBT students' experiences. The NSCS remains one of the few studies to examine the school experiences of LGBT students nationally, and its results have been vital to GLSEN's understanding of the issues that LGBT students face, thereby informing the authors' ongoing work to ensure safe and affirming schools for all.

In their 2011 survey, the authors examine the experiences of LGBT students with regard to indicators of negative school climate:

1. hearing biased remarks, including homophobic remarks, in school;
2. feeling unsafe in school because of personal characteristics, such as sexual orientation, gender expression, or race/ethnicity;
3. missing classes or days of school because of safety reasons; and
4. experiencing harassment and assault in school.

They also examine:

1. the possible negative effects of a hostile school climate on LGBT students' academic achievement, educational aspirations, and psychological well-being;
2. whether or not students report experiences of victimization to school officials or to family members and how these adults address the problem; and
3. how the school experiences of LGBT students differ by personal and community characteristics.

In addition, they demonstrate the degree to which LGBT students have access to supportive resources in school, and they explore the possible benefits of these resources, including:

1. Gay-Straight Alliances (GSAs) or similar clubs;
2. anti-bullying/harassment school policies and laws;
3. supportive school staff; and
4. curricula that are inclusive of LGBT-related topics.

OLWEUS BULLYING PREVENTION PROGRAM:
SCOPE AND SEQUENCE

Publisher Catalogue Description

What Is the Olweus Bullying Prevention Program?

The Olweus Bullying Prevention Program (OBPP) is the most researched and best-known bullying prevention program available today. With over thirty-five years of research and successful implementation all over the world, OBPP is a whole-school program that has been proven to prevent or reduce bullying throughout a school setting.

OBPP is used at the school, classroom, and individual levels and includes methods to reach out to parents and the community for involvement and support. School administrators, teachers, and other staff are primarily responsible for introducing and implementing the program. These efforts are designed to improve peer relations and make the school a safer and more positive place for students to learn and develop.

What Are the Goals of OBPP?

The goals of the program are

- to reduce existing bullying problems among students
- to prevent the development of new bullying problems
- to achieve better peer relations at school

For Whom Is OBPP Designed?

OBPP is designed for students in elementary, middle, and junior high schools (students ages five to fifteen years old). All students participate in most aspects of the program, while students identified as bullying others, or as targets of bullying, receive additional individualized interventions.

With some adaptation, the program can also be used in high schools, although research has not measured the program's effectiveness beyond tenth grade. In addition, classroom support materials are not currently available for high school students. Chapter 17 of the program's Schoolwide Guide talks about adapting the program for use in a high school setting.

WHITE HOUSE REPORT/BULLYING—AND THE POWER OF PEERS

Promoting Respectful Schools
Philip Rodkin

Using Peers to Intervene

In a review of bullying-reduction programs, Farrington and Ttofi (2009) found that interventions that involve peers, such as using students as peer mediators or engaging bystanders to disapprove of bullying and support victims of harassment, were associated with *increases* in victimization! In fact, of 20 program elements included in 44 school-based programs, work with peers was the *only* program element associated with significantly *more* bullying and victimization. (In contrast, there were significant and positive effects for parent training and school meetings in reducing bullying.) Still other reviews of bullying intervention programs have found generally weak effects (Merrell, Gueldner, Ross, & Isava, 2008).

These disheartening results speak to the fact that peer influences can be a constructive or destructive force on bullying and need to be handled with knowledge, skill, and care. Antisocial peer groups can undermine behavioral interventions. For peer mediation to be effective, students who are chosen to be peer mediators should probably be popular and prosocial (Pellegrini et al., 2010; Pepler et al., 2010; Vaillancourt et al., 2010).

Some of the most innovative, intensive, grassroots uses of peer relationships to reduce bullying, such as the You Have the Power! program in Montgomery County, Maryland, have not been scientifically evaluated. The final verdict awaits on some promising programs that take advantage of peer relationships to combat bullying, such as the Finnish program KiVa (Salmivalli et al., 2010), which has a strong emphasis on influencing onlookers to support the victim rather than encourage the bully, and the Steps to Respect program (Frey et al., 2010), which works at the elementary school level.

Teachers can ask what *kind* of bully they face when dealing with a victimization problem. Is the bully a member of a group, or is he or she a group leader? How are bullies and victims situated in the peer ecology? Educators who exclusively target peripheral, antisocial cliques as the engine of school violence problems may leave intact other groups that are more responsible for mainstream peer support of bullying. A strong step educators could take would be to periodically ask students about bullying and their social relationships. (See "What Teachers Can Do.")

• • •

5   The task ahead is to better integrate bullies and the children they harass into the social fabric of the school and better inform educators of how to recognize,

understand, and help guide children's relationships. With guidance from caring, engaged adults, youth can organize themselves as a force that makes bullying less effective as a means of social connection or as an outlet for alienation.

What Teachers Can Do

- **Ask students about bullying.** Survey students regularly on whether they are being harassed or have witnessed harassment. Make it easier for students to come to an adult in the school to talk about harassment by building staff-student relationships, having suggestion boxes where students can provide input anonymously, or administering schoolwide surveys in which students can report confidentially on peers who bully and on the children whom they harass. Consider what bullying accomplishes for a bully. Does the bully want to gain status? Does the bully use aggression to control others?

- **Ask students about their relationships.** Bullying is a destructive, asymmetric relationship. Know whom students hang out with, who their friends are, and whom they dislike. Know whom students perceive to be popular and unpopular. Connect with students who have no friends. School staff members vary widely in their knowledge of students' relationships and tend to underestimate the level of aggression among peers.

- **Build democratic classroom and school climates.** Identify student leaders who can encourage peers to stand against bullying. Assess whether student social norms are *really* against bullying. Train teachers to better understand and manage student social dynamics and handle aggression with clear, consistent consequences. Master teachers not only promote academic success, but also build relationships, trust, and a sense of community.

- **Be an informed consumer of antibullying curriculums.** Antibullying interventions can be successful, but there are significant caveats. Some bullies would benefit from services that go beyond bullying-reduction programs. Some programs work well in Europe, but not as well in the United States. Most antibullying programs have not been rigorously evaluated, so be an informed consumer when investigating claims of success. Even with a well-developed antibullying curriculum, understanding students' relationships at your school is crucial.

- **Remember that bullying is also a problem of values.** Implement an intellectually challenging character education or socioemotional learning curriculum. Teach students how to achieve their goals by being assertive rather than aggressive. Always resolve conflicts with civility among and between staff and students. Involve families.

MyWritingLab™

Exercise 5.5

Critical Reading for Synthesis

Having read the selections related to bullying, pages 139–143, write a one-sentence summary of each. On the same page, list two or three topics that you think are common to several of the selections. Beneath each topic, list the authors who have something to say on that topic and briefly note what they have to say. Finally, for each topic, jot down what *you* have to say. Now regard your effort: With each topic you have created a discussion point suitable for inclusion in a paper. (Of course, until you determine the claim of such a paper, you won't know to what end you might put the discussion.) Write a paragraph or two in which you introduce the topic, and then conduct a brief conversation among the interested parties (including yourself).

THE ARGUMENT SYNTHESIS

5.2 Write an argument synthesis.

Before drafting your argument synthesis, you should consider your purpose, develop a claim, decide how to use your source materials, plan your essay, and formulate an argument strategy.

Consider Your Purpose

Your specific purpose in writing an argument synthesis is crucial. What exactly you want to do will affect your claim and how you organize the evidence. Your purpose may be clear to you before you begin research, or it may not emerge until after you have completed your research. Of course, the sooner your purpose is clear to you, the fewer wasted motions you will make. On the other hand, the more you approach research as an exploratory process, the likelier that your conclusions will emerge from the sources themselves rather than from preconceived ideas. Each new writing project will have its own rhythm in this regard. Be flexible in your approach: Through some combination of preconceived structures and invigorating discoveries, you will find your way to the source materials that will yield a promising paper.

Let's say that while reading these four (and additional) sources related to bullying, you share the concern of many who believe that bullies traumatize too many vulnerable children and prevent them from feeling safe at school. Perhaps you believe that bullying is fundamental to human nature, or at least to some people's human nature, and that laws will do little to change the behavior. Perhaps you believe that laws shape, or at least constrain, human behavior all the time: the laws against murder or theft, for instance, or, more mundanely, speeding. You may believe that laws *do* have a role to play in lessening if not preventing bullying and that we should be willing to sacrifice some freedom of speech to prevent bullies from menacing their victims through text messages and online postings.

Most people will bring at least some personal history to this topic, and personal history is often a good place to begin. Mine that history for insights, and use them if they're able to guide you in posing questions and in developing arguments. Your purpose in writing, then, emerges from these kinds of responses to the source materials you find.

Making a Claim: Formulate a Thesis

As we indicated in the introduction to this chapter, one useful way of approaching an argument is to see it as making a *claim*. A claim is a proposition, a conclusion you have made, that you are trying to prove or demonstrate. If your purpose is to argue that bullies can learn to moderate their behavior if they are integrated into a healthy peer group, then that claim (generally expressed in one-sentence form as a *thesis*) is at the heart of your argument. You will draw support from your sources as you argue logically for your claim.

Not every piece of information in a source is useful for supporting a claim. You must read with care and select the opinions, facts, and statistics that best advance your position. You may even find yourself drawing support from sources that make claims entirely different from your own. For example, in researching the subject of bullying prevention, you may come across an anti-bullying program that you know has been proven ineffective by researchers; yet that source's presentation of statistics concerning the prevalence of bullying may be sound, and you may end up using those statistics in your argument. Perhaps you will find information in these sources to help support your own contrary arguments.

You might use one source as part of a *counterargument*— an argument opposing your own—so that you can demonstrate its weaknesses and, in the process, strengthen your own claim. On the other hand, the author of one of your sources may be so convincing in supporting a claim that you adopt it yourself, either partially or entirely. The point is that *the argument is in your hands.* You must devise it yourself and use your sources in ways that will support the claim you present in your thesis.

You may not want to divulge your thesis until the end of the paper, thereby drawing the reader along toward your conclusion, allowing the thesis to flow naturally out of the argument and the evidence on which it is based. If you do this, you are working *inductively.* Or you may wish to be more direct and (after an introduction) *begin* with your thesis, following the thesis statement with evidence and reasoning to support it. If you do this, you are working *deductively.* In academic papers, deductive arguments are far more common than inductive ones.

Based on your reactions to reading sources—and perhaps also on your own inclinations as a student—you may find yourself essentially in sympathy with a view of anti-bullying programs shared by several of your sources: that despite being required by the states' anti-bullying legislation, these programs do not work because they prescribe a one-size-fits-all approach to a complex problem. At the same time, you may feel that the suffering bullies cause is too great to do nothing. Most important, you conclude that a local approach to bullying makes sense, one that builds on the wisdom of parents, teachers, and community leaders who know the children involved and who know the local culture in which bullying occurs. You review your sources and begin working on a thesis. After a few tries, you develop this thesis:

> A blend of local, ground-up strategies and state-mandated programs and laws promises to be the best approach to dealing with bullying in American schools.

Decide How You Will Use Your Source Material

Your claim commits you to introducing the problem of bullying, explaining top-down anti-bullying legislation and its limitations, explaining ground-up strategies and their limitations, and arguing for a combined approach to changing the behavior of bullies. The sources (some provided here, some located elsewhere) offer information and ideas—evidence—that will allow you to support your claim. For instance, the catalogue description of the *Olweus Bullying Prevention Program* (OBPP) establishes the principles of a widely adopted one-size-fits-all approach to bullying prevention. Yet the "White House Report" by Rodkin cautions that "some programs [like Olweus] work well in Europe, but not as well in the United States." (These and several other sources not included in this chapter will be cited in the model argument paper.)

Develop an Organizational Plan

Having established your overall purpose and your claim, having developed a thesis (which may change as you write and revise the paper), and having decided how to draw upon your source materials, how do you logically organize your paper? In many cases, a well-written thesis will suggest an organization. In the case of the bullying project, the first part of your paper would define the problem of bullying and discuss the legislative response. The second part would argue that there are problems associated with anti-bullying legislation. The third part would introduce a solution to these problems. Sorting through your material and categorizing it by topic and subtopic, you might compose the following outline:

I. Introduction
    A. Graphic example of bullying
    B. Background: Who is bullied
    C. Cyberbullying
        1. Definition
        2. Suicides
    D. Anti-bullying laws
        1. Laws criminalize bullying
        2. Laws mandate education to reduce bullying
  Thesis

II. Problems with anti-bullying laws
    A. Laws implemented in a rush (after Columbine)
    B. Elements of some laws unconstitutional
    C. Laws don't follow standard definitions
    D. Effectiveness of anti-bullying programs uneven

III. An alternate solution to the problem of bullying
    A. Rationale and blueprint for alternate approach
    B. A local "ground-up" solution
        1. Emily Bazelon

2. Lee Hirsch and Cynthia Lowen
3. Philip Rodkin
C. Concession
   1. Local solutions possibly flawed
   2. Local solutions should be evaluated

IV. Conclusion: Blended approach needed

Formulate an Argument Strategy

The argument that emerges through this outline will build not only on evidence drawn from sources but also on the writer's assumption that a top-down legislative approach can be combined with a bottom-up grassroots approach to achieve a meaningful reduction in bullying behaviors. Some readers may disagree.

Those who believe that local solutions to complex problems are preferable to broad, one-size-fits-all solutions would likely want to emphasize school-specific initiatives for combating the problem of bullying. They would place more confidence in parents and educators on the ground to devise effective solutions than they would in statewide laws designed to combat bullying.

By contrast, those who believe that laws are the proper vehicle to address deep-rooted social problems (for instance, racism) would likely have more confidence in the legislative process—that is, in broad, system-wide fixes. On learning that laws intending to address bullying aren't working, they would be more inclined to fix the one-size-fits-all laws rather than risk implementing hundreds of local solutions that could not be readily evaluated for effectiveness. So people on both sides of the argument might not only reject an approach that runs counter to their own position on the top-down/ground-up spectrum, but might also be wary of a recommendation to blend approaches. It will be the writer's job to convince skeptics that a combined approach is workable. Everyone wants to prevent bullying, but different views on one key assumption will determine which solutions are pursued.

Writers can accept or partially accept an opposing assumption by making a *concession,* in the process establishing themselves as reasonable and willing to compromise (see p. 163). The *claim* of the argument about the best way to combat bullying is primarily a claim about *policy,* about actions that should (or should not) be taken. An argument can also concern a claim about *facts* (Does X exist? How can we define X? Does X lead to Y?), a claim about *value* (What is X worth?), or a claim about *cause and effect* (Why did X happen?).

The present argument rests to some degree on a dispute about cause and effect. No one disputes that bullying remains an intractable problem, but many have disputed how and why bullying occurs and how it is best handled. After the events at Columbine in 1999 and following the suicides of teenagers who suffered the torments of bullies, states rushed to enact tough anti-bullying legislation. But research has shown that the link between suicide and being bullied is not at all clear and that suicide, very likely, is influenced by other factors. Still, legislators were quick to enact laws assuming that the cause-and-effect relationship was clear.

Lawmakers also assumed that anti-bullying education would reduce bullying behavior, but research shows that this is not happening in any substantial way. So there is plenty of room for argument on this topic. Essentially, the argument reduces to this question: Which causes (which anti-bullying programs) will lead to the most desirable effects (a reduction in bullying)?

Draft and Revise Your Synthesis

The final draft of an argument synthesis, based on the outline above, follows. Thesis and topic sentences are highlighted. A note on documentation: While the topic leans more toward the social sciences than it does the humanities, the writer—completing a research assignment for a freshman composition class—has used Modern Language Association (MLA) documentation style as his instructor requested. MLA style is used most often in the humanities.

A cautionary note: When writing syntheses, it is all too easy to become careless in properly crediting your sources. Before drafting your paper, review the sections on Avoiding Plagiarism (pp. 49–50 and pp. 229–232).

MODEL ARGUMENT SYNTHESIS

Simmons 1

Peter Simmons

Professor Lettelier

Composition 201

8 November 2014

Responding to Bullies

(1)   On the school bus the nerdy kid with glasses tries to keep his head down. A group of older, bigger kids gets on. One of the older kids sits next to the nerdy kid, who asks, hopefully, "You're my buddy, right?" The other kid turns to him and says, "I'm not your buddy. I will f—g end you. I will shove a broomstick up your a—. You're going to die in so much pain." Another day, the nerdy kid is repeatedly punched by a kid across the aisle, who then jabs him in the arm with the point of a pencil. These scenes from the recent documentary film *Bully* are repeated in some form or other thousands of times every day.

(2)   According to some estimates, more than thirteen million school-aged children, one in five students, are bullied each year in the United States. Nearly two-thirds of bullying behavior goes unreported, and of those who suffer, a disproportionate number are the most vulnerable of children, those with learning disabilities or those who dare to break social norms, such as LGBT [lesbian, gay, bisexual, and transgender] youth (Pacer's; Kosciw et al.).

At one time, victims could find some relief at home or in the summer—away from school busses, corridors, and playgrounds where bullies lurk. The Internet has taken even that refuge away. Bullies now follow their victims online with hateful instant messages and post-ings on Facebook. Tyler Clementi, a Rutgers freshman, jumped off the George Washington Bridge after his roommate remotely recorded and posted online a private, consensual, same-sex encounter. In another horrifying case, a twelve-year-old girl jumped from an abandoned silo to her death after two classmates, twelve and fourteen, urged her to "drink bleach and die." Subsequently, one of the harassers posted a message on Facebook admitting, "Yes, I bullied Rebecca and she killed herself but IDGAF [I don't give a ----]." Bullying is a harsh and routine fact of life for school-age kids all over the country. What do we, as a society, propose to do about this? Are tough anti-bullying laws the answer?

Over the last fifteen years, responding to bully-related suicides and the horrors of Columbine, state governments have passed two-part anti-bullying laws. The first part of the law makes it a crime to commit especially vicious behaviors associated with bul-lying; the second, educational part requires school districts to implement anti-bullying programs. On its face, a two-part program that punishes bullies and teaches behaviors designed to reduce bullying seems sensible. But is it effective? The answer, unfortunately, is "no"—at least for the moment. Laws that punish the worst offenders with prison time or juvenile detention may make parents and legislators feel as if they're getting tough. But, in fact, bullying remains widespread, and relatively few cases rise to the level of criminal behavior. At the same time, several key initiatives introduced in local school dis-tricts seem to be showing some promise in addressing this difficult problem. In the end, a blend of local, ground-up strategies and state-mandated programs and laws promises to be the best approach to dealing with bullying in American schools.

The first state to adopt anti-bullying legislation was Georgia, in 1999, in response to the Columbine tragedy earlier that year when Dylan Klebold and Eric Harris killed a teacher and twelve classmates and left twenty-one wounded. The assault triggered a national outcry and a demand to understand what happened. Eva Porter, author of *Bully Nation*, argues that the media too-quickly (and incorrectly) pegged the shooters as young men who'd been bullied and retaliated with lethal force. "The nation," she writes, "fearing a repeat of the tragedy—adopted a zero-tolerance attitude toward many normal, albeit painful, aspects of childhood behavior and development, and defined them as bullying."

③

④

⑤   Understandably, legislators wanted to prevent bullied kids from becoming Klebold- and Harris-like killers. In the eleven years following the attack, a span that included several highly publicized teen suicides associated with bullying, forty-nine state legislatures adopted 120 anti-bullying bills ("School"). This rush to action was so hasty that experts began wondering about the extent to which these legislative measures were "informed by research, not singular high profile incidents" like Columbine (Patchin) or prompted by "the perceived urgent need to intervene" (Smith et al.).

⑥   No one can doubt the good intentions of legislators who want to reduce bullying. Yet the laws they enacted may be too blunt an instrument to deal with the most common forms of bullying. Civil rights activists are concerned that anti-cyberbullying laws, in particular, could curtail freedom of speech (Bazelon, "Anti"). In 2011, responding to the bully-related suicide of fourteen-year-old Jamey Rodemeyer, the Make It Better Project argued that "[c]riminalizing bullying is not the answer" (Gay-Straight Alliance). Writing about the case, Daniel Villarreal explains why: "While some . . . bullying could even rise to the level of criminal harassment, criminalizing bullying overall could result in over-reaching laws that punish any student who 'causes emotional harm' or 'creates a hostile environment'—two vague, subjective criteria that could well qualify any online insult or cafeteria put down as a criminal offense." Villarreal could have been predicting the future. In 2012, the Missouri Supreme Court struck down part of an anti-bullying law (enacted after a bullying-related suicide) that violated free speech ("Mo. High Court"). LGBT youth are easy targets for bullies. When a national organization that supports LGBT youth opposes anti-bullying laws intended to help them, the wisdom of such laws is put into serious question.

⑦   The second problem with anti-bullying legislation is that states do not generally follow "research-based definitions of bullying" (Sacco 3–8), even though most researchers have adopted a definition crafted by Dan Olweus, the Norwegian psychologist credited with conducting the first large-scale, controlled study of bullying in 1978. According to Olweus, a "person is bullied when he or she is exposed, repeatedly and over time, to negative actions on the part of one or more other persons, and he or she has difficulty defending himself or herself." Olweus introduced the element of an "imbalance of power" that results from bullies using their physical strength or social position to inflict emotional or physical harm ("Bullying").

⑧   "[A]t least ten different definitions" are being used in state laws, according to Emily Bazelon, author of *Sticks and Stones: Defeating the Culture of Bullying*—and, for her, that's a problem. A frequent commentator on the subject, Bazelon argues that "'bullying' isn't the same as garden-variety teasing or a two-way conflict. The word is being overused," she writes, "expanding, accordionlike, to encompass both appalling violence or harassment and a few mean words" ("Defining"). Anti-bullying researchers at Harvard and New York University note that teens take care to distinguish "drama"—the more typical verbal and emotional jousting among teenagers—from bullying. Drama can be more easily shrugged off as "so high school" and helps teens avoid thinking of themselves as hapless victims (Boyd and Marwick). When school-based programs fail to realize that what some students dismiss as "drama" is really "bullying," the effectiveness of anti-bullying programs is in doubt as schools may miss a lot of hurtful behaviors. "To me this is an issue about reporting, under-reporting specifically," says educational psychologist Philip Rodkin. "It's also about teenagers wanting to diminish the importance of some negative interaction, which sometimes is exactly the right thing to do, sometimes not at all the right thing" (Personal). At the same time, there is also the danger that too many harmless behaviors can be labeled as bullying. As one superintendent who is implementing the tough, new anti-bullying law in New Jersey says: "students, or their parents, will find it easier to label minor squabbles bullying than to find ways to work out their differences" (Dolan, qtd. in Hu).

A third problem with anti-bullying laws—and perhaps the most serious—is that they require school districts to adopt anti-bullying programs of unproven value. Educators are rushing to comply with these laws, and they are adopting pre-made, one-size-fits-all programs that have not been shown to work. In an analysis of forty-two studies, researchers at Texas A&M International University evaluated the effectiveness of school-based anti-bullying efforts. The combined studies involved 34,713 elementary, middle, and high school students and "measure[d] some element of bullying behavior or aggression toward peers" (Ferguson et al. 407). The researchers concluded that "school-based anti-bullying programs are not practically effective in reducing bullying or violent behaviors in the schools" (410). Another review of sixteen anti-bullying studies involving 15,386 K–12 students concluded "that school bullying interventions may produce modest positive outcomes...[but] are more likely to influence knowledge, attitudes, and self-perceptions rather than actual bullying behaviors" (Merrell et al.). These are "disheartening" results (Swearer et al. 42; Rodkin).

The world's most well-known anti-bullying program, the Olweus Bullying Prevention Program (OBPP), is a "whole-school" approach that "is used at the school, classroom, and individual levels and includes methods to reach out to parents and the community for

⑨

⑩

involvement and support" (Hazelden). Backed by thirty-five years of research, Olweus has demonstrated the effectiveness of his approach in Norwegian schools. Schools worldwide, including many in the United States, have used OBPP. But researchers have been unable to show that the Olweus program is consistently effective outside of Norway. A University of Washington study found that in American schools OBPP had "no overall effect" in preventing bullying (Bauer, Lozano, and Rivera). With their larger class sizes and racial, ethnic, and economic diversity, American schools may differ too greatly from Norwegian schools for OBPP to succeed. Or the Olweus program may need to be adapted in ways that have not yet been developed.

⑪   To sum up, definitions in anti-bullying laws are inconsistent; the effectiveness of anti-bullying programs is unproven; and cyberbullying laws may threaten free speech. Still, bullying persists and we must respond. Each day, 160,000 children skip school because they don't want to confront their tormentors (National). Even bullies are at risk: "Nearly 60 percent of boys whom researchers classified as bullies in grades six through nine were convicted of at least one crime by the age of 24. Even more dramatic, 40 percent of them had three or more convictions by age 24" (Fox et al. 2). While bullying in childhood may not be the sole or even main *cause* of later criminal behavior (another possibility: there may be abuse in the home), these statistics provide all the more reason to intervene in the bully/victim relationship. Both victims and bullies require our help.

⑫   Fresh approaches to the problem of bullying are needed, and Rodkin suggests a sensible, potentially fruitful direction: "The task ahead," he writes in a report presented at a 2011 White House Conference on Bullying Prevention, "is to better integrate bullies and the children they harass into the social fabric of the school and better inform educators of how to recognize, understand, and help guide children's relationships." Rodkin's recommendations favor an on-the-ground, local approach with individual students rather than a broad, mandated program. Mary Flannery of the National Education Association agrees that, ultimately, bullies and their victims must be engaged one on one:

> Many bullying programs apply a one-size-fits-all approach to problems on campus.
> They train teachers and support professionals to be watchful and consistent (often
> at a high price). But while it's critically important for every adult on campus to
> recognize and stop bullying, Colby College professor Lyn Mikel Brown, co-director
> of the nonprofit Hardy Girls, Healthy Women, believes most of these "top-down"
> programs look promising, but don't go far enough.

"You really have to do this work with students," Brown says. "Those programs don't allow for the messy, on-the-ground work of educating kids. That's what has to happen and it looks different in different schools and communities."

When legislators criminalize bullying and require schools to implement anti-bullying programs, they take the kind of top-down approach that Mikel Brown believes doesn't go far enough. The researchers who conducted the comprehensive "Overview of State Anti-Bullying Legislation" agree: "legal responses and mandates can at their best only facilitate the harder non-legal work that schools must undertake to create a kinder, braver world" (Sacco 22).

What might this "harder non-legal" work look like?

In *Sticks and Stones,* Bazelon advises an approach that involves children, parents, and educators working in local school- and child-specific settings. She advises bullied kids to confide in a sympathetic adult or a trusted group. Those being harassed online should contact Web sites to remove offensive content. To those who witness bullying, she suggests that dramatic action (stepping in to break up a fight) isn't necessary—though private, low-key action, like sending a supportive note, may be. Bazelon advises educators to conduct surveys to clearly define the problem of bullying at their school (309–19) and make "an on-going annual, monthly, weekly, even daily commitment" to reducing bullying (317).

In their companion book to the widely praised documentary film *Bully* (2011), Lee Hirsch and Cynthia Lowen offer an action plan for fostering an inclusive and safe school environment. Their guidelines help parents to distinguish between appropriate and inappropriate use of the Internet and urge parents to discuss bullying openly, along with strategies for reporting bullying to school authorities and promoting responsible behavior. Hirsch and Lowen provide educators with checklists to help determine whether or not effective anti-cyberbullying policies are in place. They also encourage explicit conversations among teachers about the nature and extent of the bullying problem in their school, and they suggest specific prevention and intervention strategies (159–70).

Like Bazelon, Rodkin recommends surveying students about bullying to gain a clear sense of the problem. He also recommends identifying students with no friends and finding ways to involve them in student life; encouraging peer groups to reject bullying; evaluating anti-bullying programs; and promoting character education that teaches students to be "assertive rather than aggressive" (White House).

18 All of these approaches involve "messy, on-the-ground work" that employs local experts to respond to local problems. Until researchers determine that one or another top-down approach to the problem of bullying will succeed in a wide variety of school environments, it seems best to develop a school-by-school, ground-up approach. This kind of grass-roots strategy could help integrate both bullied children and bullies into the broader school culture. Of course, there's no guarantee that the ground-up approach to combating bullying will work any better than top-down, comprehensive programs like OBPP. Leaving large social problems like bullying for locals to resolve may result in uneven and unacceptable solutions. A parallel case: Challenged by President Kennedy to rid this country of racist Jim Crow laws, many advocates of local "solutions" who had no interest in changing the status quo argued that people on the ground, in the local communities, know best. "Leave the problem to us," they said. "We'll fix it." They didn't, of course, and it took courageous action by people like Martin Luther King, Jr., and President Lyndon Johnson to force a comprehensive solution.

19 Racism may still be with us, but not to the extent it was in the 1960s, and we have (at least in part) a top-down, national approach to thank for that. It's clear that local approaches to bullying can be inept. To take one example from the movie *Bully*, a principal tries making a victim shake hands with his tormentor as if that, alone, would end the problem. It didn't. So researchers must evaluate the effectiveness of local solutions as rigorously as they do top-down solutions. If evaluations show that local solutions aren't effective, we should expect that community leaders, parents, and teachers will search for solutions that work. To the extent that they don't and bullying persists, state and federal authorities should step in with their own solutions, but only after their top-down, one-size-fits-all programs can be shown to work.

20 We should be pushing for anti-bullying programs that blend the top-down approach of state-mandated programs and the ground-up approach that tailors programs to the needs of specific communities. The state has the right to insist that every child be safe in a school environment and be free from the threat of bullying. At the same time, local teachers, parents, and administrators are often in the best position to know what approaches will show the greatest benefits in their own communities. Such a blended approach could well yield the best set of solutions to the complex and pervasive problem of bullying. And then, perhaps, the nerdy kid could ride the school bus in peace—or even in friendly conversation with his former tormentors.

Simmons 8

Works Cited

Bauer, N. S., et al. "The Effectiveness of the Olweus Bullying Prevention Program In Public
    Middle Schools: A Controlled Trial." *Journal of Adolescent Health*, vol. 40, no. 3,
    2007, pp. 266–74. *PubMed*, www.ncbi.nlm.nih.gov/pubmed/17321428.

Bazelon, Emily. "Anti-Bully Laws Get Tough with Schools." Interview by Scott
    Simon. *NPR*, 17 Sept. 2011, www.npr.org/2011/09/17/140557573/
    anti-bullying-laws-get-tough-with-schools.

---. "Defining Bullying Down." *The New York Times*. 11 Mar. 2013, www.nytimes.com/
    2013/03/12/opinion/defining-bullying-down.html.

---. *Sticks and Stones: Defeating the Culture of Bullying and Rediscovering the Power of
    Character and Empathy*. Random House, 2013.

Boyd, Danah, and Alice Marwick. "Bullying as True Drama." *The New York Times*, 22 Sept.
    2011, www.nytimes.com/2011/09/23/opinion/why-cyberbullying-rhetoric-misses-
    the-mark.html.

Bully. Directed by Lee Hirsch, The Weinstein Company, 2011. *Netflix*. Accessed 17 Oct. 2014.

"Bullying Definition." *Stopbullying.gov*. U.S. Department of Health & Human Services,
    www.stopbullying.gov/what-is-bullying/definition/index.html.

Copeland, William E., et al. "Adult Psychiatric Outcomes of Bullying and Being Bullied by
    Peers in Childhood and Adolescence." *JAMA Psychiatry*, vol. 70, no. 4, 2013,
    pp. 419–26, archpsyc.jamanetwork.com/article.aspx?articleid=1654916.

Ferguson, Christopher J., et al. "The Effectiveness of School-Based Anti-Bullying
    Programs: A Meta-Analytic Review." *Criminal Justice Review*, vol. 32, no. 4,
    2007, pp. 401–14. *Sage Publications*, cjr.sagepub.com/content/32/4/401.
    short?rss=1&ssource=mfc.

Flannery, Mary Ellen. "Bullying: Does It Get Better?" *National Education Association*,
    Jan./Feb. 2011, www.nea.org/home/41620.htm.

Fox, James Alan, et al. "Bullying Prevention Is Crime Prevention." *Fight
    Crime: Invest in Kids*, 2003, posted 22 July 2009, www.fightcrime.org/
    bullying-prevention-is-crime-prevention-2003/.

Gay-Straight Alliance Project. "Make It Better." *GSANetwork*, 26 Sept. 2011, gsanetwork.org/
    news/spotlight/make-it-better-project.

Hirsch, Lee, Cynthia Lowen, and Dina Santorelli, editors. *Bully: An Action Plan for Teachers
    and Parents to Combat the Bullying Crisis*. Weinstein Books, 2012.

Simmons 9

Hu, Winnie. "Bullying Law Puts New Jersey Schools on Spot." *The New York Times*,
    20 Aug. 2011, www.nytimes.com/2011/08/31/nyregion/bullying-law-puts-new-
    jersey-schools-on-spot.html.

Kosciw, Joseph G., et al. *The 2011 National School Climate Survey: The Experiences of
    Lesbian, Gay, Bisexual and Transgender Youth in Our Nation's Schools.* Gay, Lesbian
    and Straight Education Network, 2012.

Merrell, Kenneth W., et al. "How Effective are School Bullying Intervention Programs? A
    Meta-analysis of Intervention Research." *School Psychology Quarterly*, vol. 23, no. 1,
    2008, pp. 26–42.

"Mo. High Court Strikes Down Part of Harassment Law." *Associated Press*, 30 May 2012,
    www.firstamendmentcenter.org/mo-high-court-strikes-down-part-of-harassment-law.

"Nation's Educators Continue Push for Safe, Bully-free Environments." *NEA*, National
    Education Association, 8 Oct. 2012, www.nea.org/home/53298.htm.

Olweus, Dan. *Bullying at School: What We Know and What We Can Do.* Blackwell, 1993.

"Olweus Bullying Prevention Program: Scope and Sequence." *Violence Prevention Works*,
    Hazelden Foundation, 2007, www.violencepreventionworks.org/public/olweus_scope.page.

Pacer's National Bullying Prevention Center. "Bullying Statistics." *Pacer.org*, 2012,
    www.pacer.org/bullying/about/media-kit/stats.asp.

Patchin, Justin W. "Cyberbullying and a Student's Suicide." *The New York Times*,
    The Opinion Pages/Room for Debate, 30 Sept. 2010, www.nytimes.com/
    roomfordebate/2010/09/30/cyberbullying-and-a-students-suicide.

Porter, Susan Eva. "Overusing the Bully Label: Unfriendliness, Exclusion, and
    Unkind Remarks Aren't Necessarily Bullying." *Los Angeles Times*. Tribune
    Company, 15 Mar. 2013, http://articles.latimes.com/2013/mar/15/opinion/
    la-oe-porter-bullying-20130315.

Rodkin, Philip C. Personal Interview. 15 Oct. 2014.

---. "White House Report/Bullying—And the Power of Peers." *Educational Leadership:
    Promoting Respectful Schools*, vol. 69 no. 1, 2011, pp. 10–16. *ASCD*, www.ascd.org/
    publications/educational-leadership/sept11/vol69/num01/Bullying%E2%80%94And-
    the-Power-of-Peers.aspx.

Sacco, Dena, et al. *An Overview of State Anti-Bullying Legislation and Other Related Laws.*
    Berkman Center for Internet and Society, 2012.

Simmons 10

"School Bullying Laws Exist in Most States, U.S. Department of Education Reports Analysis
of Policies." *The Huffington Post*, HuffPost Education, 10 Aug. 2012, www.
huffingtonpost.com/2011/12/06/school-bullying-laws-exis_n_1132634.html.

Smith, J., David, et al. "The Effectiveness of Whole-School Antibullying Programs: A
Synthesis of Evaluation Research." *School Psychology Review*, vol. 33, no. 4, 2004,
pp. 547–60.

Swearer, Susan M., et al. "What Can Be Done About School Bullying? Linking Research to
Educational Practice." *Educational Researcher*, vol. 39, no. 1, 2010, pp. 38–47. *Sage
Publications*, edr.sagepub.com/content/39/1/38.abstract.

Villarreal, Daniel. "Jamey Rodemeyer's Bullies Are Happy He's Dead, But Is It a Bad Idea
to Prosecute Them?" *Queerty*, 27 Sept. 2011, www.queerty.com/jamey-rodemeyers-
bullies-are-happy-hes-dead-but-is-it-a-bad-idea-to-prosecute-them-20110927.

The Strategy of the Argument Synthesis

In his argument synthesis, Peter Simmons attempts to support a *claim*—one that
favors blending local and statewide solutions to combat the problem of bullying—
by offering *support* in the form of facts: statistics establishing bullying as an ongoing problem despite anti-bullying laws, news of a court's rejecting elements of an
anti-bullying law, and studies concluding that anti-bullying programs are largely
ineffective. Simmons also supports his claim with expert opinions like those of
Bazelon, Rodkin, and the authors of a Harvard study who state that anti-bullying
laws can "only facilitate the harder non-legal work" of reducing bullying. However,
recall that Simmons's claim rests on an *assumption* about the value of local solutions
to broad problems when system-wide solutions (that is, laws) aren't working. His
ability to change our minds about bullying depends partially on the extent to which
we, as readers, share his assumption. Readers who distrust local solutions may not
be swayed. (See our discussion of assumptions in Chapter 2, pp. 64–66.)

Recall that an assumption, sometimes called a warrant, is a generalization or
principle about how the world works or should work—a fundamental statement
of belief about facts or values. Assumptions are often deeply rooted in people's
psyches, sometimes derived from lifelong experiences and observations and, yes,
prejudices. Assumptions are not easily changed, even by the most logical of arguments. Simmons makes explicit his assumption about the limitations of laws and
the usefulness of local solutions. Though you are under no obligation to do so,
stating assumptions explicitly will clarify your arguments to readers.

A discussion of the model argument's paragraphs, along with the argument
strategy for each, follows. Note that the paper devotes one or more paragraphs to

developing each section of the outline on pages 146–147. Note also that Simmons avoids plagiarism by the careful attribution and quotation of sources.

- **Paragraph 1:** Simmons opens with a heart-wrenching example of bullying from the documentary film *Bully* and states that the example is, unfortunately, repeated throughout the United States on a daily basis.

    Argument strategy: Opening with an anecdote can engage the emotions of readers. In a paper treating a problem as emotionally sensitive as bullying, this is an effective strategy.

- **Paragraph 2:** Simmons then uses statistics to establish that bullying is a pervasive problem that afflicts our most vulnerable children, and he introduces the digital age's contribution to such aggression: cyberbullying. He relates the tragic end of a college freshman who took his life in response to being bullied. Simmons poses questions to the reader: How should we respond? Are tough laws the answer?

    Argument strategy: Simmons prepares the ground of his argument with statistics and by extending bullying to the Internet. The tragic story of Clementi further engages readers emotionally. He then moves to include readers among the "we": What are *we*, readers included, going to do about the problem of bullying?

- **Paragraph 3:** Simmons answers the question raised by the Clementi suicide. What we, as a society, have done about bullying is to adopt two-part anti-bullying legislation that makes especially vicious behaviors unlawful and obligates schools to adopt anti-bullying programs. Simmons states, directly, that the laws are ineffective. At the same time, he points to local, ground-up initiatives that have shown promise in combating bullying. The critique of top-down laws, on the one hand, and the suggested promise of local initiatives, on the other, sets up his thesis advocating a *blended* solution to the problem.

    Argument strategy: This is the first instance of Simmons declaring his position on the problem of bullying. In the first two paragraphs, he establishes the groundwork that prepares him to take a stand here. His thesis is clear, assertive, and arguable and suggests that two broad sections will follow: a review of problems associated with broad anti-bullying laws and suggested local solutions that will come "from the ground up."

- **Paragraphs 4–5:** These paragraphs explain how anti-bullying laws came into being after the events of Columbine. Simmons quotes a school administrator's critique of what she thought was hasty and flawed thinking that prompted the laws (that Klebold and Harris were bullied kids out for revenge). Well-intentioned legislators, enacting laws to prevent other such atrocities, criminalized ordinary, if painful, behaviors associated with bullying. This was a "rush to action," writes Simmons, based more on high-profile media accounts than on research.

    Argument strategy: Simmons understands the need to take preventative action in response to the Columbine shootings. However, that action may have been based on an incomplete or faulty understanding of what actually happened at Columbine. If legislators didn't fully understand the problem facing them, then it's little surprise the laws they drafted are proving ineffective. Simmons supports this powerful critique with the opinions of three experts.

- **Paragraphs 6–10:** These paragraphs constitute the section of the paper detailing three major problems with anti-bullying laws. Paragraph 6 addresses the first problem: Tough cyberbullying laws have in at least one case been shown to violate freedom of speech. The rush to keep bullies from traumatizing victims online may have ineffectively balanced the right to protect victims and the right of everyone, bullies included, to say what they want online. Paragraphs 7 and 8 address what Simmons identifies as the second problem associated with anti-bullying laws, that they misunderstand the definition of bullying. Here Simmons introduces the distinction between bullying and drama. Simmons devotes Paragraphs 9 and 10 to what in his view is the most serious problem concerning anti-bullying legislation: that in their rush to comply with the educational mandates of the legislation, school districts and teachers are reaching for broad, one-size-fits-all solutions like the Olweus Bullying Prevention Program. The problem, writes Simmons, is that anti-bullying programs don't work—a claim he supports with several scholarly studies.

  Argument strategy: Simmons devotes these paragraphs to arguments against current anti-bullying laws. He is persuasive in using a gay advocacy organization, which might be expected to support anti-bullying laws on hateful speech, to argue that such laws may jeopardize civil liberties. By focusing on inconsistent definitions of bullying, Simmons shrewdly questions how legislators can solve a problem they can't define. And by using research to cast doubt on the effectiveness of one-size-fits-all anti-bullying programs, he strikes at the heart of anti-bullying legislation that seeks both to punish and to educate. Simmons must do an effective job in these paragraphs, for readers who aren't convinced that anti-bullying laws are sufficiently flawed won't agree that we need to search for new solutions. By the time readers finish Paragraph 10, Simmons has prepared them for the turn in the argument to his proposed local solutions.

- **Paragraph 11:** In this transitional paragraph, Simmons reviews the ways in which anti-bullying laws don't work. He summarizes the three main problems with these laws, and he restates how damaging bullying can be both for victims and bullies.

  Argument strategy: This paragraph marks the pivot point in the argument and provides a rationale for considering another approach to the problem of bullying.

- **Paragraphs 12 –14:** Simmons explicitly states the need for a new approach to the problem of bullying and introduces two key sources (Rodkin and Flannery) to provide expert support for the position that an on-the-ground, local solution is needed. Paragraph 12 opens with a quotation from Philip Rodkin, whose approach relies not on broad, system-wide actions but on integrating particular bullies into the "social fabric of the school." In the same paragraph, Mary Flannery quotes a Colby College professor who introduces a key distinction: "top-down" and "on-the-ground." Simmons emphasizes this distinction in Paragraph 13 by quoting Harvard researchers who claim that anti-bullying laws can "only facilitate" a solution and are not themselves the answer. Paragraph 14 poses a brief, crucial question that Simmons devotes the rest of the argument to answering.

Argument strategy: These three paragraphs turn the paper toward local solutions to the problem of bullying. To help make this turn, Simmons introduces perhaps his most important source, the Colby College professor quoted by Flannery. Simmons adopts Mikel Brown's language—"one-size-fits-all," "top-down," and "on-the-ground"—as his own. These terms help focus his argument: The legislative approach to bullying is a top-down, one-size-fits-all solution; what's needed are on-the-ground (local) solutions.

- **Paragraphs 15–19:** In these paragraphs, Simmons makes his argument for a local, ground-up response to bullying. His research has directed him to the work of four writers—Bazelon, Hirsch and Lowen, and Rodkin—whose policy recommendations favor addressing problems through direct interaction with victims and with bullies. These experts focus on the local approach and offer a clear alternative to the system-wide, top-down approach that Simmons has argued against in the first half of the paper. Simmons gives a paragraph each to Bazelon (#15), Hirsch and Lowen (#16), and Rodkin (#17). Then, in Paragraphs 18 and 19, he raises an argument against his own position and concedes that researchers should assess local, ground-up solutions for effectiveness just as they do one-size-fits-all solutions like the Olweus program.

  Argument strategy: In these paragraphs, Simmons argues in favor of his solution, relying on expert opinion to do so. It's a wise choice, for he's had no direct experience working with victims of bullying or with bullies themselves. He makes an important concession to would-be critics by insisting that researchers evaluate local solutions for effectiveness just as they do broad, system-wide solutions. He appreciates that there's nothing inherently superior about "local wisdom" and provides an example of a flawed local solution from the documentary film *Bully*. He also concedes there will be an important role for system-wide solutions once they are proven to be effective.

- **Paragraph 20:** In his conclusion, Simmons leaves room for a blended approach to the problem of bullying: guidance from the top informed by the on-the-ground perspective of local experts. He appreciates the role the state has to play in keeping students safe. Ultimately he is migrating to a position of compromise. He ends with an echo of his lead-in example, suggesting that one day the bullied might be able to coexist peaceably with the bully.

  Argument strategy: Simmons has given his readers a clear argument, one with a debatable thesis. He has supported his thesis with carefully researched facts and expert opinions. His tone throughout is reasonable, and he makes the effort to understand the motives of those who might disagree with him. His conclusion reinforces this conciliatory spirit by suggesting that one day, when there are more successful top-down approaches, a "blended" solution may emerge. There is wisdom to be gained from all sides in the debate.

Another approach to an argument synthesis based on the same and additional sources could argue that anti-bullying laws are not yet working in the intended manner and should be changed. Such a position could draw on exactly the same support, both facts and expert opinion, that Simmons uses to demonstrate the inadequacies of current laws. But instead of making a move to local solutions, the writer could assert that a problem as widespread and significant as bullying must be addressed at the state and federal levels. Whatever your approach to a subject, in first *critically examining* the various sources and then *synthesizing* them to support a position about which you feel strongly, you are engaging in the kind of critical thinking that is essential to success in a good deal of academic and professional work.

DEVELOPING AND ORGANIZING THE SUPPORT FOR YOUR ARGUMENTS

5.3 Use various strategies to develop and support your arguments.

Experienced writers seem to have an intuitive sense of how to develop and present supporting evidence for their claims; this sense is developed through much hard work and practice. Less-experienced writers wonder what to say first and, having decided on that, wonder what to say next. There is no single method of presentation, but the techniques of even the most experienced writers often boil down to a few tried and tested arrangements.

As we've seen in the model synthesis in this chapter, the key to devising effective arguments is to find and use those kinds of support that most persuasively strengthen your claim. Some writers categorize support into two broad types: *evidence* and *motivational appeals*. Evidence, in the form of facts, statistics, and expert testimony, helps make the appeal to reason. Motivational appeals—appeals grounded in emotion and upon the authority of the speaker—are employed to get people to change their minds, to agree with the writer or speaker, or to decide upon a plan of action.

Following are the most common strategies for using and organizing support for your claims.

Summarize, Paraphrase, and Quote Supporting Evidence

In most of the papers and reports you will write in college and in the professional world, evidence and motivational appeals derive from your summarizing, paraphrasing, and quoting of material in sources that either have been provided to you or that you have independently researched. For example, in Paragraph 12 of the model argument synthesis, Simmons uses a long quotation from a writer at the National Education Association to introduce three key terms into the synthesis: "one-size-fits-all," "top-down," and "on-the-ground." You will find a number of brief quotations woven into sentences throughout. In addition, you will find summaries and paraphrases. In each case, Simmons is careful to cite the source.

Provide Various Types of Evidence and Motivational Appeals

Keep in mind that you can use appeals to both reason and emotion. The appeal to reason is based on evidence that consists of a combination of *facts* and *expert testimony.* For example, the sources by the Pacer organization and Kosciw (in Paragraph 1) and by Fox and the National Education Association (in Paragraph 11) factually establish the extent of bullying in America. Simmons draws on expert testimony by incorporating the opinions of Bazelon and others who argue that current anti-bullying programs are not working as intended.

Use Climactic Order

Climactic order is the arrangement of examples or evidence in order of anticipated impact on the reader, least to greatest. Organize by climactic order when you plan to offer a number of categories or elements of support for your claim. Recognize that some elements will be more important—and likely more persuasive—than others. The basic principle here is that you should *save the most important evidence for the end* because whatever you say last is what readers are likely to remember best. A secondary principle is that whatever you say first is what they are *next* most likely to remember. Therefore, when you have several reasons to offer in support of your claim, an effective argument strategy is to present the second most important, then one or more additional reasons, and finally the most important reason. Paragraphs 7–11 of the model synthesis do exactly this.

Use Logical or Conventional Order

Using a logical or conventional order involves using as a template a pre-established pattern or plan for arguing your case.

- One common pattern is describing or arguing a *problem/solution.* The model synthesis uses this pattern: You begin with an introduction in which you typically define the problem (perhaps explaining its origins), offer one or more solutions, then conclude. In the case of the model synthesis, Paragraphs 1–3 introduce the problem, Paragraphs 4–10 establish shortcomings of current solutions, and (after a transition) Paragraphs 12–19 suggest solutions.

- Another common pattern presents *two sides of a controversy.* Using this pattern, you introduce the controversy and (in an argument synthesis) your own point of view or claim; then you explain the other side's arguments, providing reasons why your point of view should prevail.

- A third common pattern is *comparison-and-contrast*. This pattern is so important that we will discuss it separately in the next section.

The order in which you present elements of an argument is sometimes dictated by the conventions of the discipline in which you are writing. For example, lab reports and experiments in the sciences and social sciences often follow this pattern: *Opening* or *Introduction, Methods and Materials* (of the experiment or study), *Results, Discussion.* Legal arguments often follow the so-called IRAC format: *Issue, Rule, Application, Conclusion.*

Present and Respond to Counterarguments

When developing arguments on a controversial topic, you can effectively use *counterargument* to help support your claims. When you use counterargument, you present an argument *against* your claim and then show that this argument is weak or flawed. The advantage of this technique is that you demonstrate that you are aware of the other side of the argument and that you are prepared to answer it.

Here is how a counterargument is typically developed:

  I. Introduction and claim
 II. Main opposing argument
III. Refutation of opposing argument
 IV. Main positive argument

Use Concession

Concession is a variation of counterargument. As in counterargument, you present an opposing viewpoint, but instead of dismissing that position, you *concede* that it has some validity and even some appeal, although your own position is the more reasonable one. This concession bolsters your standing as a fair-minded person who is not blind to the virtues of the other side. In the model synthesis, Simmons acknowledges that local solutions to the problem of bullying may rely too heavily on folk wisdom that may be inept or just plain wrong. Bullies and victims, for instance, cannot just shake hands and make the problem go away. Simmons recommends evaluating local solutions rigorously; he also acknowledges that state and federal, top-down solutions may have a role to play—but only after these programs have been proven effective. In his conclusion, he moves to a compromise position that "blends" top-down and ground-up, local solutions.

Given the structure of his argument, Simmons held off making his concession until the end of his paper. Here is an outline for a more typical concession argument:

  I. Introduction and claim
 II. Important opposing argument

   III. Concession that this argument has some validity

   IV. Positive argument(s) that acknowledge the counterargument and (possibly) incorporate some elements of it

Sometimes, when you are developing a counterargument or concession argument, you may become convinced of the validity of the opposing point of view and change your own views. Don't be afraid of this happening. Writing is a tool for learning. To change your mind because of new evidence is a sign of flexibility and maturity, and your writing can only be the better for it.

DEVELOPING AND ORGANIZING SUPPORT FOR YOUR ARGUMENTS

- *Summarize, paraphrase, and quote supporting evidence.* Draw on the facts, ideas, and language in your sources.
- *Provide various types of evidence and motivational appeal.*
- *Use climactic order.* Save the most important evidence in support of your argument for the *end,* where it will have the most impact. Use the next most important evidence *first.*
- *Use logical or conventional order.* Use a form of organization appropriate to the topic, such as problem/solution; sides of a controversy; comparison/contrast; or a form of organization appropriate to the academic or professional discipline, such as a report of an experiment or a business plan.
- *Present and respond to counterarguments.* Anticipate and evaluate arguments against your position.
- *Use concession.* Concede that one or more arguments against your position have some validity; reassert, nonetheless, that your argument is the stronger one.

Avoid Common Fallacies in Developing and Using Support

In Chapter 2, in the section on critical reading, we considered criteria that, as a reader, you may use for evaluating informative and persuasive writing (see pp. 53, 55–62). We discussed how you can assess the accuracy, the significance, and the author's interpretation of the information presented. We also considered the importance in good argument of clearly defined key terms and the pitfalls of emotionally loaded language. Finally, we saw how to recognize such logical fallacies as either/or reasoning, faulty cause-and-effect reasoning, hasty generalization, and false analogy. As a writer, no less than as a critical reader, you need to be aware of these common problems and how to avoid them.

   Be aware, also, of your responsibility to cite source materials appropriately. When you quote a source, double- and triple-check that you have done so accurately. When you summarize or paraphrase, take care to use your own language and sentence structures (though you can, of course, also quote within these forms). When you refer to someone else's idea—even if you are not quoting, summarizing, or paraphrasing it—give the source credit. By being ethical about the use of sources, you uphold the highest standards of the academic community.

THE COMPARISON-AND-CONTRAST SYNTHESIS

5.4 Use comparison-and-contrast, where appropriate, to develop your argument synthesis.

A particularly important type of argument synthesis is built on patterns of comparison and contrast. Techniques of comparison and contrast enable you to examine two subjects (or sources) in terms of one another. When you compare, you consider *similarities*. When you contrast, you consider *differences*. By comparing and contrasting, you perform a multifaceted analysis that often suggests subtleties that otherwise might not have come to your (or your reader's) attention.

To organize a comparison-and-contrast argument, you must carefully read sources in order to discover *significant criteria for analysis*. A *criterion* is a specific point to which both of your authors refer and about which they may agree or disagree. (For example, in a comparative report on compact cars, criteria for *comparison and contrast* might be road handling, fuel economy, and comfort of ride.) The best criteria are those that allow you not only to account for obvious similarities and differences—those concerning the main aspects of your sources or subjects—but also to plumb deeper, exploring subtle yet significant comparisons and contrasts among details or subcomponents, which you can then relate to your overall thesis.

Note that comparison-and-contrast is frequently not an end in itself but serves some larger purpose. Thus, a comparison-and-contrast synthesis may be a component of a paper that is essentially a critique, an explanatory synthesis, an argument synthesis, or an analysis.

Organizing Comparison-and-Contrast Syntheses

Two basic approaches to organizing a comparison-and-contrast synthesis are organization by *source* and organization by *criteria*.

Organizing by Source or Subject

You can organize a comparative synthesis by first summarizing each of your sources or subjects and then discussing the significant similarities and differences between them. Having read the summaries and become familiar with the distinguishing features of each source, your readers will most likely be able to appreciate the more obvious similarities and differences. In the discussion, your task is to consider both the obvious and the subtle comparisons and contrasts, focusing on the most significant—that is, on those that most clearly support your thesis.

Organization by source or subject works best with passages that can be briefly summarized. If the summary of your source or subject becomes too long, your readers might have forgotten the points you made in the first summary when they are reading the second. A comparison-and-contrast synthesis organized by source or subject might proceed like this:

I. Introduce the paper; lead to thesis.

II. Summarize source/subject A by discussing its significant features.

III. Summarize source/subject B by discussing its significant features.

IV. Discuss in a paragraph (or two) the significant points of comparison and contrast between sources or subjects A and B. Alternatively, begin the comparison-and-contrast in Section III as you introduce source/subject B.

V. Conclude with a paragraph in which you summarize your points and, perhaps, raise and respond to pertinent questions.

Organizing by Criteria

Instead of summarizing entire sources one at a time with the intention of comparing them later, you could discuss two sources simultaneously, examining the views of each author point by point (criterion by criterion), comparing and contrasting these views in the process. The criterion approach is best used when you have a number of points to discuss or when passages or subjects are long and/or complex. A comparison-and-contrast synthesis organized by criteria might look like this:

I. Introduce the paper; lead to thesis.

II. Criterion 1
   A. Discuss what author #1 says about this point. Or present situation #1 in light of this point.
   B. Discuss what author #2 says about this point, comparing and contrasting #2's treatment of the point with #1's. Or present situation #2 in light of this point and explain its differences from situation #1.

III. Criterion 2
   A. Discuss what author #1 says about this point. Or present situation #1 in light of this point.
   B. Discuss what author #2 says about this point, comparing and contrasting #2's treatment of the point with #1's. Or present situation #2 in light of this point and explain its differences from situation #1.

And so on, proceeding criterion by criterion until you have completed your discussion. Be sure to arrange criteria with a clear method. Knowing how the discussion of one criterion leads to the next will ensure smooth transitions throughout your paper. End by summarizing your key points and perhaps raising and responding to pertinent questions.

However you organize your comparison-and-contrast synthesis, keep in mind that comparing and contrasting are not ends in themselves. Your discussion should point to a conclusion, an answer to the question "So what—why bother to compare and contrast in the first place?" If your discussion is part of a larger synthesis, point to and support the larger claim. If you write a stand-alone comparison-and-contrast synthesis, though, you must by the final paragraph answer the "Why bother?" question. The model comparison-and-contrast synthesis that follows does exactly this.

MyWritingLab™

Exercise 5.6

Comparing and Contrasting

Over the course of two days, go online to the Web sites of three daily news outlets and follow how each, in its news pages, treats a particular story of national or international significance. One news outlet should be a local city outlet—perhaps the Web site of your hometown newspaper. (Note: The reporting should originate not with a syndicated newswire, like the Associated Press, but with the outlet's own staff writer.) One news outlet should have a national readership, like the *Wall Street Journal* or the *New York Times*. The third outlet should be any news source of your choice (and it needn't exist in print).

Develop a comparison-and-contrast synthesis that leads to an argument about the news coverage. In making notes toward such a synthesis, you'll want to do the following:

- Define the news story: the who, what, when, where of the issue.

- Develop at least three criteria with which to compare and contrast news coverage. Possible criteria: Do the outlets report the same facts? Do the outlets color these facts with an editorial slant? Do the outlets agree on the significance of the issue?

- As you take notes, point to specific passages.

- Review your notes. What patterns emerge? Can you draw any conclusions? Write a thesis that reflects your assessment.

- Using your notes and guided by your thesis, write a comparison-and-contrast-paper.

- Be sure that your paper answers the "So what?" question. What is the point of your synthesis?

A Case for Comparison-and-Contrast: World War I and World War II

Let's see how the principles of comparison-and-contrast can be applied to a response to a final examination question in a course on modern history. Imagine that, having attended classes involving lecture and discussion and having read excerpts from John Keegan's *The First World War* and Tony Judt's *Postwar: A History of Europe Since 1945*, you were presented with this examination question:

> Based on your reading to date, compare and contrast the two world wars in light of any four or five criteria you think significant. Once you have called careful attention to both similarities and differences, conclude with an observation. What have you learned? What can your comparative analysis teach us?

Comparison-and-Contrast Organized by Criteria

Here is a plan for a response, essentially a comparison-and-contrast synthesis, organized by *criteria* and beginning with the thesis—and the *claim*.

> *Thesis:* In terms of the impact on cities and civilian populations, the military aspects of the two wars in Europe, and their aftermaths, the differences between World War I and World War II considerably outweigh the similarities.

I. Introduction. World Wars I and II were the most devastating conflicts in history. *Thesis*

II. Summary of main similarities: causes, countries involved, battlegrounds, global scope

III. First major difference: Physical impact of war
    A. WWI was fought mainly in rural battlegrounds.
    B. In WWII cities were destroyed.

IV. Second major difference: Effect on civilians
    A. WWI fighting primarily involved soldiers.
    B. WWII involved not only military but also massive noncombatant casualties: Civilian populations were displaced, forced into slave labor, and exterminated.

V. Third major difference: Combat operations
    A. WWI, in its long middle phase, was characterized by trench warfare.
    B. During the middle phase of WWII, there was no major military action in Nazi-occupied Western Europe.

VI. Fourth major difference: Aftermath
    A. Harsh war terms imposed on defeated Germany contributed significantly to the rise of Hitler and WWII.
    B. Victorious allies helped rebuild West Germany after WWII but allowed Soviets to take over Eastern Europe.

VII. Conclusion. Since the end of World War II, wars have been far smaller in scope and destructiveness, and warfare has expanded to involve stateless combatants committed to acts of terror.

The following model exam response, a comparison-and-contrast synthesis organized by criteria, is written according to the preceding plan. (Thesis and topic sentences are highlighted.)

MODEL EXAM RESPONSE

World War I (1914–18) and World War II (1939–45) were the most catastrophic and destructive conflicts in human history. For those who believed in the steady but inevitable progress of civilization, it was impossible to imagine that two wars in the first half of the twentieth century could reach levels of barbarity and horror that would outstrip those of any previous era. Historians estimate that more than 22 million people, soldiers and civilians, died in World War I; they estimate that between 40 and 50 million died in World War II. In many ways, these two conflicts were similar: They were fought on many of the same European and Russian battlegrounds, with more or less the same countries on opposing sides. Even many of the same people were involved: Winston Churchill and Adolf Hitler figured in both wars. And the main outcome in each case was the same: total defeat for Germany. However, in terms of the impact on cities and civilian populations, the military aspects of the two wars in Europe, and their aftermaths, the differences between World Wars I and II considerably outweigh the similarities.

①

The similarities are clear enough. In fact, many historians regard World War II as a continuation—after an intermission of about twenty years—of World War I. One of the main causes of each war was Germany's dissatisfaction and frustration with what it perceived as its diminished place in the world. Hitler launched World War II partly out of revenge for Germany's humiliating defeat in World War I. In each conflict Germany and its allies (the Central Powers in WWI, the Axis in WWII) went to war against France, Great Britain, Russia (the Soviet Union in WWII), and, eventually, the United States. Though neither conflict included literally the entire world, the participation of countries not only in Europe but also in the Middle East, the Far East, and the Western Hemisphere made both conflicts global in scope. And, as indicated earlier, the number of casualties in each war was unprecedented in history, partly because modern technology had enabled the creation of deadlier weapons—including tanks, heavy artillery, and aircraft—than had ever been used in warfare.

②

Despite these similarities, the differences between the two world wars are considerably more significant. One of the most noticeable differences was the physical impact of

③

each war in Europe and in Russia—the western and eastern fronts. The physical destruction of World War I was confined largely to the battlefield. The combat took place almost entirely in the rural areas of Europe and Russia. No major cities were destroyed in the first war; cathedrals, museums, government buildings, urban houses, and apartments were left untouched. During the second war, in contrast, almost no city or town of any size emerged unscathed. Rotterdam, Warsaw, London, Minsk, and—when the Allies began their counterattack—almost every major city in Germany and Japan, including Berlin and Tokyo, were flattened. Of course, the physical devastation of the cities created millions of refugees, a phenomenon never experienced in World War I.

④ The fact that World War II was fought in the cities as well as on the battlefields meant that the second war had a much greater impact on civilians than did the first war. With few exceptions, the civilians in Europe during WWI were not driven from their homes, forced into slave labor, starved, tortured, or systematically exterminated. But all of these crimes happened routinely during WWII. The Nazi occupation of Europe meant that the civilian populations of France, Belgium, Norway, the Netherlands, and other conquered lands, along with the industries, railroads, and farms of these countries, were put into the service of the Third Reich. Millions of people from conquered Europe—those who were not sent directly to the death camps—were forcibly transported to Germany and put to work in support of the war effort.

⑤ During both wars, the Germans were fighting on two fronts—the western front in Europe and the eastern front in Russia. But while both wars were characterized by intense military activity during their initial and final phases, the middle and longest phases—at least in Europe—differed considerably. The middle phase of the First World War was characterized by trench warfare, a relatively static form of military activity in which fronts seldom moved, or moved only a few hundred yards at a time, even after major battles. By contrast, in the years between the German conquest of most of Europe by early 1941 and the Allied invasion of Normandy in mid-1944, there was no major fighting in Nazi-occupied Western Europe. (The land battles then shifted to North Africa and the Soviet Union.)

⑥ And of course, the two world wars differed in their aftermaths. The most significant consequence of World War I was that the humiliating and costly war reparations imposed on the defeated Germany by the terms of the 1919 Treaty of Versailles made possible the rise of Hitler and thus led directly to World War II. In contrast, after the end of the Second World War in 1945, the Allies helped rebuild West Germany (the portion of a divided Germany that it controlled), transformed the new country into a democracy, and helped make it one of the most thriving economies of the world. But perhaps the most significant difference in the aftermath of each war involved Russia. That country, in a considerably weakened state, pulled out of World War I a year before hostilities ended so that it could consolidate its 1917 Revolution. Russia then withdrew into itself and took no significant part in European affairs until the Nazi invasion of the Soviet Union in 1941. In contrast, it was the Red Army in World War II that was most responsible for the crushing defeat of Germany. In recognition of its efforts and of its enormous sacrifices, the Allies allowed the Soviet Union to take control of the countries of Eastern Europe after the war, leading to fifty years of totalitarian rule—and the Cold War.

⑦ While the two world wars that devastated much of Europe were similar in that, at least according to some historians, they were the same war interrupted by two decades and similar in that combatants killed more efficiently than armies throughout history ever had, the differences between the wars were significant. In terms of the physical impact of the fighting, the impact on civilians, the action on the battlefield at mid-war, and the aftermaths, World Wars I and II differed in ways that matter to us decades later. The wars in Iraq, Afghanistan, and Bosnia have involved an alliance of nations pitted against single nations, but we have not seen, since the two world wars, grand alliances moving vast armies across continents. The destruction implied by such action is almost unthinkable today. Warfare is changing, and "stateless" combatants like Hamas and Al Qaeda wreak destruction of their own. But we may never again see, one hopes, the devastation that follows when multiple nations on opposing sides of a conflict throw millions of soldiers—and civilians—into harm's way.

The Strategy of the Exam Response

The general strategy of this argument is an organization by *criteria*. The writer argues that although the two world wars exhibited some similarities, the differences between the two conflicts were more significant. Note that the writer's thesis doesn't merely state these significant differences; it also presents them in a way that anticipates both the content and the structure of the response to follow.

In argument terms, the *claim* the writer makes is the conclusion that the two global conflicts were significantly different, if superficially similar. The *assumption* is that key differences and similarities are clarified by employing specific criteria: the impact of the wars upon cities and civilian populations and the consequences of the Allied victories. The *support* comes in the form of historical facts regarding the levels of casualties, the scope of destruction, the theaters of conflict, the events following the conclusions of the wars, and so on.

- **Paragraph 1:** The writer begins by commenting on the unprecedented level of destruction of World Wars I and II and concludes with the thesis summarizing the key similarities and differences.

- **Paragraph 2:** The writer summarizes the key similarities in the two wars: the wars' causes, their combatants, their global scope, and the level of destructiveness made possible by modern weaponry.

- **Paragraph 3:** The writer discusses the first of the key differences: the battlegrounds of World War I were largely rural; the battlegrounds of World War II included cities that were targeted and destroyed.

- **Paragraph 4:** The writer discusses the second of the key differences: the impact on civilians. In World War I, civilians were generally spared from the direct effects of combat; in World War II, civilians were targeted by the Nazis for systematic displacement and destruction.

- **Paragraph 5:** The writer discusses the third key difference: Combat operations during the middle phase of World War I were characterized by static trench warfare. During World War II, in contrast, there were no major combat operations in Nazi-occupied Western Europe during the middle phase of the conflict.

- **Paragraph 6:** The writer focuses on the fourth key difference: the aftermath of the two wars. After World War I, the victors imposed harsh conditions on a defeated Germany, leading to the rise of Hitler and the Second World War. After World War II, the Allies helped Germany rebuild and thrive. However, the Soviet victory in 1945 led to its postwar domination of Eastern Europe.

- **Paragraph 7:** In the conclusion, the writer sums up the key similarities and differences just covered and makes additional comments about the course of more recent wars since World War II. In this way, the writer responds to the questions posed at the end of the assignment: "What have you learned? What can your comparative analysis teach us?"

SUMMARY OF SYNTHESIS CHAPTERS

In this chapter and in Chapter 4, we've considered three main types of synthesis: the *explanatory synthesis*, the *argument synthesis*, and the *comparison-and-contrast synthesis*. Although for ease of comprehension we've placed these in separate categories, the types are not mutually exclusive. Argument syntheses often include extended sections of explanation and/or comparison-and-contrast. Explanations commonly include sections of comparison-and-contrast. Which type of synthesis you choose will depend on your *purpose* and the method that you decide is best suited to achieve this purpose.

If your main purpose is to help your audience understand a particular subject, and in particular to help them understand the essential elements or significance of this subject, then you will be composing an explanatory synthesis. If your main purpose, on the other hand, is to persuade your audience to agree with your viewpoint on a subject, or to change their minds, or to decide on a particular course of action, then you will be composing an argument synthesis. If your purpose is to clarify similarities or differences, you will compose a comparison-and-contrast synthesis—which may be a paper in itself (either an argument or an explanation) or part of a larger paper (again, either an argument or explanation).

In planning and drafting these syntheses, you can draw on a variety of strategies: supporting your claims by summarizing, paraphrasing, and quoting from your sources; using appeals to *logos*, *pathos*, and *ethos*; and choosing from among strategies such as climactic or conventional order, counterargument, and concession the approach that will best help you achieve your purpose.

The strategies of synthesis you've practiced in these two chapters will be dealt with again in Chapter 7, where we'll consider a category of synthesis commonly known as the research paper. The research paper involves all of the skills in preparing summary, critique, and synthesis, the main difference being that you won't find the sources needed to write the paper in this particular text. We'll discuss approaches to locating and critically evaluating sources, selecting material from among them to provide support for your claims, and, finally, documenting your sources in standard professional formats.

We turn, now, to analysis, which is another important strategy for academic thinking and writing. Chapter 6, "Analysis," will introduce you to a strategy that, like synthesis, draws upon all the strategies you've been practicing as you move through *Writing and Reading Across the Curriculum.*

MyWritingLab™ Visit Ch. 5 Argument Synthesis in MyWritingLab to test your understanding of the chapter objectives.

Chapter 6

Analysis

After completing this chapter, you will be able to:

6.1 Establish a principle, definition, or personal perspective as the basis for an analysis.

6.2 Write an analysis.

WHAT IS AN ANALYSIS?

6.1 Establish a principle, definition, or personal perspective as the basis for an analysis.

An *analysis* is a type of argument in which you study the parts of something—a physical object, a work of art, a person or group of people, an event, a scientific, economic, or sociological phenomenon—to understand how it works, what it means, or why it might be significant. The writer of an analysis uses an analytic tool: a *principle* or *definition* on the basis of which the subject of study can be divided into parts and examined.

Here are excerpts from two analyses of the movie version of L. Frank Baum's *The Wizard of Oz*:

> At the dawn of adolescence, the very time she should start to distance herself from Aunt Em and Uncle Henry, the surrogate parents who raised her on their Kansas farm, Dorothy Gale experiences a hurtful reawakening of her fear that these loved ones will be rudely ripped from her, especially her Aunt (Em—M for Mother!).[1]

---

[1] Harvey Greenberg, *The Movies on Your Mind* (New York: Dutton, 1975).

[*The Wizard of Oz*] was originally written as a political allegory about grass-roots protest. It may seem harder to believe than Emerald City, but the Tin Woodsman is the industrial worker, the Scarecrow [is] the struggling farmer, and the Wizard is the president, who is powerful only as long as he succeeds in deceiving the people.[2]

As these paragraphs suggest, what you discover through analysis depends entirely on the principle or definition you use to make your insights. Is *The Wizard of Oz* the story of a girl's psychological development, or is it a story about politics? The answer is *both*. In the first example, the psychiatrist Harvey Greenberg applies the principles of his profession and, not surprisingly, sees *The Wizard of Oz* in psychological terms. In the second example, a newspaper reporter applies the political theories of Karl Marx and, again not surprisingly, discovers a story about politics.

Different as they are, these analyses share an important quality: Each is the result of a specific principle or definition used as a tool to divide an object into parts in order to see what it means and how it works. The writer's choice of analytic tool simultaneously creates and limits the possibilities for analysis. Thus, working with the principles of Freud, Harvey Greenberg sees *The Wizard of Oz* in psychological, not political, terms; working with the theories of Karl Marx, Peter Dreier understands the movie in terms of the economic relationships among the characters. It's as if the writer of an analysis who adopts one analytic tool puts on a pair of glasses and sees an object in a specific way. Another writer, using a different tool (and a different pair of glasses), sees the object differently.

WHERE DO WE FIND WRITTEN ANALYSES?

Here are just a few of the types of writing that involve analysis:

Academic Writing

- *Experimental and lab reports* analyze the meaning or implications of the study results in the Discussion section.
- *Research papers* analyze information in sources or apply theories to material being reported.
- *Process analyses* break down the steps or stages involved in completing a process.
- *Literary analyses* examine characterization, plot, imagery, or other elements in works of literature.
- *Essay exams* demonstrate understanding of course material by analyzing data using course concepts.

[2]Peter Dreier, "Oz Was Almost Reality." *Cleveland Plain Dealer* 3 Sept. 1989.

> *Workplace Writing*
>
> - *Grant proposals* analyze the issues you seek funding for in order to address them.
> - *Reviews of the arts* employ dramatic or literary analysis to assess artistic works.
> - *Business plans* break down and analyze capital outlays, expenditures, profits, materials, and the like.
> - *Medical charts* record analytic thinking and writing in relation to patient symptoms and possible options.
> - *Legal briefs* break down and analyze facts of cases and elements of legal precedents and apply legal rulings and precedents to new situations.
> - *Case studies* describe and analyze the particulars of a specific medical, social service, advertising, or business case.

You might protest: Are there as many analyses of *The Wizard of Oz* as there are people to read the book or to see the movie? Yes, or at least as many analyses as there are analytic tools. This does not mean that all analyses are equally valid or useful. Each writer must convince the reader using the power of her or his argument. In creating an analytic discussion, the writer must organize a series of related insights using the analytic tool to examine first one part and then another part of the object being studied. To read Harvey Greenberg's essay on *The Wizard of Oz* is to find paragraph after paragraph of related insights—first about Aunt Em, then the Wicked Witch, then Toto, and then the Wizard. All these insights point to Greenberg's single conclusion: that "Dorothy's 'trip' is a marvelous metaphor for the psychological journey every adolescent must make." Without Greenberg's analysis, we would probably not have thought about the movie as a psychological journey. This is precisely the power of an analysis: its ability to reveal objects or events in ways we would not otherwise have considered.

The writer's challenge is to convince readers that (1) the analytic tool being applied is legitimate and well matched to the object being studied; and (2) the analytic tool is being used systematically and insightfully to divide the object into parts and to make a coherent, meaningful statement about these parts and the object as a whole.

HOW TO WRITE ANALYSES

6.2 Write an analysis.   Let's consider a more extended example of analysis, one that approaches excessive TV watching as a type of addiction. This analytic passage illustrates the two defining features of the analysis: a statement of an analytic principle or definition and the use of that principle or definition in closely examining an object, behavior, or event. As you read, try to identify these features. An exercise with questions for discussion follows the passage.

THE PLUG-IN DRUG

Marie Winn

This analysis of television viewing as an addictive behavior appeared originally in Marie Winn's book *The Plug-In Drug: Television, Computers, and Family Life (2002)*. A writer and media critic, Winn has been interested in the effects of television on both individuals and the larger culture. In this passage, she carefully defines the term *addiction* and then applies it systematically to the behavior under study.

The word "addiction" is often used loosely and wryly in conversation. People will refer to themselves as "mystery-book addicts" or "cookie addicts." E. B. White wrote of his annual surge of interest in gardening: "We are hooked and are making an attempt to kick the habit." Yet nobody really believes that reading mysteries or ordering seeds by catalogue is serious enough to be compared with addictions to heroin or alcohol. In these cases the word "addiction" is used jokingly to denote a tendency to overindulge in some pleasurable activity.

People often refer to being "hooked on TV." Does this, too, fall into the lighthearted category of cookie eating and other pleasures that people pursue with unusual intensity? Or is there a kind of television viewing that falls into the more serious category of destructive addiction?

Not unlike drugs or alcohol, the television experience allows the participant to blot out the real world and enter into a pleasurable and passive mental state. To be sure, other experiences, notably reading, also provide a temporary respite from reality. But it's much easier to stop reading and return to reality than to stop watching television. The entry into another world offered by reading includes an easily accessible return ticket. The entry via television does not. In this way television viewing, for those vulnerable to addiction, is more like drinking or taking drugs—once you start it's hard to stop.

Just as alcoholics are only vaguely aware of their addiction, feeling that they control their drinking more than they really do ("I can cut it out any time I want—I just like to have three or four drinks before dinner"), many people overestimate their control over television watching. Even as they put off other activities to spend hour after hour watching television, they feel they could easily resume living in a different, less passive style. But somehow or other while the television set is present in their homes, it just stays on. With television's easy gratifications available, those other activities seem to take too much effort.

5   A heavy viewer (a college English instructor) observes:

> I find television almost irresistible. When the set is on, I cannot ignore it. I can't turn it off. I feel sapped, will-less, enervated. As I reach out to turn off the set, the strength goes out of my arms. So I sit there for hours and hours.

Self-confessed television addicts often feel they "ought" to do other things—but the fact that they don't read and don't plant their garden or sew or crochet or play games or have conversations means that those activities are no longer as desirable as television viewing. In a way, the lives of heavy viewers are as unbalanced by their television "habit" as drug addicts' or alcoholics' lives. They are living in a holding pattern, as it were, passing up the activities that lead to growth or development or a sense of accomplishment. This is one reason people talk about their television viewing so ruefully, so apologetically. They are aware that it is an unproductive experience, that by any human measure almost any other endeavor is more worthwhile.

It is the adverse effect of television viewing on the lives of so many people that makes it feel like a serious addiction. The television habit distorts the sense of time. It renders other experiences vague and curiously unreal while taking on a greater reality for itself. It weakens relationships by reducing and sometimes eliminating normal opportunities for talking, for communicating.

And yet television does not satisfy, else why would the viewer continue to watch hour after hour, day after day? "The measure of health," wrote the psychiatrist Lawrence Kubie, "is flexibility . . . and especially the freedom to cease when sated." But heavy television viewers can never be sated with their television experiences. These do not provide the true nourishment that satiation requires, and thus they find that they cannot stop watching.

MyWritingLab™   Exercise 6.1 ⭕

Reading Critically: Winn

In an analysis, an author first presents the analytic principle in full and then systematically applies parts of the principle to the object or phenomenon under study. In her brief analysis of television viewing, Marie Winn pursues an alternative, though equally effective, strategy by *distributing* parts of her analytic principle across the essay. Locate where Winn defines key elements of addiction. Locate where she uses each element as an analytic lens to examine television viewing as a form of addiction.

What function does paragraph 4 play in the analysis?

In the first two paragraphs, how does Winn create a funnel-like effect that draws readers into the heart of her analysis?

Recall a few television programs that genuinely moved you, educated you, humored you, or stirred you to worthwhile reflection or action. To what extent does Winn's analysis describe your positive experiences as a television viewer? (Consider how Winn might argue that from within an addicted state, a person may feel "humored, moved, or educated" but is in fact—from a sober outsider's point of view—deluded.) If Winn's analysis of television viewing as an addiction does *not* account for your experience, does it follow that her analysis is flawed? Explain.

Locate and Apply an Analytic Tool

The general purpose of all analysis is to enhance one's understanding of the subject under consideration. A good analysis provides a valuable—if sometimes unusual or unexpected—point of view, a way of *seeing*, a way of *interpreting* some phenomenon, person, event, policy, or pattern of behavior that otherwise may appear random or unexplainable. How well the analysis achieves its purpose depends upon the suitability to the subject and the precision of the analytic tools selected and upon the skill with which the writer (or speaker) applies these tools.

Each reader must determine for her- or himself whether the analysis enhances understanding or—in the opposite case—is merely confusing or irrelevant. To what extent does it enhance your understanding of *The Wizard of Oz* to view the story in psychological terms? In political terms? To what extent does it enhance your understanding of excessive TV watching to view such behavior as an addiction?

When you are faced with writing an analysis, consider these two general strategies:

- Locate an analytic tool—a principle or definition that makes a general statement about the way something works.
- Systematically apply this principle or definition to the subject under consideration.

Let's more fully consider each of these strategies.

Locate an Analytic Tool

In approaching her subject, Marie Winn finds in the definition of "addiction" a useful principle for making sense of the way some people watch TV. The word "addiction," she notes, "is used jokingly to denote a tendency to overindulge in some pleasurable activity." The question she decides to tackle is whether, in the case of watching TV, such overindulgence is harmless or whether it is destructive and thus constitutes an addiction.

Make yourself aware, as both writer and reader, of a tool's strengths and limitations. Pose these questions of the analytic principle and definitions you use:

- Are they accurate?
- Are they well accepted?
- Do you accept them?
- How successfully do they account for or throw light upon the phenomenon under consideration?
- What are the arguments against them?
- What are their limitations?

Since every principle of definition used in an analysis is the end product of an argument, you are entitled—even obligated—to challenge it. If the analytic tool is flawed, the analysis that follows from it will necessarily be flawed.

Some, for example, would question whether addiction is a useful concept to apply to television viewing. First, we usually think of addiction as applying only to substances such as alcohol, nicotine, or drugs (whether legal or illegal). Second, many people think that the word "addiction" carries inappropriate moral connotations: We disapprove of addicts and think that they have only themselves to blame for their condition. For a time, the American Psychiatric Association dropped the word "addiction" from its definitive guide to psychological disorders, the *Diagnostic and Statistical Manual of Mental Disorders* (DSM), in favor of the more neutral term "dependence." (The latest edition of the DSM has returned to the term "addiction.")

On the other hand, "addiction"—also known as "impulse control disorder"— has long been applied to behavior as well as to substances. People are said to be addicted to gambling, to shopping, to eating, to sex, even to hoarding newspapers. The editors of the new DSM are likely to add Internet addiction to the list of impulse control disorders. The term even has national implications: Many argue that this country must break its "addiction" to oil. Thus, there is considerable precedent for Winn to argue that excessive TV watching constitutes an addiction.

Apply the Analytic Tool

Having suggested that TV watching may be an addiction, Winn uses established psychological criteria[3] to identify the chief components of addictive behavior. She then applies each one of them to the behavior under consideration. In doing so, she presents her case that TV is a "plug-in drug," and her readers are free to evaluate the success and persuasiveness of her analysis.

In the body of her analysis, Winn systematically applies the component elements of addiction to TV watching. Winn does this by identifying the major components of addiction and applying them to television watching. Users:

1. Turn away from the real world.
2. Overestimate how much control they have over their addiction.
3. Lead unbalanced lives and turn away from social activities.
4. Develop a distorted sense of time.
5. Are never satisfied with their use.

Analysis Across the Curriculum

The principle that you select can be a theory as encompassing as the statement that *myths are the enemy of truth*. It can be as modest as the definition of a term such as *addiction* or *comfort*. As you move from one subject area to another, the principles and definitions you use for analysis will change, as these assignments illustrate:

Sociology: Write a paper in which you place yourself in American society by locating both your absolute position and relative rank on each single criterion of social stratification used by Lenski and Lenski. For each criterion, state whether you have attained your social position by yourself or have "inherited" that status from your parents.

Literature: Apply principles of Jungian psychology to Hawthorne's "Young Goodman Brown." In your reading of the story, apply Jung's principles of the *shadow, persona,* and *anima.*

---

[3]For example, the Web site *Addictions and Recovery*, drawing upon the *Diagnostic and Statistical Manual of Mental Disorders* (DSM) criteria, identifies seven components of substance addiction. A person who answers *yes* to three of the following questions meets the medical definition of addiction: **Tolerance** (use of drugs or alcohol increased over time); **Withdrawal** (adverse physical or emotional reactions to not using); **Difficulty controlling your use** (using more than you would like); **Negative consequences** (using even though use negatively affects mood, self-esteem, health, job, or family); **Neglecting or postponing activities** (putting off or reducing social, recreational, work in order to use); **Spending significant time or emotional energy** (spending significant time obtaining, using, concealing, planning, recovering from, or thinking about use); **Desire to cut down.**

Physics: Use Newton's second law ($F = ma$) to analyze the acceleration of a fixed pulley from which two weights hang: m_1 (.45 kg) and m_2 (.90 kg). Explain in a paragraph the principle of Newton's law and your method of applying it to solve the problem. Assume your reader is not comfortable with mathematical explanations: Do not use equations in your paragraph.

Finance: Using Guilford C. Babcock's "Concept of Sustainable Growth" [*Financial Analysis* 26 (May–June 1970): 108–14], analyze the stock price appreciation of the XYZ Corporation, figures for which are attached.

The analytic tools to be applied in these assignments must be appropriate to the discipline. Writing in response to the sociology assignment, you would use sociological principles developed by Lenski and Lenski. In your literature class, you would use principles of Jungian psychology; in physics, Newton's second law; and in finance, a particular writer's concept of "sustainable growth." But whatever discipline you are working in, the first part of your analysis will clearly state which (and whose) principles and definitions you are applying. For audiences unfamiliar with these principles, you will need to explain them; if you anticipate objections to their use, you will need to argue that they are legitimate principles capable of helping you conduct the analysis.

GUIDELINES FOR WRITING ANALYSES

Unless you are asked to follow a specialized format, especially in the sciences or the social sciences, you can present your analysis as a paper by following the guidelines below. As you move from one class to another, from discipline to discipline, the principles and definitions you use as the basis for your analyses will change, but the following basic components of analysis will remain the same.

- *Create a context for your analysis.* Introduce and summarize for readers the object, event, or behavior to be analyzed. Present a strong case for why an analysis is needed: Give yourself a motivation to write, and give readers a motivation to read. Consider setting out a problem, puzzle, or question to be investigated.

- *Locate an analytic tool: a principle or definition that will form the basis of your analysis.* Plan to devote an early part of your analysis to arguing for the validity of this principle or definition if your audience is not likely to understand it or if they are likely to think that the principle or definition is not valuable.

- *Analyze your topic by applying your selected analytic tool to the topic's component elements.* Systematically apply elements of the analytic tool to parts of the activity or object under study. You can do this by posing specific questions, based on your analytic principle or definition, about the object or phenomenon. Discuss what you find part by part (organized perhaps by question), in clearly defined subsections of the paper.

- *Conclude by stating clearly what is significant about your analysis.* When considering your analytic paper as a whole, what new or interesting insights have you made concerning the object under study? To what extent has your application of the definition or principle helped you explain how the object works, what it might mean, or why it is significant?

Formulate a Thesis

Like any other thesis, the thesis of an analysis compresses into a single sentence the main idea of your presentation. Some authors omit an explicit thesis statement, preferring to leave the thesis implied. Underlying Winn's analysis, for example, is an implied thesis: "By applying my multipart definition, we can understand television viewing as an addiction." Other authors may take two or perhaps even more sentences to articulate their thesis. But stated or implied, one sentence or more, your thesis must be clearly formulated at least in your own mind if your analysis is to hold together.

The analysis itself, as we have indicated, is a two-part argument. The first part states and establishes your use of a certain principle or definition that serves as your analytic tool. The second part applies specific parts or components of the principle or definition to the topic at hand.

Develop an Organizational Plan

You will benefit enormously in the writing of a first draft if you plan out the logic of your analysis. Turn key elements of your analytic principle or definition into questions, and then develop the paragraph-by-paragraph logic of the paper.

Turning Key Elements of a Principle or a Definition into Questions

Prepare for an analysis by phrasing questions based on the definition or principle you are going to apply and then directing those questions to the activity or object to be studied. The method is straightforward:

- State as clearly as possible the principle or definition to be applied.
- Divide the principle or definition into its parts.
- Using each part, form a question.

For example, Winn develops a multipart definition of addiction, each part of which is readily turned into a question that she directs at a specific behavior: television viewing. Her analysis of television viewing can be understood as *responses* to each of her analytic questions. Note that in her brief analysis, Winn does not first define addiction and then analyze television viewing. Rather, *as* she defines aspects of addiction, she analyzes television viewing.

Developing the Paragraph-by-Paragraph Logic of Your Paper

The following paragraph from Winn's analysis illustrates the typical logic of a paragraph in an analytic paper:

> Self-confessed television addicts often feel they "ought" to do other things—but the fact that they don't read and don't plant their garden or sew or crochet or play games or have conversations means that those activities are no longer as desirable as television viewing. In a way, the lives

of heavy viewers are as unbalanced by their television "habit" as drug addicts' or alcoholics' lives. They are living in a holding pattern, as it were, passing up the activities that lead to growth or development or a sense of accomplishment. This is one reason people talk about their television viewing so ruefully, so apologetically. They are aware that it is an unproductive experience, that by any human measure almost any other endeavor is more worthwhile.

We see in this paragraph the typical logic of an analysis:

- *The writer introduces a specific analytic tool.* Winn refers to one of the established components of addiction: the addictive behavior crowds out and takes precedence over other, more fruitful activities.
- *The writer applies this analytic tool to the object being examined.* Winn points out that people who spend their time watching television "don't read and don't plant their garden or sew or crochet or play games or have conversations...."
- *The writer uses the tool to identify and then examine the significance of some aspect of the subject under discussion.* Having applied the analytic tool to the subject of television viewing, Winn generalizes about the significance of what is revealed: "This is one reason people talk about their television viewing so ruefully, so apologetically. They are aware that it is an unproductive experience, that by any human measure almost any other endeavor is worthwhile."

An analytic paper takes shape when a writer creates a series of such paragraphs, links them with an overall logic, and draws a general conclusion concerning what was learned through the analysis. Here is the logical organization of Winn's analysis:

- **Paragraph 1:** Introduces the word "addiction" and indicates how the term is generally used.
- **Paragraph 2:** Suggests that television watching might be viewed as a "destructive addiction."
- **Paragraph 3:** Discusses the first component of the definition of addiction: an experience that "allows the participant to blot out the real world and enter into a pleasurable and passive mental state." Applies this first component to television viewing.
- **Paragraphs 4 and 5:** Discuss the second component of addiction—the participant has an illusion of control—and apply this to the experience of television viewing.
- **Paragraph 6:** Discusses the third component of addiction—because it requires so much time and emotional energy, the addictive behavior crowds out other, more productive or socially desirable activities—and applies this to the experience of television viewing.

- **Paragraph 7:** Discusses the fourth component of addiction—the negative consequences arising from the behavior—and applies this to the experience of television viewing.
- **Paragraph 8:** Discusses the fifth component of addiction—the participant is never satisfied because the experience is essentially empty—and applies this to the experience of television viewing. Note that in this paragraph, Winn brings in for support a relevant quotation by the psychiatrist Lawrence Kubie.

Draft and Revise Your Analysis

You will usually need at least two drafts to produce a paper that presents your idea clearly. The biggest changes in your paper will typically come between your first and second drafts. No paper that you write, analysis or otherwise, will be complete until you revise and refine your single compelling idea—in the case of analysis, your analytic conclusion about what the object, event, or behavior being examined means or how it is significant. You revise and refine by evaluating your first draft, bringing to it many of the same questions you pose when evaluating any piece of writing:

- Are the facts accurate?
- Are my opinions supported by evidence?
- Are the opinions of others authoritative?
- Are my assumptions clearly stated?
- Are key terms clearly defined?
- Is the presentation logical?
- Are all parts of the presentation well developed?
- Are significant opposing points of view presented?

Address these same questions to the first draft of your analysis, and you will have solid information to guide your revision.

Write an Analysis, Not a Summary

The most common error made in writing analyses—an error that is *fatal* to the form—is to present readers with a summary only. For analyses to succeed, you must *apply* a principle or definition and reach a conclusion about the object, event, or behavior you are examining. By definition, a summary (see Chapter 1) includes none of your own conclusions. Summary is naturally a part of analysis; you will need to summarize the object or activity being examined and, depending on the audience's needs, summarize the principle or definition being applied. But in an analysis, you must take the next step and share insights that suggest the meaning or significance of some object, event, or behavior.

Make Your Analysis Systematic

Analyses should give the reader the sense of a systematic, purposeful examination. Marie Winn's analysis illustrates the point: She sets out specific elements of addictive behavior in separate paragraphs and then uses each, within its paragraph, to analyze television viewing. Winn is systematic in her method, and we are never in doubt about her purpose.

Imagine another analysis in which a writer lays out four elements of a definition and then applies only two, without explaining the logic for omitting the others. Or imagine an analysis in which the writer offers a principle for analysis but directs it to only a half or a third of the object being discussed, without providing a rationale for doing so. In both cases the writer fails to deliver on a promise basic to analyses: Once a principle or definition is presented, it should be thoroughly and systematically applied.

Answer the "So What?" Question

An analysis should make readers *want* to read it. It should give readers a sense of getting to the heart of the matter, that what is important in the object or activity under analysis is being laid bare and discussed in revealing ways. If when rereading the first draft of your analysis, you cannot imagine readers saying, "I never thought of _____ this way," then something may be seriously wrong. Reread closely to determine why the paper might leave readers flat and exhausted, as opposed to feeling that they have gained new and important insights. Closely reexamine your own motivations for writing. Have *you* learned anything significant through the analysis? If not, neither will readers, and they will turn away. If you have gained important insights through your analysis, communicate them clearly. At some point, pull together your related insights and say, in effect, "Here's how it all adds up."

Attribute Sources Appropriately

In an analysis, you often work with just a few sources and apply insights from them to some object or phenomenon you want to understand more thoroughly. Because you are not synthesizing large quantities of data and because the strength of an analysis derives mostly from *your* application of a principle or definition, the opportunities for not appropriately citing sources are diminished. However, take special care to cite and quote, as necessary, those sources that you draw upon throughout the analysis.

CRITICAL READING FOR ANALYSIS

- *Read to get a sense of the whole in relation to its parts.* Whether you are clarifying for yourself a principle or a definition to be used in an analysis or you are reading a text that you will analyze, understand how parts function to create the whole. If a definition or principle consists of parts, use them to organize sections

(continues)

of your analysis. If your goal is to analyze a text, be aware of its structure: Note the title and subtitle; identify the main point and subordinate points and where they are located; break the material into sections.

- *Read to discover relationships within the object being analyzed.* Watch for patterns. When you find them, be alert—for they create an occasion to analyze, to use a principle or definition as a guide in discussing what the patterns may mean.

  In fiction, a pattern might involve responses of characters to events or to each other, the recurrence of certain words or phrasings, images, themes, or turns of plot (to name a few).

  In poetry, a pattern might involve rhyme schemes, rhythm, imagery, figurative or literal language, and more.

The challenge to you as a reader is first to see a pattern (perhaps using a guiding principle or definition to do so) and then to locate other instances of that pattern. Reading carefully in this way prepares you to conduct an analysis.

When *Your* Perspective Guides the Analysis

In some cases a writer's analysis of a phenomenon or a work of art may not result from anything as structured as a principle or a definition. It may instead follow from the writer's cultural or personal outlook, perspective, or interests. Imagine reading a story or observing the lines of a new building and being asked to analyze it—based not on someone else's definition or principle, but on your own. Your analysis of the story might largely be determined by your preference for fast pacing; intrepid, resourceful heroes; and pitiless, black-hearted villains. Among the principles you might use in analyzing the building are your admiration for curved exterior surfaces and the imaginative use of glass.

Analyses in this case continue to probe the parts of things to understand how they work and what they mean. And they continue to be carefully structured, examining one part of a phenomenon at a time. The essential purpose of the analysis, to *reveal*, remains unchanged. This goal distinguishes the analysis from the critique, whose main purpose is to *evaluate* and *assess validity*.

An intriguing example of how shifts in personal perspective over time may affect one's analysis of a particular phenomenon is offered by Terri Martin Hekker. In 1977 Hekker wrote an op-ed for the *New York Times* viewing traditional marriage from a perspective very different from that of contemporary feminists, who, she felt, valued self-fulfillment through work more than their roles as traditional housewives:

> I come from a long line of women...who never knew they were unfulfilled. I can't testify that they were happy, but they *were* cheerful.... They took pride in a clean, comfortable home and satisfaction in serving a good meal

because no one had explained to them that the only work worth doing is that for which you get paid.

Hekker's view of the importance of what she calls "housewifery"—the role of the traditional American wife and mother—derived from her own personal standards and ideals, which themselves derived from a cultural perspective that she admitted was no longer in fashion in the late 1970s.

Almost thirty years later (2006), Hekker's perspective had dramatically shifted. Her shattering experiences in the wake of her unexpected divorce had changed her view—and as a result, her analysis—of the status, value, and prospects of the traditional wife:

> Like most loyal wives of our generation, we'd contemplated eventual widowhood but never thought we'd end up divorced.... If I had it to do over again, I'd still marry the man I married and have my children.... But I would have used the years after my youngest started school to further my education. I could have amassed two doctorates using the time and energy I gave myself to charitable and community causes and been better able to support myself.

Hekker's new analysis of the role of the traditional wife derives from her changed perspective, based on her own experience and the similar experiences of a number of her divorced friends.

If you find yourself writing an analysis guided by your own insights, not by someone else's, then you owe your reader a clear explanation of your guiding principles and the definitions by which you will probe the subject under study. Continue using the Guidelines for Writing Analyses (see p. 181), modifying this advice as you think fit to accommodate your own personal outlook, perspective, or interests. Above all, remember to structure your analysis with care. Proceed systematically and emerge with a clear statement about what the subject means, how it works, or why it might be significant.

DEMONSTRATION: ANALYSIS

Linda Shanker wrote the following paper as a first-semester sophomore in response to this assignment from her sociology professor:

> Read Robert H. Knapp's "A Psychology of Rumor" in your course anthology. Use some of Knapp's observations about rumor to examine a particular rumor that you have read about in your reading during the first few weeks of this course. Write for readers much like yourself: freshmen or sophomores who have taken one course in sociology. Your object in this paper is to draw upon Knapp to shed light on how the particular rumor you select spread so widely and so rapidly.

MODEL ANALYSIS

Linda Shanker

Social Psychology 1

UCLA

17 November 2014

The Case of the Missing Kidney: An Analysis of Rumor

Rumor! What evil can surpass her speed?

In movement she grows mighty, and achieves

strength and dominion as she swifter flies...

[F]oul, whispering lips, and ears, that catch at all...

She can cling

to vile invention and malignant wrong,

or mingle with her word some tidings true.

—Virgil, *The Aeneid* (Book IV, Ch. 8)

(1) The phenomenon of rumor has been an object of fascination since ancient times. In his epic poem *The Aeneid,* Virgil noted some insidious truths about rumors: they spread quickly—especially in our own day, by means of phones, TV, e-mail, and Twitter; they can grow in strength and come to dominate conversation with vicious lies; and they are often mixed with a small portion of truth, a toxic combination that provides the rumor with some degree of credibility. In more recent years, sociologists and psychologists have studied various aspects of rumors: why they are such a common feature of any society, how they tie in to our individual and group views of the world, how and why they spread, why people believe them, and finally, how they can be prevented and contained.

(2) One of the most important studies is Robert H. Knapp's "A Psychology of Rumor," published in 1944. Knapp's article appeared during World War II (during which he was in charge of rumor control for the Massachusetts Committee of Public Safety), and many of his examples are drawn from rumors that sprang up during that conflict; but his analysis of why rumors form and how they work remains just as relevant today. First, Knapp defines rumor as an unverified statement offered about some topic in the hope that others will believe it (22). He proceeds to classify rumors into three basic types: the *pipe-dream or wish rumor,* based on what we would like to happen; the *bogie rumor,* based on our fears and anxieties; and the *wedge-driving or*

aggression rumor, based on "dividing groups and destroying loyalties" (23–24). He notes that rumors do not spread randomly through the population, but rather through certain "sub-groups and factions" who are most susceptible to believing them. Rumors spread particularly fast, he notes, when these groups do not trust officials to tell them the truth. Most important, he maintains, "rumors express the underlying hopes, fears, and hostilities of the group" (27).

Not all rumors gain traction, of course, and Knapp goes on to outline the qualities that make for successful rumors. For example, a good rumor must be "short, simple, and salient." It must be a good story. Qualities that make for a good story include "a humorous twist...striking and aesthetic detail...simplification of plot and circumstances...[and] exaggeration" (29). Knapp explains how the same rumor can take various forms, each individually suited to the groups among which it is circulating: "[n]ames, numbers, and places are typically the most unstable components of any rumor." Successful rumors adapt themselves to the particular circumstances, anxieties, prejudices of the group, and the details change according to the "tide of current swings in public opinion and interest" (30).

③

④

Knapp's insights are valuable in helping us understand why some contemporary rumors have been so frightening and yet so effective. One version of the rumor of the missing kidney, current in 1992, is recounted by Robert Dingwall, a sociologist at the University of Nottingham in England:

> A woman friend of another customer had a 17-year-old son who went to a nightclub in Nottingham, called the Black Orchid, one Friday evening. He did not come home, so she called the police, who were not very interested because they thought that he had probably picked up a girl and gone home with her. He did not come back all weekend, but rang his mother from a call box on Monday, saying he was unwell. She drove out to pick him up and found him slumped on the floor of the call box. He said that he had passed out after a drink in the club and remembered nothing of the weekend. There was a neat, fresh scar on his abdomen. She took him to the Queen's Medical Centre, the main emergency hospital in the city, where the doctors found that he had had a kidney removed. The police were called again and showed much more interest. A senior officer spoke to the mother and said that there was a secret surveillance operation going on in this club and others in the same regional chain in other East Midlands cities

because they had had several cases of the same kind and they thought that the organs were being removed for sale by an Asian surgeon. (181)

It is not clear where this rumor originated, though at around this time the missing kidney story had served as the basis of a *Law and Order* episode in 1992 and a Hollywood movie, *The Harvest,* released in 1992. In any event, within a few months the rumor had spread throughout Britain, with the name of the nightclub and other details varying according to the city where it was circulating. The following year, the story was transplanted to Mexico; a year later it was set in India. In the Indian version, the operation was performed on an English woman traveling alone who went to a New Delhi hospital to have an appendectomy. Upon returning to England, she still felt ill, and after she was hospitalized, it was discovered that her appendix was still there but that her kidney had been removed. In subsequent years the rumor spread to the United States, with versions of the story set in Philadelphia, New Orleans, Houston, and Las Vegas. In 1997, the following message, addressed "Dear Friends," was posted on an Internet message board:

I wish to warn you about a new crime ring that is targeting business travelers. This ring is well organized, well funded, has very skilled personnel, and is currently in most major cities and recently very active in New Orleans. The crime begins when a business traveler goes to a lounge for a drink at the end of the work day. A person in the bar walks up as they sit alone and offers to buy them a drink. The last thing the traveler remembers until they wake up in a hotel room bathtub, their body submerged to their neck in ice, is sipping that drink. There is a note taped to the wall instructing them not to move and to call 911. A phone is on a small table next to the bathtub for them to call. The business traveler calls 911 who have become quite familiar with this crime. The business traveler is instructed by the 911 operator to very slowly and carefully reach behind them and feel if there is a tube protruding from their lower back. The business traveler finds the tube and answers, "Yes." The 911 operator tells them to remain still, having already sent paramedics to help. The operator knows that both of the business traveler's kidneys have been harvested. This is not a scam or out of a science fiction novel, it is real. It is documented and confirmable. If you travel or someone close to you travels, please be careful. ("You've Got to Be")

Subsequent posts on this message board supposedly confirmed this story ("Sadly, this is very true"), adding different details.

Is there any truth to this rumor? None, whatsoever—not in any of its forms. Police and ⑥ other authorities in various cities have posted strenuous denials of the story in the newspapers, on official Web sites, and in internal correspondence, as have The National Business Travel Association, the American Gem Trade Association, and the Sherwin Williams Co. As reported in the rumor-reporting website Snopes.com, "the National Kidney Foundation has asked any individual who claims to have had his or her kidneys illegally removed to step forward and contact them. So far no one's showed up." The persistence and power of the missing kidney rumor can be more fully understood if we apply four of Knapp's principles of rumor formation and circulation to this particular urban legend: his notion of the "bogie"; the "striking" details that help authenticate a "good story" and that change as the rumor migrates to different populations; the ways a rumor can ride swings of public opinion; and the mingling of falsehood with truth.

The kidney rumor is first and foremost the perfect example of Knapp's bogie rumor, ⑦ the rumor that draws its power from our fears and anxieties. One source of anxiety is being alone in a strange place. (Recall the scary folktales about children lost in the forest, soon to encounter a witch.) These dreaded kidney removals almost always occur when the victim is away from home, out of town or even out of the country. Most of us enjoy traveling, but we may also feel somewhat uneasy in unfamiliar cities. We're not comfortably on our own turf, so we don't quite know our way around; we don't know what to expect of the local population; we don't feel entirely safe, or at least, we feel that some of the locals may resent us and take advantage of us. We can relate to the 17-year-old in the Nottingham nightclub, to the young English woman alone in New Delhi, to the business traveler having a drink in a New Orleans lounge.

Of course, our worry about being alone in an unfamiliar city is nothing compared to ⑧ our anxiety about being cut open. Even under the best of circumstances (such as to save our lives), no one looks forward to surgery. The prospect of being drugged, taken to an unknown facility, and having members of a crime ring remove one of our organs without our knowledge or consent—as apparently happened to the various subjects of this rumor—would be our worst nightmare. It's little wonder that this particular "bogie" man has such a powerful grip on our hearts.

Shanker 5

(9)   Our anxiety about the terrible things that may happen to us in a strange place may be heightened because of the fear that our fate is just punishment for the bad things that we have done. In the Nottingham version of the rumor, the victim "had probably picked up a girl and gone home with her" (Dingwall 181). Another version of the story features "an older man picked up by an attractive woman" (Dingwall 182). Still another version of the story is set in Las Vegas, "Sin City, the place where Bad Things Happen to the Unwary (especially the 'unwary' who were seen as deservedly having brought it upon themselves, married men intent upon getting up to some play-for-pay hanky panky)" ("You've Got to Be"). As Dingwall notes of this anxiety about a deserved fate, "[t]he moral is obvious: young people ought to be careful about nightclubs, or more generally, about any activity which takes them out of a circle of family and friends" (183).

(10)   In addition to its being a classic bogie rumor, Knapp would suggest that the missing kidney rumor persists because its "striking and aesthetic detail[s]," while false, have the ring of truth and vary from one version to another, making for a "good story" wherever the rumor spreads. Notice that the story includes the particular names of the bar or nightclub, the medical facility, and the hotel; it describes the size and shape of the scar; and it summarizes the instructions of the 911 operator to see if there is a tube protruding from the victim's back. (The detail about the bathtub full of ice and the advice to "call 911" was added to the story around 1995.) As Knapp observes, "[n]ames, numbers, and places are typically the most unstable components of any rumor" (30), and so the particular cities in which the kidney operations are alleged to have been performed, as well as the particular locations within those cities, changed as the rumor spread. Another changing detail concerns the chief villains of this story. Knapp notes that rumors adapt themselves to the particular anxieties and prejudices of the group. Many groups hate or distrust foreigners and so we find different ethnic or racial "villains" named in different cities. In the Nottingham version of the story, the operation is performed by an "Asian surgeon." The English woman's kidney was removed by an Indian doctor. In another version of the story, a Kurdish victim of the kidney operation was lured to Britain "with the promise of a job by a Turkish businessman" ("You've Got to Be").

(11)   Third, Knapp observes that successful rumors "ride the tide of current swings in public opinion and interest" (30). From news reports as well as medical and police TV dramas, many people are aware that there is a great demand for organ transplants and that such demand, combined with a short supply, has given rise to a black market for illegally obtained organs.

Shanker 6

When we combine this awareness with stories that appear to provide convincing detail about the medical procedure involved (the "neat fresh scar," the tube, the name of the hospital), it is not surprising that many people accept this rumor as truth without question. One Internet correspondent, who affirmed that "Yes, this does happen" (her sister-in-law supposedly worked with a woman whose son's neighbor was a victim of the operation), noted that the only "good" thing about this situation was that those who performed the procedure were medically trained, used sterile equipment, made "exact and clean" incisions ("You've Got to Be"), and in general took measures to avoid complications that might lead to the death of the patient.

Finally, this rumor gains credibility because, as Virgil noted, rumor "mingle[s] with her word some tidings true." Although no documented case has turned up of a kidney being removed without the victim's knowledge and consent, there have been cases of people lured into selling their kidneys and later filing charges because they came to regret their decisions or were unhappy with the size of their payment ("You Got to Be"). ⑫

Rumors can destroy reputations, foster distrust of government and other social institutions, and create fear and anxiety about perceived threats from particular groups of outsiders. Writing in the 1940s about rumors hatched during the war years, Knapp developed a powerful theory that helps us understand the persistence of rumors sixty years later. The rumor of the missing kidney, like any rumor, functions much like a mirror held up to society: it reveals anxiety and susceptibility to made-up but seemingly plausible "facts" related to contemporary social concerns. By helping us understand the deeper structure of rumors, Knapp's theories can help free us from the "domination" and the "Foul, whispering lips" that Virgil observed so accurately 2,000 years ago. ⑬

Shanker 7

Works Cited

Dingwall, Robert. "Contemporary Legends, Rumors, and Collective Behavior: Some Neglected Resources for Medical Technology." *Sociology of Health and Illness*, vol. 23, no. 2, 2001, pp. 180–202.

Knapp, Robert H. "A Psychology of Rumor." *Public Opinion Quarterly*, vol. 8, no. 1, 1944, pp. 22–37.

Shanker 8

Virgil. *The Aeneid*. Translated by Theodore C. Williams. *Perseus Digital Library*,

www.perseus.tufts.edu/hopper/text?doc=Perseus:text:1999.02.0054.

"You've Got to Be Kidneying." *Snopes.com*, 12 Mar. 2008, www.snopes.com/horrors/

robbery/kidney.asp.

MyWritingLab™   Exercise 6.2

Informal Analysis of the Model Analysis

Before reading our analysis of this model analysis, write your own informal response to the analysis. What are its strengths and weaknesses? To what extent does it follow the general Guidelines for Writing Analyses that we outlined on page 181? What function does each paragraph serve in the analysis as a whole?

THE STRATEGY OF THE ANALYSIS

- **Paragraph 1** creates a context for the analysis by introducing the phenomenon of rumor, indicating that it has been an object of fascination and study from ancient times (the poet Virgil is quoted) to the present.

- **Paragraphs 2 and 3** introduce the key principle that will be used to analyze the selected rumor, as explained by Robert H. Knapp in his article "A Psychology of Rumor." The principle includes Knapp's definition of rumor, his classification of rumors into three types, and the qualities that make for a successful rumor.

- **Paragraph 4** begins by indicating how Knapp's principles can be used to help us understand how rumor works and then presents one particular manifestation of the rumor to be analyzed, the rumor of the missing kidney. Much of the paragraph consists of an extended quotation describing one of the original versions of the rumor, set in Nottingham, England.

- **Paragraph 5** describes how the missing kidney rumor metamorphosed and spread, first throughout England and then to other countries, including Mexico, India, and the United States. A second extended quotation describes a version of the rumor set in New Orleans.

- **Paragraph 6** explains that the missing kidney rumor has no factual basis, but that its persistence and power can be accounted for by applying

Knapp's principles. The final sentence of this paragraph is the thesis of the analysis.

- **Paragraph 7** applies the first of Knapp's principles to the missing kidney rumor: It is a "bogie" rumor that "draws its power from our fears and anxieties." One such fear is that of being alone in an unfamiliar environment.

- **Paragraph 8** continues to apply Knapp's principle of the bogie rumor, this time focusing on our fears about being unwillingly operated upon.

- **Paragraph 9** discusses another aspect of the bogie rumor, the fear that what happens to us is a form of punishment for our own poor choices or immoral actions.

- **Paragraph 10** deals with a second of Knapp's principles, that the "facts" in rumors are constantly changing: Names, places, and other details change as the rumor spreads from one city to another, but the reference to specific details lends the rumor a veneer of authenticity.

- **Paragraph 11** deals with a third of Knapp's principles: that successful rumors are often based on topics of current public interest—in this case, organ transplants—and that, once again, a surface aura of facts makes the rumor appear credible.

- **Paragraph 12** returns to Virgil (cited in Paragraph 1), who notes that successful rumors also appear credible because they often mix truth with fiction.

- **Paragraph 13**, concluding the analysis, indicates why it is important to analyze rumor: Shedding light on how and why rumors like this one spread may help us counteract rumors' destructive effects.

MyWritingLab™   Visit Ch. 6 Analysis in MyWritingLab to test your understanding of the chapter objectives.

Chapter 7

Locating, Mining, and Citing Sources

After completing this chapter, you will be able to:

7.1 Explain the process involved in writing a source-based paper.

7.2 Pose a research question.

7.3 Find library and online sources and conduct interviews and surveys.

7.4 Use sources effectively for your own purpose and avoid plagiarism.

7.5 Cite sources properly in APA or MLA style.

SOURCE-BASED PAPERS

7.1 Explain the process involved in writing a source-based paper.	Research extends the boundaries of your knowledge and enables you to share your findings with others. The process of locating and working with multiple sources draws on many of the skills we have discussed in this book:

1. taking notes;
2. organizing your findings;
3. summarizing, paraphrasing, and quoting sources accurately and ethically;
4. critically evaluating sources for their value and relevance to your topic;
5. synthesizing information and ideas from several sources that best support your own critical viewpoint; and
6. analyzing topics for meaning and significance.

The model argument synthesis in Chapter 5, "Responding to Bullies" (pp. 148–157), is an example of a research paper that fulfills these requirements. The quality of your research and the success of any paper on which it is based are directly related to your success in locating relevant, significant, reliable, and current sources. This chapter will help you in that process.

WHERE DO WE FIND WRITTEN RESEARCH?

Here are just a few of the types of writing that involve research:

Academic Writing

- **Research papers** investigate an issue and incorporate results in a written or oral presentation.
- **Literature reviews** research and review relevant studies and approaches to a particular science, social science, or humanities topic.
- **Experimental reports** describe primary research and may draw on previous studies.
- **Case studies** draw upon primary and sometimes secondary research to report on or analyze an individual, a group, or a set of events.
- **Position papers** research approaches to an issue or solutions to a problem in order to formulate and advocate a new approach.

Workplace Writing

- **Reports** in business, science, engineering, social services, medicine
- **Market analyses**
- **Business plans**
- **Environmental impact reports**
- **Legal research:** memoranda of points and authorities

WRITING THE RESEARCH PAPER

Here is an overview of the main steps involved in writing research papers. Keep in mind that, as with other writing projects, writing such papers is a recursive process. For instance, you will gather data at various stages of your writing, as the list below illustrates.

Developing the Research Question

- *Find a subject.*
- *Develop a research question.* Formulate an important question that you propose to answer through your research.

Locating Sources

- *Conduct preliminary research.* Consult knowledgeable people, including academic librarians, general and specialized encyclopedias, general databases (such as *Academic Search Complete* and *JSTOR*) and discipline-specific databases

(continued)

(such as *EconLit* and *Sociological Abstracts*), and overviews and bibliographies/ references in recent books and articles. Begin your search with well-chosen keywords and pay attention to *subject tags* (keywords and phrases) assigned to the results of your search. Some of these subject tags—along with keywords and phrases in the titles, abstracts, tables of contents, and subject headings of your search results—may give you new leads in expanding or refining your search.

- *Refine your research question.* Based on your preliminary research, brainstorm about your topic and ways to answer your research question. Sharpen your focus, refining your question and planning the sources you'll need to consult.

- *Conduct focused research.* Consult books and online general and discipline-specific databases for articles in periodicals. Also consult biographical indexes, general and specialized dictionaries, government publications, and other appropriate sources. Conduct interviews and surveys, as necessary.

Mining Sources

- *Develop a working thesis.* Based on your initial research, formulate a working thesis that responds to your research question.

- *Develop a working bibliography.* Keep track of your sources, either on paper or digitally, including both bibliographic information and key points about each source. Make this bibliography easy to sort and rearrange.

- *Evaluate sources.* Determine the veracity and reliability of your sources; use your critical reading skills; check book reviews in databases like *Academic Search Complete* (or its associated databases such as *Academic Search Elite* and *Academic Search Premier*), *Alternative Press Index* (1969–present), *Periodicals Index Online* (1965–1999), *Reader's Guide Retrospective* (1890–1982), *JSTOR,* and *Project Muse.* Book reviews may also be found in *Book Review Digest, Publishers Weekly,* and Amazon.com. Look up biographies of authors, and read the "About the author" statements that often accompany scholarly articles.

- *Take notes from sources.* Paraphrase and summarize important information and ideas from your sources. Copy down important quotations. Note page numbers from sources of this quoted and summarized material.

- *Develop a working outline and arrange your notes according to your outline.*

Drafting; Citing Sources

- *Write your draft.* Write the preliminary draft of your paper, working from your notes and according to your outline.

- *Avoid plagiarism.* Take care to cite all quoted, paraphrased, and summarized source material, making sure that your own wording and sentence structure differ from those of your sources.

- *Cite sources.* Use in-text citations and a Works Cited or References list, according to the conventions of the discipline (e.g., MLA, APA, CSE).

Revising (Global and Local Changes)

- *Revise your draft.* Consider global, local, and surface revisions. Check that your thesis still reflects your paper's focus. Review topic sentences and paragraph development and logic. Use transitional words and phrases to ensure coherence. Make sure that the paper reads smoothly and clearly from beginning to end.

Editing (Surface Changes)

- *Edit your draft.* Check for style, combining short, choppy sentences and ensuring variety in your sentence structures. Check for grammatical correctness, punctuation, and spelling.

THE RESEARCH QUESTION

7.2 Pose a research question.

Pose a question to guide your research, one that interests you and allows you to fulfill the requirements of an assignment. In time, the short answer to this research question will become the thesis of your paper. By working with a question (as opposed to a thesis) early in the research process, you acknowledge that you still have ideas and information to discover before reaching your conclusions and beginning to write.

Research questions can be more or less effective in directing you to sources. Here are three suggestions for devising successful questions.

1. Pose neutral questions that open you to a variety of ideas and information. Avoid biased questions that suggest their own answers.

    EFFECTIVE How do musicians use computers to help them create songs?

    LESS EFFECTIVE Are musicians who rely on computers to compose and produce music cheating the creative process? [The use of "cheating" suggests that the researcher has already answered the question.]

2. Emphasize *how/why/what* questions that open discussion. Avoid yes-or-no questions that end discussion.

    EFFECTIVE How do software engineers create algorithms that map patterns in music?

    LESS EFFECTIVE Does music lend itself to mathematical analysis? [The yes-or-no question yields less information and leads to less understanding than the *how* question.]

3. Match the scope of your question to the scope of your paper. Avoid too-broad topics for brief papers; avoid too-narrow topics for longer papers.

    EFFECTIVE How has the use of computers affected both the production and the consumption of popular music in America?

    LESS EFFECTIVE How has the use of computers affected American popular culture? [Assuming a brief paper, the topic is too broad.]

NARROWING THE TOPIC VIA RESEARCH

If you need help narrowing a broad subject, try one or both of the following:

- Try searching for the subject heading in your library's online catalog. The catalog will show you items that match your search terms and will probably show you other subject tags on the same topic (see Fig. 7.2b, on page 203). This will give you a better idea of how to narrow down your search.

- Search by subject in an online database such as *Academic Search Premier* or *Academic OneFile*. The database may suggest different ways to break down the search into smaller or similar subjects or topics. Note subject tags (keywords and phrases) in your search results to see how the subject breaks down into components. Then narrow your search by following up on promising subject tags.

MyWritingLab™   Exercise 7.1

Constructing Research Questions

Moving from a broad topic or idea to the formulation of precise research questions can be challenging. Practice this skill by working with a small group of your classmates to construct research questions about the following topics (or come up with topics of your own). Write at least one research question that narrows each topic listed; then discuss these topics and questions with the other groups in class.

Racial or gender stereotypes in television shows

Drug addiction in the U.S. adult population

Global environmental policies

Employment trends in high-technology industries

U.S. energy policy

◎ LOCATING SOURCES ◎

7.3 Find library and online sources and conduct interviews and surveys.

Once you have a research question, find out what references are available. In your preliminary research, familiarize yourself quickly with basic issues and generate a preliminary list of sources. This will help narrow your investigations before moving to focused research.

TYPES OF RESEARCH DATA

Primary Sources

- Data gathered using research methods appropriate to a particular field

    sciences: experiments, observations

    social sciences: experiments, observations, surveys, interviews

    humanities: diaries, letters, and other unpublished documents; close reading, observation, and interpretation

Secondary Sources

- Information and ideas collected or generated by others who have conducted their own primary and/or secondary research

    library research: books, periodicals, etc.

    online research

Preliminary Research

Effective search strategies often begin with the most general reference sources: encyclopedias, biographical works, and dictionaries. Such sources are designed for people who need to familiarize themselves relatively quickly with the basic information about a particular topic. Authors of general sources assume that their readers have little or no prior knowledge of the subjects covered and of the specialized terminology of the field. By design, they cover a subject in less depth than do specialized sources. So review such comprehensive sources relatively early in your search even though you probably won't refer to them or cite them in your paper because they are so general.

Consulting Knowledgeable People

When you think of research, you may immediately think of libraries and print and online sources. But don't neglect a key reference: other people. Your *instructor* can probably suggest fruitful areas of research and some useful sources. Try to see your instructor during office hours, however, rather than immediately before or after class, so that you'll have enough time for a productive discussion.

Beyond your instructor, *academic librarians* are among the most helpful people you can find in guiding you through the research process. Your librarian can suggest which reference sources (e.g., databases, specialized encyclopedias, dictionaries, and directories) might be fruitful for your particular area of research. They can also work with you to develop search strategies; to help you choose the best keywords to describe the various facets of your topic; to use Boolean operators, truncation, and string (or phrase) searching (see Using Keywords and Boolean Logic to Refine Online Searches, pp. 214–215); to examine database results and bibliographies to find ways to extend your search; and to evaluate sources you identify through searches using the library's databases. In short, academic librarians play a significant teaching role in the process of providing access to the library's resources. Draw upon their expertise!

Familiarizing Yourself with Your Library's Resources

Knowing how to use the resources of your library is half the battle in conducting research. Among the most helpful guides to these resources are research guides, subject guides, and LibGuides. These are topically focused lists of your library's resources. LibGuides are used to note resources held or subscribed to by your library—in print and online—as well as resources freely available on the Web. Many guides also offer tips on how to search effectively within a particular field of study. Figure 7.1 shows an example of a library subject guide to world history.

Note the double row of tabs near the top of the page that offers different approaches to historical material and the "how to" guides to research (top row of tabs). The main part of the page, the large section on the right, describes key features of some of the most useful sources for research in world history.

Look for subject guides, research guides, and LibGuides on your own academic library home page. Alternatively, Google "library AND guide AND (subject word,

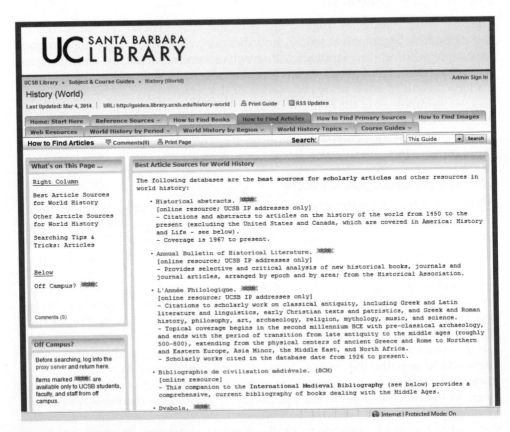

Figure 7.1   A LibGuide Screen

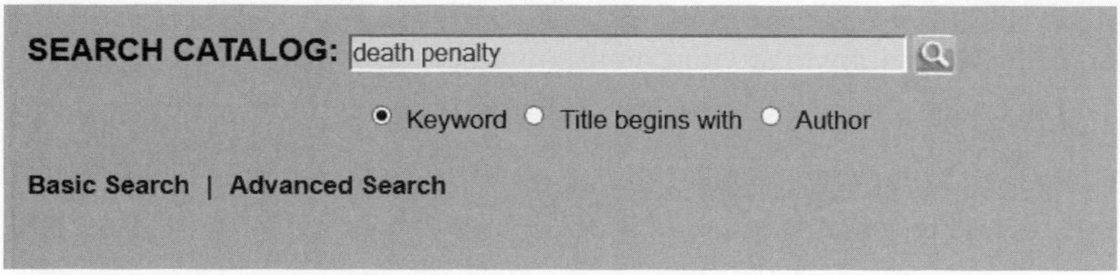

SEARCH CATALOG: death penalty   🔍

⦿ Keyword   ◯ Title begins with   ◯ Author

Basic Search | Advanced Search

Figure 7.2a   Subject Headings or Subject Tags

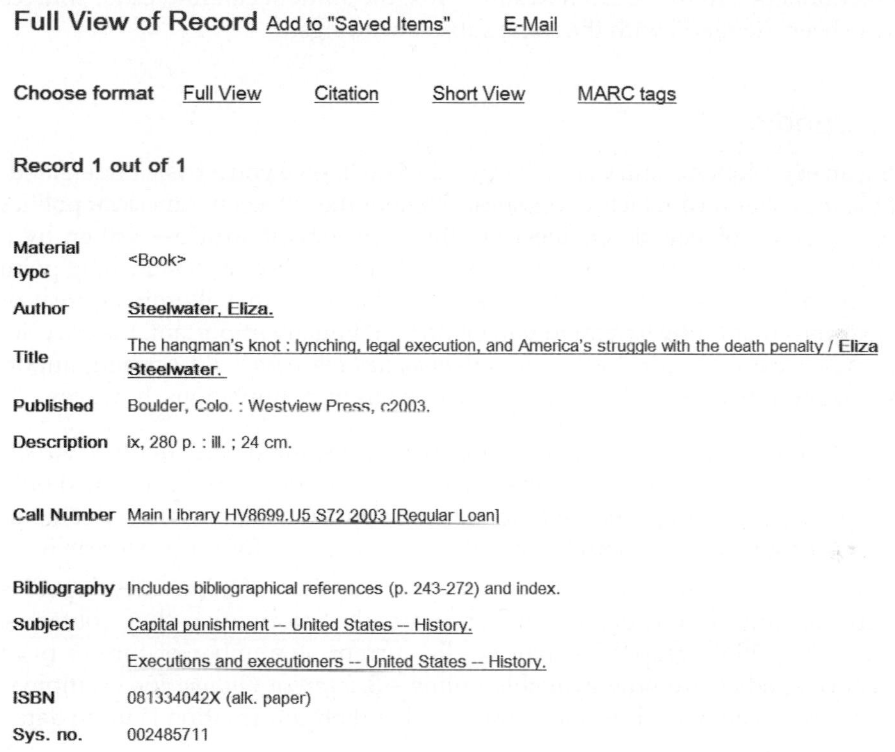

Full View of Record Add to "Saved Items"   E-Mail

Choose format   Full View   Citation   Short View   MARC tags

Record 1 out of 1

Material type	\<Book\>
Author	Steelwater, Eliza.
Title	The hangman's knot : lynching, legal execution, and America's struggle with the death penalty / Eliza Steelwater.
Published	Boulder, Colo. : Westview Press, c2003.
Description	ix, 280 p. : ill. ; 24 cm.
Call Number	Main Library HV8699.U5 S72 2003 [Regular Loan]
Bibliography	Includes bibliographical references (p. 243-272) and index.
Subject	Capital punishment -- United States -- History.
	Executions and executioners -- United States -- History.
ISBN	081334042X (alk. paper)
Sys. no.	002485711

Figure 7.2b

e.g., psychology) site:edu" to see lists of resources at other libraries—as some of these resources may be held by your home library.

Locating Preliminary Sources

- Ask your instructor to recommend sources on the subject.
- Scan the "Suggestions for Further Reading" sections of your textbooks. Ask your college librarian for useful reference tools in your subject area.
- Read an encyclopedia article on the subject and use the bibliography following the article to identify other sources.

- Read the introduction to a recent book on the subject and review that book's bibliography to identify more sources.
- Use an online database or search engine to explore your topic. Type in different keyword or search term combinations and browse the sites you find for ideas and references to sources you can look up later (see the box on pp. 214–215 for details).

Searching for sources on the death penalty, the student finds a relevant book. By clicking on the assigned subject headings ("Capital punishment" or "Executions and Executioners") in the "Search Results" box, the student can find other sources that have been "tagged" with the same subject headings.

Encyclopedias

Reading an encyclopedia entry about your subject will give you a basic understanding of the most significant facts and issues. Whether the subject is American politics or the mechanics of genetic engineering, the encyclopedia article—written by a specialist in the field—offers a broad overview that may serve as a launching point to more specialized research in a particular area. The article may illuminate areas or raise questions that motivate you to pursue further. Equally important, the encyclopedia article frequently concludes with an *annotated bibliography* describing important books and articles on the subject. Encyclopedias have limitations, however.

1. Most professors don't accept encyclopedia articles—and particularly *Wikipedia* articles (see below)—as legitimate sources for academic papers. You should use encyclopedias primarily to familiarize yourself with (and to select a particular aspect of) the subject area and as a springboard for further research.

2. Because new editions of the diminishing numbers of print encyclopedias appear only once every five or ten years, the information they contain—including bibliographies—may not be current. A number of former print encyclopedias are now available online—*Britannica Online*, for example—and this may mean, but not guarantee, that their information is up to date.

Among the well-known general encyclopedias (mostly available only online) are:

Academic American Encyclopedia

Encyclopedia.com (a compendium of more than 100 encyclopedias and dictionaries)

Encyclopedia Americana

Funk and Wagnalls New World Encyclopedia

New Encyclopaedia Britannica (or *Britannica Online*)

Wikipedia (online) [But see "Let the Buyer Beware" note below.]

But you will likely find it more helpful to consult *specialized* encyclopedias, such as the *Grove* encyclopedias of art and architecture, the *McGraw-Hill Encyclopedia of Science and Technology, Digital World Biology*, and Corsini's *Encyclopedia of Psychology*. Specialized encyclopedias restrict themselves to a particular disciplinary area, such as chemistry, law, or film, and are considerably more detailed in their treatment of a subject than are general encyclopedias.

WIKIPEDIA: LET THE BUYER BEWARE

Perhaps the Web's most widely used site for general information is *Wikipedia* (http://www.wikipedia.org). According to *Wikipedia* itself, the site contains 30 million articles in 287 languages, 4.3 million of them in the English edition. Launched in 2001 by the Internet entrepreneur Jimmy Wales and philosopher Larry Sanger, *Wikipedia* bills itself as "the free encyclopedia that anyone can edit." This site is thoroughly democratic: Not only can anyone write articles for *Wikipedia*, anyone can edit articles others have written.

At the same time and for the same reasons, these articles can be of doubtful accuracy and reliability. Authors of *Wikipedia* articles need no qualifications to write on their chosen subject, and their entries are subject to no peer review or fact-checking. (On numerous occasions, vandals have written or rewritten defamatory articles.)

The bottom line on *Wikipedia*? It can be a source of useful information not readily available elsewhere, but *caveat emptor*: Let the buyer beware. Even if researchers can't always be sure of the reliability of *Wikipedia* entries, however, many articles conclude with a section of footnote references and "External Links." These references and links often provide access to sources of established reliability, such as government agencies or academic sites.

MyWritingLab™

Exercise 7.2

Exploring Specialized Encyclopedias

Go to the reference section of your campus library and locate several specialized encyclopedias within your major or area of interest. Conduct an "advanced search" in the library's catalog, using a word that describes the broader discipline encompassing the topic (e.g., "film," "chemistry," or "law," along with the word "encyclopedia*" OR "dictionary*". (See p. 213 in "Searching Databases Effectively" on the use of truncation symbols like asterisks.) Look through the encyclopedias, noting their organization, and read entries on topics that interest you. Jot down notes describing the kinds of information you find. You might look for important concepts or terms related to your topic or for the names of important people associated with the topic or for events, dates, or definitions. These can make up the sets of words (keywords) that you subsequently take to the library catalog or article databases.

In addition, browse the reference section, especially right around the area where you found a particularly useful encyclopedia or book. Because of the way that books are arranged in the library (whether according to the Library of Congress system or the Dewey Decimal System), you'll be able to find books on similar topics near each other. For example, the books on drug abuse should be clustered near each other. Browsing can be a powerful tool for finding unexpectedly useful material.

Biographical Sources

Your preliminary research may prompt you to look up information on particular people. In these cases, consult biographical sources, which can be classified in several ways: by person (living or dead), geography, subject area, gender, race, or historical period.

Here are examples of biographical sources:

Biography in Context (a general biographical reference, incorporating numerous previously separate specialized biographical guides)

Black Americans in Congress, 1870–2007, 3rd ed.

Contemporary Authors

Current Biography (magazine) and *Current Biography Yearbook*

Notable American Women: A Biographical Dictionary (5 vols.)

Who's Who in America

Who's Who in the Arab World

These online biographical sources are included in the database collections of many academic libraries:

American National Biography Online

Biography and Genealogy Master Index

Biography Reference Bank: Contemporary Authors

Dictionary of Literary Biography

Oxford Dictionary of National Biography (replaces and extends *Dictionary of National Biography*)

Almanacs and Yearbooks

Once you settle on a broad topic still in need of narrowing, you may want to consult almanacs and yearbooks, which are generally issued annually and provide facts, lists of data, and chronologies of events. Titles include the following:

Almanac of American Politics (also a good source for biographical information)

CQ Almanac (formerly *Congressional Quarterly Almanac*, available both in print and online versions)

State of the World's Children (published by UNICEF)

World Almanac

World Trade Organization Annual Report

You can also find facts, lists of data, and chronologies by conducting an advanced search in the library's catalog, using a word that describes the broader discipline that encompasses the topic (e.g., "history," "sociology," or "medicine") along with the phrase "almanac* OR yearbook*". In addition, consult the online library guide accessible from your own library's home page (see LibGuide graphic on p. 202). See what you can find, for example, in the way of social science statistics available at your library.

Literature Guides and Handbooks

Guides to the literature of a certain subject area or handbooks can help you locate useful sources. Pay particular attention to how these guides break broad topics into subtopics—a matter of particular interest to researchers in the early stages of their work. You may become interested in a particular subtopic for your research paper. Here are examples:

The Basic Business Library: Core Resources and Services

Bearing Witness: A Resource Guide to Literature and Videos by Holocaust Victims and Survivors

CRC Handbook of Chemistry and Physics

Gallup public opinion polls (there are numerous Gallup polls; search by subject matter and year)

Guide to Everyday Economic Indicators

Information Resources in the Humanities and the Arts

Voice of the Shuttle (UCSB-based online guide to resources in the humanities, the social sciences, the sciences, and law): vos.ucsb.edu

Overviews and Bibliographies

If your professor or a bibliographic source directs you to an important recent book on your topic, skim the introductory (and possibly concluding) material, along with the table of contents, for an overview of key issues. Check also for a bibliography, Works Cited, and/or References list. These lists are extremely valuable resources for locating material for research. For example, Robert Dallek's 2003 book *An Unfinished Life: John Fitzgerald Kennedy, 1917–1963,* includes a seven-page bibliography of reference sources on President Kennedy's life and times.

Subject-Heading Guides

Seeing how a general subject (e.g., education) is broken down (e.g., into math instruction/public schools/Massachusetts/K8) in other sources also could stimulate research in a particular area. In subject-heading guides, general subjects are divided into secondary subject headings. The most well-known subject-heading guide is the *Library of Congress Subject Headings* catalog. You might also consult the *Propaedia* volume of the *Encyclopaedia Britannica* (2007) and the "Syntopicon" volumes of the *Great Books of the Western World* set. Online, look for these subject directories:

IPL2, Internet Public Library (http://www.ipl.org/)

Librarians' Index to the Internet (http://lii.org)

WWW Virtual Library (http://www.vlib.org for general subject directory)

Having used such tools to narrow the scope of your research to a particular topic and having devised an interesting research question, you're ready to undertake more-focused investigations.

FOCUSED RESEARCH

Once you have completed preliminary research, your objective becomes learning as much as you can about your topic. By the end of your inquiries, you'll have read enough to become something of an expert on your topic—or, if that's not possible given time constraints, you will at least have become someone whose critical viewpoint is based solidly on the available evidence. The following pages will suggest how to find sources for this kind of focused research.

In most cases, your research will be *secondary* in nature, based on (1) books; (2) print and online articles found through online databases; and (3) specialized reference sources. In certain cases, you may gather your own *primary* research, using (perhaps) interviews, surveys, structured observations, diaries, letters, and other unpublished sources.

Databases

Much of the information that is available in print—and a good deal that is not—is also available in digital form. Today, researchers typically access magazine, newspaper, and journal articles and reports, abstracts, and other forms of information through *online databases*, some of them freely available on the Web (e.g., Google Scholar) and some of them available to subscribers or subscriber institutions only. In rare instances, databases are accessed via *CD-ROM*. One great advantage of using databases (as opposed to print indexes) is that you can search several years' worth of different periodicals at the same time. In addition, many databases allow you to download and/or print the full text of articles.

Your library may offer access to hundreds of general and subject-specific databases, including the following:

General Databases:

Academic Search Complete (and *Academic Search Elite, Academic Search OneFile,* or *Academic Search Premiere)* (multidisciplinary range of academic journals)

Alternative Press Index

EBSCOhost (EBSCO is a vendor offering hundreds of individual databases of articles, e-books, and e-journals)

InfoTrac (database of more than 5,000 journals, magazines, and newspapers)

JSTOR (digital library of academic journals, books, and primary sources)

LexisNexis (general and legal databases)

Periodicals Index Online

Project Muse (humanities and social science articles from nonprofit publishers)

ProQuest (newspapers and periodicals)
Reader's Guide Retrospective (covers 1890–1982)

Subject-Specific Databases:

Anthropology: *Anthropology Plus*

Art: *Art Full Text* (fine, decorative, and commercial art; photography; folk art; film; architecture; etc.)
Art Index Retrospective

Biology: *Biosis* (biology and life sciences)
Biological Science Database

Business: *ABI/Inform*
Business Source Complete
EconLit

Classics: *Le Année Philologique*

Education: *ERIC*

English and Other Literatures: *MLA International Bibliography*

History: *America: History and Life*
Historical Abstracts

Law: *LexisNexis*

Medicine: *MEDLINE*
PubMed

Music: *Music Index Online*
RILM Abstracts of Music Literature

Political Science: *PAIS International* (political science, administration of justice, education, environment, labor conditions, military policy, etc.)
Worldwide Political Science Abstracts (political science, international relations, law, public administration/policy)
ProQuest Congressional (public policy, law, social, economic issues)

Psychology: *PsycINFO* and *PsycARTICLES* (psychology, behavioral sciences, and mental health)

Religion: *ATLA*

Sociology: *Sociological Abstracts*

News Databases:

Access World News
Historical New York Times
New York Times
The Times (London)
Wall Street Journal

Smartphones and Database Searching

Not everyone accesses online databases using desktops, laptops, or tablets; some use their smartphones, which have smaller screens. Fortunately, some database vendors offer interfaces that are viewable and usable on smartphones. Others, such as JSTOR and EBSCO, have apps that can be downloaded to smartphones to allow for direct access. Fig. 7.3 shows a search screen for the database JSTOR, as seen on a smartphone.

As you can see, the format of the search screen is simplified so as to be easily viewed on a small screen. Yet many of the same features of the Web version of the database are still available, such as the Advanced Search function and the ability to browse by subject. The results screen is similarly resized to fit on a smartphone screen.

The JSTOR app not only allows users to access the full text of the articles, but also allows them to restrict the search to articles, books, pamphlets, or only those articles that are accessible full-text.

Smartphone technology has also changed how to access the library Web sites through which you search these databases. Many Web sites are now scalable for smartphone screens, and some college and university library Web sites have their own apps, through which you may use the library catalog and find library information. Some specific groups of journals, such as those published by the American Psychological Association, have their own apps. See if your favorite database has a smartphone app. Such apps change constantly, so it's a good idea to check regularly for updates as well as for new offerings.

Figure 7.3   Smartphone Search Results (MyJSTOR App)

Discovery Services

Your library's Web site may be using a *discovery service*. This service may have a name like Primo (as it is called at the University of Idaho, which uses Ex Libris's Primo product). Or it may have a catchy name, such as Smart Search (which the University of Iowa gives its discovery service). Or, as at Seton Hall University, the service may not be a name at all: You may see just a search box and be given the option to "search everything," an option that utilizes the discovery service.

The discovery service operates by searching several databases at the same time. The search also includes hits from the library's online catalog, online journals, and any e-books the library may have. This can be a powerful tool, locating a vast number of resources quickly and highlighting the variety of tools at your fingertips. In addition, it offers a friendly interface that you are probably used to seeing in other contexts.

When using a discovery service, however, keep certain things in mind:

- Each individual database is unique and has its own strengths. For example, PsycARTICLES allows users to restrict searches to articles that have quantitative research. But discovery services cannot access these unique elements; they are generally restricted to limiting searches by subject headings, dates, call number ranges, or other more general elements. If you know your specific needs, you may get better results in a specific database.

- The number of results you get from a search in a discovery service can be overwhelming. You must develop good search strategies (see below, under "Searching Databases Effectively") in order to retrieve a reasonable number of hits.

In some cases, you may find exactly what you are looking for via a discovery service. In other instances, the discovery tool may serve as a gateway, giving you ideas for terms to use for effective searching and steering you toward databases where you can do more targeted searches.

Figure 7.4   A Discovery Service Search Box

Web Searches

The *World Wide Web* offers print, graphic, and video content that can be enormously helpful to your research. Keep in mind, however, that search engines like Google and Bing are only tools and that your own judgment in devising a precise search query will determine how useful these tools will be to your inquiries. Good queries yield good results; poor queries, poor results—or as the early programmers termed it, GIGO (garbage in/garbage out).

CONSTRUCTING AN EFFECTIVE DATABASE SEARCH QUERY

Up to now most of your online searches have likely been through such search engines as Google or Bing. While the World Wide Web has vast quantities of information, a good deal of it (apart from information on federal and state government sites) is of questionable reliability and usefulness for academic research. The Web itself has far fewer good resources than your academic library. Why? Your library subscribes to resources that aren't publicly available. Someone has to pay to see them. As a student, you have already paid for access to this greater pool of good resources. So why search the smaller, poorer Web pool?

One good general Web source is Google Scholar, which offers free, full-text access to articles in the scholarly literature (and references to books) in a broad range of disciplines. You may also find it useful to explore scholarly Web portals, such as the *Voice of the Shuttle* and *INFOMINE* (both multidisciplinary) as well as the *Internet Public Library* and *Librarians' Index to the Internet*. Sources referenced in Web sites like these have a better-than-average likelihood of being reliable.

Effective database searches are built on well-chosen keywords or phrases that you enter into a search engine's query box before clicking the Search button. A well-constructed query will return a list of useful Web sites. Use the following tips.

1. **Focus on a noun: a person, place, or thing.** The most important terms in your query should be *objects*—that is, tangible "things." The thing (or person or place) you want to learn more about is the center of your search, your subject.

2. **Narrow the search with another noun or a modifier.** Some search engines, such as Google, assume that all of the terms that you are searching for are joined together by the word AND. That means you are searching for *all* of the terms you typed in. When you qualify your search terms by combining them in meaningful ways, database searches become more pointed and useful. You could create a more productive search by narrowing the keyword "computers" to "computers music" or "computers music culture." See the section below on Boolean logic (pp. 213–215) for more information on this topic.

3. **Try substituting words if the search is not working.** When a search does not yield useful information, change your search terms. Think of synonyms for keywords in your query. For nonacademic topics, you might use a thesaurus to locate synonyms. For example, you might substitute "cardiac" for "heart" and "aircraft" for "plane."

4. *Re*-**search.** Librarians sometimes describe the process of library research as one of *re*-searching. A student will search with one set of words, get some good results, along with ideas of other words to use when searching, then vary the set of search words, get some more good results, and so on.

5. **Use "advanced" features to refine your search.** Search engines typically provide a "refine" function—sometimes called an "advanced" or "power" search tool—that allows you to narrow a search by date, type of publication, and type of Web site. You might instruct the engine to search only the sites of organizations, the government, or the military. You can also search in fields such as title, author, industry code, reviews, and so on. Refining your searches is easy: Locate the advanced feature option and fill in (or, in some cases, click to check) a box.

Searching Databases Effectively

Database systems in use today are still pretty dumb—that is, they are literal. They will return only the specific information requested and nothing more, however closely related. If we search for sources on AIDS, we will get lots on AIDS, but we will miss those items in the database that specify, instead, HIV or "acquired immune deficiency syndrome" or other ways of saying, basically, AIDS.

So we need to start the research process by thinking of the variety of ways an experienced researcher writing on our topic might refer to the different facets of our topic. We may be looking for articles on *college* students, but a scholar might write about *university* students. We may be looking for articles on *children*, but a scholar might write about *boys* OR *girls* OR *adolescents*.

Effective database searches are conducted according to the rules of Boolean logic. Fig. 7.5 (p. 214) illustrates such logic. Substitute for "cats" and "dogs" terms appropriate to your search and you will find yourself with an effective search strategy, one that yields a high number of relevant results while eliminating a high number of irrelevant results.

In addition to Boolean operators, researchers use truncation—often an asterisk (*), sometimes a question mark (?)—immediately following the search term (no space) as a "wild card." A search for the word "children" will identify items in which the title or abstract or subject tags include the word *children*, but we will not see items that instead refer to *childhood* or to the *child*. A truncated search for "child*" will yield results in which any variation of *child-* appears: *child, childhood, childish, childlike, children*, and so on.

Researchers also do string or phrase searching. If, for instance, we search in many databases using the words "United" and "States," we will (as one would expect) identify items on the United States of America. But since most database search engines merely search for the occurrence of each word we specify, we might also turn up things on altered *states* of consciousness in the *United* Kingdom (Brits under the influence). To help the database know specifically what we want, we can use quotation marks around the search phrase "United States."

Boolean Operators help define the relationship between search terms. When searching in a database, Boolean operators help you narrow or broaden your set of search results. The three Boolean operators are **AND**, **OR**, and **NOT**.

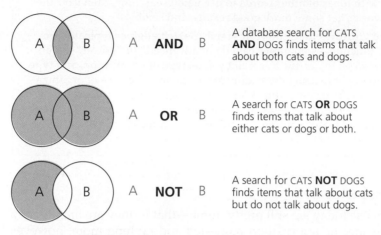

A **AND** B	A database search for CATS **AND** DOGS finds items that talk about both cats and dogs.
A **OR** B	A search for CATS **OR** DOGS finds items that talk about either cats or dogs or both.
A **NOT** B	A search for CATS **NOT** DOGS finds items that talk about cats but do not talk about dogs.

Figure 7.5   Boolean Operators

USING KEYWORDS AND BOOLEAN LOGIC TO REFINE ONLINE SEARCHES

You'll find more—and more relevant—sources on Internet search engines and library databases if you carefully plan your search strategies.

Note: Some online databases have their own systems for searching, so review the "Help" section of each database or search engine and use "Advanced Search" options where available. The following tips are general guidelines, and their applicability in different search engines may vary somewhat.

1. *Identify multiple keywords:*

   Write down your topic and/or your research question, and then brainstorm synonyms and related terms for the words in that topic/question.

   Sample topic: Political activism on college campuses

   Sample research question: What kinds of political activism are college students involved in today?

   Keywords: Political activism; college students

   Synonyms and related terms: politics; voting; political organizations; protests; political issues; universities; colleges; campus politics

2. *Conduct searches using different combinations of synonyms and related terms.*
3. *Find new terms in the sources you locate and search with them.*
4. *Use quotation marks around words you want linked:* "political activism"

5. *Use "Boolean operators" to link keywords:*

The words AND, OR, and NOT are used in "Boolean logic" to combine search terms and get more precise results than using keywords alone.

AND: Connecting keywords with AND narrows a search by retrieving only those sources that contain *both* keywords:

political activism AND college students

OR: Connecting keywords with OR broadens a search by retrieving all sources that contain at least one of the search terms. This operator is useful when you have a topic/keyword for which there are a number of synonyms. Linking synonyms with OR will lead you to the widest array of sources:

political activism OR protests OR political organizing OR voting OR campus politics college OR university OR campus OR students

AND and OR: You can use these terms in combination, by putting the OR phrase in parentheses:

(political activism OR protests) AND (college OR university)

NOT: Connecting keywords with NOT (or, in some cases, AND NOT) narrows a search by excluding certain terms. If you want to focus on a very specific topic, NOT can be used to limit what the search engine retrieves; however, this operator should be used carefully as it can cause you to miss sources that may actually be relevant:

college students NOT high school

political activism NOT voting

Evaluating Web Sources

The Web makes it possible for people at home, work, or school to gain access to corporate, government, and personal Web pages. Academic researchers are obligated to read Web-based material just as critically as they read print-based material. Chapter 2, Critical Reading and Critique, offers criteria for evaluating the quality and reliability of information and ideas in *any* source (pp. 53–62). Web sources are no exception, particularly self-published Web pages that are not subject to editorial review.

Reference librarians Jan Alexander and Marsha Tate have offered useful guidelines for helping researchers assess Web sources. First, they point out, it's important to determine what *type* of Web page you are dealing with. Web pages generally fall into one of five types, each with a different purpose:

1. business/marketing
2. reference/information
3. news
4. advocacy of a particular point of view or program
5. personal page

The purpose of a Web site—to sell, persuade, entertain—has a direct bearing on the objectivity and reliability of the information presented. When evaluating a site and determining its reliability for use in a research project, apply the same general criteria that you apply to print sources: (1) accuracy, (2) authority, (3) objectivity, (4) currency, (5) coverage. You might pose these questions in an effort to assess reliability:

- What's the likelihood that the information has been checked by anyone other than the author?
- What are the author's qualifications to write on the subject?
- What is the reputation of the publisher?
- Who is the author?
- What are the biases—stated or unstated—of the Web site?
- How current is the site?
- Which topics are included (and not included) in the site? To what extent are the topics covered in depth?

Pose these questions and determine, as you would for any non-Web source, reliability and suitability for your research project.

Other Pitfalls of Web Sites

Because reliable sites may include links to other sites that are inaccurate or out-dated, users cannot rely on the link as a substitute for evaluating the five criteria just outlined. Web pages are also notoriously unstable, frequently changing and even disappearing without notice.

Remember: As a researcher working in an academic setting, you should apply the same critical reading skills to all your sources—no matter what types they are or where you found them, including on the Web.

MyWritingLab™   Exercise 7.3

Exploring Online Sources

Go online and access one of the search engines or academic/professional data-bases discussed in this chapter. Select a topic/research question that interests you. Review the box on pages 214–215 and try different combinations of keywords and Boolean operators to see what sources you can find for your topic. Jot down notes describing the kinds of sources you find and which terms seem to yield the best results.

MyWritingLab™   Exercise 7.4

Practice Evaluating Web Sources

To practice applying the evaluation criteria discussed in the section on Web sources, go to an Internet search engine and look for sources addressing a topic of interest to you (perhaps after completing Exercise 7.3). Try to locate one source representing each of the five types of Web pages (business/marketing, reference/information, news, advocacy, and personal). Print the home page of each source and bring the copies to class. In small groups of classmates, look over the sites each student found and make notes on each example's (1) accuracy, (2) authority, (3) objectivity, (4) currency, and (5) coverage.

Periodicals: General

Because many more periodical articles than books are published every year, you are likely (depending on the subject) to find more information in periodicals than in books. General periodicals are the magazines and newspapers that are usually found on newsstands or in bookstores, such as the *New York Times, Time,* and the *New Yorker.* Periodicals often have Web sites where many of their current articles are available online; you can also subscribe to these periodicals via e-readers. By their nature, recent general periodical articles are more current than books. For example, the best way to find out about a political party's position on Social Security reform is to look for current articles in periodicals and newspapers. But periodical articles may have less critical distance than books, and like books, they may become dated, to be superseded by more recent articles.

Magazines

General periodicals such as *The Atlantic,* the *New Republic,* and *The Nation* are intended for nonspecialists. Their articles, which tend to be highly readable, may be written by staff writers, freelancers, or specialists. But they usually don't provide citations or other indications of sources, so they're of limited usefulness for scholarly research. Increasingly, texts and abstracts of articles in general sources are available in online databases.

Newspapers

News stories, feature stories, and editorials (even letters to the editor) may be important sources of information. Your college library may have indexes to *The New York Times* and other important newspapers such as *The Washington Post,* the *Los Angeles Times,* the *Chicago Tribune, The Wall Street Journal,* and *The Christian Science Monitor.* It is also entirely possible that your library opts to forego print indexes in favor of online databases such as *EBSCO Newspaper Source Plus* or ProQuest's *New York Times* interface.

Periodicals: Specialized

Some professors will expect at least some of your research to be based on articles in specialized periodicals or scholarly journals. So instead of (or in addition to) relying on an article from *Psychology Today* (considered a general periodical even though its subject is somewhat specialized) for an account of the effects of crack cocaine on mental functioning, you might also rely on an article from the *Journal of Abnormal Psychology*. If you are writing a paper on the satirist Jonathan Swift, in addition to a recent reference to him that may have appeared in *The New Yorker*, you may need to locate a relevant article in *Eighteenth-Century Studies*.

Articles in such journals are normally written by specialists and professionals in the field rather than by staff writers or freelancers, and the authors will assume that their readers already understand the basic facts and issues concerning the subject. Other characteristics of scholarly journals:

- They tend to be heavily researched, as indicated by their numerous notes and references.
- They are generally published by university presses.
- Most of the authors represented are university professors.
- The articles, which have a serious, formal, and scholarly tone (and so are less reader-friendly than those in general magazines), are generally peer reviewed by other scholars in the field.

To find articles in specialized periodicals, you'll use specialized databases (see pp. 208–209)—that is, databases for particular disciplines, such as *ProQuest Education Plus* and *Business Source Complete*. You may also find it helpful to refer to *abstracts*, such as *Sociological Abstracts*. Like specialized databases, abstracts list articles published in a particular discipline over a given period, but they also provide summaries of the articles listed. They can save you a lot of time in determining which articles you should read and which ones you can safely skip. Don't treat abstracts alone as sources for research, however; when you find useful material in an abstract, locate the article to which it applies and use that as the source you reference. You will also find a lot of information on periodicals of all types via online databases. These databases run the gamut from those that provide bibliographic indexing or abstracting information, such as *Alternative Press Index* and *Sociological Abstracts*, to full-text databases such as *Academic Search Premier* that provide access to the full-length article.

One caution: Students too often think that they can simply browse their way to enough sources to write their papers. But this would be a hit-or-miss approach. To be a successful (more purposeful and systematic) browser, try instead to use the article databases in your discipline to identify one or two or twelve potentially interesting sources; then browse within those issues of journals to see if anything else seems interesting.

MyWritingLab™

Exercise 7.5

Exploring Specialized Periodicals

Visit your campus library and locate online or print specialized periodical indexes for your major or area of interest (ask a reference librarian for help). Use your online catalog or ask a librarian for assistance in finding your library's print periodicals, if they are available. Note the call numbers for specialized periodicals (also called academic journals) in your field, and visit the section of the library where recent editions of academic journals are usually housed. If your library keeps its journals in call number order, browse the area where the journals are located, and look at journals around it. If periodicals are listed alphabetically, do a keyword search in the catalog for journal names, and find where those journals are located in the library. If your library does not keep its journals accessible in print form, do a search in a database on your topic. Look at the titles of the journals that come up in your search results. Look through the specialized periodicals in your field. The articles you find in these journals represent some of the most recent scholarship in the field—the kind of scholarship many of your professors are busy conducting. Write half a page or so describing the articles you find interesting and why.

Books

Books are useful for providing both the breadth and depth of coverage of a subject. Because they are generally published at least a year or two after the events treated, they also tend to provide the critical distance that is sometimes missing from articles. Conversely, this delay in coverage means that the information in books won't be as current as the information you find in periodicals. Any piece of writing, books included, may be inaccurate, outdated, or biased.

Book Reviews

One way to determine the reliability and credibility of a book you may want to use is to look up the reviews published in resources such as *Publishers Weekly*, *Library Journal*, or *The New York Times Book Review*. You can also look at book reviews either in the online *Book Review Digest* or on *Amazon.com*. Reviews may often be searched for by:

- author
- title
- subject
- keyword

The online *Book Review Digest* offers brief descriptions of thousands of books and, more importantly, provides excerpts from (and references to) reviews. Another useful list of print and online resources for book reviews in the humanities is available at the UCSB library guide site (search: "guides library ucsb book reviews"). If a book receives bad reviews, you don't necessarily have to avoid it (the book may still have something useful to offer, and the review itself may be unreliable). But you should take any negative reaction into account when using that book as a source.

Government Publications and Other Statistical Sources

The collection, organization, and analysis of data take us into the realm of statistics, where researchers typically focus on changing patterns of numbers and percentages. How much money did consumers spend on entertainment last year—as opposed to the year before? How has the makeup of immigrant population changed over the past twenty years? Is the divorce rate rising or falling? How much money was spent on Head Start during the past five years? Since 1878, researchers looking for statistical information about the United States have relied heavily upon the *Statistical Abstracts of the United States*, produced by the Statistical Compendia program of the U.S. Census Bureau. For budgetary reasons, the *Statistical Abstracts* and related resources were terminated in 2011. As an alternative, the Census Bureau recommended that researchers looking for this kind of statistical information refer to the organizations cited in the source notes of the most recent (2012) *Statistical Abstracts* (http://www.census.gov/compendia/statab/). In addition, ProQuest, the publisher of a general database, announced that it will take over publication for updating and releasing its own version of *Statistical Abstracts* in print and online formats (http://cisupa .proquest.com).

Beyond the *Statistical Abstracts*, a huge quantity of reference information (both statistical and nonstatistical) is available on government Web sites. A valuable tool for finding online government information is USA.gov (http://www.usa .gov). This site is an online portal for the U.S. government and allows users to search the Web sites of all the federal government's Web sites; in addition, users can find information on state and federal Web sites.

A useful (and free) Web site for medical information is *MedlinePlus*, produced by the National Institutes of Health (NIH) (http://www.nlm.nih.gov/medlineplus). This Web site is not only a source of reliable medical information, but it also provides access to medical studies, dictionaries, publications from the National Library of Medicine, and health news.

Among other databases of government publications:

American Statistics Index (a guide and index to U.S. government statistical publications)

Congressional Information Service (legislative and statistical works recently acquired by ProQuest)

A good list of social sciences data and statistics sources may be found by searching "guides and library and ucsb and socialsci stats." Statistical data on politics may be found by searching "guides and library and ucsb and politics."

Historical statistics may be found in the following sources:

Historical Statistics of the United States (online and print)

International Historical Statistics: Africa, Asia and Oceania, 1750–2000 (print)

International Historical Statistics: The Americas, 1750–2000 (print)

International Historical Statistics: Europe, 1750–2000 (print)

U.S. Census Bureau—Historical Census Browser (University of Virginia)
(http://mapserver.lib.virginia.edu)

U.S. Census Bureau—Census of Population and Housing
(http://www.census.gov/prod/www/decennial.html) [digitized copies of print volumes, 1790–2010]

For current information on a subject as of a given year, consult an *almanac* (such as *World Almanac*). For annual updates of information, consult a *yearbook* (such as *The Statesman's Yearbook*). For maps and other geographic information, consult an *atlas* (such as *The New York Times Atlas of the World*). Often, simply browsing through the reference shelves for data on your general subject—such as biography, public affairs, psychology—will reveal valuable sources of information.

Interviews and Surveys

Depending on the subject of your paper, you may want to *interview* your professors, your fellow students, or other individuals knowledgeable about your subject. Additionally, or alternatively, you may wish to conduct *surveys* via *questionnaires* (see the related box). When well prepared and insightfully interpreted, such tools can produce valuable information about the ideas or preferences of a group of people.

GUIDELINES FOR CONDUCTING INTERVIEWS

- Become knowledgeable about the subject before the interview so that you can ask intelligent questions. Prepare most of your questions beforehand.

- Ask "open-ended" questions designed to elicit meaningful responses, rather than "forced-choice" questions that can be answered with a word or two or "leading questions" that presume a particular answer. For example, instead of asking, "Do you think that male managers should be more sensitive to women's concerns for equal pay in the workplace?" ask, "To what extent do you see evidence that male managers are insufficiently sensitive to women's concerns for equal pay in the workplace?"

- Ask follow-up questions to elicit additional insights or details.

- If you record the interview (in addition to or instead of taking notes), get your subject's permission, preferably in writing.

GUIDELINES FOR CONDUCTING SURVEYS AND DESIGNING QUESTIONNAIRES

- Determine your *purpose* in conducting the survey: what kind of *information* you seek and *whom* (i.e., what subgroup of the population) you intend to survey.

- Decide whether you want to collect information on the spot or have people send their responses back to you. (You will get fewer responses if they are sent back to you, but those you do get will likely be more complete than surveys conducted on the spot.)

- Devise and word questions carefully so that they (1) are understandable and (2) don't reflect your own biases. For example, for a survey on attitudes toward capital punishment, if you ask, "Do you believe that the state should endorse legalized murder?" you've loaded the question to influence people to answer in the negative.

- Devise short-answer or multiple-choice questions; open-ended questions encourage responses that are difficult to quantify. (You may want to leave space, however, for "additional comments.") Conversely, yes-or-no responses or rankings on a five-point scale are easy to quantify.

- It may be useful to break out the responses by as many meaningful categories as possible—for example, gender, age, ethnicity, religion, education, geographic locality, profession, and income.

○ MINING SOURCES ○

7.4 Use sources effectively for your own purpose and avoid plagiarism.

Having located your sources (or at least having begun the process), you'll proceed to "mining" them—that is, extracting from them information and ideas that you can use in your paper. Mining sources involves three important tasks:

- Compiling a working bibliography to keep track of what information you have and how it relates to your research question.

- Taking notes on your sources and evaluating them for reliability and relevance.

- Developing some kind of *outline*—formal or informal—that allows you to see how you might subdivide and organize your discussion and at which points you might draw on relevant sources.

CRITICAL READING FOR RESEARCH

- *Use all the critical reading tips we've suggested thus far.* The tips contained in the boxes Critical Reading for Summary on pages 6–7, Critical Reading for Critique on pages 75–76, Critical Reading for Synthesis on page 129, and Critical Reading for Analysis on pages 185–186 are all useful for the kinds of reading engaged in when conducting research.

- *Read for relationships to your research question.* How does the source help you formulate and clarify your research question?

- *Read for relationships among sources.* How does each source illustrate, support, expand upon, contradict, or offer an alternative perspective to those of your other sources?

- *Consider the relationship between your source's form and content.* How does the form of the source—specialized encyclopedia, book, article in a popular magazine, article in a professional journal—affect its content, the manner in which that content is presented, and its relationship to other sources?

- *Pay special attention to the legitimacy of Internet sources.* Consider how the content and validity of the information on the Web page may be affected by the purpose of the site. Assess Web-based information for its (1) accuracy, (2) authority, (3) objectivity, (4) currency, and (5) coverage (see pp. 215–216).

THE WORKING BIBLIOGRAPHY

As you conduct your research, keep a *working bibliography,* a record of bibliographic information on all the sources you're likely to use in preparing the paper. If you are careful to record *full* bibliographic information—author(s), title, publisher, and so on—you'll spare yourself the frustration of hunting for it during the composition of your paper.

In addition to a working bibliography, it's a good idea to keep a *research log.* As you search, keep note of which database you are searching and which words you use in each search. Note significant sources that you find (your "working bibliography"), but also note new words or phrases or concepts that you might use on subsequent searches. By keeping a running research log, you can go back to previously searched databases with new search strategies—without risking running the same search over and over again.

Online catalogs and databases make it easy to copy and paste your sources' (or potential sources') bibliographic information into a document or to e-mail citations to yourself for cutting and pasting later. A more traditional but still very efficient way to compile bibliographic information is on 3" × 5" cards. (Note, also, that certain software programs allow you to create sortable digital records.) Using any of these methods, you can easily add, delete, and rearrange individual bibliographic records as your research progresses. Whether you keep bibliographic information on 3" × 5" cards or in a digital document, be sure to record the following:

- The author or editor (last name first) and, if relevant, the translator
- The title (and subtitle) of the book or article
- The publisher (if a book) or the title of the periodical
- The date and/or year of publication; if a periodical, volume and issue number

- The date you accessed an online source, if you think this will help you locate it again
- The edition number (of a book beyond its first edition)
- The inclusive page numbers (if an article)
- The specific page number of a quotation or other special material you might paraphrase

You'll also find it helpful to include this additional information:

- The URL or DOI (digital object identifier) of an online source
- A brief description of the source (to help you recall it later in the research process)
- A code number, which you can use as a shorthand reference to the source in your notes (see the sample note records below)

Here's an example of a working bibliography record:

> Gorham, Eric B. *National Service, Political Socialization, and Political Education*. SUNY P, 1992.
>
> Argues that the language government uses to promote national service programs betrays an effort to "reproduce a postindustrial, capitalist economy in the name of good citizenship." Chap. 1 provides a historical survey of national service.

Here's an example of a working bibliography record for an article:

> Gergen, David. "A Time to Heed the Call." *U.S. News & World Report*, 24 Dec. 2001, pp. 60–61.
>
> Argues that in the wake of the surge of patriotism that followed the September 11 terrorist attacks, the government should encourage citizens to participate in community and national service. Supports the McCain-Bayh bill.

Here's an example of a working bibliography record for an online source:

> Bureau of Labor Statistics. "Table 1: Volunteers by Selected Characteristics, September 2009." 27 Jan. 2010, www.bls.gov/news.release/volun.t01.htm.
>
> Provides statistical data on volunteerism in the U.S.

Some instructors may ask you to prepare—either in addition to or instead of a research paper—an *annotated bibliography*. This is a list of relevant works on a subject, with the contents of each work briefly described or assessed. The sample bibliography records above could become the basis for three entries in an annotated bibliography on national service. Annotations differ from abstracts in that annotations aren't comprehensive summaries; rather, they indicate how the items may be useful to the researcher.

Note-Taking

People have their favorite ways of note-taking. Some use legal pads or spiral notebooks; others type notes into a laptop or tablet computer, perhaps using a database program. Some prefer 4" × 6" cards for note-taking. Such cards have some of the same advantages that 3" × 5" cards have for working bibliographies: They can easily be added to, subtracted from, and rearranged to accommodate changing organizational plans. Also, discrete pieces of information from the same source can easily be arranged (and rearranged) into subtopics. Whatever your preferred approach, consider including the following along with the note:

- a topic or subtopic label corresponding to your outline (see below)
- a code number, corresponding to the number assigned the source in the working bibliography
- a page reference at the end of the note

Here's a sample note record for the table "Volunteers by Selected Characteristics, September 2009" from the Bureau of Labor Statistics (bibliographic record above):

Pervasiveness of Volunteerism (I)   7

Shows that 26.8 percent of Americans age 16 and older, 63.3 million in all, devote time to community service.

Here's a note record for the periodical article by Gergen (see bibliography note on the previous page):

Beneficial Paid Volunteer Programs (II)   12

Says that both the community and the individual benefit from voluntary service programs. Cites Teach for America, Alumni of City Year, Peace Corps as programs in which participants receive small stipends and important benefits (60). "Voluntary service when young often changes people for life. They learn to give their fair share." (60)

Both note records are headed by a topic label followed by the tentative location (indicated by a Roman numeral) in the paper outline where the information may be used. The number in the upper right corner corresponds to the number you assigned to the source in your bibliography note. The note in the first record uses *summary*. The note in the second record uses *summary* (sentence 1), *paraphrase* (sentence 2), and *quotation* (sentence 3). Notice the inclusion of page references, which the writer will reference in the paper itself (if the note is used). For hints on when to choose summary, paraphrase, and quotation, see Chapter 1, page 47.

Remember: Use quotation marks to distinguish between your language and the source author's language. Cite page references when you note an author's exact language *or* ideas. If you're careful to keep the distinctions between your language and that of authors clear, you'll avoid plagiarizing your sources. See the discussion of plagiarism on pages 49–50 and later in this chapter for more details.

Getting the Most from Your Reading

Fig. 7.6 presents some tips to help you determine how useful particular books will be in answering your research question.

In evaluating your sources, whether print or online, whether in book, article, or statistical form, try using the mnemonic "A-CRAB" to remember to pose a series of questions (see Fig. 7.7).

HOW TO READ A BOOK (OR ANY OTHER SOURCE)

First, don't read it word for word. Not yet.

Flip through the book to see how it is organized. Look for a TABLE OF CONTENTS and an INDEX. Do these seem to indicate that your topic is covered in enough depth to be useful?

Skim through the book's PREFACE or INTRODUCTION. For a journal article, read the ABSTRACT if there is one. What does the author say she accomplishes in this work? Do her claims appear to be grounded in fact? Or is this opinion or propaganda? Skim the first and last paragraphs of each chapter; these will reveal major points the author makes along the way. For an article, skim the introductory and concluding paragraphs. Note HEADINGS and SUBHEADINGS within chapters that can guide your progress in reading. Look for tables, charts, graphs, diagrams, maps, photographs, and any other VISUAL RESOURCES that can help you understand the author's train of thought.

Sample the author's writing as you skim the work. Does the level of information she presents appear to be appropriate for your needs? Is the author either too general or too technical in covering your topic? Do the author's claims appear to be backed by sound reasoning? Is there enough evidence presented to back up the author's point of view? Check the author's FOOTNOTES and CITATIONS to see if they appear relevant to your topic. Does the author cite solid, scholarly sources to support her points of view?

If, after this quick review, it appears to be a useful source ... **Read the Book!**

Figure 7.6   How to Read a Book

Credibility of Sources

WHILE YOU READ … THINK LIKE **A-CRAB**	**A**uthority	Ask yourself, who wrote this? Do the author's credentials, education, past writings, and experience impress you? Does the author cite credible, authoritative sources?
	Currency	When was it written? Is the source current and up-to-date for your topic?
	Relevance	Is the information useful to you? Is the source extensive or marginal in its coverage of your topic?
	Audience	Who is the intended reader? Is this source written for a popular audience? Or a scholarly audience?
	Bias	Does the author have a specific bias? Is the author trying to persuade the reader to accept a particular point of view?

Figure 7.7   Credibility of Sources

GUIDELINES FOR EVALUATING SOURCES

- *Skim the source.* With a book, look over the table of contents, the introduction and conclusion, and the index; zero in on passages that your initial survey suggests are important. With an article, skim the introduction and the headings.
- *Be alert for references* in your sources to other important sources, particularly to sources that several authors treat as important.
- Other things being equal, the *more recent* the source, the better. Recent work usually incorporates or refers to important earlier work.
- If you're considering making multiple references to a book, look up the reviews in the *Book Review Digest* or via articles found using online databases. Also, check the author's credentials in a source such as *Contemporary Authors* or *Current Biography Illustrated.* If an author is not listed in either of these sources, you may choose to do a Web search for the author and look for online résumés, online portfolios, or references to the author's work.

ARRANGING YOUR NOTES: THE OUTLINE

You won't use all the notes you take during the research process. Instead, you'll need to do some selecting, which requires you to distinguish more important from less important (and unimportant) material. Using your original working thesis (see Chapter 3)—or a new thesis that you have developed during the course of data gathering and invention—you can begin constructing a *preliminary outline* of your paper. This outline will indicate which elements of the topic you intend to discuss and in what order. You can then arrange relevant note cards (or digital files) accordingly and remove, to a separate location, notes that will not likely find their way into the paper.

Some people prefer not to develop an outline until they have more or less completed their research. At that point they look over their notes, consider the relationships among the various pieces of evidence, possibly arrange notes or cards into separate piles, and then develop an outline based on their perceptions and insights about the material. Subsequently, they rearrange and code the notes to conform to their outline—an informal outline indicating just the main sections of the paper and possibly one level below that.

The model paper on bullying (see Chapter 5) could be informally outlined as follows:

> **Introduction:** Examples of bullying (physical and cyber), who is bullied, anti-bullying laws
>
> **Thesis:** A blend of local, ground-up strategies and state-mandated programs and laws promises to be the best approach to dealing with bullying in American schools.
>
> **Problems with anti-bullying laws:** Rushed, some elements unconstitutional, some laws ignore standard definitions, often ineffective
>
> **Alternate solution needed:** Think local
>
> **Limits of local solutions:** Flaws, difficulty evaluating
>
> **Conclusion**

Such an outline will help you organize your research and should not be an unduly restrictive guide to writing.

The *formal outline* is a multilevel plan with Roman and Arabic numerals and uppercase and lowercase lettered subheadings that can provide a useful blueprint for composition as well as a guide to revision. See pages 146–147 in Chapter 5 for a formal outline of the paper on bullying. Here is one section of that outline. Compare its level of detail with the level of detail in the informal outline immediately above:

> I. An alternate solution to the problem of bullying
>   A. Rationale and blueprint for alternate approach
>   B. A local "ground-up" solution
>   1. Emily Bazelon
>   2. Lee Hirsch and Cynthia Lowen
>   3. Philip Rodkin

Outlining your draft after you have written it may help you discern structural problems: illogical sequences of material, confusing relationships between ideas, poor unity or coherence, or unevenly developed content.

Instructors may require that a formal outline accompany the finished research paper. Formal outlines are generally of two types: *topic outlines* and *sentence outlines.* In the topic outline, headings and subheadings are words or phrases. In the sentence outline, each heading and subheading is a complete sentence. Both topic and sentence outlines are typically preceded by the thesis.

RESEARCH AND PLAGIARISM

All too easily, research can lead to plagiarism. See Chapter 1, pages 49–50, for a definition and examples of plagiarism. The discussion here will suggest ways of avoiding plagiarism.

None of the situations that lead to plagiarism discussed below assumes the plagiarist is a bad person. All kinds of pressures can cause someone to plagiarize. By understanding those pressures, you may come to recognize them and take corrective action before plagiarism seems like a reasonable option.

Time Management and Plagiarism

The problem: You do not allocate time well and face crushing deadlines. Work, sports, and family responsibilities are the kinds of commitments that can squeeze the time needed to conduct research and write.

A solution: Learn time management. If you do not manage time well, admit that and seek help (it will be a further asset when you graduate). Consider taking three steps:

1. Begin the paper on the day it is assigned. Work on the paper for a set amount of time each day.
2. Visit the on-campus learning-skills center and enroll in a time management class. (Most schools offer this on a noncredit basis. If your school has no such class, you can readily find one online.)
3. When (despite your best efforts) you discover that you will not make a deadline, explain the situation to your instructor and seek an extension *before* the paper is due. State that you are seeking help and do not expect the problem to recur. Do not ask for a second extension.

Confidence and Plagiarism

The problem: You lack the confidence to put forward your ideas.

A solution: Understand that knowledge about your topic, and your confidence to present it in your own words, will increase in direct proportion to your research. Suggestions:

1. Stop worrying and begin. The longer you wait, the greater will be the pressure to plagiarize.
2. Seek out the on-campus writing center and let a trained tutor help you break the assignment into manageable parts. Then you can sit down to research or write one part of your paper at a time. Complete enough parts, and you will have finished the assignment.

Note-Taking and Plagiarism

The problem: Inaccurate note-taking results in plagiarism: You neglect to place quotation marks around quoted language and later copy the note into the paper without using quotation marks.

   A solution: Develop careful note-taking skills. Some useful approaches and techniques:

1. Enroll in a study skills class on working with sources, in which you will learn techniques for improving the accuracy and efficiency of note-taking.

2. Make certain to gather bibliographic information for every source and to link every note with a source.

3. Photocopy sources when possible, making sure to include publication information. When you use a source in a paper, check your language against the original language. Make corrections and add quotation marks as needed.

4. Learn the difference between quotation, summary, and paraphrase (see Chapter 1).

Digital Life and Plagiarism

The problem: Plagiarism has never been easier, given the volume of information on the Internet and the ease of digital copying and pasting.

   A solution: Recall some of the reasons you are in college:

1. to improve your ability to think critically
2. to learn how to think independently
3. to discover your own voice as a thinker and writer

Borrowing the work of others without giving due credit robs you of an opportunity to pursue these goals. Don't allow the ease of plagiarism in the digital age to compromise your ethics. Easily managed or not, plagiarism is cheating.

DETERMINING COMMON KNOWLEDGE

Note one exception to the rule that you must credit sources: when ideas and information are considered common knowledge. You can best understand common knowledge through examples:

General Lee commanded the Confederate forces during the Civil War.

Mars is the fourth planet from the sun.

Ernest Hemingway wrote *The Sun Also Rises*.

These statements represent shared, collective information. When an idea or item of information is thus shared, or commonly known, you do not need to cite it even though you may have learned of that information in a source. What is considered common knowledge changes from subject area to subject area. When in doubt, ask your instructor.

The key issue underlying the question of common knowledge is the likelihood of readers mistakenly thinking that a certain idea or item of information originated with you when, in fact, it did not. If there is *any* chance of such a mistake occurring, cite the source.

A Guideline for Determining Common Knowledge

If the idea or information you intend to use can be found unattributed (that is, *not* credited to a specific author) in three or more sources, then you can consider that material common knowledge. But remember: If you quote a source (even if the material could be considered common knowledge), you must use quotation marks and give credit.

Here is an example of a paragraph in which the writer summarizes one source, quotes another, and draws on common knowledge twice. Only the summary and the quotation need to be cited.

> Very soon, half of America will communicate via e-mail, according to analysts (Singh 283). We can only assume that figure will grow—rapidly—as children who have matured in the Internet era move to college and into careers. With e-mail becoming an increasingly common form of communication, people are discovering and conversing with one another in a variety of ways that bring a new twist to old, familiar patterns. Using e-mail, people meet "to exchange pleasantries and argue, engage in intellectual discourse, conduct commerce, exchange knowledge, share emotional support, make plans, brainstorm, gossip, feud, [and] fall in love" (Chenault). That is, through e-mail, people do what they have always done: communicate. But the medium of that communication has changed, which excites some people and concerns others.

In both places where the writer draws on common knowledge, sources that could have been cited were not because evidence for the statements appeared in at least three sources.

PLAGIARISM, THE INTERNET, AND FAIR USE

The Internet is a medium like paper, television, or radio. Intellectual property (stories, articles, pictures) is transmitted through the medium. *The same rules that apply to not plagiarizing print sources also apply to not plagiarizing Internet sources.* Any content posted on the Internet that is not your original work is the intellectual property of others. Doing either of the following constitutes plagiarism:

- Copying and pasting digital content from the Internet into your document without citing the source.
- Buying a prewritten or custom-written paper from the Internet.[1]

---

[1]Buying or using any part(s) of a paper written by another person is considered plagiarism, regardless of its source.

Internet Paper Mills

Online "paper mills" merit special attention, for they make available prewritten papers on almost any topic. Remember that instructors know how to use Internet search engines to find the same papers and identify cases of plagiarism.

FAIR USE AND DIGITAL MEDIA

U.S. copyright law permits "fair use" of copyrighted materials—including print (paper- and digital-based), images, video, and sound—for academic purposes. As long as you fully credit your sources, you may quote "excerpts in a review or criticism for purposes of illustration or comment; [and]... short passages in a scholarly or technical work."[2] The key to fair use of any material relies on the extent to which you have "transformed" the original work for your purposes. Thus:

- It is illegal for a student to copy a song from a CD and place it on a peer-to-peer file sharing network.

- It would be legal to "transform" that same song by including it as the background track to a digital movie or podcast that includes other media elements created by the student, so long as it is created for educational purposes and cited on a bibliography page.

○ CITING SOURCES ○

7.5 Cite sources properly in APA or MLA style.

When you refer to or quote the work of another, you are obligated to credit or cite your source properly. There are two types of citations—*in-text citations* in the body of a paper and *full citations* (Works Cited or References) at the end of the paper—and they work in tandem.

Many academic libraries (and writing centers) maintain brief guides to APA, MLA, and other format styles. Students can find these easily by Googling "MLA AND guide site:.edu."

The *Purdue Online Writing Lab* (OWL) maintains an excellent online guide to APA, Chicago, and MLA (http://owl.english.purdue.edu/owl/).

TYPES OF CITATIONS

- In-text citations indicate the source of quotations, paraphrases, and summarized information and ideas. These citations, generally limited to author's last name, relevant page number, and publication date of source, appear *in the text,* within parentheses.

- Full citations appear in an alphabetical list of "Works Cited" (MLA) or "References" (APA) *at the end of the paper,* always starting on a new page. These citations provide full bibliographical information on the source.

---

[2]"Fair Use." U.S. Copyright Office. May 2009. Web. 23 Mar. 2010.

If you are writing a paper in the humanities, you will probably be expected to use the Modern Language Association (MLA) format for citation. This format is fully described in the *MLA Handbook*, 8th ed. (Modern Language Association of America, 2016). A paper in the social sciences will probably use the American Psychological Association (APA) format. This format is fully described in the *Publication Manual of the American Psychological Association*, 6th ed. (Washington, D.C.: American Psychological Association, 2010).

In the following section, we provide a brief guide to the major MLA and APA citation types you will use when researching and writing a paper. Look online for format guidance when citing sources not listed here. And bear in mind that instructors often have their own preferences. Check with your instructor for the preferred documentation format if this is not specified in the assignment.[3]

APA DOCUMENTATION BASICS

APA In-Text Citations in Brief

When quoting or paraphrasing, place a parenthetical citation in your sentence that includes the author, publication year, and page or paragraph number.

Direct quotation, author and publication year not mentioned in sentence

> Research suggests that punishing a child "promotes only momentary compliance" (Berk & Ellis, 2002, p. 383).

Paraphrase, author and year mentioned in the sentence

> Berk and Ellis (2002) suggest that punishment may be ineffective (p. 383).

Direct quotation from Internet source

> Others have noted a rise in "problems that mimic dysfunctional behaviors" (Spivek, Jones, & Connelly, 2006, Introduction section, para. 3).

---

[3]Some instructors require the documentation style specified in the *Chicago Manual of Style*, 16th ed. (Chicago: University of Chicago Press, 2010). This style is similar to the American Psychological Association style, except that publication dates are not placed within parentheses. Instructors in the sciences often follow the Council of Science Editors (CSE) formats, one of which is a number format: Each source listed on the bibliography page is assigned a number, and all text references to the source are followed by the appropriate number within parentheses. Some instructors prefer the old MLA style, which called for footnotes and endnotes.

APA References List in Brief

On a separate, concluding page titled "References," alphabetize sources by author, providing full bibliographic information for each.

Article from a Journal   Conclude your entry with the digital object identifier—the article's unique reference number. When a DOI is not available and you have located the article on the Web, conclude with *Retrieved from* and the URL of the home page. For articles located through a database such as *LexisNexis*, do not list the database in your entry.

ARTICLE (WITH VOLUME AND ISSUE NUMBERS) LOCATED VIA PRINT OR DATABASE

Ivanenko, A., & Massie, C. (2006). Assessment and management of sleep

disorders in children. *Psychiatric Times, 23*(11), 90–95.

ARTICLE (WITH DOI AND VOLUME NUMBER) LOCATED VIA PRINT OR DATABASE

Jones, K. L. (1986). Fetal alcohol syndrome. *Pediatrics in Review,* 8,

122–126. doi:10.1542/10.1542/pir.8-4-122

ARTICLE LOCATED VIA WEB

Ivanenko, A., & Massie, C. (2006). Assessment and management of sleep

disorders in children. *Psychiatric Times, 23*(11), 90–95. Retrieved from

http://www.psychiatrictimes.com

Article from a Magazine

ARTICLE (WITH VOLUME AND ISSUE NUMBERS) LOCATED VIA PRINT OR DATABASE

Landi, A. (2010, January). Is beauty in the brain of the beholder? *ARTnews,*

109(1), 19–21.

ARTICLE LOCATED VIA WEB

Landi, A. (2010, January). Is beauty in the brain of the beholder? *ARTnews,*

109(1). Retrieved from http://www.artnews.com

Article from a Newspaper

ARTICLE LOCATED VIA PRINT OR DATABASE

Wakabayashi, D. (2010, January 7). Sony pins future on a 3-D revival.

The Wall Street Journal, pp. A1, A14.

ARTICLE LOCATED VIA WEB

Wakabayashi, D. (2010, January 7). Sony pins future on a 3-D revival.

The Wall Street Journal. Retrieved from http://www.wsj.com

Book

BOOK LOCATED VIA PRINT

Mansfield, R. S., & Busse, T. V. (1981). *The psychology of creativity and discovery: Scientists and their work. Chicago*, IL: Nelson-Hall.

BOOK LOCATED VIA WEB

Freud, S. (1920). *Dream psychology: Psychoanalysis for beginners* (M. D. Elder, Trans.). Retrieved from http://www.gutenberg.org

SELECTION FROM AN EDITED BOOK

Halberstam, D. (2002). Who we are. In S. J. Gould (Ed.), *The best American essays 2002* (pp. 124–136). New York, NY: Houghton Mifflin.

LATER EDITION

Samuelson, P., & Nordhaus, W. D. (2005). *Economics* (18th ed.). Boston, MA: McGraw-Hill Irwin.

MLA DOCUMENTATION BASICS

When writers document sources clearly and consistently, readers can more easily access those sources and draw their own conclusions about them. As participants in an ongoing conversation between writers and readers, writers have a responsibility to ensure that readers have the essential information they need in order to access sources—without bogging them down in unnecessary details. Accordingly, the Modern Language Association's guidelines for documenting sources emphasize the need for capturing the core information about a source, no matter how that source is delivered—whether in print, digitally, or by another means.

MLA style is designed for simplicity and consists of two steps: brief in-text citations and a complete list of works cited. Writers provide detailed information for each source in the Works Cited list, as well as brief citations in the text that direct readers to the related works-cited entry.

MLA In-Text Citations in Brief

When referring to a source, use parentheses to enclose a page number reference. Include the author's name if you do not mention it in your sentence.

> From the beginning, the AIDS test has been "mired in controversy" (Bayer 101).

Or if you name the author in the sentence:

> Bayer claims the AIDS test has been "mired in controversy" (101).

MLA Works Cited List in Brief

Writers whose projects use the MLA style of documentation include (or link to) a list of works cited. This list provides expanded information for readers about each source. Each item in the Works Cited list includes a number of what MLA calls *core elements*, given in a specific order, with each element followed by the punctuation shown in the following list:

- Author.
- Title of source.
- Title of container,
- Other contributors,
- Version,
- Number,
- Publisher,
- Publication date,
- Location.

To clarify some terms in the preceding list, the MLA defines a *container* as a larger element that holds a source. For example, a container might be a periodical that holds an article, an anthology that holds a poem or short story, or a Web site that contains a posting. Sometimes a container is actually nested within an even larger container, such a a journal that is stored in a digital database. The MLA defines *location* as the specific place a source can be found—page numbers in a print source, or the URL or DOI (digital object identifier) of an online source. For a thorough discussion of MLA style and detailed examples, refer to the *MLA Handbook*, 8th ed., or go to https://style.mla.org/. Following are examples of some of the most common types of source citations in MLA format.

Magazine or Newspaper Article

ARTICLE IN A PRINT MAGAZINE OR NEWSPAPER

>   Packer, George. "The Choice." *The New Yorker*, 28 Jan. 2008, pp. 28–35.

- Include the article *The* if it is included in the masthead of the publication, as it is for *The New Yorker*.

ARTICLE LOCATED ONLINE

>   Packer, George. "The Choice." *The NewYorker*, Condé Nast, 28 Jan. 2008,
>
>   www.newyorker.com/magazine/2008/01/28/the-choice-6.

Scholarly Article

SCHOLARLY ARTICLE IN A PRINT JOURNAL

> Ivanenko, Anna, and Clifford Massie. "Assessment and Management of Sleep
> Disorders in Children." *Psychiatric Times*, vol. 23, no. 11, 2006,
> pp. 90–95.

SCHOLARLY ARTICLE LOCATED ONLINE

> Ivanenko, Anna, Valerie MacLaughlin Crabtree, and David Gozal. *Pediatric
> Clinics of North America*, vol. 51, no. 1, pp. 51–68, doi:10.1016/
> s0031-3955(03)00181-0.

Book

BOOK IN PRINT

> James, William. *The Varieties of Religious Experience: A Study in Human
> Nature; Being the Gifford Lectures on Natural Religion Delivered at
> Edinburgh in 1901–1902*. Longmans, Green, 1902.

BOOK FOUND ONLINE OR IN A DATABASE

> James, William. *The Varieties of Religious Experience: A Study in Human
> Nature; Being the Gifford Lectures on Natural Religion Delivered at
> Edinburgh in 1901–1902*. Longmans, Green, 1902. *Archive.org*, archive.
> org/details/varietiesofrelig00jameuoft.

WEB-BASED ARTICLE ON A LARGER SITE

> White, Veronica. "Gian Lorenzo Bernini." *Heilbrunn Timeline of Art History*.
> Metropolitan Museum of Art, New York, 2009, www.metmuseum.org/
> toah/hd/bern/hd_bern.htm.

BLOG

> Wong, Kristin. "How to Prepare Your Pets for a Big Move."
> *Lifehacker*, 7 Apr. 2016. 4:00 a.m., lifehacker.com/
> how-to-prepare-your-pets-for-a-big-move-1769552628.

MyWritingLab™   Visit Ch. 7 Locating, Mining, and Citing Sources in MyWritingLab
to test your understanding of the chapter objectives.

Part

Brief Takes

In this section, you'll practice the skills you've learned in summary, critique, synthesis, and analysis. These three "brief take" chapters are—as their name suggests—shorter than the five chapters that make up the main part of the anthology (Part III of this book) and feature a more limited number of writing assignments. In two of these chapters, assignments are sequenced so that the early ones, such as summary and critique, can be incorporated into the more complex later ones, such as analysis and argument synthesis.

The subject matters of these short chapters—musical covers, ethical dilemmas, and "tiger moms"—span the academic disciplines. Each chapter includes six to nine articles. After reading them, you'll be asked to create various kinds of papers that draw upon the skills you have learned in Part I of this book.

Your reading and writing will help firm up the skills you've learned earlier in the course and will prepare you both for the lengthier reading and writing assignments of Part III and for the assignments of your other courses. Beyond the value of that preparation, we hope that you'll find yourself pleasantly absorbed by the subject matter. The "conversations" you are about to enter are fascinating.

"Stormy Weather" and the Art of the Musical Cover

The earliest manmade musical instrument—a flute constructed out of mammoth ivory and bird bone—dates back more than 40,000 years. But long before there were flutes, there were other instruments: Our feet stomping the ground. Our hands clapping. Our own voices. It's quite likely that human beings have been making music for as long as there have been human beings.

Today, music remains part of many of our most important rites and ceremonies—such as weddings and religious events—but music also accompanies our road trips, our runs, our meals in restaurants, our movies and video games and TV shows. We put on music during the highest and lowest points in our days. We listen to music that matches our mood, and we listen to music in order to *change* our mood. We download MP3s, we share YouTube clips with friends, we hang out with music on and dance to it. For many of us, our musical lives are inseparable from our social lives. In fact, *who we are* is to some degree defined by the music we listen to.

And yet for something so ubiquitous, music can be difficult to write about. Unlike poetry or fiction, for example, music is a nonverbal art form. (Even when a song has lyrics, those lyrics tell only part of the story.) When we love a song, we often do so not for any intellectual reason, but rather because of the way the song somehow finds an express route to our deepest emotional selves. It hits us in the gut. It makes us feel.

Now, the same can be said of poetry or fiction—they can hit us in the gut, too—but poetry and fiction are based in language. The challenge of writing about music, then, is to take an art form that isn't language-based and to describe it using language. Yet it's a challenge well worth embarking on, because if you can learn to describe *how* something goes about producing an emotional effect, then you are demonstrating a very high degree of thought and understanding.

This chapter focuses attention on the "cover song," a new version of a previously recorded song, redone by a singer or a band. Cover songs are nothing new, though they aren't all that old, either. In the early days of sound recording, most performers didn't write their own songs, and there was far less of a sense that a song "belonged" to any particular singer. Then, at the beginning of the rock-and-roll era, cover songs were mainly the product of white musicians re-recording songs first recorded by black musicians and releasing them to a larger white audience in order to eclipse the market—an insidious practice that critics have called "hijacking hits."

Today, the term "cover song" no longer has a negative connotation. It refers more generally to a recording artist creating a new version of someone else's previously recorded song. When we hear Tori Amos's version of Nirvana's biggest hit song, "Smells Like Teen Spirit," no one is thinking that Amos is trying to pass off Nirvana's song as her own, or trying to eclipse their record sales. Rather, we are interested in seeing how Amos, an artsy pianist/vocalist, is able to put her unique spin on the classic grunge song.

This notion of originality and interpretation lies at the heart of why songs get covered—an artist bringing his or her own talents and imagination to an older song and making it anew. One song that has been "covered" again and again through the years is "Stormy Weather," written by Harold Arlen and Ted Koehler. We'll begin by exploring some of the numerous versions of "Stormy Weather" available on YouTube, which will give you a clearer sense of the astounding range of musical styles in which artists have presented this classic song. To help you become familiar with the specialized language of musical description, we offer a glossary of key musical terms that you'll find useful in developing your own analyses. In the online version of the glossary, musician Greg Blair explains and demonstrates each of the seventeen musical terms you'll find defined in the text. You will also read a model paper by Blair that examines three particular covers of "Stormy Weather." Not all covers are successful, of course. In "Why Do Some Covers Disappoint?" critic Jeff Turrentine offers a set of standards for you to consider and apply (if you agree with him) as you begin your review of cover songs.

We then take up a second example of covers—this time, of Leonard Cohen's celebrated "Hallelujah." You'll review and analyze the unique styles of several major covers of what has come to be known as the "*Shrek* song," by John Cale, Jeff Buckley, and others. Finally, for your listening enjoyment, we'll provide you with some listings of "The Greatest Covers of All Time." Drawing upon these resources, you'll be able to write an informed paper examining two or more covers of a song of your own choosing.

A CLOUDFUL OF "STORMY WEATHER"

Harold Arlen and Ted Koehler

"Stormy Weather," written in 1933 by Harold Arlen and Ted Koehler, is one of the most enduring songs in The Great American Songbook.[1] It is a classic "torch song"—one in which the artist sings longingly and disappointedly about her (or his) lost or unrequited love. The song was first sung in public by Ethel Waters at Harlem's Cotton Club, to the accompaniment of Duke Ellington and his orchestra. Waters's version of "Stormy Weather" became famous, but the song has been recorded by numerous other artists, including Lena Horne, Billie Holliday, Francis Langford, Glenn Miller (an orchestral version), Frank Sinatra, Sarah Vaughan, Etta James, Shirley Bassey, Joni Mitchell, the Muppets, and at least two finalists on *American Idol*.

To get some idea of the wide range of moods the same song can convey when performed by musicians with their own very personal interpretations, listen to the following three distinctive covers of "Stormy Weather": Go to YouTube and search for "stormy weather lena horne." Play this version, and you'll hear a classic performance by a great singer of Arlen and Koehler's enduring song. Next, search for "stormy weather art tatum" and you'll be treated to an astounding piano rendition of the same melody. Finally, to hear how "Stormy Weather" comes across when "punked," search for "stormy weather reigning sound."

This kind of exhilaratingly creative reinterpretation of song is the phenomenon we will be exploring in this chapter.

"Stormy Weather" has a standard AABA form, which simply means that it begins with a verse (the first A section) that gets repeated (the second A section). The song continues with a "bridge"—the B section—which has a different melody than the A section, followed by a return to the final A section.[2]

Thousands of popular songs take this form. Think of "Rudolph, the Red-Nosed Reindeer," for example, or "Somewhere Over the Rainbow," and sing the verses to yourself, one at a time, with this AABA form in mind. When you listen to the various versions of "Stormy Weather," you'll notice that many artists take liberties with this basic form that become part of their own interpretations.

---

[1]"The Great American Songbook" is a term used to indicate popular songs, mainly from musical theater and musical films, that were written and performed from the 1920s to the 1950s. Among the most popular composers of such songs were Irving Berlin, Sigmund Romberg, George Gershwin, Cole Porter, Jerome Kern, Harold Arlen, Richard Rodgers, Hoagy Carmichael, Johnny Green, Johnny Mercer, Herman Hupfield, Billy Strayhorn, Duke Ellington, Sammy Fain, Frank Loesser, Henry Mancini, Harry Ruby, Arthur Schwartz, Jule Styne, Frederick Lowe, Jimmy van Heusen, Harry Warren, Dorothy Fields, Naio Herb Brown, and Victor Young.

[2]For a better understanding of musical concepts and terminology, see the next selection—and the accompanying videos—by Greg Blair.

5   To continue your exploration of "Stormy Weather," go to YouTube and search for "stormy weather ellington instrumental" (the length is 3:04). As you listen to this classic rendition, identify each section as Duke Ellington's band plays it.

• • •

Note first that the band plays an introduction to the song, working in fragments of the main melody. The first A section actually begins at 00:15 (i.e., 15 seconds into the song), with the trumpet playing the main melody. The second A section begins at 00:38, with another trumpet—muted this time—playing the melody in a different style. After an extra line at the end of the second A section, the B section begins at 1:07, with a trombone picking up the melody. The third A section begins at 1:29, with the trombonist continuing to carry the melody. A second bridge (B section) begins at 1:58, and a final A section begins at 2:19, with a clarinet this time playing the melody. Note that the last line of this final A section is repeated three times before the song draws to a close.

Having heard the instrumental version, hear (and see) how this same orchestra performs "Stormy Weather," this time with a vocalist. Search for "stormy weather ellington anderson." You'll find another version of "Stormy Weather" that Ellington made a few months after the instrumental version; but this time singer Ivie Anderson accompanies the band. View and listen to this performance and see if you can tell where the various A and B sections begin and end. Compare the instrumental version with the vocal version. Which did you prefer? Why?

• • •

In this first section, then, we'd like you to listen to (and in some cases watch) some of the numerous covers of "Stormy Weather" in the cloud. First, we'll offer some specific listening suggestions. Then we'll invite you to explore the "Stormy Weather" cloud on your own. We promise that no matter how many times you hear this remarkable song, you'll never grow tired of it. And if you do, you must be in a bad mood!

Listening Suggestions

Go to YouTube and type in "stormy weather" followed by the name of the lead artist. (Remember that YouTube search boxes are not case sensitive, so all lowercase letters are fine.) In some cases, we have specified a video of a particular length to differentiate between two or more covers of the song by the same artist.

10   *Note:* If you feel that you need a better grounding in the elements of music to listen with fuller awareness to these covers, see the next selection by Greg Blair and watch his videos before proceeding with this section.

Otherwise, listen now to some of the most well-known covers of "Stormy Weather":

Ethel Waters
Ella Fitzgerald
Lena Horne
Billie Holiday
Judy Garland
Frank Sinatra [*4:15 and 3:38 versions*]
Louis Armstrong

Next, sample some of the following additional covers:

Ted Lewis
Coleman Hawkins
Glenn Miller
Frances Langford
Charlie and his Orchestra [*Nazi propaganda version!*]
Art Tatum
Peggy Lee
Liberace [*"Mr. Showmanship"*]
Carmen Cavallaro
Etta James
Sarah Reid and Alex Serra
Amos Milburn
Charles Mingus [*3:19*]
Kay Starr
Eydie Gormé
Keely Smith
Willie Nelson and Shelby Lynne
The Spaniels
Elizabeth Welch
The Muppets
Reigning Sound [*punk version*]
Royal Crown Revue [*L.A. band: 3:31 and 3:49*]
Barbara Dennerlein
Oscar Peterson and Itzhak Perlman
Liza Minnelli
Joni Mitchell
Shirley Bassey
George Benson
Fantasia [*5:40 and 3:30*]

Finally, you may find it interesting to sample covers of "Stormy Weather" by other artists. Just type in "stormy weather" and scroll through some of your results. For example, try Vanessa Williams, Sal Grippaldi's 2013 trumpet solo, or the duet by Tony Bennett and Natalie Cole.

● **Discussion and Writing Suggestions**   MyWritingLab™

1. Which of these versions do you like the best? Which the least? Explain the reasons for your preferences.

2. Compare Judy Garland's cover of "Stormy Weather" to that of her daughter, Liza Minnelli. What similarities and differences in style and sound do you find between these two versions of the song?

3. Listen to the three piano versions of "Stormy Weather": those by Art Tatum, Liberace, and Carmen Cavallaro. (Add Barbara Dennerlein's organ to the mix, if you wish.) What makes them sound different? How do these different performances affect the mood of the song?

4. Both Lena Horne's and Elisabeth Welch's covers of "Stormy Weather" are staged versions, involving a set and other characters who interact with the performer. Compare and contrast these performances in style and mood.

5. How well, in your view, does the "punk" sound of Reigning Sound's 2002 performance of "Stormy Weather" fit with the music and lyrics of the song? Why do you think the band might have chosen to record this particular song? How does their interpretation compare with that of the Spaniels' 1957 performance?

6. How do the gravelly voice of Louis Armstrong and the smooth voice of Frank Sinatra bring out different qualities of "Stormy Weather"?

7. Compare and contrast Ethel Waters and Fantasia (or two other singers of your choice) as interpreters of "Stormy Weather." Note: this is less a matter of determining which singer is "better," but rather, how the singers convey different moods and interpretations.

8. Shirley Bassey's cover of "Stormy Weather" is offered as a "tribute" to Lena Horne's. Compare and contrast the two performances.

9. From your review of these covers, can you draw some preliminary conclusions about which qualities make for the most successful covers? Do you find yourself being more interested in the versions that stick closer to the original song and its mood, or to versions that depart significantly from the original?

How To Talk—And Write—About Popular Music

Greg Blair

People in any profession talk shop, and when they do they often use "in-house" language. By this we mean the specialized vocabulary of a trade. Carpenters use the words "plumb" and "square." Software designers use the acronym "GUI" (for graphical user interface). Musicians also have their specialized language, and in the glossary that follows we'll introduce you to several key terms that should help you identify and then compare and contrast notable elements of songs and their covers. This glossary, written in nontechnical language, isn't meant to be exhaustive. Rather, it's limited to fundamental musical concepts that will help you consider the songs you hear and write about them with greater nuance and precision.

You'll probably find the companion video glossary to be especially helpful. In these videos, musician Greg Blair demonstrates each glossary term with a musical instrument.

Glossary

Accompaniment refers to everything that happens musically in support of the melody, or main tune. In many types of Western music (rock, country, jazz, pop, etc.), it is typical for an accompaniment to consist of a percussive beat, perhaps from drums, bass guitar, and chords being played on the guitar or piano. However, any instrument playing anything at all besides the melody can contribute to a song's accompaniment.

Dynamics means, quite simply, volume—specifically, it refers to the use of volume as an expressive performance element. When a musician or group of musicians play their instruments at a low or soft dynamic level, they are playing quietly. An elevated dynamic level means that the musicians are playing their instruments loudly. A piece of music can be described as having a narrow or wide "dynamic range," depending on how big the changes in dynamics are.

Note that "dynamics" refers only to the music as it is performed, and not how the listener plays the music on his or her speakers. If you were to crank up your speakers to make a soft part loud, you haven't changed the dynamics of the work itself.

Harmony is the result of multiple notes being played or sung simultaneously to form chords. Unless we are listening to a solo performer, we are typically hearing harmony in music all the time. Harmony is an essential element of musical accompaniment, the function of which is to support the melody. Harmony is used to evoke various moods throughout a piece, and different harmonies can radically change the way a melody sounds and the mood it evokes.

Over time, musicians have codified various types of harmonies and the ways in which one moment of harmony moves to the next; these are called "chord progressions." The "twelve-bar blues" is a popular progression of one set of harmonies—or chords—to the next, meaning that many different blues songs have the same underlying harmonies.

Instrumentation refers both to the number and type of instruments chosen for a performance of a piece of music. Music can have a large instrumentation (symphony orchestra), small (string quartet), or anywhere in between. A diverse instrumentation would be one with many different instruments, and a uniform instrumentation would feature multiple musicians playing the same instrument. In a choral piece for which the only musicians are the singers, there is only one "instrument," but there can be many or few of them. In this way, an instrumentation can be diverse or uniform regardless of the size of the group.

Typical Instrumentations:

Rock/Pop/Blues Band: Lead vocals, backup vocals, guitar(s), electric bass, keyboard, drums, and sometimes other instruments such as saxophone, trumpet, violin, or synthesizer.

Big Band: Clarinet(s), 5 saxes, 5 trumpets, 5 trombones, and piano, bass, and drums. Sometimes a lead singer is added to this instrumentation.

Orchestra: Large instrumentation typically comprised of strings (violins, violas, cellos, double bass), woodwinds (flutes, clarinets, oboes, bassoons), brass (trumpet, trombone, French horn, tuba), and percussion (timpani, cymbals, etc.).

Jazz Combo: Trumpet or saxophone (or both), piano, upright bass, and drums.

Bluegrass: Mandolin, fiddle, acoustic guitar, upright bass, and singers.

There are, of course, as many options for instrumentation as there are instruments and musicians who play them. This list is only a selection of some common instrumentations used in American music.

Improvisation occurs when a performer creates music—either a new melody or, for an instrument like piano, both melody and accompaniment—that has not previously been written down or planned ahead of time. This can take the form of embellishments to a melody or a departure altogether from the melody. The essential ingredient of improvisation is its spontaneity, though such spontaneity is typically rooted in a high degree of musical knowledge and practice.

Not every genre of music has improvisation as an element. For instance, in most classical music, the musicians perform a precisely written part. However, other musical genres, especially jazz, feature the heavy use of improvisation. In fact, the quality of a jazz musician is partly based on how well he or she improvises.

Usually, only one musician improvises at a time, while the others play an accompaniment to the improvised melody.

Legato notes are held for maximum duration and connected to one another without a noticeable break between them. They thicken and smooth out the texture of the music being played. (The opposite of "legato" is "staccato," defined below.)

"Legato" and "staccato" are terms that are independent of dynamic level—that is, one can play legato/staccato notes loudly or softly. Additionally, legato and staccato do not refer to the number of notes being played, or the speed at which they are played. A musician can play one note by itself or many fast ones in a row. As long as the note or notes sound long and connected, then they are being played legato. If they sound short and separated, then they are being played staccato.

A **melody** is a collection of notes played in a certain order and is typically the most recognizable part of a song. When many notes are being played at once, the melody is the lead or most prominent line. The melody is particularly easy to identify in music with a vocalist, because it is often the part of the music to which the principle lyrics are set—and the part that the lead singer sings.

Pitch refers to how "high" or "low" a note is and is sometimes used synonymously with "note." A piccolo plays high pitches, while a tuba plays low ones, and every instrument (except for some percussion instruments) play a range of pitches. Technically, the pitch of a note has a frequency that can be measured as the number of vibrations or "beats" per second. For instance, when an orchestra tunes to "Concert A," that pitch corresponds precisely to 440 beats per second. When a guitar gets tuned, the musician is adjusting the instrument so that each string corresponds to a specific pitch. When musicians are imprecise with their pitches, the result is an unpleasant, muddy sound—though some musicians intentionally adjust or "bend" their pitch to create a bluesy, gritty effect.

Rhythm Generally speaking, musical notes are comprised of two main elements: "pitch," which corresponds to how high or low the notes are, and "rhythm," which corresponds to their duration, emphasis, and the time between one note and the next. For example, if you were to tap out the melody of "Happy Birthday" on your tabletop, you would be playing the song's rhythm. In fact, it's possible that somebody walking by and hearing you would *recognize* the song as "Happy Birthday" even though you aren't playing any pitches at all.

If a flute and a tuba were to play the same melody, the pitches would be quite different—the flute's pitch would be much higher than the tuba's—but the rhythms played by the two instruments would be the same.

"Rhythm" is also used to describe a song's metrical sound more generally and is frequently used synonymously with "beat," "meter," and "tempo."

A band's "rhythm section" is comprised of instruments whose primary purpose is to create and sustain the song's beat—typically, drums and bass guitar.

Riffs are brief, memorable melodies that often recur throughout a piece of music. They can either be part of the main melody or part of the accompaniment that momentarily jumps out to the forefront. In pop music, riffs are often called "hooks," as they "hook" the listener's ear and help the song stick in the listener's head.

A **rubato** section is a part of a piece of music that temporarily breaks from the established beat or tempo. Rubato sections allow the instrumentalist or singer to add a personal, often dramatic touch to a piece of music. These sections are often found at the very beginning or end of a piece, or at the end of a particularly dramatic section of music, though they can occur anywhere.

A **staccato** note is one that is played in a short, punctuated manner. Staccato notes have the effect of sounding clipped and succinct, and often thin the texture of the music being played. The opposite of "staccato" is "legato." (See definition above.)

Tempo is the Italian word for "time." It is fitting, then, that the tempo of a piece of music has to do with how fast it moves through time—specifically, its "speed" or "pace." A fast tempo (or "up-tempo") song is one with a fast beat, and a slow tempo song has a slow beat. The exact tempo of a piece of music can be described by its "beats per minute" (bpm). The higher the bpm, the faster the tempo.

Timbre (pronounced TAM-ber) most closely translates to "tone color." Any individual instrument or sound has a timbre, and a collection of instruments or sounds playing together also has a timbre.

Think of the difference between an electric guitar and a violin, or between an opera singer and the lead singer of a rock band. Even when they all play the same notes, all of these instruments or voices produce sounds with distinct tone qualities, or timbres.

Words often used to describe timbre include: warm, harsh, dark, bright, thin, velvety.

Note that "loud" and "soft" are not descriptions of timbre. Rather, they are dynamics. (See "dynamics," defined above.)

Vibrato, loosely translated as "vibration," is a technique that musicians use to make a note seem to waver or vibrate. It involves changing the dynamic of the note very quickly between soft and loud. This is often accompanied by a subtle upwards and downwards bending of a pitch. Many, though not all, singers use vibrato to some degree. While most instruments can be played with vibrato, several of them (violin, cello, flute) are almost always played with vibrato by expert musicians, while others (clarinet and most brass instruments) are less often played with vibrato. It is not possible to achieve vibrato on most percussion instruments (except, notably, on the vibraphone, named for its characteristic vibrato).

A vibrato can be wide—sometimes called "fat"—and dramatic, with a noticeable bending of a note and large dynamic changes (something more common in older instrumental and operatic music), or it can be narrow and subtle, or even nonexistent.

Music Glossary Videos

Visit MyWritingLab or go to YouTube and search for "WRAC Music Glossary Videos." Select from this group those individual videos you wish to see. Individual videos may also be found by typing key search terms in YouTube's search box; e.g., "elements music blair rhythm"

COMPARING AND CONTRASTING THREE COVERS OF "STORMY WEATHER"

Greg Blair

The following paper compares and contrasts three very different versions of the song "Stormy Weather." The paper demonstrates how to write about music in a way that's descriptive, analytical, and comparative.

You can find all three versions of the song on YouTube by searching on the following terms:

Lena Horne: "lena horne stormy weather 1943"
Royal Crown Revue: "stormy weather royal crown revue" (3:31 version)
Kooks: "stormy weather kooks sinatra" (3:50 version)

Although you don't need to be a musician to read and understand this paper, it contains certain musical terms that might be unfamiliar to you. When reading the paper—and later, when writing your own musical analyses—you'll probably find it helpful to refer to the musical glossary created especially for this chapter. The text version begins on page 247, and the online version, featuring videos that demonstrate each term, is available in MyWritingLab or on the "WRAC Music Glossary Videos" YouTube channel.

Greg Blair is a saxophonist, arranger, and composer—and licensed sailing instructor—living in Amherst, MA. He has a degree in music from the University of Massachusetts, Amherst.

One of the more enduring songs of the last eighty years is Harold Arlen and Ted Koehler's now-classic "Stormy Weather." It is a narrative about lost love in which the singer explains that she and her "man ain't together" and, because of that, it "keeps raining all the time." The singer Ethel Waters debuted "Stormy Weather" at New York's famous Cotton Club in 1933, and both she and Frances Langford recorded it that year—as did composer and bandleader Duke Ellington in a purely instrumental arrangement. Vocalists and instrumentalists, hundreds by this point, have been reinterpreting the song ever since. We get a sense of the variety of these covers by examining three very different approaches: recordings by singer Lena Horne and by the bands Royal Crown Revue and The Kooks.

Lena Horne's version of "Stormy Weather" appears in the 1943 movie of the same name. This early performance, set in a nightclub, includes trumpets, trombones, saxophones, and clarinet in addition to the usual rhythm section of piano, upright bass, and drums—a classic "big band" accompaniment. From the outset, the sound of this iconic instrumentation transports the listener back in time to the jazz age of the '30s and '40s. This was a time when hundreds of couples in ballrooms danced to the swing rhythms of the big bands led by bandleaders like Benny Goodman, Paul Whiteman, and Ted Lewis. Following the intro, Ms. Horne launches into the melody of the song at 0:30, at a gentle yet steady tempo in which she mourns the breakup with her man in a performance that is dramatic and sincere. The band's accompaniment—warm and lush, with legato playing from all instruments—gracefully sustains this musical lament. It isn't until almost halfway through the song (2:49) that we finally hear some short, punctuated staccato hits from the band that change the texture of the accompaniment and create a sense of emotional urgency, as if the singer has reached a point of crisis in this tale of broken love. At 2:58, the group enters a rubato section in which the band breaks from a steady tempo to achieve a moment of reflection before the main melody returns for the last time. At 3:13, the original tempo returns and the song ends at 3:48, when the orchestra abruptly transitions to the next piece of music in their program. Throughout, Ms. Horne's vocal timbre is slightly nasal but warm, velvety, and rich in vibrato. This is characteristic of much of the popular music of the time and contributes to the song's mournful mood.

One might think that a tale of broken love can only be mournful, but Royal Crown Revue's 1998 cover of "Stormy Weather" proves otherwise. Royal Crown Revue is a band from Los Angeles, formed in 1989. Improbably, their performance of the song is an up-tempo, finger-snapping version. It opens with a sharp, gun-like burst of drums that gives way to swinging saxophone riffs, announcing a peppy, sassy take on the song. This version is borne out with the condensed, modern instrumentation of electric guitar and bass, drums, trumpet, saxophone, and vocals, further differentiating it from the expansive instrumentation of Ms. Horne's version. At 0:08 the lead singer enters with the melody, with a warm vocal timbre and just a touch of vibrato. This is not the mournful, soul-searching vocal we hear from Horne. Rather, lead singer Eddie Nichols sounds slightly amused as he sings "...can't get my poor self together," as if he knows that this spell of stormy weather is precisely what he deserves and that he might as well enjoy it. At 0:34, the melody repeats with the addition of background vocals, which support the lead singer and add a new texture to the musical and emotional landscape. We hear a new riff from the trumpet, sax, and guitar at 0:57, and at 1:23 there is a return to both the main melody and the riff that we've heard previously. A unique feature of this version of the song is the sax solo at 1:49. The saxophonist plays with a rough, thick, growling tone, which is typical of the upbeat and sassy swing style of music the group is playing. At 2:57, the band uses a common tactic of repeating the last phrase of the melody ("rainin' all the time") several times. This is known as "tagging" the ending. Following the tag, the band plays a few rubato hits to end the song.

The Kooks, a British band formed in 2004, have yet another distinctive take on "Stormy Weather." The overall feel of their recording is swampy and earthy, certainly more raw sounding than the other two versions. It features only acoustic guitar, harmonica (heard at 0:16 in the intro and for a solo at 2:47), and a singer, with his raspy, rock-and-roll vocal timbre. The tempo of this version is on the slow side, similar to Ms. Horne's version, and as such it shares with the Horne version an earnestness that contrasts with Royal Crown Revue's slicker, more ironic version. The Kooks add some simple but pleasing vocal harmonies beginning at 1:33. These harmonies add a welcome yet brief change in texture, breathing fresh air into the arrangement. At 1:57, drums enter softly, lending more forward drive without changing the overall melancholy mood. The drums become louder at 2:24, then softer again for the harmonica solo at 2:47. These small changes in instrumentation and dynamics provide just enough variation in this stripped-down version to keep it from becoming predictable. The ending is simple but effective—the singer and guitarist slow down a bit on the last phrase of the song, and the guitarist strums the final chord.

5   From the number and types of instruments, to decisions about tempo and dynamics, to the singer's distinctive approach to the melody, these three versions of "Stormy Weather" demonstrate the wide range of options musicians have when covering a song. Whether it's Royal Crown Revue upping the tempo and adding recurring riffs, the Kooks paying special attention to dynamics, or Horne employing a thick vibrato that soars above the lush big band accompaniment, each version finds unique ways to interpret Harold Arlen and Ted Koehler's song. In fact, these versions, taken together, pay tribute to Arlen and Koehler's classic song by revealing just how rich in potential it remains even after eight decades.

WHY DO SOME COVERS DISAPPOINT?

Jeff Turrentine

Why do so many singers look to The Great American Songbook later in their recording careers, and why do so many of their efforts fall flat? In the following essay, critic Jeff Turrentine offers a theory and makes several thought-provoking assertions about what constitutes a "good" cover of somebody else's song. The articles editor for *OnEarth* magazine and a former editor at *Architectural Digest*, Turrentine is also a frequent contributor to the *Washington Post*, the *New York Times Book Review*, and *Slate*, where this essay was posted on February 28, 2012.

The latest album by Paul McCartney, a collection of pop standards by the likes of Harold Arlen, Irving Berlin, Johnny Mercer, and Frank Loesser, was released three weeks ago today to generally positive reviews. In the *New York Times*, critic Stephen Holden went through two purple ink cartridges as he described how the album "floats over you like a light mist on a cool spring morning in an English garden as the sun glints through the haze. You want to inhale the fresh air, taste the fragrance of buds blooming, as the sky clears to a serene deep blue." In *Rolling Stone*, a somewhat more measured Will Hermes said of *Kisses on the Bottom* (the title is lifted from the lyrics to the Fats Waller song that opens the record) that it is "the sound of a musician joyfully tapping his roots…it's fun, and touching, to hear [McCartney] crooning his way through the great American songbook."

Kisses on the Bottom is McCartney's 16th solo album, and the first to be composed almost entirely of songs written by others. By choosing material from the great American songbook, McCartney joins a group of 1960s and '70s pop singers who have discovered just how rewarding—musically, critically, and commercially—this particular sentimental journey can be. Rod Stewart, Carly Simon, Natalie Cole, and Linda Ronstadt have recorded, between them, no fewer than a dozen such albums. For each of the singers, these releases have served as well-timed career-resuscitators, allowing the aging artists—whose hit-making days have, for the most part, long since passed—to earn platinum sales and sell out giant arenas.

In interviews and press releases, these artists invariably describe having "grown up" with this music; often they hint at an innocent youth spent in some prelapsarian Tin Pan Eden, where they learned these songs at their daddy's knee before getting older and guiltily partaking of the rock-and-roll apple. But there's another, more self-serving reason that a particular type of superannuated rocker likes to put out an album of standards. These songs—penned by Cole Porter, the Gershwins, Rodgers & Hart (or Hammerstein) to name just a few of their most famous composers—represent the sturdy foundation on which all popular music is based. If you're a pop singer or songwriter concerned about your legacy, linking yourself to the great American songbook confers a kind of late-stage artisanal legitimacy onto your entire career. It shows that you, too, have always possessed a deep and sophisticated understanding of authentic songcraft. If you're worried that the world may remember you primarily for wearing Spandex pants and snarling "Do Ya Think I'm Sexy?" what better penance than to croon "Isn't It Romantic?" in a rakish coat and tie, carried along by a lush string section?

With few exceptions, however, these albums of standards by pop superstars *d'un certain âge* fall flat. I confess that even the McCartney album, *pace* Holden, leaves me shrugging my shoulders and wondering if it was really worth all the trouble. Why is this? The source material is unquestionably superb. (McCartney, to his great credit, has chosen to cover several lesser-known songs that would fly right under the radar of a Stewart or a Simon, who tend to go straight for the crowd-pleasers.) No one would deny that the artists themselves have real talent. So: good songs, good singers—where do things go wrong?

5   The answer, I think, is in the over-reverent and/or unimaginative way in which the songs themselves are typically approached. The queen of songbook revivalism, Linda Ronstadt, deserves enormous credit for convincing her manager and record label to let her record *What's New* (1983), the first of three standards albums she released consecutively during the 1980s. At the time, Ronstadt was still arguably a hit-maker in the pop/soft-rock vein, and by aligning herself with pre-rock-era music she was taking something of a risk. That risk paid off commercially and critically: The albums did extraordinarily well by any measure, and went a long way toward sparking a new interest in jazz and swing among listeners who'd previously thought of these songs as someone else's (i.e, their parents', or grandparents').

But listen to the albums today, even with their wonderful Nelson Riddle arrangements, and one is struck by the anodyne safeness of these numbers, their meticulous fealty to an abstracted, supper-club definition of "good taste." These are fetishistic period pieces, not interpretations. And as such they call into question the whole purpose of covering a "standard" in the first place. Jazz greats, including vocalists, have always understood that a standard is simply a vessel into which an artist pours her unique essence. Think John Coltrane's hypnotic, inimitable version of "My Favorite Things," or Bill Evans' glistening "What Is This Thing Called Love?" or Sarah Vaughan's jaw-droppingly gorgeous "Embraceable You"—a marriage of singer and song so divinely blessed that it was recorded in one single, miraculous take. These artists weren't paying homage to any person or era. They were *being themselves*—utterly and magnificently.

Compare these recordings to practically any song taken at random from Rod Stewart's ever-metastasizing catalog of standards, now hurtling inexorably toward its sixth CD. Over artless cruise-ship arrangements, Stewart attempts to capture some of Sinatra's loose-tied, fedora-hatted magic from the mid-1950s, but doesn't even come close. Like his musical accompaniment, his vocals are phoned in, which means that the songs—many of which were written using a double-entendre-heavy "code," of which Cole Porter was the undisputed master—are all but stripped of their wit and subtext, their musical and lyrical richness streamlined into bland, repetitive sonic wallpaper. Which is almost certainly the point of this decade-long exercise: Ultimately, Stewart's songbook is a five-album soundtrack for a night of sixtysomething romance, music meant to be played at a low volume while cologned…husbands pour Champagne and prepare dinner for their beloveds.

But when a rock-era pop star is willing to take some chances, magical things can happen. One of the earliest examples of the songbook revival genre, Harry Nilsson's *A Little Touch of Schmilsson in the Night*, still has the power to astound nearly 40 years after its release. Arranged by the legendary Gordon Jenkins—who had worked, in his prime, with Ella Fitzgerald, Billie Holiday, and Judy Garland, among many others—the album is constructed as a moody song cycle that capitalizes on the weird disconnect between Jenkins' soaring orchestration and Nilsson's broken, halting vocals. Another idiosyncratic vocalist, Rickie Lee Jones, managed to infuse old standards with new mystery and melancholy in her inexcusably overlooked gem, *Pop Pop*, from 1991.

Eight years later, with his album *As Time Goes By*, Roxy Music frontman Bryan Ferry rather effortlessly did what Rod Stewart only *thinks* he's been doing for the last 10 years, which is to say he translated his louche persona into a performance that the swinging, lady-killing Sinatra of the 1950s would have recognized and admired. The next year saw the release of Joni Mitchell's haunting *Both Sides Now*, which marked a kind of turning point for the artist, formalizing the completion of her metamorphosis from guitar-strumming coffeehouse chanteuse to dark jazz prophetess. She hovers over the whole affair like some mystical cross between Cassandra and Nina Simone.

10   *Kisses On The Bottom*, like just about everything else Paul McCartney has ever done, is marked by a game, high-spirited optimism that's pretty hard to hate. A few of the songs on it—like his lilting and graceful "More I Cannot Wish You," from Frank Loesser's *Guys and Dolls*—are truly beautiful, offering ample

proof that Macca's own remarkable body of work is as firmly rooted in classic, pre-rock pop as it is in Little Richard and everything that came afterward. But even he can't escape the curse that befalls so many of these respectful, well-intentioned projects. It's the curse of pleasantness, of innocuousness, of valedictory tribute. It threatens to turn the best songs ever written into easily forgettable ditties. Thankfully, these songs are also the most durable—they're "standards," after all—and will always be a good deal stronger than their weakest renditions. They can't take that away from us.

Discussion and Writing Suggestions   MyWritingLab™

1. Turrentine's essay assumes that there is more artistry involved in reimagining a song than in rerecording it with the hope of making a precise copy. Do you agree? To what extent is it possible for a musician to perform a faithful rendition of someone else's song and still bring something of him- or herself to the effort?

2. Turrentine believes that covers of old standards by aging pop superstars often "fall flat" because of "the over-reverent and/or unimaginative way" in which the singers approach them. Can you think of covers of either old standards or more recent songs that fail for either reason? Explain. Refer to specific songs, if possible, in developing your answer.

3. Turrentine celebrates cover artists who in recording their versions of old standards are "*being themselves*—utterly and magnificently." He calls for "interpretations," not "fetishistic period pieces." He scorns cover artists who are too "respectful," who play it safe and don't "take some chances." And yet as Turrentine himself acknowledges in his article, many people derive great enjoyment from these old standards as sung by artists like Paul McCartney and Rod Stewart. To what extent do you agree with Turrentine's criteria for evaluating a cover? If you're acquainted with one of Stewart's or McCartney's covers (or any cover of a classic song), discuss it as you develop your answer.

4. Turrentine writes about the "safeness" of Linda Rondstadt's cover albums and "their meticulous fealty to an abstracted, supper-club definition of 'good taste.'" He is making an implicit argument about music being more valuable—being better—when it is less safe and less palatable. What do you think? How would you define "safe" music? "Dangerous" music? To what extent do you agree with Turrentine that musical "safeness" and "good taste" are things to be avoided in a cover song—or in any song for that matter?

5. Choose one of your favorite songs and imagine that you are about to record a cover of it. What would you change? What would you keep? Write a letter to your record company explaining your decisions and the reasons for them.

A HEARTFUL OF "HALLELUJAH"

Leonard Cohen

More than half a century after the composition of "Stormy Weather," songwriter Leonard Cohen wrote "Hallelujah" (1984), consistently ranked as one of the greatest songs of recent decades. With its haunting melody and compelling lyrics, "Hallelujah" has attracted numerous cover artists (*Wikipedia* lists some 170 of them).

The four most influential covers are those by the following artists:

> **Leonard Cohen**
> **John Cale**
> **Jeff Buckley**
> **Rufus Wainwright**

Other noteworthy covers have been produced by these artists or groups:

> **K. D. Lang**
> **Bono** *(a highly idiosyncratic treatment)*
> **Bob Dylan**
> **Willie Nelson**
> **Over the Rhine**
> **Ari Hest**
> **Brandi Carlile**
> **Justin Timberlake**
> **Regina Spektor**
> **Alendra Burke with Elton John**
> **Casey Pitel**
> **Beirut**
> **Amanda Palmer**
> **Imogen Heap**
> **Kathryn Williams**
> **Damien Rice**
> **Keren Ann**
> **Jake Shimabukuru** *(guitar version)*

You can listen to some of these covers—as well as Leonard Cohen's original—on YouTube. Search by using the song name and the artist's name; e.g., *"hallelujah buckley."* You can also find many of these covers on *Paste Magazine's* Web site by entering *"paste great hallelujah covers"* into your search engine.

Which of these versions do you like best? Why? Which—perhaps using criterial suggested by Jeff Turrentine in the preceding selection—do you consider misfires? Why?

5   Consider also the question we asked of the "Stormy Weather" covers: "From your review, can you draw some preliminary conclusions about which qualities make for the most successful covers? Do you find yourself being more interested in the versions that stick closer to the original song and its mood, or to versions that depart significantly from the original?"

The various covers of "Hallelujah" have been given insightful book-length treatment by Alan Light in *The Holy or the Broken: Leonard Cohen, Jeff Buckley, and the Unlikely Ascent of "Hallelujah"* (2012). We have drawn upon Light's remarks about the various "Hallelujah" covers in the following questions.

● **Discussion and Writing Suggestions**   MyWritingLab™

1. Write a comparative analysis of any three versions of "Hallelujah," using Greg Blair's comparative analysis of "Stormy Weather" covers as a model.

2. In Alan Light's interviews with the producer John Lissauer and others concerning the recording of and reactions to Cohen's "Hallelujah," we find emotionally loaded expressions like "makes me feel good"; "uplifting"; "blessed"; "sincerity"; and "struggle, conflict, and resignation." What has emotion to do with music? Discuss one of your favorite songs—or one of its covers—in terms of your emotional responses to the particular performance. How does emotion attach itself to, and in what sense is it *in*, the song?

3. Light writes about John Cale's editing of Cohen's "Hallelujah": "Despite his implication that he avoided the spiritual dimension of the song, Cale sensed the elemental power of the biblical stories and languages, and returned them to the position of the song's entry point, but then undercut them with the lyrics focused on . . . longing and tragic romance." Light is saying that in interpreting Cohen's song, Cale in some sense re- or co-created it. How is this possible? Again selecting one of your favorite songs, explain how a cover artist brings a song that is already in existence into existence (again).

4. Light writes that in recording many takes of "Hallelujah," Jeff Buckley searched "for the subtleties and nuances he wanted, for a precise shading in the ultimate delivery of this song that he had come to inhabit so fully." Think of a particular song that you love. In what sense do you "inhabit" it? In what sense does the song, which someone else has written, become "yours"? If you were, or are, a musician, how might your answers to these questions influence the cover you might do of this song? That is, on what basis, or by what right, do you have to sing someone else's song *your* way?

5. Consider Light's description of Jeff Buckley's "Hallelujah" cover: "Where the older Cohen and Cale sang the words with a sense of experience and perseverance, of hard lessons won, this rising star delivered the lyrics with swooning emotion, both fragile and indomitable." In drawing upon such subjective vocabulary, Light does not use objective or technical terms of music (like the ones you'll find in this chapter's glossary) to describe Buckley's cover. Still, his description is effective in helping you understand the distinctive flavor and power of a particular cover. How so?

THE GREATEST COVERS OF ALL TIME

Ranking artistic works is a very subjective, and controversial, matter. For example, in 2012, Alfred Hitchcock's 1958 thriller *Vertigo* was ranked first in *Sight and Sound's* once-in-a-decade list of the greatest films of all time. But in the American Film Institute's comparable listing, this same film was ranked sixty-first. So much for critical consensus on the greatest film of all time.

Despite—or perhaps because of—such disagreements, ranking artistic efforts is both a pleasurable and useful exercise. It's pleasurable because in the process of such ranking we enjoy the work again and therefore reexperience those qualities that so appealed to us in the first place. And it's useful because it requires us to exercise our judgment and to justify our choices to others, thereby sharpening our critical faculties.

So let's take the phrase "the greatest covers of all time" with a grain of salt and admit, first, that all such listings represent the personal preferences of individuals or groups of individuals and, second, that *we* may assemble a very different list based on differences of taste. But let's also agree that such listings are a starting point for some great listening and some interesting conversations/arguments. As a practical matter for the assignments in this chapter, they provide an extensive set of resources from which you can select and discuss your own favorite covers.

We'll begin by presenting a *Rolling Stone* listing (compiled by Andy Greene) of reader-selected best cover songs[3]:

1. Jimi Hendrix - 'All Along The Watchtower'

Last weekend we asked our readers to pick their favorite cover song of all time. Unlike previous readers' polls, the top vote getter won by a gigantic margin. Your favorite cover (with no close second) is Jimi Hendrix's take on Bob Dylan's "All Along The Watchtower." Released six months after Dylan's original appeared on *John Wesley Harding* in December 1967, Hendrix's version radically re-arranged Dylan's acoustic original. Dylan didn't play the song live until 1974, and said Hendrix's rendition made him reconsider how to approach the song.

"[Hendrix] could find things inside a song and vigorously develop them," Dylan told the *Fort Lauderdale Sun Sentinel* in 1995. "He found things that other people wouldn't think of finding in there. He probably improved upon it by the spaces he was using. I took license with the song from his version, actually, and continue to do it to this day."

2. Johnny Cash - 'Hurt'

Trent Reznor remembers the first time he saw the video for Johnny Cash's cover of his 1994 song "Hurt." "Tears started welling up," he said. "I realized it wasn't

---

[3]http://www.rollingstone.com/music/pictures/rolling-stone-readers-pick-the-top-10-greatest-cover-songs-20110302

really my song anymore. It just gave me goose bumps up and down my spine. It's an unbelievably powerful piece of work. After he passed away I remember feeling saddened, but being honored to have framed the end of his life in something that is very tasteful."

3. Jeff Buckley - 'Hallelujah'

Leonard Cohen's career was at a low point when he wrote "Hallelujah" in the early Eighties, and his record label had no interest in even releasing the track or the rest of the songs that eventually came out on 1984's *Various Positions*. The track was a fan favorite, but it didn't receive much love until the Velvet Underground's John Cale created a stripped-down piano version for a 1991 Leonard Cohen tribute album.

Jeff Buckley used Cale's version as the basis for his stunningly beautiful version of the song on his 1994 LP *Grace*. The track wasn't a single, but after Buckley's tragic death in 1997 the song slowly started to become recognized as a classic.

4. Joe Cocker - 'With A Little Help From My Friends'

It's one of the most indelible images from Woodstock: Joe Cocker, looking so stoned he can barely stand upright, belting out The Beatles classic "With A Little Help From Friends" like it was an old soul standard. The performance became a key part of 1971's Woodstock documentary, instantly turning the radical re-imagining of the tune into Cocker's signature song. In the late Eighties, when the producers of *The Wonder Years* needed a single song to represent the Sixties, they went with this.

5. Nirvana - 'The Man Who Sold The World'

Until Nirvana taped their *MTV Unplugged* special in late 1993, "The Man Who Sold The World" was known only as one of David Bowie's earliest hits. After Kurt Cobain's suicide the song became his, and the tale of a man who had the world and gave it away seemed eerily prophetic. When Bowie revived the song on his 1995 tour with Nine Inch Nails many of the young fans in the audience had no idea it was his song, assuming he was doing a special Nirvana tribute.

6. The Beatles - 'Twist and Shout'

The Beatles cut their 1963 LP *Please Please Me* in a single day, so when it came time for John Lennon to sing a cover of the Isley Brothers' "Twist And Shout" near the end of the session his voice was shredded. He rallied by gargling milk and swallowing cough drops before nailing the song in just two takes. He was unhappy with how his voice sounded, but the raw sound is part of what makes the track so memorable.

7. The White Stripes - 'Jolene'

Dolly Parton's 1973 classic song "Jolene" is hardly a feminist anthem. Inspired by a true story, the song is in the voice of a desperate woman begging a more attractive woman to not steal her man. Not a single word is reserved for the man in the love triangle. The White Stripes recorded a snarling, feedback-laden cover of it in 2000, and it was a highlight of their live show through their last tour in 2007.

8. Nirvana - 'Where Did You Sleep Last Night'

Unlike most *Unplugged* specials, Nirvana did very few of their hits at the TV taping. They opted mainly for deep cuts and covers of songs by the Vaselines, David Bowie, and the Meat Puppets – as well as this 19th-century folk standard that was popularized by folk legend Lead Belly. A 1990 home demo of the song appears on Nirvana's 2004 box set *With The Lights Out*, but the definitive version (with the screaming final verse) is on *Unplugged*.

9. Guns N' Roses - 'Knockin' On Heaven's Door"

Originally written for the soundtrack to *Pat Garrett and Billy The Kid*, "Knockin' On Heaven's Door" gave Bob Dylan a much-needed hit after years of being written off as a washed-up Sixties relic. The song was covered by everybody from Eric Clapton to U2, but in 1990 Guns N' Roses recorded it for the *Days of Thunder* soundtrack and introduced it to an entirely new generation. [It became a staple of their live show.]

10. Muse - 'Feeling Good'

Written for the widely forgotten 1965 Broadway musical *The Roar of the Greasepaint - The Smell of the Crowd*, "Feeling Good" has been covered by Nina Simone, Bobby Darin, Frank Sinatra, George Michael, and countless others. Muse recorded a popular version for their 2001 LP *Origin of Symmetry*, which has recently gotten a lot of play in America in a commercial for Virgin Airlines.

Here are some additional best cover lists you may enjoy browsing through. YouTube provides links to many of the songs listed:

Search for: "100 best songs of the past twenty five years"

"15 best song covers ever"

"10 most covered songs"

"jack whites best classic rock cover songs"

"rolling stones top greatest cover songs"

"24 greatest cover versions of all time"

"top ten cover songs that are better than the original"

"top forty cover songs from the movies"

"top 21 cover songs that make you realize how amazing the originals were"

"unexpected cover songs 20 unique renditions of famous tunes"

"elvis hound dog among best 11 cover songs of all time"

"20 bob dylan songs deserve a listen"

ASSIGNMENT   MyWritingLab™

Select your favorite song from among those cited in the *Rolling Stone* list or one of the other lists referenced at the end of this selection. Or, if you prefer, choose a song that is not on any of these lists, but one that has generated at least two notable covers. If you happen to prefer the old standards from "The Great American Songbook," you might even choose another song from the "Stormy Weather" period, such as "As Time Goes By" or "That Old Black Magic." If you like Broadway shows, go to YouTube and try searching, for example, for covers of "If I Were a Rich Man" (from *Fiddler on the Roof*) or "Feeling Good" (from *The Roar of the Greasepaint—The Smell of the Crowd*), particularly the covers by Nina Simone and Muse.

In a few paragraphs, discuss the performance of this song by the original artist. For a model of such a discussion, review Greg Blair's discussion of "Stormy Weather." Draw also upon the terminology discussed by Greg Blair in his glossary to indicate what is happening musically as the song progresses. You may also wish to rewatch one or more of Blair's videos on YouTube. At the end of this section of your paper, draw conclusions about the overall impact of the original song and how it achieves its distinctive mood and voice and its emotional power.

Next, select at least two covers of this song performed by other artists. In the same manner as you described the song performed by the original artist(s), explain how the cover artists reinterpret this song in a way that retains (to some extent) the identity of the original while transmuting it into a different form. Draw comparisons and contrasts, as necessary.

As you work toward a conclusion, discuss which version of the song you like best and/or least, offering reasons for your preferences. How did the musical artist(s) get it just right for you? How did other versions fall short? In your discussion of the relative merits of these covers, you may want to draw on the observations of Turrentine, who, as you've read, is unafraid to slam covers he finds unimaginative. (If you're not completely satisfied with any of the covers, suggest what you would do differently were *you* the cover artist.) Finally, what do you conclude about the qualities that make for successful musical covers?

MyWritingLab™   Visit Ch. 8 "Stormy Weather" and the Art of the Musical Cover in MyWritingLab to test your understanding of the chapter objectives.

Ethical Dilemmas in Everyday Life

The word "ethics" is connected intrinsically with questions of correct conduct within society. Etymologically, "ethics" comes from the Greek "ethos," meaning "character," which indicates a concern for virtuous people, reliable character, and proper conduct. "Morality" is derived from "mores" or custom—the rules of conduct of a group or society. An initial definition of ethics, then, is *the analysis, evaluation, and promotion of correct conduct and/or good character, according to the best available standards.*

Ethics asks what we should do in some circumstance, or what we should do as participants in some form of activity or profession. Ethics is not limited to the acts of a single person. Ethics is also interested in the correct practices of governments, corporations, professionals and many other groups. To these issues, ethics seeks a reasoned, principled, position. An appeal to existing practice or the command of a powerful leader is not sufficient.... Some ethical questions will require reflection on our basic values and the purpose of human society.

Ethics is best conceived of as something we "do," a form of on-going inquiry into practical problems. Ethics is the difficult practical task of applying norms and standards to ever new and changing circumstances.

—Stephen J. A. Ward, "Ethics in a Nutshell"

In the spring of 2013, Edward Snowden, a former employee of the CIA and former technical contractor for the National Security Agency, leaked to the press thousands of documents detailing top-secret U.S. mass-surveillance programs. Snowden's actions rocked the national security establishment and divided the country. Some saw him as a hero performing a great public service in tearing the veil of secrecy from such programs and making them known to the American public. Others viewed him as a traitor who had violated his oath and endangered the security of his country. Snowden saw himself as following in the footsteps of others who believed that they were acting honorably in what they regarded as the public interest—such as Private Bradley Manning, who in 2010 passed classified national defense information to the Web site *Wikileaks*, and Daniel Ellsberg, who in 1971 released to the *New York Times* the "Pentagon Papers," a secret Department of Defense history of the Vietnam War, which was raging at the time.

Honorable men or traitors? How we view such people depends upon the ethical standards we bring to bear upon their actions. Are the social benefits of releasing classified information in the interest of transparency outweighed by the harm that may result from these releases? Is it so inherently wrong to violate laws covering official secrecy that there can be no justification for such acts?

To answer such questions, we rely upon ethical frameworks, belief systems forged by our culture, our religion, our parents, our teachers, and our life experience. Sometimes we respond to weighty questions like "Is abortion acceptable under any circumstances?" or "Was the United States justified in dropping the atomic bomb on Japan in 1945 to end World War II?" Generally, though, the ethical dilemmas we face are more mundane: What do we do about a friend we see shoplifting? A family member who makes a racist, sexist, or simply inconsiderate remark? A coworker who habitually arrives late and leaves early and ignores your protests on the subject? How are we to act—and what do our actions say about us?

Large or small, the ethical dilemmas we face can be vexing. In this practice chapter, you'll get to work through a series of (mostly hypothetical) dilemmas, guided by distinct ethical principles that will help you clarify what, in your view, is a proper course of action. You'll learn about classic theories of ethics: the utilitarian approach, the rights approach, the fairness approach, and the virtues approach. You'll also learn how stages of moral development affect the way we judge behavior, our own and that of others. You'll draw upon all these approaches, alone and in combination, to help resolve the ethical dilemmas inherent in the example cases.

Your main assignment in this chapter is to write an argument that synthesizes your own insights on one or more ethical dilemmas along with what various authors have written. In preparation, you will complete several briefer exercises that require you to draw on your sources. During this progression of assignments, you will write a combination of summaries, paraphrases, critiques, and explanations that will prepare you for—and that will produce sections of—your more ambitious argument synthesis. In this respect, the assignments here are typical of other writing you will do in college: While at times you will be called on to write a stand-alone critique or a purely explanatory paper, you will also write papers that blend the basic forms of college writing that you have studied in this text. Both your critiques and your explanations will rely in part on summaries—or partial summaries—of specific articles. Your arguments may rely on summaries, critiques, and explanations. The assignments in this chapter will therefore help prepare you for future academic research tasks while broadening your understanding of the world of ethical analysis.

Read; Prepare to Write

As you read these selections, prepare for the assignments by marking up the texts: Write notes to yourself in the margins, and comment on what the authors have said.

To prepare for the more ambitious of the assignments that follow—the explanatory and argument syntheses—consider drawing up a topic list of your sources as you read. For each topic about which two or more authors have something to say, jot down notes and page (or paragraph) references. Here's an example entry concerning one type of ethical dilemma you will read about in this chapter:

To speak up—or not—when you see something wrong

- The director of safety in the "Collapsed Mine"—De George, par. 1, p. 271
  He sees a safety problem, reports it to his boss, boss ignores it, safety director is told to say nothing more—and mine collapses.

- Should a doctor violate doctor/patient confidentiality? par. 1, p. 291
  A doctor promises he will keep a patient's confession in confidence. This confession reveals that an innocent man has gone to jail. Should the doctor violate his promise and speak up to save the falsely imprisoned man?

Such a topic list, keyed to your sources, will spare you the frustration of reading these three sources and flipping through them later, saying, "Now where did I read that?" At this early point, you don't need to know how you might write a paper based on this or any other topic. But a robust list with multiple topics and accurate notes for each lays the groundwork for your own discussion later and puts you in a good position to write a synthesis.

The sample entry above should be useful for responding to one of the explanatory synthesis assignments that follows the readings: to explain what an ethical dilemma is. In your reading of the various theories of ethics and the casebook of dilemmas that follow, you may decide to explain ethical dilemmas in part by explaining *types* of dilemmas—one of which would be "speaking up or not." There would be others, for instance killing (or letting another die) for the greater good and choosing to protect life over enforcing a law. Creating a topic list with multiple entries like the example above will add to your reading time, but it will save time as you prepare to write.

GROUP ASSIGNMENT #1: MAKE A TOPIC LIST

Working in groups of three or four, create a topic list for the selections in this chapter, jotting down notes and page (or paragraph) references. Try several of the following topics to get you started. Find and take notes on other topics common to two or more sources. When you are done, share your topic lists with fellow group members.

- Definition of ethics
- Examples of consequence-based (teleological) ethical dilemmas/decisions
- Examples of morality-based (deontological) ethical dilemmas/decisions
- Examples of Kohlberg's stages of moral development
- Using intuition vs. formal ethics to make decisions
- When both sides are right (or wrong)

(continued)

- Difference between what is legal and what is ethical
- When must rules be overridden?
- Individual conscience vs. social order

GROUP ASSIGNMENT #2: CREATE A TOPIC WEB

Before dividing the group into three subgroups, all group members should read the selection by Ronald White. That done, each subgroup should take charge of re-reading a particular ethical theory in the selection: rule-based ethics (deontology), consequence-based ethics (teleology), and virtue-based ethics. Now, reconvened as a large group, choose an ethical dilemma featured in this chapter (see pages 289–295) and discuss it from the three formal ethical perspectives. Each subgroup can present its understanding of the dilemma from one of the three ethical perspectives. Then open the discussion: To what extent do these perspectives, applied to the dilemma, suggest different courses of action? Discuss as well the differences between formal and informal responses to ethical dilemmas.

GROUP ASSIGNMENT #3: DECIDE FOR YOURSELF

Two cases in this chapter come with clear arguments about ethical action(s) to be taken: "No Edit" and "Should I Protect a Patient?" Read these cases and discuss each as a group. Do you agree with the positions these authors take? Develop a logic for your responses. Provide reasons for suggesting a particular course of action.

Following an introduction to the study of ethical dilemmas as "thought experiments," you'll read a number of cases that challenge you to decide upon a fair and reasonable course of action. What counts as "fair" and "reasonable," of course, depends on your standard of fairness and the logic you use to apply that standard. Change the standard and you may well change your decision. So we also provide in this chapter a review of formal ethical theories, or standards, that you can draw on to guide your decision making about each case. Look as well for search engine keywords that will point you to YouTube presentations of ethical dilemmas. Whether written, acted out in an episode of *Grey's Anatomy*, or reduced to a provocative animation, the ethical dilemmas that you encounter in the pages to follow will call on you to decide, if only in your mind's eye, and to defend your decision.

THE READINGS AND VIDEOS

What If ...

Daniel Sokol

"Is there a difference between killing someone and letting them die? Are consequences all that matter, or are there some things we should never do, whatever the outcome?" Such questions lie at the heart of "thought experiments" like the four famous ones posed by Daniel Sokol in the following article (and indeed in the rest of this chapter). How we respond to such scenarios, some admittedly farfetched, provides some insight into the moral perspectives from which we make choices every day. This piece first appeared on the *BBC News* Web site on May 2, 2006. Dr. Daniel K. Sokol is a medical ethicist at Imperial College in London and a barrister at King's Bench Walk Chambers. A regular contributor to the BBC, he is also a columnist (the "Ethics Man") for the *British Medical Journal* and the author of the book *Doing Clinical Ethics*, published in 2012.

Suppose you could save five lives by taking one—what would be the correct thing to do? Such ethical dilemmas provide classic "experiments" for philosophers. Here [BBC News presents] four such quandaries and asks readers to vote on what they think is right....

Like scientists, philosophers use experiments to test their theories. Unlike scientists, their experiments do not require sophisticated laboratories, white-robed technicians or even rodents. They occur in the mind, and start with 'What if....'

These "thought experiments" help philosophers clarify their understanding of certain concepts and intuitions. In the field of ethics, thought experimenters typically present a dilemma, examine the most popular "intuitive" response and then show the implications for real-world issues.

But such experiments are rarely tested on large numbers of people. So to reach a larger group, here are four typical experiments. Readers are invited to vote on how they think they would act in each case.

5   Here is a well-known example:

1. Thomson's Violinist

One day, you wake up in hospital. In the nearby bed lies a world famous violinist who is connected to you with various tubes and machines.

To your horror, you discover that you have been kidnapped by the Music Appreciation Society. Aware of the maestro's impending death, they hooked you up to the violinist.

If you stay in the hospital bed, connected to the violinist, he will be totally cured in nine months. You are unlikely to suffer harm. No one else can save him. Do you have an obligation to stay connected?

The creator of the experiment, Judith Thomson, thinks the answer is "no." It would be generous if you did, she claims, but there is no obligation to stay, even if that means the violinist will die.

So how is this bizarre scenario related to the real world? Thomson used the experiment to show that a pregnant woman need

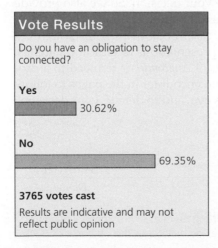

Vote Results

Do you have an obligation to stay connected?

Yes

30.62%

No

69.35%

3765 votes cast

Results are indicative and may not reflect public opinion

not go to full term with her baby, as long as she had taken reasonable steps to avoid getting pregnant. It is thus a "pro-choice" argument.

The violinist represents the baby, and you—in the hospital bed—play the role of the mother. If you think unhooking yourself from the violinist is acceptable, but aborting an unwanted foetus is not, what are the moral differences between the two cases? In both situations, you could save a person by bearing a great burden for nine months.

One major flaw with thought experiments, especially in ethics, is that they are rarely tested on people. The sample size is minuscule. The philosopher will simply assume that most people think that one option is right (or wrong).

10   Philippa Foot, a renowned British philosopher, believed that if a doctor, about to save a patient's life with a large dose of a scarce drug, was suddenly interrupted by the arrival of five patients each in need of one fifth of the drug (without which death would be certain), then the doctor should give it to the five. It is, after all, better to let one person die than five.

Elizabeth Anscombe, another prominent philosopher, disagreed: "There seems to me nothing wrong with giving the single patient the massive dose and letting the others die." As these assumptions about people's intuition are central to the arguments of many philosophers, and as these assumptions can be tested, why not do so?

2. The Runaway Trolley Car

One of the most famous thought experiments in ethics is "the runaway trolley." It aims to clarify how we should distinguish right from wrong.

Here is the scenario with two well-known variations.

A runaway trolley car is hurtling down a track. In its path are five people who will definitely be killed unless you, a bystander, flip a switch which will divert it on to another track, where it will kill one person. Should you flip the switch?

3. The Fat Man and the Trolley Car

The runaway trolley car is hurtling down a track where it will kill five people. You are standing on a bridge above the track and, aware of the imminent disaster, you decide to jump on the track to block the trolley car. Although you will die, the five people will be saved.

Vote Results

Should you flip the switch?

Yes
76.85%

No
23.15%

3814 votes cast

Results are indicative and may not reflect public opinion

Vote Results

Should you push the fat man?

Yes
26.88%

No
73.12%

20320 votes cast

Results are indicative and may not reflect public opinion

Just before your leap, you realise that you are too light to stop the trolley. Next to you, a fat man is standing on the very edge of the bridge. He would certainly block the trolley, although he would undoubtedly die from the impact. A small nudge and he would fall right onto the track below. No one would ever know. Should you push him?

Philippa Foot would say that everyone ("without hesitation") would choose to flip the switch in the first trolley case, but that most of us would be appalled at the idea of pushing the fat man.

15   The philosophical puzzle is this: Why is it acceptable to sacrifice the one person in The Runaway Trolley Car but not in The Fat Man case? Can it ever be morally acceptable to kill an innocent person if that is the only way to save many? Should some actions—such as deliberately killing innocent people against their wishes—never be done? The last thought experiment explores this idea:

4. The Cave Explorers

An enormous rock falls and blocks the exit of a cave you and five other tourists have been exploring. Fortunately, you spot a hole elsewhere and decide to let "Big Jack" out first. But Big Jack, a man of generous proportions, gets stuck in the hole. He cannot be moved and there is no other way out.

The high tide is rising and, unless you get out soon, everyone but Big Jack (whose head is sticking out of the cave) will inevitably drown. Searching through your backpack, you find a stick of dynamite. It will not move the rock, but will certainly blast Big Jack out of the hole. Big Jack, anticipating your thoughts, pleads for his life. He does not want to die, but neither do you and your four companions. Should you blast Big Jack out?

If the roles were reversed, what would you advise your trapped companions to do?

Thought experiments, although abstract, possibly implausible and open to different interpretations, can have important repercussions on the way we think and act as individuals. They raise thorny questions about morality in medicine, war, politics and indeed in everyday life.

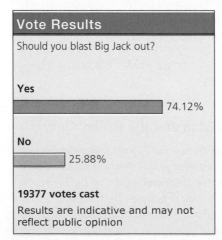

Vote Results

Should you blast Big Jack out?

Yes

74.12%

No

25.88%

19377 votes cast

Results are indicative and may not reflect public opinion

Is there a difference between killing someone and letting them die? Are consequences all that matter, or are there some things we should never do, whatever the outcome?

By pointing out inconsistencies in our thinking, or simply encouraging us to reflect on issues we usually ignore, they can sharpen our intellect and enrich our moral lives. They also make for great conversation topics at the dinner table or at the pub. But be warned: you may lose friends as a result. And stay away from caves and bridges.

VIDEO LINK: THE TROLLEY CAR

The trolley problem discussed by Sokol and referenced in numerous books and articles on ethics has also been treated in several YouTube videos. Here's one of the best. You may want to look at others as well, to get an idea of the various perspectives from which this particular scenario can be viewed.

Go to: YouTube

Search terms: *"presentation part 1 trolley problem"*

THE CASE OF THE COLLAPSED MINE*

Richard T. De George

Business ethics is an important subcomponent of the broader study of ethics, with many business schools requiring students to take at least one course on the subject. Studying business ethics can make one sensitive to issues and questions that might otherwise have escaped notice. A business situation fraught with dilemmas for one person might for another be simply business as usual. And this is the problem: One person sees a conflict of values; another sees none. So here is a selection that demonstrates how someone who is sensitive to ethical dilemmas would approach a particular incident. In "The Case of the Collapsed Mine," Richard T. De George presents a case study and then raises a series of questions that, in effect, provides an overview of business ethics. For instance, De George takes up questions on the value of human life as measured against the cost of designing very safe or relatively safe products and on the need to restructure systems that reward loyalty at the expense of morality. You may be surprised by the number of questions De George can draw from this case. As you begin to think like an ethicist, you, too, will recognize and pose such questions.

Richard T. De George is University Distinguished Professor of Philosophy and Courtesy Professor of Management at the University of Kansas. He is the author or editor of more than fifteen books and more than one hundred scholarly articles on business ethics.

The following case illustrates the sorts of questions that might arise in business ethics and various ways to approach them. Consider the case of the collapsed mine shaft. In a coal mining town of West Virginia, some miners were digging coal in a tunnel thousands of feet below the surface. Some gas buildup had been detected during the two preceding days. This had been reported by the director of safety to the mine manager. The buildup was sufficiently serious to have closed down operations until it was cleared. The owner of the mine decided that the buildup was only marginally dangerous, that he had coal orders to fill, that he could not afford to close down the mine, and that he would take the chance that the gas would dissipate before it exploded. He told the director of safety not to say anything about the danger. On May 2nd, the gas exploded. One section of the tunnel collapsed, killing three miners and trapping eight others in a pocket. The rest managed to escape.

---

*De George, Richard T., *Business Ethics*, 6th Ed., © 2006. Reprinted and Electronically reproduced by permission of Pearson Education, Inc., Upper Saddle River, New Jersey.

The explosion was one of great force and the extent of the tunnel's collapse was considerable. The cost of reaching the men in time to save their lives would amount to several million dollars. The problem facing the manager was whether the expenditure of such a large sum of money was worth it. What, after all, was a human life worth? Whose decision was it and how should it be made? Did the manager owe more to the stockholders of the corporation or to the trapped workers? Should he use the slower, safer, and cheaper way of reaching them and save a large sum of money or the faster, more dangerous, and more expensive way and possibly save their lives?

He decided on the latter and asked for volunteers. Two dozen men volunteered. After three days, the operation proved to be more difficult than anyone had anticipated. There had been two more explosions and three of those involved in the rescue operation had already been killed. In the meantime, telephone contact had been made with the trapped men who had been fortunate enough to find a telephone line that was still functioning. They were starving. Having previously read about a similar case, they decided that the only way for any of them to survive long enough was to draw lots, and then kill and eat the one who drew the shortest straw. They felt that it was their duty that at least some of them should be found alive; otherwise, the three volunteers who had died rescuing them would have died in vain.

After twenty days the seven men were finally rescued alive; they had cannibalized their fellow miner. The director of safety who had detected the gas before the explosion informed the newspapers of his report. The manager was charged with criminal negligence; but before giving up his position, he fired the director of safety. The mine eventually resumed operation.

5   There are a large number of issues in the above account....

The director of safety is in some sense the hero of the story. But did he fulfill his moral obligation before the accident in obeying the manager and in not making known either to the miners, the manager's superior, or to the public the fact that the mine was unsafe? Did he have a moral obligation after the explosion and rescue to make known the fact that the manager knew the mine was unsafe? Should he have gone to the board of directors of the company with the story or to someone else within the company rather than to the newspapers? All these questions are part of the phenomenon of worker responsibility. To whom is a worker responsible and for what? Does his moral obligation end when he does what he is told? Going public with inside information such as the director of safety had is commonly known as "blowing the whistle" on the company. Frequently those who blow the whistle are fired, just as the director of safety was. The whole phenomenon of whistle blowing raises serious questions about the structure of companies in which employees find it necessary to take such drastic action and possibly suffer the loss of their jobs. Was the manager justified in firing the director of safety?

The manager is, of course, the villain of the story. He sent the miners into a situation which he knew was dangerous. But, he might argue, he did it for the good of the company. He had contracts to fulfill and obligations to the owners of the company to show a profit. He had made a bad decision. Every manager has to take risks. It just turned out that he was unlucky. Does such a defense sound plausible? Does a manager have an obligation to his workers as well as to the owners of a company? Who should take precedence and under what conditions does one group or the other become more important? Who is to decide and how?

The manager decided to try to save the trapped miners even though it would cost the company more than taking the slower route. Did he have the right to spend more of the company's money in this way? How does one evaluate human life in comparison with expenditure of money? It sounds moral to say that human life is beyond all monetary value. In a sense it is. However, there are limits which society and people in it can place on the amount they will, can, and should spend to save lives. The way to decide, however, does not seem to be to equate the value of a person's life with the amount of income he would produce in his remaining years, if he lives to a statistically average age, minus the resources he would use up in that period. How does one decide? How do and should people weigh human lives against monetary expenditure? In designing automobiles, in building roads, in making many products, there is a trade-off between the maximum safety that one can build into the product and the cost of the product. Extremely safe cars cost more to build than relatively safe cars. We can express the difference in terms of the number of people likely to die driving the relatively safe ones as opposed to the extremely safe ones. Should such decisions be made by manufacturers, consumers, government, or in some other way?

The manager asked for volunteers for the rescue work. Three of these volunteers died. Was the manager responsible for their deaths in the same way that he was responsible for the deaths of the three miners who had died in the first mine explosion? Was the company responsible for the deaths in either case? Do companies have obligations to their employees and the employees' families in circumstances such as these, or are the obligations only those of the managers? If the manager had warned the miners that the level of gas was dangerous, and they had decided that they wanted their pay for that day and would work anyway, would the manager have been responsible for their deaths? Is it moral for people to take dangerous jobs simply to earn money? Is a system that impels people to take such jobs for money a moral system? To what extent is a company morally obliged to protect its workers and to prevent them from taking chances?

10   The manager was charged with criminal negligence under the law. Was the company responsible for anything? Should the company have been sued by the family of the dead workers? If the company were sued and paid damages to the families, the money would come from company profits and hence from the profits of the shareholders. Is it fair that the shareholders be penalized for an incident they had nothing to do with? How is responsibility shared and/or distributed in a company, and can companies be morally responsible for what is done in their name? Are only human beings moral agents and is it a mistake to use moral language with respect to companies, corporations, and businesses?

The decision of the trapped miners to cast lots to determine who would be killed and eaten also raises a number of moral issues. Our moral intuitions can provide in this case no ready answer as to whether their decision was morally justifiable, since the case is not an ordinary one. How to think about such an issue raises the question of how moral problems are to be resolved and underscores the need for some moral theory as guidelines by which we can decide unusual cases. A number of principles seem to conflict—the obligation not to kill, the consideration that it is better for one person to die rather than eight, the fact noted by the miners that three persons had already died trying to rescue them, and so on. The issue here is not one peculiar to business ethics, but it is rather a moral dilemma that requires some technique of moral argument to solve.

The case does not tell us what happened to either the manager or the director of safety. Frequently the sequel to such cases is surprising. The managers come off free and ultimately rewarded for their concern for the company's interest, while the whistle blower is black-balled throughout the industry. The morality of such an outcome seems obvious—justice does not always triumph. What can be done to see that it triumphs more often is a question that involves restructuring the system.

Business ethics is sometimes seen as conservative and is also used as a defense of the status quo. Sometimes it is seen as an attack on the status quo and hence viewed as radical. Ideally it should be neither. It should strive for objectivity. When there are immoral practices, structures, and actions occurring, business ethics should be able to show that these actions are immoral and why. But it should also be able to supply the techniques with which the practices and structures that are moral can be defended as such. The aim of business ethics is neither defense of the status quo nor its radical change. Rather it should serve to remedy those aspects or structures that need change and protect those that are moral. It is not a panacea. It can secure change only if those in power take the appropriate action. But unless some attention is paid to business ethics, the moral debate about practices and principles central to our society will be more poorly and probably more immorally handled than otherwise.

A FRAMEWORK FOR THINKING ETHICALLY
Manual Velasquez, Dennis Moberg, Michael J. Meyer et al.

Some people confronted with an ethical dilemma might find no dilemma at all: They seem to instinctively know which is the right choice (for them) and to act upon it. Others find themselves in the archetypal predicament of having a devil perched on one shoulder and an angel on the other, with devil and angel offering conflicting advice. In some situations, there may be a devil on *each* side, with the choice being between two terrible alternatives—the worst of these being known as a "Sophie's Choice" dilemma, a reference to the main character of William Styron's novel, forced to choose which of her two children will be executed at a Nazi concentration camp.

Although ethics can offer little useful guidance in such worst-case scenarios, it can, in most everyday situations, offer a framework that will help people make choices they can feel good about. One such framework is offered in the following selection, produced by the Markkula Center for Applied Ethics. After explaining what ethics is *not*, the authors provide an overview of the main approaches to ethical decision making: the utilitarian approach, the rights approach, the fairness or justice approach, and so on. The authors conclude with a series of questions that, when answered, will help people make ethical choices based on which approach they find most useful.

The Markkula Center for Applied Ethics, based at Santa Clara University, a Jesuit institution south of San Francisco, "seeks to encourage dialogue on the ethical dimensions of current issues." This piece appears on the center's Web site. Throughout the chapter, we will refer to this selection as the "Markkula framework."

This document is designed as an introduction to thinking ethically. We all have an image of our better selves—of how we are when we act ethically or are "at our best." We probably also have an image of what an ethical community, an ethical business, an ethical government, or an ethical society should be. Ethics really has to do with all these levels—acting ethically as individuals, creating ethical organizations and governments, and making our society as a whole ethical in the way it treats everyone.

What Is Ethics?

Simply stated, ethics refers to standards of behavior that tell us how human beings ought to act in the many situations in which they find themselves—as friends, parents, children, citizens, businesspeople, teachers, professionals, and so on.

It is helpful to identify what ethics is NOT:

• Ethics is not the same as feelings. Feelings provide important information for our ethical choices. Some people have highly developed habits that make them feel bad when they do something wrong, but many people feel good even though they are doing something wrong. And often our feelings will tell us it is uncomfortable to do the right thing if it is hard.

• Ethics is not religion. Many people are not religious, but ethics applies to everyone. Most religions do advocate high ethical standards but sometimes do not address all the types of problems we face.

• Ethics is not following the law. A good system of law does incorporate many ethical standards, but law can deviate from what is ethical. Law can become ethically corrupt, as some totalitarian regimes have made it. Law can be a function of power alone and designed to serve the interests of narrow groups. Law may have a difficult time designing or enforcing standards in some important areas, and may be slow to address new problems.

• Ethics is not following culturally accepted norms. Some cultures are quite ethical, but others become corrupt or blind to certain ethical concerns (as the United States was to slavery before the Civil War). "When in Rome, do as the Romans do" is not a satisfactory ethical standard.

• Ethics is not science. Social and natural science can provide important data to help us make better ethical choices. But science alone does not tell us what we ought to do. Science may provide an explanation for what humans are like. But ethics provides reasons for how humans ought to act. And just because something is scientifically or technologically possible, it may not be ethical to do it.

Why Identifying Ethical Standards Is Hard

There are two fundamental problems in identifying the ethical standards we are to follow:

1. On what do we base our ethical standards?
2. How do those standards get applied to specific situations we face?

5   If our ethics are not based on feelings, religion, law, accepted social practice, or science, what are they based on? Many philosophers and ethicists have helped us answer this critical question. They have suggested at least five different sources of ethical standards we should use.

Five Sources of Ethical Standards

The Utilitarian Approach

Some ethicists emphasize that the ethical action is the one that provides the most good or does the least harm, or, to put it another way, produces the greatest balance of good over harm. The ethical corporate action, then, is the one that produces the greatest good and does the least harm for all who are affected—customers, employees, shareholders, the community, and the environment. Ethical warfare balances the good achieved in ending terrorism with the harm done to all parties through death, injuries, and destruction. The utilitarian approach deals with consequences; it tries both to increase the good done and to reduce the harm done.

The Rights Approach

Other philosophers and ethicists suggest that the ethical action is the one that best protects and respects the moral rights of those affected. This approach starts from the belief that humans have a dignity based on their human nature per se or on their ability to choose freely what they do with their lives. On the basis of such dignity, they have a right to be treated as ends and not merely as means to other ends. The list of moral rights—including the rights to make one's own choices about what kind of life to lead, to be told the truth, not to be injured, to a degree of privacy, and so on—is widely debated; some now argue that non-humans have rights, too. Also, it is often said that rights imply duties—in particular, the duty to respect others' rights.

The Fairness or Justice Approach

Aristotle and other Greek philosophers have contributed the idea that all equals should be treated equally. Today we use this idea to say that ethical actions treat all human beings equally—or if unequally, then fairly based on some standard that is defensible. We pay people more based on their harder work or the greater amount that they contribute to an organization, and say that is fair. But there is a debate over CEO salaries that are hundreds of times larger than the pay of others; many ask whether the huge disparity is based on a defensible standard or whether it is the result of an imbalance of power and hence is unfair.

The Common Good Approach

The Greek philosophers have also contributed the notion that life in community is a good in itself and our actions should contribute to that life. This approach suggests that the interlocking relationships of society are the basis of ethical reasoning and that respect and compassion for all others—especially the vulnerable—are requirements of such reasoning. This approach also calls attention to the common conditions that are important to the welfare of everyone. This may be a system of laws, effective police and fire departments, health care, a public educational system, or even public recreational areas.

The Virtue Approach

10   A very ancient approach to ethics is that ethical actions ought to be consistent with certain ideal virtues that provide for the full development of our humanity. These virtues are dispositions and habits that enable us to act according to the highest potential of our character and on behalf of values like truth and beauty. Honesty, courage, compassion, generosity, tolerance, love, fidelity, integrity, fairness, self-control, and prudence are all examples of virtues. Virtue ethics asks of any action, "What kind of person will I become if I do this?" or "Is this action consistent with my acting at my best?"

Putting the Approaches Together

Each of the approaches helps us determine what standards of behavior can be considered ethical. There are still problems to be solved, however.

The first problem is that we may not agree on the content of some of these specific approaches.

We may not all agree to the same set of human and civil rights.

We may not agree on what constitutes the common good. We may not even agree on what is a good and what is a harm.

15   The second problem is that the different approaches may not all answer the question "What is ethical?" in the same way. Nonetheless, each approach gives us important information with which to determine what is ethical in a particular circumstance. And much more often than not, the different approaches do lead to similar answers.

Making Decisions

Making good ethical decisions requires a trained sensitivity to ethical issues and a practiced method for exploring the ethical aspects of a decision and weighing the considerations that should impact our choice of a course of action. Having a method for ethical decision making is absolutely essential. When practiced regularly, the method becomes so familiar that we work through it automatically without consulting the specific steps.

The more novel and difficult the ethical choice we face, the more we need to rely on discussion and dialogue with others about the dilemma. Only by careful exploration of the problem, aided by the insights and different perspectives of others, can we make good ethical choices in such situations.

We have found the following framework for ethical decision making a useful method for exploring ethical dilemmas and identifying ethical courses of action.

A Framework for Ethical Decision Making

Recognize an Ethical Issue

1. Could this decision or situation be damaging to someone or to some group? Does this decision involve a choice between a good and bad alternative, or perhaps between two "goods" or between two "bads"?
2. Is this issue about more than what is legal or what is most efficient? If so, how?

Get the Facts

3. What are the relevant facts of the case? What facts are not known? Can I learn more about the situation? Do I know enough to make a decision?
4. What individuals and groups have an important stake in the outcome? Are some concerns more important? Why?
5. What are the options for acting? Have all the relevant persons and groups been consulted? Have I identified creative options?

Evaluate Alternative Actions

6. Evaluate the options by asking the following questions:
   - Which option will produce the most good and do the least harm? (The Utilitarian Approach)
   - Which option best respects the rights of all who have a stake? (The Rights Approach)
   - Which option treats people equally or proportionately? (The Justice Approach)
   - Which option best serves the community as a whole, not just some members? (The Common Good Approach)
   - Which option leads me to act as the sort of person I want to be? (The Virtue Approach)

Make a Decision and Test It

7. Considering all these approaches, which option best addresses the situation?
8. If I told someone I respect—or told a television audience—which option I have chosen, what would they say?

Act and Reflect on the Outcome

9. How can my decision be implemented with the greatest care and attention to the concerns of all stakeholders?
10. How did my decision turn out and what have I learned from this specific situation?

This framework for thinking ethically is the product of dialogue and debate at the Markkula Center for Applied Ethics at Santa Clara University. Primary contributors include Manuel Velasquez, Dennis Moberg, Michael J. Meyer, Thomas Shanks, Margaret R. McLean, David DeCosse, Claire André, and Kirk O. Hanson. It was last revised in May 2009.

Moral Inquiry

Ronald F. White

In the following selection, Ronald F. White provides a closer examination of some of the major approaches to ethical decision making that are discussed in the Markkula framework. Don't be intimidated by White's terminology: What he calls "teleological approaches" is essentially the same as what the authors of "A Framework for Thinking Ethically" call "the utilitarian approach." And when White contrasts teleological theories with "deonotological theories," he's actually making the same distinction as Daniel Sokol ("What If . . ."), who asks: "Are consequences all that matter, or are there some things we should never do, whatever the outcome?" The first question is a teleological one; the second is deontological. White fleshes out these distinct approaches with his discussions of particular examples.

White is a professor of philosophy at the College of St. Joseph in Cincinnati. With specialties in health care ethics, business ethics, and societal and political philosophy, he has written numerous essays and book reviews for professional journals. This selection is an excerpt from his unpublished book *Moral Inquiry* (available online).

Whatever Truth is, we do know that our beliefs about it have a tendency to change over time. I used to believe in Santa Claus, the Easter Bunny, and governmental efficiency. Scientists used to believe that the earth is the center of the universe, and that bloodletting cures insanity. Based on the flow of history, it is safe to assume that most of what we believe to be true today will eventually be regarded as either imprecise or false. We also know that human beliefs concerning Truth vary between individuals, groups of individuals, and between cultures. Generally speaking, we deal with this *cognitive dissonance* by summarily dismissing beliefs that conflict with our own. Our beliefs are true, theirs are false.

Human beings also believe that some human behavior is good and praiseworthy, and that other behavior is bad and blameworthy. It is true that human beings murder each other, steal from each other, drive too fast, and fart in elevators. Under most circumstances, none of these behaviors are considered to be good or praiseworthy, although there may be particular circumstances when they might be. Farting is a perfectly natural phenomenon open to descriptive inquiry. It can be explained in terms of the laws of human physiology, (the production of nitrogenous waste) and the laws of physics: our knowledge of both sets of laws change over time. Killing and stealing can also be explained in biological terms. But many philosophers argue that there is a difference between inquiring into whether something is true and/or whether it is good.

•   •   •

All moral theories address the questions of what is Good, why it's Good, and where the Good is located? If there is anything "easy" about moral inquiry it's the fact that there are only three basic kinds of prescriptive moral theories: *teleological theories, deontological theories, and virtue-based theories.* Unfortunately, they often (but not always) provide different and mostly conflicting answers to these basic questions.

Teleological Ethical Theories

Teleological moral theories locate moral goodness in the consequences of our behavior and not the behavior itself. According to teleological (or *consequentialist*) moral theory, all rational human actions are teleological in the sense that we reason about the *means* of achieving certain *ends*. Moral behavior, therefore, is goal-directed. I have ice in my gutters right now. I am deliberating about when and how to get that ice out in order to prevent water damage inside the house. There are many strategies (means) that I might employ to remove that ice (end). Should I send my oldest son, Eli, up on the icy roof today? After careful deliberation I finally decided not send him on the roof because it is slippery and he might fall. How did I decide? Well, I took into account the possible consequences. There is nothing inherently wrong with climbing on the roof. What made roof climbing the morally wrong thing to do at this particular time and place were the possible consequences. The issue has moral significance in so far as it affects persons. So from the teleological point of view, human behavior is neither right nor wrong in and of itself. What matters is what might happen as a consequence of those actions in any given context. Thus, it is the contextualized consequences that make our behavior, good or bad, right or wrong. In the case of roof climbing in the winter, I decided to climb up on the roof myself, because it's dangerous. Eli might fall off and get hurt. If that happened, my wife would blame me and so would the community. But if I fell off the roof, I would be judged to be imprudent, but not necessarily immoral.

5   From a teleological standpoint, stealing, for example, could not be judged to be inherently right or wrong independent of the context and the foreseeable consequences. Suppose I am contemplating stealing a loaf of bread from the neighborhood grocery store. Many moral theorists would argue that morality requires an analysis of my motives (or intent) that brought about that behavior. However, from a teleological perspective, motives really have nothing to do with the rightness or wrongness of the act. What really matters lies in the potential pains and pleasures associated with the short-term and long-term consequences. If my children were starving, and if stealing a loaf of bread would immediately prevent them from starving, then I might seriously consider stealing. But I'd have to know if the consequences would significantly harm the grocery store. What would be the odds of getting caught? If I got caught, what would happen to me? Would I go to jail? Get fined? If I went to jail, who would take care of my children? Therefore, even if my motive (preventing my children from starving) was praiseworthy, the act of stealing might still be wrong because other actions might be more cost-effective in bringing about the desired consequences. Perhaps I'd be better off signing up for food stamps or asking the storeowner

to give me day-old bread. On the other hand, suppose that there were no other options and that I invented a foolproof system for stealing bread. Would I be wrong for doing it? If you think about the consequences of your actions when you make moral decisions, you are applying teleological moral theory.

• • • •

Deontological Theories

There are many philosophers who reject the entire teleological agenda by arguing that moral goodness has nothing to do with…consequences. *Deontological theories* are by definition *duty-based*. That is to say, that morality, according to deontologists, consists in the fulfillment of moral *obligations,* or *duties.* Duties, in the deontological tradition, are most often associated with obeying *absolute moral rules.* Hence, human beings are morally required to do (or not to do) certain acts in order to uphold a rule or law. The rightness or wrongness of a moral rule is determined independent of its consequences or how happiness or pleasure is distributed as a result of abiding by that rule, or not abiding by it.

It's not difficult to see why philosophers would be drawn to this position.… In early nineteenth-century America, many members of the anti-slavery movement argued that slavery was wrong, even though slaveholders and southern society in general, economically benefited from it. Suppose, also that the slaveholders were also able to condition the slaves to the point where they actually enjoyed living under slavery. From a teleological perspective, slavery might appear to be an ideal economic institution. Everybody is happy!

A deontologist, however, would argue that even if the American government conducted a detailed cost/benefit analysis of slavery and decided that it created more pleasure in society than pain, it would still be wrong. Therefore, deontologists believe that right and wrong have nothing to do with pleasure, pain, or consequences. Morality is based on whether acts conflict with moral rules or not, and the motivation behind those acts. An act is therefore good if and only if it was performed out of a desire to do one's duty and obey a rule. In other words, act out of a good will. Hence, slavery is wrong, not because of its negative consequences, but because it violates an absolute moral rule. The problem here is: "How does one distinguish absolute moral rules from mere convention, prudence, or legality…?"

• • •

Virtue-Based Moral Theories

In the Western world (and the Eastern World) there is a venerable system of moral reasoning based on the idea of virtue. Let's call those various systems *virtue-based moral systems.* In the history of Western moral theory, there are two different types of virtue-based systems. The nonsecular line of inquiry relies on divine command theory in order to discern moral virtues from vices, as illustrated by the Judeo-Christian moral tradition. The secular line of inquiry relies primarily on reason and experience, and not divine command theory. It goes back to the ancient Greeks, via the writings of Homer, Hesiod, Plato, and Aristotle....

10   All virtue-based moral systems focus on big questions such as: "What is the 'Good Life?'" And "How do I go about living the 'Good Life?'" Therefore, they tend to focus on how to live one's life over the long run, rather than how to address particular issues that pop up at any given time. In short, virtue-based systems focus on character development within harmonious communities. These systems also tend to rely on moral exemplars, or role models. Once a person has internalized the virtue of kindness, then that person will exemplify that virtue in his/her actions.

All virtue-based moral systems differentiate between virtues (good behavior) and vices (bad behavior). Ultimately, non-secular virtue-based theories differentiate between virtues and vices based on religions authorities, usually traced back to the authority of the Bible and/or its official interpreters. The Christian authorities have identified *faith, hope*, and *charity* as its primary virtues. If you pursue these ideals over the course of your lifetime, you'll lead a "good life."

Aristotle believed moral virtue consists in choosing the mean between the extremes of excess and deficiency within any given sphere of action. The vice of excess consists in choosing too much of a good thing and the vice of deficiency consists of not enough. Excellence is found midway between the two. For example, the virtue of bravery can be found midway between the vices of cowardice and foolhardiness.

VIDEO LINK: GREY'S ANATOMY (A MEDICAL DILEMMA)

Go to: YouTube

Search terms: "greys anatomy presentation" (length: 9:32)

HEINZ'S DILEMMA: KOHLBERG'S SIX STAGES OF MORAL DEVELOPMENT*

William Crain

A distinctly different take on ethical decision making is provided by William Crain in the following selection, which discusses the theory of Lawrence Kohlberg (1927–87), a psychologist at the Department of Psychology at the University of Chicago and the Graduate School of Education at Harvard University. Kohlberg was much influenced by the work of Swiss psychologist Jean Piaget (1896–1980), who studied the cognitive and moral development of children. Kohlberg studied both children and adolescents in developing his own approach

*Crain, William, *Theories of Development: Concepts and Applications*, 6th Ed., © 2011, pp. 159–165. Reprinted and Electronically reproduced by permission of Pearson Education, Inc., Upper Saddle River, New Jersey.

to moral development. It was in his 1958 doctoral dissertation, based upon his interviews with boys and girls from the United States and around the world, that he first expounded his six stages of moral development, each showing a different and progressively more complex approach to moral reasoning and decision making.

In the following selection, Crain discusses Kohlberg's six stages of moral development, focusing on how they apply to his famous example of the Heinz dilemma ("Heinz steals the drug"). You should be able to draw upon Crain's discussion of Kohlberg's stages and Heinz's dilemma when you later attempt to analyze the choices represented in other cases in this chapter.

This selection is drawn from Crain's *Theories of Development: Concepts and Applications*.

Kohlberg's Method

Kohlberg's (1958a) core sample was comprised of 72 boys, from both middle- and lower-class families in Chicago. They were ages 10, 13, and 16. He later added to his sample younger children, delinquents, and boys and girls from other American cities and from other countries (1963, 1970).

The basic interview consists of a series of dilemmas such as the following:

Heinz Steals the Drug

> In Europe, a woman was near death from a special kind of cancer. There was one drug that the doctors thought might save her. It was a form of radium that a druggist in the same town had recently discovered. The drug was expensive to make, but the druggist was charging ten times what the drug cost him to make. He paid $200 for the radium and charged $2,000 for a small dose of the drug. The sick woman's husband, Heinz, went to everyone he knew to borrow the money, but he could only get together about $1,000 which is half of what it cost. He told the druggist that his wife was dying and asked him to sell it cheaper or let him pay later. But the druggist said: "No, I discovered the drug and I'm going to make money from it." So Heinz got desperate and broke into the man's store to steal the drug for his wife. Should the husband have done that? (Kohlberg, 1963, p. 19)

Kohlberg is not really interested in whether the subject says "yes" or "no" to this dilemma but in the reasoning behind the answer. The interviewer wants to know why the subject thinks Heinz should or should not have stolen the drug. The interview schedule then asks new questions which help one understand the child's reasoning. For example, children are asked if Heinz had a right to steal the drug, if he was violating the druggist's rights, and what sentence the judge should give him once he was caught. Once again, the main concern is with the reasoning behind the answers. The interview then goes on to give more dilemmas in order to get a good sampling of a subject's moral thinking. [See the Video Link following this reading (p. 289) for two videos dealing with the Heinz dilemma.]

Once Kohlberg had classified the various responses into stages, he wanted to know whether his classification was *reliable*. In particular, he wanted to know if others would score the protocols in the same way. Other judges independently scored a sample of responses, and he calculated the degree to which all raters agreed. This procedure is called *interrater reliability*. Kohlberg found these agreements to be high, as he has in his subsequent work, but whenever investigators use Kohlberg's interview, they also should check for interrater reliability before scoring the entire sample.

Kohlberg's Six Stages

Level 1. Preconventional Morality

5   **Stage 1. Obedience and Punishment Orientation.** Kohlberg's stage 1 is similar to Piaget's first stage of moral thought. The child assumes that powerful authorities hand down a fixed set of rules which he or she must unquestioningly obey. To the Heinz dilemma, the child typically says that Heinz was wrong to steal the drug because "It's against the law," or "It's bad to steal," as if this were all there were to it. When asked to elaborate, the child usually responds in terms of the consequences involved, explaining that stealing is bad "because you'll get punished" (Kohlberg, 1958b).

Although the vast majority of children at stage 1 oppose Heinz's theft, it is still possible for a child to support the action and still employ stage 1 reasoning. For example, a child might say, "Heinz can steal it because he asked first and it's not like he stole something big; he won't get punished" (see Rest, 1973). Even though the child agrees with Heinz's action, the reasoning is still stage 1; the concern is with what authorities permit and punish.

Kohlberg calls stage 1 thinking "preconventional" because children do not yet speak as members of society. Instead, they see morality as something external to themselves, as that which the big people say they must do.

Stage 2. Individualism and Exchange. At this stage children recognize that there is not just one right view that is handed down by the authorities. Different individuals have different viewpoints. "Heinz," they might point out, "might think it's right to take the drug, the druggist would not." Since everything is *relative*, each person is free to pursue his or her *individual* interests. One boy said that Heinz might steal the drug if he wanted his wife to live, but that he doesn't have to if he wants to marry someone younger and better-looking (Kohlberg, 1963, p. 24). Another boy said Heinz might steal it because maybe they had children and he might need someone at home to look after them. But maybe he shouldn't steal it because they might put him in prison for more years than he could stand (Colby and Kauffman, 1983, p. 300).

What is right for Heinz, then, is what meets his own self-interests.

10   You might have noticed that children at both stages 1 and 2 talk about punishment. However, they perceive it differently. At stage 1 punishment is tied up in the child's mind with wrongness; punishment "proves" that disobedience is wrong. At stage 2, in contrast, punishment is simply a risk that one naturally wants to avoid.

Although stage 2 respondents sometimes sound amoral, they do have some sense of right action. This is a notion of *fair exchange* or fair deals. The philosophy is one of returning favors—"If you scratch my back, I'll scratch yours." To the Heinz story, subjects often say that Heinz was right to steal the drug because the druggist was unwilling to make a fair deal; he was "trying to rip Heinz off." Or they might say that he should steal for his wife "because she might return the favor some day" (Gibbs et al., 1983, p. 19).

Respondents at stage 2 are still said to reason at the preconventional level because they speak as isolated individuals rather than as members of society. They see individuals exchanging favors, but there is still no identification with the values of the family or community.

Level II. Conventional Morality

Stage 3. Good Interpersonal Relationships. At this stage children—who are by now usually entering their teens— see morality as more than simple deals. They believe that people should live up to the expectations of the family and community and behave in "good" ways. Good behavior means having good motives and interpersonal feelings such as love, empathy, trust, and concern for others. Heinz, they typically argue, was right to steal the drug because "He was a good man for wanting to save her," and "His intentions were good, that of saving the life of someone he loves." Even if Heinz doesn't love his wife, these subjects often say, he should steal the drug because "I don't think any husband should sit back and watch his wife die" (Gibbs et al., 1983, pp. 36–42; Kohlberg, 1958b).

If Heinz's motives were good, the druggist's were bad. The druggist, stage 3 subjects emphasize, was "selfish," "greedy," and "only interested in himself, not another life." Sometimes the respondents become so angry with the druggist that they say that he ought to be put in jail (Gibbs et al., 1983, pp. 26–29, 40–42). A typical stage 3 response is that of Don, age 13:

> It was really the druggist's fault, he was unfair, trying to overcharge and letting someone die. Heinz loved his wife and wanted to save her. I think anyone would. I don't think they would put him in jail. The judge would look at all sides, and see that the druggist was charging too much. (Kohlberg, 1963, p. 25)

15   We see that Don defines the issue in terms of the actors' character traits and motives. He talks about the loving husband, the unfair druggist, and the understanding judge. His answer deserves the label "conventional morality" because it assumes that the attitude expressed would be shared by the entire community—"anyone" would be right to do what Heinz did (Kohlberg, 1963, p. 25).

As mentioned earlier, there are similarities between Kohlberg's first three stages and Piaget's two stages. In both sequences there is a shift from unquestioning obedience to a relativistic outlook and to a concern for good motives. For Kohlberg, however, these shifts occur in three stages rather than two.

Stage 4. Maintaining the Social Order. Stage 3 reasoning works best in two-person relationships with family members or close friends, where one can make a real effort to get to know the other's feelings and needs and try to help. At stage 4, in contrast, the respondent becomes more broadly concerned with *society as a whole*. Now the emphasis is on obeying laws, respecting authority, and performing one's duties so that the social order is maintained. In response to the Heinz story, many subjects say they understand that Heinz's motives were good, but they cannot condone the theft. What would happen if we all started breaking the laws whenever we felt we had a good reason? The result would be chaos; society couldn't function. As one subject explained,

> I don't want to sound like Spiro Agnew,[1] law and order and wave the flag, but if everybody did as he wanted to do, set up his own beliefs as to right and wrong, then I think you would have chaos. The only thing I think we have in civilization nowadays is some sort of legal structure which people are sort of bound to follow. [Society needs] a centralizing framework. (Gibbs et al., 1983, pp. 140–41)

Because stage 4, subjects make moral decisions from the perspective of society as a whole, they think from a full-fledged member-of-society perspective (Colby and Kohlberg, 1983, p. 27).

You will recall that stage 1 children also generally oppose stealing because it breaks the law. Superficially, stage 1 and stage 4 subjects are giving the same response, so we see here why Kohlberg insists that we must probe into the reasoning behind the overt response. Stage 1 children say, "It's wrong to steal" and "It's against the law," but they cannot elaborate any further, except to say that stealing can get a person jailed. Stage 4 respondents, in contrast, have a conception of the function of laws for society as a whole—a conception which far exceeds the grasp of the younger child.

Level III. Postconventional Morality

20 **Stage 5. Social Contract and Individual Rights.** At stage 4, people want to keep society functioning. However, a smoothly functioning society is not necessarily a good one. A totalitarian society might be well-organized, but it is hardly the moral ideal. At stage 5, people begin to ask, "What makes for a good society?" They begin to think about society in a very theoretical way, stepping back from their own society and considering the rights and values that a society ought to uphold. They then evaluate existing societies in terms of these prior considerations. They are said to take a "prior-to-society" perspective (Colby and Kohlberg, 1983, p. 22).

Stage 5 respondents basically believe that a good society is best conceived as a social contract into which people freely enter to work toward the benefit of all. They recognize that different social groups within a society will have different values, but they believe that all rational people would agree on two points. First they would all want certain basic *rights*, such as liberty and life, to be protected.

---

[1] Spiro Agnew, vice president of the United States (1969–73) under President Richard M. Nixon, was famous (or notorious) for his blistering attacks on antigovernment protestors and counterculture types. He characterized one group of opponents as "an effete corps of impudent snobs who characterize themselves as intellectuals" and was given to alliterative insults like "pusillanimous pussyfooters" and "nattering nabobs of negativism." Agnew resigned the vice presidency in 1973 just before pleading no contest to criminal charges of tax evasion for accepting bribes while serving as governor of Maryland.

Second, they would want some *democratic* procedures for changing unfair law and for improving society.

In response to the Heinz dilemma, stage 5 respondents make it clear that they do not generally favor breaking laws; laws are social contracts that we agree to uphold until we can change them by democratic means. Nevertheless, the wife's right to live is a moral right that must be protected. Thus, stage 5 respondents sometimes defend Heinz's theft in strong language:

> It is the husband's duty to save his wife. The fact that her life is in danger transcends every other standard you might use to judge his action. Life is more important than property.

This young man went on to say that "from a moral standpoint" Heinz should save the life of even a stranger, since to be consistent, the value of a life means any life. When asked if the judge should punish Heinz, he replied:

> Usually the moral and legal standpoints coincide. Here they conflict. The judge should weight the moral standpoint more heavily but preserve the legal law in punishing Heinz lightly. (Kohlberg, 1976, p. 38)

Stage 5 subjects, then, talk about "morality" and "rights" that take some priority over particular laws. Kohlberg insists, however, that we do not judge people to be at stage 5 merely from their verbal labels. We need to look at their social perspective and mode of reasoning. At stage 4, too, subjects frequently talk about the "right to life," but for them this right is legitimized by the authority of their social or religious group (e.g., by the Bible). Presumably, if their group valued property over life, they would too. At stage 5, in contrast, people are making more of an independent effort to think out what any society ought to value. They often reason, for example, that property has little meaning without life. They are trying to determine logically what a society ought to be like (Kohlberg, 1981, pp. 21–22; Gibbs et al., 1983, p. 83).

25   **Stage 6: Universal Principles.** Stage 5 respondents are working toward a conception of the good society. They suggest that we need to (a) protect certain individual rights and (b) settle disputes through democratic processes. However, democratic processes alone do not always result in outcomes that we intuitively sense are just. A majority, for example, may vote for a law that hinders a minority. Thus, Kohlberg believes that there must be a higher stage—stage 6—which defines the principles by which we achieve justice.

Kohlberg's conception of justice follows that of the philosophers Kant and Rawls, as well as great moral leaders such as Gandhi and Martin Luther King. According to these people, the principles of justice require us to treat the claims of all parties in an impartial manner, respecting the basic dignity of all people as individuals. The principles of justice are therefore universal; they apply to all. Thus, for example, we would not vote for a law that aids some people but hurts others. The principles of justice guide us toward decisions based on an equal respect for all.

In actual practice, Kohlberg says, we can reach just decisions by looking at a situation through one another's eyes. In the Heinz dilemma, this would mean that all parties—the druggist, Heinz, and his wife—take the roles of the others. To do this in an impartial manner, people can assume a "veil of ignorance" (Rawls, 1971), acting as if they do not know which role they will eventually occupy. If the druggist did this, even he would recognize that life must take priority over property; for he wouldn't want to risk finding himself in the wife's shoes with property valued over life. Thus, they would all agree that the wife must be saved—this would be the fair solution. Such a solution, we must note, requires not only impartiality, but the principle that everyone is given full and equal respect. If the wife were considered of less value than the others, a just solution could not be reached.

Until recently, Kohlberg had been scoring some of his subjects at stage 6, but he has temporarily stopped doing so. For one thing, he and other researchers had not been finding subjects who consistently reasoned at this stage. Also, Kohlberg has concluded that his interview dilemmas are not useful for distinguishing between stage 5 and stage 6 thinking. He believes that stage 6 has a clearer and broader conception of universal principles (which include justice as well as individual rights), but feels that his interview fails to draw out this broader understanding. Consequently, he has temporarily dropped stage 6 from his scoring manual, calling it a "theoretical stage" and scoring all postconventional responses as stage 5 (Colby and Kohlberg, 1983, p. 28).

Theoretically, one issue that distinguishes stage 5 from stage 6 is civil disobedience. Stage 5 would be more hesitant to endorse civil disobedience because of its commitment to the social contract and to changing laws through democratic agreements. Only when an individual right is clearly at stake does violating the law seem justified. At stage 6, in contrast, a commitment to justice makes the rationale for civil disobedience stronger and broader. Martin Luther King, for example, argued that laws are only valid insofar as they are grounded in justice, and that a commitment to justice carries with it an obligation to disobey unjust laws. King also recognized, of course, the general need for laws and democratic processes (stages 4 and 5), and he was therefore willing to accept the penalties for his actions. Nevertheless, he believed that the higher principle of justice required civil disobedience (Kohlberg, 1981, p. 43).

Summary

30 At stage 1 children think of what is right as that which authority says is right. Doing the right thing is obeying authority and avoiding punishment. At stage 2, children are no longer so impressed by any single authority; they see that there are different sides to any issue. Since everything is relative, one is free to pursue one's own interests, although it is often useful to make deals and exchange favors with others.

At stages 3 and 4, young people think as members of the conventional society with its values, norms, and expectations. At stage 3, they emphasize being a good person, which basically means having helpful motives toward people close to one. At stage 4, the concern shifts toward obeying laws to maintain society as a whole.

At stages 5 and 6 people are less concerned with maintaining society for its own sake, and more concerned with the principles and values that make for a good society. At stage 5 they emphasize basic rights and the democratic processes that give everyone a say, and at stage 6 they define the principles by which agreement will be most just.

VIDEO LINK: THE HEINZ DILEMMA

There are many treatments on the Heinz Dilemma on YouTube. Among the best:

Go to: YouTube

Search terms: *"heinz dilemma kohlbergs theory moral development"* (select video with length: 3:00)

"kohlbergs moral development theory" (select video with length: 4:17)

A CASEBOOK OF ETHICAL DILEMMAS

This section presents an array of cases, both real and hypothetical, that invite you to decide on an ethical course of action. In making your decision, you should be guided not only by your innate sense of what is the right thing to do, but also by the kind of ethical frameworks discussed in Velasquez et al., White, and Crain's treatment of Kohlberg's stages of moral development. Consider, for example, the "lifeboat" case, in which ten people want to climb into a lifeboat that can only hold six. In choosing, for example, whether to allow either a lifeguard or an elementary school teacher into the lifeboat, should utilitarian considerations prevail? Considerations of justice or of rights? And in the Klosterman scenario, is it better for a doctor to respect the right of a patient to have his doctor maintain confidentiality or the right of an innocent man not to have to rot in jail?

THE LIFEBOAT

Rosetta Lee

This case, a version of the familiar lifeboat scenario, was developed by Rosetta Lee as an assignment for The Seattle Girls' School. Note that while this scenario is quite specific, it has applications in a variety of other contexts. For example, which of several candidates should be first in line for an organ transplant? How do we decide who gets the vaccine when only limited supplies are available?

Note: You can see an intriguing dramatization of the issues posed in "The Lifeboat" (and at least one of the other scenarios in this chapter, such as "The Runaway Trolley") in the 2014 film *After the Dark*, which poses the question: Which 10 of 21 individuals should be allowed to enter a survival bunker after a nuclear apocalypse has destroyed most human life on earth?

The ship is sinking and the seas are rough. All but one lifeboat has been destroyed. The lifeboat holds a maximum of six people. There are ten people (listed below) that want to board the lifeboat. The four individuals who do not board the boat will certainly die.

Woman who thinks she is six months pregnant

Lifeguard

Two young adults who recently married

Senior citizen who has fifteen grandchildren

Elementary school teacher

Thirteen year old twins

Veteran nurse

Captain of the ship

LIFEBOAT ETHICS: THE CASE AGAINST HELPING THE POOR

Garrett Hardin

The following selection is excerpted from the first part of Garrett Hardin's essay of the same name, which first appeared in *Psychology Today* in September 1974. Hardin (1915–2003) was an often-controversial ecologist who taught at the University of California, Santa Barbara, from 1963 to 1978. His most well-known paper was "The Tragedy of the Commons" (1963), which drew attention to "the damage that innocent actions by individuals can inflict on the environment." In particular, he warned against the dangers of human overpopulation in a world of limited resources. Hardin is the author of numerous articles and several books, including *The Limits of Altruism: An Ecologist's View of Survival* (1977), *Filters Against Folly: How to Survive Despite Economists, Ecologists, and the Merely Eloquent* (1985), and *The Ostrich Factor: Our Population Myopia* (1999).

   Note: This passage is not a case, per se, but takes the "lifeboat" scenario and extrapolates the situation onto a global scale to argue against helping the poor—that is, against bringing people onto the "lifeboat."

If we divide the world crudely into rich nations and poor nations, two thirds of them are desperately poor, and only one third comparatively rich, with the United States the wealthiest of all. Metaphorically each rich nation can be seen as a lifeboat full of comparatively rich people. In the ocean outside each lifeboat swim the poor of the world, who would like to get in, or at least to share some of the wealth. What should the lifeboat passengers do?

   First, we must recognize the limited capacity of any lifeboat. For example, a nation's land has a limited capacity to support a population and as the current energy crisis has shown us, in some ways we have already exceeded the carrying capacity of our land.

Adrift in a Moral Sea

So here we sit, say 50 people in our lifeboat. To be generous, let us assume it has room for 10 more, making a total capacity of 60. Suppose the 50 of us in the lifeboat see 100 others swimming in the water outside, begging for admission to our boat or for handouts. We have several options: we may be tempted to try to live by the Christian ideal of being "our brother's keeper," or by the Marxist ideal of "to each according to his needs." Since the needs of all in the water are the same, and since they can all be seen as "our brothers," we could take them all into our boat, making a total of 150 in a boat designed for 60. The boat swamps, everyone drowns. Complete justice, complete catastrophe.

Since the boat has an unused excess capacity of 10 more passengers, we could admit just 10 more to it. But which 10 do we let in? How do we choose? Do we pick the best 10, "first come, first served"? And what do we say to the 90 we exclude? If we do let an extra 10 into our lifeboat, we will have lost our "safety factor," an engineering principle of critical importance. For example, if we don't leave room for excess capacity as a safety factor in our country's agriculture, a new plant disease or a bad change in the weather could have disastrous consequences.

5   Suppose we decide to preserve our small safety factor and admit no more to the lifeboat. Our survival is then possible although we shall have to be constantly on guard against boarding parties.

While this last solution clearly offers the only means of our survival, it is morally abhorrent to many people. Some say they feel guilty about their good luck. My reply is simple: "Get out and yield your place to others." This may solve the problem of the guilt-ridden person's conscience, but it does not change the ethics of the lifeboat. The needy person to whom the guilt-ridden person yields his place will not himself feel guilty about his good luck. If he did, he would not climb aboard. The net result of conscience-stricken people giving up their unjustly held seats is the elimination of that sort of conscience from the lifeboat.

This is the basic metaphor within which we must work out our solutions.... The harsh ethics of the lifeboat become even harsher when we consider the reproductive differences between the rich nations and the poor nations. The people inside the lifeboats are doubling in numbers every 87 years; those swimming around outside are doubling, on the average, every 35 years, more than twice as fast as the rich. And since the world's resources are dwindling, the difference in prosperity between the rich and the poor can only increase.

SHOULD I PROTECT A PATIENT AT THE EXPENSE OF AN INNOCENT STRANGER?*

Chuck Klosterman

The following selection originally appeared in "The Ethicist" column of the *New York Times Magazine* on May 10, 2013. In addition to regularly writing this column for the *Times*, Klosterman has also been a columnist for *Esquire*. He has also published several essay

*From the *New York Times*, May 10, 2013 © 2013 New York Times. All rights reserved. Used by permission and protected by the Copyright Laws of the United States. The printing, copying, redistribution, or retransmission of this Content without express written permission is prohibited.

collections (including *Sex, Drugs, and Cocoa Puffs: A Low Culture Manifesto* [2004]), two novels, and eight books on American popular culture, including *I Wear the Black Hat: Grappling with Villains (Real and Imagined)* (2013).

> I am a physician. Years ago, I saw a young patient with headaches, who disclosed—reluctantly—that he had committed a serious crime and that somebody else took the fall for it. I believe he was telling me the truth (his headaches soon resolved after the confession). Before his admission, I assured him that whatever he told me would not leave the room. Later, without giving specifics, I consulted our hospital lawyer, who told me that we were under no obligation to report the incident, because the patient wasn't in danger of hurting himself or others. But the future of an innocent man hinges on two people's consciences, my patient's and my own. I feel like a coward, hiding behind the Hippocratic oath, doing nothing. —NAME WITHHELD

I'm (obviously) not a doctor, and I assume some doctors will vehemently disagree with what I'm about to write. But I feel that the first thing we need to recognize is that the Hippocratic oath represents the ideals of a person who died in the historical vicinity of 370 B.C. Now, this doesn't make it valueless or inherently flawed. It's a good oath. But we're dealing with a modern problem, so I would separate the conditions of that concept from this discussion. And even if you refuse to do that—even if you feel your commitment to this symbolic oath supersedes all other things keep in mind that one of its cornerstones is to "do no harm." Are you latently doing harm by allowing someone to be penalized for a crime he did not commit? This is not exactly a medical issue, but your relationship to the problem is still an extension of your position as a physician.

Here is the root of the problem: You promised a man that you would keep his secret in confidence, only to have him tell you something you now view as too important to remain unspoken. The stakes are pretty high; the possibility of someone's being convicted of a crime that he did not commit is awful. But you've painted yourself into a corner. You should not tell someone "Whatever you tell me will never leave this room" if that promise only applies to anecdotes you deem as tolerable. It doesn't matter if you're a physician or anyone else. The deeper question, of course, is whether breaking this commitment is ethically worse than allowing someone to go to jail for no valid reason. On balance, I have to say it is not.

I would advise the following: Call the patient back into your office. Urge him to confess what happened to the authorities and tell him you will assist him in any way possible (helping him find a lawyer before going to the police, etc.). If he balks, you will have to go a step further; you will have to tell him that you were wrong to promise him confidentiality and that your desire for social justice is greater than your personal integrity as a professional confidant. There is, certainly, danger in doing this. I don't know what the real impact will be (considering the circumstances, it seems as if it would be easy for him to claim his confession came under mental distress and that you coerced or misinterpreted his admission but the information still might help the innocent man's case).

This is a situation in which I'm personally uncomfortable with my own advice. If I told someone "Whatever you tell me will never leave this room," it would be almost impossible for me to contradict that guarantee, regardless of whatever insane thing the person proceeded to tell me. That is my own human weakness. But given the advantage of detached objectivity, it's very difficult to argue that the significance of your promise to a guilty stranger is greater than an innocent stranger's freedom from wrongful prosecution. You should not have made the original promise, and you should not allow that bad promise to stand. But keep in mind I'm only looking at this from a civilian perspective. The conditions of doctor-patient privilege might make this untenable. I'm merely weighing the two evils and deeming one to be greater, at least in this specific case.

No Edit

Randy Cohen

A writer and humorist, Randy Cohen preceded Chuck Klosterman as the writer of the *New York Times*' "Ethicist" column. He has written articles for the *Village Voice* and the online magazine *Slate*. He has also written for several TV shows, including *TV Nation, The Rosie O'Donnell Show*, and (for 950 episodes) *The David Letterman Show*. Among his books are *Diary of a Flying Man* (1989), a collection of humor pieces; *The Good, The Bad, & The Difference: How to Tell Right from Wrong in Everyday Situations* (2002); and *Be Good: How to Navigate the Ethics of Everything* (2012). He currently hosts the public radio show *Person Place Thing*.

> As a high-school English teacher, I am frequently asked to proofread and make rewriting suggestions for students' college-application essays. I decline on the grounds that admissions officers assume that these essays accurately represent the students' work. Other teachers argue that our students lose the editing advantage many students receive. Is it ethical for me to read student essays? —NAME WITHHELD

The all-the-kids-are-doing-it defense? Unpersuasive. A teacher may read student essays but not write them. You should eschew anything as hands-on as editing or proofreading and instead find ways to guide students toward producing first-rate work that is their own.

This is a more conservative stance than that of at least one person who will judge the finished product. Jeffrey Brenzel, dean of undergraduate admissions at Yale, says, "I would think it foolish of a student not to have an essay proofed for spelling, grammar and syntax by someone competent to do so."

As to your concern—and mine—that such direct involvement by the teacher can mislead a college about a student's language skills and undermine the student's integrity and sense of accomplishment, Brenzel replies: "We are not looking to take the measure of writing ability, genius or cleverness. We simply want to know something about personal outlook and perspective—how a student sees things or what a student has learned from his or her experiences."

Admissions offices are wise to use these essays as a way to learn more about applicants but disingenuous to suggest that they are uninfluenced by the quality of the writing. How could they not be?

5   Your challenge is to help your students without distorting their voices or misrepresenting their abilities. One technique recommended by College Summit, a nonprofit organization that helps public-school systems increase

college enrollment, is to ask students probing questions about their essays—why did you spend your summer vacation in that shark tank? Is there a word in standard English that is clearer than "aieeee"?—but not proffer answers. That is, help a student identify a problem, but let the student solve it.

THE TORTURED CHILD

Kelley L. Ross

"The Tortured Child" was developed by Kelley L. Ross for his Web site *Some Moral Dilemmas*. Ross is retired from the Department of Philosophy at Los Angeles Valley College in Van Nuys, California. The moral dilemmas he discusses are adapted from those provided in Victor Grassian's *Moral Reasoning: Ethical Theory and Some Contemporary Moral Problems* (1981).

Dostoyevsky...imagines a classic right vs. good dilemma:

> "Tell me yourself—I challenge you: let's assume that you were called upon to build the edifice of human destiny so that men would finally be happy and would find peace and tranquility. If you knew that, in order to attain this, you would have to torture just one single creature, let's say the little girl who beat her chest so desperately in the outhouse, and that on her unavenged tears you could build that edifice, would you agree to do it? Tell me and don't lie!"

> "No I would not," Alyosha said softly. [Fyodor Dostoevsky, *The Brothers* Karamazov, 1880, translated by Andrew H. MacAndrew, Bantam Books, 1970, p. 296]

This could stand as a *reductio ad absurdum* of Utilitarianism; but Dostoyevsky himself cites one innocent person who is indeed sacrificed to build an "edifice" of "peace and tranquility," namely Jesus Christ. Jesus went to his fate willingly, unlike the little girl of the example here; but those who sent him there had something else in mind. Dostoyevsky's thought experiment was developed into a science fiction short story, "The Ones Who Walk Away from Omelas" [1973], by Ursula K. Le Guin. Le Guin, however, originally credited the device to William James, having read it in James and forgotten that it was in Dostoyevsky.

THE ONES WHO WALK AWAY FROM OMELAS

Ursula Le Guin

In "The Tortured Child" (previous selection), Kelley L. Ross indicates that Ursula Le Guin's 1973 short story "The Ones Who Walk Away from Omelas" was derived from Dostoyevsky's "classic right vs. good dilemma" from *The Brothers Karamazov*. Le Guin's beautifully written and yet disturbing story is available online. It evokes in the most vivid manner possible the ethical dilemma that is briefly suggested by Dostoyevsky. After you read it, you may find yourself turning to the ethical approaches discussed by authors like White, Velasquez et al., and Crain to make moral sense of the choices made by both those who remain in Omelas and those who walk away.

Ursula Le Guin (1929–) is a prolific author of children's books, novels, and short stories focusing on science fiction and fantasy. Among her books are *Planet of Exile*

(1966), *A Wizard of Earthsea* (1968), *The Dispossessed: An Ambiguous Utopia* (1974), *The Compass Rose* (1982), *Always Coming Home* (1985), *The Other Wind* (2001), and *Lavinia* (2008).

Online you'll discover many analyses of Le Guin's story. You may or may not want to read them—but either way, the fun and the benefit of this "case" derive from thinking through the ethical dilemmas yourself and discussing them with your classmates.

Go to: Google or Bing

Search terms: *"pdf the ones who walk away from omelas"*

VIDEO LINK: *THE DROWNING CHILD* BY PETER SINGER

Australian philosopher and ethicist Peter Singer (1946–), author of *Animal Liberation* (1975) and now a professor of bioethics at Princeton University and Laureate Professor of Philosophy at the University of Melbourne, poses an ethical question that appears to point to an obvious choice—until he adds a twist.

Go to: YouTube

Search terms: *"drowning child singer"* (1:58 or 3:18 version; shorter version includes visuals)

A CALLOUS PASSERBY

Kelley L. Ross

Roger Smith, a quite competent swimmer, is out for a leisurely stroll. During the course of his walk he passes by a deserted pier from which a teenage boy who apparently cannot swim has fallen into the water. The boy is screaming for help. Smith recognizes that there is absolutely no danger to himself if he jumps in to save the boy; he could easily succeed if he tried. Nevertheless, he chooses to ignore the boy's cries. The water is cold and he is afraid of catching a cold—he doesn't want to get his good clothes wet, either. "Why should I inconvenience myself for this kid?" Smith says to himself and passes on. Does Smith have a moral obligation to save the boy? If so, should he have a legal obligation ["Good Samaritan" laws] as well?

 SUMMARY   MyWritingLab™

Summarize "What If..." by Sokol. In preparing your summary, consult the Guidelines for Writing Summaries on pages 7–8.

ALTERNATE SUMMARY ASSIGNMENT   MyWritingLab™

> In preparation for writing an argument about Ursula Le Guin's "The Ones Who Walk Away from Omelas," summarize this short story.

A work of fiction is based on narrative logic, not the expository logic of facts and opinions you find in most writing—in Sokol, for instance. For this reason, summarizing a work of fiction differs from summarizing a selection that explains and argues. So for this assignment, you won't be relying on the Guidelines for Writing Summaries.

Instead, briefly relate the main events of the story, providing an account of both the characters and action. Make notes as you read and prepare to summarize "Omelas." A useful strategy is to respond to a journalist's questions: *who* (is the story about), *what* (happens), *where* (does it happen), *when* (does it happen), and *why* (does it happen).

Try using this typical common opening in summarizing a narrative: "*X* tells the story of a _____ who _____." Consult your notes (who, what, etc.) and follow with your account of the broad action of the story and the motivations of its main actors. Write the summary of a narrative using present-tense verbs, as in these examples:

> The happiness of Omelas is conditional on the imprisonment and torture of a single person.

> Periodically, some citizens decide to leave Omelas.

When used in summarizing works of fiction, the present tense is referred to as the "historical" present tense. This tense suggests that the action of a story is always present to readers each time they return to the story. However often we read *The Great Gatsby*, we find Jay Gatsby staring across the water at a green light at the end of a dock. The actors in that and any other fiction are continually present to us, no matter how often we visit with them—as if they are frozen in an eternal *now*.

If you choose to develop the first alternate assignment for the Argument assignment that follows, you'll put this summary to use in the larger paper. Note that, on occasion, you may need to vary your use of the present tense to clarify sequences of events.

CRITIQUE   MyWritingLab™

> Critique Garrett Hardin's use of the lifeboat metaphor to argue against helping the poor.

In writing this critique, develop both an introduction and a conclusion as well as the main body of the critique. See Chapter 2 for advice on critical reading. See particularly the Guidelines for Writing Critiques box on page 68, along with the hints on incorporating quoted material into your own writing on pages 43–49. In general, follow the advice above for developing a critique. Organize and develop the body of your evaluation around specific points, each of which you will develop in one or more paragraphs:

- State each point of evaluation as a clear topic sentence.
- Cite specific examples in the article that illustrate this observation.
- Discuss these examples in two or three follow-on sentences in one paragraph or at greater length in two or more paragraphs.

In preparing to write, consider the following questions. Your responses may help you formulate elements of your critique:

- Classify Hardin's thinking as primarily *teleological* (consequence-based ethics) or *deontological* (morality-based ethics). To help you make this classification, see the selection by Ronald White.
- What assumptions does Hardin make about the ability of progress in technology to make the lifeboat bigger and able to accommodate more people?
- What assumptions does Hardin make about the possibilities of human cooperation to accommodate more people in the lifeboat?
- What assumptions does Hardin make about the worthiness of people who already find themselves *in* the lifeboat? By what right do they find themselves in the boat? Do they deserve to be there? Why?
- To what extent do you agree that the lifeboat metaphor is an appropriate one on which to base policies dealing with the poor? Explain.
- What other metaphor can you think of to describe the obligations of a nation to its citizens and those who wish to become citizens? Does this alternate metaphor suggest policies different than the ones Hardin recommends?
- In what ways can a metaphor (such as Hardin's lifeboat) both open and limit a conversation?
- What evidence do you see of "lifeboat" thinking in congressional debates today?

EXPLANATORY SYNTHESIS   MyWritingLab™

> Explain—in no more than two pages—an ethical dilemma that you've faced in
> your life and the choice you eventually made to resolve it.

This assignment requires you to answer a key question: *What* is an ethical dilemma? Start by defining both parts of that term. Several sources in the chapter define ethics, including the introduction to this chapter. Consider developing explanations for *types* of ethical dilemmas. For a definition of *dilemma*, review the many examples in the chapter and infer a definition; review also what the Velasquez et al. (of the Markkula Center) and White write on the matter.

In relating your experience, be sure to identify all participants in the dilemma and their stakes in the outcome; the issues or values in conflict; the course of action you chose; and the ramifications of that choice. This explanation will form the first part of a later analysis (should you choose the alternate assignment for Analysis). Try to bring real richness to your explanation. Help your readers *feel* the tension of a difficult decision.

In developing your explanation, consult the Guidelines for Writing Syntheses on pages 102–103. More specifically, consider the following:

Suggestions for Developing the Assignment

Develop your explanation systematically, remembering throughout that you're a *story-teller*. Be true to your experience, but at the same time think of your readers. Dilemmas involve conflict; conflict creates tension. How do you plan to create tension for readers so that they'll want to keep reading and learn what you did (or did not do)? How vividly can you describe the participants?

- Provide the who, when, and where of the situation.
- What was the dilemma?
- *Why* was it a dilemma? To answer this question, provide a definition of *dilemma*.
- How did this dilemma involve ethics? To answer this question, start with a clear definition of *ethics*—and you can draw on sources in the chapter, including the chapter introduction, to do so.
- *What choices* did you have?
- Devote a paragraph or two to discussing the choice you made when faced with the dilemma. There's no need to analyze that decision—assessing whether or not you did the right thing. (You may choose to do that later as a part of an analysis assignment.) Instead, focus on your choice. Since this was a dilemma, which means there were (at least) two courses of action open to you, discuss the tension involved in making that choice. What forces were in play—for instance, religious or parental training/rules, the advice of friends or teachers, the expectations of coaches?

Keep in mind that this brief paper is an explanation—not, at this point, an analysis of your decision or a consideration of whether or not you did the right thing. The success of this paper is based on how carefully you can pre-sent your experience in a way that enables readers to appreciate an ethical dilemma. In defining this dilemma, draw on the sources in this chapter. Be sure to set up your references to those sources (whether summaries, paraphrases, or quotations) by using appropriate citation format, most likely MLA (see pp. 232–238).

ANALYSIS   MyWritingLab™

> Choose an ethical dilemma from this chapter (from either the casebook or
> Sokol's article—The Runaway Trolley, The Cave Explorers, Thomson's Violinist).
> Analyze this dilemma using two (or more) ethical principles as discussed in
> White's "Moral Inquiry" or the Markkula framework (Velasquez et al.).

This is a *comparative* analysis. That is, you will be applying at least two principles to a particular case in order to reveal insights that will suggest (possibly) different courses of action. As a conclusion, recommend one course of action over another and justify this recommendation. In organizing your thoughts and then writing the analysis, follow either the Guidelines for Writing Analyses on page 181 in Chapter 6 or the Markkula framework (Velasquez et al.) on pages 274–279.

Suggestions for Developing the Assignment

This assignment requires two parallel analyses of a single case—and a follow-on comparison-and-contrast. Before beginning, you may find it useful to review the discussion of comparison-and-contrast on pages 165–172. We recommend the following structure for organizing your paper:

- Paragraph 1: Summarize the case and provide a context for its analysis. Let readers know why they should care about the case and your discussion.
- Paragraph 2: Define the first analytic tool or principle—for instance, teleological (consequence-based) ethics or deontological (morality-based) ethics. Recall that there are other analytic tools, or principles, discussed in the readings.
- Paragraphs 3–4: Apply the first principle to the case, concluding with a course of action consistent with that principle.
- Paragraph 5: Define the second analytic tool or principle.
- Paragraphs 6–7: Apply the second principle to the case, concluding with a course of action consistent with that principle.
- Paragraphs 8–10: Compare and contrast your applications of the ethical principles. Use the "criteria" approach for comparison-and-contrast. (See pp. 166–167.) Choose three criteria, or key points, for comparison and contrast and discuss the two ethical principles and their applications to the case.
- Paragraph 11+: Argue that one ethical principle and the decision following from it makes for the better outcome.

 ALTERNATE ANALYSIS ASSIGNMENT   MyWritingLab™

Explain an ethical dilemma that you've faced in your life and the choice you made. (See the assignment for Explanatory Synthesis.) Analyze that choice based on at least two ethical principles discussed in this chapter, using the Markkula framework (Velasquez et al.) to conduct the analysis. Conclude by assessing whether or not you "did the right thing." Would you change your decision today, had you to decide all over again?

ARGUMENT   MyWritingLab™

Suppose a friend in another class looked over the cases you've been studying in this chapter and asserted that many of the dilemmas they presented—the runaway trolley, for example—were so farfetched and unrealistic that they were useless as a guide to ethical decision making. Your classmate also raised questions about the ethical frameworks themselves, contending that they were too complicated for most people to apply in everyday situations. Develop an argument responding to these assertions—one expressing agreement, disagreement, or something in between.

Suggestions for Developing the Assignment

- A paragraph or so laying out in somewhat greater detail the situation outlined in the assignment above.

- A paragraph or two briefly describing some of (1) the cases presented in this chapter and (2) the ethical frameworks. Cite examples that appear, at least on the surface, to support your friend's assertions.

- *Thesis:* A paragraph detailing your own response to your friend's assertions. Conclude this paragraph with a clearly worded statement—your thesis—explaining the extent to which you agree and/or disagree with your friend.

- Several paragraphs in which you systematically respond to your friend's assertions. Discuss some of the representative cases presented in the chapter in light of the argument that they are (or are not) useful as guides to ethical decision making. Explain why the particularly "farfetched" examples may (or may not) be useful for this purpose. Note, for example, Sokol's explanation of the significance of the Thomson's violinist scenario. Do you find this explanation plausible? Discuss also some of the ethical frameworks presented in the chapter in light of how easy (or how difficult) they might be in helping to resolve ethical dilemmas in everyday life.

- A paragraph of counterargument, in which you concede that others might justifiably find fault with your central argument. Explain your concession.

- A "nevertheless" section, in which you respond to the counterargument(s) and reaffirm your own position.

- A paragraph or two of conclusion. See Chapter 3 (pp. 89–95) for advice on concluding your argument.

It's up to you to decide *where* you place the individual elements of this argument synthesis. It's also up to you to decide which sources to use and what logic to present in defense of your claim. See pages 144–148 and pages 161–167 for help in thinking about structuring and supporting your argument.

ALTERNATE ARGUMENT ASSIGNMENT #1 MyWritingLab™

Read Ursula Le Guin's "The Ones Who Walk Away from Omelas" and decide whether or not you would be one of the people who walked away. Draw on other selections in this chapter to argue for your choice. Use your summary of Le Guin from the earlier alternate summary assignment if you chose that assignment. As you put that summary to use in your argument, you'll have to change its form a bit, presenting the summary in parts:

- a main section, early in the paper, which relates the overall arc of the story, its actors, and its main themes.
- *brief* summaries of individual parts of the story, which call your reader's attention to particular scenes that you will discuss, each in its turn.

 ALTERNATE ARGUMENT ASSIGNMENT #2 MyWritingLab™

Two cases in this chapter turn on the rightness of a person's decision to speak up or remain silent when confronted with an apparent ethical lapse: the "Collapsed Mine" (p. 271) and "Should I Protect a Patient" (p. 291).

Building on the ethical principles you've learned about in this chapter, develop guidelines to help *you* decide when to speak or remain silent when confronted with dilemmas. That is, choose among ethical principles or combine them as you see fit; then shape them into a personal approach. Argue in support of this approach, showing its strengths—and acknowledging its weaknesses—as you apply it to some or all of the cases just mentioned. If you're feeling ambitious, apply your approach to the case of Edward Snowden, alluded to briefly in the introduction to this chapter (page 264). You'll find detailed accounts of Snowden's leaks in online news sources.

A Note on Incorporating Quotations and Paraphrases

Identify those sources that you intend to use in your synthesis. Working with a phrase, sentence, or brief passage from each, use a variety of the techniques discussed in the Incorporating Quotations into Your Sentences section (pp. 43–49) to advance your argument. Some of these sentences should demonstrate the use of ellipses and brackets. (See pp. 45–48 in Chapter 1.) Paraphrase passages as needed, incorporating the paraphrases into your paragraphs.

MyWritingLab™   Visit Ch. 9 Ethical Dilemmas in Everyday Life in MyWritingLab to test your understanding of the chapter objectives.

Chapter 10

The Roar of the Tiger Mom

In January 2011, an op-ed adapted from Yale Law School professor Amy Chua's book *Battle Hymn of the Tiger Mother* ignited a furious national debate over parenting methods. The online edition of the newspaper in which the excerpt appeared records over 8,800 responses to the initial op-ed in which Chua lists the activities she does not allow her children to do (including attend a sleepover, watch TV or play computer games, or get any grade less than A). In the piece, Chua also describes her efforts to motivate her children to excellence (by calling one child "garbage," rejecting an amateurish birthday card as unworthy, and driving her 7-year-old to tears after she is unable, after hours of practice, to perfectly execute a complex piano piece). A cover story in *Time* magazine reports that when Chua appeared on the *Today* show, "the usually sunny host Meredith Viera could hardly contain her contempt as she read aloud a sample of viewer comments: 'She's a monster'; 'The way she raised her kids is outrageous'; 'Where is the love, the acceptance?'"

But Chua's ideas and methods resonated with many readers. At a time when American students are ranked seventeenth in the world in reading, twenty-third in science, and thirty-first in math, can the country settle for anything less than excellence? Can American citizens hope to compete with China and other rising economies in the global marketplace if they find academic mediocrity acceptable? And on the personal level, are parents helping their children if they accept anything less than the best, if they strive, in "Western" manner, not to damage their children's unearned self-esteem and to protect them from the consequences of failure?

And yet—what are the psychological consequences of the "Chinese" parenting methods advocated by Chua? To what extent should we allow children a childhood that is filled with play and exploration, not rigid goals? What is Chua's goal beyond strictly defined academic excellence? Does academic excellence correspond with success in one's profession? With one's broader happiness in life? Does a relentless focus on academic excellence in any way limit developing social skills? (The final selection in this chapter, new to this edition, reports on a recent study that provided some answers to these questions.)

These issues are the subject of the readings that follow. You'll be asked to consider such questions as you prepare several writing assignments of the type discussed in the previous chapters. These assignments will culminate in an argument synthesis, a paper that will draw upon what you have already written for the summary, the critique, the explanatory synthesis, and the analysis.

Preceding the reading selections is a group of activities that will help prepare you for the writing assignments to come. The writing assignments themselves follow the readings.

READ; PREPARE TO WRITE

As you read these selections, prepare for the assignments by marking up the texts: Write notes to yourself in the margins and comment on what the authors have said.

And to prepare for the more ambitious of the assignments that follow—the explanatory and argument syntheses—consider drawing up a topic list of your sources as you read. For each topic about which two or more authors have something to say, jot down notes and page references. Here's an example entry:

> *Shaming/threatening children who underperform*
>
> Amy Chua: Sophia incident ("garbage") (p. 306); Lulu incidents ("Little White Donkey") (p. 308)
>
> Hanna Rosin: birthday card; rejection of Chua's approach (p. 310)
>
> Elizabeth Kolbert: Kolbert's sons' reaction to the Sophia episode (p. 318)

Such a topic list, keyed to your sources, will spare you the frustration of reading eight or nine sources and flipping through them later, saying, "Now where did I read that?" In the sample entry, we see four authors speaking to the wisdom of shaming or threatening underperforming children. At this early point, you don't need to know how you might write a paper based on this or any other topic. But a robust list with multiple topics and accurate notes for each lays the groundwork for your own discussion later and puts you in a good position to write a synthesis.

As it happens, the sample entry above should come in handy when you're preparing to write your own explanatory and argument syntheses on the subject of tiger moms. Creating a topic list with multiple entries will take you a bit more time as you read, but it will save you time as you write.

GROUP ASSIGNMENT #1: MAKE A TOPIC LIST

Working in groups of three or four, create a topic list for the selections in this chapter, making sure to jot down notes and page references for each. Here are some entries to get you started; find other topics common to two or more sources.

(continued)

- overriding importance of children excelling academically—and musically
- importance for children in not wasting time (according to Chua) on nonacademic activities
- importance of practice and hard work for a child's sense of achievement and self-esteem
- effects of relentless academic focus on a child's creativity and/or social skills
- factors contributing to American competitiveness (or decline) in a global economy

GROUP ASSIGNMENT #2: CREATE A TOPIC WEB

Working in groups of three or four, create a network, or web, of connections among selected topics. That is, determine which topics relate or "speak" to other topics.

Articulate these connections in a series of different webs, understanding that not all topics will be connected to each web. For example, draw a line from one topic (say, the overriding importance of children excelling academically) to another (say, factors contributing to American competitiveness in a global economy). How are these topics related? As a group, generate as many topic webs as possible and, for each, as many connections as possible. At the conclusion of the session, you'll have in hand not only the fruits of Assignment #1, multiple authors discussing common topics, but you'll also have a potential connection *among* topics—basically, the necessary raw material for writing your syntheses.

Note that one synthesis—a single paper—couldn't possibly refer to every topic, or every connection among topics, that you have found. Your skill in preparing and writing a synthesis depends on your ability to *identify* closely related topics and to make and develop a claim that links and is supported by these topics.

The readings on "tiger moms" follow. After the readings, you will find a series of linked assignments that will lead you to write some combination of summary, critique, analysis, explanatory synthesis, and argument synthesis.

ADAPTED FROM BATTLE HYMN OF THE TIGER MOTHER

Amy Chua

Amy Chua, a professor at Yale Law School, is the author of *The World on Fire: How Exporting Free Market Democracy Breeds Ethnic Hatred and Global Instability* (2002), *Day of Empire: How Hyperpowers Rise to Global Dominance—and Why They Fall* (2007), and *Battle Hymn of the Tiger Mother* (2011), from which the following selection was excerpted as a newspaper op-ed on January 8, 2011. The editors of the newspaper gave the excerpt a controversial title, referenced in the responses that follow Chua's piece, most likely in an attempt (a successful one) to attract attention and encourage controversy.

A lot of people wonder how Chinese parents raise such stereotypically successful kids. They wonder what these parents do to produce so many math whizzes and music prodigies, what it's like inside the family, and whether they could do it too. Well, I can tell them, because I've done it. Here are some things my daughters, Sophia and Louisa, were never allowed to do:

- attend a sleepover
- have a playdate
- be in a school play
- complain about not being in a school play
- watch TV or play computer games
- choose their own extracurricular activities
- get any grade less than an A
- not be the No. 1 student in every subject except gym and drama
- play any instrument other than the piano or violin
- not play the piano or violin.

I'm using the term "Chinese mother" loosely. I know some Korean, Indian, Jamaican, Irish and Ghanaian parents who qualify too. Conversely, I know some mothers of Chinese heritage, almost always born in the West, who are not Chinese mothers, by choice or otherwise. I'm also using the term "Western parents" loosely. Western parents come in all varieties.

All the same, even when Western parents think they're being strict, they usually don't come close to being Chinese mothers. For example, my Western friends who consider themselves strict make their children practice their instruments 30 minutes every day. An hour at most. For a Chinese mother, the first hour is the easy part. It's hours two and three that get tough.

Despite our squeamishness about cultural stereotypes, there are tons of studies out there showing marked and quantifiable differences between Chinese and Westerners when it comes to parenting. In one study of 50 Western American mothers and 48 Chinese immigrant mothers, almost 70% of the Western mothers said either that "stressing academic success is not good for children" or that "parents need to foster the idea that learning is fun." By contrast, roughly 0% of the Chinese mothers felt the same way. Instead, the vast majority of the Chinese mothers said that they believe their children can be "the best" students, that "academic achievement reflects successful parenting," and that if children did not excel at school then there was "a problem" and parents "were not doing their job." Other studies indicate that compared to Western parents, Chinese parents spend approximately 10 times as long every day drilling academic activities with their children. By contrast, Western kids are more likely to participate in sports teams.

Adapted from *Battle Hymn of the Tiger Mother* by Amy Chua, copyright © 2011 by Amy Chua. Used by permission of The Penguin Press, a division of Penguin Group (USA) LLC.

5   What Chinese parents understand is that nothing is fun until you're good at it. To get good at anything you have to work, and children on their own never want to work, which is why it is crucial to override their preferences. This often requires fortitude on the part of the parents because the child will resist; things are always hardest at the beginning, which is where Western parents tend to give up. But if done properly, the Chinese strategy produces a virtuous circle. Tenacious practice, practice, practice is crucial for excellence; rote repetition is underrated in America. Once a child starts to excel at something—whether it's math, piano, pitching or ballet—he or she gets praise, admiration and satisfaction. This builds confidence and makes the once not-fun activity fun. This in turn makes it easier for the parent to get the child to work even more.

Chinese parents can get away with things that Western parents can't. Once when I was young—maybe more than once—when I was extremely disrespectful to my mother, my father angrily called me "garbage" in our native Hokkien dialect. It worked really well. I felt terrible and deeply ashamed of what I had done. But it didn't damage my self-esteem or anything like that. I knew exactly how highly he thought of me. I didn't actually think I was worthless or feel like a piece of garbage.

As an adult, I once did the same thing to Sophia, calling her garbage in English when she acted extremely disrespectfully toward me. When I mentioned that I had done this at a dinner party, I was immediately ostracized. One guest named Marcy got so upset she broke down in tears and had to leave early. My friend Susan, the host, tried to rehabilitate me with the remaining guests.

The fact is that Chinese parents can do things that would seem unimaginable—even legally actionable—to Westerners. Chinese mothers can say to their daughters, "Hey fatty— lose some weight." By contrast, Western parents have to tiptoe around the issue, talking in terms of "health" and never ever mentioning the f-word, and their kids still end up in therapy for eating disorders and negative self-image. (I also once heard a Western father toast his adult daughter by calling her "beautiful and incredibly competent." She later told me that made her feel like garbage.)

Chinese parents can order their kids to get straight As. Western parents can only ask their kids to try their best. Chinese parents can say, "You're lazy. All your classmates are getting ahead of you." By contrast, Western parents have to struggle with their own conflicted feelings about achievement, and try to persuade themselves that they're not disappointed about how their kids turned out.

10   I've thought long and hard about how Chinese parents can get away with what they do. I think there are three big differences between the Chinese and Western parental mindsets.

First, I've noticed that Western parents are extremely anxious about their children's self-esteem. They worry about how their children will feel if they fail at something, and they constantly try to reassure their children about how good they are notwithstanding a mediocre performance on a test or at a recital. In other words, Western parents are concerned about their children's psyches. Chinese parents aren't. They assume strength, not fragility, and as a result they behave very differently.

For example, if a child comes home with an A-minus on a test, a Western parent will most likely praise the child. The Chinese mother will gasp in horror and ask what went wrong. If the child comes home with a B on the test, some Western parents will still praise the child. Other Western parents will sit their child down and express disapproval, but they will be careful not to make their child feel inadequate or insecure, and they will not call their child "stupid," "worthless" or "a disgrace." Privately, the Western parents may worry that their child does not test well or have aptitude in the subject or that there is something wrong with the curriculum and possibly the whole school. If the child's grades do not improve, they may eventually schedule a meeting with the school principal to challenge the way the subject is being taught or to call into question the teacher's credentials.

If a Chinese child gets a B—which would never happen—there would first be a screaming, hair-tearing explosion. The devastated Chinese mother would then get dozens, maybe hundreds of practice tests and work through them with her child for as long as it takes to get the grade up to an A.

Chinese parents demand perfect grades because they believe that their child can get them. If their child doesn't get them, the Chinese parent assumes it's because the child didn't work hard enough. That's why the solution to sub-standard performance is always to excoriate, punish and shame the child. The Chinese parent believes that their child will be strong enough to take the shaming and to improve from it. (And when Chinese kids do excel, there is plenty of ego-inflating parental praise lavished in the privacy of the home.)

15   Second, Chinese parents believe that their kids owe them everything. The reason for this is a little unclear, but it's probably a combination of Confucian filial piety and the fact that the parents have sacrificed and done so much for their children. (And it's true that Chinese mothers get in the trenches, putting in long grueling hours personally tutoring, training, interrogating and spying on their kids.) Anyway, the understanding is that Chinese children must spend their lives repaying their parents by obeying them and making them proud.

By contrast, I don't think most Westerners have the same view of children being permanently indebted to their parents. My husband, Jed, actually has the opposite view. "Children don't choose their parents," he once said to me. "They don't even choose to be born. It's parents who foist life on their kids, so it's the parents' responsibility to provide for them. Kids don't owe their parents anything. Their duty will be to their own kids." This strikes me as a terrible deal for the Western parent.

Third, Chinese parents believe that they know what is best for their children and therefore override all of their children's own desires and preferences. That's why Chinese daughters can't have boyfriends in high school and why Chinese kids can't go to sleepaway camp. It's also why no Chinese kid would ever dare say to their mother, "I got a part in the school play! I'm Villager Number Six. I'll have to stay after school for rehearsal every day from 3:00 to 7:00, and I'll also need a ride on weekends." God help any Chinese kid who tried that one.

Don't get me wrong: It's not that Chinese parents don't care about their children. Just the opposite. They would give up anything for their children. It's just an entirely different parenting model.

Here's a story in favor of coercion, Chinese-style. Lulu was about 7, still playing two instruments, and working on a piano piece called "The Little White Donkey" by the French composer Jacques Ibert. The piece is really cute—you can just imagine a little donkey ambling along a country road with its master—but it's also incredibly difficult for young players because the two hands have to keep schizophrenically different rhythms.

20   Lulu couldn't do it. We worked on it nonstop for a week, drilling each of her hands separately, over and over. But whenever we tried putting the hands together, one always morphed into the other, and everything fell apart. Finally, the day before her lesson, Lulu announced in exasperation that she was giving up and stomped off.

"Get back to the piano now," I ordered.
"You can't make me."
"Oh yes, I can."

Back at the piano, Lulu made me pay. She punched, thrashed and kicked. She grabbed the music score and tore it to shreds. I taped the score back together and encased it in a plastic shield so that it could never be destroyed again. Then I hauled Lulu's dollhouse to the car and told her I'd donate it to the Salvation Army piece by piece if she didn't have "The Little White Donkey" perfect by the next day. When Lulu said, "I thought you were going to the Salvation Army, why are you still here?" I threatened her with no lunch, no dinner, no Christmas or Hanukkah presents, no birthday parties for two, three, four years. When she still kept playing it wrong, I told her she was purposely working herself into a frenzy because she was secretly afraid she couldn't do it. I told her to stop being lazy, cowardly, self-indulgent and pathetic.

25   Jed took me aside. He told me to stop insulting Lulu—which I wasn't even doing, I was just motivating her—and that he didn't think threatening Lulu was helpful. Also, he said, maybe Lulu really just couldn't do the technique—perhaps she didn't have the coordination yet—had I considered that possibility?

"You just don't believe in her," I accused.
"That's ridiculous," Jed said scornfully. "Of course I do."
"Sophia could play the piece when she was this age."
"But Lulu and Sophia are different people," Jed pointed out.

30   "Oh no, not this," I said, rolling my eyes. "Everyone is special in their special own way," I mimicked sarcastically. "Even losers are special in their own special way. Well don't worry, you don't have to lift a finger. I'm willing to put in as long as it takes, and I'm happy to be the one hated. And you can be the one they adore because you make them pancakes and take them to Yankees games."

I rolled up my sleeves and went back to Lulu. I used every weapon and tactic I could think of. We worked right through dinner into the night, and I wouldn't let Lulu get up, not for water, not even to go to the bathroom. The house became a war zone, and I lost my voice yelling, but still there seemed to be only negative progress, and even I began to have doubts.

Then, out of the blue, Lulu did it. Her hands suddenly came together—her right and left hands each doing their own imperturbable thing—just like that.

Lulu realized it the same time I did. I held my breath. She tried it tentatively again. Then she played it more confidently and faster, and still the rhythm held. A moment later, she was beaming.

"Mommy, look—it's easy!" After that, she wanted to play the piece over and over and wouldn't leave the piano. That night, she came to sleep in my bed, and we snuggled and hugged, cracking each other up. When she performed "The Little White Donkey" at a recital a few weeks later, parents came up to me and said, "What a perfect piece for Lulu—it's so spunky and so *her*."

35   Even Jed gave me credit for that one. Western parents worry a lot about their children's self-esteem. But as a parent, one of the worst things you can do for your child's self-esteem is to let them give up. On the flip side, there's nothing better for building confidence than learning you can do something you thought you couldn't.

There are all these new books out there portraying Asian mothers as scheming, callous, overdriven people indifferent to their kids' true interests. For their part, many Chinese secretly believe that they care more about their children and are willing to sacrifice much more for them than Westerners, who seem perfectly content to let their children turn out badly. I think it's a misunderstanding on both sides. All decent parents want to do what's best for their children. The Chinese just have a totally different idea of how to do that.

Western parents try to respect their children's individuality, encouraging them to pursue their true passions, supporting their choices, and providing positive reinforcement and a nurturing environment. By contrast, the Chinese believe that the best way to protect their children is by preparing them for the future, letting them see what they're capable of, and arming them with skills, work habits and inner confidence that no one can ever take away.

MOTHER INFERIOR?

Hanna Rosin

Hanna Rosin is a contributing editor at the *Atlantic* and is working on a book based on her recent *Atlantic* cover story, "The End of Men." "Mother Inferior?" first appeared in the *Wall Street Journal* on January 15, 2011.

The other day I was playing a game called "Kids on Stage" with my 2-year-old. I had to act out "tiger," so I got down on all fours and roared. He laughed, so I roared even louder, which only made him laugh more. Eventually he came up to me, patted my head and said "kitty kat" with benevolent condescension. This perfectly sums up my status in the animal pack of mothers defined by Amy Chua's *Battle Hymn of the Tiger Mother*. There are the fierce tigers who churn out child prodigies, and then there are the pussycats who waste their afternoons playing useless board games and get bested by their own toddlers.

In pretty much every way, I am the weak-willed, pathetic Western parent that Ms. Chua describes. My children go on playdates and sleepovers; in fact

I wish they would go on more of them. When they give me lopsided, hastily drawn birthday cards, I praise them as if they were Matisse, sometimes with tears in my eyes. (Ms. Chua threw back one quickly scribbled birthday card, saying "I reject this," and told her daughters they could do better.) My middle son is skilled at precisely the two extracurricular activities Ms. Chua most mocks: He just got a minor part in the school play as a fisherman, and he is a master of the drums, the instrument that she claims leads directly to using drugs (I'm not sure if she is joking or not).

I would be thrilled, of course, if my eldest child made it to Carnegie Hall at 14, which is the great crescendo of the Chua family story (although I would make sure to tell my other two children that they were fabulous in other ways!). But the chances that I would threaten to burn all her stuffed animals unless she played a piano piece perfectly, or to donate her favorite doll house to the Salvation Army piece by piece, as Ms. Chua did with her daughter, are exactly zero. It's not merely that such vigilant attention to how my daughter spends every minute of her afternoon is time-consuming and exhausting; after all, it takes time to play "Kids on Stage" and to drive to drum lessons, too. It's more that I don't have it in me. I just don't have the demented drive to pull it off.

Many American parents will read *Battle Hymn of the Tiger Mother* and feel somewhat defensive and regretful. *Well, I do make my Johnny practice his guitar twice a week! Or, Look, I have this nice discipline chart on my refrigerator with frowny faces for when he's rude at dinner!* But I don't feel all that defensive. In fact, I think Ms. Chua has the diagnosis of American childhood exactly backward. What privileged American children need is not more skills and rules and math drills. They need to lighten up and roam free, to express themselves in ways not dictated by their upright, over-invested parents. Like Ms. Chua, many American parents suffer from the delusion that, with careful enough control, a child can be made perfect. Ms. Chua does it with Suzuki piano books and insults, while many of my friends do it with organic baby food and playrooms filled with fully curated wooden toys. In both cases, the result is the same: an excess of children who are dutiful proto-adults, always responsible and good, incapable of proper childhood rebellion.

5   In the days since Ms. Chua's book has come out, the media have brought up horror stories of child prodigies gone bad, including this 16-year-old who stabbed her mother to death after complaining that her Chinese immigrant parents held her to impossibly high standards. Most prodigy stories, I imagine, involve more complicated emotions. (The Amy Chua of the book, by the way, is more seductive than the distilled media version. She is remarkably self-aware. "The truth is, I'm not good at enjoying life," she writes, and she never hesitates to tell stories that she knows make her look beastly. It's worth noting that, in TV and radio interviews about the book, she's been trending more pussycat).

"Mother Inferior?" by Hanna Rosin, January 16, 2011. Reprinted by permission of the *Wall Street Journal*, Copyright © 2011 Dow Jones & Company, Inc. All rights reserved Worldwide. License number 2897151259352.

I have a good friend who was raised by a Chinese-style mother, although her parents were actually German. Her mother pushed her to practice the violin for eight hours a day, and she rarely saw other people her age. Now she is my age, and she does not hate her mother or even resent her. She is grateful to her mother for instilling in her a drive and focus that she otherwise would have lacked. What she does hate is music, because it carries for her associations of loneliness and torture. She hasn't picked up the violin in a decade, and these days, she says, classical music leaves her cold. It's not an uncommon sentiment among prodigies: "I hate tennis," Andre Agassi says on the first page of his autobiography, "Open," "hate it with a dark and secret passion, and always have."

The oddest part of Ms. Chua's parenting prescription is that it exists wholly apart from any passion or innate talent. The Chua women rarely express pure love of music; instead they express joy at having mastered it. Ms. Chua writes that she listened to CDs of Itzhak Perlman to figure out "why he sounded so good." This conception of child prodigies is not just Chinese. It is the extreme expression of the modern egalitarian notion of genius, as described by Malcolm Gladwell in *Outliers*. Anyone can be a genius, if they just put in 10,000 hours of practice! It doesn't matter if they can carry a tune or have especially limber fingers. They don't even have to like music.

But why not wait for your children to show some small spark of talent or interest in an activity before you force them to work at it for hours a day? What would be so bad if they followed their own interests and became an expert flutist, or a soccer star or even a master tightrope walker? What's so special about the violin and the piano?

Ms. Chua's most compelling argument is that happiness comes from mastery. "What Chinese parents understand is that nothing is fun until you're good at it." There is some truth to this, of course. But there is no reason to believe that calling your child "lazy" or "stupid" or "worthless" is a better way to motivate her to be good than some other more gentle but persistent mode. There is a vast world between perfection and loserdom. With her own children, Ms. Chua does not just want them to be good at what they do; she wants them to be better than everyone else.

10   "Children on their own never want to work," Ms. Chua writes, but in my experience this is not at all true. Left to their own devices, many children of this generation still have giant superegos and a mad drive to succeed. They want to run faster than their siblings, be smarter than their classmates and save the world from environmental disaster. In my household, it's a struggle to get my children to steal a cookie from the cookie jar without immediately confessing.

Before I had children, I worried about all the wrong things. I was raised by (immigrant) parents who did not have a lot of money, and so I spent my childhood roaming the streets of Queens looking for an open handball court. My children, by contrast, have been raised by relatively well-off parents who can afford to send them to good schools and drum lessons. I wanted them to be coddled and never to experience hardship. But childhood, like life, doesn't work that way. Privilege does not shield a child from being painfully shy or awkward around peers or generally ostracized. There are a thousand ways a child's life can be difficult, and it's a parent's job to help them navigate through them.

Because Ms. Chua really likes bullet points, I will offer some of my own:

- Success will not make you happy.
- Happiness is the great human quest.
- Children have to find happiness themselves.
- It is better to have a happy, moderately successful child than a miserable high-achiever.

"Western parents," Ms. Chua writes, "have to struggle with their own conflicted feelings about achievement and try and persuade themselves that they're not disappointed in how their kids turned out." With that, she really has our number. At the present moment in Western parenting, we believe that our children are special and entitled, but we do not have the guts or the tools to make that reality true for them. This explains, I think, a large part of the fascination with Ms. Chua's book.

But *Battle Hymn of the Tiger Mother* will lead us down the wrong path. The answer is not to aim for more effective child-perfecting techniques; it is to give up altogether on trying to perfect our children. Now I look upon those aimless days wandering the streets of Queens with fondness, because my life since then, starting the moment I entered a competitive high school, has been one ladder rung after another.

15   In her book, Ms. Chua refers, with some disdain, to her mother-in-law's belief that childhood should be full of "spontaneity, freedom, discovery and experience." My mother-in-law believes that, too, and she is especially gifted at facilitating it with whatever tools are at hand: a cardboard box, some pots and pans, torn envelopes. One afternoon I watched her play with my then-2-year old daughter for hours with some elephant toothpick holders and Play-Doh. I suppose that I could quantify what my daughter learned in those few hours: the letter E, the meaning of "pachyderm," who Hannibal was and how to love her grandmother 2% more. But the real point is that they earned themselves knee scabs marching across those imaginary Alps, and pretty soon it was time for a nap.

Amy Chua Is a Wimp

David Brooks

David Brooks is a columnist for the *New York Times* and a commentator on the PBS News Hour and National Public Radio. He has written for the *Wall Street Journal* and the *Washington Times* and has been an editor for the *Weekly Standard*, the *Atlantic*, and *Newsweek*. His books include the anthology *Backward and Upward: The New Conservative Writing* (1996), a book of cultural commentary, *Bobos in Paradise: The New Upper Class and How They Got There* (2000), and *On Paradise Drive: How We Live Now (And Always Have) in the Future Tense* (2004). This article appeared in the *New York Times* on January 17, 2011.

Sometime early last week, a large slice of educated America decided that Amy Chua is a menace to society. Chua, as you probably know, is the Yale professor who has written a bracing critique of what she considers the weak, cuddling American parenting style.

Chua didn't let her own girls go out on play dates or sleepovers. She didn't let them watch TV or play video games or take part in garbage activities like crafts. Once, one of her daughters came in second to a Korean kid in a math competition, so Chua made the girl do 2,000 math problems a night until she regained her supremacy. Once, her daughters gave her birthday cards of insufficient quality. Chua rejected them and demanded new cards. Once, she threatened to burn all of one of her daughter's stuffed animals unless she played a piece of music perfectly.

As a result, Chua's daughters get straight As and have won a series of musical competitions.

In her book, *Battle Hymn of the Tiger Mother*, Chua delivers a broadside against American parenting even as she mocks herself for her own extreme "Chinese" style. She says American parents lack authority and produce entitled children who aren't forced to live up to their abilities.

5   The furious denunciations began flooding my in-box a week ago. Chua plays into America's fear of national decline. Here's a Chinese parent working really hard (and, by the way, there are a billion more of her) and her kids are going to crush ours. Furthermore (and this Chua doesn't appreciate), she is not really rebelling against American-style parenting; she is the logical extension of the prevailing elite practices. She does everything over-pressuring upper-middle-class parents are doing. She's just hard core.

Her critics echoed the familiar themes. Her kids can't possibly be happy or truly creative. They'll grow up skilled and compliant but without the audacity to be great. She's destroying their love for music. There's a reason Asian-American women between the ages of 15 and 24 have such high suicide rates.

I have the opposite problem with Chua. I believe she's coddling her children. She's protecting them from the most intellectually demanding activities because she doesn't understand what's cognitively difficult and what isn't.

Practicing a piece of music for four hours requires focused attention, but it is nowhere near as cognitively demanding as a sleepover with 14-year-old girls. Managing status rivalries, negotiating group dynamics, understanding social norms, navigating the distinction between self and group—these and other social tests impose cognitive demands that blow away any intense tutoring session or a class at Yale.

"Amy Chua Is a Wimp" by David Brooks from the *New York Times*, January 17, 2011. © 2011 New York Times. All rights reserved. Used by permission and protected by the Copyright Laws of the United States. The printing, copying, redistribution, or retransmission of this Content without express written permission is prohibited.

Yet mastering these arduous skills is at the very essence of achievement. Most people work in groups. We do this because groups are much more efficient at solving problems than individuals (swimmers are often motivated to have their best times as part of relay teams, not in individual events). Moreover, the performance of a group does not correlate well with the average I.Q. of the group or even with the I.Q.'s of the smartest members.

10   Researchers at the Massachusetts Institute of Technology and Carnegie Mellon have found that groups have a high collective intelligence when members of a group are good at reading each others' emotions—when they take turns speaking, when the inputs from each member are managed fluidly, when they detect each others' inclinations and strengths.

Participating in a well-functioning group is really hard. It requires the ability to trust people outside your kinship circle, read intonations and moods, understand how the psychological pieces each person brings to the room can and cannot fit together.

This skill set is not taught formally, but it is imparted through arduous experiences. These are exactly the kinds of difficult experiences Chua shelters her children from by making them rush home to hit the homework table.

Chua would do better to see the classroom as a cognitive break from the truly arduous tests of childhood. Where do they learn how to manage people? Where do they learn to construct and manipulate metaphors? Where do they learn to perceive details of a scene the way a hunter reads a landscape? Where do they learn how to detect their own shortcomings? Where do they learn how to put themselves in others' minds and anticipate others' reactions?

These and a million other skills are imparted by the informal maturity process and are not developed if formal learning monopolizes a child's time.

15   So I'm not against the way Chua pushes her daughters. And I loved her book as a courageous and thought-provoking read. It's also more supple than her critics let on. I just wish she wasn't so soft and indulgent. I wish she recognized that in some important ways the school cafeteria is more intellectually demanding than the library. And I hope her daughters grow up to write their own books, and maybe learn the skills to better anticipate how theirs will be received.

TIGER MOTHER STIRS REFLECTIONS ON PARENTHOOD

Tina Griego

Tina Griego reports for the *Denver Post*, where this article first appeared on January 20, 2011.

Yes, of course, I read the Tiger Mother in *The Wall Street Journal*. I'm a modern-day mother of two children, one in middle school, one in third grade. By definition, this makes me neurotic.

Naturally, I'm compelled to read a newspaper article called 'Why Chinese Mothers Are Superior'—a headline that author and Tiger Mother Amy Chua complained about, but for which she should be giving an unknown copy editor a cut of her book profits.

The modern-day neurotic parent gravitates toward that which is guaranteed to shake confidence in his or her parenting ability. We are expert self-flagellators. Typically, this is offset by a similar pull toward that which makes us feel superior in our parenting skills, the cool balm of sanctimony. Chua offered one-stop shopping. Self-doubt undone by horror. Her teenage daughter played Carnegie Hall! She called her daughter garbage!

5   A million words have been written in response to the *Journal* excerpt, most amounting to what we all already know: Balance in all things. Which is boring.

I have to wonder, not for the first time, what my grandmothers would make of all this churning of the parental waters. I figure they'd understand Chua, or, at the very least, share her confidence. Grandmas Jacquez and Griego were not, as Chua is, born of immigrants, but they were children of the Depression, children of laborers, and parental doubt was a self-indulgence. You work hard. Your children obey, and if, with the imposition of the values of obedience and duty to family, childhood is fleeting, so it must be. When the children are old enough, they will work hard. If you've taught them well, they will succeed and, in turn, take care of you.

In fact, my grandmothers' view was not long ago expressed to me by a 20-something refugee from Bhutan, Deg Adhikari. 'My parents, they do not have school. They just work and work for us. Now it is our job to make them happy and to work for the coming generations.'

How long do you think it will be before the Adhikari family and its descendants succumb to the lure of the more individualistic, more hedonistic culture that will surround them here? If you think you detect a strain of lament in the question, you would not be mistaken. Yeah, your kids are obedient and respectful now, a Chicano friend once teased a Mexican immigrant friend, but just wait until the U.S. gets ahold of them.

What's been most interesting about the discussion Chua provoked is not whether she's a good parent or bad parent. No, I'm more intrigued by how she has chosen to operate within the currents of her culture, economic class and generational expectation, in the way she negotiated the sometimes-competing values of the three. Most parents engage in this negotiation. It's inevitable. People are shaped, though not bound, by their culture, class and time, and the influences of each rise and fall.

10   A small example: I come from small-town, Catholic, been-here-forever Latino New Mexico. I grew up and away from the communal values of my family. The times holding sway over culture. I moved, only for a year, to a village in Japan and a culture much like my grandparents': patriarchal, disciplined, consensus-oriented, shame-conscious and so averse to risk.

We went out for pancakes when I returned. But this was the conversation in the car as we left the airport. Dad: 'Let's go get huevos rancheros.' Sisters and brothers in the back seat, drowning out Dad: 'No-o-o-o.' Tina sitting next to siblings, shaken by their lack of respect: 'What are you doing? Let Dad decide.' Culture holding sway over time.

And no, it didn't last. Nothing is that neat, and the currents move fast. They inform and hinder and bless me, and as aware, ridiculously so, as I am of what influences me as a parent, my kids are not. Why should they be? My job is to keep the boat straight, give them safe harbor, to love and guide and prepare them as best as I know how for the day they take the oars.

TIGER MOM VS. TIGER MAILROOM

Patrick Goldstein

Patrick Goldstein writes "The Big Picture," a *Los Angeles Times* column dealing with the film industry. This article first appeared in the *Times* on February 6, 2011.

It's hard to go anywhere these days, especially if you're a parent with young kids, where the conversation doesn't eventually turn to Amy Chua's red-hot child-rearing memoir, *Battle Hymn of the Tiger Mother*. It offers a provocative depiction of Chinese-style extreme parenting—her daughters are not allowed to watch TV, have playdates or get any grade below an A, all as preparation for success in life, beginning with getting into an Ivy League school, like their Tiger Mom, who went to Harvard and now teaches at Yale Law School.

But of all the heated reaction to Chua's parenting strategy, none was as compelling as what former Harvard President Larry Summers had to say when he discussed parenting with Chua at the recent World Economic Forum in Davos, Switzerland. Summers made a striking point, arguing that the two Harvard students who'd had the most transformative impact on the world in the past 25 years were Bill Gates and Mark Zuckerberg, yet neither had, ahem, graduated from college. If they had been brought up by a Tiger Mom, Summers imagined, she would've been bitterly disappointed.

I have no beef with Chua's parenting code, which hardly seems any more extreme than the neurotic ambitions of mothers and fathers I'm exposed to living on the Westside of Los Angeles. But if Chua wants a radically different perspective on the relationship between higher education and career achievement, she should spend some time in Hollywood, a place that's been run for nearly a century by men who never made it through or even to college. The original moguls were famously uneducated, often having started as peddlers and furriers before finding their perches atop the studio dream factories. But even today, the industry is still dominated by titanic figures, both on the creative and on the business side, who never got anywhere near Harvard Yard.

A short list of the industry leaders who never finished or even attended college would include Steve Jobs, David Geffen, Steven Spielberg, Jeffrey Katzenberg, James Cameron, Clint Eastwood, Barry Diller, Ron Meyer, Peter Jackson, Harvey Weinstein, Scott Rudin and Quentin Tarantino. Some of this is clearly a generational thing, since everyone on that list is over 40. On the other hand, the younger new-media icons seem as likely to be degree-free as their Hollywood brethren, whether it's Zuckerberg or the founders of Twitter, who didn't graduate from college either. (Though it's true that Zuckerberg might not have even thought of Facebook if he hadn't been in the sexually charged freshman swirl at Harvard.)

Common Thread

5 But in showbiz, you learn by doing. If there is a common denominator to all of those success stories, it's that they were all men in a hurry, impatient with book learning, which could only take them so far in the rough-and-tumble world of Hollywood. Ron Meyer, a founder of Creative Artists Agency and now president of Universal Studios, dropped out of high school, served in the Marines and proudly notes on his résumé that his first job was as a messenger boy for the Paul Kohner Agency.

"The truth is that if you have a particular talent and the will to succeed, you don't really need a great education," Meyer told me last week. "In showbiz, your real college experience is working in a talent agency mail-room. That's the one place where you can get the most complete understanding of the arena you're playing in and how to deal with the complicated situations you'll come across in your career."

There are plenty of successful lawyers and MBAs in Hollywood, but the raw spirit of can-do invention and inspiration will take people further than the ability to read a complex profit and loss statement. Years ago, Geffen, who dropped out of night school at Brooklyn College before eventually landing a job in the William Morris mail-room, once told me that his early success was rooted in the ability to develop relationships. "It's not about where you went to college or how good-looking you are or whether you could play football—it's about whether you can create a relationship."

To produce a film or create a TV show or found a company requires the same kind of raw entrepreneurial zeal that it must have taken the '49ers who came west in search of gold. "You often feel like you're surrounded by a do-it-yourself ethic, almost a pioneer spirit," says Michael De Luca, producer of *The Social Network*, who dropped out of NYU four credits short of graduation to take a job at New Line Cinema, where he rose to become head of production. "All those successful guys you're talking about—they had an intense desire to create something big, new and different. They didn't need to wait around for the instruction manual."

In David Rensin's wonderful oral history *The Mailroom: Hollywood History From the Bottom Up*, survivors of the Mike Ovitz-era CAA experience tell war stories about how, as mail-room flunkies, they had to replenish Ovitz's candy dishes, stock his jars with raw cashews and fill his water jar with Evian. It seemed like hellish drudgery but, as the agents recalled, it prepared you for all the craziness of later Hollywood life, where multimillion-dollar movie star deals could fall a part if someone's exercise trainer or makeup specialist wasn't provided.

Do the Hustle

10 Even today, people in Hollywood are far more impressed by, say, your knack for finding new talent than by what your grades were like. "Show business is all

about instinct and intuition," says Sam Gores, head of the Paradigm Agency, who went to acting school but never to college, having joined a meat-cutters' union by the time he was 18. "To succeed, you need to have a strong point of view and a lot of confidence. Sometimes being the most well-informed person in your circle can almost get in your way."

In show business, charm, hustle and guile are the aces in the deck. When *New York Times* columnist David Brooks was dissecting Chua's book recently, he argued that "managing status rivalries, negotiating group dynamics, understanding social norms, navigating the distinction between self and group" imposed the kind of cognitive demands that far exceed what's required of students in a class at Yale. He probably picked that up reading a fancy sociology text, but it was a letter-perfect description of the skill set for a gifted filmmaker, agent or producer.

In Hollywood, whether you were a C student or *summa cum laude*, it's a level playing field. "When you're working on a movie set, you've got 50 film professors to learn from, from the sound man to the cinematographer," says producer David Permut, who dropped out of UCLA to work for Roger Corman. "I've never needed a résumé in my whole career. All you need is a 110-page script that someone is dying to make and you're in business."

AMERICA'S TOP PARENT

Elizabeth Kolbert

Elizabeth Kolbert is a staff writer for the *New Yorker*, where this article first appeared on January 20, 2011. Kolbert has also written for the *New York Times* and is the author of *Field Notes from a Catastrophe: Man and Nature and Climate Change* (2006).

"Call me garbage."

The other day, I was having dinner with my family when the subject of Amy Chua's new book, *Battle Hymn of the Tiger Mother* (Penguin Press; $25.95), came up. My twelve-year-old twins had been read an excerpt from the book by their teacher, a well-known provocateur. He had been sent a link to the excerpt by another teacher, who had received it from her sister, who had been e-mailed it by a friend, and, well, you get the point. The excerpt, which had appeared in the *Wall Street Journal* under the headline "WHY CHINESE MOTHERS ARE SUPERIOR," was, and still is, an Internet sensation—as one blogger put it, the "Andromeda Strain of viral memes." Within days, more than five thousand comments had been posted, and "Tiger Mother" vaulted to No. 4 on Amazon's list of best-sellers. Chua appeared on NPR's "All Things Considered" and on NBC's "Nightly News" and "Today" show. Her book was the topic of two columns in last week's Sunday *Times*, and, under the racially neutral headline "IS EXTREME PARENTING EFFECTIVE?," the subject of a formal debate on the paper's Web site.

Thanks to this media blitz, the basic outlines of *Tiger Mother*'s story are by now familiar. Chua, the daughter of Chinese immigrants, is a Yale Law School professor. She is married to another Yale law professor and has two daughters, whom she drives relentlessly. Chua's rules for the girls include: no sleepovers, no playdates, no grade lower than an A on report cards, no choosing your own extracurricular activities, and no ranking lower than No. 1 in any subject. (An exception to this last directive is made for gym and drama.)

In Chua's binary world, there are just two kinds of mother. There are "Chinese mothers," who, she allows, do not necessarily have to be Chinese. "I'm using the term 'Chinese mothers' loosely," she writes. Then, there are "Western" mothers. Western mothers think they are being strict when they insist that their children practice their instruments for half an hour a day. For Chinese mothers, "the first hour is the easy part." Chua chooses the instruments that her daughters will play—piano for the older one, Sophia; violin for the younger, Lulu—and stands over them as they practice for three, four, sometimes five hours at a stretch. The least the girls are expected to do is make it to Carnegie Hall. Amazingly enough, Sophia does. Chua's daughters are so successful—once, it's true, Sophia came in second on a multiplication test (to a Korean boy), but Chua made sure this never happened again—that they confirm her thesis: Western mothers are losers. I'm using the term "losers" loosely.

5   Chua has said that one of the points of the book is "making fun of myself," but plainly what she was hoping for was to outrage. Whole chapters of "Tiger Mother"—admittedly, many chapters are only four or five pages long—are given over to incidents like that of the rejected smiley face.

"I don't want this," she tells Lulu, throwing back at her a handmade birthday card. "I want a better one."

In another chapter, Chua threatens to take Lulu's doll house to the Salvation Army and, when that doesn't work, to deny her lunch, dinner, and birthday parties for "two, three, four years" because she cannot master a piece called "The Little White Donkey." The kid is seven years old. In a third chapter, Chua tells Sophia she is "garbage." Chua's own father has called her "garbage," and she finds it a highly effective parenting technique. Chua relates this at a dinner party, and one of the guests supposedly gets so upset that she breaks down in tears. The hostess tries to patch things up by suggesting that Chua is speaking figuratively.

"You didn't actually call Sophia garbage," the hostess offers.

"Yes, I did," Chua says.

10   When the dinner-party episode was read in class, my sons found it hilarious, which is why they were taunting me. "Call me garbage," one of the twins said again. "I dare you."

"O.K.," I said, trying, for once, to be a good mother. "You're garbage."

If Chua's tale has any significance—and it may not—it is as an allegory. Chua refers to herself as a Tiger because according to the Chinese zodiac she was born in the Year of the Tiger. Tiger people are "powerful, authoritative, and magnetic," she informs us, just as tigers that walk on four legs inspire "fear and respect." The "tiger economies" of Asia aren't mentioned in the book, but they growl menacingly in the background.

It's just about impossible to pick up a newspaper these days—though who actually *picks up* a newspaper anymore?—without finding a story about the rise of the East. The headlines are variations on a theme: "SOLAR PANEL MAKER MOVES WORK TO CHINA"; "CHINA DRAWING HIGH-TECH RESEARCH FROM U.S."; "IBM CUTTING 5,000 SERVICE JOBS; MOVING WORK TO INDIA." What began as an outflow of manufacturing jobs has spread way beyond car parts and electronics to include information technology, legal advice, even journalism. (This piece could have been written much more cost-effectively by a team in Bangalore and, who knows, maybe next month it will be.)

On our good days, we tell ourselves that our kids will be all right. The new, global economy, we observe, puts a premium on flexibility and creativity. And who is better prepared for such a future than little Abby (or Zachary), downloading her wacky videos onto YouTube while she texts her friends, messes with Photoshop, and listens to her iPod?

15   "Yes, you can brute-force any kid to learn to play the piano—just precisely like his or her billion neighbors" is how one of the comments on the *Wall Street Journal's* Web site put it. "But you'll never get a Jimi Hendrix that way."

On our bad days, we wonder whether this way of thinking is, as Chua might say, garbage. Last month, the results of the most recent Programme for International Student Assessment, or PISA, tests were announced. It was the first time that Chinese students had participated, and children from Shanghai ranked first in every single area. Students from the United States, meanwhile, came in seventeenth in reading, twenty-third in science, and an especially demoralizing thirty-first in math. This last ranking put American kids not just behind the Chinese, the Koreans, and the Singaporeans but also after the French, the Austrians, the Hungarians, the Slovenians, the Estonians, and the Poles.

"I know skeptics will want to argue with the results, but we consider them to be accurate and reliable," Arne Duncan, the U.S. Secretary of Education, told the *Times*. "The United States came in twenty-third or twenty-fourth in most subjects. We can quibble, or we can face the brutal truth that we're being out-educated."

Why is this? How is it that the richest country in the world can't teach kids to read or to multiply fractions? Taken as a parable, Chua's cartoonish narrative about browbeating her daughters acquires a certain disquieting force. Americans have been told always to encourage their kids. This, the theory goes, will improve their self-esteem, and this, in turn, will help them learn.

After a generation or so of applying this theory, we have the results. Just about the only category in which American students outperform the competition is self-regard. Researchers at the Brookings Institution, in one of their frequent studies of education policy, compared students' assessments of their abilities in math with their scores on a standardized test. Nearly forty per cent of American eighth graders agreed "a lot" with the statement "I usually do well in mathematics," even though only seven per cent of American students actually got enough correct answers on the test to qualify as advanced. Among Singaporean students, eighteen per cent said they usually did well in math; forty-four per cent qualified as advanced. As the Brookings researchers pointed out, even the least self-confident Singaporean students, on average, outscored the most self-confident Americans. You can say it's sad that kids in Singapore are so beaten down that they can't appreciate their own accomplishments. But you've got to give them this: at least they get the math right.

20   Our problems as a country cannot, of course, be reduced to our problems as educators or as parents. Nonetheless, there is an uncomfortable analogy. For some time now, the U.S. has, in effect, been drawing crappy, smiley-face birthday cards and calling them wonderful. It's made us feel a bit better about ourselves without improving the basic situation. As the cover story on China's ascent in this month's *Foreign Policy* sums things up: "American Decline: This Time It's Real."

It's hard to believe that Chua's book would be causing quite as much stir without the geopolitical subtext. (Picture the reaction to a similar tale told by a Hungarian or an Austrian über-mom.) At the same time, lots of people have clearly taken "Tiger Mother" personally.

Of the zillions of comments that have been posted on the Web, many of the most passionate are from scandalized "Western" mothers and fathers, or, as one blogger dubbed them, "Manatee dads." Some have gone as far as to suggest that Chua be arrested for child abuse. At least as emotional are the posts from Asians and Asian-Americans.

"Parents like Amy Chua are the reason why Asian-Americans like me are in therapy," Betty Ming Liu, who teaches journalism at N.Y.U., wrote on her blog.

"What's even more damning is her perpetuation of the media stereotypes of Asian-Americans," Frank Chi, a political consultant, wrote in the Boston *Globe's* opinion blog.

25   "Having lived through a version of the Chinese Parenting Experience, and having been surrounded since birth with hundreds of CPE graduates, I couldn't not say something," a contributor to the Web site Shanghaiist wrote after the *Wall Street Journal* excerpt appeared. "The article actually made me feel physically ill."

Chua's response to some of the unkind things said about her—she has reported getting death threats—has been to backpedal. "RETREAT OF THE 'TIGER MOTHER' " was the headline of one *Times* article. (It, too, quickly jumped to the top of the paper's "most e-mailed" list.) Chua has said that it was not her plan to write a parenting manual: "My actual book is not a how-to guide." Somehow or other, her publisher seems to be among those who missed this. The back cover spells out, in black and red type, "How to Be a Tiger Mother."

According to Chua, her "actual book" is a memoir. Memoir is, or at least is supposed to be, a demanding genre. It requires that the author not just narrate his or her life but reflect on it. By her own description, Chua is not a probing person. Of her years studying at Harvard Law School, she writes:

> I didn't care about the rights of criminals the way others did, and I froze whenever a professor called on me. I also wasn't naturally skeptical and questioning; I just wanted to write down everything the professor said and memorize it.

Battle Hymn of the Tiger Mother exhibits much the same lack of interest in critical thinking. It's breezily written, at times entertaining, and devoid of anything approaching introspection. Imagine your most self-congratulatory friend holding forth for two hours about her kids' triumphs, and you've more or less got the narrative. The only thing that keeps it together is Chua's cheerful faith that whatever happened to her or her daughters is interesting just because it happened to happen to them. In addition to all the schlepping back and forth to auditions, there are two chapters on Chua's dogs (Samoyeds named Coco and Pushkin), three pages of practice notes that she left behind for Lulu when she could not be there to berate her in person, and a complete list of the places that she had visited with her kids by the time they were twelve and nine:

> London, Paris, Nice, Rome, Venice, Milan, Amsterdam, The Hague, Barcelona, Madrid, Málaga, Liechtenstein, Monaco, Munich, Dublin, Brussels, Bruges, Strasbourg, Beijing, Shanghai, Tokyo, Hong Kong, Manila, Istanbul, Mexico City, Cancún, Buenos Aires, Santiago, Rio de Janeiro, São Paulo, La Paz, Sucre, Cochabamba, Jamaica, Tangier, Fez, Johannesburg, Cape Town, and the Rock of Gibraltar.

Chua's husband is not Chinese, in either sense of the word. He makes occasional appearances in the book to try—ineffectually, it seems—to shield the girls. Chua has said that she wrote more about their arguments, but her husband didn't like those passages, so they've been cut. Perhaps had more of his voice been included it would have provided some grit and at least the semblance of engagement. As it is, though, it's just her. "I'm happy to be the one hated," she tells her husband at one point, and apparently she means it.

30   Parenting is hard. As anyone who has gone through the process and had enough leisure (and still functioning brain cells) to reflect on it knows, a lot of it is a crapshoot. Things go wrong that you have no control over, and, on occasion, things also go right, and you have no control over those, either. The experience is scary and exhilarating and often humiliating, not because you're disappointed in your kids, necessarily, but because you're disappointed in yourself.

Some things do go wrong in Chua's memoir. Her mother-in-law dies; her younger sister develops leukemia. These events get roughly the same amount of space as Coco and Pushkin, and yet they are, on their own terms, moving. More central to the story line is a screaming fit in a Moscow restaurant during which a glass is thrown. The upshot of the crisis is that Lulu is allowed to take up tennis, which Chua then proceeds to micromanage.

Chua clearly wants to end her book by claiming that she has changed. She knows enough about the conventions of memoir-writing to understand that some kind of transformation is generally required. But she can't bring herself to do it. And so in the final pages she invokes the Founding Fathers. They, too, she tells her daughters, would not have approved of sleepovers.

*TIGER MOMS DON'T RAISE SUPERIOR KIDS,
SAYS NEW STUDY*

Susan Adams

The previous selections in this chapter are all, essentially, opinion-based: that is, they argue particular positions on the subject of tiger mothers, based on the writers' own personal viewpoints or experiences. In contrast, the following article reports upon an empirical, fact-based, study that researchers used to test the truth of the thesis that the kind of rigorous, demanding parenting advocated by Chua results in more highly accomplished children. Susan Adams is on the staff of *Forbes* online magazine. This article was first posted on May 8, 2013.

When Yale Law School professor Amy Chua's piece, "Why Chinese Mothers Are Superior," appeared in the *Wall Street Journal* two years ago, I was especially interested because my son, now 16, goes to Stuyvesant High School in Manhattan, an academically rigorous test-in school where 72% of the 3,300 students are of Asian descent. According to Chua, who expounded on her ideas in a popular book, *Battle Hymn of the Tiger Mother*, the typical Asian mom prioritizes academics and musical accomplishment (in classical piano and violin only) over typical fun kid stuff like sleepovers and playdates. Chua wrote that she would never allow her daughters to watch TV, play computer games or be in a school play.

Though Chua's piece had a humorous tone, she made it clear that she thought Western parents like me were too soft, producing young people who are undisciplined and less accomplished than the children of so-called tiger mothers. Indeed, my son plays jazz saxophone, is on the tennis team, occasionally plays Xbox, hangs out with friends on the weekends and participates in several clubs, like Model UN. If my husband and I were more like Chua's stereotypical Asian mother, I have wondered, would our son get better grades and ultimately be more successful in life?

Chua's book also struck a chord for Su Yeong Kim, an associate professor of human development and family sciences at the University of Texas, who had been studying more than 300 Chinese-American families for a decade. Last month Kim, working with three graduate students and one undergrad, published her results in the *Asian American Journal of Psychology* (*Slate* has an interesting article today on the study).

Chua and her fans may find the paper surprising. The kids of strict tiger parents had lower grades, were more troubled emotionally and were more estranged from their families than kids whose parents were what Kim categorizes as "supportive" and "easygoing." Also, despite the now-popular belief that most Asian parents are tigers, the majority of parents in Kim's study turned out to fit a supportive parenting style.

5   According to Kim, since the 1980s, academics have divided parenting styles into four categories—authoritative, authoritarian, permissive and negligent. Authoritative parents are responsive to their children's needs and desires but they also exercise their power while negotiating with their kids. Studies have shown that in white families, this style produces high-achieving young people who don't tend to be depressed. (I'd like to think this is the way my husband and I parent.) Authoritarian parents are more coercive and less responsive; their kids have lower self-esteem and more depression. Permissive parents are warm but they don't exercise much control over their kids. This style, not surprisingly, produces young people who achieve less than the kids of authoritarian and authoritative parents. Negligent parents don't control their kids and they also exude little warmth or caring.

Kim, who is Korean-American, didn't think that any of those categories matched the kind of parenting she saw around her as she was growing up. "Researchers think Asian-American parents are authoritarian parents," she says. "It was perplexing to me that Asian-American parents were characterized this way but the developmental outcomes of their kids weren't the same as [the outcomes of] European-American [kids, who tended to have] lower GPAs and more social and emotional problems."

For her study, Kim expanded on the categories, coming up with profiles that more closely matched what she knew about East Asian families. She started with eight different parenting attributes, four positive and four negative, including one she says is prevalent in Asian-American homes while not widespread among white families—shaming, where parents point out how their kids are failing to behave as well as other more successful children.

The other attributes included positives like warmth; inductive reasoning, where parents explain the reasons for their rules; and monitoring, where parents track their kids' whereabouts away from home. Negative attributes besides shaming included hostility and punishing without explanation. To do the study, Kim and her team asked the children and parents in the 300 families about each of these eight attributes at three different stages in the kids' lives—in middle school, high school, and upon graduation from college. The families all live in Northern California and they are not especially well off, with median incomes that range from $30,000 to $45,000. After gathering the data, Kim and her team ran the categories and answers through a computer and did what's called a latent profile analysis to come up with four parenting styles.

After the data-gathering was done, Chua had come out with her book, so Kim and her team decided to label one of the styles "tiger." These parents score high on all eight categories, positive and negative. They're warm and they monitor their kids closely, while also demonstrating hostility toward bad behavior, at times punishing their children with no explanation, and using shame as a way to try to mold behavior.

10   "Harsh" parents also use shame, punish with no explanation, are hostile when they disapprove of behavior and they wield psychological control by changing the subject when their children try to speak and by not meeting their gaze. Harsh parents don't exhibit any positive attributes like warmth. By contrast, supportive parents are warm, explain their reasons for exercising discipline, track their children's whereabouts and give their kids some autonomy in discussions and behavior, and score low on negative attributes like shaming and punitive discipline. Easygoing parents have low scores in all eight categories. They aren't hostile, punitive and shaming but they also don't bother to monitor their kids or explain the reasoning behind their rules.

After all the categorizing, years of surveying and number crunching, to Kim's surprise, the team found that the greatest number of Chinese-American families in the study turned out to have supportive parents whose children did well academically while not feeling oppressed by the pressure. Those kids also felt close to their families. Tiger families and easygoing families ranked second, with about the same number in each category. Kids of easygoing parents did the second-best after the kids of supportive parents when it came to academic achievement and emotional well-being. The tiger kids did worse academically and socially. Harsh families made up the smallest group and their kids had the worst academic performance and the highest levels of depression.

Kim says she was surprised by the study's results because the idea that Asian-American parents fit the tiger mold has become so pervasive following Chua's book, not just among the general public but in the academy as well. "Tiger parenting has become the most common profile," she says. "Our study shows a different result."

So if my son's classmates aren't the children of tiger parents, why do Asian-American kids so dominate at Stuyvesant, the public school that has the highest bar to admission in the city, while Asian-American students make up only around 14% of the city's total public school population? Are Asian-American parents more supportive than other ethnic groups? Why are there virtually no Hispanic students at Stuyvesant, the greatest share of the city's public school population, at more than 40%? "I don't have an answer for you," says Kim." That will have to be the subject of my next study."

SUMMARY   MyWritingLab™

Following the guidelines in Chapter 1, particularly the Guidelines for Writing Summaries box (pp. 7–8), summarize the excerpt adapted from *Battle Hymn of the Tiger Mother* by Amy Chua. In preparation for writing the summary, review the model summary (pp. 20–21) and consult the advice on note-taking (pp. 15–16).

As an alternative, summarize one of the other selections in this chapter. The article by Kolbert would also be a good subject for summary.

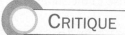

CRITIQUE   MyWritingLab™

Following the guidelines in Chapter 2, particularly the Guidelines for Writing Critiques box (p. 68), write a critique of Chua's op-ed. The early part of the critique should draw upon the summary of Chua that you prepared for the previous assignment. In preparation for writing the critique, review the model critique (p. 70–75).

You've probably already noticed that most of the articles following Chua are to some extent critiques of either the excerpt adapted from *Battle Hymn of the Tiger Mother* or the book as a whole. Some authors argue with her basic premise, some support it, though perhaps with reservations, and others discuss related issues such as the preparedness of America's youth to compete with their counterparts in China. In developing your own critique, you're free to draw upon these other authors; but you should also stake out your own position based upon your own observations and experience and your own understanding of the issues Chua discusses. Doing so will help ensure that your critique isn't merely a compendium of other authors' observations and arguments.

Begin preparing for the critique by reflecting on your own observations and experiences in relation to Chua's main assumption (expressed in the two sentences that open ¶ 5): "What Chinese parents understand is that nothing is fun until you're good at it. To get good at anything you have to work, and children on their own never want to work, which is why it is crucial to override their preferences." Ask yourself:

- To what extent do you agree that "nothing is fun until you're good at it"? Do your own experiences and the experiences of your friends and relatives bear out this assumption? What have you read that supports or refutes it?
- Do you agree that "children on their own never want to work"? Cite examples in support or to the contrary.
- Consider the proposition that it is crucial for parents to override children's natural disinclination to work, in light of your own experiences, observations, and reading.

Throughout Chua's op-ed, you'll encounter controversial statements such as those in the first two bullet points above, along with anecdotes about the ways she has driven her children, sometimes mercilessly, in pursuit of her standards of excellence and success. And you'll find numerous comparisons between "Chinese" and "Western" approaches to child rearing. Your assessment of these statements should provide a rich source of material for your own critique.

Here's a suggested organizational plan for your critique:

1. An introduction, setting the issue in context (see Chapter 3 for advice on creating introductions)
2. A summary of Chua's op-ed (a brief version of your response to the summary assignment above)
3. An evaluation of Chua's piece for clarity, logic, and/or fairness (the Question #1 topics in Chapter 2, p. 52)
4. An account of your own agreement or disagreement with Chua's argument (the Question #2 topics in Chapter 2, pp. 63–66)
5. A conclusion (see Chapter 3 for advice on creating conclusions)

In preparing your critique, follow the advice in Chapter 2, see particularly the Guidelines for Writing Critiques box (p. 68), along with the hints in Chapter 1 on incorporating summaries, paraphrases, and quoted material into your own writing (pp. 43–45).

EXPLANATORY SYNTHESIS   MyWritingLab™

Based on the readings in this chapter, write an explanatory synthesis that you might use in a broader argument on the subject of varying approaches to child rearing and preparing children to be competitive in the workplace of the future. The synthesis should each consist of three to five well-developed paragraphs on the following topics: (1) an account of the controversy over Chua's op-ed and the book from which it was drawn; (2) an account of the two different approaches to parenting represented by the "Chinese" and "Western" models; and (3) an account of the different approaches to preparing children to be competitive in the current and future marketplace. Follow the guidelines in Chapter 4, particularly the Guidelines for Writing Syntheses box (pp. 102–103); review also the model explanatory synthesis (pp. 122–128), though your assignment here calls for a considerably briefer paper. In your synthesis, take into account the results of the study by Kim and her fellow researchers, as reported by Susan Adams.

Key requirements for the explanatory synthesis:

- Craft a thesis for your paper, a single statement that will guide the writing of the paragraphs of explanation that follow.

- Begin each paragraph of explanation that follows the explanatory thesis with a clear topic sentence.

- Refer in each paragraph of explanation to *at least two* different sources. Set up the references carefully, using an appropriate citation format, most likely MLA (see the "Quick Index" at the end of this text).

- In developing your explanatory synthesis, draw on facts, examples, statistics, and expert opinions from your sources.

ANALYSIS   MyWritingLab™

Select a principle or definition discussed in one of the readings in "The Roar of the Tiger Mom" and apply this principle or definition to either (1) a particular situation of which you have personal knowledge or (2) a situation that you have learned about in the course of your reading. Follow the guidelines in Chapter 6, particularly the Guidelines for Writing Analyses box (p. 181); review also the model analysis (pp. 188–194).

First, review the topic list you created in Group Assignment #1 after reading the selections in this chapter. At least one of the items on the list may point the way to an analytic principle that resonates with you. If so, follow through by locating a particular quotation that articulates this principle. Here are some examples of such quotations from the readings:

- "But as a parent, one of the worst things you can do for your child's self-esteem is to let them give up. On the flip side, there's nothing better for building confidence than learning you can do something you thought you couldn't." (Chua, p. 309)

- "What privileged American children need is not more skills and rules and math drills. They need to lighten up and roam free, to express themselves in ways not dictated by their uptight, over-invested parents." (Rosin, p. 310)

- "Managing status rivalries, negotiating group dynamics, understanding social norms, navigating the distinction between self and group—these and other social tests impose cognitive demands that blow away any intense tutoring session or a class at Yale." (Brooks, p. 313).

- "For some time now, the U.S. has, in effect, been drawing crappy, smiley-faced birthday cards and calling them wonderful." (Kolbert, p. 321)

- "You work hard. Your children obey, and if, with the imposition of the values of obedience and duty to family, childhood is fleeting, so it must be." (Griego, p. 315)

Consider using the following structure for your analysis:

1. An introductory paragraph that sets a context for the topic and presents the claim you intend to support in the analysis that follows. Your claim (your thesis) distills the conclusions you've drawn from your analysis. Your claim may appear at the end of the introductory paragraph (or introductory section).

2. A paragraph or two introducing the analytic tool or principle you intend to use and discussing its key components. Suppose you decided to use Brooks's quotation as an analytic principle. You would need to explain what he means by one or more of these skills: "[m]anaging status rivalries," "negotiating group dynamics," "understanding social norms," and "navigating the distinction between self and group." You would also need to explain how successfully managing such social tests imposes "cognitive demands that blow away any intense tutoring session or a class at Yale." Note, however, that you're not required to establish that one set of tasks is *more* difficult or important than the other. It may be sufficient for your purpose to establish simply that the social skills are at least *as* important as the academic skills. Once you establish this analytic principle, you can proceed with the analysis.

3. A paragraph or two describing the situation that you will analyze—drawn from your own personal experience or observation or from your reading.

4. Several paragraphs (this is the heart of your analysis) in which you systematically apply the key components of the principle you have selected to the situation you have described. Staying with Brooks, you would apply such key components as managing status rivalries, negotiating group dynamics, and so on to the situation you have described. As you apply these key components each in turn, in separate paragraphs or groupings of paragraphs, you would discuss why such skills are, if not *more* difficult than undergoing a demanding class or tutoring session, then at least *as valuable* for success in later life as academic skills.

5. A conclusion in which you argue that, based on the insights gained through your analysis, the experience or situation in question can now be understood more deeply. See Chapter 3 (pp. 89–95) for advice on concluding your papers.

○ ARGUMENT   MyWritingLab™

> Write an argument synthesis based upon the selections in "The Roar of the Tiger Mom." You may find it useful to draw upon the products of your earlier assignments in this section on summary, critique, explanatory synthesis, and analysis. In your synthesis, take into account the results of the study by Kim and her fellow researchers, as reported by Susan Adams.
>
> Follow the guidelines in Chapter 5 and reference the Guidelines for Writing Synthesis box in Chapter 4 (pp. 102–103); review also the model argument synthesis (pp. 148–157).

In planning your synthesis, review the master list of topics and notes that you and your classmates generated for Group Assignment #1 above (pp. 303–304), and draw upon what the authors of the passages have written about these topics in developing your outline. Devise a claim, a thesis that distills your argument to a sentence or two. Plan to support your claim with facts, opinions, and statistics from the passages.

Note that one synthesis—a single paper—could not possibly refer to every topic, or every connection among authors, that you have found. The craft of preparing and writing a synthesis depends on your ability to select closely related topics and then to make and develop a claim that links and can be supported by them. You don't have to refer to all of the selections in this chapter while developing your paper; but you will likely want to refer to most. You may even want to research additional sources.

In formulating arguments on a controversial issue—for example, immigration, abortion, the size of government, or capital punishment—the immediate temptation is to adopt one strong (and uncompromising) position or to adopt its counterpart on the opposite side. Many commentators on Chua's book or op-ed tend to divide themselves into pro-Chua or anti-Chua camps: she's either dead right about her approach to parenting or she's dead wrong. Arguments supporting such polarized positions may be forceful, even eloquent, but seldom persuade those predisposed to the opposite point of view. (See "The Limits of Argument" in Chapter 5, pp. 137–138.)

After considering all the facts and the assertions, strive yourself for a more nuanced approach. This doesn't necessarily mean adopting a straight-down-the-middle/split-the-difference position, which is likely to persuade no one. It does mean acknowledging opposing arguments and dealing with them in good faith. (See "Present and Respond to Counterarguments" in Chapter 5, p. 163.) It does mean considering the issue afresh, thinking about the implications of the problems and the possible solutions, and coming up with your own insights, your own distinctive take on the subject. Such thought, such nuance, should be reflected in your thesis. (See "Writing a Thesis" in Chapter 3, pp. 78–79.)

Without writing your thesis for you, we'll suppose for the sake of example that the subject of your argument synthesis concerns how the debate over Chua's ideas clarifies how parents can best help their children succeed as they prepare for adulthood. An arguable claim on the subject would likely state which approach to child rearing, in your opinion, would best prepare children. Here's one way of structuring such an argument synthesis:

- An introductory paragraph that sets a context for the topic—in the example above, the debate over Chua's op-ed and the best pathway to success—and presents the claim you intend to support in the argument that follows. Your claim (that is, your argumentative thesis) may appear at the end of this paragraph (or introductory section).

- A paragraph or two summarizing Chua's ideas. This section may be an abbreviated version of the summary you wrote earlier.

- One to three paragraphs discussing some of the commentary on Chua's ideas, organized by topic, rather than author. That is, identify two or three main categories of response to Chua—favorable, unfavorable, and neutral—and take up each category in turn. You may have created topic webs for these categories when preparing to write. See Group Assignments #1 and #2.

- A paragraph or two discussing your own assessment of the best pathway (or pathways) to success, supported in part by the comments of some of the authors in this chapter. Relate this assessment to ideas contained within the articles by Chua and her critics. For this section you may want to draw upon your responses to the earlier analysis or critique assignments. You may even elect to consult additional sources on the subject.

- A counterargument section, in which you concede the validity of positions on the subject different from your own and acknowledge the ideas of authors in this section with whom you disagree.

- A "nevertheless" section, in which you respond to the counterarguments and reaffirm your own position.

- A paragraph or two of conclusion. See Chapter 3 (pp. 89–95) for advice on concluding your papers.

Where you place the various elements of this argument synthesis will be your decision as writer. Which sources to use and what logic to present in defense of your claim is also yours to decide. See pages 161–165 for help in thinking about structuring and supporting your argument.

A Note on Incorporating Quotations and Paraphrases

Identify the sources you intend to use for your synthesis. Working with a phrase, sentence, or brief passage from each, use a variety of the techniques discussed in the section Incorporating Quotations into Your Sentences, Chapter 1 (pp. 43–48), to write sentences that you can use to advance your argument. Some of these sentences should demonstrate the use of ellipsis marks and brackets. See pages 45–48 in Chapter 1. Paraphrase passages, as needed, and incorporate these as well into your papers.

MyWritingLab™   Visit Ch. 10 The Roar of the Tiger Mom in MyWritingLab to test your understanding of the chapter objectives.

Part III

An Anthology of Readings

First Impressions: The Art and Craft of Storytelling

> "So now, get up."
>   Felled, dazed, silent, he has fallen; knocked full length on the cobbles of the yard. His head turns sideways; his eyes are turned toward the gate, as if someone might arrive to help him out. One blow, properly placed, could kill him now.

These are the first words of *Wolf Hall*, the first book of Hilary Mantel's trilogy about Thomas Cromwell, counselor to Henry VIII. Imagine you just bought the book based on a friend's recommendation.

Would you keep reading? Or would you keep reading a novel with this opening sentence:

> If you really want to hear about it, the first thing you'll probably want to know is where I was born, and what my lousy childhood was like, and how my parents were occupied and all before they had me, and all that David Copperfield kind of crap, but I don't feel like going into it, if you want to know the truth.
>
> —J. D. Salinger: *The Catcher In The Rye* (1951)

Who *is* this narrator? And if he isn't going into his "lousy childhood," then what *is* he going into?

Aspiring novelists are often told that they must grab readers by the end of the first chapter—ideally, by the end of the first scene or even the first page. That's putting a lot of weight on that first impression, but this is good advice. We readers are busy people, and even when we aren't busy, we're being bombarded constantly with potential distractions. A novelist who expects complete strangers to spend ten or fifteen or twenty hours reading her work has the formidable task of making us want to put aside everything else in our lives except for the book in front of us. In that first chapter, she must convince us to read the second one. She must convince us that our time spent reading her novel will be put to good use.

As you must already know, novels begin in strikingly different ways. From the writer's perspective, however, first chapters typically have a number of similar objectives. In relatively few pages, they must introduce the main characters, reveal the premise, get the plot moving, establish the time and place, set the tone and mood, and establish the voice or writing style. Perhaps the most important goal for the first chapter is to convince the reader to keep reading. After all, unless the novel is a school assignment, the reader always has the option of closing the book or shutting off the e-reader and finding some other way to spend his or her time.

So those opening pages of a novel, then, are crucial. And book publishers know it, which is why so many of them make the first chapters of novels available for free online: they need to hook the reader.

Effective opening "chapters" are just as important in movies as in novels, and for the same reasons. Consider the opening scene of *Vertigo*, directed by Alfred Hitchcock. A crook clutches a rail on an iron ladder attached to a building, pulls himself up onto the roof, and runs away. A second later, a uniformed cop climbs up after him and heads in the same direction as the crook. A moment after that, a plainclothes cop (James Stewart) also climbs onto the roof and runs in the same direction. From a distance, we see the three on the roof, the crook in the lead, the two cops following. The crook jumps across the opening between adjacent buildings, grabs onto a steeply banked roof, and keeps climbing until he reaches the top, then continues to run. The uniformed cop does the same. The plainclothes cop tries to follow but loses his grip and falls, hanging precariously from the sagging rain gutter. He looks down several stories and almost blanks out from vertigo. The uniformed cop abandons the pursuit and tries to help the other cop. But in reaching down to grab his arm, he loses his footing and falls to his death. The plainclothes cop looks on helplessly, still holding on to the gutter for dear life. The scene fades out.

Film openings can set "hooks" into an audience just as effectively as the openings to novels can. Recall the opening scene of *The Wizard of Oz*, showing Dorothy frantically running home after wicked Miss Gulch has threatened to sic the sheriff on Toto. Recall the opening scene of Stanley Kubrick's *2001: A Space Odyssey*, with three heavenly bodies—sun, moon, and earth—aligning vertically, to the accompaniment of the pounding chords of Richard Strauss's *Thus Spoke Zarathustra*. Watch the opening scene of *The Social Network*, showing Facebook founder-to-be Mark Zuckerberg managing to thoroughly alienate his date as he attempts to demonstrate his brilliance. As portrayed by Jesse Eisenberg, Zuckerberg is an obnoxious genius, but a character so compelling that he makes us want to see just how he came to create one of the most celebrated and influential companies of recent decades.

In this chapter, you'll read the first chapters of several novels and view the openings of several movies so that you can assess what qualities do—or don't—pique your interest and propel you into a story. As tools for your inquiry, we include three essays by contemporary novelists: K. M. Weiland introduces the concept of "the hook," the question the writer sets in the reader's mind to create a compelling need to continue reading. Michael Kardos discusses the story elements fiction writers must establish in those crucial opening pages. And Tim O'Brien likens writing fiction to performing magic and offers insights into the mysteries of character and plot.

You may well have it in you to write your own novel or shoot your own film one day. If you do, we hope you'll send us a copy! For the moment, though, you'll be working with the materials here to write analyses, not fiction. That is, you'll be applying the insights of Weiland, Kardos, and O'Brien to assorted Chapter Ones and Scene Ones in order to understand how these openings achieve their effects. So happy reading—and viewing! Here's the lineup of Chapter Ones:

- *Emma* (1815) by Jane Austen (1775–1817). Austin's fourth published novel chronicles the intrusive matchmaking of a privileged young woman, Emma Woodhouse, in nineteenth-century England.
- *Wuthering Heights* (1847) by Emily Brontë (1818–1848). Set on the English moors, this novel explores love and revenge and madness through the love story of Catherine Earnshaw and Mr. Heathcliff.
- *Jane Eyre* (1847) by Charlotte Brontë (1816–1855). This coming-of-age novel chronicles the life of its title character from unhappy childhood to marriage.
- *Great Expectations* (1860) by Charles Dickens (1812–1870). Often considered Dickens's finest novel, this is the coming-of-age story of an English orphan named Pip.
- *The Sign of the Four* (1890) by Sir Arthur Conan Doyle. This is Doyle's second novel starring Sherlock Holmes, the world's "only unofficial consulting detective."
- *The Red Badge of Courage* (1895) by Stephen Crane. Set in Virginia in 1863, Crane's second novel depicts a young man, Henry Fleming, who is fighting for the Union army during the American Civil War.
- *Dracula* (1897) by Bram Stoker. This is the classic vampire novel to which all subsequent vampire novels and movies are indebted.

Here's the lineup of openings to some classic films, which you can readily find online or through Amazon, Netflix, or iTunes rentals. Your instructor may also make these films available to you, either by showing them in class or by placing them on reserve. Watch and enjoy. Use the questions following both the Chapter Ones and the introductions to the films to prompt discussions with classmates. Use these same questions and others (on pp. 426–428) as prompts for formulating your own thoughts on what makes for effective openings.

- *Jane Eyre* (1943) directed by Robert Stevenson. This is only one—but an influential one—of numerous film versions of Brontë's romantic novel.

- *Great Expectations* (1946) directed by David Lean. Lean's version of the terrifying encounter on an English marsh between Dickens's young Pip and the escaped convict has never been surpassed.

- *Emma* (1996) directed by Robert McGrath, and *Clueless* (1995) directed by Amy Heckerling. Here are two versions of Austen's classic novel—the first a period piece, like Austen's novel, set in the county of Surrey, England; the second is set in Beverly Hills.

- *Dracula* (1931) directed by Tod Browning, and *Bram Stoker's Dracula* (1992) directed by Francis Ford Coppola. Here are two film versions of Bram Stoker's classic vampire story, created more than sixty years apart by directors with very different artistic visions.

- *The Red Badge of Courage* (1951) directed by John Huston. Crane's novel of a Civil War soldier wondering how he will act in battle is faithfully filmed—and then heavily edited by the studio bosses.

- *Citizen Kane* (1941) directed by Orson Welles. This is the work most frequently cited as the greatest film of all time. Whether or not you agree, the opening scene of a newspaper magnate's final moments make for compelling viewing.

- *Brief Encounter* (1945) directed by David Lean. This is one of the greatest romantic dramas ever filmed—in a typically restrained British fashion.

- *Shane* (1953) directed by George Stevens. In many ways, this is the archetypal Western: Set against magnificent Wyoming scenery, the film depicts an epic battle between a reluctant gunfighter and a rancher trying to drive homesteaders off their land.

- *The Godfather, Part One* (1972) directed by Francis Ford Coppola. The greatest gangster film ever made is also a family drama—which begins at a wedding celebration.

- *Sleepless in Seattle* (1993) directed by Nora Ephron. In the tradition of classic romantic dramas, Ephron focuses on two people thousands of miles apart gravitating (haltingly) toward each other.

- *Do the Right Thing* (1989) directed by Spike Lee. A simmering racial conflict on the hottest day of the year in the Bedford-Stuyvesant neighborhood of Brooklyn is the focus of Spike Lee's controversial film.

- *The Devil in a Blue Dress* (1995) directed by Carl Franklin. The classic private detective formula is re-imagined along racial lines in Carl Franklin's story of an unemployed African-American World War II veteran tasked to find the missing girlfriend of a Los Angeles mayoral candidate.

- *Chicago* (2002) directed by Rob Marshall. Kander and Ebb's scintillating musical about two female murderers begins with two knockout songs set partially in the characters' heads.

- *The Hurt Locker* (2008) directed by Kathryn Bigelow. This tense film chronicles the daily life-and-death struggles of a bomb disposal unit during the Iraq War.
- *Gravity* (2013) directed by Alfonso Cuarón. This visually stunning film about an astronaut trying to return to earth after a catastrophic accident kept audiences on the edge of their seats.
- *12 Years a Slave* (2013) directed by Steve McQueen. A brutally intense drama about a free black man sold into slavery is unforgettably depicted in McQueen's film, which won the Academy Award for Best Picture of 2013.

THE ART AND CRAFT OF STARTING YOUR STORY

Like a lens you hold up to a leaf or to the back of your hand, revealing details invisible to the unaided eye, a good question or a carefully defined concept can help you read a book or watch a film and see things you might otherwise overlook. Exactly *how* does an opening scene of a film or chapter of a novel engage your interest and move you from living in your world to imaginatively inhabiting a fictional one? Writers and directors don't leave the answering of such important questions to chance. They employ time-tested techniques to grab your attention and prepare you for what is to come. Whether or not they succeed is for you to decide.

The three selections that open this chapter provide the questions and concepts you can use to read deeply and view deeply the Chapter Ones and Scene Ones we've gathered for your analysis. Novelist K. M. Weiland begins by defining "The Hook" and emphasizing the importance of questions. Novelist Michael Kardos alerts you to the art of how stories make a favorable first impression on the reader, emphasizing conflict and the disclosing of key information. And in comparing writing to performing magic, novelist Tim O'Brien emphasizes *mystery* in his discussion of plot and character: that is, the mystery of what happens next and the mystery of "the other"—the fictional person whose history and nature we will explore through the medium of the storyteller.

Read these selections with care, and you'll have the tools to write with authority about what makes for an effective Chapter One or Scene One.

THE HOOK

K. M. Weiland

Among the numerous handbooks offering practical advice to aspiring novelists, K. M. Weiland's *Structuring Your Novel* (2013) stands out. Weiland is a prolific writer of books and audios on the craft of writing, including *Outlining Your Novel* (2011) and *Structuring Your Novel*, in which the present selection appears. She is also the author of a Western, *A Man Called Outlaw* (2007); a medieval epic, *Behold the Dawn* (2009); and the epic fantasy *Dreamlander* (2012). *Writer's Digest* has listed Weiland's Web site, "Helping Writers Become Authors," as one of the "101 Best Websites for Writers." She's a prolific blogger on matters of craft, and you may visit her site <www.helpingwritersbecomeauthors.com> to read posts like this one:"Why Protagonists Must Suffer to Be Interesting."

Readers are like fish. Smart fish. Fish who know authors are out to get them, reel them in, and capture them for the rest of their seagoing lives. Like all self-respecting fish, readers aren't caught easily. They aren't about to surrender themselves to the lure of your story unless you've presented them with an irresistible hook.

Our discussion of story structure very naturally begins at the beginning—and the beginning of any good story is its hook. Unless you hook readers into your story from the very first chapter, they won't swim in deep enough to experience the rest of your rousing adventure, no matter how amazing it is.

The hook comes in many forms, but stripped down to its lowest common denominator, it's nothing more or less than a question. If we can pique our readers' curiosity, we've got 'em. Simple as that.

The beginning of every story should present character, setting, and conflict. But, in themselves, none of these represent a hook. We've created a hook only when we've convinced readers to ask the general question, "What's going to happen?" because we've also convinced them to ask a more specific question— "What scary reptilian monster killed the worker?" (*Jurassic Park* by Michael Crichton) or "How does a city hunt?" (*Mortal Engines* by Philip Reeve).

5   Your opening question might be explicit: perhaps you open with the character wondering something, which will hopefully make readers wonder the same thing. But more often, the question is implicit, as it is, for example, in Elizabeth Gaskell's short story "Lizzie Leigh," which opens with a dying man's last words to his wife. All he says is, "I forgive her, Anne! May God forgive me." Readers have no idea whom the man is forgiving, or why he might need to beg God's forgiveness in turn. The very fact that we don't know what he's talking about makes us want to read on to find the answers.

The important thing to remember about presenting this opening question is that it cannot be vague. Readers have to understand enough about the situation to mentally form a specific question. *What the heck is going on here?* does not qualify as a good opening question.

It's not necessary for the question to remain unanswered all the way to the end of the story. It's perfectly all right to answer the question in the very next paragraph, so long as you introduce another question, and another and another, to give readers a reason to keep turning those pages in search of answers.

Beginnings are the sales pitch for your entire story. Doesn't matter how slam-bang your finish is, doesn't matter how fresh your dialogue is, doesn't matter if your characters are so real they tap dance their way off the pages. If your beginning doesn't fulfill all its requirements, readers won't get far enough to discover your story's hidden merits.

Although no surefire pattern exists for the perfect opening, most good beginnings share the following traits:

- **They don't open *before* the beginning.** Mystery author William G. Tapley points out, "Starting before the beginning…means loading up your readers with background information they have no reason to care about." Don't dump your backstory into your reader's lap right away, no matter how vital it is to the plot. How many of us want to hear someone's life story the moment after we meet him?

- **They open with characters, preferably the protagonist.** Even the most plot-driven tales inevitably boil down to characters. The personalities that inhabit your stories are what will connect with readers. If you fail to connect them with the characters right off the bat, you can cram all the action you want into your opening, but the intensity and the drama will still fall flat.

- **They open with conflict.** No conflict, no story. Conflict doesn't always mean nuclear warheads going off, but it does demand your characters be at odds with someone or something right from the get-go. Conflict keeps the pages turning, and turning pages are nowhere more important than in the beginning.

- **They open with movement.** Openings need more than action, they need motion. Motion gives readers a sense of progression and, when necessary, urgency. Whenever possible, open with a scene that allows your characters to keep moving, even if they're just checking the fridge.

- **They establish the setting.** Modern authors are often shy of opening with description, but a quick, incisive intro of the setting serves not only to ground readers in the physicality of the story, but also to hook their interest and set the stage. Opening lines "that hook you immediately into the hero's dilemma almost always follow the hook with a bit of stage setting," and vice versa.

- **They orient readers with an "establishing" shot.** Anchoring readers can often be done best by taking a cue from the movies and opening with an "establishing" shot. If done skillfully, you can present the setting and the characters' positions within it in as little as a sentence or two.

- **They set the tone.** Because your opening chapter sets the tone for your entire story, you need to give readers accurate presuppositions about the type of tale they're going to be reading. Your beginning needs to set the stage for the denouement—without, of course, giving it away.

10   If you can nail all these points in your opening chapter, your readers will keep the pages turning into the wee hours of the morning.

Five Elements of a Riveting First Line

Because your ability to convince readers to keep reading is dependent on your hook, you will need to present it as early as possible in your first scene. In fact, if you can get it into your first line, so much the better. However, the hook *must be organic*. Teasing readers with a killer opening line ("Mimi was dying again") only to reveal all is not as it seems (turns out Mimi is an actress performing her 187th death scene) both negates the power of your hook and betrays readers' trust. And readers don't like to be betrayed. Not one little bit.

The opening line of your book is your first (and, if you don't take advantage of it, *last*) opportunity to grab your readers' attention and give them a reason to read your story. That's a gargantuan job for a single sentence. But if we analyze opening lines, we discover a number of interesting things. One of the most surprising discoveries is that very few opening lines are memorable.

Say *what?*

Before you start quoting the likes of "Call me Ishmael" and "Happy families are all alike," take a moment to think about the last few books you read and loved. Can you remember the opening lines?

15   The very fact that these unremembered lines convinced us to keep reading until we loved the books means they did their jobs to sparkly perfection. I looked up the first lines of five of my favorite reads from the last year:

> When I wake up, the other side of the bed is cold. (*The Hunger Games* by Suzanne Collins)
>
> When he woke in the woods in the dark and the cold of the night he'd reach out to touch the child sleeping beside him. (*The Road* by Cormac McCarthy)
>
> It was night again. The Waystone Inn lay in silence, and it was a silence of three parts. (*The Name of the Wind by Patrick Rothfuss*)
>
> They used to hang men at Four Turnings in the old days. (*My Cousin Rachel* by Daphne du Maurier)
>
> On the night he had appointed his last among the living, Dr. Ben Givens did not dream, for his sleep was restless and visited by phantoms who guarded the portal to the world of dreams by speaking relentlessly of this world. (*East of the Mountains* by David Guterson)

What makes these lines work? What about them makes us want to read on? Let's break them down into five parts.

1. **Inherent Question**. To begin with, they all end with an invisible question mark. Why is the other side of the bed cold? Why are these characters sleeping outside in bad weather? How can silence be divided into three separate parts? Whom did they hang in the old days—and why don't they hang them anymore? And why and how has Ben Givens appointed the time of his death? You can't just tell readers what's going on in your story; you have to give them enough information to make *them* ask the questions—so you can then answer them.
2. **Character**. Most of these opening lines give us a character (and the rest introduce their characters in the sentences that follow). The first line is the first opportunity readers have to meet and become interested in your main character. Guterson ramps this principle to the max by naming his character, which allows readers that many more degrees of connection.
3. **Setting**. Most of these lines also offer a sense of setting. In particular, McCarthy, du Maurier, and Rothfuss use their settings to impart a deep sense of foreboding and to set the tone of the book. The opening line doesn't have to stand alone. It is supported by and leads into the scaffolding of all the sentences and paragraphs that follow.

4. **Sweeping Declaration**. Only one of our example books (du Maurier's) opens with a declaration. Some authors feel this is another technique that's fallen by the wayside, along with the omniscient narrators of Melville and Tolstoy. But the declaration is still alive and well, no matter what point of view you're operating from. The trick is using the declaration to make readers ask that all-important inherent question. "The sky is blue" or "a stitch in time saves nine" are the kind of yawn-infested declarations that lead nowhere. But if you dig a little deeper—something along the lines of William Gibson's "The sky above the port was the color of television, tuned to a dead channel"—you find not only a bit of poetry, but also a sense of tone and the question of *why?* that makes readers want to keep going.

5. **Tone**. Finally, in every one of our examples readers can find the introduction of tone. Your first line is your "hello." Don't waste it. Set the tone of your story right from the start. Is your book funny, snarky, wistful, sad, or poetic? Make sure we find that core element in your opening line. Don't hand them a joke at the beginning if your story is a lyrical tragedy.

Opening lines offer authors their first and best opportunity to make a statement about their stories. Play around until you find something that perfectly introduces your story's character, plot, setting, theme, and voice. Your opening line may be as short as Suzanne Collins's. It may be longer than David Guterson's. It may be flashy, or it may be straightforward. Whatever the case, it needs to be an appropriate starting line for the grand adventure that is your story.

Examples From Film and Literature

Now that we have a basic idea of what a hook is and where it belongs, let's consider a few examples. I've selected two movies and two novels (two classics and two recent), which we'll use as examples throughout the book, so you can follow the story arc as presented in popular and successful media. Let's take a look at how the professionals hook us so effectively we never realize we've swallowed the worm.

- *Pride & Prejudice* **by Jane Austen (1813):** Austen begins by masterfully hooking us with her famous opening line, "It is a truth universally acknowledged, that a single man in possession of a good fortune must be in want of a wife." The subtle irony gives us a sense of conflict from the very first and lets us know that neither the wife in search of the fortune nor the man in search of the wife will find their goals so easily. Austen deepens the pull of her hook in her opening paragraph by further highlighting the juxtaposition of her opening statement with the realities of her plot. She deepens it still further throughout the opening scene, which introduces readers to the Bennet family in such a way that we not only grow interested in the characters, but also realize both the thrust of the plot and the difficulties of the conflict.

- *It's a Wonderful Life* **directed by Frank Capra (1947):** Capra opens with a framing device that hooks viewers with a sneak peek of the Climax. The movie opens at the height of the main character's troubles and has us wondering why George Bailey is in such a fix that the whole town is praying for him. Next thing we know, we're staring at an unlikely trio of angels, manifested as blinking constellations. The presentation not only fascinates us with its unexpectedness, it also succinctly expresses the coming conflict and stakes and engages readers with a number of specific need-to-know questions.

- *Ender's Game* **by Orson Scott Card (1977):** The opening line to Card's acclaimed science-fiction novel is packed with hooking questions: "I've watched through his eyes, I've listened through his ears, and I tell you he's the one. Or at least as close as we're going to get." Just like that, Card's got us wondering how the speaker is watching and listening through someone else's mind, who is "the one," what is "the one" supposed to do, and why are they settling for a "one" who is less than perfect? He then successfully builds his killer opening into a scene that introduces his unlikely hero, six-year-old Ender Wiggin, just as his life is about to be turned upside down.

- *Master and Commander: The Far Side of the World* **directed by Peter Weir (2004):** As a brilliant adaptation of Patrick O'Brian's beloved Aubrey/Maturin series, this movie is unusual in a number of areas, not least in its non-formulaic tone and plot. Nevertheless, it follows the requirements of structure to a T, beginning with the stark opening that shows the morning ritual aboard the man of war HMS *Surprise*. Aside from arousing our natural curiosity about the unique setting, the hook doesn't appear until a minute or so into the film when one of the midshipmen spots what might be an enemy ship. The film never slows to explain the situation to the viewers. It carries them through a few tense moments of uncertainty and indecision, then, almost without warning, plunges them into the midst of a horrific sea battle. We are hooked almost before we see the hook coming.

Takeaway Value

So what can we learn from these masterful hooks?

1. Hooks should be inherent to the plot.
2. Hooks don't always involve action, but they always set it up.
3. Hooks never waste time.
4. Hooks almost always pull double or triple duty in introducing character, conflict, and plot—and even setting and theme.

20   Your hook is your first chance to impress readers, and like it or not, first impressions will make you or break you. Plan your hook carefully and wow readers so thoroughly they won't ever forget your opening scene.

● **Review Questions**   MyWritingLab™

1. Weiland claims that questions play a central role in setting a narrative hook. How so?

2. In what ways does an explicit hook-related question differ from an implicit one?

3. What important elements do successful openings share?

4. Why is a novel's first line so important, and why *doesn't* it need to be memorable?

5. What kinds of information can first lines convey?

● **Discussion and Writing Suggestions**   MyWritingLab™

1. Reread the final section of Weiland, on "Takeaway Value." Choose one such value and discuss how it emerges from the opening to either of the two novels or two films she analyzes. For instance, how can Value #1 ("Hooks should be inherent to the plot") be observed at work in *Pride and Prejudice*?

2. Weiland compares readers to "smart fish." In your experience, how well does this image describe your situation as you settle down to read a book or view the opening of a film? For instance, when you read a book or view a film, do you feel hooked and "reeled" into the action? Do you sense that the writer or director has gone "fishing" for you? Suggest another image that could illuminate the relationship between a reader/viewer and an opening chapter/scene.

3. Weiland's lists concerning effective openings and first lines are descriptive. That is, she has read numerous books and seen numerous movies and distilled her observations into succinct lists. Imagine you're a novelist. How readily do you think the process could work in reverse? Guided by Weiland's lists, how readily could you write a successful opening to a novel? Give it a go! Write a great opening line or paragraph, try it out on your friends, and then analyze its effectiveness according to Weiland's criteria.

4. In her discussion of narrative openings, Weiland emphasizes *questions* and the corresponding need for answers. Consider this need to know about the lives of strangers on the page and on the screen. Why are we remotely interested? After all, there are plenty of *living, breathing* people surrounding us every day in our actual, lived lives. Why should fictional characters make any claim at all on our curiosity?

STARTING YOUR STORY

Michael Kardos

What tasks must the beginning of a novel accomplish? Why should stories sometimes begin in the middle of the action, rather than at the beginning? These and other questions are treated by novelist Michael Kardos in his book *The Art and Craft of Fiction* (2013). Kardos is also the author of the story collection *One Last Good Time* (2011) and the novel *The Three-Day Affair* (2012), named by *Esquire* as a best book of 2012. His most recent novel is *Before He Finds Her* (2015). His stories have appeared in such journals as *The Southern Review*, *Crazyhorse*, and *Prairie Schooner*, and his essays about fiction have been published in *The Writer's Chronicle* and *Writer's Digest*. Kardos received his BA from Princeton, his MFA. from Ohio State, and his PhD from the University of Missouri. He currently lives in Starkville, Mississippi, where he codirects the creative writing program at Mississippi State. The following material is reprinted from *The Art and Craft of Fiction: A Writer's Guide,* by Michael Kardos (michaelkardos.com), published by Bedford/St. Martin's, © 2013. The content is Chapter 3: Starting Your Story (pp. 25–41). To learn more about the book, see bedfordstmartins.com/kardos/catalog.

 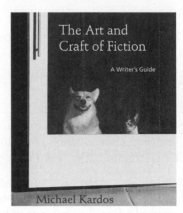

Author Michael Kardos and *The Art and Craft of Fiction*, published by Bedford/St. Martin's © 2013.

There's an old Head & Shoulders shampoo ad campaign with the tagline "You never get a second chance to make a first impression."

And what's true for shampoo is generally true for fiction.

The beginning of a story presents a world of possibilities for a writer, and each beginning will make a different first impression. The first sentence matters because a story has exactly one of them. The same is true about a first paragraph and a first scene.

What Beginnings Do

Beyond making a favorable first impression on the reader, the beginning of a story typically needs to complete certain narrative tasks. Before long, a story must

- Introduce the characters and the relationships among them
- Present the underlying situation and the beginning of conflict
- Establish the tone, voice, and point of view (its storytelling approach)
- Establish the setting
- Give us a reason to keep reading

5   This might sound like a lot—and it is—but it needn't be overly complicated. Consider fairy tales. The Brothers Grimm began many of their fairy tales by conveying just this sort of information:

> Once upon a time, in a large forest, close to a village, stood the cottage where the Teddy Bear family lived. They were not really proper Teddy Bears, for Father Bear

was very big, Mother Bear was middling in size, and only Baby Bear could be described as a Teddy Bear.

Right away, we're told the story's setting—its time (the past, when magical things happened) and place (the cottage, the village, the forest). We're introduced to the Bear family, their relationships, and their key characteristics. We're also introduced to the storytelling approach—it is being told to us by an all-knowing third-person narrator, in a fairly formal storytelling voice.

Here's another one:

> Next to a great forest there lived a poor woodcutter with his wife and his two children. The boy's name was Hansel and the girl's name was Gretel. He had but little to eat, and once, when a great famine came to the land, he could no longer provide even their daily bread.

As with "Goldilocks and the Three Bears," the beginning of "Hansel and Gretel" lays out its setting as well as its principal characters and their relationships to one another. It also immediately reveals the family's predicament: A famine has made this already poor family desperate for food.

Notice the similarities between the storytelling approach taken by the Brothers Grimm and Kevin Brockmeier in his 2008 story "A Fable with Slips of White Paper Spilling from the Pockets":

> Once there was a man who happened to buy God's overcoat. He was rummaging through a thrift store when he found it hanging on a rack by the fire exit, nestled between a birch-colored fisherman's sweater and a cotton blazer with a suede patch on one of the elbows.

10 Here, too, we're introduced immediately to the main character (the man), the story's initial setting (a thrift store), and its time ("once"—like the Grimm fairy tale, some unspecified time in the past). The narrative voice is somewhat less formal than in the Grimm tale. The phrase "who happened to buy" sounds casual, and even a little comic in the way it downplays what a reader would assume is an extraordinary event. We also get a sense of the story's underlying *situation* and its *conflict*. A man has bought God's overcoat. Surely this fact must lead to something.

Brockmeier's beginning illustrates one other thing that story openings do:

- The beginning of a story gives the reader a sense of what *kind* of story the story is going to be. It lays out the rules of the game.

When I was growing up, most board games printed their rules on the inside of the box. Nowadays, board games usually come with instruction manuals. In any event, when you buy a new game, first you learn the rules and then you play the game.

Stories don't work that way. Stories—all stories—have "rules," but the rules get revealed *as* the game is being played. As we read the beginning of a story, we come to understand the story's rules—what sort of things are permissible in the story's world, and what aren't. We also start to determine such things as whether the story will be sincere, or ironic, or comic, or somber, and whether the prose will be lyrical or workmanlike.

This laying out of a story's own rules is sometimes referred to as a "contract"—that this, the story establishes a contract with its readers. A highly realistic story in which, on page 10, the mother ship lands and beams all the characters aboard would be said to be *violating the story's contract*.

15   From Brockmeier's first two sentences, we anticipate a story that in terms of content and tone will resemble a fable or fairy tale ("Once there was a man …"), but one that also is rooted in the real, modern-day world of thrift stores with fire exits. A story like Brockmeier's includes highly realistic characters and also fantastical elements, such as God's overcoat, without violating the contract or breaking the rules, whichever phrase you prefer.

Reveal Key Information (Spill the Beans)

The opening sentence of "A Fable with Slips of White Paper Spilling from the Pockets" is a wonderful example of the following maxim: *It's a good idea to reveal key information, especially hard-to-swallow information, as soon as possible.*

By telling us immediately that this is "God's overcoat," we, the readers, aren't allowed to argue the point. We can't say, "No, it isn't." Because it is. We're told it is and must accept that fact as part of the story's premise.

Perhaps the best example of front-loading hard-to-swallow information is the first sentence of Franz Kafka's 1915 novella *The Metamorphosis*:

> Gregor Samsa awoke one morning from unsettled dreams to find that he had turned into a giant cockroach.

When we begin reading Kafka's novella, we don't think: "No, Gregor didn't. People can't turn into cockroaches." Of course we don't. Rather, we accept the situation as presented and keep reading. Why? Because we're told about it up front. The author is making a first impression that says, "My story features a man-cockroach. Deal with it."

20   So one answer to the question "How do I begin?" is to begin with whatever information the reader needs most in order to appreciate—or simply believe—your story.

The corresponding advice is that you shouldn't withhold vital information as a secret until the end of your story. Sometimes new writers like to "surprise" the reader at the end with shocking facts. The two characters are really a single character with multiple personalities! The whole story was actually just a dream! These sort of "surprises" (I put the word in quotation marks because they rarely surprise) will disappoint all but the most naïve reader.

Rather than mislead or trick the reader, give us the important information up front. Make us care, and go from there.

Even stories that do not feature heavenly outerwear or giant, sentient insects often front-load information that the reader needs in order to appreciate and care about what happens. Here is how Sherman Alexie begins his story "This Is What It Means to Say Phoenix, Arizona":

> Just after Victor lost his job at the BIA, he also found out that his father had died of a heart attack in Phoenix, Arizona. Victor hadn't seen his father in a few years, only talked to him on the telephone once or twice, but there still was a genetic pain, which was soon to be pain as real and immediate as a broken bone.
>
> Victor didn't have any money. Who does have money on a reservation, except the cigarette and fireworks salespeople? His father had a savings account waiting to be claimed, but Victor needed to find a way to get to Phoenix. Victor's mother was just as poor as he was, and the rest of his family didn't have any use at all for him. So Victor called the Tribal Council.

Notice how this opening quickly establishes its characters, setting, and tone. But beyond that, it gives us the story's underlying *situation* (Victor must deal with the practicalities of the death of his father, with whom he didn't have a close relationship, a problem compounded by his lack of funds to get to Phoenix). Finally, this paragraph ends with the promise of immediate *conflict*, specifically an uncomfortable meeting between Victor and the Tribal Council. Surely the council won't simply agree to give Victor all the money he needs. That would be too easy.

25   Notice, too, that in revealing certain information, Alexie arouses our curiosity. We know that Victor hasn't seen his father in a few years, but we know nothing of the nature of their rift. We know that Victor's family "didn't have any use at all for him," but we don't know why that is. By providing us with information, Alexie causes us to ask questions about the story that we hope will be answered before long.

The opening to Richard Bausch's story "The Man Who Knew Belle Starr" looks, at first, like a relatively straightforward paragraph of exposition in which basic information about McRae's situation is revealed. Yet the story withholds just enough information to create little mysteries that make us want to keep reading:

> On his way west McRae picked up a hitcher, [1] a young woman carrying a paper bag[2] and a leather purse, wearing jeans and a shawl—which she didn't take off, though it was more than ninety degrees out and McRae had no air-conditioning. [3] He was driving an old Dodge Charger with a bad exhaust system and one long crack in the wraparound windshield. He pulled over for her, and she got right in, put the leather purse on the seat between them, and settled herself with a paper bag on her lap between her hands.[4] He had just crossed into Texas from Oklahoma. This was the third day of the trip.

This opening raises a number of questions:

1. Why is McRae heading west? And why does he pick up the hitch-hiker?
2. What is in the bag?

3. Why won't she take off her shawl?

4. Seriously, what's in the paper bag? It's been mentioned twice already. She sure is protective of it. Must be important.

Establish the Story's Stakes

Readers need a reason to keep reading. They need to see fairly quickly why what they're reading matters. A story's stakes are what make a story matter to the story's characters and to the reader.

"This Is What It Means to Say Phoenix, Arizona" immediately provides reasons to care about Victor and to understand why he wants what he wants. The story matters to us because it matters to Victor, and because we sense that Victor's quest will not be an easy one. I'm not just referring to his lack of money. I mean that already, in the story's first paragraphs, we see Victor's ambivalence. On the one hand, he and his father weren't close. That should make the man's death a little easier on Victor. On the other hand, Victor feels "a genetic pain, which was soon to be pain as real and immediate as a broken bone." Before the end of the story, Victor will have to deal with his conflicting feelings about his father—and that internal voyage is what pulls us into the story at least as much as the prospect of his trip to Phoenix.

CHECKLIST:

Set the Stakes

- What does your main character have to gain or lose in your story? What is at stake for him or her?
- How can you introduce the stakes early in your story?

30   Tim O'Brien takes a different approach toward presenting the stakes at the beginning of his story "On the Rainy River" a direct appeal to the reader:

> This is one story I've never told before.

Quite simply, this sentence appeals to our desire to know somebody else's intimate secrets. After reading that sentence, we naturally want to know (1) the story that's been kept secret and (2) why it's been kept secret.

But the paragraph doesn't end there. The stakes get raised:

> Not to anyone. Not to my parents, not to my brother or sister, not even to my wife. To go into it, I've always thought, would only cause embarrassment for all of us, a sudden need to be elsewhere, which is the natural response to a confession.

So the narrator isn't simply revealing a long-held secret—he's making a confession. Confessions, as we know, tend to be juicy and worth sticking around for.

The paragraph continues:

> Even now, I'll admit, the story makes me squirm. For more than twenty years I've had to live with it, feeling the shame, trying to push it away, and so by this act of remembrance, by putting the facts down on paper, I'm hoping to relieve at least some of the pressure on my dreams.

Considering that he's kept the story from his wife and family for twenty years, we can assume that this is no run-of-the-mill, I-forgot-to-take-out-the-trash confession. This narrator seems thoughtful and honest, and he has a secret that has been weighing heavily on him for *twenty years*. Now, finally, he's going to come clean and reveal his secret in the hopes of unburdening himself.

35   That's something we'll stick around to hear.

Start with a Break From Routine

Imagine a story that begins like this:

> When the alarm clock went off at 6:30 a.m., Phil hit the snooze button. Nine minutes later, same as every weekday morning, he hit it again. Finally he arose from his bed and went into the bathroom to brush his teeth. He took a long, hot shower, got dressed in his suit and tie, and went downstairs to brew a pot of his favorite coffee—hazelnut. He sat at the kitchen table and looked out the window. The sun was just coming up. A neighborhood kid rode his bike past the house, a stack of newspapers under his arm. Phil didn't receive a paper. He read all his news online. After draining two cups of coffee, Phil put on his shoes and left the house. He arrived at the office eleven minutes later, same as always. He said hello to his co-workers and went into his office, where he began to check his email. Phil was an insurance broker, and he received dozens of emails a day—most, it seemed, from angry clients. When he looked up from his computer, his colleague, Sean, was standing in the doorway wearing a giraffe suit.

QUESTION: Where does this story actually begin?
CLUE: Where does Phil's story diverge from his ordinary routine?

Phil's story does not begin with the alarm clock going off. Beginning writers often confuse the beginning of a character's *day* with the beginning of a character's *story*. They are not the same.

In the sample story opening above, Phil's morning routine is just that—routine. It isn't news. Part of the problem is that nothing particularly distinguishes Phil's morning from that of millions of other hardworking citizens. The bigger problem, though, is that it isn't even unusual for *him*. He awakes, he showers, he drinks coffee, he drives to work. Does it matter that he prefers hazelnut-flavored coffee to a basic French roast? Probably not. (If it does, we can certainly work that detail into the story later.)

Just as it's a mistake to begin this story in bed with the alarm clock going off, it would be a mistake to start it with Phil's drive to work. The drive, like the hot shower and cup of coffee, is just a preface to what really matters.

40   The giraffe suit? Now that's news:

> One Thursday morning, Phil looked up from his computer terminal to find his colleague, Sean, standing in the doorway wearing a giraffe suit.

Or:

> "So what do you think?" asked Sean, standing in the doorway of Phil's office dressed in a giraffe suit. Like Phil, Sean was an insurance broker. The office had a strict dress code: suit, tie. No facial hair.
> "What do I think about what?" Phil asked.

Or:

> Yesterday it was a gorilla suit. The day before, an elephant. Sean's wife had left him over the weekend, and now all week he'd been coming to the office dressed as one large mammal or another. Phil, who had always considered Sean to be one of the more boring brokers at Midwest Insurance, couldn't decide if he was more amused or annoyed. He had dozens of emails to return and calls to make. Time was money. Still, it was always interesting to see a fellow human being crack open like an egg.

The story possibilities, and the ways of telling them, are endless. But they all begin after Phil's morning routine is over, at the moment when his routine gets disrupted.

Stories, with few exceptions, are about *the day that's different*—the day that a man happens to buy God's overcoat. The day that Victor loses his job, learns about his father's death, and decides he must travel to Phoenix, Arizona. They are about the disruption from one's ordinary routine. A wise place to begin, therefore, is at the moment when this disruption first announces itself. (In *The Metamorphosis*, this difference actually does announce itself in Gregor's bed, because that's when he realizes that he has turned into a giant cockroach. In that one example, the beginning of a character's day happens to coincide with the beginning of his story. But Gregor's morning, we can safely assume, will be far from routine.)

Karen Russell's story "St. Lucy's Home for Girls Raised by Wolves" takes place over a large portion of a school year. Rather than beginning at home, or on the long drive to the academy, the story begins at the institution. The opening paragraph reveals just how out-of-place the girls are upon arriving at their new school. It reveals, too, how at first the narrator considers herself one of a pack. There is no "I" perspective, but rather a "we," something that will begin to shift later in the story as the narrator, Claudette, develops her own identity apart from the pack:

> At first, our pack was all hair and snarl and floor-thumping joy. We forgot the barked cautions of our mothers and fathers, all the promises we'd made to be civilized and

ladylike, couth and kempt. We tore through the austere rooms, overturning dresser drawers, pawing through the neat piles of the Stage 3 girls' starched underwear, smashing light bulbs with our bare fists. Things felt less foreign in the dark. The dim bedroom was windowless and odorless. We remedied this by spraying exuberant yellow streams all over the bunks. We jumped from bunk to bunk, spraying. We nosed each other midair, our bodies buckling in kinetic laughter. The nuns watched us from the corner of the bedroom, their tiny faces pinched with displeasure.

The place you start your story has a lot to do with what your story is ultimately about. Karen Russell could have started her story the day that Claudette first learns that there will be a dance with the boys' school—when Claudette first understands that her socialization will be put to the test. Or it could have begun even later, at the dance itself. Instead, Russell begins when the girls first arrive at their school. The story therefore covers months instead of days or hours, making it less about a single event and more about the steady erosion of Claudette's ties to her roots—her pack—as she becomes indoctrinated into "civilized" society.

•   •   •

Consider Starting *in Medias Res*

45 Brockmeier's and Alexie's stories both begin with the narrator providing necessary information to the reader using exposition. This is what the third example of the giraffe-suit story does, as well:

> Yesterday it was a gorilla suit. The day before, an elephant. Sean's wife had left him over the weekend, and now all week he'd been coming to the office dressed as one large mammal or another.

However, a story that begins *in medias res*, a Latin phrase meaning "into the middle of things," drops us—well, into the middle of things. Here are a few stories that do just that from the first sentence:

> He had been reading to her from Rilke, a poet he admired, when she fell asleep with her head on his pillow.
>
> —RAYMOND CARVER, "The Student's Wife"

> I read about it in the paper, in the subway, on my way to work.
>
> —JAMES BALDWIN, "Sonny's Blues"

> I was popular in certain circles, says Aunt Rose.
>
> —GRACE PALEY, "Goodbye and Good Luck"

> In walks these three girls in nothing but bathing suits.
>
> —JOHN UPDIKE, "A & P"

Look back at the first paragraph of "St. Lucy's Home for Girls Raised by Wolves." Even though that story begins at the start of the school year, Karen Russell's story begins *in medias res*, dropping us into the middle of the action. Who are the "Stage 3 girls"? What are the nuns doing there? And what, exactly, is this "pack" being referred to? These questions will all get sorted out—but not right away.

The practice of beginning a story *in medias res* isn't new: Homer did it in both the *Iliad* and the *Odyssey*. More recently, so did George Lucas in the original *Star Wars* movie—which, we're told right away, is "episode four" and therefore truly the middle of things. *Star Wars* begins with a thrilling battle scene before we have any clue who is fighting or what the battle is about. Because we haven't yet been introduced to the characters and situation, a story that begins *in medias res* often causes momentary confusion. Yet it has the benefit of urgency and, done well, can generate in the reader an oddly satisfying sensation of not quite keeping up with the story. Most action/adventure films begin *in medias res* because of a need to hook the viewer with something immediately thrilling. *Raiders of the Lost Ark* begins with Indiana Jones skillfully evading a booby-trapped cave, then stealing a huge jewel, then running like mad when a giant boulder threatens to crush him. At this point, we don't know anything about the characters or the plot, but we're intrigued because the events themselves are so gripping.

A story that begins *in medias res* eventually will need to supply the missing pieces. A reader (or viewer) will be willing to remain confused for only so long before becoming frustrated. The second scene in *Raiders of the Lost Ark* features Indiana Jones back on safer ground, at the university where he teaches anthropology. In this second scene, we learn all the necessary information that would have been supplied up front in a "once upon a time" opening.

50   Becky Hagenston begins her story "Midnight, Licorice, Shadow" *in medias res*. A "once upon a time" beginning might read:

> Donna and Jeremy, her boyfriend of three weeks, were trying to name their new cat. The cat used to belong to a woman they'd robbed and killed. Now it was theirs. They were holed up in a motel room now, and Donna was feeling an increased urgency to name the cat. That was because Jeremy had said, "If we don't have a name by tomorrow morning, it's bye-bye, Mister Kitty." He didn't like when something didn't have a name. He felt it was bad luck.

Instead, Hagenston drops us into the middle of things:

> "Midnight, Licorice, Shadow," she says. "Cocoa, Casper, Dr. Livingston."
> "Alfred Hitchcock," he says. "Dracula. Vincent Price."
> They have had the cat for nearly three days.
> "Cinderblock?" she tries. "Ice bucket?"
> It's useless. The harder they try to think of a name, the more elusive it becomes.

"Tomorrow, then," Jeremy says. "If we don't have a name by tomorrow morning, it's bye-bye, Mr. Kitty. No offense, Cupcake," he tells the cat, and gives it a quick rub on the head.

Donna looks at the animal, sprawled on the orange motel carpet like a black bearskin rug. One of his fangs is showing. His monkey paws are kneading at the air.

We don't learn for seven paragraphs that they're in a motel room, and we won't learn for several pages about the murder, or about Jeremy's superstition about things not having names. The story as Hagenston begins it emphasizes the oppressiveness of the relationship between Donna and Jeremy, and the urgency they feel, especially Donna. She's desperate to name that cat. Why? we wonder, and we keep reading to find out.

Whose Perspective Should You Choose?

Knowing what you want to write about isn't the same as knowing whose perspective to tell it from. Your choice will inform just about every other aspect of your story, just as your version of the first day of school is no doubt different from your teacher's.

CHECKLIST:

Decide on a Perspective

Here are some things to consider:

- Who has the most at stake? The most to gain or lose? Whoever is most heavily invested in the outcome of your story might well be the natural character to designate as your point-of-view character.

- On the other hand, some characters don't make especially good narrators, such as very young children and those with extremely limited perspectives or communication skills. A point-of-view character who is (1) delusional, (2) drunk, or (3) a dog presents challenges that are extremely hard to overcome. In the novel *The Great Gatsby,* Gatsby doesn't tell his own story. He is no slouch, but he can't tell his own story because he would have neither the words nor the perspective. (Plus, by the end of the novel he's dead.) Nick Carraway tells Gatsby's story because Nick possesses the narrative and interpretive skills that Gatsby lacks, as well as the capacity to change.

- Is your story less about a single character than about several people or a community? If so, then your story might best be told from several characters' perspectives, as in Jill McCorkle's story "Magic Words."

Other Information to Convey Sooner Rather Than Later

Early on in your story—probably within the first page or two—it's usually a good idea to provide some basic information about the characters.

CHECKLIST:

Establish the Basics

- **Your main character's name.** Yes, some stories never name their characters, using "he" or "she" or "the man" or "the women" throughout. Ernest Hemingway's story "Hills Like White Elephants" is a commonly cited example. However, the decision not to name your character should be just that—a decision—rather than an oversight. (The main character in Kevin Brockmeier's story "A Fable with Slips of White Paper Spilling from the Pockets" goes unnamed. Why do you think that is?) In general, readers like to know the names of the characters in a story, and not naming them will not make them more universal.

- **Your main character's sex.** It can be very disorienting for a reader to assume that a story's main character is female and then, on page 9, to learn that he is male.

- **The basic relationships between characters.** A story that begins

> Bill kissed Brittany on the cheek and went off with Sonya to get married.

is confusing because we don't yet know Brittany's relationship to Bill or Sonya. Instead, consider something like:

> Bill kissed Brittany, his youngest sister, on the cheek and went off with Sonya to get married.

Or:

> Bill kissed Brittany, his girlfriend of eleven years, on the cheek and went off with Sonya to get married.

These are two entirely different stories. Readers deserve to know which it is so that we will create the proper picture in our minds.

Ultimately, It's Your Call

55 When does your character's routine get interrupted? What are your story's stakes? What key information needs to be revealed? What are the benefits of beginning either "once upon a time" or *in medias res*? Once you've given these matters some thought, you'll be well on your way to making a strong—and strongly favorable—first impression.

Whenever you work on a new story, bear in mind that the beginning might well change. As you write, your understanding of your own story grows, and that requires a rethinking of the beginning. You might change the point of view or change the tense from present to past. You might change the voice, making it more formal or less formal. Sometimes, the beginning—the first page or section—will end up staying in place all the way through to the final draft. But maybe not. You might end up using the first attempt elsewhere in the story, or maybe it will need to get cut completely once you realize that a different beginning would be better. Always, though, you'll learn something about your story from that first attempt—so the effort isn't ever wasted.

The good news about fiction writing is that you can unmake or revisit your decisions as you continue to work. Nothing is irreversible. Remember: We aren't performing surgery. We aren't defusing bombs. If we make a misstep, nobody is going to die. In fact, we *will* make missteps, guaranteed. Most of the time, they aren't actually missteps. They're necessary steps—that is, necessary parts of a creative process.

So start your story already!

● Review Questions   MyWritingLab™

1. Which key story elements are revealed in the opening lines to the Grimms' classic "Goldilocks and the Three Bears"?

2. Kardos introduces the terms *rules* and *contract* to discuss the opening scenes of a story. Define these terms.

3. What is "spilling the beans," and what function does it serve in the opening of a story? By contrast, what is the "withholding of information," and how can such an act contribute to the successful opening of a story?

4. Authors must establish "stakes" for their characters. Define the term and explain its significance for successful story openings.

5. "Stories … are about *the day that's different*." What does Kardos mean?

6. Define *in medias res* and the reasons authors use this technique.

● Discussion and Writing Suggestions   MyWritingLab™

1. Inform and convince. Go online and find a weird news story, something that is factually true but doesn't seem plausible. (You can even Google "weird news.") Then write the first paragraph of a short story, based on the news piece, that readers must believe.

2. Kardos's "Starting Your Story" constitutes one chapter of a guide to fiction writing. In one of the exercises accompanying this chapter, Kardos writes: "As with so many other aspects of fiction writing, our best teachers are the stories and novels we read." What does he mean? What can you learn from stories that you cannot learn, or perhaps not learn as easily, from guides such as Kardos's?

3. The audience for Kardos's *The Art and Craft of Fiction* consists of would-be writers: readers who will take his advice and turn to writing their own stories. You can put Kardos's advice to a different use by applying his discussion to the openings of novels and films. You'll do that soon enough when you turn to assignments for writing analyses and syntheses later in this chapter. For now, think of one story or film you know well—the opening of which you can recall vividly. Select one or more of Kardos's terms and apply it to this opening. How does his vocabulary help you see the story in new, perhaps more revealing, ways?

4. Reread Kardos's analysis of the opening to "Goldilocks and the Three Bears" and "Hansel and Gretel" (pp. 344–345). An experienced writer and teacher, Kardos is able to glean a great deal of information from just a few lines. Try your hand at this exercise. Locate a fairy tale online. Read and reread the opening paragraph or two and make a bullet-point list of all that you learn. Review this list. What have you learned? As a variation of this exercise, read the same fairy tale opening as a friend who's working on this same assignment. Compare your lists and discuss the similarities and differences.

5. In some ways, the opening line and paragraph of a story, or the first few minutes of a film, serve as a bridge from your world to the story's world. The writer, or filmmaker, creates this bridge and you travel it. Reflect for a moment on the ways in which you (in particular) need to have this bridge built. What does the author/filmmaker need to do to command *your* attention? What are the surest signs that as a reader and viewer you are making the transition from one world to the next?

THE MAGIC SHOW

Tim O'Brien

In the following selection, novelist Tim O'Brien discusses how writing a story is like performing an act of magic. And he explains how mystery functions as a crucial aspect of storytelling. O'Brien (b. 1946) is the author of two enduring novels of the Vietnam era, *The Things They Carried* (1990) and *Going After Cacciato* (winner of the National Book Award, 1978). He is also the author of *If I Die in a Combat Zone* (1973), *Northern Lights* (1975), *The Nuclear Age* (1985), *In the Lake of* the *Woods* (1994), and *July, July* (2002). His short stories have appeared nationally in magazines such as the *Atlantic* and the *New Yorker*. O'Brien has been honored by the American Academy of Arts and Letters and the National Endowment for the Arts and now teaches creative writing at Texas State University. "The Magic Show" is excerpted from an essay that first appeared in *Crafting Fiction: In Theory, In Practice* (2001) by Marvin Diogenes and Clyde Moneyhun.

As a kid, through grade school and into high school, my hobby was magic. I enjoyed the power; I liked making miracles happen. In the basement, where

I practiced in front of a stand-up mirror, I caused my mother's silk scarves to change color. I used a scissors to cut my father's best tie in half, displaying the pieces, and then restored it whole. I placed a penny in the palm of my hand, made my hand into a fist, made the penny into a white mouse. This was not true magic. It was trickery. But I sometimes pretended otherwise, because I was a kid then, and because pretending was the thrill of magic, and because for a time what seemed to happen became a happening in itself. I was a dreamer. I liked watching my hands in the mirror, imagining how someday I might perform much grander magic, tigers becoming giraffes, beautiful girls levitating like angels in the high yellow spotlights, naked maybe, no wires or strings, just floating.

It was illusion, of course—the creation of a new and improved reality. What I enjoyed about this peculiar hobby, at least in part, was the craft of it: learning the techniques of magic and then practicing those techniques, alone in the basement, for many hours and days. That was another thing about magic. I liked the aloneness, as God and other miracle makers must also like it—not lonely, just alone. I liked shaping the universe around me. I liked the power. I liked the tension and suspense when, for example, the magician displays a guillotine to the audience, demonstrating its cutting power by slicing a carrot in half; the edgy delight when a member of the audience is asked to place his hand in the guillotine hole; the hollow silence when, very slowly, the magician raises up the blade. Believe me, *there* is drama. And when the blade slams down, if it's *your* hand in the hole, you have no choice but to believe in miracles.

When practiced well, however, magic goes beyond a mere sequence of illusions. It becomes art. In the art of magic, as opposed to just doing tricks, there is a sense of theater and drama and continuity and beauty and wholeness. Take an example. Someone in the audience randomly selects a card from a shuffled deck—the Ace of Diamonds. The card is made to vanish, then a rabbit is pulled out of a hat, and the hat collapses into a fan, and the magician uses the fan to fan the rabbit, and the rabbit is transformed into a white dove, and the dove flies into the spotlights and returns a moment later with a playing card in its beak—the Ace of Diamonds. With such unity and flow, with each element contributing as both cause and effect, individual tricks are blended into something whole and unified, something indivisible, which is in the nature of true art.

Beyond anything, though, what appealed to me about this hobby was the abiding mystery at its heart. Mystery everywhere—permeating mystery—even in the most ordinary objects of the world: a penny becomes a white mouse. The universe seemed both infinite and inexplicable. Anything was possible. The old rules were no longer binding, the old truths no longer true. If my father's tie could be restored whole, why not someday use my wand to wake up the dead?

5   It's pretty clear, I suppose, where all this is headed. I stopped doing magic—at least of that sort. I took up a new hobby, writing stories. But without straining

too much, I can suggest that the fundamentals seemed very much the same. Writing fiction is a solitary endeavor. You shape your own universe. You practice all the time, then practice some more. You pay attention to craft. You aim for tension and suspense, a sense of drama, displaying in concrete terms the actions and reactions of human beings contesting problems of the heart. You try to make art. You strive for wholeness, seeking continuity and flow, each element performing both as cause and effect, always hoping to create, or to re-create, the great illusions of life.

Above all, writing fiction involves a desire to enter the mystery of things: that human craving to know what cannot be known. In the ordinary world, for instance, we have no direct access to the thoughts of other human beings—we cannot *hear* those thoughts—yet even in the most "realistic" piece of fiction we listen as if through a stethoscope to the innermost musings of Anna Karenina and Lord Jim and Huck Finn. We know, in these stories, what cannot be known. It's a trick, of course. (And the tricks in these stories have been elevated into art.) In the ordinary sense, there *is* no Huck Finn, and yet in the extraordinary sense, which is the sense of magic, there most certainly *is* a Huck Finn and always will be. When writing or reading a work of fiction, we are seeking access to a kind of enigmatic "otherness"—other people and places, other worlds, other sciences, other souls. We give ourselves over to what is by nature mysterious, imagining the unknowable, and then miraculously knowing by virtue of what is imagined. There are new standards of knowing, new standards of reality. (Is Huck Finn real? No, we would say, by ordinary standards. Yes, by extraordinary standards.) For a writer, and for a reader, the process of imaginative knowing does not depend upon the scientific method. Fictional characters are not constructed of flesh and blood, but rather of words, and those words serve as explicit incantations that invite us into and guide us through the universe of the imagination. Language is the apparatus—the magic dust—by which a writer performs his miracles. Words are uttered: "By and by," Huck says, and we hear him. Words are uttered: "We went tiptoeing along a path amongst the trees," and we see it. Beyond anything, I think, a writer is someone entranced by the power of language to create a magic show of the imagination, to make the dead sit up and talk, to shine light into the darkness of the great human mysteries.

•   •   •

[T]he story, the novel … must ultimately represent and explore those same mysteries. … [I]t is my view that good storytelling involves, in a substantive sense, a plunge … into mystery of the grandest order. Briefly, almost in summary form, I want to examine this notion through two different windows of craft— plot and character.

It is my belief that plot revolves around certain mysteries of fact, or what a story represents as fact. What happened? What will happen? Huck and Jim hop on a raft (fact) and embark on a journey (fact) and numerous events occur along the way (facts). On the level of plot, this narrative appeals to our curiosity about where the various facts will lead. As readers, we wonder and worry about what may befall these two human beings as they float down a river in violation of the ordinary social conventions. We are curious about facts still to come. In this sense, plot involves the inherent and riveting mystery of the *future*. What next? What are the coming facts? By its very nature, the future compels and intrigues us—it holds promise, it holds terror—and plot relies for its power on the essential cloudiness of things to come. We don't know. We want to know.

In a magic act, as in a story, there is the reporting (or purporting) of certain facts. The guillotine *is* sharp, it *does* cut the carrot, the man's hand *does* enter the guillotine's hole, the blade *does* slam down. For an audience, the mystery has entirely to do with future facts. What will become of this poor man? Will he lose his hand? Will he weep? Will the stump bleed as stumps tend to do?

10   Without some concept of the future, these questions would be both impossible and irrelevant. It is the mystery of the future, at least in part, that compels us to turn the pages of a novel, or of a story, or of our own lives. Unlike the animals, we conceive of tomorrow. And tomorrow fascinates us. Tomorrow matters—maybe too much—and we spend a great portion of our lives adjusting the present in hope of shaping the future. In any case, we are driven to care and to be curious about questions of fate and destiny: we can't help it, we're human.

On one level, then, I am arguing in defense of old-fashioned plot—or in defense of plot in general—which is so often discredited as a sop to some unsophisticated and base human instinct. But I see nothing base in the question, "What will happen next?" I'm suggesting that plot is grounded in a high—even noble—human craving to *know*, a craving to push into the mystery of tomorrow.

·   ·   ·

About real people, we sometimes say: "Well, she's a mystery to me," or "I wonder what makes him tick." Such comments represent, I think, a deep and specific desire for the miraculous: to enter another human soul, to read other minds and hearts, to find access to what is by nature inaccessible. A person lives in his own skin. All else is other, and otherness is suspect. If we see a man laugh, for instance, we might guess that he is experiencing elation or giddiness or joy of some sort. But perhaps not. Maybe it's ironic laughter, or nervous laughter, or the laughter of the insane. Again, who knows? In a story called *The Lady with the Pet Dog*, Chekhov has one of his characters muse as follows: "Judging others by himself, he did not believe what he saw, and always fancied that every man led his real, most interesting life under cover of secrecy as under cover of night." It is easy to sympathize with this view. Like Chekhov's character, we can "judge others by ourselves," but we cannot directly experience their loves and pains and joys. We know our own thoughts—we know by the act of thinking—but we cannot think those "other" thoughts. The mystery of otherness seems permanent and binding, a law of the universe, and yet *because* it is a mystery, *because* it binds, we find ourselves clawing at the darkness of human nature in an effort to know what cannot be known. "I love you," someone says, and we begin to wonder. "Well, how much?" we say, and when the answer comes, "With my whole heart," we then wonder about the wholeness of that heart. We probe and probe again. Along with Chekhov, we fancy that there is some secret lodged inside a human personality, hidden as if under cover of night, and that if light could be cast into the darkness of another's heart, we would find there the "real" human being. Such curiosity seems to me both inevitable and misdirected. Judging from what I know of myself, the human "character," if there is such a thing, seems far too complex and fluid and contradictory ever to pin down with much solidity or specificity. To really know a human character, to expose a single "secret," strikes me as beyond reach. In a sense, we "know" human character—maybe even our own—in the same way we know black holes: by their effects on the external world.

· · ·

The magician's credo is this: don't give away your secrets. Once a trick is explained—once a secret is divulged—the world moves from the magical to the mechanical. Similarly, with plot and character, the depletion of mystery robs a story of the very quality that brings us to pursue fiction in the first place. We might admire the cleverness of the writer. But we forget the story. Because there is no miracle to remember. The object of storytelling, like the object of magic, is not to explain or to resolve, but rather to create and to perform miracles of the imagination. To extend the boundaries of the mysterious. To push into the unknown in pursuit of still other unknowns. To reach into one's own heart, down into that place where the stories are, bringing up the mystery of oneself.

● Discussion and Writing Suggestions   MyWritingLab™

1. In this selection, O'Brien draws a parallel between magicians and writers. Both the magician and the writer are creators, he claims; both work largely alone; both concern themselves with "the abiding mystery" of things; both shape universes; both ponder the drama of what will happen next; both are artists. O'Brien's linkage of magicians and novelists is fresh and probably surprising to you. What do you make of it? Discuss.

2. Recall a magic show you've seen and the sense of wonder it evoked. Now recall a story or film and the experience of coming to know, and perhaps care about, a fictional character. Compare and contrast watching magic and reading/viewing a story. What are the similarities? The differences? (O'Brien writes from the point of view of the magician/novelist. You should respond to this question from the point of view of a reader or audience member.)

3. Plot, writes O'Brien, appeals to our curiosity concerning "the inherent and riveting mystery of the future." Recall a story you know well: a novel or a film. Now consider that story purely from the perspective of plot, as O'Brien defines it. How does the writer or filmmaker engage your interest in the mystery of what will happen next? Why do you feel the *need* to know what will happen to these fictional characters in a made-up situation?

4. In writing about character, O'Brien reflects on the mystery of "the other" and the impossibility of directly knowing anyone else's thoughts and sensations. Fiction, he writes, creates the illusion of access. But it's a "trick." Do you agree? Is there any sense in which your knowledge of characters in fiction is *more* intimate than your knowledge of people in actual life? Explain.

5. If you had to reduce O'Brien's essay on magic and fiction to a single word, it would probably be *mystery*. A "writer," he says, "is someone entranced by the power of language to create a magic show of the imagination." With respect to the word *mystery*, what does O'Brien mean?

6. O'Brien is struck by the mysteries of this world. Often enough, we aren't especially aware of mystery. Why not? Why might we need magicians, writers, and filmmakers to evoke a sense of mystery?

CHAPTER ONES: THE NOVELS

Here we invite you to read the first chapter of seven classic novels. As you read, consider how the authors go about creating their fictional worlds: What details do they give the reader about characters, plot, and setting? What information do the authors refrain from giving us? What do you find yourself thinking about—and feeling—as you read? Perhaps most importantly, how do these authors, in just a handful of pages, go about making us care about the lives of made-up people in made-up situations?

The Discussion and Writing Suggestions assume that you have only read the first chapters of these novels. That said, if a first chapter intrigues you, then by all means seek out the whole novel—they are all available on Project Gutenberg, a Web site that offers free versions of work that is in the public domain: <http://www.gutenberg.org>

EMMA

Jane Austen

Jane Austen, born in 1775, began writing at a young age and completed several novels before *Sense and Sensibility* was published in 1811, followed by *Pride and Prejudice* (1813) and *Mansfield Park* (1814). First published in 1815, *Emma* was the author's last novel to be published before her death two years later at the age of forty-one. (Two more novels were published posthumously.) Notably, Austen's work was published anonymously; her identity wasn't revealed until after her death.

Emma tells the story of Emma Woodhouse and her fondness for matchmaking and generally inserting herself into others' affairs. It is a gently satirical novel that sheds light on the various social classes in England, and particularly the dependence that women of the day had on marriage for their social standing and financial security. The novel has been adapted many times for stage, TV, and film. One of the most interesting adaptions is the 1995 movie *Clueless* (see pp. 406–407), which sets Emma's story in modern-day Beverly Hills, California.

Chapter 1

Emma Woodhouse, handsome, clever, and rich, with a comfortable home and happy disposition, seemed to unite some of the best blessings of existence; and had lived nearly twenty-one years in the world with very little to distress or vex her.

She was the youngest of the two daughters of a most affectionate, indulgent father; and had, in consequence of her sister's marriage, been mistress of his house from a very early period. Her mother had died too long ago for her to have more than an indistinct remembrance of her caresses; and her place had been supplied by an excellent woman as governess, who had fallen little short of a mother in affection.

Sixteen years had Miss Taylor been in Mr. Woodhouse's family, less as a governess than a friend, very fond of both daughters, but particularly of Emma. Between *them* it was more the intimacy of sisters. Even before Miss Taylor had ceased to hold the nominal office of governess, the mildness of her temper had hardly allowed her to impose any restraint; and the shadow of authority being now long passed away, they had been living together as friend and friend very mutually attached, and Emma doing just what she liked; highly esteeming Miss Taylor's judgment, but directed chiefly by her own.

The real evils, indeed, of Emma's situation were the power of having rather too much her own way, and a disposition to think a little too well of herself; these were the disadvantages which threatened alloy to her many enjoyments. The danger, however, was at present so unperceived, that they did not by any means rank as misfortunes with her.

5   Sorrow came—a gentle sorrow—but not at all in the shape of any disagreeable consciousness.—Miss Taylor married. It was Miss Taylor's loss which first brought grief. It was on the wedding-day of this beloved friend that Emma first sat in mournful thought of any continuance. The wedding over, and the bride-people gone, her father and herself were left to dine together, with no prospect of a third to cheer a long evening. Her father composed himself to sleep after dinner, as usual, and she had then only to sit and think of what she had lost.

The event had every promise of happiness for her friend. Mr. Weston was a man of unexceptionable character, easy fortune, suitable age, and pleasant manners; and there was some satisfaction in considering with what self-denying, generous friendship she had always wished and promoted the match; but it was a black morning's work for her. The want of Miss Taylor would be felt every hour of every day. She recalled her past kindness—the kindness, the affection of sixteen years— how she had taught and how she had played with her from five years old—how she had devoted all her powers to attach and amuse her in health—and how nursed her through the various illnesses of childhood. A large debt of gratitude was owing here; but the intercourse of the last seven years, the equal footing and perfect unreserve which had soon followed Isabella's marriage, on their being left to each other, was yet a dearer, tenderer recollection. She had been a friend and companion such as few possessed: intelligent, well-informed, useful, gentle, knowing all the ways of the family, interested in all its concerns, and peculiarly interested in herself, in every pleasure, every scheme of hers—one to whom she could speak every thought as it arose, and who had such an affection for her as could never find fault.

How was she to bear the change?—It was true that her friend was going only half a mile from them; but Emma was aware that great must be the difference between a Mrs. Weston, only half a mile from them, and a Miss Taylor in the house; and with all her advantages, natural and domestic, she was now in great danger of suffering from intellectual solitude. She dearly loved her father, but he was no companion for her. He could not meet her in conversation, rational or playful.

The evil of the actual disparity in their ages (and Mr. Woodhouse had not married early) was much increased by his constitution and habits; for having been a valetudinarian all his life, without activity of mind or body, he was a much older man in ways than in years; and though everywhere beloved for the friendliness of his heart and his amiable temper, his talents could not have recommended him at any time.

Her sister, though comparatively but little removed by matrimony, being settled in London, only sixteen miles off, was much beyond her daily reach; and many a long October and November evening must be struggled through at Hartfield, before Christmas brought the next visit from Isabella and her husband, and their little children, to fill the house, and give her pleasant society again.

10   Highbury, the large and populous village, almost amounting to a town, to which Hartfield, in spite of its separate lawn, and shrubberies, and name, did really belong, afforded her no equals. The Woodhouses were first in consequence there. All looked up to them. She had many acquaintance in the place, for her father was universally civil, but not one among them who could be accepted in lieu of Miss Taylor for even half a day. It was a melancholy change; and Emma could not but sigh over it, and wish for impossible things, till her father awoke, and made it necessary to be cheerful. His spirits required support. He was a nervous man, easily depressed; fond of every body that he was used to, and hating to part with them; hating change of every kind. Matrimony, as the origin of change, was always disagreeable; and he was by no means yet reconciled to his own daughter's marrying, nor could ever speak of her but with compassion, though it had been entirely a match of affection, when he was now obliged to part with Miss Taylor too; and from his habits of gentle selfishness, and of being never able to suppose that other people could feel differently from himself, he was very much disposed to think Miss Taylor had done as sad a thing for herself as for them, and would have been a great deal happier if she had spent all the rest of her life at Hartfield. Emma smiled and chatted as cheerfully as she could, to keep him from such thoughts; but when tea came, it was impossible for him not to say exactly as he had said at dinner,

"Poor Miss Taylor!—I wish she were here again. What a pity it is that Mr. Weston ever thought of her!"

"I cannot agree with you, papa; you know I cannot. Mr. Weston is such a good-humoured, pleasant, excellent man, that he thoroughly deserves a good wife;—and you would not have had Miss Taylor live with us for ever, and bear all my odd humours, when she might have a house of her own?"

"A house of her own!—But where is the advantage of a house of her own? This is three times as large.—And you have never any odd humours, my dear."

"How often we shall be going to see them, and they coming to see us!—We shall be always meeting! *We* must begin; we must go and pay wedding visit very soon."

15   "My dear, how am I to get so far? Randalls is such a distance. I could not walk half so far."

"No, papa, nobody thought of your walking. We must go in the carriage, to be sure."

"The carriage! But James will not like to put the horses to for such a little way;— and where are the poor horses to be while we are paying our visit?"

"They are to be put into Mr. Weston's stable, papa. You know we have settled all that already. We talked it all over with Mr. Weston last night. And as for James, you may be very sure he will always like going to Randalls, because of his daughter's being housemaid there. I only doubt whether he will ever take us anywhere else. That was your doing, papa. You got Hannah that good place. Nobody thought of Hannah till you mentioned her—James is so obliged to you!"

"I am very glad I did think of her. It was very lucky, for I would not have had poor James think himself slighted upon any account; and I am sure she will make a very good servant: she is a civil, pretty-spoken girl; I have a great opinion of her. Whenever I see her, she always curtseys and asks me how I do, in a very pretty manner; and when you have had her here to do needlework, I observe she always turns the lock of the door the right way and never bangs it. I am sure she will be an excellent servant; and it will be a great comfort to poor Miss Taylor to have somebody about her that she is used to see. Whenever James goes over to see his daughter, you know, she will be hearing of us. He will be able to tell her how we all are."

20   Emma spared no exertions to maintain this happier flow of ideas, and hoped, by the help of backgammon, to get her father tolerably through the evening, and be attacked by no regrets but her own. The backgammon-table was placed; but a visitor immediately afterwards walked in and made it unnecessary.

Mr. Knightley, a sensible man about seven or eight-and-thirty, was not only a very old and intimate friend of the family, but particularly connected with it, as the elder brother of Isabella's husband. He lived about a mile from Highbury, was a frequent visitor, and always welcome, and at this time more welcome than usual, as coming directly from their mutual connexions in London. He had returned to a late dinner, after some days' absence, and now walked up to Hartfield to say that all were well in Brunswick Square. It was a happy circumstance, and animated Mr. Woodhouse for some time. Mr. Knightley had a cheerful manner, which always did him good; and his many inquiries after "poor Isabella" and her children were answered most satisfactorily. When this was over, Mr. Woodhouse gratefully observed, "It is very kind of you, Mr. Knightley, to come out at this late hour to call upon us. I am afraid you must have had a shocking walk."

"Not at all, sir. It is a beautiful moonlight night; and so mild that I must draw back from your great fire."

"But you must have found it very damp and dirty. I wish you may not catch cold."

"Dirty, sir! Look at my shoes. Not a speck on them."

25   "Well! that is quite surprising, for we have had a vast deal of rain here. It rained dreadfully hard for half an hour while we were at breakfast. I wanted them to put off the wedding."

"By the bye—I have not wished you joy. Being pretty well aware of what sort of joy you must both be feeling, I have been in no hurry with my congratulations; but I hope it all went off tolerably well. How did you all behave? Who cried most?"

"Ah! poor Miss Taylor! 'Tis a sad business."

"Poor Mr. and Miss Woodhouse, if you please; but I cannot possibly say 'poor Miss Taylor.' I have a great regard for you and Emma; but when it comes to the question of dependence or independence!—At any rate, it must be better to have only one to please than two."

"Especially when *one* of those two is such a fanciful, troublesome creature!" said Emma playfully. "That is what you have in your head, I know—and what you would certainly say if my father were not by."

30   "I believe it is very true, my dear, indeed," said Mr. Woodhouse, with a sigh. "I am afraid I am sometimes very fanciful and troublesome."

"My dearest papa! You do not think I could mean *you*, or suppose Mr. Knightley to mean *you*. What a horrible idea! Oh no! I meant only myself. Mr. Knightley loves to find fault with me, you know—in a joke—it is all a joke. We always say what we like to one another."

Mr. Knightley, in fact, was one of the few people who could see faults in Emma Woodhouse, and the only one who ever told her of them: and though this was not particularly agreeable to Emma herself, she knew it would be so much less so to her father, that she would not have him really suspect such a circumstance as her not being thought perfect by every body.

"Emma knows I never flatter her," said Mr. Knightley, "but I meant no reflection on any body. Miss Taylor has been used to have two persons to please; she will now have but one. The chances are that she must be a gainer."

"Well," said Emma, willing to let it pass—"you want to hear about the wedding; and I shall be happy to tell you, for we all behaved charmingly. Every body was punctual, every body in their best looks: not a tear, and hardly a long face to be seen. Oh no; we all felt that we were going to be only half a mile apart, and were sure of meeting every day."

35   "Dear Emma bears every thing so well," said her father. "But, Mr. Knightley, she is really very sorry to lose poor Miss Taylor, and I am sure she *will* miss her more than she thinks for."

Emma turned away her head, divided between tears and smiles. "It is impossible that Emma should not miss such a companion," said Mr. Knightley. "We should not like her so well as we do, sir, if we could suppose it; but she knows how much the marriage is to Miss Taylor's advantage; she knows how very acceptable it must be, at Miss Taylor's time of life, to be settled in a home of her own, and how important to her to be secure of a comfortable provision, and therefore cannot allow herself to feel so much pain as pleasure. Every friend of Miss Taylor must be glad to have her so happily married."

"And you have forgotten one matter of joy to me," said Emma, "and a very considerable one—that I made the match myself. I made the match, you know, four years ago; and to have it take place, and be proved in the right, when so many people said Mr. Weston would never marry again, may comfort me for any thing."

Mr. Knightley shook his head at her. Her father fondly replied, "Ah! my dear, I wish you would not make matches and foretell things, for whatever you say always comes to pass. Pray do not make any more matches."

"I promise you to make none for myself, papa; but I must, indeed, for other people. It is the greatest amusement in the world! And after such success, you know!—Every body said that Mr. Weston would never marry again. Oh dear, no! Mr. Weston, who had been a widower so long, and who seemed so perfectly comfortable without a wife, so constantly occupied either in his business in town or among his friends here, always acceptable wherever he went, always cheerful—Mr. Weston need not spend a single evening in the year alone if he did not like it. Oh no! Mr. Weston certainly would never marry again. Some people even talked of a promise to his wife on her deathbed, and others of the son and the uncle not letting him. All manner of solemn nonsense was talked on the subject, but I believed none of it.

40 "Ever since the day—about four years ago—that Miss Taylor and I met with him in Broadway Lane, when, because it began to drizzle, he darted away with so much gallantry, and borrowed two umbrellas for us from Farmer Mitchell's, I made up my mind on the subject. I planned the match from that hour; and when such success has blessed me in this instance, dear papa, you cannot think that I shall leave off match-making."

"I do not understand what you mean by 'success,'" said Mr. Knightley. "Success supposes endeavour. Your time has been properly and delicately spent, if you have been endeavouring for the last four years to bring about this marriage. A worthy employment for a young lady's mind! But if, which I rather imagine, your making the match, as you call it, means only your planning it, your saying to yourself one idle day, 'I think it would be a very good thing for Miss Taylor if Mr. Weston were to marry her,' and saying it again to yourself every now and then afterwards, why do you talk of success? Where is your merit? What are you proud of? You made a lucky guess; and *that* is all that can be said."

"And have you never known the pleasure and triumph of a lucky guess?—I pity you.—I thought you cleverer—for, depend upon it a lucky guess is never merely luck. There is always some talent in it. And as to my poor word 'success,' which you quarrel with, I do not know that I am so entirely without any claim to it. You have drawn two pretty pictures; but I think there may be a third—a something between the do-nothing and the do-all. If I had not promoted Mr. Weston's visits here, and given many little encouragements, and smoothed many little matters, it might not have come to any thing after all. I think you must know Hartfield enough to comprehend that."

"A straightforward, open-hearted man like Weston, and a rational, unaffected woman like Miss Taylor, may be safely left to manage their own concerns. You are more likely to have done harm to yourself, than good to them, by interference."

"Emma never thinks of herself, if she can do good to others," rejoined Mr. Woodhouse, understanding but in part. "But, my dear, pray do not make any more matches; they are silly things, and break up one's family circle grievously."

45 "Only one more, papa; only for Mr. Elton. Poor Mr. Elton! You like Mr. Elton, papa,—I must look about for a wife for him. There is nobody in Highbury who deserves him—and he has been here a whole year, and has fitted up his house so comfortably, that it would be a shame to have him single any longer—and I thought when he was joining their hands to-day, he looked so very much as if he would like to have the same kind office done for him! I think very well of Mr. Elton, and this is the only way I have of doing him a service."

"Mr. Elton is a very pretty young man, to be sure, and a very good young man, and I have a great regard for him. But if you want to shew him any attention, my dear, ask him to come and dine with us some day. That will be a much better thing. I dare say Mr. Knightley will be so kind as to meet him."

"With a great deal of pleasure, sir, at any time," said Mr. Knightley, laughing, "and I agree with you entirely, that it will be a much better thing. Invite him to dinner, Emma, and help him to the best of the fish and the chicken, but leave him to chuse his own wife. Depend upon it, a man of six or seven-and-twenty can take care of himself."

Discussion and Writing Suggestions   MyWritingLab™

1. These opening pages dramatize the relationship between Emma Woodhouse and her father. Describe this relationship. What are the characters' respective concerns and fears?

2. The novel begins with high praise of its title character: "Emma Woodhouse, handsome, clever, and rich, with a comfortable home and happy disposition, seemed to unite some of the best blessings of existence..." As the chapter unfolds, do you detect any flaws in Emma's character? If so, what might they be?

3. Why does Emma seem so upset by the recent wedding and departure of her governess? Does Emma's distress seem reasonable to you, given what the chapter reveals about her life up to that point?

4. Emma states to her father and Mr. Knightly that matchmaking is "the greatest amusement in the world." What does she seem to enjoy about the activity? What does this enjoyment say about her? What does it say about the range of activities that are available to her?

5. Have you ever tried to set anyone up? How did it go? What are the potential joys and pitfalls of playing the role of matchmaker?

WUTHERING HEIGHTS

Emily Brontë

Emily Brontë was born in northern England in 1818, the second of three daughters, who all became writers. When she was only three, her mother died, and the three daughters were moved from school to school until they eventually were educated at home by their father and an aunt. *Wuthering Heights* is Emily Brontë's only novel, published in 1847 when the author was twenty-nine. Because women writers in the nineteenth century were not typically taken as seriously as their male counterparts, Brontë published under the pen name Ellis Bell. Emily Brontë was not revealed to be the real author of *Wuthering Heights* until after her death. Set on the English moors, the novel explores passion and revenge and madness through the love story of Catherine Earnshaw and Mr. Heathcliff. This first chapter depicts a meeting between Mr. Heathcliff and his tenant, Mr. Lockwood.

Chapter 1

1801.—I have just returned from a visit to my landlord—the solitary neighbour that I shall be troubled with. This is certainly a beautiful country! In all England, I do not believe that I could have fixed on a situation so completely removed from the stir of society. A perfect misanthropist's heaven: and Mr. Heathcliff and I are such a suitable pair to divide the desolation between us. A capital fellow! He little imagined how my heart warmed towards him when I beheld his black eyes withdraw so suspiciously under their brows, as I rode up, and when his fingers sheltered themselves, with a jealous resolution, still further in his waistcoat, as I announced my name.

'Mr. Heathcliff?' I said.

A nod was the answer.

'Mr. Lockwood, your new tenant, sir. I do myself the honour of calling as soon as possible after my arrival, to express the hope that I have not inconvenienced you by my perseverance in soliciting the occupation of Thrushcross Grange: I heard yesterday you had had some thoughts—'

5   'Thrushcross Grange is my own, sir,' he interrupted, wincing. 'I should not allow any one to inconvenience me, if I could hinder it—walk in!'

The 'walk in' was uttered with closed teeth, and expressed the sentiment, 'Go to the Deuce:' even the gate over which he leant manifested no sympathising movement to the words; and I think that circumstance determined me to accept the invitation: I felt interested in a man who seemed more exaggeratedly reserved than myself.

When he saw my horse's breast fairly pushing the barrier, he did put out his hand to unchain it, and then sullenly preceded me up the causeway, calling, as we entered the court,—'Joseph, take Mr. Lockwood's horse; and bring up some wine.'

'Here we have the whole establishment of domestics, I suppose,' was the reflection suggested by this compound order. 'No wonder the grass grows up between the flags, and cattle are the only hedge-cutters.'

Joseph was an elderly, nay, an old man: very old, perhaps, though hale and sinewy. 'The Lord help us!' he soliloquised in an undertone of peevish displeasure, while relieving me of my horse: looking, meantime, in my face so sourly that I charitably conjectured he must have need of divine aid to digest his dinner, and his pious ejaculation had no reference to my unexpected advent.

10   Wuthering Heights is the name of Mr. Heathcliff's dwelling. 'Wuthering' being a significant provincial adjective, descriptive of the atmospheric tumult to which its station is exposed in stormy weather. Pure, bracing ventilation they must have up there at all times, indeed: one may guess the power of the north wind blowing over the edge, by the excessive slant of a few stunted firs at the end of the house; and by a range of gaunt thorns all stretching their limbs one way, as if craving alms of the sun. Happily, the architect had foresight to build it strong: the narrow windows are deeply set in the wall, and the corners defended with large jutting stones.

Before passing the threshold, I paused to admire a quantity of grotesque carving lavished over the front, and especially about the principal door; above which, among a wilderness of crumbling griffins and shameless little boys, I detected the date '1500,' and the name 'Hareton Earnshaw.' I would have made a few comments, and requested a short history of the place from the surly owner; but his attitude at the door appeared to demand my speedy entrance, or complete departure, and I had no desire to aggravate his impatience previous to inspecting the penetralium.

One stop brought us into the family sitting-room, without any introductory lobby or passage: they call it here 'the house' pre-eminently. It includes kitchen and parlour, generally; but I believe at Wuthering Heights the kitchen is forced to retreat altogether into another quarter: at least I distinguished a chatter of tongues, and a clatter of culinary utensils, deep within; and I observed no signs of roasting, boiling, or baking, about the huge fireplace; nor any glitter of copper saucepans and tin cullenders on the walls. One end, indeed, reflected splendidly both light and heat from ranks of immense pewter dishes, interspersed with silver jugs and tankards, towering row after row, on a vast oak dresser, to the very roof. The latter had never been under-drawn: its entire anatomy lay bare to an inquiring eye, except where a frame of wood laden with oatcakes and clusters of legs of beef, mutton, and ham, concealed it. Above the chimney were sundry villainous old guns, and a couple of horse-pistols: and, by way of ornament, three gaudily-painted canisters disposed along its ledge. The floor was of smooth, white stone; the chairs, high-backed, primitive structures, painted green: one or two heavy black ones lurking in the shade. In an arch under the dresser reposed a huge, liver-coloured bitch pointer, surrounded by a swarm of squealing puppies; and other dogs haunted other recesses.

The apartment and furniture would have been nothing extraordinary as belonging to a homely, northern farmer, with a stubborn countenance, and stalwart limbs set out to advantage in knee-breeches and gaiters. Such an individual seated in his arm-chair, his mug of ale frothing on the round table before him, is to be seen in any circuit of five or six miles among these hills, if you go at the right time after dinner. But Mr. Heathcliff forms a singular contrast to his abode and style of living. He is a dark-skinned gipsy in aspect, in dress and manners a gentleman: that is, as much a gentleman as many a country squire: rather slovenly, perhaps, yet not looking amiss with his negligence, because he has an erect and handsome figure; and rather morose. Possibly, some people might suspect him of a degree of under-bred pride; I have a sympathetic chord within that tells me it is nothing of the sort: I know, by instinct, his reserve springs from an aversion to showy displays of feeling—to manifestations of mutual kindliness. He'll love and hate equally under cover, and esteem it a species of impertinence to be loved or hated again. No, I'm running on too fast: I bestow my own attributes over-liberally on him. Mr. Heathcliff may have entirely dissimilar reasons for keeping his hand out of the way when he meets a would-be acquaintance, to those which actuate me. Let me hope my constitution is almost peculiar: my dear mother used to say I should never have a comfortable home; and only last summer I proved myself perfectly unworthy of one.

While enjoying a month of fine weather at the sea-coast, I was thrown into the company of a most fascinating creature: a real goddess in my eyes, as long as she took no notice of me. I 'never told my love' vocally; still, if looks have language, the merest idiot might have guessed I was over head and ears: she understood me at last, and looked a return—the sweetest of all imaginable looks. And what did I do? I confess it with shame—shrunk icily into myself, like a snail; at every glance retired colder and farther; till finally the poor innocent was led to doubt her own senses, and, overwhelmed with confusion at her supposed mistake, persuaded her mamma to decamp. By this curious turn of disposition I have gained the reputation of deliberate heartlessness; how undeserved, I alone can appreciate.

15   I took a seat at the end of the hearthstone opposite that towards which my landlord advanced, and filled up an interval of silence by attempting to caress the canine mother, who had left her nursery, and was sneaking wolfishly to the back of my legs, her lip curled up, and her white teeth watering for a snatch. My caress provoked a long, guttural gnarl.

'You'd better let the dog alone,' growled Mr. Heathcliff in unison, checking fiercer demonstrations with a punch of his foot. 'She's not accustomed to be spoiled—not kept for a pet.' Then, striding to a side door, he shouted again, 'Joseph!'

Joseph mumbled indistinctly in the depths of the cellar, but gave no intimation of ascending; so his master dived down to him, leaving me *vis-à-vis* the ruffianly bitch and a pair of grim shaggy sheep-dogs, who shared with her a jealous guardianship over all my movements. Not anxious to come in contact with their fangs, I sat still; but, imagining they would scarcely understand tacit insults, I unfortunately indulged in winking and making faces at the trio, and some turn of my physiognomy so irritated madam, that she suddenly broke into a fury and leapt on my knees. I flung her back, and hastened to interpose the table between us. This proceeding aroused the whole hive: half-a-dozen four-footed fiends, of various sizes and ages, issued from hidden dens to the common centre. I felt my heels and coat-laps peculiar subjects of assault; and parrying off the larger combatants as effectually as I could with the poker, I was constrained to demand, aloud, assistance from some of the household in reestablishing peace.

Mr. Heathcliff and his man climbed the cellar steps with vexatious phlegm: I don't think they moved one second faster than usual, though the hearth was an absolute tempest of worrying and yelping. Happily, an inhabitant of the kitchen made more despatch: a lusty dame, with tucked-up gown, bare arms, and fire-flushed cheeks, rushed into the midst of us flourishing a frying-pan: and used that weapon, and her tongue, to such purpose, that the storm subsided magically, and she only remained, heaving like a sea after a high wind, when her master entered on the scene.

'What the devil is the matter?' he asked, eyeing me in a manner that I could ill endure, after this inhospitable treatment.

20 'What the devil, indeed!' I muttered. 'The herd of possessed swine could have had no worse spirits in them than those animals of yours, sir. You might as well leave a stranger with a brood of tigers!'

'They won't meddle with persons who touch nothing,' he remarked, putting the bottle before me, and restoring the displaced table. 'The dogs do right to be vigilant. Take a glass of wine?'

'No, thank you.'

'Not bitten, are you?'

'If I had been, I would have set my signet on the biter.' Heathcliff's countenance relaxed into a grin.

25 'Come, come,' he said, 'you are flurried, Mr. Lockwood. Here, take a little wine. Guests are so exceedingly rare in this house that I and my dogs, I am willing to own, hardly know how to receive them. Your health, sir?'

I bowed and returned the pledge; beginning to perceive that it would be foolish to sit sulking for the misbehaviour of a pack of curs; besides, I felt loth to yield the fellow further amusement at my expense; since his humour took that turn. He—probably swayed by prudential consideration of the folly of offending a good tenant—relaxed a little in the laconic style of chipping off his pronouns and auxiliary verbs, and introduced what he supposed would be a subject of interest to me,—a discourse on the advantages and disadvantages of my present place of retirement. I found him very intelligent on the topics we touched; and before I went home, I was encouraged so far as to volunteer another visit to-morrow. He evidently wished no repetition of my intrusion. I shall go, notwithstanding. It is astonishing how sociable I feel myself compared with him.

● **Discussion and Writing Suggestions**   MyWritingLab™

1. When the novel opens, Mr. Lockwood thinks of himself and Mr. Heathcliff as "a suitable pair." Why might he think so? How does he feel about Mr. Heathcliff? Characterize their relationship with evidence from the chapter.

2. The novel is titled *Wuthering Heights*, which is the name of the manor in the opening chapter. What can you deduce about the manor and the people who work for Mr. Heathcliff?

3. Would you return to your unfriendly landlord's house after his pack of wild dogs nearly attacked you? Why do you think that Mr. Lockwood would agree to return for a second visit?

4. From this chapter, to what extent to you believe that you understand the motivations of Mr. Lockwood and Mr. Heathcliff? To what extent are their motivations mysterious?

JANE EYRE

Charlotte Brontë

Charlotte Brontë (1816–1855) was the eldest of the three novelist sisters, including *Wuthering Heights* author Emily Brontë. After the death of her mother, she and her sisters spent a great deal of time together inventing their own fictional words, which set the stage for a lifetime of imaginative writing. After leaving home and going to school, Charlotte Brontë worked as a teacher and governess, experiences that would find their way into her fiction. *Jane Eyre* (1847), Brontë's first published novel, chronicles the life of its title character from childhood to marriage. Upon publication, the novel was well received by critics and readers but was considered controversial because of its calling into question the traditional roles of gender and social class. It remains a classic of nineteenth-century English literature and has been adapted for film and television many times.

Charlotte Brontë went on to publish two subsequent novels during her lifetime: *Shirley* and *Villette*. Like her sisters, she published her work under a male pen name in order for the work to be taken seriously; the name she used was Currer Bell. She died tragically—pregnant and newly married—at age 38.

Chapter 1

There was no possibility of taking a walk that day. We had been wandering, indeed, in the leafless shrubbery an hour in the morning; but since dinner (Mrs. Reed, when there was no company, dined early) the cold winter wind had brought with it clouds so sombre, and a rain so penetrating, that further out-door exercise was now out of the question.

I was glad of it: I never liked long walks, especially on chilly afternoons: dreadful to me was the coming home in the raw twilight, with nipped fingers and toes, and a heart saddened by the chidings of Bessie, the nurse, and humbled by the consciousness of my physical inferiority to Eliza, John, and Georgiana Reed.

The said Eliza, John, and Georgiana were now clustered round their mama in the drawing-room: she lay reclined on a sofa by the fireside, and with her darlings about her (for the time neither quarrelling nor crying) looked perfectly happy. Me, she had dispensed from joining the group; saying, "She regretted to be under the necessity of keeping me at a distance; but that until she heard from Bessie, and could discover by her own observation, that I was endeavouring in good earnest to acquire a more sociable and childlike disposition, a more attractive and sprightly manner— something lighter, franker, more natural, as it were—she really must exclude me from privileges intended only for contented, happy, little children."

"What does Bessie say I have done?" I asked.

5   "Jane, I don't like cavillers or questioners; besides, there is something truly forbidding in a child taking up her elders in that manner. Be seated somewhere; and until you can speak pleasantly, remain silent."

A breakfast-room adjoined the drawing-room, I slipped in there. It contained a bookcase: I soon possessed myself of a volume, taking care that it should be one stored with pictures. I mounted into the window-seat: gathering up my feet, I sat cross-legged, like a Turk; and, having drawn the red moreen curtain nearly close, I was shrined in double retirement.

Folds of scarlet drapery shut in my view to the right hand; to the left were the clear panes of glass, protecting, but not separating me from the drear November day. At intervals, while turning over the leaves of my book, I studied the aspect of that winter afternoon. Afar, it offered a pale blank of mist and cloud; near a scene of wet lawn and storm-beat shrub, with ceaseless rain sweeping away wildly before a long and lamentable blast.

I returned to my book—Bewick's History of British Birds: the letterpress thereof I cared little for, generally speaking; and yet there were certain introductory pages that, child as I was, I could not pass quite as a blank. They were those which treat of the haunts of sea-fowl; of "the solitary rocks and promontories" by them only inhabited; of the coast of Norway, studded with isles from its southern extremity, the Lindeness, or Naze, to the North Cape—

> Where the Northern Ocean, in vast whirls,
> Boils round the naked, melancholy isles
> Of farthest Thule; and the Atlantic surge
> Pours in among the stormy Hebrides.

10   Nor could I pass unnoticed the suggestion of the bleak shores of Lapland, Siberia, Spitzbergen, Nova Zembla, Iceland, Greenland, with "the vast sweep of the Arctic Zone, and those forlorn regions of dreary space,—that reservoir of frost and snow, where firm fields of ice, the accumulation of centuries of winters, glazed in Alpine heights above heights, surround the pole, and concentre the multiplied rigours of extreme cold." Of these death-white realms I formed an idea of my own: shadowy, like all the half-comprehended notions that float dim through children's brains, but strangely impressive. The words in these introductory pages connected themselves with the succeeding vignettes, and gave significance to the rock standing up alone in a sea of billow and spray; to the broken boat stranded on a desolate coast; to the cold and ghastly moon glancing through bars of cloud at a wreck just sinking.

I cannot tell what sentiment haunted the quite solitary churchyard, with its inscribed headstone; its gate, its two trees, its low horizon, girdled by a broken wall, and its newly-risen crescent, attesting the hour of eventide.

The two ships becalmed on a torpid sea, I believed to be marine phantoms.

The fiend pinning down the thief's pack behind him, I passed over quickly: it was an object of terror.

So was the black horned thing seated aloof on a rock, surveying a distant crowd surrounding a gallows.

15   Each picture told a story; mysterious often to my undeveloped understanding and imperfect feelings, yet ever profoundly interesting: as interesting as the tales Bessie sometimes narrated on winter evenings, when she chanced to be in good humour; and when, having brought her ironing-table to the nursery hearth, she allowed us to sit about it, and while she got up Mrs. Reed's lace frills, and crimped her nightcap borders, fed our eager attention with passages of love and adventure taken from old fairy tales and other ballads; or (as at a later period I discovered) from the pages of Pamela, and Henry, Earl of Moreland.

With Bewick on my knee, I was then happy: happy at least in my way. I feared nothing but interruption, and that came too soon. The breakfast-room door opened.

"Boh! Madam Mope!" cried the voice of John Reed; then he paused: he found the room apparently empty.

"Where the dickens is she!" he continued. "Lizzy! Georgy! (calling to his sisters) Joan is not here: tell mama she is run out into the rain—bad animal!"

"It is well I drew the curtain," thought I; and I wished fervently he might not discover my hiding-place: nor would John Reed have found it out himself; he was not quick either of vision or conception; but Eliza just put her head in at the door, and said at once—

20   "She is in the window-seat, to be sure, Jack."

And I came out immediately, for I trembled at the idea of being dragged forth by the said Jack.

"What do you want?" I asked, with awkward diffidence.

"Say, 'What do you want, Master Reed?'" was the answer. "I want you to come here;" and seating himself in an arm-chair, he intimated by a gesture that I was to approach and stand before him.

John Reed was a schoolboy of fourteen years old; four years older than I, for I was but ten: large and stout for his age, with a dingy and unwholesome skin; thick lineaments in a spacious visage, heavy limbs and large extremities. He gorged himself habitually at table, which made him bilious, and gave him a dim and bleared eye and flabby cheeks. He ought now to have been at school; but his mama had taken him home for a month or two, "on account of his delicate health." Mr. Miles, the master, affirmed that he would do very well if he had fewer cakes and sweetmeats sent him from home; but the mother's heart turned from an opinion so harsh, and inclined rather to the more refined idea that John's sallowness was owing to over-application and, perhaps, to pining after home.

25   John had not much affection for his mother and sisters, and an antipathy to me. He bullied and punished me; not two or three times in the week, nor once or twice in the day, but continually: every nerve I had feared him, and every morsel of flesh in my bones shrank when he came near. There were moments when I was bewildered by the terror he inspired, because I had no appeal whatever against either his menaces or his inflictions; the servants did not like to offend their young master by taking my part against him, and Mrs. Reed was blind and

deaf on the subject: she never saw him strike or heard him abuse me, though he did both now and then in her very presence, more frequently, however, behind her back.

Habitually obedient to John, I came up to his chair: he spent some three minutes in thrusting out his tongue at me as far as he could without damaging the roots: I knew he would soon strike, and while dreading the blow, I mused on the disgusting and ugly appearance of him who would presently deal it. I wonder if he read that notion in my face; for, all at once, without speaking, he struck suddenly and strongly. I tottered, and on regaining my equilibrium retired back a step or two from his chair.

"That is for your impudence in answering mama awhile since," said he, "and for your sneaking way of getting behind curtains, and for the look you had in your eyes two minutes since, you rat!"

Accustomed to John Reed's abuse, I never had an idea of replying to it; my care was how to endure the blow which would certainly follow the insult.

"What were you doing behind the curtain?" he asked.

30   "I was reading."

"Show the book."

I returned to the window and fetched it thence.

"You have no business to take our books; you are a dependent, mama says; you have no money; your father left you none; you ought to beg, and not to live here with gentlemen's children like us, and eat the same meals we do, and wear clothes at our mama's expense. Now, I'll teach you to rummage my bookshelves: for they *are* mine; all the house belongs to me, or will do in a few years. Go and stand by the door, out of the way of the mirror and the windows."

I did so, not at first aware what was his intention; but when I saw him lift and poise the book and stand in act to hurl it, I instinctively started aside with a cry of alarm: not soon enough, however; the volume was flung, it hit me, and I fell, striking my head against the door and cutting it. The cut bled, the pain was sharp: my terror had passed its climax; other feelings succeeded.

35   "Wicked and cruel boy!" I said. "You are like a murderer—you are like a slave-driver—you are like the Roman emperors!"

I had read Goldsmith's History of Rome, and had formed my opinion of Nero, Caligula, etc. Also I had drawn parallels in silence, which I never thought thus to have declared aloud.

"What! what!" he cried. "Did she say that to me? Did you hear her, Eliza and Georgiana? Won't I tell mama? but first—"

He ran headlong at me: I felt him grasp my hair and my shoulder: he had closed with a desperate thing. I really saw in him a tyrant, a murderer. I felt a drop or two of blood from my head trickle down my neck, and was sensible of somewhat pungent suffering: these sensations for the time predominated over fear, and I received him in frantic sort. I don't very well know what I did with my hands, but he called me "Rat! Rat!" and bellowed out aloud. Aid was near him: Eliza and Georgiana had run for Mrs. Reed, who was gone upstairs: she now came upon the scene, followed by Bessie and her maid Abbot. We were parted: I heard the words—

"Dear! dear! What a fury to fly at Master John!"

40   "Did ever anybody see such a picture of passion!"

Then Mrs. Reed subjoined—

"Take her away to the red-room, and lock her in there." Four hands were immediately laid upon me, and I was borne upstairs.

● Discussion and Writing Suggestions   MyWritingLab™

1. How is the weather described at the beginning of the novel? What mood does it set up?

2. From the opening chapter, what can you infer about Jane's personality? In what ways is she different from the others living in the house?

3. While reading the book *The History of British Birds*, Jane "feared nothing but interruption." Why does reading and not being interrupted seem so important to her?

4. Why do you think this first chapter includes the fight between Jane and John Reed? What does the fight, and the family's reaction to it, suggest about Jane's status in the family? Why is she, rather than Master John, punished for fighting?

5. Do your own feelings about Jane differ from how the other characters in the novel (like Mrs. Reed and John Reed) feel about her? If so, in what ways?

6. We're told, at the end of the chapter, that Jane is being banished to the "red room." But we don't yet know what this room is. What other mysteries does this first chapter introduce? What do you most want to know more about in chapter two and beyond?

GREAT EXPECTATIONS

Charles Dickens

Charles Dickens was born on England's southern coast and at age ten moved with his family to London. He attended school until age twelve, at which point his father was imprisoned for bad debt, forcing Charles to take a job at a boot-polishing factory. He later worked as an office boy before beginning to write for several newspapers, which marked the beginning of an extremely prolific and successful literary career. By the time *Great Expectations* was published in 1860, Dickens had already published over a dozen novels, delivered lectures across America, and become on two continents what many consider to be the first modern celebrity. Like several of Dickens's novels, *Great Expectations* was originally published in serial form, with new chapters appearing every week in the magazine *All the Year Round*. Often considered Dickens's finest novel, *Great Expectations* is a classic "bildungsroman"— that is, a "novel of formation" or, more simply, a coming-of-age novel. Specifically, *Great Expectations* chronicles the life of a poor orphan named Pip who gradually matures to become a gentleman. In this opening chapter, Pip describes in his own words the first significant event that he can remember.

Chapter 1

My father's family name being Pirrip, and my Christian name Philip, my infant tongue could make of both names nothing longer or more explicit than Pip. So, I called myself Pip, and came to be called Pip.

I give Pirrip as my father's family name, on the authority of his tombstone and my sister,—Mrs. Joe Gargery, who married the blacksmith. As I never saw my father or my mother, and never saw any likeness of either of them (for their days were long before the days of photographs), my first fancies regarding what they were like were unreasonably derived from their tombstones. The shape of the letters on my father's, gave me an odd idea that he was a square, stout, dark man, with curly black hair. From the character and turn of the inscription, "Also Georgiana Wife of the Above," I drew a childish conclusion that my mother was freckled and sickly. To five little stone lozenges, each about a foot and a half long, which were arranged in a neat row beside their grave, and were sacred to the memory of five little brothers of mine,—who gave up trying to get a living, exceedingly early in that universal struggle,—I am indebted for a belief I religiously entertained that they had all been born on their backs with their hands in their trousers-pockets, and had never taken them out in this state of existence.

Ours was the marsh country, down by the river, within, as the river wound, twenty miles of the sea. My first most vivid and broad impression of the identity of things seems to me to have been gained on a memorable raw afternoon towards evening. At such a time I found out for certain that this bleak place overgrown with nettles was the churchyard; and that Philip Pirrip, late of this parish, and also Georgiana wife of the above, were dead and buried; and that Alexander, Bartholomew, Abraham, Tobias, and Roger, infant children of the aforesaid, were also dead and buried; and that the dark flat wilderness beyond the churchyard, intersected with dikes and mounds and gates, with scattered cattle feeding on it, was the marshes; and that the low leaden line beyond was the river; and that the distant savage lair from which the wind was rushing was the sea; and that the small bundle of shivers growing afraid of it all and beginning to cry, was Pip.

"Hold your noise!" cried a terrible voice, as a man started up from among the graves at the side of the church porch. "Keep still, you little devil, or I'll cut your throat!"

5   A fearful man, all in coarse gray, with a great iron on his leg. A man with no hat, and with broken shoes, and with an old rag tied round his head. A man who had been soaked in water, and smothered in mud, and lamed by stones, and cut by flints, and stung by nettles, and torn by briars; who limped, and shivered, and glared, and growled; and whose teeth chattered in his head as he seized me by the chin.

"Oh! Don't cut my throat, sir," I pleaded in terror. "Pray don't do it, sir."

"Tell us your name!" said the man. "Quick!"

"Pip, sir."

"Once more," said the man, staring at me. "Give it mouth!"

10 "Pip. Pip, sir."

"Show us where you live," said the man. "Point out the place!"

I pointed to where our village lay, on the flat in-shore among the alder-trees and pollards, a mile or more from the church.

The man, after looking at me for a moment, turned me upside down, and emptied my pockets. There was nothing in them but a piece of bread. When the church came to itself,—for he was so sudden and strong that he made it go head over heels before me, and I saw the steeple under my feet,—when the church came to itself, I say, I was seated on a high tombstone, trembling while he ate the bread ravenously.

"You young dog," said the man, licking his lips, "what fat cheeks you ha' got."

15 I believe they were fat, though I was at that time undersized for my years, and not strong.

"Darn me if I couldn't eat em," said the man, with a threatening shake of his head, "and if I han't half a mind to't!"

I earnestly expressed my hope that he wouldn't, and held tighter to the tombstone on which he had put me; partly, to keep myself upon it; partly, to keep myself from crying.

"Now lookee here!" said the man. "Where's your mother?"

"There, sir!" said I.

20 He started, made a short run, and stopped and looked over his shoulder.

"There, sir!" I timidly explained. "Also Georgiana. That's my mother."

"Oh!" said he, coming back. "And is that your father alonger your mother?"

"Yes, sir," said I; "him too; late of this parish."

"Ha!" he muttered then, considering. "Who d'ye live with,—supposin' you're kindly let to live, which I han't made up my mind about?"

25 "My sister, sir,—Mrs. Joe Gargery,—wife of Joe Gargery, the blacksmith, sir."

"Blacksmith, eh?" said he. And looked down at his leg.

After darkly looking at his leg and me several times, he came closer to my tombstone, took me by both arms, and tilted me back as far as he could hold me; so that his eyes looked most powerfully down into mine, and mine looked most helplessly up into his.

"Now lookee here," he said, "the question being whether you're to be let to live. You know what a file is?"

"Yes, sir."

30 "And you know what wittles is?"

"Yes, sir."

After each question he tilted me over a little more, so as to give me a greater sense of helplessness and danger.

"You get me a file." He tilted me again. "And you get me wittles." He tilted me again. "You bring 'em both to me." He tilted me again. "Or I'll have your heart and liver out." He tilted me again.

I was dreadfully frightened, and so giddy that I clung to him with both hands, and said, "If you would kindly please to let me keep upright, sir, perhaps I shouldn't be sick, and perhaps I could attend more."

35 He gave me a most tremendous dip and roll, so that the church jumped over its own weathercock. Then, he held me by the arms, in an upright position on the top of the stone, and went on in these fearful terms:—

"You bring me, to-morrow morning early, that file and them wittles. You bring the lot to me, at that old Battery over yonder. You do it, and you never dare to say a word or dare to make a sign concerning your having seen such a person as me, or any person sumever, and you shall be let to live. You fail, or you go from my words in any partickler, no matter how small it is, and your heart and your liver shall be tore out, roasted, and ate. Now, I ain't alone, as you may think I am. There's a young man hid with me, in comparison with which young man I am a angel. That young man hears the words I speak. That young man has a secret way pecooliar to himself, of getting at a boy, and at his heart, and at his liver. It is in wain for a boy to attempt to hide himself from that young man. A boy may lock his door, may be warm in bed, may tuck himself up, may draw the clothes over his head, may think himself comfortable and safe, but that young man will softly creep and creep his way to him and tear him open. I am a keeping that young man from harming of you at the present moment, with great difficulty. I find it wery hard to hold that young man off of your inside. Now, what do you say?"

I said that I would get him the file, and I would get him what broken bits of food I could, and I would come to him at the Battery, early in the morning.

"Say Lord strike you dead if you don't!" said the man.

I said so, and he took me down.

40 "Now," he pursued, "you remember what you've undertook, and you remember that young man, and you get home!"

"Goo-good night, sir," I faltered.

"Much of that!" said he, glancing about him over the cold wet flat. "I wish I was a frog. Or a eel!"

At the same time, he hugged his shuddering body in both his arms,—clasping himself, as if to hold himself together,—and limped towards the low church wall. As I saw him go, picking his way among the nettles, and among the brambles that bound the green mounds, he looked in my young eyes as if he were eluding the hands of the dead people, stretching up cautiously out of their graves, to get a twist upon his ankle and pull him in.

When he came to the low church wall, he got over it, like a man whose legs were numbed and stiff, and then turned round to look for me. When I saw him turning, I set my face towards home, and made the best use of my legs. But presently I looked over my shoulder, and saw him going on again towards the river, still hugging himself in both arms, and picking his way with his sore feet among the great stones dropped into the marshes here and there, for stepping-places when the rains were heavy or the tide was in.

45 The marshes were just a long black horizontal line then, as I stopped to look after him; and the river was just another horizontal line, not nearly so broad nor

yet so black; and the sky was just a row of long angry red lines and dense black lines intermixed. On the edge of the river I could faintly make out the only two black things in all the prospect that seemed to be standing upright; one of these was the beacon by which the sailors steered—like an unhooped cask upon a pole—an ugly thing when you were near it; the other, a gibbet, with some chains hanging to it which had once held a pirate. The man was limping on towards this latter, as if he were the pirate come to life, and come down, and going back to hook himself up again. It gave me a terrible turn when I thought so; and as I saw the cattle lifting their heads to gaze after him, I wondered whether they thought so too. I looked all round for the horrible young man, and could see no signs of him. But now I was frightened again, and ran home without stopping.

● Discussion and Writing Suggestions   MyWritingLab™

1. From their tombstones, Pip determines that his father was "a square, stout, dark man, with curly black hair" and that his mother was "freckled and sickly." Do you suppose the descriptions are accurate? How do these supposed details about the family Pip never knew help characterize him?

2. What does this chapter's setting—specifically, the location and the weather—do for the chapter's overall mood?

3. This first chapter depicts Pip's "first most vivid and broad impression of the identity of things." If you were to narrate your own life story, what would your "first most vivid and broad impression" be?

4. Dickens describes the escaped convict as "a man who had been soaked in water, and smothered in mud, and lamed by stones, and cut by flints, and stung by nettles, and torn by briars." What does this description reveal about the man? What does it reveal about the way Dickens describes his characters?

5. The convict mentions a second man, far crueler than himself, who is presumably listening in on their conversation. Do you think this second man really exists? Why does the convict mention him?

6. What do we learn about Pip from the way he deals with the escaped convict?

7. Does this chapter make you want to go on and read Chapter 2? If so, what elements in the chapter hook you in?

THE SIGN OF THE FOUR

Arthur Conan Doyle

You've probably already heard of Sherlock Holmes—if not from Sir Arthur Conan Doyle's novels, then from one of the many film adaptations (the most recent starring Robert

Downey as Holmes and Jude Law as Watson), or perhaps the 2010 TV show starring Bene-dict Cumberbatch and Martin Freeman, or maybe for the simple reason that the name itself has become inseparable from the notions of deductive reasoning and logic. Conan Doyle (1859–1930) was trained as a physician. He wrote his stories and novels when there were no patients in his office, until he was making enough money with his writing to quit medi-cine. In addition to his detective novels, he published historical and supernatural fiction, as well as poetry and nonfiction. Sherlock Holmes was by far the author's most beloved character—so much so that after killing him off in one novel, public outcry, and the financial rewards earned by authoring literature's most famous detective, convinced the author to resurrect the character for a new novel several years later.

The Sign of the Four, published in 1890, is Conan Doyle's second novel (his first was *A Study in Scarlet*, mentioned in paragraph 13) starring Holmes, the world's only "unofficial consulting detective." In this opening chapter, the sheer oddness of Holmes's personality, coupled with his brilliance, reveals why he has intrigued so many readers and spawned so many adaptations over the years.

Chapter I: The Science of Deduction

Sherlock Holmes took his bottle from the corner of the mantel-piece and his hy-podermic syringe from its neat morocco case. With his long, white, nervous fin-gers he adjusted the delicate needle, and rolled back his left shirt-cuff. For some little time his eyes rested thoughtfully upon the sinewy forearm and wrist all dot-ted and scarred with innumerable puncture-marks. Finally he thrust the sharp point home, pressed down the tiny piston, and sank back into the velvet-lined arm-chair with a long sigh of satisfaction.

Three times a day for many months I had witnessed this performance, but custom had not reconciled my mind to it. On the contrary, from day to day I had become more irritable at the sight, and my conscience swelled nightly within me at the thought that I had lacked the courage to protest. Again and again I had registered a vow that I should deliver my soul upon the subject, but there was that in the cool, nonchalant air of my companion which made him the last man with whom one would care to take anything approaching to a liberty. His great powers, his masterly manner, and the experience which I had had of his many extraordinary qualities, all made me diffident and backward in crossing him.

Yet upon that afternoon, whether it was the Beaune which I had taken with my lunch, or the additional exasperation produced by the extreme deliberation of his manner, I suddenly felt that I could hold out no longer.

"Which is it to-day?" I asked,—"morphine or cocaine?"

5   He raised his eyes languidly from the old black-letter volume which he had opened. "It is cocaine," he said,—"a seven-per-cent. solution. Would you care to try it?"

"No, indeed," I answered, brusquely. "My constitution has not got over the Afghan campaign yet. I cannot afford to throw any extra strain upon it."

He smiled at my vehemence. "Perhaps you are right, Watson," he said. "I suppose that its influence is physically a bad one. I find it, however, so transcen-dently stimulating and clarifying to the mind that its secondary action is a mat-ter of small moment."

"But consider!" I said, earnestly. "Count the cost! Your brain may, as you say, be roused and excited, but it is a pathological and morbid process, which involves increased tissue-change and may at last leave a permanent weakness. You know, too, what a black reaction comes upon you. Surely the game is hardly worth the candle. Why should you, for a mere passing pleasure, risk the loss of those great powers with which you have been endowed? Remember that I speak not only as one comrade to another, but as a medical man to one for whose constitution he is to some extent answerable."

He did not seem offended. On the contrary, he put his finger-tips together and leaned his elbows on the arms of his chair, like one who has a relish for conversation.

10   "My mind," he said, "rebels at stagnation. Give me problems, give me work, give me the most abstruse cryptogram or the most intricate analysis, and I am in my own proper atmosphere. I can dispense then with artificial stimulants. But I abhor the dull routine of existence. I crave for mental exaltation. That is why I have chosen my own particular profession,—or rather created it, for I am the only one in the world."

"The only unofficial detective?" I said, raising my eyebrows.

"The only unofficial consulting detective," he answered. "I am the last and highest court of appeal in detection. When Gregson or Lestrade or Athelney Jones are out of their depths— which, by the way, is their normal state—the matter is laid before me. I examine the data, as an expert, and pronounce a specialist's opinion. I claim no credit in such cases. My name figures in no newspaper. The work itself, the pleasure of finding a field for my peculiar powers, is my highest reward. But you have yourself had some experience of my methods of work in the Jefferson Hope case."

"Yes, indeed," said I, cordially. "I was never so struck by anything in my life. I even embodied it in a small brochure with the somewhat fantastic title of 'A Study in Scarlet.'"

He shook his head sadly. "I glanced over it," said he. "Honestly, I cannot congratulate you upon it. Detection is, or ought to be, an exact science, and should be treated in the same cold and unemotional manner. You have attempted to tinge it with romanticism, which produces much the same effect as if you worked a love-story or an elopement into the fifth proposition of Euclid."

15   "But the romance was there," I remonstrated. "I could not tamper with the facts."

"Some facts should be suppressed, or at least a just sense of proportion should be observed in treating them. The only point in the case which deserved mention was the curious analytical reasoning from effects to causes by which I succeeded in unraveling it."

I was annoyed at this criticism of a work which had been specially designed to please him. I confess, too, that I was irritated by the egotism which seemed to demand that every line of my pamphlet should be devoted to his own special doings. More than once during the years that I had lived with him in Baker Street I had observed that a small vanity underlay my companion's quiet and didactic manner. I made no remark, however, but sat nursing my wounded leg.

I had a Jezail bullet through it some time before, and, though it did not prevent me from walking, it ached wearily at every change of the weather.

"My practice has extended recently to the Continent," said Holmes, after a while, filling up his old brier-root pipe. "I was consulted last week by Francois Le Villard, who, as you probably know, has come rather to the front lately in the French detective service. He has all the Celtic power of quick intuition, but he is deficient in the wide range of exact knowledge which is essential to the higher developments of his art. The case was concerned with a will, and possessed some features of interest. I was able to refer him to two parallel cases, the one at Riga in 1857, and the other at St. Louis in 1871, which have suggested to him the true solution. Here is the letter which I had this morning acknowledging my assistance." He tossed over, as he spoke, a crumpled sheet of foreign notepaper. I glanced my eyes down it, catching a profusion of notes of admiration, with stray "magnifiques," "coup-de-maitres," and "tours-de-force," all testifying to the ardent admiration of the Frenchman.

"He speaks as a pupil to his master," said I.

20 "Oh, he rates my assistance too highly," said Sherlock Holmes, lightly. "He has considerable gifts himself. He possesses two out of the three qualities necessary for the ideal detective. He has the power of observation and that of deduction. He is only wanting in knowledge; and that may come in time. He is now translating my small works into French."

"Your works?"

"Oh, didn't you know?" he cried, laughing. "Yes, I have been guilty of several monographs. They are all upon technical subjects. Here, for example, is one 'Upon the Distinction between the Ashes of the Various Tobaccoes.' In it I enumerate a hundred and forty forms of cigar-, cigarette-, and pipe-tobacco, with colored plates illustrating the difference in the ash. It is a point which is continually turning up in criminal trials, and which is sometimes of supreme importance as a clue. If you can say definitely, for example, that some murder has been done by a man who was smoking an Indian lunkah, it obviously narrows your field of search. To the trained eye there is as much difference between the black ash of a Trichinopoly and the white fluff of bird's-eye as there is between a cabbage and a potato."

"You have an extraordinary genius for minutiae," I remarked.

"I appreciate their importance. Here is my monograph upon the tracing of footsteps, with some remarks upon the uses of plaster of Paris as a preserver of impresses. Here, too, is a curious little work upon the influence of a trade upon the form of the hand, with lithotypes of the hands of slaters, sailors, corkcutters, compositors, weavers, and diamond-polishers. That is a matter of great practical interest to the scientific detective,—especially in cases of unclaimed bodies, or in discovering the antecedents of criminals. But I weary you with my hobby."

25 "Not at all," I answered, earnestly. "It is of the greatest interest to me, especially since I have had the opportunity of observing your practical application of it. But you spoke just now of observation and deduction. Surely the one to some extent implies the other."

"Why, hardly," he answered, leaning back luxuriously in his arm-chair, and sending up thick blue wreaths from his pipe. "For example, observation shows me that you have been to the Wigmore Street Post-Office this morning, but deduction lets me know that when there you dispatched a telegram."

"Right!" said I. "Right on both points! But I confess that I don't see how you arrived at it. It was a sudden impulse upon my part, and I have mentioned it to no one."

"It is simplicity itself," he remarked, chuckling at my surprise,—"so absurdly simple that an explanation is superfluous; and yet it may serve to define the limits of observation and of deduction. Observation tells me that you have a little reddish mould adhering to your instep. Just opposite the Seymour Street Office they have taken up the pavement and thrown up some earth which lies in such a way that it is difficult to avoid treading in it in entering. The earth is of this peculiar reddish tint which is found, as far as I know, nowhere else in the neighborhood. So much is observation. The rest is deduction."

"How, then, did you deduce the telegram?"

30   "Why, of course I knew that you had not written a letter, since I sat opposite to you all morning. I see also in your open desk there that you have a sheet of stamps and a thick bundle of post-cards. What could you go into the post-office for, then, but to send a wire? Eliminate all other factors, and the one which remains must be the truth."

"In this case it certainly is so," I replied, after a little thought. "The thing, however, is, as you say, of the simplest. Would you think me impertinent if I were to put your theories to a more severe test?"

"On the contrary," he answered, "it would prevent me from taking a second dose of cocaine. I should be delighted to look into any problem which you might submit to me."

"I have heard you say that it is difficult for a man to have any object in daily use without leaving the impress of his individuality upon it in such a way that a trained observer might read it. Now, I have here a watch which has recently come into my possession. Would you have the kindness to let me have an opinion upon the character or habits of the late owner?"

I handed him over the watch with some slight feeling of amusement in my heart, for the test was, as I thought, an impossible one, and I intended it as a lesson against the somewhat dogmatic tone which he occasionally assumed. He balanced the watch in his hand, gazed hard at the dial, opened the back, and examined the works, first with his naked eyes and then with a powerful convex lens. I could hardly keep from smiling at his crestfallen face when he finally snapped the case to and handed it back.

35   "There are hardly any data," he remarked. "The watch has been recently cleaned, which robs me of my most suggestive facts."

"You are right," I answered. "It was cleaned before being sent to me." In my heart I accused my companion of putting forward a most lame and impotent excuse to cover his failure. What data could he expect from an uncleaned watch?

"Though unsatisfactory, my research has not been entirely barren," he observed, staring up at the ceiling with dreamy, lack-lustre eyes. "Subject to your correction, I should judge that the watch belonged to your elder brother, who inherited it from your father."

"That you gather, no doubt, from the H. W. upon the back?"

"Quite so. The W. suggests your own name. The date of the watch is nearly fifty years back, and the initials are as old as the watch: so it was made for the last generation. Jewelry usually descends to the eldest son, and he is most likely to have the same name as the father. Your father has, if I remember right, been dead many years. It has, therefore, been in the hands of your eldest brother."

40   "Right, so far," said I. "Anything else?"

"He was a man of untidy habits,—very untidy and careless. He was left with good prospects, but he threw away his chances, lived for some time in poverty with occasional short intervals of prosperity, and finally, taking to drink, he died. That is all I can gather."

I sprang from my chair and limped impatiently about the room with considerable bitterness in my heart.

"This is unworthy of you, Holmes," I said. "I could not have believed that you would have descended to this. You have made inquires into the history of my unhappy brother, and you now pretend to deduce this knowledge in some fanciful way. You cannot expect me to believe that you have read all this from his old watch! It is unkind, and, to speak plainly, has a touch of charlatanism in it."

"My dear doctor," said he, kindly, "pray accept my apologies. Viewing the matter as an abstract problem, I had forgotten how personal and painful a thing it might be to you. I assure you, however, that I never even knew that you had a brother until you handed me the watch."

45   "Then how in the name of all that is wonderful did you get these facts? They are absolutely correct in every particular."

"Ah, that is good luck. I could only say what was the balance of probability. I did not at all expect to be so accurate."

"But it was not mere guess-work?"

"No, no: I never guess. It is a shocking habit,—destructive to the logical faculty. What seems strange to you is only so because you do not follow my train of thought or observe the small facts upon which large inferences may depend. For example, I began by stating that your brother was careless. When you observe the lower part of that watch-case you notice that it is not only dinted in two places, but it is cut and marked all over from the habit of keeping other hard objects, such as coins or keys, in the same pocket. Surely it is no great feat to assume that a man who treats a fifty-guinea watch so cavalierly must be a careless man. Neither is it a very far-fetched inference that a man who inherits one article of such value is pretty well provided for in other respects."

I nodded, to show that I followed his reasoning.

50   "It is very customary for pawnbrokers in England, when they take a watch, to scratch the number of the ticket with a pin-point upon the inside of the case. It is more handy than a label, as there is no risk of the number being lost or transposed. There are no less than four such numbers visible to my lens on the inside of this case. Inference,—that your brother was often at low water. Secondary inference,—that he had occasional bursts of prosperity, or he could not have redeemed

the pledge. Finally, I ask you to look at the inner plate, which contains the key-hole. Look at the thousands of scratches all round the hole,—marks where the key has slipped. What sober man's key could have scored those grooves? But you will never see a drunkard's watch without them. He winds it at night, and he leaves these traces of his unsteady hand. Where is the mystery in all this?"

"It is as clear as daylight," I answered. "I regret the injustice which I did you. I should have had more faith in your marvellous faculty. May I ask whether you have any professional inquiry on foot at present?"

"None. Hence the cocaine. I cannot live without brain-work. What else is there to live for? Stand at the window here. Was ever such a dreary, dismal, unprofitable world? See how the yellow fog swirls down the street and drifts across the dun-colored houses. What could be more hopelessly prosaic and material? What is the use of having powers, doctor, when one has no field upon which to exert them? Crime is commonplace, existence is commonplace, and no qualities save those which are commonplace have any function upon earth."

I had opened my mouth to reply to this tirade, when with a crisp knock our landlady entered, bearing a card upon the brass salver.

"A young lady for you, sir," she said, addressing my companion.

55 "Miss Mary Morstan," he read. "Hum! I have no recollection of the name. Ask the young lady to step up, Mrs. Hudson. Don't go, doctor. I should prefer that you remain."

● Discussion and Writing Suggestions MyWritingLab™

1. What initial impression does the novel give us of Sherlock Holmes? Why might the author have chosen to begin his novel with its title character injecting himself with cocaine?

2. What do you make of Holmes's claim as to why he is using drugs? Do you think he is telling the truth? Is he trying to deceive Watson? Trying to deceive himself?

3. How would you characterize the relationship between Sherlock Holmes and Dr. Watson? What values do they share? In what ways do their values differ?

4. Sherlock Holmes says of his work, "I claim no credit in such cases. My name figures in no newspaper. The work itself, the pleasure of finding a field for my peculiar power, is my highest reward." How does Holmes's refusal to take credit for his work square with your own experience of how most people are? That is, do you find that people tend to take more pleasure in the work itself or in taking the credit?

5. What indications do you find that Holmes might be fully aware of the effect his revelations about the watch might have upon Watson?

6. Does your impression of Holmes change from the beginning of the chapter to the end? What moments in the chapter make you rethink your feelings about him?

THE RED BADGE OF COURAGE

Stephen Crane

Stephen Crane was born in 1871 in New Jersey, the youngest of fourteen children. He attended college for two years before moving to New York City to work as a journalist and gather material for his fiction. *The Red Badge of Courage,* published in 1895 when he was only twenty-four, was Crane's second novel. Set in Virginia in 1863, it depicts a young man, Henry Fleming, who is fighting for the Union army during the American Civil War. The novel became a fast commercial and critical success and was thought to be unique among war novels of the day not only for its realistic depictions of battle, but also because of its focus on a single, low-ranking soldier's subjective experiences rather than on the broader war, with its grand strategies and tactics.

Crane was a prolific writer who published novels, short fiction, and poetry before dying of tuberculosis in 1900 at the age of twenty-eight. This opening chapter from *The Red Badge of Courage* depicts Henry Fleming and his internal dilemma—his deep fear of running away cowardly when the bullets start flying.

Chapter 1

The cold passed reluctantly from the earth, and the retiring fogs revealed an army stretched out on the hills, resting. As the landscape changed from brown to green, the army awakened, and began to tremble with eagerness at the noise of rumors. It cast its eyes upon the roads, which were growing from long troughs of liquid mud to proper thoroughfares. A river, amber-tinted in the shadow of its banks, purled at the army's feet; and at night, when the stream had become of a sorrowful blackness, one could see across it the red, eyelike gleam of hostile camp-fires set in the low brows of distant hills.

Once a certain tall soldier developed virtues and went resolutely to wash a shirt. He came flying back from a brook waving his garment bannerlike. He was swelled with a tale he had heard from a reliable friend, who had heard it from a truthful cavalryman, who had heard it from his trustworthy brother, one of the orderlies at division headquarters. He adopted the important air of a herald in red and gold.

"We're goin' t' move t'morrah—sure," he said pompously to a group in the company street. "We're goin' 'way up the river, cut across, an' come around in behint 'em."

To his attentive audience he drew a loud and elaborate plan of a very brilliant campaign. When he had finished, the blue-clothed men scattered into small arguing groups between the rows of squat brown huts. A negro teamster who had been dancing upon a cracker box with the hilarious encouragement of twoscore soldiers was deserted. He sat mournfully down. Smoke drifted lazily from a multitude of quaint chimneys.

5   "It's a lie! that's all it is—a thunderin' lie!" said another private loudly. His smooth face was flushed, and his hands were thrust sulkily into his trouser's pockets. He took the matter as an affront to him. "I don't believe the derned old

army's ever going to move. We're set. I've got ready to move eight times in the last two weeks, and we ain't moved yet."

The tall soldier felt called upon to defend the truth of a rumor he himself had introduced. He and the loud one came near to fighting over it.

A corporal began to swear before the assemblage. He had just put a costly board floor in his house, he said. During the early spring he had refrained from adding extensively to the comfort of his environment because he had felt that the army might start on the march at any moment. Of late, however, he had been impressed that they were in a sort of eternal camp.

Many of the men engaged in a spirited debate. One outlined in a peculiarly lucid manner all the plans of the commanding general. He was opposed by men who advocated that there were other plans of campaign. They clamored at each other, numbers making futile bids for the popular attention. Meanwhile, the soldier who had fetched the rumor bustled about with much importance. He was continually assailed by questions.

"What's up, Jim?"

10   "Th'army's goin' t' move."

"Ah, what yeh talkin' about? How yeh know it is?"

"Well, yeh kin b'lieve me er not, jest as yeh like. I don't care a hang."

There was much food for thought in the manner in which he replied. He came near to convincing them by disdaining to produce proofs. They grew much excited over it.

There was a youthful private who listened with eager ears to the words of the tall soldier and to the varied comments of his comrades. After receiving a fill of discussions concerning marches and attacks, he went to his hut and crawled through an intricate hole that served it as a door. He wished to be alone with some new thoughts that had lately come to him.

15   He lay down on a wide bunk that stretched across the end of the room. In the other end, cracker boxes were made to serve as furniture. They were grouped about the fireplace. A picture from an illustrated weekly was upon the log walls, and three rifles were paralleled on pegs. Equipments hung on handy projections, and some tin dishes lay upon a small pile of firewood. A folded tent was serving as a roof. The sunlight, without, beating upon it, made it glow a light yellow shade. A small window shot an oblique square of whiter light upon the cluttered floor. The smoke from the fire at times neglected the clay chimney and wreathed into the room, and this flimsy chimney of clay and sticks made endless threats to set ablaze the whole establishment.

The youth was in a little trance of astonishment. So they were at last going to fight. On the morrow, perhaps, there would be a battle, and he would be in it. For a time he was obliged to labor to make himself believe. He could not accept with assurance an omen that he was about to mingle in one of those great affairs of the earth.

He had, of course, dreamed of battles all his life—of vague and bloody conflicts that had thrilled him with their sweep and fire. In visions he had seen himself in many struggles. He had imagined peoples secure in the shadow of his eagle-eyed prowess. But awake he had regarded battles as crimson blotches on the pages of the past. He had put them as things of the bygone with his thought-images of heavy crowns and high castles. There was a portion of the world's history which he had regarded as the time of wars, but it, he thought, had been long gone over the horizon and had disappeared forever.

From his home his youthful eyes had looked upon the war in his own country with distrust. It must be some sort of a play affair. He had long despaired of witnessing a Greeklike struggle. Such would be no more, he had said. Men were better, or more timid. Secular and religious education had effaced the throat-grappling instinct, or else firm finance held in check the passions.

He had burned several times to enlist. Tales of great movements shook the land. They might not be distinctly Homeric, but there seemed to be much glory in them. He had read of marches, sieges, conflicts, and he had longed to see it all. His busy mind had drawn for him large pictures extravagant in color, lurid with breathless deeds.

20   But his mother had discouraged him. She had affected to look with some contempt upon the quality of his war ardor and patriotism. She could calmly seat herself and with no apparent difficulty give him many hundreds of reasons why he was of vastly more importance on the farm than on the field of battle. She had had certain ways of expression that told him that her statements on the subject came from a deep conviction. Moreover, on her side, was his belief that her ethical motive in the argument was impregnable.

At last, however, he had made firm rebellion against this yellow light thrown upon the color of his ambitions. The newspapers, the gossip of the village, his own picturings, had aroused him to an uncheckable degree. They were in truth fighting finely down there. Almost every day the newspaper printed accounts of a decisive victory.

One night, as he lay in bed, the winds had carried to him the clangoring of the church bell as some enthusiast jerked the rope frantically to tell the twisted news of a great battle. This voice of the people rejoicing in the night had made him shiver in a prolonged ecstasy of excitement. Later, he had gone down to his mother's room and had spoken thus: "Ma, I'm going to enlist."

"Henry, don't you be a fool," his mother had replied. She had then covered her face with the quilt. There was an end to the matter for that night.

Nevertheless, the next morning he had gone to a town that was near his mother's farm and had enlisted in a company that was forming there. When he had returned home his mother was milking the brindle cow. Four others stood waiting. "Ma, I've enlisted," he had said to her diffidently. There was a short silence. "The Lord's will be done, Henry," she had finally replied, and had then continued to milk the brindle cow.

25   When he had stood in the doorway with his soldier's clothes on his back, and with the light of excitement and expectancy in his eyes almost defeating the glow of regret for the home bonds, he had seen two tears leaving their trails on his mother's scarred cheeks.

Still, she had disappointed him by saying nothing whatever about returning with his shield or on it. He had privately primed himself for a beautiful scene. He had prepared certain sentences which he thought could be used with touching effect. But her words destroyed his plans. She had doggedly peeled potatoes and addressed him as follows: "You watch out, Henry, an' take good care of yerself in this here fighting business—you watch, an' take good care of yerself. Don't go a-thinkin' you can lick the hull rebel army at the start, because yeh can't. Yer jest one little feller amongst a hull lot of others, and yeh've got to keep quiet an' do what they tell yeh. I know how you are, Henry.

"I've knet yeh eight pair of socks, Henry, and I've put in all yer best shirts, because I want my boy to be jest as warm and comf'able as anybody in the army. Whenever they get holes in 'em, I want yeh to send 'em right-away back to me, so's I kin dern 'em.

"An' allus be careful an' choose yer comp'ny. There's lots of bad men in the army, Henry. The army makes 'em wild, and they like nothing better than the job of leading off a young feller like you, as ain't never been away from home much and has allus had a mother, an' a-learning 'em to drink and swear. Keep clear of them folks, Henry. I don't want yeh to ever do anything, Henry, that yeh would be 'shamed to let me know about. Jest think as if I was a-watchin' yeh. If yeh keep that in yer mind allus, I guess yeh'll come out about right.

"Yeh must allus remember yer father, too, child, an' remember he never drunk a drop of licker in his life, and seldom swore a cross oath.

30 "I don't know what else to tell yeh, Henry, excepting that yeh must never do no shirking, child, on my account. If so be a time comes when yeh have to be kilt or do a mean thing, why, Henry, don't think of anything 'cept what's right, because there's many a woman has to bear up 'ginst sech things these times, and the Lord 'll take keer of us all.

"Don't forgit about the socks and the shirts, child; and I've put a cup of blackberry jam with yer bundle, because I know yeh like it above all things. Good-by, Henry. Watch out, and be a good boy."

He had, of course, been impatient under the ordeal of this speech. It had not been quite what he expected, and he had borne it with an air of irritation. He departed feeling vague relief.

Still, when he had looked back from the gate, he had seen his mother kneeling among the potato parings. Her brown face, upraised, was stained with tears, and her spare form was quivering. He bowed his head and went on, feeling suddenly ashamed of his purposes.

From his home he had gone to the seminary to bid adieu to many schoolmates. They had thronged about him with wonder and admiration. He had felt the gulf now between them and had swelled with calm pride. He and some of his fellows who had donned blue were quite overwhelmed with privileges for all of one afternoon, and it had been a very delicious thing. They had strutted.

35 A certain light-haired girl had made vivacious fun at his martial spirit, but there was another and darker girl whom he had gazed at steadfastly, and he thought she grew demure and sad at sight of his blue and brass. As he had walked down the path between the rows of oaks, he had turned his head and detected her at a window watching his departure. As he perceived her, she had immediately begun to stare up through the high tree branches at

the sky. He had seen a good deal of flurry and haste in her movement as she changed her attitude. He often thought of it.

On the way to Washington his spirit had soared. The regiment was fed and caressed at station after station until the youth had believed that he must be a hero. There was a lavish expenditure of bread and cold meats, coffee, and pickles and cheese. As he basked in the smiles of the girls and was patted and complimented by the old men, he had felt growing within him the strength to do mighty deeds of arms.

After complicated journeyings with many pauses, there had come months of monotonous life in a camp. He had had the belief that real war was a series of death struggles with small time in between for sleep and meals; but since his regiment had come to the field the army had done little but sit still and try to keep warm.

He was brought then gradually back to his old ideas. Greeklike struggles would be no more. Men were better, or more timid. Secular and religious education had effaced the throat-grappling instinct, or else firm finance held in check the passions.

He had grown to regard himself merely as a part of a vast blue demonstration. His province was to look out, as far as he could, for his personal comfort. For recreation he could twiddle his thumbs and speculate on the thoughts which must agitate the minds of the generals. Also, he was drilled and drilled and reviewed, and drilled and drilled and reviewed.

40   The only foes he had seen were some pickets along the river bank. They were a sun-tanned, philosophical lot, who sometimes shot reflectively at the blue pickets. When reproached for this afterward, they usually expressed sorrow, and swore by their gods that the guns had exploded without their permission. The youth, on guard duty one night, conversed across the stream with one of them. He was a slightly ragged man, who spat skillfully between his shoes and possessed a great fund of bland and infantile assurance. The youth liked him personally.

"Yank," the other had informed him, "yer a right dum good feller." This sentiment, floating to him upon the still air, had made him temporarily regret war.

Various veterans had told him tales. Some talked of gray, bewhiskered hordes who were advancing with relentless curses and chewing tobacco with unspeakable valor; tremendous bodies of fierce soldiery who were sweeping along like the Huns. Others spoke of tattered and eternally hungry men who fired despondent powders. "They'll charge through hell's fire an' brimstone t' git a holt on a haversack, an' sech stomachs ain't a'lastin' long," he was told. From the stories, the youth imagined the red, live bones sticking out through slits in the faded uniforms.

Still, he could not put a whole faith in veteran's tales, for recruits were their prey. They talked much of smoke, fire, and blood, but he could not tell how much might be lies. They persistently yelled "Fresh fish!" at him, and were in no wise to be trusted.

However, he perceived now that it did not greatly matter what kind of soldiers he was going to fight, so long as they fought, which fact no one disputed. There was a more serious problem. He lay in his bunk pondering upon it. He tried to mathematically prove to himself that he would not run from a battle.

45   Previously he had never felt obliged to wrestle too seriously with this question. In his life he had taken certain things for granted, never challenging his belief in ultimate success, and bothering little about means and roads. But here he was confronted with a thing of moment. It had suddenly appeared to him that perhaps in a battle he might run. He was forced to admit that as far as war was concerned he knew nothing of himself.

A sufficient time before he would have allowed the problem to kick its heels at the outer portals of his mind, but now he felt compelled to give serious attention to it.

A little panic-fear grew in his mind. As his imagination went forward to a fight, he saw hideous possibilities. He contemplated the lurking menaces of the future, and failed in an effort to see himself standing stoutly in the midst of them. He recalled his visions of broken-bladed glory, but in the shadow of the impending tumult he suspected them to be impossible pictures.

He sprang from the bunk and began to pace nervously to and fro. "Good Lord, what's th' matter with me?" he said aloud.

He felt that in this crisis his laws of life were useless. Whatever he had learned of himself was here of no avail. He was an unknown quantity. He saw that he would again be obliged to experiment as he had in early youth. He must accumulate information of himself, and meanwhile he resolved to remain close upon his guard lest those qualities of which he knew nothing should everlastingly disgrace him. "Good Lord!" he repeated in dismay.

50   After a time the tall soldier slid dexterously through the hole. The loud private followed. They were wrangling.

"That's all right," said the tall soldier as he entered. He waved his hand expressively. "You can believe me or not, jest as you like. All you got to do is sit down and wait as quiet as you can. Then pretty soon you'll find out I was right."

His comrade grunted stubbornly. For a moment he seemed to be searching for a formidable reply. Finally he said: "Well, you don't know everything in the world, do you?"

"Didn't say I knew everything in the world," retorted the other sharply. He began to stow various articles snugly into his knapsack.

The youth, pausing in his nervous walk, looked down at the busy figure. "Going to be a battle, sure, is there, Jim?" he asked.

55   "Of course there is," replied the tall soldier. "Of course there is. You jest wait 'til to-morrow, and you'll see one of the biggest battles ever was. You jest wait."

"Thunder!" said the youth.

"Oh, you'll see fighting this time, my boy, what'll be regular out-and-out fighting," added the tall soldier, with the air of a man who is about to exhibit a battle for the benefit of his friends.

"Huh!" said the loud one from a corner.

"Well," remarked the youth, "like as not this story'll turn out jest like them others did."

60   "Not much it won't," replied the tall soldier, exasperated. "Not much it won't. Didn't the cavalry all start this morning?" He glared about him. No one denied his statement. "The cavalry started this morning," he continued. "They say there ain't hardly any cavalry left in camp. They're going to Richmond, or some place, while we fight all the Johnnies. It's some dodge like that. The regiment's got orders, too. A feller what seen 'em go to headquarters told me a little while ago. And they're raising blazes all over camp—anybody can see that."

"Shucks!" said the loud one.

The youth remained silent for a time. At last he spoke to the tall soldier. "Jim!"

"What?"

"How do you think the reg'ment 'll do?"

65   "Oh, they'll fight all right, I guess, after they once get into it," said the other with cold judgment. He made a fine use of the third person. "There's been heaps of fun poked at 'em because they're new, of course, and all that; but they'll fight all right, I guess."

"Think any of the boys 'll run?" persisted the youth.

"Oh, there may be a few of 'em run, but there's them kind in every regiment, 'specially when they first goes under fire," said the other in a tolerant way. "Of course it might happen that the hull kit-and-boodle might start and run, if some big fighting came first-off, and then again they might stay and fight like fun. But you can't bet on nothing. Of course they ain't never been under fire yet, and it ain't likely they'll lick the hull rebel army all-to-oncet the first time; but I think they'll fight better than some, if worse than others. That's the way I figger. They call the reg'ment 'Fresh fish' and everything; but the boys come of good stock, and most of 'em 'll fight like sin after they oncet git shootin'," he added, with a mighty emphasis on the last four words.

"Oh, you think you know--" began the loud soldier with scorn.

70   The other turned savagely upon him. They had a rapid altercation, in which they fastened upon each other various strange epithets.

The youth at last interrupted them. "Did you ever think you might run yourself, Jim?" he asked. On concluding the sentence he laughed as if he had meant to aim a joke. The loud soldier also giggled.

The tall private waved his hand. "Well," said he profoundly, "I've thought it might get too hot for Jim Conklin in some of them scrimmages, and if a whole lot of boys started and run, why, I s'pose I'd start and run. And if I once started to run, I'd run like the devil, and no mistake. But if everybody was a-standing and a-fighting, why, I'd stand and fight. Be jiminey, I would. I'll bet on it."

"Huh!" said the loud one.

The youth of this tale felt gratitude for these words of his comrade. He had feared that all of the untried men possessed great and correct confidence. He now was in a measure reassured.

● Discussion and Writing Suggestions   MyWritingLab™

1. The novel begins with the dialogue and actions of low-ranking soldiers who have neither determined nor been told their battle strategy. They are essentially stuck at their camp with no information. How do these soldiers attempt to deal with their powerlessness and their boredom?

2. Using the terminology of Robert H. Knapp in his article "A Psychology of Rumor" (Chapter 13), do you think the rumor of imminent battle spread by the tall soldier is a "wish rumor," a "bogie rumor," or a "wedge-driving or aggression rumor"? What makes his rumor a particularly "good rumor"?

3. Why did Henry decide to enlist in the army? What were his expectations of being a solider? How do his expectations seem to be stacking up against his actual experiences?

4. Why do you think Stephen Crane started a war novel with a chapter depicting monotony? How does he go about depicting monotony without the story itself becoming monotonous?

5. Henry develops a fear that in the midst of battle he'll panic and run away. Though he has never been a coward before, Henry believes that "in this crisis his laws of life were useless. Whatever he had learned of himself was here of no avail. He was an unknown quantity." To what degree do you agree with this view that in crisis we become "unknown quantities"?

DRACULA

Bram Stoker

Stephanie Meyer's bestselling *Twilight* series; Anne Rice's bestselling novel *Interview with the Vampire*; the hit TV shows *True Blood* and *Buffy the Vampire Slayer*... These are only a few of the many vampire incarnations that are indebted to Bram Stoker's classic 1897 novel of gothic horror. Although *Dracula* is not the first-ever vampire novel, Stoker's particular depiction of the vampire count from Transylvania is the one that has endured for well over a century and has informed all subsequent vampire incarnations.

Bram Stoker (1847–1912) grew up in Dublin, Ireland as one of seven children, attended Trinity College in Dublin, and became interested in the theater before turning to fiction. *Dracula* is his second novel. Notably, it is comprised entirely of fictional "found" documents—diary entries, newspaper articles, letters, etc.—in an attempt to lend the work an added degree of authenticity. It is as if the novel wasn't written at all, but rather pieced together from various real scraps of printed material. The opening chapter is presented as an entry from Jonathan Harker's personal journal, as he travels from England to Hungary to meet Count Dracula for the first time.

Dracula's Guest

When we started for our drive the sun was shining brightly on Munich, and the air was full of the joyousness of early summer. Just as we were about to depart,

Herr Delbrück (the maître d'hôtel of the Quatre Saisons, where I was staying) came down, bareheaded, to the carriage and, after wishing me a pleasant drive, said to the coachman, still holding his hand on the handle of the carriage door:

'Remember you are back by nightfall. The sky looks bright but there is a shiver in the north wind that says there may be a sudden storm. But I am sure you will not be late.' Here he smiled, and added, 'for you know what night it is.'

Johann answered with an emphatic, 'Ja, mein Herr,' and, touching his hat, drove off quickly. When we had cleared the town, I said, after signalling to him to stop:

'Tell me, Johann, what is tonight?'

5   He crossed himself, as he answered laconically: 'Walpurgis nacht.'[1] Then he took out his watch, a great, old-fashioned German silver thing as big as a turnip, and looked at it, with his eyebrows gathered together and a little impatient shrug of his shoulders. I realised that this was his way of respectfully protesting against the unnecessary delay, and sank back in the carriage, merely motioning him to proceed. He started off rapidly, as if to make up for lost time. Every now and then the horses seemed to throw up their heads and sniffed the air suspiciously. On such occasions I often looked round in alarm. The road was pretty bleak, for we were traversing a sort of high, wind-swept plateau. As we drove, I saw a road that looked but little used, and which seemed to dip through a little, winding valley. It looked so inviting that, even at the risk of offending him, I called Johann to stop—and when he had pulled up, I told him I would like to drive down that road. He made all sorts of excuses, and frequently crossed himself as he spoke. This somewhat piqued my curiosity, so I asked him various questions. He answered fencingly, and repeatedly looked at his watch in protest. Finally I said:

'Well, Johann, I want to go down this road. I shall not ask you to come unless you like; but tell me why you do not like to go, that is all I ask.' For answer he seemed to throw himself off the box, so quickly did he reach the ground. Then he stretched out his hands appealingly to me, and implored me not to go. There was just enough of English mixed with the German for me to understand the drift of his talk. He seemed always just about to tell me something—the very idea of which evidently frightened him; but each time he pulled himself up, saying, as he crossed himself: 'Walpurgis nacht!'

I tried to argue with him, but it was difficult to argue with a man when I did not know his language. The advantage certainly rested with him, for although he began to speak in English, of a very crude and broken kind, he always got excited and broke into his native tongue—and every time he did so, he looked at his watch. Then the horses became restless and sniffed the air. At this he grew very pale, and, looking around in a frightened way, he suddenly jumped forward, took them by the bridles and led them on some twenty feet. I followed, and asked why he had done this. For answer he crossed himself, pointed to the spot we had left and drew his carriage in the direction of the other road, indicating a cross, and said, first in German, then in English: 'Buried him—him what killed themselves.'

---

[1] "Walpurgis Night": a folk celebration with pagan origins observed in northern Europe on April 30. Among other holiday activities, revelers drink and make loud noises to scare off evil spirits. See also paragraph 37.

I remembered the old custom of burying suicides at cross-roads: 'Ah! I see, a suicide. How interesting!' But for the life of me I could not make out why the horses were frightened.

Whilst we were talking, we heard a sort of sound between a yelp and a bark. It was far away; but the horses got very restless, and it took Johann all his time to quiet them. He was pale, and said, 'It sounds like a wolf—but yet there are no wolves here now.'

10   'No?' I said, questioning him; 'isn't it long since the wolves were so near the city?'

'Long, long,' he answered, 'in the spring and summer; but with the snow the wolves have been here not so long.'

Whilst he was petting the horses and trying to quiet them, dark clouds drifted rapidly across the sky. The sunshine passed away, and a breath of cold wind seemed to drift past us. It was only a breath, however, and more in the nature of a warning than a fact, for the sun came out brightly again. Johann looked under his lifted hand at the horizon and said:

'The storm of snow, he comes before long time.' Then he looked at his watch again, and, straightway holding his reins firmly—for the horses were still pawing the ground restlessly and shaking their heads—he climbed to his box as though the time had come for proceeding on our journey.

I felt a little obstinate and did not at once get into the carriage.

15   'Tell me,' I said, 'about this place where the road leads,' and I pointed down.

Again he crossed himself and mumbled a prayer, before he answered, 'It is unholy.'

'What is unholy?' I enquired.

'The village.'

'Then there is a village?'

20   'No, no. No one lives there hundreds of years.' My curiosity was piqued, 'But you said there was a village.'

'There was.'

'Where is it now?'

Whereupon he burst out into a long story in German and English, so mixed up that I could not quite understand exactly what he said, but roughly I gathered that long ago, hundreds of years, men had died there and been buried in their graves; and sounds were heard under the clay, and when the graves were opened, men and women were found rosy with life, and their mouths red with blood. And so, in haste to save their lives (aye, and their souls!—and here he crossed himself) those who were left fled away to other places, where the living lived, and the dead were dead and not—not something. He was evidently afraid to speak the last words. As he proceeded with his narration, he grew more and more excited. It seemed as if his imagination had got hold of him, and he ended in a perfect paroxysm of fear—white-faced, perspiring, trembling and looking round him, as if expecting that some dreadful presence would manifest itself there in the bright sunshine on the open plain. Finally, in an agony of desperation, he cried:

'Walpurgis nacht!' and pointed to the carriage for me to get in. All my English blood rose at this, and, standing back, I said:

25   'You are afraid, Johann—you are afraid. Go home; I shall return alone; the walk will do me good.' The carriage door was open. I took from the seat my oak walking-stick—which I always carry on my holiday excursions—and closed the door, pointing back to Munich, and said, 'Go home, Johann—Walpurgis nacht doesn't concern Englishmen.'

The horses were now more restive than ever, and Johann was trying to hold them in, while excitedly imploring me not to do anything so foolish. I pitied the poor fellow, he was deeply in earnest; but all the same I could not help laughing. His English was quite gone now. In his anxiety he had forgotten that his only means of making me understand was to talk my language, so he jabbered away in his native German. It began to be a little tedious. After giving the direction, 'Home!' I turned to go down the cross-road into the valley.

With a despairing gesture, Johann turned his horses towards Munich. I leaned on my stick and looked after him. He went slowly along the road for a while: then there came over the crest of the hill a man tall and thin. I could see so much in the distance. When he drew near the horses, they began to jump and kick about, then to scream with terror. Johann could not hold them in; they bolted down the road, running away madly. I watched them out of sight, then looked for the stranger, but I found that he, too, was gone.

With a light heart I turned down the side road through the deepening valley to which Johann had objected. There was not the slightest reason, that I could see, for his objection; and I daresay I tramped for a couple of hours without thinking of time or distance, and certainly without seeing a person or a house. So far as the place was concerned, it was desolation, itself. But I did not notice this particularly till, on turning a bend in the road, I came upon a scattered fringe of wood; then I recognised that I had been impressed unconsciously by the desolation of the region through which I had passed.

I sat down to rest myself, and began to look around. It struck me that it was considerably colder than it had been at the commencement of my walk—a sort of sighing sound seemed to be around me, with, now and then, high overhead, a sort of muffled roar. Looking upwards I noticed that great thick clouds were drifting rapidly across the sky from North to South at a great height. There were signs of coming storm in some lofty stratum of the air. I was a little chilly, and, thinking that it was the sitting still after the exercise of walking, I resumed my journey.

30   The ground I passed over was now much more picturesque. There were no striking objects that the eye might single out; but in all there was a charm of beauty. I took little heed of time and it was only when the deepening twilight forced itself upon me that I began to think of how I should find my way home. The brightness of the day had gone. The air was cold, and the drifting of clouds high overhead was more marked. They were accompanied by a sort of faraway rushing sound, through which seemed to come at intervals that mysterious cry which the driver had said came from a wolf. For a while I hesitated. I had said I would see the deserted village, so on I went, and presently came on a wide stretch of open country, shut in by hills all around. Their sides were covered with trees which spread down to the plain, dotting, in clumps, the gentler slopes

and hollows which showed here and there. I followed with my eye the winding of the road, and saw that it curved close to one of the densest of these clumps and was lost behind it.

As I looked there came a cold shiver in the air, and the snow began to fall. I thought of the miles and miles of bleak country I had passed, and then hurried on to seek the shelter of the wood in front. Darker and darker grew the sky, and faster and heavier fell the snow, till the earth before and around me was a glistening white carpet the further edge of which was lost in misty vagueness. The road was here but crude, and when on the level its boundaries were not so marked, as when it passed through the cuttings; and in a little while I found that I must have strayed from it, for I missed underfoot the hard surface, and my feet sank deeper in the grass and moss. Then the wind grew stronger and blew with ever increasing force, till I was fain to run before it. The air became icy-cold, and in spite of my exercise I began to suffer. The snow was now falling so thickly and whirling around me in such rapid eddies that I could hardly keep my eyes open. Every now and then the heavens were torn asunder by vivid lightning, and in the flashes I could see ahead of me a great mass of trees, chiefly yew and cypress all heavily coated with snow.

I was soon amongst the shelter of the trees, and there, in comparative silence, I could hear the rush of the wind high overhead. Presently the blackness of the storm had become merged in the darkness of the night. By-and-by the storm seemed to be passing away: it now only came in fierce puffs or blasts. At such moments the weird sound of the wolf appeared to be echoed by many similar sounds around me.

Now and again, through the black mass of drifting cloud, came a straggling ray of moonlight, which lit up the expanse, and showed me that I was at the edge of a dense mass of cypress and yew trees. As the snow had ceased to fall, I walked out from the shelter and began to investigate more closely. It appeared to me that, amongst so many old foundations as I had passed, there might be still standing a house in which, though in ruins, I could find some sort of shelter for a while. As I skirted the edge of the copse, I found that a low wall encircled it, and following this I presently found an opening. Here the cypresses formed an alley leading up to a square mass of some kind of building. Just as I caught sight of this, however, the drifting clouds obscured the moon, and I passed up the path in darkness. The wind must have grown colder, for I felt myself shiver as I walked; but there was hope of shelter, and I groped my way blindly on.

I stopped, for there was a sudden stillness. The storm had passed; and, perhaps in sympathy with nature's silence, my heart seemed to cease to beat. But this was only momentarily; for suddenly the moonlight broke through the clouds, showing me that I was in a graveyard, and that the square object before me was a great massive tomb of marble, as white as the snow that lay on and all around it. With the moonlight there came a fierce sigh of the storm, which appeared to resume its course with a long, low howl, as of many dogs or wolves. I was awed and shocked, and felt the cold perceptibly grow upon me till it seemed to grip me by the heart. Then while the flood of moonlight still fell on the marble tomb, the storm gave further evidence of renewing, as though it was returning on its track. Impelled by some sort of fascination, I approached the sepulchre to see what it was, and why such a thing stood alone in such a place. I walked around it, and read, over the Doric door, in German:

Countess Dolingen of Gratz in Styria Sought and Found Death 1801

35   On the top of the tomb, seemingly driven through the solid marble—for the structure was composed of a few vast blocks of stone—was a great iron spike or stake. On going to the back I saw, graven in great Russian letters:

'The dead travel fast.'

There was something so weird and uncanny about the whole thing that it gave me a turn and made me feel quite faint. I began to wish, for the first time, that I had taken Johann's advice. Here a thought struck me, which came under almost mysterious circumstances and with a terrible shock. This was Walpurgis Night!

Walpurgis Night, when, according to the belief of millions of people, the devil was abroad— when the graves were opened and the dead came forth and walked. When all evil things of earth and air and water held revel. This very place the driver had specially shunned. This was the depopulated village of centuries ago. This was where the suicide lay; and this was the place where I was alone—unmanned, shivering with cold in a shroud of snow with a wild storm gathering again upon me! It took all my philosophy, all the religion I had been taught, all my courage, not to collapse in a paroxysm of fright.

And now a perfect tornado burst upon me. The ground shook as though thousands of horses thundered across it; and this time the storm bore on its icy wings, not snow, but great hailstones which drove with such violence that they might have come from the thongs of Balearic slingers—hailstones that beat down leaf and branch and made the shelter of the cypresses of no more avail than though their stems were standing-corn. At the first I had rushed to the nearest tree; but I was soon fain to leave it and seek the only spot that seemed to afford refuge, the deep Doric doorway of the marble tomb. There, crouching against the massive bronze door, I gained a certain amount of protection from the beating of the hailstones, for now they only drove against me as they ricocheted from the ground and the side of the marble.

As I leaned against the door, it moved slightly and opened inwards. The shelter of even a tomb was welcome in that pitiless tempest, and I was about to enter it when there came a flash of forked-lightning that lit up the whole expanse of the heavens. In the instant, as I am a living man, I saw, as my eyes were turned into the darkness of the tomb, a beautiful woman, with rounded cheeks and red lips, seemingly sleeping on a bier. As the thunder broke overhead, I was grasped as by the hand of a giant and hurled out into the storm. The whole thing was so sudden that, before I could realise the shock, moral as well as physical, I found the hailstones beating me down. At the same time I had a strange, dominating feeling that I was not alone. I looked towards the tomb. Just then there came another blinding flash, which seemed to strike the iron stake that surmounted the tomb and to pour through to the earth, blasting and crumbling the marble, as in a burst of flame. The dead woman rose for a moment of agony, while she was lapped in the flame, and her bitter scream of pain was drowned in the thundercrash. The last thing I heard was this mingling of dreadful sound, as again I was seized in the giant-grasp and dragged away, while the hailstones beat on me, and the air around seemed reverberant with the howling of wolves. The last sight that I remembered was a vague, white, moving mass, as if all the graves around me had sent out the phantoms of their sheeted-dead, and that they were closing in on me through the white cloudiness of the driving hail.

40   Gradually there came a sort of vague beginning of consciousness; then a sense of weariness that was dreadful. For a time I remembered nothing; but slowly my senses returned. My feet seemed positively racked with pain, yet I could not move them. They seemed to be numbed. There was an icy feeling at the back of my neck and all down my spine, and my ears, like my feet, were dead, yet in torment; but there was in my breast a sense of warmth which was, by comparison, delicious. It was as a nightmare—a physical nightmare, if one may use such an expression; for some heavy weight on my chest made it difficult for me to breathe.

This period of semi-lethargy seemed to remain a long time, and as it faded away I must have slept or swooned. Then came a sort of loathing, like the first stage of sea-sickness, and a wild desire to be free from something—I knew not what. A vast stillness enveloped me, as though all the world were asleep or dead—only broken by the low panting as of some animal close to me. I felt a warm rasping at my throat, then came a consciousness of the awful truth, which chilled me to the heart and sent the blood surging up through my brain. Some great animal was lying on me and now licking my throat. I feared to stir, for some instinct of prudence bade me lie still; but the brute seemed to realise that there was now some change in me, for it raised its head. Through my eyelashes I saw above me the two great flaming eyes of a gigantic wolf. Its sharp white teeth gleamed in the gaping red mouth, and I could feel its hot breath fierce and acrid upon me.

For another spell of time I remembered no more. Then I became conscious of a low growl, followed by a yelp, renewed again and again. Then, seemingly very far away, I heard a 'Holloa! holloa!' as of many voices calling in unison. Cautiously I raised my head and looked in the direction whence the sound came; but the cemetery blocked my view. The wolf still continued to yelp in a strange way, and a red glare began to move round the grove of cypresses, as though following the sound. As the voices drew closer, the wolf yelped faster and louder. I feared to make either sound or motion. Nearer came the red glow, over the white pall which stretched into the darkness around me. Then all at once from beyond the trees there came at a trot a troop of horsemen bearing torches. The wolf rose from my breast and made for the cemetery. I saw one of the horsemen (soldiers by their caps and their long military cloaks) raise his carbine and take aim. A companion knocked up his arm, and I heard the ball whizz over my head. He had evidently taken my body for that of the wolf. Another sighted the animal as it slunk away, and a shot followed. Then, at a gallop, the troop rode forward—some towards me, others following the wolf as it disappeared amongst the snow-clad cypresses.

As they drew nearer I tried to move, but was powerless, although I could see and hear all that went on around me. Two or three of the soldiers jumped from their horses and knelt beside me. One of them raised my head, and placed his hand over my heart.

'Good news, comrades!' he cried. 'His heart still beats!'

45   Then some brandy was poured down my throat; it put vigour into me, and I was able to open my eyes fully and look around. Lights and shadows were moving among the trees, and I heard men call to one another. They drew together, uttering frightened exclamations; and the lights flashed as the others came pouring out of the cemetery pell-mell, like men possessed. When the further ones came close to us, those who were around me asked them eagerly:

'Well, have you found him?'

The reply rang out hurriedly:

'No! no! Come away quick—quick! This is no place to stay, and on this of all nights!'

'What was it?' was the question, asked in all manner of keys. The answer came variously and all indefinitely as though the men were moved by some common impulse to speak, yet were restrained by some common fear from giving their thoughts.

50   'It—it—indeed!' gibbered one, whose wits had plainly given out for the moment.

'A wolf—and yet not a wolf!' another put in shudderingly.

'No use trying for him without the sacred bullet,' a third remarked in a more ordinary manner.

'Serve us right for coming out on this night! Truly we have earned our thousand marks!' were the ejaculations of a fourth.

'There was blood on the broken marble,' another said after a pause—'the lightning never brought that there. And for him—is he safe? Look at his throat! See, comrades, the wolf has been lying on him and keeping his blood warm.'

55   The officer looked at my throat and replied:

'He is all right; the skin is not pierced. What does it all mean? We should never have found him but for the yelping of the wolf.'

'What became of it?' asked the man who was holding up my head, and who seemed the least panic-stricken of the party, for his hands were steady and without tremor. On his sleeve was the chevron of a petty officer.

'It went to its home,' answered the man, whose long face was pallid, and who actually shook with terror as he glanced around him fearfully. 'There are graves enough there in which it may lie. Come, comrades—come quickly! Let us leave this cursed spot.'

The officer raised me to a sitting posture, as he uttered a word of command; then several men placed me upon a horse. He sprang to the saddle behind me, took me in his arms, gave the word to advance; and, turning our faces away from the cypresses, we rode away in swift, military order.

60   As yet my tongue refused its office, and I was perforce silent. I must have fallen asleep; for the next thing I remembered was finding myself standing up, supported by a soldier on each side of me. It was almost broad daylight, and to the north a red streak of sunlight was reflected, like a path of blood, over the waste of snow. The officer was telling the men to say nothing of what they had seen, except that they found an English stranger, guarded by a large dog.

    'Dog! that was no dog,' cut in the man who had exhibited such fear. 'I think I know a wolf when I see one.'

    The young officer answered calmly: 'I said a dog.'

    'Dog!' reiterated the other ironically. It was evident that his courage was rising with the sun; and, pointing to me, he said, 'Look at his throat. Is that the work of a dog, master?'

    Instinctively I raised my hand to my throat, and as I touched it I cried out in pain. The men crowded round to look, some stooping down from their saddles; and again there came the calm voice of the young officer:

65   'A dog, as I said. If aught else were said we should only be laughed at.'

    I was then mounted behind a trooper, and we rode on into the suburbs of Munich. Here we came across a stray carriage, into which I was lifted, and it was driven off to the Quatre Saisons—the young officer accompanying me, whilst a trooper followed with his horse, and the others rode off to their barracks.

    When we arrived, Herr Delbrück rushed so quickly down the steps to meet me, that it was apparent he had been watching within. Taking me by both hands he solicitously led me in. The officer saluted me and was turning to withdraw, when I recognised his purpose, and insisted that he should come to my rooms. Over a glass of wine I warmly thanked him and his brave comrades for saving me. He replied simply that he was more than glad, and that Herr Delbrück had at the first taken steps to make all the searching party pleased; at which ambiguous utterance the maître d'hôtel smiled, while the officer pleaded duty and withdrew.

    'But Herr Delbrück,' I enquired, 'how and why was it that the soldiers searched for me?'

    He shrugged his shoulders, as if in depreciation of his own deed, as he replied:

70   'I was so fortunate as to obtain leave from the commander of the regiment in which I served, to ask for volunteers.'

    'But how did you know I was lost?' I asked.

    'The driver came hither with the remains of his carriage, which had been upset when the horses ran away.'

    'But surely you would not send a search-party of soldiers merely on this account?'

    'Oh, no!' he answered; 'but even before the coachman arrived, I had this telegram from the Boyar whose guest you are,' and he took from his pocket a telegram which he handed to me, and I read:

75   *Bistritz.*

          Be careful of my guest—his safety is most precious to me. Should aught happen to him, or if he be missed, spare nothing to find him and ensure his safety. He is English and therefore adventurous. There are often dangers from snow and wolves and night. Lose not a moment if you suspect harm to him. I answer your zeal with my fortune.—*Dracula*.

As I held the telegram in my hand, the room seemed to whirl around me; and, if the attentive maître d'hôtel had not caught me, I think I should have fallen. There was something so strange in all this, something so weird and impossible to imagine, that there grew on me a sense of my being in some way the sport of opposite forces—the mere vague idea of which seemed in a way to paralyse me. I was certainly under some form of mysterious protection. From a distant country had come, in the very nick of time, a message that took me out of the danger of the snow-sleep and the jaws of the wolf.

● **Discussion and Writing Suggestions**   MyWritingLab™

1. The first chapter of *Dracula* is written as an entry from Jonathan Harker's journal. How does this type of storytelling differ from some of the other first chapters you have read? In what ways does the fact that you are supposedly reading someone's journal help pull you into the story? In what ways might it make getting into the story more difficult?

2. What are some of the details in this chapter that best contribute toward setting the novel's eerie mood?

3. How do the various people that Jonathan Harker meets on his journey act toward him? How do they react upon learning that he is coming to visit the count? Do you think, as Harker does, that the locals are being overly superstitious? Or do you think, instead, that their fear is well-founded and that Jonathan Harker is being naïve? What leads you to these conclusions?

4. Significantly, the character of Dracula doesn't appear in the opening chapter. However, we do see various other characters reacting—often with great fear— to the very mention of his name. Why might the author have decided to delay the appearance of the novel's title character?

5. What mysteries or questions does this opening chapter present to the reader? How do you think they might get addressed in Chapter 2?

6. *Dracula* was first published in 1897. What dramatic elements in this first chapter seem to have influenced contemporary horror fiction? Explain.

SCENE ONES: THE FILMS

In this section we invite you to view the opening scenes of film adaptations of five of the classic novels presented earlier in this chapter, as well as the opening scenes of eleven additional films. Several of these films—including George Stevens's *Shane* and Francis Ford Coppola's *The Godfather, Part One*—are based on novels;

the rest, for the most part, are original works created for the cinema. (Two—*Brief Encounter* and *Chicago*—are based on plays.)

Scene Ones are not as clearly demarked in films as in novels, where novelists number or at least title separate chapters, so it sometimes takes a keen eye to determine where one scene of a film ends and the next begins. Typically, though, we have deemed the first scene ended when a particular line of dramatic action has reached some kind of natural conclusion or at least has come to a significant pause. In earlier times, these pauses were often signaled by fade-outs or dissolves, but such devices are now often considered old-fashioned.

For your viewing convenience, the heading of each film treated in this section concludes with an indication of how many minutes and seconds the scene lasts. So 00:00–6:33 indicates that the scene begins at the zero point—typically with the appearance of the studio logo—and ends 6 minutes and 33 seconds later. Although you may choose—and are even encouraged—to continue viewing into scene two and beyond, the Discussion and Writing Suggestions sections assume that you have watched only to the designated point. Some of these scenes (for example, the openings of Robert Stevenson's *Jane Eyre*, David Lean's *Great Expectations*, and Orson Welles's *Citizen Kane*) are available complete on YouTube. In most cases, the Web offers only a truncated version of the opening scene. But today a vast number of films are widely available for a modest rental rate from such sources as Netflix, iTunes, and Amazon streaming video. And your instructor may also make these films available to you, either by showing them in class or by placing them on reserve. We wish you pleasurable viewing—and even envy you if you are about to watch these films for the first time!

JANE EYRE (1943)

Robert Stevenson, Director
(00:00–6:33)

Charlotte Brontë's *Jane Eyre* has been adapted for film and television at least 30 times, according to the Internet Movie Database. The 1944 version, directed by Robert Stevenson, is particularly notable for Orson Welles's brooding performance as the tortured Mr. Rochester. Joan Fontaine plays Jane as an adult. The film is also impressive for its re-creation of the Yorkshire moors, though it was filmed entirely on a Hollywood backlot. The novelist Aldous Huxley was one of the three credited screenwriters, and the musical score was composed by Bernard Herrmann, who was to write the music for most of Alfred Hitchcock's American films. Stevenson later directed *Mary Poppins* (1964).

As many novels contain more material than can be comfortably contained within the 90 or 120 minutes of the typical narrative film, Stevenson's *Jane Eyre* has significant differences from Brontë's novel. The film does retain Brontë's first scene, with Mrs. Reed and her son John facing off against Jane. But it omits a major subplot that develops after Jane flees Thornfield upon discovering that Mr. Rochester already has a wife. She is eventually taken in by three siblings (who turn out to be her cousins); one of them, a clergyman who wants to do missionary work, eventually proposes to Jane and invites her to come with him to India. She is tempted, but then hears in her mind Rochester's desperate call for help.

● **Discussion and Writing Suggestions**   MyWritingLab™

1. The opening credits of the film use a common convention of the time for literary adaptations: They appear as turning pages in a book, and the last page we see is the first page of the novel: "My name is Jane Eyre. I was born in 1820, a time of harsh change in England. Money and position seemed all that mattered.... There was no proper place for the poor or the unfortunate."

   The problem is—as you can readily see by turning to p. 372, where we reprint the actual first page of *Jane Eyre*—that these are not, in fact, Brontë's opening words; they have been entirely made up by the screenwriters and are simply masquerading as the opening of the novel.

   In light of the way the novel *Jane Eyre actually* begins, why do you think the director and the screenwriters attempted to "cheat" on Brontë's own opening in this manner?

2. Compare the action of the opening of Brontë's novel with the action of the opening sequence of the film: the footman and Bessie getting Jane out of her locked closet and downstairs to confront her aunt and Mr. Brocklehurst. How do these different openings help shape our different responses to the book and to the film? Or do they not make a difference in terms of our overall "first impression" of the story?

3. How does the director Robert Stevenson use dramatic camera angles to emphasize Jane's insignificant place in the household and, on the other hand, the awesome power of a man like Brocklehurst?

4. Both Mrs. Reed and Brocklehurst view Jane as a "wicked" girl. Based on this opening segment, how would you describe her? And based upon what you have seen and heard, explain the situation in this household. Why is Mrs. Reed so determined to get rid of Jane? Why is Brocklehurst so eager to get her to come to Lowood?

GREAT EXPECTATIONS **(1946)**

David Lean, Director
(00:00–3:55)

"One of the great things about Dickens," wrote the critic Roger Ebert, "is the way his people colonize your memory." Ebert goes on to note that "[David] Lean brings Dickens's classic set-pieces to life as if he'd been reading over our shoulder: Pip's encounter with the convict Magwitch in the churchyard, Pip's first meeting with the mad Miss Havisham, and the ghoulish atmosphere in the law offices of Mr. Jaggers, whose walls are decorated with the death masks of clients he has lost to the gallows."

Like *Jane Eyre*, Dickens's *Great Expectations* has been adapted into film numerous times. The 1946 version, starring John Mills as the adult Pip, was directed by Lean, who went on to create numerous Hollywood epic films, including *The Bridge on the River*

Kwai (1957), *Lawrence of Arabia* (1962), *and Dr. Zhivago* (1965). *Great Expectations* was nominated for Five Academy Awards and won two (Best Cinematography and Best Art Direction). The visuals in the first sequence of the film, closely paralleling the descriptions in Dickens's first chapter, show why.

● Discussion and Writing Suggestions   MyWritingLab™

1. Like Robert Stevenson's film *Jane Eyre*, David Lean's *Great Expectations* opens with turning book pages and with the adult protagonist reading the first paragraph of the novel; but in this case, the words are Dickens's own. Following the credits, we see the boy Pip running along the marshes. What else do we see on the screen, and what do we hear on the soundtrack? How do these images and sounds help create a mood that is equivalent to the one evoked in the opening of Dickens's novel?

2. Stevenson the filmmaker needs to convey vital information about Pip's status as an orphan currently living with his aunt and her husband, information that is fully developed in the opening pages of the novel. What is the filmmaker's solution, and how well do you think he has solved the problem of initial exposition?

3. Compare and contrast the moment in the book when Pip first encounters the convict Magwitch with the same moment in Lean's film. Consider such matters as the role of your imagination in envisaging the convict (and how he would appear to a young boy) and the way that Dickens and Stevenson create the shock of this encounter for Pip.

EMMA **(1996)**

Douglas McGrath, Director

(00:00–10:37)

---

and

CLUELESS **(1995)**

Amy Heckerling, Director

(00:00–14:00)

Jane Austen's *Emma* has been adapted into feature films twice (both of these in 1996) and once into a TV miniseries. The version we examine here, starring Gwyneth Paltrow as Austen's matchmaking heroine, was written and directed by Douglas McGrath. (The other 1996 version, also well worth viewing, stars Kate Beckinsale and was directed by Diarmuid

Lawrence.) The McGrath film was well reviewed by critics and popular with audiences. Devotees of *The Good Wife* will note that Mr. Elton is played by a very young Alan Cumming. McGrath also directed a film version of Charles Dickens's *Nicholas Nickleby* (2002) and wrote the screenplay of Woody Allen's *Bullets Over Broadway* (1994).

Clueless, a contemporary comic version of Austen's novel, set in Beverly Hills (whose teenage residents talk "Valley Speak"—"As if!"), was written and directed by Amy Heckerling and released in 1995. Heckerling makes no attempt to closely track the events recounted in *Emma*; but her film, with its young protagonist who never hesitates to interfere with the love lives of others, is nevertheless broadly recognizable as the story originally devised by Austen. Heckerling also directed *Fast Times at Ridgemont High* (1982), *National Lampoon's European Vacation* (1985), and *Look Who's Talking* (1989).

● Discussion and Writing Suggestions   MyWritingLab™

1. Austen begins her novel *Emma* with the following sentence: "Emma Woodhouse, handsome, clever, and rich, with a comfortable home and happy disposition, seemed to unite some of the best blessings of existence; and had lived nearly twenty-one years in the world with very little to distress or vex her." To what extent do the two characters portrayed, respectively, by Gwyneth Paltrow in Douglas McGrath's film and Alicia Silverstone (who plays "Cher") in Amy Heckerling's film display these qualities? How are these same qualities dramatized at particular moments or in particular scenes during the opening sequences of the two films?

2. Describe the common elements in the two versions of *Emma*. How does Amy Heckerling attempt to modernize some of these elements for contemporary audiences? To what extent do you think she has been true to the spirit of Austen? To what extent do you believe that she has significantly distorted Austen's vision of her heroine and the world in which she lives?

3. Find the analogues to Mr. Knightley, Mr. Woodhouse, and Mr. Elton in Amy Heckerling's film. How are the two sets of characters similar? How are they different?

4. Compare and contrast the kind of humor found in Austen's novel and in Douglas McGrath's film with the kind of humor found in *Clueless*. What kinds of things are (1) Austen, (2) McGrath, and (3) Heckerling inviting us to laugh at?

5. Based on what you have seen so far, what are likely to be the main sources of major conflict in Heckerling's film? To what extent does the heroine have a character flaw that is likely to aggravate this conflict? Cite specific moments in each film that support your conclusions.

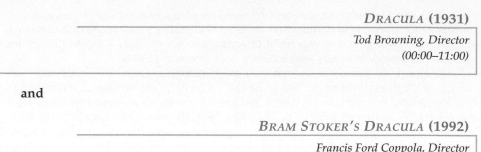

DRACULA **(1931)**

Tod Browning, Director
(00:00–11:00)

and

BRAM STOKER'S DRACULA **(1992)**

Francis Ford Coppola, Director
(00:00–15:38)

Bram Stoker's *Dracula* has been frequently adapted to film, but for sheer creepiness the original 1931 version directed by Tod Browning has never been surpassed. Newspapers reported that some members of the audience at the premiere fainted from shock. This film, directed by Tod Browning, is actually based on the 1924 play by Hamilton Deane and John Balderston, which was itself based on Stoker's novel. (An unauthorized version of the story had been filmed in 1922, as *Nosferatu*, but Stoker's widow successfully sued to get the prints destroyed; some survived.) The Hungarian actor Bela Lugosi, who makes an unforgettable impression as the vampire Count Dracula, was not the producer's first choice for the role, even though he had played the role on stage. Lugosi was later to appear in numerous other horror films, some of them comic. The visual look of the film can be credited as much to Karl Freud, Browning's cinematographer, as to the director himself. Browning made his reputation directing silent film, and *Dracula*, made just a few years into the sound era, has much of the look and the acting style (with its heightened expressions and gestures) of the silent era.

Francis Ford Coppola, director of *The Godfather* films (1972, 1974, 1990) and *Apocalypse Now* (1979), said that he wanted his 1992 version of the Dracula legend to resemble "an erotic dream." One critic, Vincent Canby of the *New York Times,* wrote, "Mr. Coppola has created his own wild dream of a movie, which looks as if it required a special pact with the Treasury Department to finance." Spurning digital effects, because he wanted the film to look old-fashioned, Coppola made significant use of old-school film techniques like rear projection, matte painting, multiple exposure, and forced perspective (also used by Peter Jackson in the *Lord of the Rings* films to make, for example, hobbits look small) to create some of his hallucinatory images. He also devoted significant resources to costume design, for which the film won an Academy Award (along with Best Makeup).

● **Discussion and Writing Suggestions**   MyWritingLab™

1. In the first chapter of his novel, Bram Stoker attempts to create an atmosphere of dread. How does Tod Browning strive to create the equivalent sense of dread in his film? Point out particular things that we see and hear that are intended to give us the shivers. To what extent do such images and sounds have the capacity to make us uneasy, or even terrified? To what extent have they become so familiar that they have lost the capacity to disturb us? (Indeed, they may even make us laugh.)

2. We don't meet Dracula in the first chapter of Stoker's novel, but we do in the opening segment of Browning's film—first, when we see him emerge from his

coffin in the crypt of the castle, next when he assumes the guise of a coach-man and conveys Renfield to the castle, and finally (in our sequence) when he descends the staircase in the great hall of the castle and bids Renfield wel-come. How do Browning and actor Bela Lugosi choose to characterize Dracula in this film interpretation of the novel? Compared to the villains of other horror films, what distinguishes this particular fiend of darkness?

3. Coppola's opening scene differs most obviously from Stevenson's in its his-torical back story. Instead of beginning (like most Draculas) with the hero traveling through a fearsome landscape toward Castle Dracula, this one begins several centuries earlier with the founding member of the Dracula vampire fam-ily. So we see how the original Dracula decides to renounce God in the wake of the suicide of his beloved Elizabeta (which rendered her damned in the eyes of the Church), and we see how blood becomes an essential part of the Dracula legend. To what extent do you think Coppola made a good choice in providing this kind of historical background as a prelude to the more modern story set in Victorian times? (Note: This background makes it possible for Dracula to later see in Harker's fiancée Mina the reincarnation of his beloved Elisabeta.)

4. Dramatic imagery is an essential component of all horror films, and certainly of all Draculas. In Tod Browning's film, we are treated to images of coffins (and rats) in moldering crypts. We also see the tuxedo-clad count descending the stone steps of his vast castle to greet his visitor. Cite images in Coppola's film that are particularly striking. How do they contribute to the mood of the story?

5. In Browning's *Dracula*, we see Renfield on his way to the castle and then be-ing welcomed by Dracula. In Coppola's film, we see him as an inmate of a mental institution, reduced to eating flies while promising to obey his unseen master. (The man traveling to the castle is Jonathan Harker.) To what extent do you think Coppola made the right choice in showing the power of Dracula over his victims before we even see the vampire himself?

6. Compare and contrast Bela Lugosi (in Browning's film) and Gary Oldman (in Coppola's). What qualities does each actor bring to his role that affect our conception of the character?

7. Compare and contrast the two *Draculas* in the way they build suspense in making us want to know what is going to happen next.

THE RED BADGE OF COURAGE (1951)

John Huston, Director
(00:00–6:54)

Unlike many other fictional masterpieces that have been filmed repeatedly—think *Jane Eyre* and *Great Expectations*—Stephen Crane's *Red Badge of Courage* has been adapted into only one feature film (1951) and one television movie (1974). There just isn't sufficient broad appeal for movie audiences in Crane's story of a private who worries that he will bolt in the heat of battle—and does, though he redeems himself toward the end. Crane is less concerned with the descriptions of exciting and heroic battles than in the psychological aspects of warfare, and such inward turmoil does not easily translate into entertaining film. Nevertheless, if any American director could succeed in adapting Crane's vision of war to film, John Huston was the person to do it.

John Huston (1906–87) directed some of the most familiar films in the American repertoire: *The Maltese Falcon* (1941), *Treasure of the Sierra Madre* (1948), *Key Largo* (1948), *The Asphalt Jungle* (1950), *Moulin Rouge* (1942), *The Misfits* (1960), *The Man Who Would Be King* (1975), and *The Dead* (1987). He began his career as a reporter and short story writer (he was also a boxer, a portrait artist, and a cavalry rider in Mexico), and a number of his films were adaptations of great fiction: Melville's *Moby Dick* (1956), James Joyce's "The Dead" (1987), and Stephen Crane's *The Red Badge of Courage* (1951).

The story behind Huston's *The Red Badge of Courage* has been told in one of the best books ever written about the making of a film: Lillian Ross's *Picture* (1952), originally published as a series of articles in the *New Yorker*. Ross describes how excited Huston was to be filming Crane's classic novel and the enormous care he took in adapting the novel to screenplay, and then casting and directing it. She also describes how Huston seemed to lose interest in the project once principal photography was completed, leaving others to work on postproduction and his producer, Gottfried Reinhardt, to argue with the studio, which was never particularly enthusiastic about the film's commercial prospects. While Huston set off to Africa to film his next project, *The African Queen,* with Humphrey Bogart and Katherine Hepburn, the studio trimmed the film's length to a mere 70 minutes and added narration to transition over the deleted material and explain (to those who weren't clear on the subject) the film's meaning.

Henry Fleming, the uncertain hero, is played by Audie Murphy, the most decorated soldier of World War II. The film also features columnist/cartoonist Bill Mauldin as "the loud soldier." *The Red Badge of Courage* flopped at the box office, though the passage of years has yielded increased respect for Huston's mutilated masterpiece.

● Discussion and Writing Suggestions   MyWritingLab™

1. The film begins with shots of columns of soldiers on the march, led by their officers. To what extent do you think these shots make for a good opening, dramatically?

2. Comment on the use and the content of the narration we hear during this opening segment, particularly in comparison to Crane's narration at the beginning of the novel.

3. How does Huston *visually* dramatize the way rumors start and spread in this opening segment? How closely does Huston follow Crane at this point?

4. After the rumor sequence, Henry writes to his pa, telling him that the regiment is going into action. "I hope my conduct on the battlefield will make you proud of being my father," he writes. In what way does this action parallel a similar sequence in Crane? Account for the differences.

CITIZEN KANE **(1941)**

Orson Welles, Director
(00:00–3:10)

For about fifty years, *Citizen Kane* (1941) topped the *Sight & Sound* list of greatest films of all time. In 2012, *Kane* was demoted from the top spot (to second place) by Alfred Hitchcock's *Vertigo*. It remains number one, however, on the American Film Institute's list of one hundred greatest American movies. (*Vertigo* is #61 on that list.)

First or second, *Citizen Kane* is certainly one of the most celebrated and influential films ever made. The character of Charles Foster Kane, the newspaper publisher who rose from poverty to enormous wealth and power—and then lost most of his fortune, as well as all of his friends—is based loosely on the life of newspaper magnate William Randolph Hearst (1863–1951), though Welles always denied the connection. Hearst and his lawyers tried to buy up all prints and negatives of the film and have them destroyed, but to its credit, the small studio RKO resisted the legal onslaughts, and *Citizen Kane* survives.

Orson Welles (1915–85) was an actor, writer, producer, and director who began his career producing Broadway plays and was one of the founders of the Mercury Theater (some of the Mercury Theater veterans worked with him on *Citizen Kane*). One of the Mercury Theater's most notorious productions was a radio adaptation of the novel *The War of the Worlds,* by H. G. Wells, which sent thousands of listeners into a panic on the night of the broadcast when they thought Martians were actually invading the earth from their landing site in Grover's Mill, New Jersey. On the strength of his reputation as a wonder boy (he was twenty-three when he produced "The War of the Worlds"), Welles was invited to Hollywood to produce and direct the movie that became *Citizen Kane*.

The movie flopped commercially (owing partially to pressure from the Hearst interests, which did not allow mention of the film in any of its newspapers) and it did not become a critical success until years later. Meanwhile, the individualistic Welles found it increasingly difficult to work within the collaborative studio system. After he shot his next film, *The Magnificent Ambersons* (based on the novel by Booth Tarkington), the studio took the film away from him and assigned others to edit and complete it. Welles completed only thirteen more films during his lifetime, including the film noir *A Touch of Evil* (1959), *Chimes at Midnight* (1965), about Shakespeare's character Falstaff, and the celebrated documentary *F is For Fake* (1973). He also acted memorably in films directed by others, including *Jane Eyre* (1943), *The Lady from Shanghai* (1947), and *The Third Man* (1949).

Citizen Kane has an unusual, nonlinear structure. The film begins by showing the death of Kane, alone (except for a nurse) in his mansion. This is followed by a newsreel announcing his death, and we then see an executive of the studio that produced the newsreel assigning a reporter to dig up more information on Kane. The reporter goes off to talk to the people who knew Kane—his former colleagues and employees and his ex- wife; and he also reads a manuscript memoir written by the lawyer who managed Kane's affairs and who knew him as a child. From these fragmentary accounts emerges a fuller—but not complete—account of the life of Charles Foster Kane.

● **Discussion and Writing Suggestions**   MyWritingLab™

I. *Citizen Kane* opens with a series of striking images, beginning with a "No Trespassing" sign posted on a wire fence. Describe some of those images and speculate about what they might reveal to us about the man who lived in the mansion and whose death concludes the scene. Three minutes into the film, what do you *already* know about Charles Foster Kane?

2. One of the favorite topics of those discussing *Citizen Kane* has been the significance of Kane's dying word, "Rosebud." Viewed in context of the immediately preceding and following images, what do *you* think "Rosebud" might mean?

3. Stylistically (the mists, the darkness, the brooding music), this scene appears to be introducing a horror film. And yet if you look at even the first few seconds or so of the following scene ("News on the March!"), the mood—and the cinematic style—changes 180 degrees. Why might the director, Orson Welles, have thought it was appropriate to begin his film about Kane in this gloomy manner?

Brief Encounter (1945)

David Lean, Director
(00:00–10:30)

For a generation or two of Anglo-American cinephiles, *the* definitive screen romance was *Brief Encounter*, the story of an intense but doomed love affair between a suburban British housewife and an idealistic doctor, both married (more or less happily) to other people. The relationship between Laura Jesson (Celia Johnson) and Alec Harvey (Trevor Howard) is told in flashback, as Laura recalls the affair while riding the train back to her hometown. David Lean's 1945 beautifully photographed black-and-white film, written by playwright, actor, composer, and singer Noel Coward (who collaborated with Lean on three other films), is based on a one-act play by Coward, *Still Life* (1936), and is forever associated with both English railway stations and their refreshment rooms and the romantic melodies of Rachmaninoff's Piano Concerto no.2, which is featured prominently in the soundtrack.

Brief Encounter was subsequently adapted as a radio play and performed numerous times (with different actors) in the years following Lean's film. It was also readapted into a full-length play and performed both in Britain and the United States. A 1974 television remake, starring Sophia Loren and Richard Burton, was not well received. In 2009, the story was adapted into a two-act opera and performed by the Houston Grand Opera, with music by Andrew Previn. But none of these versions had the emotional impact or the warm reception of Lean's 1945 film, which in 1999 was ranked second in a British Film Institute poll of greatest British films of all time. *Postscript:* In 1980 Celia Johnson and Trevor Howard were reunited on screen (as other characters) in *Staying On*, a TV movie about a British colonel and his wife choosing to remain in India after the British government granted independence to that country in 1947.

See the headnote under *Great Expectations* for information about David Lean. In addition to the films mentioned there, Lean also directed another adaptation from Dickens, *Oliver Twist* (1948); *Breaking the Sound Barrier* (1952); *Ryan's Daughter* (1970); and his final film, *A Passage to India* (1984).

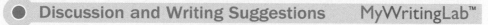

● **Discussion and Writing Suggestions**   MyWritingLab™

1. *Brief Encounter* has long been celebrated as one of the most romantic stories ever committed to film. And yet when we first see Laura Jesson and Dr. Alec Harvey in the station tearoom, we come across them almost accidentally: They are in the background, as if they were extras in a film that's really about the stationmaster and the tearoom attendant, who are having an extended conversation. If you were to watch the entire film (highly recommended!), you would see that David Lean shoots this same scene *twice*—only the second time, toward the end of the film, Laura and Alex are the principals, and the stationmaster and the tearoom attendant are in the background. And the second time around, instead of staying on Laura's friend Dolly Messiter as she orders her chocolate, we follow Laura as she departs the tearoom and walks out to the platform where Alec's train has just left. What do you think might be the dramatic logic behind this unconventional framing of a film romance?

2. Study Laura and Alec's reactions when the gossipy Dolly enters the room and joins them at the table. What can you tell about their relationship, based upon what happens in this scene, up to the time Alec departs the tearoom and Dolly orders her chocolate? How do both Laura and Alec respond to the unwelcome interruption? How does Alec say good-bye to Laura? How does Laura react when Dolly says, "I shall have to telephone Fred [Laura's husband] in the morning and make mischief"? And how do all these reactions suggest what preceded this scene?

3. Indelibly associated with this film are the melodies of Rachmaninoff's Piano Concerto no.2, which we first hear in the title sequence, and again (in a creative use of sound), when Laura and Dolly are conversing in the train. How does Lean's use of music help create the mood of these scenes—and help establish the tone of the story?

SHANE **(1953)**

George Stevens, Director
(00:00–8:52)

In some ways, *Shane* is the archetypal Western. A mysterious stranger rides into town (or onto a homestead), assesses the situation that is creating problems for the locals, deals with the problem almost singlehandedly (which inevitably involves gunfire), and then rides out again. Much as he might like to settle down and live a "normal" life, with his own family, he is—partially because of his background, partially because of his temperament—just not that kind of man and will never be accepted as such. We see this motif, in one form or another, in such films as *The Searchers* (1956) and the Clint Eastwood "man with no name films" directed by Sergio Leone—*A Fistful of Dollars* (1964), *For a Few Dollars More* (1964), *The Good, the Bad, and the Ugly* (1966)—as well as the old *Lone Ranger* TV series. In more contemporary terms, we see the same motif in Lee Child's popular "Jack Reacher" novels. Reacher is not a cowboy, of course, but an ex-military cop; like his Western analogues, he comes into town with little more than the clothes on his back, a sense of justice, and a serious capacity to kick butt. After solving the problem, he leaves as quickly as he arrived.

Shane was shot on location, near Jackson Hole, Wyoming, against the backdrop of the Grand Tetons; and the contrast between the wide-open spaces of the range and the cramped quarters of the general store and the saloon in the makeshift town is one of the motifs of the film. But the main dramatic conflict is between homesteaders like Joe Starrett and neighbors, on the one hand, and the Ryker brothers, on the other, who own the ranches and need large areas for grazing. The setting is also that of Wyoming's Johnson County War, which was also dramatized in Michael Cimono's *Heaven's Gate* (1980). In 1985 *Shane* was remade by Clint Eastwood as *Pale Rider*.

The *New York Times* critic Bosley Crowther wrote of the 1953 film, "*Shane* contains something more than the beauty and the grandeur of the mountains and plains, drenched by the brilliant Western sunshine and the violent, torrential, black-browed rains. It contains a tremendous comprehension of the bitterness and passion of the feuds that existed between the new homesteaders and the cattlemen on the open range. It contains a disturbing revelation of the savagery that prevailed in the hearts of the old gun-fighters, who were simply legal killers under the frontier code. And it also contains a very wonderful understanding of the spirit of a little boy amid all the tensions and excitements and adventures of a frontier home."

Montgomery Clift and William Holden were originally cast to play Shane and Joe Starrett, respectively; when both proved unavailable, Alan Ladd and Van Heflin were called upon to replace them. *Shane* was the film debut of Jack Palance, who plays the gunfighter Wilson. Palance was later to star as the count himself in yet another film adaptation of *Bram Stoker's Dracula* (1973). A somber postscript: Brandon de Wilde, who played Joey, was killed in a traffic accident in 1972 at the age of 30.

George Stevens was considered one of the greatest classic American filmmakers, directing numerous feature films, shorts, and documentaries (including documentary footage he took while with the troops in World War II). Among his best-known films are *Alice Adams* (1935), *Swing Time* (considered by many the best of the Astaire-Rogers musicals, 1936), *Gunga Din* (1939), *Woman of the Year* (1942), *The Talk of the Town* (1942), *I Remember Mama* (1948), *A Place in the Sun* (1951), *Giant* (1956), *and The Diary of Anne Frank* (1959). His son George Jr. became a successful Hollywood producer.

● Discussion and Writing Suggestions   MyWritingLab™

1. In what way is the first image of the film, shot against the magnificent Grand Tetons of Wyoming, representative of numerous other Westerns (including, for example, the Clint Eastwood "man with no name" films) in establishing the kind of story that is to follow?

2. The opening scene of *Shane* introduces us to some of the principals: Shane himself; the boy Joey; his parents, Joe and Marion Starrett; and Ryker, the chief antagonist, and his men. Based upon these characters' behaviors, and their interactions, what predictions can you make about the direction of the main conflict of the story and perhaps how this main conflict is a standard feature of the Western as a genre?

3. Joe Starrett's first words to his son, "Well, let him come," indicate a misapprehension on his part about Shane. But how does this misapprehension foreshadow the conflict to follow?

4. What kind of a man is Shane? What can you tell about his background? In particular, what does he say and what does he do that supports your assessment of him? Now respond to the same questions about Joe Starrett.

5. In Westerns, setting is a crucial element of the reading or viewing experience. Consider the opening segment of *Shane*, both with Joey tracking the stag and watching Shane as he rides toward the homestead, and later with Joe Starrett's account of Ryker's men and the homesteaders. Cite particular images that underline the importance of *place* in grounding the story. What, for example, is the significance of Starrett's men trampling Marian's vegetable garden as they ride away?

6. The gun is a common element of almost all Westerns. How do guns figure in this scene? How do they help set up the story to follow?

THE GODFATHER, PART ONE (1972)

Francis Ford Coppola, Director
(00:00–27:02)

The Godfather is, above all, a film about a successful American family. The family business happens to be organized crime, the family members don't always get along with one another or with people outside the family, and the family sometimes suffers catastrophic reversals as a result of bad decisions made by its members or by members of other families. Still, the family is what we primarily remember about the Corleone saga: Vito, the patriarch (played unforgettably by Marlon Brando), the hotheaded elder son Sonny (James Caan), the weak son Fredo (John Cazale), the quiet but calculating son (and future Don) Michael (Al Pacino), the naïve soon-to-be-married daughter Connie (Talia Shire), and the adopted son and consigliere Tom Hagen (Robert Duvall). All these family members—and a great many nonfamily members as well—are introduced to us in the first sequence (the wedding sequence) of *The Godfather, Part I* (1972), directed by Francis Ford Coppola and based on the novel by Mario Puzo.

It's difficult to overestimate the effect that *The Godfather* (1972) and its two sequels (1974 and 1990) had on the American consciousness. Even real mobsters started taking their cues from the way Coppola's characters talked and acted. It became the top-grossing film of 1972. The reviews were almost uniformly ecstatic. Francis Ford Coppola had put his finger on one reason the film resonated so deeply with the public: The action of the film was a metaphor for American capitalism. When Michael is courting Kay, he tells his skeptical bride-to-be that his father is no different than any other powerful man, like a senator or a president. Kay scoffs and retorts that he is being naïve: Senators and presidents don't have men killed. Michael looks at her for a moment: "Oh. Now who's being naive, Kay?" he asks.

Despite the film's secure place in the American cinematic pantheon (the American Film Institute has it in the #4 position, after *Vertigo, Citizen Kane,* and *Casablanca*), *The Godfather* did not have an easy birth. Coppola was not yet an experienced director (though he had cowritten the script for *Patton* in 1970), and the studio was reluctant to hand him the directorial reins. The studio bosses also didn't like Coppola's choices for the top acting roles: Laurence Olivier and Ernest Borgnine were considered for Vito's role; Jack Nicholson, Dustin Hoffman, and Warren Beatty for Sonny's. Coppola was able to prevail, though, as he confessed during an interview, he feared being let go at any time: "*The Godfather* was a very unappreciated movie when we were making it. They were very unhappy with it. They didn't like the cast. They didn't like the way I was shooting it. I was always on the verge of getting fired. So it was an extremely nightmarish experience. I had two little kids, and the third one was born during that. We lived in a little apartment, and I was basically frightened that they didn't like it. They had as much as said that, so when it was all over I wasn't at all confident that it was going to be successful, and that I'd ever get another job."

The film features members of Coppola's own family. Talia Shire, who played Connie, is Coppola's sister; his infant daughter, Sofia (who later became a well-regarded director in her own right), is the baby in the baptism scene; and Coppola's two sons play Tom Hagen's sons. Coppola's father, Carmine, a distinguished composer and conductor, wrote some of the material for the film, supplementing the primary (and more famous) musical score composed by Nino Rota.

Critic John Podhoretz sums up the film's achievement: It is "arguably *the* great American work of popular art."

Discussion and Writing Suggestions   MyWritingLab™

1. The opening segment of *The Godfather* alternates between scenes in Vito Corleone's office and scenes of the wedding celebration outside. How do these alternating scenes represent the two worlds of the Godfather? In what ways are these worlds separate? In what ways do they intersect? Draw upon specific moments in developing your responses.

2. The character and reputation of Vito Corleone is established not only by what he does and says, but also how others respond to what he does and says. How is this character and reputation reflected in this segment by the responses of people like his elder son, Sonny; his adopted son, Tom Hagen; the undertaker Bonasera; the pastry maker Nazorine; and his godson, the singer Johnny Fontane? How is Corleone's character and reputation further established by the story Michael tells to Kay and by the awkward behavior of his enforcer, Luca Brasi?

3. In the first minute or so of the scene between Vito Corleone and Bonasera, we see the don gesture with his hand, and we eventually hear his voice, but the director holds off showing his face until he finally reacts to the undertaker's request for vengeance. What do you think is Coppola's dramatic strategy here?

4. From this opening segment, we could draw up a set of rules of etiquette for high-level mobsters, as well as rules for interacting with the police. Explain some of these unwritten and unspoken rules that define and regulate acceptable behavior, drawing upon particular moments and interactions that you see occurring during the wedding.

5. Select one of the members of the Corleone family—Sonny, Michael, Fredo, Connie, or Tom Hagen—and write a paragraph describing his character, based upon what he or she does and says during this opening segment and by how he or she is treated by others.

SLEEPLESS IN SEATTLE (1993)

Nora Ephron, Director
(00:00–9:45)

Nora Ephron's *Sleepless in Seattle* (1993) is unique among American romantic comedies in that the two lovers (played by Tom Hanks and Meg Ryan), though gravitating toward one another for the entire film, do not actually meet until the final scene, less than three minutes from the end. Despite (or perhaps because of) this narrative quirk, the film struck a chord with audiences and with critics and was nominated for several awards (losing out to Jane Campion's *The Piano* for Best Original Screenplay). The chemistry between Hanks (who plays grieving widower Sam Baldwin) and Ryan (who plays Annie Reed, engaged to another man) is palpable. (The two were reunited in Ephron's later comedy, *You've Got Mail!* [1998].) And Ross Malinger, who plays Jonah, Sam's young, matchmaking son—a latter-day Emma—is irresistible. Insider note: Rita Wilson, who plays one of Sam's friends trying to cheer him up in this opening sequence, was and is Hanks's wife in real life.

Ephron (1941–2012) also directed *This is My Life* (1992), *Mixed Nuts* (1994), *and Julia and Julia* (about chef and cookbook author Julia Child 2009). As a director, she frequently collaborated with her screenwriter sister Delia. As a screenwriter herself, she wrote the scripts of *Silkwood* (about Karen Silkwood, the antinuclear activist, 1983), *Heartburn* (a thinly-disguised account of her failed marriage with journalist Carl Bernstein, 1986), and *When Harry Met Sally...* (another romantic comedy, with Billy Crystal, 1989).

● Discussion and Writing Suggestions   MyWritingLab™

1. How does Ephron establish the dramatic situation regarding Sam Baldwin (Tom Hanks) *visually* in the very first shot of the film?

2. In what ways does Ephron dramatize Baldwin's grief over the loss of his wife? Explain how the succession of brief scenes before the credit sequence establishes different facets of Baldwin's emotional state.

3. Based on what you have seen so far, what is likely to be the main conflict in this film? And based on what you have seen so far of Baldwin, how is he likely to deal with this conflict as the film progresses? What kind of a man does he appear to be, under his grief? What does he do or say that makes you think so?

4. In "Starting Your Story," Michael Kardos quotes a passage from Sherman Alexie's story "This Is What It Means to Say Phoenix, Arizona," about Victor,

a man who has just lost his father. In terms of what Kardos calls "establishing a story's stakes," how are Victor's and Sam Baldwin's initial situations similar? How are they different? How do these similarities and differences affect the stakes? As Kardos explains the term, "what make[s] a story matter to the story's character and to the reader[/viewer]"?

DO THE RIGHT THING (1989)

Spike Lee, Director
(00:00–13:22)

Before Spike Lee and *Do the Right Thing* (1989), American films had seldom focused seriously and extendedly on black-white relations. Black people in film were generally presented as slaves, servants or other hired help, noble victims of racial bigotry, or objects of socially forbidden desire. But Lee's film about an explosive few hours for race relations in the Bedford-Stuyvesant neighborhood of Brooklyn on the hottest day of the year was something that audiences had never seen before, something that for years to come occasioned passionate debate and discussion about such topics as "Who's right about the way to deal with racial oppression—Martin Luther King Jr. or Malcolm X?"

Spike Lee has a distinctive vision and a distinctive point of view, but this film is no mere racial polemic with cardboard characters obediently mouthing the views of the author/director. Rather, *Do the Right Thing* is a stylish and exuberant work of filmmaking that is at once passionate, funny, and thought-provoking, with fully rounded human beings who almost jump off the screen with their vividness. Mookie, the pizza delivery man (Lee); Sal, the pizzeria owner (Danny Aiello); Jade (Joie Lee); Da Mayor (Ossie Davis); Mother Sister (Ruby Dee); Buggin' Out (Giancarlo Esposite); Pino (John Turturro); Radio Raheem (Bill Nunn); Tina (Rosie Perez); Señor Love Daddy (Samuel Jackson): All these characters are conceived and brought to life by Lee and his actors with such imagination and individuality that they seem to reside in a fully realized world. But Lee didn't stop with getting the characters right; their environment, their neighborhood also had to be perfect. As Lee recalls in his journal of the film, "The block where the bulk of the film takes place should be a character in its own right. I need to remember my early years for this." Lee recalled the Mr. Softee ice cream truck playing its tune. He wanted the look of the film to be almost blindingly bright. "Everyone will be wearing shorts and cutoff jeans," he wrote. "Men will be shirtless, women in tube tops."

Lee had previously established himself as a major directorial talent with *She's Gotta Have It* (1986), about a woman with three lovers, and *School Daze* (1988), a musical about a man who wants to pledge to a fraternity at an all-black college where lines are drawn between light-skinned and dark-skinned blacks (the film was based on Lee's own experiences at college). The many films Lee directed after *Do the Right Thing* include *Mo' Better Blues* (1990)*, Jungle Fever* (1991), *Malcolm X* (1992), *Clockers* (1995), *Girl 6* (1996), *4 Little Girls* (a documentary about the terrorist bombing of an African-American church during the civil rights struggles of the 1960s [1997]), *He Got Game* (1998), *The 25th Hour* (2002), *Inside Man* (2006), *The Miracle of Anna* (2008), and *Oldboy* (2013). These films were all made by his production company, 40 Acres and a Mule. That name is an allusion to the broken promise of reparations to former slaves who had worked land before they were freed by the Emancipation Proclamation and who expected—in vain—to be compensated for their decades of forced labor.

● **Discussion and Writing Suggestions   MyWritingLab™**

1. The setting of *Do the Right Thing* is as important to the theme and the mood of this film as is the totally different wide-open-spaces setting of Wyoming in *Shane*. How does the neighborhood inhabited by the characters—first viewed when the camera pulls away from Señor Love Daddy's radio studio to focus on the street outside—become a crucial element in the way that the characters relate to one another?

2. The title sequence of his segment shows Rosie Perez (who plays Tina, Mookie's love interest in the film) dancing to the rhythms of Public Enemy's "Fight the Power." Discuss the way this unusual sequence helps set the tone of what follows.

3. Following the title sequence, we see a number of short scenes that introduce some of the main characters of *Do the Right Thing*: First, we see Señor Love Daddy, the neighborhood radio DJ, and then the elderly "Da Mayor," awakening from sleep. We see Smiley hawking his pictures of "Malcolm and Martin" and, next, pizzeria owner Sal and his two sons, Vito and Pino, arriving at their place of business. And finally we see pizza delivery man Mookie (Spike Lee) and his sister Jade as he counts his money, bothers his sister, and then sets off to work, passing through the Bed-Sty neighborhood on his way to Sal's pizzeria. Focus on one or two of those characters and indicate what we know about them, based on what they say and do (and how others behave toward them) in this opening sequence.

4. Sal and his two sons are clearly an alien presence in this neighborhood. Besides the obvious fact of their skin color, what are some of the other ways we know this? At the same time, what kind of accommodations has Sal, at least, tried to make so that his business becomes as important a part of the community as Señor Love Daddy's radio station?

THE DEVIL IN A BLUE DRESS (1995)

Carl Franklin, Director
(00:00–11:10)

The Devil in a Blue Dress is another film dealing with race relations (the hero is black; almost all of his adversaries are white). But unlike *Do the Right Thing*, *Devil* was designed to fit into the preexisting genre of the hard-boiled detective film. In this type of film, a detective (or a detective figure) assigned a relatively routine task of discovering the whereabouts of a missing person finds that the more he searches, the deeper he gets entangled in a web of deceit and corruption. One or two murders along the way are meant to deter him from pursuing his investigation any further. But our intrepid detective will not be deterred. As Thomas Schatz writes in his book *Hollywood Genres*, "the hardboiled detective is a cultural middle-man. His individual talents and street-wise savvy enable him to survive within a sordid, crime-infested city, but his moral sensibilities and deep-rooted idealism align him with the forces of social order and the promise of a utopian urban community." As indicated in the questions below, other films of this type include *The Maltese Falcon* (1941), *Double Indemnity* (1944), *The Big Sleep* (1946), *A Touch of Evil* (1958), *Chinatown* (1974), and *L.A. Confidential* (1997).

Based on the novel by Walter Mosley, Carl Franklin's film explores the situation of an African-American who loses his job after serving in World War II and, in order to save his house and continue to eat, must accept a dubious assignment. The story is ingeniously plotted and builds up a great deal of suspense as Mosley's hero, Ezekiel ("Easy") Rawlins, played by Denzel Washington, grows ever more assured, if wary, in his new role of dealing with white people on their own terms. Rawlins became so popular a detective that Mosley wrote twelve more novels about him (the last published in 2014). Carl Franklin, who is also an actor, directed *One True* Thing (1998), *High Crimes* (2002), and episodes of television series such as *Rome*, *The Pacific*, *The Newsroom*, *Homeland*, and *House of Cards*.

● Discussion and Writing Suggestions   MyWritingLab™

1. *The Devil in a Blue Dress* combines some of the features of the traditional private detective movie—from *The Maltese Falcon* to *Chinatown* to *L.A. Confidential*—with the kinds of themes underlying racially conscious movies such as *Do the Right Thing*. Point out some of the moments in this opening segment where you see these features and themes intersecting. Based on your knowledge of other "private eye" films or even TV police procedurals, where does this story seem to be heading? How will the fact that "Easy" Rawlins is African-American appear to factor into where the story is going?

2. Many private-eye films of the 1940s (when the events of this film take place) make use of the kind of voice-over narration introduced in this opening sequence. Thus, when we first see the protagonist, we hear his narration: "It was summer 1948, and I needed money..." We hear such narration periodically as Rawlins comments on what is happening. But storytellers are often warned to "show, not tell." To what extent do you feel that such voice-overs are effective ways of advancing the story or giving it significance? Would your reaction to this particular sequence be any different if there was no voice-over narration? What does the narration provide that would otherwise be difficult to "show"?

3. What do we know about Ezekiel ("Easy") Rawlins, based upon what we see in this opening sequence? What do we see that tells us about his background? What does he say and do that indicates the kind of man he is?

4. K. M. Weiland discusses the importance of setting and orienting readers and viewers with an "establishing" shot. How does Franklin create such a setting in his opening? Start with the image of the mural of Los Angeles that the camera explores under the title credits (to the sound of T-Bone Walker singing "West Side Baby"), and note other shots in this sequence that help establish the L.A. setting.

5. You may have seen Roman Polanski's *Chinatown*, another film about a private detective (played by Jack Nicholson) who seems to be on a routine job but soon enough stumbles into a web of political corruption and deadly threat. To the extent that you recall how Polanski's film opens, how do you think it compares and contrasts to the opening of *The Devil in a Blue Dress* in terms of such elements as the protagonist and the way the plot is launched?

CHICAGO (2002)

Rob Marshall, Director
(00:00–10:16)

Chicago has a long history and is based—very loosely—upon actual events. In 1924, the city of Chicago was abuzz over the sensational details of two unrelated murders committed by two women, Beulah Annan and Belva Gaertner, against the men in their lives. The stories were reported by Maurine Dallas Watkins of the *Chicago Tribune*. Watkins's columns proved so popular that she turned them into a play (original title: *Brave Little Woman*) that ran for 172 performances. The murderers were renamed Roxie Hart and Velma Kelly. The following year, Hollywood got into the act when director Cecil B. DeMille directed a silent film based on the events dramatized in the play. In 1942, Ginger Rogers, Fred Astaire's dancing partner, starred in another film version of the story, *Roxie Hart*. In the 1960s, dancer and singer Gwen Verdon read the Watkins play and urged her husband, choreographer Bob Fosse, to convert it into a musical. Watkins refused to sell the rights, but after her death, these rights were sold to Verdon and Fosse, who then commissioned John Kander and Fred Ebb to write music and lyrics. (Kander and Ebb also wrote the music and lyrics to *Cabaret*.)

The Kander/Ebb *Chicago* (set, like the original, in 1926 Chicago) premiered on Broadway in 1975 and ran for two years. The show also had a run in the West End of London, and was revived on Broadway in 1996. This revival was to become the longest-running musical revival, as well as one of the longest-running musicals, in Broadway history. In 2002, *Chicago* was readapted by director Robb Marshall into a film starring Renée Zellweger as Roxie Hart and Catherine Zeta-Jones as Velma Kelly. Richard Gere also features as the lawyer Billy Flynn, a character that is a composite of the original lawyers on the cases, William Scott Stewart and W. W. O'Brien. The columnist and playwright Maurine Dallas Watkins is transformed into Mary Sunshine (Christine Baranski) in the 2002 film.

In his latest version of *Chicago*, Marshall pays tribute to the original musical: He recreated much of Bob Fosse's original, distinctive choreography and even had one of the dancers in the opening number ("All That Jazz") made up to resemble Gwen Verdon. But otherwise, Marshall departs from the 1975 play by staging many of the musical numbers as dream (or daydream) sequences in Roxie's head. This is a technique well established by such films as Federico Fellini's *8½* (1962), David Lynch's *Mulholland Drive* (2001), Alejandro Amenabar's *The Others* (2002), and, since then, Christopher Nolan's *Inception* (2010).

Rob Marshall has also directed *Memoirs of a Geisha* (2005), based on the novel by Arthur Golden; *9* (2009), a sequel of sorts to Federico Fellini's *8½*, and *Pirates of the Caribbean: On Stranger Tides* (2011).

● Discussion and Writing Suggestions   MyWritingLab™

1. *Chicago* opens with a close-up of a pair of eyes that becomes an extreme close-up of a single eye. This shot is mirrored later on in the sequence. At what point does this second eye shot occur, and what does it signify for Roxie's state of mind, both at this particular moment and in terms of the film as a whole and the dramatic approach of the songs in this sequence ("All That Jazz" and "Funny Honey")?

2. We first meet Velma Kelly when she emerges from the cab; the camera then follows her as she enters the club, rushes upstairs to her dressing room, and puts on her costume in preparation for her performance. We have not yet seen her face (and won't until the spotlight falls upon her face in the "All That Jazz" number), but the director has already given us crucial information about this character. What do we see and hear during this pre-song sequence that helps establish who Roxie is and what she has done?

3. By the end of this opening sequence, both Velma Kelly and Roxie Hart have been arrested and jailed for separate murders. How does the director Rob Marshall indicate that these women are dramatically tied together? In particular, how does he use song and dance to help establish their relationship, both when they are in the club and when Roxie has gone with her lover to her apartment?

4. Musicals are always balancing precariously on the edge of credibility, because audiences, particularly modern audiences, have a hard time believing that characters will suddenly break out into song and dance when the impulse hits them. How does Marshall attempt to solve this problem, particularly in his staging of Roxie's "Funny Honey" song? How do reality and dramatic artifice blend here? To what extent did you find this solution effective?

THE HURT LOCKER (2008)

Kathryn Bigelow, Director
(00:00–9:58)

Conventional war films, even those as psychologically oriented as *The Red Badge of Courage*, typically feature set-piece battles between opposing armies or perhaps special missions by a "dirty dozen" or so of soldiers sent to destroy a key enemy fortress. Kathryn Bigelow's *The Hurt Locker* (2008) features no such battles or triumphant missions: It follows an army EOD (explosive ordinance disposal) team for several months in Bagdad in the aftermath of the U.S. invasion of Iraq (2003 and the years following). Based on the experiences of journalist Mark Boal (who also served as screenwriter) when he was embedded with U.S. troops in Iraq, *The Hurt Locker* shows how small bomb-disposal teams attempt to defuse bombs in an urban setting before they explode, killing and maiming civilians and the bomb-disposal personnel themselves. Sometimes they succeed; sometimes they don't.

The film stars Jeremy Renner as Sergeant First Class William James, a team leader. Though we don't see James in this first segment, we do see the bomb-disposal mission that made him the new team leader, and therefore we view the new kind of war that American soldiers were fighting in Iraq. Nothing quite like this had been seen before in an American feature film. (One precursor was *Danger UXB*, a 1979 British television series about a bomb-disposal unit that defused unexploded bombs that fell on London during the German blitz of World War II.) But the film resonated with both audiences and critics. *New York Times* critic A. O. Scott wrote: "You may emerge from *The Hurt Locker* shaken, exhilarated and drained, but you will also be thinking....The movie is a viscerally exciting, adrenaline-soaked tour de force of suspense and surprise, full of explosions and hectic scenes of combat, but it blows a hole in the condescending assumption that such effects are just empty spectacle or mindless noise." *The Hurt Locker* won six Academy Awards, including Best Picture, Best Director, Best Original Screenplay, and Best Editing, Sound Editing, and Sound Mixing.

One of the film's editors, Chris Innis, said of its method: "This movie is kind of like a horror film where you're unable to see the killer. You know a bomb could go off at any minute, but you never know just when it's going to happen, so the ideas of [Alfred] Hitchcock—about making your audience anxious[1]—were influential for us when we did the editing."

Educated at the San Francisco Art Institute and later at Columbia University Film School, Bigelow directed *Point Break* (1991) and *Strange Days, K-19: The Widowmaker* before making *The Hurt Locker*. She has since directed *Zero Dark Thirty* (2012), about the CIA team that hunted down and planned the killing of Osama bin Laden.

● Discussion and Writing Suggestions   MyWritingLab™

1. Note the epigraph to the film by journalist Chris Hedges at the outset. How does the director, Kathryn Bigelow, begin to demonstrate the truth of this epigraph during the first scene?

2. Discuss some of the ways the director builds suspense. Consider, in particular, how, cinematically, she ratchets up the tension toward the end of the segment before and during the explosion of the bomb.

3. How does the director reveal the relationship between the soldiers of the bomb-disposal group and the surrounding populace as the scene proceeds? In what ways does this relationship drive the main conflict within this opening segment?

4. In what ways are the various emotions experienced by the bomb-disposal team, including Sergeant Thompson, dramatized during this scene?

5. In what ways do elements of the setting—the buildings, the street, the vehicles (the "bot," the Humvee, the helicopter) play a dramatic role in this segment? Note in particular the first shot of the film. Why open with such a shot?

---

[1]Alfred Hitchcock (1899–1980), director of numerous suspense films including *Rear Window, North by Northwest, Vertigo,* and *Psycho,* once explained the difference between surprise and suspense: Surprise, he said, is when you see a bus driving off, and then a bomb on the bus suddenly explodes. Suspense is when you know there's a bomb on the bus, but you don't know when, or if, it's going to go off. He asked his interviewer which technique he thought was the best for sustaining a film.

GRAVITY **(2013)**

Alfonso Cuarón, Director
(00:00-13:08)

Many science fiction films set in outer space take for granted the vastly different environmental and existential differences between earth and space. In the *Star Wars* and *Star Trek* films, vessels of every size and shape hurtle through the void, and their human passengers move on and off them and then land on their destination planets as if all of this were a logistical problem no more complex—or hazardous—than getting on and off the bus. The hokey adventures and thrilling battles they experience might just as well be taking place on earth, or over the blue skies of our planet.

A few films set in outer space have not taken the realities of space travel for granted. They have focused their action on the sheer wonder of the experience, on the sense of isolation experienced by space travelers, and on the extreme danger of the environment and the potentially catastrophic effects of something going wrong (for instance, an equipment malfunction). In this category we find Stanley Kubrick's *2001: A Space Odyssey* (1968). We also find *Marooned* (1969), *Apollo 13* (1995), *and Moon* (2009), all of which deal with the psychological problems caused by isolation in space and the frightening sense of being cut off from the rest of humanity, as well as the physical dangers of being a thin wall of metal or glass away from annihilation.

Alfonso Cuarón's *Gravity* (2013) was for many viewers as revelatory and exhilarating a space film experience as was *2001* in its time. Like Kubrick's film, *Gravity* is also a visual feast. We see broad—and deep—vistas of space stations and astronauts. We are dazzled by the artful and often beautiful technology, shown in precise and loving detail, necessary to sustain life and allow scientific activity. All this is both delightful and scary to watch. And like both *2001* and *Apollo 13*, *Gravity* is a story about survival in the face of almost insurmountable odds. In fact, one can reach much further back, to the beginning of narrative, to find story analogs: *Gravity* is like Homer's *Odyssey* in that both are stories about a protagonist who finds him/herself far from home and who must carefully negotiate a series of dangerous obstacles using his/her wits and whatever physical and emotional resources she/he can summon to surmount the obstacles and succeed in safely returning home. The relatively few critics who complained about *Gravity* having no story seemed unaware that the film was following the path of one of the oldest –and most resonant—stories of all.

Gravity, released in 3D, was hugely popular with both audiences and critics. Justin Chang, of *Variety*, for example, wrote that the film "restores a sense of wonder, terror and possibility to the big screen that should inspire awe among critics and audiences worldwide." By April 2014, *Gravity* had grossed almost $300 million in North America and almost $450 million in other countries. It won seven Academy Awards, including Best Director, Best Cinematography, Best Visual Effects, and Best Film Editing.

One of the many notable features of *Gravity* is that it contains fewer shots and longer shots than almost any other film of its length. Cuarón choreographed both his camera and his actors so as to follow the action as long as possible. The first shot of the film is a tour de force of camera and human choreography. The camera runs continuously for more than thirteen minutes from the first moment that we see the curve of the earth to the moment we see the image of Dr. Stone, separated from her tether, hurtling head over heels away from us.

Alfonso Cuarón is one of Mexico's premier film directors, one of the "three amigos" of Mexican cinema (along with Guillermo del Toro and Alejandro González Iñárritu). Often working with his brother Carlos and his son Jonás, Cuarón has also directed *Y Tu Mamá También (2001), Harry Potter and the Prisoner of Azkaban (2004),* and *Children of Men* (2006). He also directed a film adaptation of Dickens's *Great Expectations*, with Gwyneth Paltrow, in 1998.

● Discussion and Writing Suggestions   MyWritingLab™

1. Michael Kardos points out that two of the goals of the story opening are to reveal key information and to establish the story's stakes. How does Cuarón attempt to achieve these goals in the first thirteen minutes of *Gravity*? Kardos also notes that good story openings "start with a break from routine." To what extent does Cuarón observe this rule? To what extent does he ignore it? More specifically, what use does Cuarón make of routine at the outset of the story?

2. *Gravity* is a visual spectacle, but the director and screenwriter are careful to establish the differing personalities of the two main characters from the outset. In this first long sequence, what do we find out about the characters of Dr. Ryan Stone and Commander Matt Kowalski? What do they say and do that helps establish their characters?

3. The setting of *Gravity*—"600 kilometers above planet Earth"—is perhaps the most important element of the film. Point out particular moments in this first scene that indicate how the setting helps establish the essential plotline of the story, the development of character, and the shape of the conflict.

4. The astonishing single shot that makes up this opening sequence involves numerous complicated camera movements. How does Cuarón use the camera to follow the action and the characters from one point of view to another to develop the story in a logical and dramatically effective order?

---

12 YEARS A SLAVE (2013)

Steve McQueen, Director

(00:00–6:00)

The film epic *Gone With the Wind* (1939) opens with scenes of slaves picking cotton. They seem happy enough, if not exactly whistling while they work. As the credits roll, we are told by the narrator that what should distress us about this opening is that it represents a way of life that has ceased to exist. In other words, to the makers of *Gone With the Wind*, the distressing fact is not slavery itself, but rather that the gracious life of the old South that depended for its existence on slave labor is no more:

> There was a land of Cavaliers and Cotton Fields called the old South.... Here in this pretty world, Gallantry took its last bow.... Here was the last ever to be seen of Knights and their Ladies Fair, of Master and of Slave.... Look for it only in books for it is no more than a dream remembered. A Civilization gone with the wind.

In the years that followed, Hollywood continued to portray slaves in movies set before the Civil War, though not quite in so elegiac a manner. The injustice was recognized, if not directly confronted. It was not until a 1976 television miniseries called *Roots* (based upon Alex Haley's novel about slavery in the United States) that American viewers were given their first hard look at the realities of slavery. Some feature films treated slavery more or less honestly: *Glory* (1989), *Jefferson in Paris* (1995), *Amistad* (1997), *Beloved* (1998), and *Lincoln* (2012). But until Steve McQueen's *12 Years a*

Slave (2013), no film had presented the day-to-day reality of slavery in all of its ugly brutality—the daily humiliations and savage beatings, the separation of husband from wife and parents from children, the appalling living and working conditions, the inhumanity of the slave masters.

The film *12 Years a Slave* is based on the memoir of Solomon Northrop, a free man, a musician, living in New York State with his wife and family. After he had been lured to Washington D.C. on the pretext of a temporary job performing music, Northrop was drugged and sold into slavery. As a slave, he worked on Louisiana plantations for twelve years before he was released through the intervention of friends in the North. The film won three Academy Awards, including Best Picture of 2013.

In an interview with NPR (National Public Radio), director Steve McQueen explained what impelled him to make the film: "I read this book, and I was totally stunned. At the same time I was pretty upset with myself that I didn't know this book. I live in Amsterdam where Anne Frank is a national hero, and for me this book read like Anne Frank's diary but written 97 years before—a firsthand account of slavery. I basically made it my passion to make this book into a film." McQueen, who is British, has directed many short films. In addition to *12 Years a Slave*, he directed two other feature films, *Hunger* (2008) and *Shame* (2011).

● Discussion and Writing Suggestions   MyWritingLab™

1. What is the dramatic situation at the beginning of *12 Years a Slave*? Consider the role of dialogue in this opening segment in establishing the dramatic situation, as opposed to visual detail and what we hear on the soundtrack. Cite two or three key visual details in particular shots that help vividly create this dramatic situation.

2. What hints of future developments for main character Solomon Northrop do you detect in this opening? How does the director contrast Northrop's present with his past? To what extent does he make use of the narrative technique of *in medias res*? (See Kardos, pp. 351–353.)

3. Based on what you see of him in this opening segment, what kind of man does Northrop appear to be? How does he respond to the situation in which he finds himself?

4. Compare the treatment of slavery in this film opening to the treatment in other films you have seen that have depicted slavery: for instance, *The Birth of a Nation*, *Gone With the Wind*, *Amistad*, *Beloved*, and *Django Unchained*.

◯ SYNTHESIS QUESTIONS

1. Discuss one of the Chapter Ones in terms of how it meets (or does not meet) the criteria for effective openings as discussed by Michael Kardos and K. M. Weiland.

2. If you didn't particularly care for one of the Chapter Ones, then take on the role of editor. Write an "editorial memo" back to the author in which you advise him or her how to revise the first chapter in order to improve it. In making your case, refer to the criteria offered by Weiland, Kardos, and O'Brien. And please remember that authors are people, too—so you'll want your memo to be honest yet diplomatic.

3. Readers who love a particular novel are frequently disappointed with the film adaptation. Why do you think this might be so? Choose the Chapter One you liked most and explain what would be easiest and hardest about adapting the chapter for film. If the novel you choose has already been adapted for film (many of them have, several times over), go ahead and watch the opening scene—or better still, the full movie—and report on the results.

4. Weiland, Kardos, and O'Brien have offered advice for writing successful fiction. There are hundreds, perhaps thousands, of such guides, and it's safe to say that no one offers definitive advice. Perhaps you have some insights not mentioned by Weiland, Kardos, or O'Brien about what makes for an effective opening. If so, define these criteria clearly and illustrate them by referring to several of the Chapter Ones you've read here.

5. Discuss one of the film openings discussed in this chapter in terms of how it meets (or does not meet) the criteria for effective openings covered by Michael Kardos and K. M. Weiland in their chapters.

6. Select two film openings that seem to you to represent entirely different modes of presenting character, plot, or setting. Compare and contrast the apparent strategies of the filmmakers, referring as necessary to the articles by Weiland, Kardos, and O'Brien.

7. Compare and contrast the two film versions of *Emma*. Or compare and contrast the two film versions of *Dracula*. Consider how each film of your selected pair introduces its main character—either Emma or Dracula. How does each presentation affect your initial impression of the character? Compare and contrast also the dramatic situations of the first sequence of each film—that is, the introduction to the plot. Finally, compare and contrast the settings in each film and the way in which the setting contributes to the emotional power of the introduction. Which film in either of these pairs do you prefer, and why? Feel free to compare and contrast the first scene of each film with the first scene in the novel by Jane Austen or by Bram Stoker.

8. Decide which of these film openings appeals to you most, and then watch the entire movie. Watch a second time and keep careful notes on how the questions raised in the opening scene resonate throughout the film. That resonance may involve character, plot, mood, theme, or some other element essential to the film's success. Write an explanatory paper in which you carefully "deconstruct"—or break down element by element—the opening scene and then trace its impact throughout the rest of the film.

9. Assuming you have watched four or five of the opening scenes presented in this chapter, think "large" and argue that two or three qualities you will define and discuss are essential to making an opening succeed. You will have to define "success." You will also need to define the elements you will be putting forward as essential. As evidence for your argument, refer generously to scenes (or partial scenes). As needed, draw upon the work of O'Brien, Kardos, or Weiland to help you make your case.

MyWritingLab™   Visit Ch. 11 First Impressions in MyWritingLab to test your understanding of the chapter objectives.

The Changing Landscape of Work in the Twenty-First Century

You attend college for many reasons, but perhaps none is so compelling as the hope and expectation that higher education offers a passport to a better future, a future based on meaningful employment and financial independence—especially in an uncertain economy.

As fate would have it, you will enter the American workforce at a particularly dynamic and (most would acknowledge) stressful time. The "Great Recession" of January 2007–June 2009 continues to roil the economy. But long before the recession took hold, the twin forces of globalization and computer-driven technology began to alter the workplace of your future. If the wisdom of the analysts and economists collected in this chapter could be reduced to a single statement of advice, it would be this: Think strategically about your future working life.

As you begin, some recent history can provide perspective. In the second half of the twentieth century, since the end of World War II, the labor market rewarded the educated, conferring on those who attended college an "education premium." Even as the forces of globalization reshaped the American economy and workers began losing manufacturing jobs to competitors offshore in China and India, college-educated workers were generally spared major career disruptions. Today, higher education no longer promises such protection. The relentless search for cheap labor and plentiful raw materials, together with advances in technology, has opened the information-based service economy to foreign competition. Increasingly, the American college-educated workforce will face the same relentless pressures that decades ago unsettled the automotive and manufacturing sectors. Employers are already offshoring computer coding, certain types of accounting, and medical consultation (the reading of X-rays, MRIs, CT scans, and such)—services that require extensive training. Experts predict that more American jobs will be lost to foreign competition and fewer will entail a lifelong commitment between employer and employee. What are the implications of these developments for you and your intended career? Will they affect the courses you take, the major (and minors) you choose, the summer jobs and internships you pursue? Could you investigate *now* how to anticipate and avoid major disruptions to your working life tomorrow?

This chapter offers insights into what economists, policy analysts, sociologists, educators, statisticians, and journalists are forecasting about the world of work in the twenty-first century. You'll find selections presented in three topic clusters, beginning with **The Puzzling U.S. Labor Market**. First is Jenna Brager's "A Post-College Flow Chart of Misery and Pain," a cartoon that might cut a little close to the bone for those pursuing a humanities degree. Next, reporter Hadley Malcolm takes a snapshot of job prospects for graduates in May 2014, concluding that for "young Americans…the recession never ended." Writing for the *Wall Street Journal*, business professor Peter Cappelli acknowledges the tough job market for college grads, appreciates the impulse to gain hands-on skills, but questions the wisdom of turning the college years into narrowly focused vocational training. To read analyses that set the U.S. labor market in a broader context, economist and former presidential advisor Alan Blinder traces the migration of service jobs (even those requiring a college degree) away from American shores. Finally, journalist Don Peck investigates the role of big data in the hiring process of the near future. (You may be playing a video game as part of the interview process—at the end of which a computer will forecast the likelihood of your success as an employee.)

We continue with a second cluster, **Data on the U.S. Labor Market**. Here you will find charts, graphs, and tables that provide a snapshot of the conditions you can expect to encounter when looking for work. You'll learn, among other things, how graduates in different majors are faring in their search for jobs—and what they're earning when hired. We've drawn upon three sources for graphical data: Pew Research, Georgetown Public Policy Institute, and United States Bureau of Labor Statistics.

We conclude with selections that respond to a question on the minds of many young men and women entering the workforce: **Should You Do What You Love?** Steve Jobs answered that question with a resounding *yes* in his celebrated commencement address at Stanford University in June 2005. In the years since, others have sharply disagreed, and for varying reasons. We include three critiques of Jobs's opinion, along with an invitation that you grapple with the question yourself. Jeff Haden explores why "[t]elling someone to follow their passion…has probably resulted in more failed businesses than all the recessions combined." Next, Carl McCoy argues that working at what you love leaves unanswered an important question about "why the work should be done" at all. Perhaps more young people would be happier in their jobs if "love [was] a consequence of meaningful work instead of…the motivation for it." Finally, art historian Miya

Tokumitsu brings a socialist critique to the debate, arguing that people who work for love of the job are ripe for exploitation.

The job market you'll be entering is doubly uncertain as it struggles to emerge from a long recession and responds to economic and technological forces that will continue to play out in the years to come. As you search for employment now and in the near future, the selections in this chapter may help inform your choices.

THE PUZZLING U.S. LABOR MARKET

That perfect job: It's out there, you hope—even in these distressed times. And now, you're taking the first steps to get it. In part, isn't this why you've come to college—to acquire skills that will lead to satisfying, well-paid work? You know the economy is uncertain, and you're more than curious: Just what are the job prospects these days for new college graduates?

This first component of readings will help provide some answers. We begin with a provocative teaser—"A Post-College Flow Chart of Misery and Pain" by Jenna Brager, who writes a weekly webcomic for curmudgeoncomic .com. In this satiric look at job possibilities for American Lit and Philosophy types, Brager raises an important question: If the job market is so tough for humanities majors, why would anyone study the humanities? People do, of course—for many reasons, not always related to employability. This graphic first appeared on the shareable.com Web site and in its online book *Share or Die: Youth in Recession*.

Four selections round out this opening cluster. Writing for *USA Today* on May 19, 2014, "Young Money" reporter Hadley Malcolm opens with the sobering news that "the nation's job market continues to force college graduates to take jobs they're overqualified for, jobs outside their major, and generally delay their career." Still, good jobs are out there and, for the most part, employment figures have been trending favorably. In challenging times, students may be tempted to focus narrowly on specific skills likely (so they believe) to impress employers post-graduation. Writing for the *Wall Street Journal* on November 15, 2013, Wharton Business School professor Peter Cappelli advises against specializing too narrowly, for the job market is unstable enough that specific jobs trained for today may disappear tomorrow. Economist Alan Blinder advises students against pursuing jobs likely to be shipped overseas—including jobs that require college (and even graduate-school) degrees. Finally, journalist Don Peck investigates the role of big data in the future workplace, specifically in the hiring process.

A Post-College Flow Chart of Misery and Pain

Jenna Brager

JOB OUTLOOK FOR 2014 GRADS PUZZLING

Hadley Malcolm

Dear Class of 2014: We regret to inform you that the nation's job market continues to force college graduates to take jobs they're overqualified for, jobs outside their major, and generally delay their career to the detriment of at least a decade's worth of unearned wages. Good luck on your continued job search.

A job rejection letter to this year's graduates, who are now supposed to be starting their first truly independent adult years, might as well go something like that.

The latest jobs report for April gave grads a puzzling picture. Employers added the most jobs in more than two years, 288,000. Unemployment dropped from 6.7% to 6.3%, the first time it was that low since September 2008. Young adults still face higher unemployment, but the rate for 25–29 year-olds fell from 7.5% in March to 6.9%. The unemployment rate for those 20–24 dropped from 12.2% to 10.6%.

Still, the portion of Americans 25–34 who were working in April fell to a five-month low of 75.5%, down from 75.9% in March.

5   "The entire drop (in unemployment) was due to people dropping out of the labor force, in particular young people," says Heidi Shierholz, a labor market economist who writes an annual report on the state of employment for young adults for Economic Policy Institute.

And despite the number of jobs added last month, Shierholz calls the gradual improvement "agonizingly slow."

Seniors who graduate over the next several weeks are poised to be yet another product of a depressing economic cycle that isn't their fault, but that they may never fully recover from. They and other recent graduating classes entered college and subsequently the labor market amidst a panoply of converging circumstances that will inevitably set them back: rising tuition, their parents' decreasing ability to pay that tuition, fewer jobs after graduation, and lower wages for the jobs that are available.

In Shierholz's paper on this year's graduates, released early this month, she and her colleagues write that "the Class of 2014 will be the sixth consecutive graduating class to enter the labor market during a period of profound weakness."

'Never been this bad'

High unemployment for young adults during and after recessions is not a new phenomenon. Bureau of Labor Statistics data compiled by EPI show that the unemployment rate for those under 25 is typically at least twice the national average, because they are so new to the job market, lack experience, and may be the first let go when a company has to downsize in hard economic times. Still, previous generations didn't experience the fallout as harshly or for nearly as long as the current one, Shierholz says.

10 "It's never been this bad," she says. "How long we've had elevated unemployment is unprecedented."

That hasn't dampened students' spirits at least. A majority, or 84%, of this year's graduating class expects to find a job in their chosen field, according to an employment survey released this month by consulting firm Accenture.

That seems to align with attitudes on campuses. Lisa Severy, director of career services at University of Colorado Boulder, says this year's class is less anxious than past year's graduates about their job prospects, and has been more eager to attend career events.

"They seem more excited, hopeful, and enthusiastic," she says.

Their optimism may only be slightly warranted. A survey on recruitment trends by the Collegiate Employment Research Institute at Michigan State University finds hiring for bachelor's degrees this year is up 7%. That's relatively in line with increases in previous years though. The research institute calls the 3% overall growth in the college labor market "modest."

15 And many employers continue to seek students whose skills tend to be in high demand no matter what: business, engineering, and accounting majors.

Madison Piercy, a senior double majoring in electrical engineering and computer science at Boulder, had her fair share of suitors this year. The 21 year-old was pursued by Intel, Microsoft, and Noble Energy before accepting a position at MIT Lincoln Laboratory, a federally funded research center at Massachusetts Institute of Technology.

But most grads aren't in Piercy's position.

In the two years since Rebecca Mersiowsky graduated from Radford University in Radford, Va., she's worked at a beach club on Martha's Vineyard, as a substitute teacher in Fredericksburg, Va., and as a sales associate at a boutique in Boston, where she lives now.

The 24 year-old, who graduated with a degree in communications, has had no luck finding a job in public relations.

20 In the meantime, she convinced her employer at the boutique in Beacon Hill to let her take on the shop's blog and social media. She works up to 35 hours a week as a sales associate and blogger, but the shop can't afford to hire her full-time.

"I don't think frustrated even begins to describe it," Mersiowsky says of her plight. "It's really scary when I think about my graduating class and how now, two more of those classes have come out and have entered the workforce and that puts me behind them. I feel like I am being set back with every passing day."

Life-long consequences to late career start

As so many students approach graduation without a job, moving back home has become a given, as opposed to a last resort. Taylor Maycan, a former USA TODAY intern, graduated early from Northwestern University in March and moved home to Houston to live with her parents while she looks for a job. Until then, she babysits and does other odd jobs to make money.

"It's stressful. No one wants to graduate and not have a job lined up," she says. "You want to be able to say, I graduated and here's what I'm doing next.

It's kind of tough to say, I graduated from this great school and I have no idea what I'm doing now."

Hers is a reality many college students have come to accept as the logical next step after graduation. Evan Feinberg, president of youth advocacy organization Generation Opportunity, says it's "probably the most difficult compromise my generation has been forced to make. It's really hard to get started on your own."

25   Maycan still has a hopeful attitude about finding employment and has accepted she may have to adjust her expectations about her first job.

Still, the consequences of a late career start could be life-long. Studies show that entering the labor market during a recession can affect your earnings for the next 10–15 years, depending on the industry you work in and how long you are unemployed or underemployed. And Shierholz says even that time estimate may be optimistic, given most studies on so-called "wage scarring" are on graduates who entered the labor market during the early 1980s recession, which was "long and severe" but "nothing like the one we're in," she says.

Severy sees evidence that the market may be improving, at least in some areas. The career center at Boulder has received so many job postings from employers this year, sometimes between 100 and 150 a day, that Severy hired one of this year's graduates to manage the postings full time.

As a whole though, graduates continue to struggle.

"Unfortunately for young Americans," Feinberg says, "the recession never ended."

WHY FOCUSING TOO NARROWLY IN COLLEGE COULD BACKFIRE

Peter Cappelli

A job after graduation. It's what all parents want for their kids.

So, what's the smartest way to invest tuition dollars to make that happen?

The question is more complicated, and more pressing, than ever. The economy is still shaky, and many graduating students are unable to find jobs that pay well, if they can find jobs at all.

The result is that parents guiding their children through the college-application process—and college itself—have to be something like venture capitalists. They have to think through the potential returns from different paths, and pick the one that has the best chance of paying off.

5   For many parents and students, the most-lucrative path seems obvious: be practical. The public and private sectors are urging kids to abandon the liberal arts, and study fields where the job market is hot right now.

Schools, in turn, are responding with new, specialized courses that promise to teach skills that students will need on the job. A degree in hospital financing? Casino management? Pharmaceutical marketing?

Little wonder that business majors outnumber liberal-arts majors in the U.S. by two-to-one, and the trend is for even more focused programs targeted to niches in the labor market.

It all makes sense. Except for one thing: It probably won't work. The trouble is that nobody can predict where the jobs will be—not the employers, not the schools, not the government officials who are making such loud calls for vocational training. The economy is simply too fickle to guess way ahead of time, and any number of other changes could roil things as well. Choosing the wrong path could make things worse, not better.

So, how should the venture-capitalist parents proceed? What should they weigh as they decide where to put their limited capital to get the biggest bang? Here are some things to consider.

Does the Product Get Out the Door?

10   You can pick the perfect school in terms of courses and location and price and ambience. But none of it does a student any good if he or she doesn't end up with a degree. After all, college improves job prospects only if a student graduates. That is why it is crucial to scrutinize the graduation rates at various schools.

What's more, it is also important to look at how *long* it takes students to graduate. Only about 60% of Division 1 university students graduate in six years, for example.

Many parents and students don't realize that even top schools differ greatly in their ability to get students out the door to graduation on time. Consider the difference between an elite private university like Stanford University and an elite public university like the University of California, Berkeley. My colleague Robert Zemsky found that the private school has a much wider array of support services—counseling, tutoring and so forth—that vastly improve the odds that a student will actually graduate, and will do so in four years. An expensive, private school may end up being cheaper if a student doesn't have to be there as long.

Probably the most important statistics to scrutinize are job-placement rates for graduates, but they are often hard to get and easy to fudge. Are we measuring jobs at graduation, or within a year after? Do internships count as a "job"?

Statistics about starting salaries, to judge the quality of those jobs, can be even more elusive. In the absence of good data, visit the school's career center and see which employers are actually interviewing students and for what jobs.

15   Parents and students should push to require schools to post graduation rates, job-placement rates and other information on the outcomes for their graduates—especially considering how many students are now using government-backed loans to pay for their education. It is not in the public interest for students to use public funds for vocational degrees that don't have a good chance of paying off.

Today's Jobs Aren't Necessarily Tomorrow's

The trend toward specialized, vocational degrees is understandable, with an increasing number of companies grumbling that graduates aren't coming out of school qualified to work.

But guessing about what will be hot tomorrow based on what's hot today is often a fool's errand.

The problem is that the job market can change rapidly for unforeseeable reasons. Today, we frequently hear that computers and information technology are and will be the hot fields, but both have gone from boom to bust over time. Students poured into IT programs in the late 1990s, responding to the Silicon Valley boom, only to graduate after 2001 into the tech bust.

Changes in regulations, meanwhile, can rapidly create and kill fields. For instance, the Sarbanes-Oxley Act amped up the demand for accountants. Emerging technologies can be just as disruptive—applicant-tracking software eliminates jobs in recruiting, while cellphones create programming jobs in mobile technology. Developments like these are almost impossible to anticipate.

20　　It gets even more complicated than that. Let's say governments and colleges *could* tell what the demand would be for a particular occupation years out. The problem for someone making an investment in that occupation is that everyone else has the same information. That means students will rush to train in that field, the supply of potential workers goes up, and the jobs are no longer so attractive.

Consider an email that Texas A&M University sent to this year's class of incoming petroleum engineers, the hottest job in the U.S. in terms of starting wages.

The message reminded students that the job market for engineers has always been competitive and cyclical, and warned, "Recent data suggests that some concern about the sustainability of the entry-level job market during a time of explosive growth in the number of students studying petroleum engineering in U.S. universities may be prudent."

Unfortunately, that kind of caution isn't common. Schools want to get as many applicants as possible, and to get the best ones to attend. Showing parents and students all the caveats that go with the impressions they create about future jobs may conflict with those interests.

The Danger of Specialization

Another important caveat that doesn't get discussed much: It may be worse to have the *wrong* career focus in college than having *no* career focus—because skills for one career often can't be used elsewhere.

25　　Let's say a student spends four years learning to market pharmaceuticals. But what can he or she do with that degree if the drug companies aren't hiring? The skills don't transfer easily anyplace else.

That may even be true *within* a field. Anthony Carnevale, of Georgetown's Center on Education and the Workforce, calculates that the unemployment rate among recent IT graduates at the moment is actually twice that of theater majors. Despite the constant complaints from IT employers about skill shortages, only *certain* skills within IT are hot at the moment, such as those associated with mobile communications.

Focusing on a very specific field also means that you miss out on courses that might broaden your abilities. Courses that teach, say, hospitality management or sports medicine may crowd out a logic class that can help students learn to improve their reasoning or an English class that sharpens their writing. Both of those skills can help in any field, unlike the narrowly focused ones.

Beyond those concerns, a narrow educational focus forces students to pick a career at age 17, before they know much of anything about their interests and abilities. And if they choose incorrectly, it can be very difficult for them to start over once they're older.

Researchers Eric A. Hanushek, Ludger Woessmann and Lei Zhang find that more vocationally focused education in high school appears to limit adaptability to changing labor markets later in life. The same thing may be true in college.

30   All that said, practical degrees do have value. But they're not nearly as valuable as boosters say.

Yes, in some fields, like engineering, the only way in is with a specialized degree. Other things being equal, students with one of these degrees will have an easier time getting their first job in the field than students with liberal-arts degrees. After the first job, though, it is not clear how much advantage that practical degree has.

Certainly, some matter in part because they are prestigious—such as a Wharton M.B.A.—but for those that aren't prestigious, and where the degree isn't required or common, a degree may not matter at all.

Also consider that what companies really want hires to have is actual work experience. If they have a choice between hiring someone fresh out of a hospitality-degree program or someone who doesn't have that degree but who has run a restaurant, they will choose the latter.

The Way Forward

So, what are the practical lessons for the venture-investor parent and their child?

35   Students that go the practical route should delay choosing majors and specialized courses as long as possible, so that there is likely to be a better match between course work and employer interests. Students can rely on real-time information from the career office to gauge demand. Because of the need to adjust, it also helps to be at a school where switching majors is easy. Small programs with limited resources mean that students may have to stay more than four years to get all the courses that are required for a new major.

Naturally, it is good to know the job-placement rates for graduates. But as we've seen, those numbers may not be available. So, beyond visiting the school's career center, they should see what ties the school has to employers and what its reputation is in their child's prospective industry.

If specialized education seems too limited or risky, there is another path to consider, one that often gets short shrift these days: go to college to get a well-rounded education and worry about the job market after graduation.

It may seem impractical, given the state of the economy and the scramble for jobs that many liberal-arts graduates face. But remember that work experience is what really is important to employers—and graduates without vocational training can now get that experience from a number of programs.

Bootcamp Education's DevBootcamp provides an experience that mimics a real job. Participants learn by working on real projects, and the company helps them build leads to employers. General Assembly offers hands-on learning and partners with companies to develop curriculum and create hiring relationships for graduates.

40   Education providers like Dartmouth's Tuck Business School are also getting into the act. Tuck has a nondegree certificate Business Bridge program aimed at juniors, seniors and recent graduates in a nonbusiness degree of study. The program offers a general management curriculum as well as career development to enter the job market.

More people than parents should pay attention to this shift toward vocational college degrees. A lot of taxpayer money supports these programs, and in states like Texas, the pressure is on to steer even more students toward them. It is an expensive and inefficient way to provide the practical skills that employers want for the first job out of school, though, as well as being a big, risky bet for parents to underwrite.

There should be better alternatives. One might be for employers to rethink whether they could go back to providing some of the initial training and work experience college grads used to get in entry-level jobs a generation ago.

Review Questions   MyWritingLab™

1. Summarize Jenna Brager's "A Post-College Flow Chart of Misery and Pain."

2. According to Hadley Malcolm's article in *USA Today*, how have graduates in 2014 fared in comparison with those graduating in the preceding four years?

3. Summarize Hadley Malcolm's assessment of the job market for graduating college seniors. What evidence does Malcolm provide to back her assessment?

4. Peter Cappelli suggests that those paying college tuition should think like "venture capitalists" and examine pertinent data closely. Why? What data should be examined in deciding which college to attend?

5. According to Cappelli, what is the danger of specialization—focusing narrowly on a specific skill set as an undergraduate—with the expectation of landing a job post-graduation?

Discussion and Writing Suggestions   MyWritingLab™

1. The topic of marginal job prospects for college graduates is no laughing matter. Yet Brager's "A Post-College Flow Chart of Misery and Pain" should provoke a smile. Why? What's the role of humor in Brager's "flow chart"? Reread your summary of Brager. Which format—prose or graphic—is more compelling, and why? How does the graphic convey Brager's observations on job prospects in a way that (1) your summary and (2) Hadley Malcolm's article in *USA Today* do not?

2. Brager's cartoon chronicles the misery and pain of humanities majors in the current job market. Based on what you've read in Malcolm and Cappelli, to what extent has this misery and pain extended beyond the humanities?

3. Peter Cappelli writes: "Schools want to get as many applicants as possible, and to get the best ones to attend. Showing parents and students all the caveats that go with the impressions they create about future jobs may conflict with those interests." Here Cappelli addresses a potential conflict of interest in the college applications business: That is, even as they encourage students to apply and attend (and pay the requisite fees), colleges may not be able to deliver jobs to their graduates. To what extent do you believe that colleges have a responsibility to be more forthright to students about prospects for jobs after graduation?

4. If Peter Cappelli could talk to Jenna Brager, what might he say about her "Flowchart of Misery and Pain?" After all, he has advised the readers of his *Wall Street Journal* column against the dangers of undergraduate specialization. And while "practical degrees do have value," he writes, "they're not nearly as valuable as boosters say." At the same time, the odds are reasonably good that the humanities student has devoted time to reasoning, writing, and speaking—skills that can be easily adapted regardless of job sector. Assume you are Cappelli and have come across Berger's "Flowchart." Write her a quick e-mail or a comment on the Web site where the flow chart first appeared.

5. Brager premises her "Flow Chart" on a trend obvious to many who major in the humanities: Finding a job can be difficult when one hasn't learned an immediately applicable skill such as accounting or engineering. Why, then, do you think that students continue to major in the humanities?

WILL YOUR JOB BE EXPORTED?

Alan S. Blinder

Alan S. Blinder is the Gordon S. Rentschler Memorial Professor of Economics at Princeton University. He has served as vice chairman of the Federal Reserve Board and was a member of President Clinton's original Council of Economic Advisers. This article, published originally as "Outsourcing: Bigger Than You Thought," first appeared in the *American Prospect* in October 2006.

The great conservative political philosopher Edmund Burke, who probably would not have been a reader of *The American Prospect*, once observed, "You can never plan the future by the past."[1] But when it comes to preparing the American workforce for the jobs of the future, we may be doing just that.

---

[1]Edmund Burke (1729–1797) was a conservative British statesman, philosopher, and author. *The American Prospect*, in which "Will Your Job Be Exported?" first appeared in the November 2006 issue, describes itself as "an authoritative magazine of liberal ideas."

For about a quarter-century, demand for labor appears to have shifted toward the college-educated and away from high school graduates and drop-outs. This shift, most economists believe, is the primary (though not the sole) reason for rising income inequality, and there is no end in sight. Economists refer to this phenomenon by an antiseptic name: skill-biased technical progress. In plain English, it means that the labor market has turned ferociously against the low skilled and the uneducated.

In a progressive society, such a worrisome social phenomenon might elicit some strong policy responses, such as more compensatory education, stepped-up efforts at retraining, reinforcement (rather than shredding) of the social safety net, and so on. You don't fight the market's valuation of skills; you try to mitigate its more deleterious effects. We did a bit of this in the United States in the 1990s, by raising the minimum wage and expanding the Earned Income Tax Credit.[2] Combined with tight labor markets, these measures improved things for the average worker. But in this decade, little or no mitigation has been attempted. Social Darwinism has come roaring back.[3]

With one big exception: We have expended considerable efforts to keep more young people in school longer (e.g., reducing high-school dropouts and sending more kids to college) and to improve the quality of schooling (e.g., via charter schools and No Child Left Behind[4]). Success in these domains may have been modest, but not for lack of trying. You don't have to remind Americans that education is important; the need for educational reform is etched into the pub-lic consciousness. Indeed, many people view education as the silver bullet. On hearing the question "How do we best prepare the American workforce of the future?" many Americans react reflexively with: "Get more kids to study science and math, and send more of them to college."

5   Which brings me to the future. As I argued in a recent article in *Foreign Affairs* magazine, the greatest problem for the next generation of American workers may not be lack of education, but rather "offshoring"—the movement of jobs overseas, especially to countries with much lower wages, such as India and China. Manufacturing jobs have been migrating overseas for decades. But the new wave of offshoring, of *service* jobs, is something different.

Traditionally, we think of service jobs as being largely immune to foreign competition. After all, you can't get your hair cut by a barber or your broken arm

---

[2]The Earned Income Tax Credit, an antipoverty measure enacted by Congress in 1975 and revised in the 1980s and 1990s, provides a credit against federal income taxes for any filer who claims a depen-dent child.

[3]Social Darwinism, a largely discredited philosophy dating from the Victorian era and espoused by Herbert Spenser, asserts that Charles Darwin's observations on natural selection apply to human societies. Social Darwinists argue that the poor are less fit to survive than the wealthy and should, through a natural process of adaptation, be allowed to die out.

[4]Charter schools are public schools with specialized missions to operate outside of regulations that some feel restrict creativity and performance in traditional school settings. The No Child Left Behind Act of 2001 (NCLB) mandates standards-based education for all schools receiving federal fund-ing. Both the charter schools movement and NCLB can be understood as efforts to improve public education.

set by a doctor in a distant land. But stunning advances in communication technology, plus the emergence of a vast new labor pool in Asia and Eastern Europe, are changing that picture radically, subjecting millions of presumed-safe domestic service jobs to foreign competition. And it is not necessary actually to move jobs to low-wage countries in order to restrain wage increases; the mere threat of offshoring can put a damper on wages.

Service-sector offshoring is a minor phenomenon so far, Lou Dobbs notwithstanding; probably well under 1 percent of U.S. service jobs have been outsourced.[5] But I believe that service-sector offshoring will eventually exceed manufacturing-sector offshoring by a hefty margin—for three main reasons. The first is simple arithmetic: There are vastly more service jobs than manufacturing jobs in the United States (and in other rich countries). Second, the technological advances that have made service-sector offshoring possible will continue and accelerate, so the range of services that can be moved offshore will increase ineluctably. Third, the number of (e.g., Indian and Chinese) workers capable of performing service jobs offshore seems certain to grow, perhaps exponentially.

I do not mean to paint a bleak picture here. Ever since Adam Smith and David Ricardo, economists have explained and extolled the gains in living standards that derive from international trade.[6] Those arguments are just as valid for trade in services as for trade in goods. There really *are* net gains to the United States from expanding service-sector trade with India, China, and the rest. The offshoring problem is not about the adverse nature of what economists call the economy's eventual equilibrium. Rather, it is about the so-called transition—the ride from here to there. That ride, which could take a generation or more, may be bumpy. And during the long adjustment period, many U.S. wages could face downward pressure.

Thus far, only American manufacturing workers and a few low-end service workers (e.g., call-center operators) have been competing, at least potentially, with millions of people in faraway lands eager to work for what seems a pittance by U.S. standards. But offshoring is no longer limited to low-end service jobs. Computer code can be written overseas and e-mailed back to the United States. So can your tax return and lots of legal work, provided you do not insist on face-to-face contact with the accountant or lawyer. In writing and editing this article, I communicated with the editors and staff of *The American Prospect* only by telephone and e-mail. Why couldn't they (or I, for that matter) have been in India? The possibilities are, if not endless, at least vast.

10   What distinguishes the jobs that cannot be offshored from the ones that can? The crucial distinction is not—and this is the central point of this essay—the required levels of skill and education. These attributes have been critical

---

[5]Lou Dobbs, a conservative columnist and former political commentator for CNN, is well known for his anti-immigration views.
[6]Adam Smith (1723–1790), Scottish author of *An Inquiry into the Nature and Causes of the Wealth of Nations* (1776), established the foundations of modern economics. David Ricardo (1772–1823) was a British businessman, statesman, and economist who founded the classical school of economics and is best known for his studies of monetary policy.

to labor-market success in the past, but may be less so in the future. Instead, the new critical distinction may be that some services either require personal delivery (e.g., driving a taxi and brain surgery) or are seriously degraded when delivered electronically (e.g., college teaching—at least, I hope!), while other jobs (e.g., call centers and keyboard data entry) are not. Call the first category personal services and the second category impersonal services. With this terminology, I have three main points to make about preparing our workforce for the brave, new world of the future.

First, we need to think about, plan, and redesign our educational system with the crucial distinction between personal service jobs and impersonal service jobs in mind. Many of the impersonal service jobs will migrate offshore, but the personal service jobs will stay here.

Second, the line that divides personal services from impersonal services will move in only one direction over time, as technological progress makes it possible to deliver an ever-increasing array of services electronically.

Third, the novel distinction between personal and impersonal jobs is quite different from, and appears essentially unrelated to, the traditional distinction between jobs that do and do not require high levels of education.

For example, it is easy to offshore working in a call center, typing transcripts, writing computer code, and reading X-rays. The first two require little education; the last two require quite a lot. On the other hand, it is either impossible or very difficult to offshore janitorial services, fast-food restaurant service, college teaching, and open-heart surgery. Again, the first two occupations require little or no education, while the last two require a great deal. There seems to be little or no correlation between educational requirements (the old concern) and how "offshorable" jobs are (the new one).

15   If so, the implications could be startling. A generation from now, civil engineers (who must be physically present) may be in greater demand in the United States than computer engineers (who don't). Similarly, there might be more divorce lawyers (not offshorable) than tax lawyers (partly offshorable). More imaginatively, electricians might earn more than computer programmers. I am not predicting any of this; lots of things influence relative demands and supplies for different types of labor. But it all seems within the realm of the possible as technology continues to enhance the offshorability of even highly skilled occupations. What does seem highly likely is that the relative demand for labor in the United States will shift away from impersonal services and toward personal services, and this shift will look quite different from the familiar story of skill-biased technical progress. So Burke's warning is worth heeding.

I am *not* suggesting that education will become a handicap in the job market of the future. On the contrary, to the extent that education raises productivity and that better-educated workers are more adaptable and/or more creative, a wage premium for higher education should remain. Thus, it still makes sense to send more of America's youth to college. But, over the next generation, the kind of education our young people receive may prove to be more important than how much education they receive. In that sense, a college degree may lose its exalted "silver bullet" status.

Looking back over the past 25 years, "stay in school longer" was excellent advice for success in the labor market. But looking forward over the next 25 years, more subtle occupational advice may be needed. "Prepare yourself for a high-end personal service occupation that is not offshorable" is a more nuanced message than "stay in school." But it may prove to be more useful. And many non-offshorable jobs—such as carpenters, electricians, and plumbers—do not require college education.

The hard question is how to make this more subtle advice concrete and actionable. The children entering America's educational system today, at age 5, will emerge into a very different labor market when they leave it. Given gestation periods of 13 to 17 years and more, educators and policy-makers need to be thinking now about the kinds of training and skills that will best prepare these children for their future working lives. Specifically, it is essential to educate America's youth for the jobs that will actually be available in America 20 to 30 years from now, not for the jobs that will have moved offshore.

Some of the personal service jobs that will remain in the United States will be very high-end (doctors), others will be less glamorous though well paid (plumbers), and some will be "dead end" (janitor). We need to think long and hard about the types of skills that best prepare people to deliver high-end personal services, and how to teach those skills in our elementary and high schools. I am not an education specialist, but it strikes me that, for example, the central thrust of No Child Left Behind is pushing the nation in exactly the wrong direction. I am all for accountability. But the nation's school system will not build the creative, flexible, people-oriented workforce we will need in the future by drilling kids incessantly with rote preparation for standardized tests in the vain hope that they will perform as well as memory chips.

20   Starting in the elementary schools, we need to develop our youngsters' imaginations and people skills as well as their "reading, writing, and 'rithmetic." Remember that kindergarten grade for "works and plays well with others"? It may become increasingly important in a world of personally delivered services. Such training probably needs to be continued and made more sophisticated in the secondary schools, where, for example, good communications skills need to be developed.

More vocational education is probably also in order. After all, nurses, carpenters, and plumbers are already scarce, and we'll likely need more of them in the future. Much vocational training now takes place in community colleges; and they, too, need to adapt their curricula to the job market of the future.

While it is probably still true that we should send more kids to college and increase the number who study science, math, and engineering, we need to focus on training more college students for the high-end jobs that are unlikely to move offshore, and on developing a creative workforce that will keep America incubating and developing new processes, new products, and entirely new industries. Offshoring is, after all, mostly about following and copying. America needs to lead and innovate instead, just as we have in the past.

Educational reform is not the whole story, of course. I suggested at the outset, for example, that we needed to repair our tattered social safety net and turn it into a retraining trampoline that bounces displaced workers back into productive employment. But many low-end personal service jobs cannot be turned into more attractive jobs simply by more training—think about janitors, fast-food workers, and nurse's aides, for example. Running a tight labor market would help such workers, as would a higher minimum wage, an expanded Earned Income Tax Credit, universal health insurance, and the like.

Moving up the skill ladder, employment is concentrated in the public or quasi-public sector in a number of service occupations. Teachers and health-care workers are two prominent examples. In such cases, government policy can influence wages and working conditions directly by upgrading the structure and pay of such jobs—developing more professional early-childhood teachers and fewer casual daycare workers for example—as long as the taxpayer is willing to foot the bill. Similarly, some service jobs such as registered nurses are in short supply mainly because we are not training enough qualified personnel. Here, too, public policy can help by widening the pipeline to allow more workers through. So there are a variety of policy levers that might do some good—if we are willing to pull them.

25   But all that said, education is still the right place to start. Indeed, it is much more than that because the educational system affects the entire population and because no other institution is nearly as important when it comes to preparing our youth for the world of work. As the first industrial revolution took hold, America radically transformed (and democratized) its educational system to meet the new demands of an industrial society. We may need to do something like that again. There is a great deal at stake here. If we get this one wrong, the next generation will pay dearly. But if we get it (close to) right, the gains from trade promise coming generations a prosperous future.

The somewhat inchoate challenge posed here—preparing more young Americans for personal service jobs—brings to mind one of my favorite Churchill quotations: "You can always count on Americans to do the right thing—after they've tried everything else." It is time to start trying.

Review Questions   MyWritingLab™

1. What is "offshoring"? Why have service jobs been thought "immune to foreign competition"?

2. Explain Blinder's distinction between "personal services" and "impersonal services." Why is this distinction important?

3. In the past twenty-five years, what role has education played in preparing people for work? How does Blinder see that role changing in the coming decades?

4. What advice does Blinder offer young people preparing for future work in the coming decades?

5. Why will the United States eventually lose more service-sector than manufacturing-sector jobs?

● Discussion and Writing Suggestions   MyWritingLab™

1. Identify a worker (real or imagined) in a job that may be at risk for offshoring, according to Blinder. Write a letter to that person, apprising him or her of the potential danger and offering advice you think appropriate.

2. What is your reaction to Blinder's claim that educational achievement, in and of itself, will be less of a predictor of job quality and security than it once was?

3. Describe a well-paying job that would not require a college education but that should, according to Blinder, be immune to offshoring. Compare your responses to those of your classmates.

4. What work can you imagine doing in ten years? Describe that work in a concise paragraph. Now analyze your description as Blinder might. How secure is your future job likely to be?

5. Approach friends who have not read the Blinder article with his advice on preparing for future work (see Review Question 4). Report on their reactions.

6. What were your *emotional* reactions to Blinder's article? Did the piece leave you feeling hopeful, anxious, apprehensive, excited? Explain.

THEY'RE WATCHING YOU AT WORK: THE JOB INTERVIEW

Don Peck

In this next piece, Don Peck investigates the ways computer-based statistical analyses may come to dominate the hiring and assessment of American workers. Already, "analytics" is used to measure the performance of baseball players. The trend may be spreading. By the time you graduate, you may find yourself in a job interview being asked to play a video game while a computer records your every move and predicts your likely success as an employee. This article first appeared in the *Atlantic* in December 2013. In addition to being a deputy editor of that magazine, Don Peck is the author of *Pinched: How the Great Recession Has Narrowed Our Futures and What We Can Do About It* (2011).

In 2003, thanks to Michael Lewis and his best seller *Moneyball*, the general manager of the Oakland A's, Billy Beane, became a star. The previous year, Beane had turned his back on his scouts and had instead entrusted player-acquisition decisions to mathematical models developed by a young, Harvard-trained statistical wizard on his staff. What happened next has become baseball lore. The A's, a small-market team with a paltry budget, ripped off the longest winning streak in American League history and rolled up 103 wins for the season. Only the mighty Yankees, who had spent three times as much on player salaries, won as many games. The team's success, in turn, launched a revolution. In the years that followed, team after team began to use detailed predictive models to assess players' potential and monetary value, and the early adopters, by and large, gained a measurable competitive edge over their more hidebound peers.

That's the story as most of us know it. But it is incomplete. What would seem at first glance to be nothing but a memorable tale about baseball may turn out to be the opening chapter of a much larger story about jobs. Predictive statistical analysis, harnessed to big data, appears poised to alter the way millions of people are hired and assessed.

Yes, unavoidably, *big data*. As a piece of business jargon, and even more so as an invocation of coming disruption, the term has quickly grown tiresome. But there is no denying the vast increase in the range and depth of information that's routinely captured about how we behave, and the new kinds of analysis that this enables. By one estimate, more than 98 percent of the world's information is now stored digitally, and the volume of that data has quadrupled since 2007. Ordinary people at work and at home generate much of this data, by sending e-mails, browsing the Internet, using social media, working on crowd-sourced projects, and more—and in doing so they have unwittingly helped launch a grand new societal project. "We are in the midst of a great infrastructure project that in some ways rivals those of the past, from Roman aqueducts to the Enlightenment's Encyclopédie,"[1] write Viktor Mayer-Schönberger and Kenneth Cukier in their recent book, *Big Data: A Revolution That Will Transform How We Live, Work, and Think*. "The project is datafication. Like those other infrastructural advances, it will bring about fundamental changes to society."

Some of the changes are well known, and already upon us. Algorithms that predict stock-price movements have transformed Wall Street. Algorithms that chomp through our Web histories have transformed marketing. Until quite recently, however, few people seemed to believe this data-driven approach might apply broadly to the labor market.

5   But it now does. According to John Hausknecht, a professor at Cornell's school of industrial and labor relations, in recent years the economy has witnessed a "huge surge in demand for workforce-analytics roles." Hausknecht's own program is rapidly revising its curriculum to keep pace. You can now find dedicated analytics teams in the human-resources departments of not only huge corporations such as Google, HP, Intel, General Motors, and Procter & Gamble, to name just a few, but also companies like McKee Foods, the Tennessee-based maker of Little Debbie snack cakes. Even Billy Beane is getting into the game. Last year he appeared at a large conference for corporate HR executives in Austin, Texas, where he reportedly stole the show with a talk titled "The Moneyball Approach to Talent Management." Ever since, that headline, with minor modifications, has been plastered all over the HR trade press.

---

[1]The ancient Romans built aqueducts to deliver water from remote sources to population centers, a practice that made possible the construction of great cities throughout the empire. Seventeen hundred years later, Denis Diderot's *Encyclopédie*, with more than 70,000 articles authored by nearly 150 scholars, became one of the great intellectual achievements of the Enlightenment. It attempted to record, in one place, the output of a world exploding with knowledge. Both the aqueducts and encyclopedia were "infrastructure" projects in the sense that they enabled major growth: one of cities, the other of knowledge. According to Schönberger and Cukier, big data and the use we will make of it takes its place alongside these two historic developments.

The application of predictive analytics to people's careers—an emerging field sometimes called "people analytics"—is enormously challenging, not to mention ethically fraught. And it can't help but feel a little creepy. It requires the creation of a vastly larger box score of human performance than one would ever encounter in the sports pages, or that has ever been dreamed up before. To some degree, the endeavor touches on the deepest of human mysteries: how we grow, whether we flourish, what we become. Most companies are just beginning to explore the possibilities. But make no mistake: during the next five to 10 years, new models will be created, and new experiments run, on a very large scale. Will this be a good development or a bad one—for the economy, for the shapes of our careers, for our spirit and self-worth?

• • •

Consider Knack, a tiny start-up based in Silicon Valley. Knack makes app-based video games, among them Dungeon Scrawl, a quest game requiring the player to navigate a maze and solve puzzles, and Wasabi Waiter, which involves delivering the right sushi to the right customer at an increasingly crowded happy hour. These games aren't just for play: they've been designed by a team of neuroscientists, psychologists, and data scientists to suss out human potential. Play one of them for just 20 minutes, says Guy Halfteck, Knack's founder, and you'll generate several megabytes of data, exponentially more than what's collected by the SAT or a personality test. How long you hesitate before taking every action, the sequence of actions you take, how you solve problems—all of these factors and many more are logged as you play, and then are used to analyze your creativity, your persistence, your capacity to learn quickly from mistakes, your ability to prioritize, and even your social intelligence and personality. The end result, Halfteck says, is a high-resolution portrait of your psyche and intellect, and an assessment of your potential as a leader or an innovator.

When Hans Haringa heard about Knack, he was skeptical but intrigued. Haringa works for the petroleum giant Royal Dutch Shell—by revenue, the world's largest company last year. For seven years he's served as an executive in the company's GameChanger unit: a 12-person team that for nearly two decades has had an outsize impact on the company's direction and performance. The unit's job is to identify potentially disruptive business ideas. Haringa and his team solicit ideas promiscuously from inside and outside the company, and then play the role of venture capitalists, vetting each idea, meeting with its proponents, dispensing modest seed funding to a few promising candidates, and monitoring their progress. They have a good record of picking winners, Haringa told me, but identifying ideas with promise has proved to be extremely difficult and time-consuming. The process typically takes more than two years, and less than 10 percent of the ideas proposed to the unit actually make it into general research and development.

When he heard about Knack, Haringa thought he might have found a short-cut. What if Knack could help him assess the people proposing all these ideas, so that he and his team could focus only on those whose ideas genuinely deserved close attention? Haringa reached out, and eventually ran an experiment with the company's help.

10   Over the years, the GameChanger team had kept a database of all the ideas it had received, recording how far each had advanced. Haringa asked all the idea contributors he could track down (about 1,400 in total) to play Dungeon Scrawl and Wasabi Waiter, and told Knack how well three-quarters of those people had done as idea generators. (Did they get initial funding? A second round? Did their ideas make it all the way?) He did this so that Knack's staff could develop game-play profiles of the strong innovators relative to the weak ones. Finally, he had Knack analyze the game-play of the remaining quarter of the idea generators, and asked the company to guess whose ideas had turned out to be best.

When the results came back, Haringa recalled, his heart began to beat a little faster. Without ever seeing the ideas, without meeting or interviewing the people who'd proposed them, without knowing their title or background or academic pedigree, Knack's algorithm had identified the people whose ideas had panned out. The top 10 percent of the idea generators as predicted by Knack were in fact those who'd gone furthest in the process. Knack identified six broad factors as especially characteristic of those whose ideas would succeed at Shell: "mind wandering" (or the tendency to follow interesting, unexpected offshoots of the main task at hand, to see where they lead), social intelligence, "goal-orientation fluency," implicit learning, task-switching ability, and conscientiousness. Haringa told me that this profile dovetails with his impression of a successful innovator. "You need to be disciplined," he said, but "at all times you must have your mind open to see the other possibilities and opportunities."

What Knack is doing, Haringa told me, "is almost like a paradigm shift." It offers a way for his GameChanger unit to avoid wasting time on the 80 people out of 100—nearly all of whom look smart, well-trained, and plausible on paper—whose ideas just aren't likely to work out. If he and his colleagues were no longer mired in evaluating "the hopeless folks," as he put it to me, they could solicit ideas even more widely than they do today and devote much more careful attention to the 20 people out of 100 whose ideas have the most merit.

Haringa is now trying to persuade his colleagues in the GameChanger unit to use Knack's games as an assessment tool. But he's also thinking well beyond just his own little part of Shell. He has encouraged the company's HR executives to think about applying the games to the recruitment and evaluation of all professional workers. Shell goes to extremes to try to make itself the world's most innovative energy company, he told me, so shouldn't it apply that spirit to developing its own "human dimension"?

"It is the whole man The Organization wants," William Whyte wrote back in 1956, when describing the ambit of the employee evaluations then in fashion. Aptitude, skills, personal history, psychological stability, discretion, loyalty— companies at the time felt they had a need (and the right) to look into them all. That ambit is expanding once again, and this is undeniably unsettling. Should the ideas of scientists be dismissed because of the way they play a game? Should job candidates be ranked by what their Web habits say about them? Should the "data signature" of natural leaders play a role in promotion? These are all live questions today, and they prompt heavy concerns: that we will cede one of the most subtle and human of skills, the evaluation of the gifts and promise of other people, to machines; that the models will get it wrong; that some people will never get a shot in the new workforce.

15   It's natural to worry about such things. But consider the alternative. A mountain of scholarly literature has shown that the intuitive way we now judge professional potential is rife with snap judgments and hidden biases, rooted in our upbringing or in deep neurological connections that doubtless served us well on the savanna but would seem to have less bearing on the world of work.

● Review Questions   MyWritingLab™

1. What is "big data"?

2. Explain "people analytics."

3. Why does Peck believe that people analytics has moved beyond the idea stage and has arrived in corporate America?

4. How do the video games Dungeon Scrawl and Wasabi Waiter relate to the discussion of personal analytics?

5. What did Hans Haringa of Dutch Shell discover about assessing talent from the start-up Knack?

● Discussion and Writing Suggestions   MyWritingLab™

1. Peck writes that "the endeavor [to mine employee data] touches on the deepest of human mysteries: how we grow, whether we flourish, what we become." Do you approve of the application of big data to these "human mysteries"?

2. Big data applied to the Oakland A's baseball team produced stunning results and revolutionized the sport. Do you think the application of big data beyond the ball field has similar potential? For instance, is work life sufficiently analogous to performance on a ball field to make you comfortable that big data could be used in recognizing *your* talent as a prospective employee?

3. The people analytics generated by Dungeon Scrawl and Wasabi Waiter convinced one executive at Royal Dutch Shell that computer gaming can identify talent with greater efficiency than people can. Are you surprised? What could be the limitations of computer gaming in identifying talent?

4. In reporting the efforts of Hans Haringa to persuade the human resources department of Royal Dutch Shell to use Knack's gaming programs to recruit and evaluate workers, Peck writes: "Shell goes to extremes to try to make itself the world's most innovative energy company…, so shouldn't it apply that spirit to developing its own "human dimension"? Do you detect any ironies here? Discuss.

5. Peck writes: "Should the ideas of scientists be dismissed because of the way they play a game? Should job candidates be ranked by what their Web habits say about them? Should the "data signature" of natural leaders play a role in promotion?" Choose one of these questions and develop an answer.

DATA ON THE U.S. LABOR MARKET: CHARTS, GRAPHS, TABLES

What do we know about the hundreds of occupations you might pursue—for instance, how much they pay, the education and training needed to land an interview, their prospects for growth? You don't have to guess at answers because clear, reliable information exists—much of it summarized in graphical form. We have gathered some of that data here for a closer look.

- Five graphs measure, as the title says, "The Rising Cost of Not Going to College"—information that first appeared in a February 2014 report by the Pew Research Center. The Pew Center describes itself as "a nonpartisan fact tank that informs the public about the issues, attitudes and trends shaping America and the world."

- Next, a table from the Georgetown Public Policy Institute and Center for Education and the Workforce summarizes unemployment rates and earnings, by major field of study, for recent college graduates, experienced graduates, and holders of advanced degrees. The Georgetown Center "seeks to inform and educate federal, state, and local policymakers and stakeholders on ways to better align education and training with labor market demand and qualifications."

- We conclude with charts and tables from the Bureau of Labor Statistics (BLS): "Earnings and Unemployment Rates by Educational Attainment"; "Projected Annual Employment Rate of Change by Major Industry Sector, 2012–2022"; and "Projected Rate of Employment Change by Major Occupational Group, 2012–2022."

- The final table is a representation of the BLS "Occupation Finder" from its *Occupational Outlook Handbook* (go to http://www.bls.gov/ooh/occupation-finder.htm). This powerful, interactive resource allows you to search the projected outlook for 580 different jobs by combining five categories: entry-level education, availability of on-the-job training, projected number of new jobs, projected growth rate, and median pay (as of 2012). A division of the U.S. Department of Labor, the BLS "is the principal Federal agency responsible for measuring labor market activity, working conditions, and price changes in the economy." It releases ten-year employment projections every two years for the benefit of those looking for, or changing, jobs.

If you don't find the information you need on the job market in the fifteen graphs, charts, and tables that follow, enter the pertinent term in a search engine, followed by the word "statistics." Your search will very likely yield hundreds of potential sources.

Rising Earnings Disparity Between Young Adults with And Without a College Degree

Median annual earnings among full-time workers ages 25 to 32, in 2012 dollars

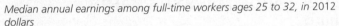

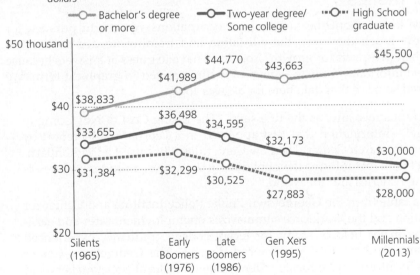

Note: Median annual earnings are based on earnings and work status during the calendar year prior to interview and limited to 25- to 32-year-olds who worked full time during the previous calendar year and reported positive earnings. "Full time" refers to those who usually worked at least 35 hours a week last year.

Source: Pew Research Center tabulations of the 2013,1995,1986,1979 and 1965 March Current Population Survey (CPS) Integrated Public Use Micro Samples

Pew Research Center

From "The Rising Cost of Not Going to College," February 11, 2014.

Disparity among Millennials Ages 25–32 By Education Level in Teams of Annual Earnings ...

(median among full-time workers, in 2012 dollars)

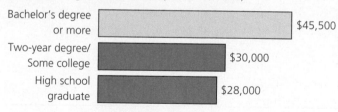

Bachelor's degree or more — $45,500
Two-year degree/Some college — $30,000
High school graduate — $28,000

Unemployment Rate ...

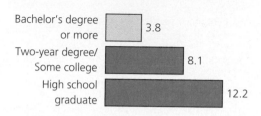

Bachelor's degree or more — 3.8
Two-year degree/Some college — 8.1
High school graduate — 12.2

And Share Living in Poverty ...

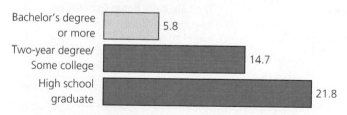

Bachelor's degree or more — 5.8
Two-year degree/Some college — 14.7
High school graduate — 21.8

Notes: Median annual earnings are based on earnings and work status during the calendar year prior to interview and limited to 25- to 32-year-olds who worked full time during the previous calendar year and reported positive earnings. "Full time" refers to those who usually worked at least 35 hours a week last year. The unemployment rate refers to the share of the labor force (those working or actively seeking work) who are not employed. Poverty is based on the respondent's family income in the calendar year preceding the survey.

Source: Pew Research Center tabulations of the 2013 March Current Population Survey (CPS) Integrated Public Use Micro Sample

Pew Research Center

Education and Views About Work

% of employed adults ages 25 to 32 with each level of education saying ...

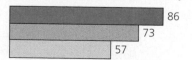

■ Bachelor's degree or more
☐ Two-year degree/Some college
☐ High school grad or less

... they have a career/career-track job

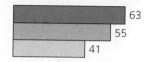

86
73
57

... they have enough education and training to get ahead in their job

63
55
41

... they are "very satisfied" with current job

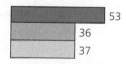

53
36
37

... their education was "very useful" in preparing them for a job or career

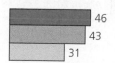

46
43
31

Notes: Based on currently employed 25- to 32-year-olds (n = 509).

Pew Research Center   **Q34,28,2c,20**

Percentage of Generation in Poverty, by Educational Attainment

	All	College graduate	Two-year degree/ Some college	High school graduate
Millennials in 2013	16	6	15	22
Gen Xers in 1995	13	3	10	15
Late Boomers in 1986	12	4	8	12
Early Boomers in 1979	8	3	6	7

Notes: "All" includes those who are not high school graduates. Poverty is based on the respondent's family income in the calendar year preceding the survey. Silent generation not shown because poverty measures are not available before 1968.

Pew Research Center

The Generations Defined

The Millennial Generation
Born: After 1980
Age of adults in 2013: 18 to 32*

Generation X
Born: 1965 to 1980
Age in 2013: 33 to 48

The Late Baby Boom Generation
Born: 1955 to 1964
Age in 2013: 49 to 58

The Early Baby Boom Generation
Born: 1946 to 1954
Age in 2013: 59 to 67

The Silent Generation
Born: 1928 to 1945
Age in 2013: 68 to 85

* The youngest Millennials are in their teens. No chronological end point has been set for this group.

Note: The "Greatest Generation," which includes those born before 1928, is not included in the analysis due to the small sample size.

Pew Research Center

Usefulness of Major, by Field of Study

% of majors in each area who say their current job is...
related to their major in college or graduate school

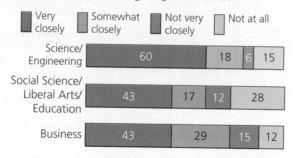

- ■ Very closely
- ■ Somewhat closely
- ■ Not very closely
- ■ Not at all

	Very closely	Somewhat closely	Not very closely	Not at all
Science/Engineering	60	18	6	15
Social Science/Liberal Arts/Education	43	17	12	28
Business	43	29	15	12

Note: Based on those with at least a bachelor's degree who are employed full time or part time (n = 606). "Don't know/Refused" responses not shown.

Pew Research Center   Q40

Unemployment and Earnings for College Majors

MAJOR	UNEMPLOYMENT RATES			EARNINGS		
	RECENT COLLEGE GRADUATE	EXPERIENCED COLLEGE GRADUATE	GRADUATE DEGREE HOLDER	RECENT COLLEGE GRADUATE	EXPERIENCED COLLEGE GRADUATE	GRADUATE DEGREE HOLDER
Agriculture & Natural Resources	6.1%	3.4%	2.3%	$33,000	$51,000	$67,000
Science-Life/Physical	7.3%	4.8%	2.1%	$30,000	$60,000	$90,000
Architecture	12.8%	9.3%	6.9%	$36,000	$65,000	$72,000
Humanities and Liberal Arts	9.0%	6.3%	3.9%	$30,000	$51,000	$66,000
Communications & Journalism	7.8%	6.0%	4.2%	$33,000	$54,000	$64,000
Computers & Mathematics	9.1%	4.8%	3.6%	$45,000	$76,000	$91,000
Education	5.7%	4.0%	2.0%	$33,000	$44,000	$57,000
Engineering	7.4%	4.4%	3.0%	$54,000	$83,000	$101,000
Law and Public Policy	9.2%	4.8%	4.1%	$33,000	$56,000	$70,000
Social Science	10.3%	4.6%	4.0%	$36,000	$61,000	$84,000
Industrial Arts	8.2%	2.6%	—	$41,000	$71,000	—
Health	6.1%	2.6%	2.0%	$43,000	$65,000	$81,000
Psychology & Social Work	8.8%	6.6%	3.4%	$30,000	$46,000	$60,000
Recreation	5.2%	4.5%	—	$29,000	$50,000	—
Arts	9.8%	6.9%	5.6%	$30,000	$48,000	$55,000
Business	7.5%	5.2%	4.3%	$39,000	$63,000	$83,000

Source: http://cew.georgetown.edu/unemployment2013

From *Hard Times: College Majors, Unemployment and Earnings.* Anthony P. Carnevale and Ban Cheah, Georgetown Public Policy Institute /Center for Education and the Workforce, May 29, 2013.

Earnings and Unemployment Rates by Educational Attainment

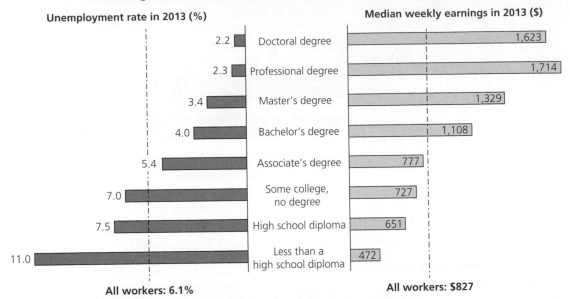

Unemployment rate in 2013 (%)

Median weekly earnings in 2013 ($)

2.2	Doctoral degree	1,623
2.3	Professional degree	1,714
3.4	Master's degree	1,329
4.0	Bachelor's degree	1,108
5.4	Associate's degree	777
7.0	Some college, no degree	727
7.5	High school diploma	651
11.0	Less than a high school diploma	472

All workers: 6.1%

All workers: $827

Note: Data are for persons age 25 and over. Earnings are for full-time wage and salary workers.
Source: Current Populations survey, U.S. Bureau of Labor Statistics, U.S. Department of Labor, March, 24, 2014, http://www.bls.gov/emp/ep_chart_001.htm

Earnings and Unemployment Rates by Educational Attainment

Education attained	Unemployment rate in 2013 (Percent)	Median weekly earnings
Doctoral degree	2.2	$1,623
Professional degree	2.3	1,714
Master's degree	3.4	1,329
Bachelor's degree	4.0	1,108
Associate's degree	5.4	777
Some college, no degree	7.0	727
High school diploma	7.5	651
Less than a high school diploma	11.0	472

Note: Data are for persons age 25 and over. Earnings are for full-time wage and salary workers.

Source: Current Population Survey, U.S. Department of Labor, U.S. Bureau of Labor Statistics, http://www.bls.gov/emp/ep_table_001.htm

These education categories reflect only the highest level of education attained. They do not take into account completion of training programs in the form of apprenticeships and other on-the-job training, which may also influence earnings and unemployment rates.

Projected Annual Employment Rate of Change by Major Industry Sector, 2012–22

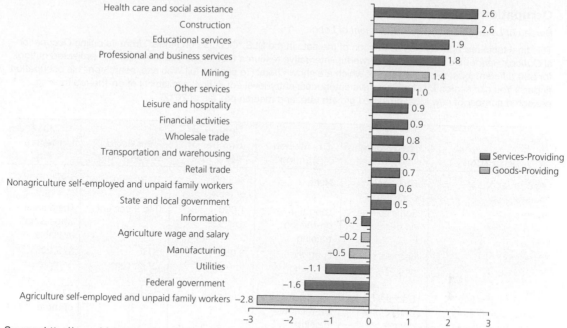

Source: http://www.bls.gov/news.release/pdf/ecopro.pdf
From Bureau of Labor Statistics, *Employment Projections 2012–2022*, December 19, 2013.

Projected Rate of Employment Change by Major Occupational Group, 2012–22

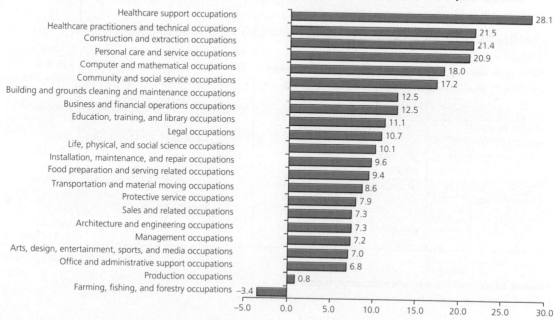

Source: http://www.bls.gov/news.release/pdf/ecopro.pdf

Occupation Finder

Bureau of Labor Statistics, US Department of Labor

This final table reproduces a small fraction of the data in the BLS "Occupation Finder" from its online *Occupational Outlook Handbook*. The OOH is a powerful, interactive resource that allows you to search the projected outlook for 580 different jobs, the first twelve of which are shown here. (To see the full Web site, search on "bls occupation finder.") You can search by combining five categories: entry-level education, availability of on-the-job training, projected number of new jobs, projected growth rate, and median pay (as of 2012).

Occupation	Entry-Level Education	On-The-Job-Training	Projected Number Of New Jobs	Projected Growth Rate	2012 Median Pay
Accountants and auditors	Bachelor's degree	None	50,000 or more	10 to 19 percent	$55,000 to $74.999
Actors	Some college, no degree	Long-term on-the-job training	1,000 to 4,999	0 to 9 percent	The annual wage is not available.
Actuaries	Bachelor's degree	Long-term on-the-job training	5,000 to 9,999	20 to 29 percent	$75,000 or more
Administrative law judges, adjudicators, and hearing officers	Doctoral or professional degree	Short-term on-the-job training	Declining	Declining	$75,000 or more
Administrative services managers	Bachelor's degree	None	10,000 to 49,999	10 to 19 percent	$75,000 or more
Adult basic and secondary education and literacy teachers and instructors	Bachelor's degree	Internship / residency	5,000 to 9,999	0 to 9 percent	$35,000 to $54.999
Advertising and promotions managers	Bachelor's degree	None	1,000 to 4,999	0 to 9 percent	$75,000 or more
Advertising sales agents	High school diploma or equivalent	Moderate-term on-the-job training	Declining	Declining	$35,000 to $54,999
Aerospace engineering and operations technicians	Associate's degree	None	0 to 999	0 to 9 percent	$55,000 to $74,999
Aerospace engineers	Bachelor's degree	None	5,000 to 9,999	0 to 9 percent	$75,000 or more
Agricultural and food science technicians	Associate's degree	Moderate-term on-the-job training	0 to 999	0 to 9 percent	$25,000 to $34,999
Agricultural engineers	Bachelor's degree	None	0 to 999	0 to 9 percent	$55,000 to $74,999

Published January 8, 2014

Source: http://www.bls.gov/ooh/occupation-finder.htm

● Review Questions · MyWritingLab™

1. Summarize any two of the graphs, tables, or charts in this section.

2. Make a claim about health care workers that is supported by data from more than one graph, chart, or table.

3. Based on the graphs, tables, and charts in this section, support a claim about the relationship of education to employability, earning potential, and the likelihood of living below the poverty line.

4. Two of the graphs from the Bureau of Labor Statistics represent *projections*— that is, educated guess about changes coming to the American labor force. As such, they are not yet facts. Still, you'll find some agreement between labor data projected by the BLS and data reported by Pew Research and Georgetown Public Policy Institute. Identify one such area of agreement.

5. What do employers care about most and least when evaluating college graduates for a new job?

● Discussion and Writing Suggestions · MyWritingLab™

1. The Georgetown Public Policy Institute's table "Unemployment and Earnings for College Majors" indicates relatively high unemployment rates of recently graduated majors in architecture, the social sciences, and humanities. Notice what happens to the unemployment rates after further education that leads to a graduate degree. What conclusions do you draw, and what effect might these conclusions have on your consideration of potential majors?

2. In this section's graphs, charts, and tables, locate industries and/or majors you find interesting. Pay special attention to the BLS projections in these same areas. What are the job prospects both at present and in the (projected) future? How would you use this data to help you decide about the types of work you want to pursue after graduation?

3. Both in terms of income and the likelihood of living in poverty, the relative impact of attaining a college degree on one's working life has changed substantially in the past fifty years. (On this point, see especially the first Pew Research graph.) How do you respond to this development? What's lost and what's gained when a college degree is all but required for economic advancement? In developing your answer, you might reflect on the jobs and economic situations of your parents and grandparents.

4. Use the graphical information in this section to plot a purely data-driven decision about which major and which career(s) you will pursue. Now review your decision. Are you happy with it? Could you devote your career to your chosen field? Why or why not?

5. Go to the Bureau of Labor Statistics' "Occupation Finder" (go to http://www .bls.gov/ooh/occupation-finder.htm or search "bls occupation finder"). This powerful tool offers a wealth of information about virtually any type of work you may be considering. Aside from summarizing key elements of the jobs (each job is hyperlinked to a "Summary" page), you'll learn about education needed, training opportunities, salary ranges, and projected jobs and growth rates. Spend ten minutes on the page, experimenting with different searches.[1] Write a one-page summary of the key results of your search.

6. Consider this scenario: A parent or other concerned figure presents you with the BLS projected employment rates by major industry and major industry group, 2012–2022. Pointing to the occupational groups that are likely to see the biggest gains, this person advises you to choose a course of study that prepares you for one of these significantly expanding occupational areas. What do you say?

7. As you review the charts, graphs, and tables, what data point stands out to you as the biggest surprise? What did you learn in reviewing this data that you did not know before? Discuss.

DEBATE: SHOULD YOU DO WHAT YOU LOVE?

One of the fundamental questions to ask in preparing for a lifetime of work is this: "Should I do what I love?" The (often) unspoken addendum: "...even if following my passion means that I'll earn less or have a difficult time finding work?" There it is, the tough choice: to work for money or to work for love? The question itself inclines us to think that the alternatives are mutually exclusive. But as with many either/or questions, this one obscures other possibilities, such as working a job that *needs* doing or a job that is meaningful (however this word is defined). And then there's the option of working at a not particularly interesting job to earn income for a greater good: to support a family, for instance, or to finance a child's education. Couldn't this effort bring satisfaction?

---

[1]Note: You have the option of beginning your search by selecting search categories rather than particular jobs. For instance, using the drop-down menus, you can instruct the Web site to show you all jobs that (1) require an Associate's degree—that is, a two year degree—for which there is projected to be (2) a large increase in positions in a field that is (3) growing quickly and will pay (4) up to $55,000. Seven jobs are listed. Or you can search the list of 580 specific jobs.

Perhaps meaning needn't come through work at all. Perhaps a job is just a job, a way to make money, and one's identity and self-worth come from activities *outside* the workplace. ("This is just my day job," says the waiter who during his off-hours works on his screenplay.) Though you may feel the need to make a single, fateful decision now as you contemplate your choice of major and future job prospects, the truth is that you'll be puzzling through these questions for a lifetime. Still, the decisions you make now *are* consequential, and so it's a good idea to be informed about the job market and to be mindful of your own priorities.

Earlier readings in this chapter have kept you abreast of changing data on the job market. This final cluster will give you a chance to ponder what it is you *want* from work.

DO WHAT YOU LOVE

Steve Jobs

On June 12, 2005, Steve Jobs (1955–2011), Apple cofounder and towering figure in the computer revolution, set off something of a chain reaction when he advised the graduating class of Stanford University to "find what you love"—that is, to find work about which you can be passionate. Was this good advice? The three writers who follow him in this cluster don't think so—though for differing reasons.

Steve Jobs was a technology pioneer who brought a ferocious focus on aesthetics to the world of computers, insisting that they be beautiful, intuitive, and accessible to a broad public, not just to engineers. He cofounded Apple in 1976 with Steve Wozniak, was forced out of that company in 1985, and a year later cofounded the computer animation company Pixar (creator of Toy Story [1995]). Apple rehired Jobs in 1997 (a year after Pixar was sold for more than $7 billion). In 2001, he introduced the iPod, two years later announcing the iTunes streaming music store that would revolutionize the music industry. Jobs was diagnosed with pancreatic cancer in 2003. Working through his illness, he introduced the touch-screen iPhone in 2007 and, three years later, the iPad, technologies that have profoundly transformed our interactions with the digital world. He finally succumbed to his illness on October 5, 2011. Not three weeks later Walter Isaacson's biography, titled Steve Jobs, was published to wide acclaim. As Isaacson points out in his introduction, the book is about "the roller coaster life and searingly intense personality of a creative entrepreneur whose passion for perfection and ferocious drive revolutionized six industries: personal computers, animated movies, music, phones, tablet computers, and digital publishing."

To read Steve Job's speech, available via the *Stanford News*, go online and use these search terms: "jobs stanford speech." You can also watch Jobs give this commencement address on YouTube.

● Discussion and Writing Suggestions   MyWritingLab™

1. Jobs advises the graduating class at Stanford "to find what you love"—advice roundly rejected by the three writers remaining in this chapter. Before you read their critiques of the Do What You Love (DWYL) philosophy, decide for yourself: Is DWYL *good* advice? How centrally will it figure in *your* search for a job?

2. Jobs calls dropping out of college "one of the best decisions I ever made." He explains that the decision was "scary" at the time but later proved to be the right one because he could take courses that interested him without suffering through ones that didn't. Do you think his decision to quit college was courageous? How might one drop out of college in a *non*courageous way? What do you think would be the differences?

3. Jobs says: "You have to trust in something—your gut, destiny, life, karma, whatever. This approach has never let me down." Do you think that you're capable of such deep, intuitive trust? Or is it only the talented few who can trust as Jobs did, leaving the safe path for the riskier one? What do *you* trust—and how will that factor into decisions about which jobs to pursue?

4. Given your inclination to DWYL on the one hand and the realities of data about the job market on the other, what do you expect will drive your decision about choosing a career? Are you inclined to dismiss the employment data and trust that your love of art history or nineteenth-century British literature (for instance) will eventually land you on your feet? How do you navigate between passion and practicality?

5. Jobs writes that sometimes "life hits you in the head with a brick. Don't lose faith." Dropping out of college, he says, was one of the "best" decisions he ever made. And getting fired from Apple was "the best thing that could have ever happened to me. . . . It freed me to enter one of the most creative periods of my life." Do you think Jobs's talent for finding positives in what many might call negatives can be learned? Could *you* learn it? How?

6. The last of the three "stories" Jobs shares with the graduating seniors concerns the ways that death sets life in perspective. That knowledge remained hypothetical until he was diagnosed with pancreatic cancer. With death a more tangible prospect, Jobs found the advice "Live every day as if it was your last" compelling. To what extent do you find it compelling? How would your answer affect the kind of work you will seek upon graduation?

7. The words adorning the final issue of *The Whole Earth Catalogue*: "Stay Hungry. Stay Foolish." Jobs found this to be good advice. Do you?

Do What You Love? #@&** That!

Jeff Haden

Jeff Haden is ghostwriter of more than three dozen books, many on business. He is also a columnist for CBS MoneyWatch.com, the *Shenandoah Business Journal*, and *Inc.* magazine and Inc.com, where the following appeared on November 14, 2012.

Imagine you've agreed to give advice to a group of business students but you can't think of a theme. Here's a guaranteed winner: Go with "Follow your passions...and do what you love!"

That's advice everyone loves to hear. You'll *kill*.

You'll also be wrong.

"Telling someone to follow their passion—from an entrepreneur's point of view—is disastrous," says Cal Newport, Georgetown University professor and author of *So Good They Can't Ignore You: Why Skills Trump Passion in the Search For Work You Love*. "That advice has probably resulted in more failed businesses than all the recessions combined...because that's not how the vast majority of people end up owning successful businesses."

5   "Passion is not something you follow," he adds. "Passion is something that will follow you as you put in the hard work to become valuable to the world."

Here's why.

Career Passions Are Rare

It's easy to confuse a hobby or interest for a profound passion that will result in career and business fulfillment. The reality is, that type of preexisting passion is rarely valuable.

Don't believe me? Think about something you're passionate about. Or were passionate about when you were in high school. Write it down.

Then apply this test: Will people pay you for it? Will they pay you a *lot* for it?

10   "Money matters, at least in a relative sense," Newport says. "Money is a neutral indicator of value. Potential customers don't care about your passion. Potential customers care about giving up money."

A passion people won't pay you for is hardly the basis for a career. It's a hobby. You can still love your hobbies—just love them in your spare time.

The key as an entrepreneur is to identify a *relevant* passion.

Passion Takes Time

The "hobby" passion is much different from the kind of passion you hope to find in your business career.

"Producing something important, gaining respect for it, feeling a sense of control over your life, feeling a connection to other people—that gives people a real sense of passion," Newport says.

15   Roughly speaking, work can be broken down into a job, a career, or a calling. A job pays the bills; a career is a path towards increasingly better work; a calling is work that is an important part of your life and a vital part of your identity. (Clearly most people want their work to be a calling.)

According to research, what is the strongest predictor of a person seeing her work as a calling?

The number of years spent on the job. The more experience you have the more likely you are to love your work.

Why? The more experience you have the better your skills and the greater your satisfaction in having those skills. The more experience you have the more you can see how your work has benefited others. And you've had more time to develop strong professional and even personal relationships with some of your employees, vendors, and customers.

Where business success is concerned, passion is almost always the result of time and effort. It's not a prerequisite.

Passion Is a Side Effect of Mastery

20   "The myth of the virtuoso is also a problem," Newport says. "In the majority of cases, people didn't think of someone who became a virtuoso as having unusual talent when they were very young."

Instead, most highly skilled people were exposed to something in a way that made it interesting. Take music: Something (a song, an instrument, a teacher, etc.) initially inspired them. They started learning and then benefited from what Newport describes as a feedback effect.

"If you practice hard, soon you might find you're the best in your group of students," he says. "That's great feedback and it motivates you to keep practicing. Then you're one of the best in a larger group and that's motivating too. Practice and achievement is a gradual, self-reinforcing process."

If the work is interesting and you think there's a market—meaning people will pay you for that work—that's enough to get started. Then the work itself will give you the feedback you need. Creating a viable product will motivate you to develop your skills so you can refine that product or create more products. Landing one customer will motivate you to develop more skills so you can land more customers.

The satisfaction of achieving one level of success spurs you on to gain the skills to reach the next level, and the next, and the next.

25   And one day you wake up feeling incredibly fulfilled.

"The satisfaction of improving is deeply satisfying, as eons of craftspeople will attest," Newport says. "The process of becoming really good at something valuable is a fulfilling and satisfying process in itself…and is the foundation for a great entrepreneurial career."

Working Right Trumps Finding the Right Work

Want to love what you do? Pick something interesting. Pick something financially viable—something people will pay you to do or provide.

Then work hard. Improve your skills, whether at managing, selling, creating, implementing—whatever skills your business requires. Use the satisfaction and fulfillment of small victories as motivation to keep working hard.

And as you build your company, stay focused on creating a business that will eventually provide you with a sense of respect, autonomy, and impact.

30   "Don't focus on the value your work offers *you*," Newport says. "That's the passion mindset. Instead focus on the value you produce through your work: how your actions are important, how you're good at what you do, and how you're connected to other people."

When you do, the passion will follow—and if you work hard enough, someday you'll be so good they can't ignore you.

● Discussion and Writing Suggestions   MyWritingLab™

1. Haden quotes Georgetown University professor Cal Newport: "Passion is not something you follow. Passion is something that will follow you as you put in the hard work to become valuable to the world." This conclusion is very different than Jobs's DWYL insistence that that passion *precedes* work. Which view has greater emotional appeal? Logical appeal? Cultural appeal (in the sense that one formulation is perceived as more popular or "hip" than the other)? How does the passion/mastery debate prompt differing responses to these questions?

2. Imagine yourself sitting in the audience at Stanford on June 12, 2005, when Steve Jobs delivered his famous commencement address. (If you haven't already done so, you may want to go to YouTube to watch and listen to the address: search "commencement jobs stanford.") How might the Jobs's DWYL approach be daunting to many people? How might Haden's passion-follows-mastery approach offer an easier entry to the world of work?

3. To what extent are there limits to the passion-follows-mastery formulation? Think of a job that seems tremendously *un*appealing to you but at the same time is work that is socially useful, that people would pay for, and that you could master. Could you see passion eventually emerging from such work?

4. Haden discusses a feedback loop that builds confidence in workers: Practice and early success is praised, praise induces the worker to work harder, which results in more praise, and so on until "one day you wake up feeling incredibly fulfilled." Assuming that the path Haden describes actually leads to fulfillment, consider two questions: Is fulfillment in work a sufficient goal for you? To what extent is fulfillment the same thing as passion? Use these questions to reflect on what it is you *want* from work.

5. "Don't focus on the value your work offers *you*," Newport says. "That's the passion mindset. Instead focus on the value you produce through your work: how your actions are important, how you're good at what you do, and how you're connected to other people." Does the work experience of anyone you know validate Newport's view? Explain.

6. "Working right trumps finding the right work." What does Haden mean? Do you agree?

DEAR GRADS: DON'T DO WHAT YOU LOVE

Carl McCoy

Carl McCoy is a Boston-based writer and musician who studied at Tufts University, Oxford University, and the Johns Hopkins School of Advanced International Studies. This selection first appeared in the *Wall Street Journal* on May 28, 2013.

This month, commencement speakers across the country are exhorting graduates not to settle. They are urged instead to find their passion—to "do what you love." But is this the best advice for college students entering a tough labor market?

For those grads who do get jobs, the work will often be low-paying, with little in the way of long-term prospects. Some will soon go on to better jobs, but many will stay in these "day jobs" for years, waiting for their big break, waiting to be discovered—or simply waiting to find out what exactly it is that they truly love.

"Do what you love" is an important message, but it's unwise to build a career on the notion that we should all be paid for our passions. The advice captures only part of the story. It tells us how excellent work might be accomplished—by loving it—but it doesn't tell us why the work should be done. What is the point of all the effort? What is being worked toward?

The answer lies in working with a deeper sense of purpose or vocation. You don't need to be a religious or spiritual person to tap into this higher purpose; it can be derived from a sense of community and a desire to pull together. Yet without such a higher purpose where all this love and ambition can be directed, we don't have a very useful guidepost for meaningful success. We simply have a call to discover what it is that we love, and then to do it.

5   Sure, there are many people doing what they genuinely love. But how many of us love just one thing? It's romantic to imagine that each person is destined for a particular career path, one capable of being discovered with sufficient soul-searching. But most people have multifaceted interests and abilities and could probably be successful and happy in several fields.

Then there are those who love things that will never pay very well. As someone who has tried living as a starving artist, I can attest that there's nothing romantic or noble about being impoverished in pursuit of doing what you love. When you're working two or three jobs, and you can't pay your bills, it doesn't matter how much you love any of them. You just get worn out.

Maybe there's another way to encourage new college graduates to think about their careers. Maybe all those commencement speakers would send more young people into the world likelier to be happy in their jobs if the speakers talked about love as a consequence of meaningful work instead of as the motivation for it.

Does the doctor love going into the hospital to see a patient in the middle of the night? Does the firefighter love entering a burning building? Does the teacher love trying to control a classroom full of disrespectful children? Not likely. But the work is performed with a sense of purpose that "love" doesn't capture.

We don't all have to become first responders or social workers. And we can't all find jobs with such obvious benefits to society. When diplomas are being handed out, though, it might be worthwhile for graduates—and the rest of us—if the popular "do what you love" message were balanced with a more timeless message to find work that, even in some small way, truly matters.

● Discussion and Writing Suggestions   MyWritingLab™

1. McCoy writes that "work [can be] performed with a sense of purpose that 'love' doesn't capture." What does he mean? What are the differences between working for "love" and working for a "purpose"?

2. To what extent is the work McCoy advocates focused on the world and its needs (call it outer-directed)? To what extent is this work driven by passion focused on the worker (call it inner-directed)? Is a particular job inherently more interesting to you or more worthy of your interest? Explain.

3. Commencement speakers often urge graduates not to *settle* (see McCoy's first paragraph). Given a tough job market, is it reasonable to hold out for what McCoy calls "work that, even in some small way, truly matters"? What if the only job open to you pays the rent and your student loans but doesn't address your need for meaning and/or passion? In what other endeavors might you seek meaning and passion?

4. How important is finding a job "that, even in some small way, truly matters" to you? Do you believe that one can find meaning, even nobility, in *any* job? Have you observed someone you know finding such meaning in what most would consider a routine, even menial job?

In the Name of Love

Miya Tokumitsu

Miya Tokumitsu holds a doctorate in art history from the University of Pennsylvania. Her critique of the Do-What-You-Love approach to work generated a great deal of media coverage on its publication in early 2014. "In the Name of Love" first appeared in *Jacobin* magazine, "a leading voice of the American left, offering socialist perspectives on politics, economics, and culture."

This essay is challenging but worth the effort, as it offers a smart, politically charged analysis of who actually gets to "do what they love" in our economy. Notably, Tokumitsu's reasons for disagreeing with the much-quoted advice of Steve Jobs differ from those of Jeff Haden and Carl McCoy. Considered together, these three critics offer a formidable front against the view of work that Jobs encourages; but Jobs, of course, a famously opinionated man, can hold his own. What is your view? We've glossed difficult vocabulary and formulations in Tokumitsu to ease your way.

There's little doubt that "do what you love" (DWYL) is now the unofficial work mantra for our time. The problem is that it leads not to salvation, but to the devaluation of actual work, including the very work it pretends to elevate—and more importantly, the dehumanization of the vast majority of laborers.[1]

Superficially, DWYL is an uplifting piece of advice, urging us to ponder what it is we most enjoy doing and then turn that activity into a wage-generating enterprise. But why should our pleasure be for profit? Who is the audience for this dictum? Who is not?

By keeping us focused on ourselves and our individual happiness, DWYL distracts us from the working conditions of others while validating our own choices and relieving us from obligations to all who labor, whether or not they love it. It is the secret handshake of the privileged and a worldview that disguises its elitism as noble self-betterment. According to this way of thinking, labor is not something one does for compensation, but an act of self-love. If profit doesn't happen to follow, it is because the worker's passion and determination were insufficient. Its real achievement is making workers believe their labor serves the self and not the marketplace.[2]

5   Aphorisms have numerous origins and reincarnations, but the generic and hackneyed nature of DWYL confounds precise attribution. Oxford Reference[3] links the phrase and variants of it to Martina Navratilova and François Rabelais,[4]

---

[1]This is Tokumitsu's thesis. As you read, bear in mind the following question: In what ways does working at what you love devalue work and/or dehumanize workers?

[2]This key paragraph is worth reading several times, until you are confident you understand each sentence. Much of the rest of the argument rests on what Tokumitsu states here. Of special note is Tokumitsu's phrase "act of self-love." Jobs worked so hard at getting Apple products right less out of *self*-love than because he had a passion to get the products just right—for him an act of love, but love of the task and the final product, not love of himself.

[3]Oxford Reference: an online database of Oxford University Press's dictionaries and encyclopedias.

[4]Martina Navratilova and François Rabelais: respectively, a famous twentieth- and twenty-first-century tennis player and a famous sixteenth-century French Renaissance writer and doctor. Tokumitsu is saying, in effect, that we can't pinpoint the origins of the expression DWYL.

among others. The internet frequently attributes it to Confucius, locating it in a misty, Orientalized past. Oprah Winfrey and other peddlers of positivity have included it in their repertoires for decades, but the most important recent evangelist of the DWYL creed is deceased Apple CEO Steve Jobs.

His graduation speech to the Stanford University class of 2005 provides as good an origin myth as any, especially since Jobs had already been beatified as the patron saint of aestheticized work[5] well before his early death. In the speech, Jobs recounts the creation of Apple, and inserts this reflection:

> You've got to find what you love. And that is as true for your work as it is for your lovers. Your work is going to fill a large part of your life, and the only way to be truly satisfied is to do what you believe is great work. And the only way to do great work is to love what you do.

In these four sentences, the words "you" and "your" appear eight times. This focus on the individual is hardly surprising coming from Jobs, who cultivated a very specific image of himself as a worker: inspired, casual, passionate—all states agreeable with ideal romantic love. Jobs telegraphed the conflation of his besotted worker-self with his company so effectively that his black turtleneck and blue jeans became metonyms for all of Apple and the labor that maintains it.[6]

But by portraying Apple as a labor of his individual love, Jobs [ignored] the labor of untold thousands in Apple's factories, conveniently hidden from sight on the other side of the planet — the very labor that allowed Jobs to actualize his love.

The violence of this erasure needs to be exposed. While "do what you love" sounds harmless and precious, it is ultimately self-focused to the point of narcissism. Jobs' formulation of "do what you love" is the depressing antithesis to Henry David Thoreau's utopian vision of labor for all. In "Life Without Principle," Thoreau wrote,

> . . . . it would be good economy for a town to pay its laborers so well that they would not feel that they were working for low ends, as for a livelihood merely, but for scientific, even moral ends. Do not hire a man who does your work for money, but him who does it for the love of it.

10   Admittedly, Thoreau had little feel for the proletariat (it's hard to imagine someone washing diapers for "scientific, even moral ends," no matter how well-paid).[7] But he nonetheless maintains that society has a stake in making work well-compensated and meaningful. By contrast, the twenty-first-century Jobsian view demands that we all turn inward. It absolves us of any obligation to or

---

[5]That is, work in which one finds beauty and meaning.

[6]"Besotted" means drunk or obsessed. In this context Tokumitsu suggests that Jobs was intoxicated with the idea of himself as a passionate worker. "Metonym" is an object that stands in place for, and suggests, some other object, entity, or idea. For instance, a scepter suggests a king or queen. One look at Jobs's black turtleneck and jeans and people thought Apple Computer.

[7]The "proletariat": the working-class wage earner who, according to Karl Marx, does not own property.

acknowledgment of the wider world, underscoring its fundamental betrayal of all workers, whether they consciously embrace it or not.

One consequence of this isolation is the division that DWYL creates among workers, largely along class lines. Work becomes divided into two opposing classes: that which is lovable (creative, intellectual, socially prestigious) and that which is not (repetitive, unintellectual, undistinguished). Those in the lovable work camp are vastly more privileged in terms of wealth, social status, education, society's racial biases, and political clout, while comprising a small minority of the workforce.

For those forced into unlovable work, it's a different story. Under the DWYL credo, labor that is done out of motives or needs other than love (which is, in fact, most labor) is not only demeaned but erased. As in Jobs' Stanford speech, unlovable but socially necessary work is banished from the spectrum of consciousness altogether.

Think of the great variety of work that allowed Jobs to spend even one day as CEO: his food harvested from fields, then transported across great distances. His company's goods assembled, packaged, shipped. Apple advertisements scripted, cast, filmed. Lawsuits processed. Office wastebaskets emptied and ink cartridges filled. Job creation goes both ways. Yet with the vast majority of workers effectively invisible to elites busy in their lovable occupations, how can it be surprising that the heavy strains faced by today's workers (abysmal wages, massive child care costs, et cetera) barely register as political issues even among the liberal faction of the ruling class?

In ignoring most work and reclassifying the rest as love, DWYL may be the most elegant anti-worker ideology around. Why should workers assemble and assert their class interests if there's no such thing as work?[8]

15   "Do what you love" disguises the fact that being able to choose a career primarily for personal reward is an unmerited privilege, a sign of that person's socioeconomic class. Even if a self-employed graphic designer had parents who could pay for art school and cosign a lease for a slick Brooklyn apartment, she can self-righteously bestow DWYL as career advice to those covetous of her success.

If we believe that working as a Silicon Valley entrepreneur or a museum publicist or a think-tank acolyte is essential to being true to ourselves — in fact, to loving ourselves — what do we believe about the inner lives and hopes of those who clean hotel rooms and stock shelves at big-box stores? The answer is: nothing.

Yet arduous, low-wage work is what ever more Americans do and will be doing. According to the U.S. Bureau of Labor Statistics, the two fastest-growing

---

[8]Here Tokumitsu is referencing labor movements in which workers with common interests band together ("assemble") to assert their rights and win concessions such as improved wages, health care, and so on. The relatively few DWYL workers in principle have no reason to protest working conditions because they love their work. To focus on the relatively few DWYL workers, however, ignores most workers—for instance, the very people who assemble iPhones for Apple Inc. These workers *do* have grievances and could stand improvements in the working conditions. But if only DWYL work gets talked about and honored, if only DWYL work is the work that matters culturally, then the rest of the workforce, with its very real needs, gets ignored. Ultimately, this is an "anti-worker ideology" says Tokumitsu. It's a political problem that divides workers along class lines: those who have the resources to do DWYL work, and those who don't.

occupations projected until 2020 are "Personal Care Aide" and "Home Care Aide," with average salaries of $19,640 per year and $20,560 per year in 2010, respectively. Elevating certain types of professions to something worthy of love necessarily denigrates the labor of those who do unglamorous work that keeps society functioning, especially the crucial work of caregivers.

• • •

Ironically, DWYL reinforces exploitation even within the so-called lovable professions where off-the-clock, underpaid, or unpaid labor is the new norm: reporters required to do the work of their laid-off photographers, publicists expected to Pin and Tweet on weekends, the 46 percent of the workforce expected to check their work email on sick days. Nothing makes exploitation go down easier than convincing workers that they are doing what they love.

Instead of crafting a nation of self-fulfilled, happy workers, our DWYL era has seen the rise of…the unpaid intern—people persuaded to work for cheap or free, or even for a net loss of wealth. This has certainly been the case for all those interns working for college credit or those who actually purchase ultra-desirable fashion-house internships at auction. (Valentino and Balenciaga are among a handful of houses that auctioned off month-long internships. For charity, of course.) The latter is worker exploitation taken to its most extreme, and as an ongoing ProPublica[9] investigation reveals, the unpaid intern is an ever larger presence in the American workforce.

20   It should be no surprise that unpaid interns abound in fields that are highly socially desirable, including fashion, media, and the arts. These industries have long been accustomed to masses of employees willing to work for social currency instead of actual wages, all in the name of love. Excluded from these opportunities, of course, is the overwhelming majority of the population: those who need to work for wages. This exclusion not only calcifies economic and professional immobility, but insulates these industries from the full diversity of voices society has to offer.[10]

• • •

Do what you love and you'll never work a day in your life! Before succumbing to the intoxicating warmth of that promise, it's critical to ask, "Who, exactly, benefits from making work feel like non-work?" "Why *should* workers feel as if they aren't working when they are?" Historian Mario Liverani reminds us that

---

[9]From the ProPublica Web site: "ProPublica is an independent, non-profit newsroom that produces investigative journalism in the public interest."

[10]Here Tokumitsu argues that people who need to earn money can't afford to work as unpaid interns at jobs associated most often with DWYL. One result: Social immobility, as wage earners can't cross the divide to "lovable" work, at least not as interns. Another result: Companies that hire unpaid interns suffer from cultural uniformity—they don't get to hear and learn from diverse, fresh voices frozen out of the intern market.

"ideology has the function of presenting exploitation in a favorable light to the exploited, as advantageous to the disadvantaged."[11]

In masking the very exploitative mechanisms of labor that it fuels, DWYL is, in fact, the most perfect ideological tool of capitalism. It shunts aside the labor of others and disguises our own labor to ourselves. It hides the fact that if we acknowledged all of our work as work, we could set appropriate limits for it, demanding fair compensation and humane schedules that allow for family and leisure time.

And if we did that, more of us could get around to doing what it is we *really* love.

---

[11]In this essay, Tokumitsu has characterized DWYL as an "ideology"—that is, as a belief system. As any belief system, this one has consequences for the people who adopt it. In a capitalist system, writes Tokumitsu (who quotes historian Liverani to make her point), the DWYL "ideology" favors the employer who can underpay (or, in the case of interns, *not* pay) workers who themselves accept the proposition that as long as they are doing what they love, they don't really *need* to get paid. The workers are duped into thinking they actually benefit from the arrangement, but they are actually being exploited. Their "disadvantage" is being sold to them as an "advantage." As for the wage laborers who don't work at DWYL jobs, the ideology ignores them altogether. Culturally, they disappear.

● Review Questions   MyWritingLab™

1. According to Tokumitsu, how can DWYL make us insensitive to the working conditions of others?

2. How does DWYL divide workers along class lines?

3. Tokumitsu writes: "labor that is done out of motives or needs other than love (which is, in fact, most labor) is not only demeaned but erased." What does she mean?

4. DWYL is ultimately an "anti-worker ideology," according to Tokumitsu. Why?

5. Tokumitsu quotes Historian Mario Liverani: "ideology has the function of presenting exploitation in a favorable light to the exploited, as advantageous to the disadvantaged." What does Liverani mean?

● Discussion and Writing Suggestions   MyWritingLab™

1. Early on, Tokumitsu asks, "Why should our pleasure be for profit?" It's a good question. Why or why not?

2. Tokumitsu claims that only the wealthy can afford to be self-actualized at work—and to do what they love. Do you agree? Explain.

3. Tokumitsu asks us to consider that while the privileged few are doing what they love, an entire army of low-wage workers is supporting them: truck drivers

delivering goods, day laborers picking fruit, custodians cleaning bathrooms, food preparers making our meals, and so on. Such labor is largely invisible to us, says Tokumitsu. Have you ever found yourself wondering about the daily lives of those who make it possible for you to enjoy yourself, either at work or at leisure? Discuss.

4. Tokumitsu writes: "If we believe that working as a Silicon Valley entrepreneur or a museum publicist or a think-tank acolyte is essential to being true to ourselves—in fact, to loving ourselves—what do we believe about the inner lives and hopes of those who clean hotel rooms and stock shelves at big-box stores? The answer is: nothing." This is an explosive accusation. Do you agree? Discuss.

5. Have you ever worked as an intern, unpaid or otherwise? Did you feel exploited? Did your internship "disguise" your own labor to you in any sense? (See Tokumitsu's last paragraph.)

6. Tokumitsu presents a radical thesis. Restate it as directly as you can and discuss it with classmates. To what extent do you agree with her? Provide reasons to defend your position.

SYNTHESIS ACTIVITIES   MyWritingLab™

1. Write an explanatory synthesis that reviews the impacts of globalization and technology, especially "big data," on the twenty-first-century workplace. What jobs are most—and least—at risk from these two forces? In developing your paper, draw especially on the selections by Blinder and Peck.

    Write an explanatory synthesis that reviews the current trends in the contemporary job market. In developing this paper, draw upon the material in this chapter—especially the graphs, charts, and tables and the selections by Malcolm, Cappelli, and Blinder.

2. Steve Jobs was able to parlay doing what he loved into one of the largest fortunes in the country, largely because there turned out to be such huge demand for the products he loved imagining and developing. But for most young people contemplating occupations for which the demand is limited or minimal, this will not be the case. Imagine the woman who loves hiking in the great outdoors and wants to be a park ranger or the man who gets a thrill going on anthropological digs. For them, there will be no financial bonanza—even if they're successful in the work they love, assuming they're fortunate enough to find work. Many young people who follow their passion, as Jobs advises, will earn a modest living. So the question for each individual is, how important is the daily job in providing meaning and satisfaction in life?

    Should you do what you love and accustom yourself to a modest lifetime wage or, worse, risk perpetual financial uncertainty? Or should you take a job that pays well but does not particularly excite you, and then seek meaning and fulfillment elsewhere—say, in family, an absorbing avocation, a faith community, or volunteer work? Write an argument that takes a position on the

Do What You Love debate, using the sources in this chapter to support your claim. See especially the Steve Jobs commencement speech and the responses to it by Haden, McCoy, and Tokumitsu.

3. In terms of getting a well-paying job, a college degree is now more necessary than ever. (On this point, see especially the first Pew Research graph.) What are the pluses and minuses of this new reality? In developing your answer, you might reflect on the jobs and economic situations of your parents and grandparents.

4. Alan Blinder writes that current trends in the job market suggest that "[m]ore vocational education is probably . . . in order." Peter Cappelli writes that the "trend toward specialized, vocational degrees is understandable, with an increasing number of companies grumbling that graduates aren't coming out of school qualified to work. . . . But guessing about what will be hot tomorrow based on what's hot today is often a fool's errand."

   The difference of opinion here concerns the wisdom of specialized training. If you train too narrowly and choose the wrong field, you run the risk of the job market leaving you behind. But if you train too broadly, you may lack the specific skills to qualify you for available jobs. (Just ask an art history major.) Having read the selections in this chapter, how would you advise a recent high school graduate trying to decide between a two-year vocational school and a four-year college? Write that person a letter, and support the advice you offer by referring to the selections in this chapter.

5. How do the selections in this chapter illustrate the serious reality underlying "A Post-College Flow Chart of Misery and Pain" by Jenna Brager? The graphic prompts both a smile and a groan. Why? At the risk of destroying a good laugh by analyzing it to death, how can the selections by Blinder, Cappelli, Tokumitsu, and/or Malcolm and the chapter's graphs, charts, and tables help you appreciate Brager's humor? Note that this explanatory synthesis requires summarizing Brager's graphic and analyzing her humor.

6. What kind of workers are likeliest to succeed in the new economy? Write an explanatory synthesis that presents the likely attributes for success as suggested in the chapter's graphs, charts, and tables and as discussed by Blinder, Malcolm, Cappelli, Peck, and Tokumitsu. (Concerning Peck, how comfortable are you in allowing computers to assess these attributes?) In the second part of your paper, analyze your own prospects for workplace success based on these same attributes. Respond, particularly, to two questions: To what extent do you currently possess these attributes? And to what extent will your intended course of study prepare you to develop these attributes?

7. Many analysts agree with British sociologist Richard Sennett, who writes that "a young American with at least two years of college can expect to change jobs at least eleven times in the course of working, and change his or her skill base at least three times during those forty years of labor." Assuming the accuracy of this claim, how can a college student like you prepare for a life of work in which change is constant?

Address the following tension in your paper: On the one hand, you can major in a subject that leads you to master a particular skill (like engineering) that's in current demand in the workplace. (On this point, see Malcolm and the chapter's graphs, charts, and tables.) On the other hand, assuming that the economy will require you to change skill sets (see Cappelli), you'll need broader training. What mix of specific and general skills will you seek in order to prepare yourself for the labor force of the twenty-first century? Develop your response into an argument synthesis.

8. The graphs, tables, and charts in this chapter make clear that students who major in the liberal arts have more trouble finding jobs post-graduation than do those who major in more skills-specific subjects, like engineering. Moreover, when liberal arts majors do find work, they tend to earn less than their counterparts. Why, then, do you think that, against all current employment trends, students continue to major in the liberal arts? What's the value of such an education in a work environment such as the one you now face? Develop your answer into an argument synthesis. Draw on the authors in this chapter—especially Brager, Cappelli, Jobs, Haden, Tokumitsu, and McCoy—to help you make your case. (As part of your argument, consider referencing Sennett's observation about changing "skill sets," as detailed in Synthesis Activity 7.)

9. Draw upon the selections in this chapter to identify a job that will (a) not likely be lost to outsourcing, (b) not likely be lost to computerization, and (c) pay reasonably well. To make this selection, draw upon the graphs, charts, and tables gathered in the chapter.

   Having identified this job, devote some time to understanding it: What's the industry sector, what's the product, what are the responsibilities, the skill sets required, and so on? (A good place to begin this review would be the "Occupation Finder" on the Bureau of Labor Statistics Web site.) Then, following Jeff Haden's argument that passion follows mastery, discuss whether or not you could see yourself pursuing this job, mastering it, and, in time, becoming passionate about it. Write a two-part paper that explains the process of defining the job and then argues for the wisdom (and/or practicality) of actually pursuing it.

RESEARCH ACTIVITIES   MyWritingLab™

1. Interview several workers you know who are in their forties or, preferably, in their fifties. Ask them to describe changes they've seen in the workplace and how they're adapting to these changes. Frame the results of your interview in the context of several of the readings in this chapter. That is, use the readings to help make sense of the information you record in the interviews. Your research paper could take the form of an argument or an analysis.

2. Take a thorough accounting of the "Occupational Outlook Handbook" at the Bureau of Labor Statistics Web site. Prepare a report that presents

(1) the range of information available at the OOH site and closely linked sites; (2) a strategy for mining useful information. Essentially, you will be preparing a "user's guide" to the OOH.

3. Find a copy of Studs Terkel's *Working*, select one of the interviewees reporting on his or her experiences at a particular job, and research the current status of this job or career field at the Bureau of Labor Statistics Web site. Compare and contrast the experiences of the Terkel subject (mid-1970s) with those of a present-day worker.

4. Visit the career counseling office at your school; interview one or more of the staff people there, and survey the publications available at the office to determine facts about the interests and employment prospects of the student body at your school. Write a report on the success your fellow students have had in securing internships at local businesses or job placements with local employers.

5. Research the impact "big data" is having on the workplace. You might begin by reading Viktor Mayer-Schönberger's and Kenneth Cukier's *Big Data: A Revolution That Will Transform How We Live, Work, and Think* (2013).

6. Trace the changing attitudes toward work in Western culture. Authors of interest will likely include Herbert Applebaum, Melvin Kranzberg and Joseph Gies, Richard Donkin, and Joanne Ciulla.

7. Research the origins of the Puritan work ethic and its persistence in American culture. Puritans, writes Melvin Kranzberg, "regard[ed] the accumulation of material wealth through labor as a sign of God's favor as well as of the individual's religious fervor." Be sure, in your research, to look at *The Protestant Ethic and the Spirit of Capitalism* by economist and sociologist Max Weber.

8. Research and report on one jobs-related aspect of the "Great Recession" of December 2007–June 2009, the most significant downturn in the American economy since the Great Depression of the 1930s. Here are five jobs-related topics on which you might report: "underemployment"; the fate of older laid-off workers; the impact of the recession on American youth employment; job losses in the industries and businesses hardest hit by the recession; the emergence of "Top 10" (or 8 or 20, etc.) lists of "recession-proof" jobs.

MyWritingLab™   Visit Ch. 12 Work in the Twenty-First Century in MyWritingLab to test your understanding of the chapter objectives.

Chapter 13

Have You Heard This?
The Latest on Rumor

Beneath the streets of New York City, countless alligators live in the sewers. Entire packs of these menacing reptiles roam the subterranean waterways, waiting to swallow unsuspecting citizens above. These are no ordinary alligators. Flushed down toilets after growing too large for their owners, fed on an endless supply of New York City rats and trash shoved from the streets into grates, they are huge, fearsome creatures. No one has actually seen these nightmarish beasts, but they are certainly lurking below, their sharp teeth just hidden from view.

The alligator rumor might be the high concept for a horror movie if it were true. But of course it isn't. This classic story is a quintessential rumor, having developed over the decades into urban legend. As it circulated and gradually took hold of public consciousness, it became, for many, as good as fact. Then, both New Yorkers and tourists began nervously watching their toes as they approached sewer grates.

How fast do rumors spread? Consider a math problem: On January 1, you tell a story to a couple of your friends. On January 2, each of your friends tells two others. On January 3, each of these tells two more. And so on, for twenty days. The spread of the rumor during the first two days can be diagrammed as follows (P = person):

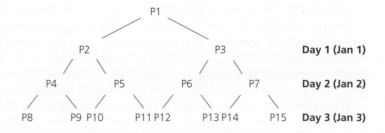

By the 20th of January, how many people will know the rumor? Answer: 2,097,151.

At some moment, a spreading rumor eventually crosses what rumor expert Cass Sunstein calls a "tipping point," the point at which so many people believe the story that it's hard to separate rumor from reality. The alligator rumor began in the 1920s but didn't reach that key moment until it hit fever pitch in the early 1980s. Of course, during the first few decades of this intervening period, there was no TV, much less cable news, and the Internet didn't become an efficient agent of rumor spreading until the '90s. Otherwise, the tipping point for the Big Apple's subterranean alligators would likely have been reached much earlier.

Reconsider the math problem above, which assumes one-day-at-a-time distribution via word of mouth. How would the same problem work in the digital age? In 2012, we can e-mail an entire address book with a simple touch of the "Send" button or "share" with all of our Facebook friends with a quick tap of "Enter." Within seconds, minutes, or hours, a rumor can "go viral," moving from a whispered piece of gossip to an e-mail chain, a Twitter feed, or a recurring story on cable news. As the transition from rumor to perceived reality becomes near-instantaneous, rumors become virtually uncontrollable, both by those who originate them and those who are targeted.

What do rumors tell us about those who start and spread them? Or, as psychologist Nicholas DiFonzo asks, "What is it about being human that sets the stage for rumor activity?" As you will discover in this chapter, rumors can be understood as expressions of our collective fears, hopes, and attitudes about the community and the world we live in. They are outward signs of the way we view one another, individually and in groups. They help us make sense of a sometimes confusing or threatening world by confirming the truth of our world views or our beliefs about how particular groups of people behave. Some rumors encapsulate what Robert H. Knapp calls our "pipe dreams"—our fervent, if unrealistic, hopes. Others offer thinly veiled covers for our anxieties, our concerns about the bad things that might happen. They often confirm what we already believe to be true (even if it isn't). They also drive further apart individuals and groups who are already suspicious of one another. In examining rumors, we discern the psychological, emotional, and intellectual life of our personal and business relationships, our popular culture, our politics, and our society.

Consider political rumors, which often arise out of fears about what a president or political party might do unless stopped. During the health care debate of 2009, so many rumors were competing for public attention (among them, the government's "death panels") that the White House eventually created a Web site to attempt to set the record straight. Two years later, President Obama felt compelled to release his long-form birth certificate to put to rest the stubbornly persistent rumor that he was not born in the United States. But as *Los Angeles Times* columnist Gregory Rodriguez explains, once we accept as true a rumor that is supported by our own belief system, even hard evidence is unlikely to sway us. The release of the president's birth certificate counted for nothing to some of his opponents, who went to great lengths to explain why the released document was not real or was of suspect origin.

The falsehoods about Barack Obama's citizenship are the most prominent recent manifestations of rumor in American presidential politics. As former John

McCain presidential campaign manager Richard H. Davis explains, political rumors have long been a feature of American history. During the 1828 presidential campaign, supporters of Andrew Jackson spread a rumor that his opponent, incumbent president John Quincy Adams, had procured an American woman to provide sexual services for the czar of Russia. Later that century, rumors circulated that Abraham Lincoln was actually the illegitimate son of a Smoky Mountain man named Abram Elroe. Other presidential rumors are rooted in religious bigotry: that Lincoln was a Catholic, that Franklin Roosevelt was a Jew, that Barack Obama is a Muslim. Among the more bizarre recent political rumors was the Clinton "body count," a list of more than fifty suspicious deaths of colleagues, friends, advisors, and other citizens who were allegedly preparing to testify against the Clintons in the wake of the Monica Lewinsky scandal.

Rumors driven by anxiety, fear, and prejudice also proliferate in the immediate wake of national disasters. After the Japanese attack on Pearl Harbor in December 1941, rumors spread that Roosevelt and Churchill had actually plotted the raids as a pretext for U.S. entry into World War II, and even that some of the attacking airplanes were piloted by British and American flyers. After 9/11, rumors spread that the American and Israeli governments were involved in planning the attacks on the World Trade Center and the Pentagon, and that 4,000 Jews stayed home from work that day because they had been told in advance of the targeting of the twin towers. (In fact, such beliefs are almost conventional wisdom among many in the Middle East.)

Many other rumors are focused on the personal—on what is happening, or what could happen, to ordinary people: Dave and his next door neighbor are having a fling; the company where we work is closing down next month (or, if actually scheduled to close down, will stay in business, after all); school jobs in the community are being given to illegal aliens from Jamaica; vaccinations cause autism (or cancer); or—to look back at our model analysis in Chapter 6—travelers abroad who are rash enough pick up sexual companions in lounges risk having their kidneys surgically removed.

In the following pages, then, we explore this problematic but ubiquitous phenomenon of rumor. Among our chief concerns:

- How and why do rumors start?
- How do rumors spread? What are their mechanisms, and what can we do to stop them—or at least to neutralize them?
- Why do rumors spread? Why are people apt to believe them, even when the evidence suggests they are false? How may rumors confirm what people already believe or suspect to be true?
- In what ways do people use rumors for professional or personal gain?
- What do our rumors suggest about *us*?

The chapter consists of three types of selections: works of art or literature, case studies of particular rumors, and theoretical or reflective pieces that attempt to explain how rumors work. The works of art serve as bookends to the chapter.

We begin with the famous *Saturday Evening Post* cover "The Gossips" by the beloved American painter Norman Rockwell, which vividly—and humorously—illustrates the communal spread of rumor. We end by directing readers online to a short story by John Updike, famed chronicler of twentieth-century middle-class suburban angst. In "The Rumor," Updike creates a tale of a long-married couple dealing in unexpected ways with an amusing but potentially damaging rumor.

The case studies offer extended examples of particular rumors. "Frankenchicken," from the popular myth-debunking Web site Snopes.com, discusses one of the first Internet-fueled rumors, the supposedly genetically modified chicken offered by a popular fast food chain. In "The Runaway Grandmother," Jan Harold Brunvand discusses numerous versions of an urban legend about what happened to grandma after her body was mounted on top of the car. In "Fighting that Old Devil Rumor," Sandra Salmans explores the supposed satanic logo of a major American company. And Ian Glenn's "Paul is Dead (said Fred)" traces the life of a Beatle rumor.

The theoretical selections attempt to explain how and why rumors work and how they can be fought. In "Anatomy of a Rumor: It Flies on Fear," Daniel Goleman discusses the role of anxiety in rumor creation and propagation, particularly concerning the spread of rumors about disease and death. In "Truth is in the Ear of the Beholder," Gregory Rodriguez examines how we accept rumors that confirm our world view and reject facts that don't. The classic "A Psychology of Rumor" by Robert H. Knapp explores three particular types of rumor and their causes and responds to the question "What are the qualities that make for a good rumor?" In "How and Why Rumors Work—And How to Stop Them," psychologist Nicholas DiFonzo explores the ways in which rumors help us make sense of a complex and sometimes threatening world. And, finally, to follow up on our set of political rumors, Jesse Singal discusses in "How to Fight a Rumor" the evolutionary basis of the kinds of rumors that have long plagued politicians and other public figures, along with some suggestions for fighting them.

Together, these selections should help you understand rumors in many of their forms and venues: why they're created, how they work, and how we all contribute to their enduring power.

THE GOSSIPS

Norman Rockwell

As children, most of us have played the "telephone game." One person shares a piece of information with a friend, who tells it to another, who tells it to another, and so on. By the time the last person hears the news, the original story has changed into something else entirely. "The sky is blue" can turn somewhere along the line into "the sky is going to fall on you." In the painting below, which originally appeared as the cover of the March 6, 1948, edition of the *Saturday Evening Post*, Norman Rockwell (1894–1978) humorously traces this kind of error-compounding pattern.

One of America's most beloved artists, Rockwell created quintessential, wholesome, and often whimsical images of American life, many of them originally appearing in the *Saturday Evening Post* (322 of his paintings were published as *Post* covers over a period of 47 years). As his career progressed, Rockwell began to explore the complex issues of his time: civil rights, poverty, and even space travel. His critics sometimes accused him of idealizing and sentimentalizing American life; but Rockwell's reputation has grown in recent years, culminating with exhibitions in art museums in New York, Washington, Raleigh, Chicago, Phoenix, Tacoma, and San Diego, as well as in the White House. Whether depicting an archetypal Thanksgiving meal, a father seeing his son off to military service, or a young African-American girl accompanied by federal marshals as she enrolls in a previously all-white school, Rockwell's work indelibly memorialized mainstream American life. In "The Gossips," he shows the sometimes amusing, sometimes insidious play of that most mainstream of American, indeed human, activities—rumor.

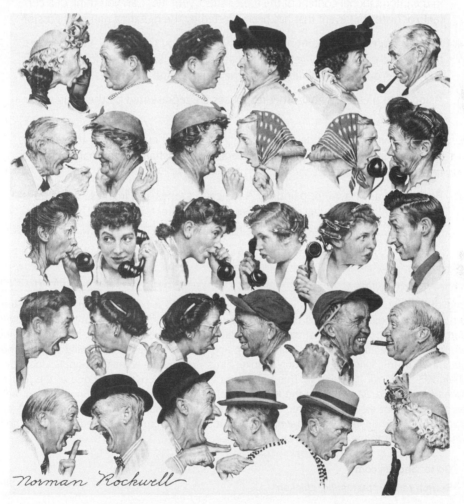

Printed by permission of the Norman Rockwell Family Agency, Copyright © 1948 The Norman Rockwell Family Entities.

● Discussion and Writing Suggestions   MyWritingLab™

1. Rockwell's painting is called "The Gossips." In your own mind and experience, what are the main similarities and differences between gossip and rumor?

2. Most of us have found ourselves in a situation similar to the one Rockwell portrays here, at least once in our lives. Where was your placement in the line? How did the initial message change during the course of the communication?

3. When a piece of information is transmitted on a wave of gossip, the content of that information—its meaning and implications—often changes drastically. Think about an event from your own life affected by a rumor. In what ways did changes in the informational content of the rumor affect your life? Can you think of a current (or historical) event that has been affected by the mutating nature of gossip?

4. Several figures in this painting are clearly pleased by the gossip. Why do you think some people enjoy getting and passing along salacious information (of sometimes dubious reliability) about their friends and neighbors?

5. Aside from pleasure, what other responses are represented by the figures in the painting?

6. The last two figures in the painting suggest that the end result of the gossip is negative. Can you think of any *positive* aspects of sharing information in this manner?

7. Rockwell was known for painting "American" scenes and images. What does this particular piece suggest about American culture—at least in the era (the late 1940s) when this painting was created?

FRANKENCHICKEN

One of life's guilty pleasures is occasionally digging into a plate of crispy fried chicken. But suppose someone told you that what you were eagerly ingesting wasn't really chicken, but a "frankenfood" bird, genetically engineered to have shrunken bones, no beak, and no feet and to be technologically optimized for preparing and cooking? According to the rumor described in the following selection, frankenbirds are exactly what the popular fast food chain KFC uses for its chicken. This rumor has the distinction of being one of the first to spread worldwide via e-mail. In the following selection, the popular site Snopes.com tackles this rampant early Internet rumor and explains why it was just that—a rumor, not the truth. A vast cornucopia of fascinating rumor lore, Snopes.com was formed in 1995 to help Web surfers get to the bottom of online rumors.

Go to: Snopes.com

Search terms: *"tastes like chicken"*

● Review Questions   MyWritingLab™

1. As it worked its way across the Internet, many people accepted this apparently absurd rumor without question. Why did they find it so plausible? What "facts" were offered in support?

2. What elements of the story (e.g., about corporate practices and corporate deception) seemed reasonable to readers and to those spreading the rumor?

3. While this rumor implies a distrust of corporate practices, how does it also reflect a lack of faith in government?

4. In what ways did contemporary scientific developments contribute to this particular rumor?

● Discussion and Writing Suggestions   MyWritingLab™

1. Reading about this rumor in hindsight can make it seem absurd. But plenty of people believed it when it worked its way across the Internet. Why do you think that people found it so plausible?

2. The piece alludes to other popular fast food restaurant rumors, including worms at McDonald's and roaches at Taco Bell. What other restaurant-focused rumors have you heard? Did you believe them? Why or why not?

3. Snopes.com offers some reasons for the spread of this rumor. Which reason seems most persuasive—and why? What might motivate someone to help spread a rumor like this?

4. Considering how quickly Internet stories can spread, a company can find itself on the wrong side of a rumor in the blink of an eye. If you were running a business, how would you respond to this sort of rumor? (For instance, would you respond at all?)

5. Clearly, the KFC rumor may have affected the public's eating patterns—or at least those of a segment of the population. Have you ever altered your behavior based on a rumor? Tell the story—in a paragraph.

6. What does the wide reach of this particular rumor suggest about rumor transmission in general?

TRUTH IS IN THE EAR OF THE BEHOLDER

Gregory Rodriguez

In this op-ed, published on September 28, 2009, in the *Los Angeles Times*, columnist Gregory Rodriguez argues that rumors thrive because those who hear them are
"predisposed to believe them." Drawing upon rumor theorists such as Robert H. Knapp
and Cass Sunstein, represented later in this chapter, he explores the ways in which
rumors emerge from our anxieties and belief systems. Rumors that support and validate our prior convictions are hard to disprove, even when countered with cold hard
facts and solid reasoning. A founding director of Arizona State University's Center for
Social Cohesion, Rodriguez writes about civic engagement and political and cultural
trends.

Rumors and conspiracy theories can only thrive in the minds of people who are
predisposed to believe them. Successful propagators of fringe theories don't just
send random balloons into the atmosphere. Rather, they tap into the preexisting
beliefs and biases of their target audiences.

   Plenty of studies have shown that people don't process information in a
neutral way—"biased assimilation" they call it. In other words, rather than
our opinions being forged by whatever information we have available, they
tend to be constructed by our wants and needs. With all their might, our minds
try to reduce cognitive dissonance—that queasy feeling you get when you are
confronted by contradictory ideas simultaneously. Therefore, we tend to reject
theories and rumors—and facts and truths—that challenge our worldview and
embrace those that affirm it.

   It's easy to assume that lack of education is the culprit when it comes to
people believing rumors against logic and evidence—for instance, that Barack
Obama, whose mother was an American citizen and whose state of birth has
repeatedly said his birth records are in good order, isn't a legitimate American
citizen. But one 1994 survey on conspiracy theories found that educational
level or occupational category were not factors in whether you believed in
them or not.

   What was significant? Insecurity about employment. That finding ties into
psychologist Robert H. Knapp's 1944 thesis that rumors "express and gratify the
emotional needs" of communities during periods of social duress. They arise,
in his view, to "express in simple and rationalized terms the uncertainties and
hostilities which so many feel."

5   If, on the one hand, you think you should blame rumormongers and rumor
believers for not doing their homework, you can, on the other hand, give them
credit for striving pretty hard to explain phenomena they find threatening.
Rumors and conspiracy theories often supply simplified, easily digestible explanations (and enemies) to sum up complex situations. However crass, they're both
fueled by a desire to make sense of the world.

Can false rumors and off-the-wall theories be corrected by broadcasting the truth? Sometimes, but not always. Access to information, evidently, is not a silver bullet. In his just-published book, *On Rumors*, legal scholar (and new head of the White House Office of Information and Regulatory Affairs) Cass R. Sunstein argues that efforts at correcting rumors can sometimes even hurt the cause of truth.

He cites a 2004 experiment in which liberals and conservatives were asked to examine their views on the existence of weapons of mass destruction in Iraq. After reading a statement that declared that Iraq had WMD, the subjects were asked to reveal their views on a five-point scale, from "strongly agree" to "strongly disagree."

Then they were handed a mock news article in which President George W. Bush defended the war, in part by suggesting that Saddam Hussein had weapons of mass destruction. After reading that article, participants were also asked to read about the CIA's Duelfer report, which showed that the Bush administration was wrong to think Iraq had such weapons. Finally, they were again asked their opinion of the original statement on the same five-point scale.

What the researchers found is that the outcome depended on the participants' political point of view. The liberals shifted in the direction of greater disagreement, while the conservatives showed a significant shift in agreeing with the original statement. As the researchers put it, "The correction backfired— conservatives who received the correction telling them that Iraq did not have WMD were more likely to believe that Iraq had WMD."

10   Are you scared yet? I am.

Sunstein's book goes on to explore ways that society can hold rumor-mongers accountable without eliciting a chilling effect on the freedom of speech. He's concerned that crazy rumors in the Internet Age can gum up the machinery of democracy itself.

I applaud the effort, but I'd prefer to do away with the insecurity and uncertainty that feed wacko theories and rumors in the first place. A modicum of stability, a fair and functioning economy and polity—those have to be what we strive for.

But in the meantime, don't forget psychologist Knapp. "To decry the ravages of rumor-mongering is one thing," he wrote, "to control it is yet an other." Pass it on.

Review Questions   MyWritingLab™

1. Define "biased assimilation."

2. Which factors concerning rumors were found *not* to be of importance, according to a 1994 study? Which *were* found significant?

3. In what ways are the views of psychologist Robert H. Knapp supported by the 1994 findings discussed here?

4. How did researchers draw a connection between the political stance of participants and their beliefs about the justification for the Iraq War?

● Discussion and Writing Suggestions   MyWritingLab™

1. Rodriguez suggests that when confronted with information that flies in the face of our personal ideologies, we often ignore the new information and stick with what we already believe. Discuss an occasion when you changed your mind on a subject based on new information or—conversely—a time when you ignored or rationalized away new data in order to justify sticking with your existing belief or set of values.

2. Rodriguez describes a 2004 study concerning participants' changing views about the justification of the U.S. war in Iraq—both before and after participants were presented with the "facts" about Iraq's weapons of mass destruction. What other recent events or controversies have sparked broad, vocal opinions about "facts" that have since been discredited? Consider stories such as the controversies over the president's birth certificate and religious beliefs. In these or other like cases, to what extent do you find that facts, when eventually revealed, make a difference to people's convictions?

3. Rodriguez summarizes Cass Sunstein's view that trying to correct false rumors is often counterproductive. Cite examples of situations in which attempts to clarify a rumor only reinforces it.

4. How does the Internet affect both the spread and the attempted refutation of rumors? What seem to you the differences between reading a correction online, reading a correction in a traditional print source, and being given the correction face-to-face by another person?

5. Discussing those who don't change their opinions after being confronted with the facts, Rodriguez says that we can at least "give them credit for striving pretty hard to explain phenomena they find threatening." What does he mean? To what extent do you agree?

ANATOMY OF A RUMOR: IT FLIES ON FEAR

Daniel Goleman

The following selection offers a concise introduction to the world of rumors. Psychologist Daniel Goleman provides numerous examples of rumors in the modern world, particularly those concerning death and disease, and explains how such stories are spread by the anxiety and fear of those who hear or read about them. He also offers advice on the best strategy for fighting rumors. Goleman is a psychologist and science journalist. He has been a visiting faculty member at Harvard and lectures frequently on college campuses and to business and professional groups. His many books include *The Varieties of Meditative Experience* (1977), *Emotional Intelligence* (1995), *Primal Leadership* (2001), and *Social Intelligence: The New Science of Human Relationships* (2006). A two-time Pulitzer Prize nominee, Goleman won a Career Achievement Award for journalism from the American Psychological Association. For twelve years he wrote articles for the *New York Times* on psychology and brain sciences. This selection originally appeared in the *Times* on June 4, 1991.

Did you hear?

This woman trying on a coat in a department store put her hand in the pocket and was bitten by a snake. See, the coat had been made in Taiwan where a viper laid eggs in the pocket. The woman died.

Oh, and then a man in New York City on business went to a bar for a drink and woke up the next morning in Central Park, feeling so terrible he went to the hospital. The doctor found a long, neat scar up the man's back: someone had removed one of the man's kidneys and neatly sewn him up again.

And did you hear that you shouldn't swim in public swimming pools because you can get AIDS from them? It happened to a little girl in Pittsburgh. Or maybe it was a little boy in St. Louis.

5   None of this is true, of course. But each of these stories is circulating as a rumor. They are specimens from the collection of Dr. Allan J. Kimmel, a psychologist at Fitchburg State College in Fitchburg, Mass., who is among the social scientists studying the anatomy of rumors in order to find better ways to control them.

The results suggest rumors are a kind of opportunistic information virus, thriving because of their ability to create the very anxieties that make them spread, and to mutate to fit new situations. Some rumors have survived for centuries, simply changing their targets as they traveled around the globe.

The need for effective ways to combat rumors is becoming ever more apparent. The AIDS rumors, for instance, heighten anxieties while making the work of public health officials more difficult. Racial tensions and riots are almost always fed by rumors. Businesses targeted by rumors have lost millions of dollars in sales.

The Role of Anxiety

The new research highlights the role of anxiety in giving life to rumors. For instance, people are much more likely to pass on a rumor that is about something they are already anxious about, studies have found. Repeating the rumor serves to reassure people that they understand something that troubles and perplexes them, psychologists say.

"A rumor is a kind of hypothesis, a speculation that helps people make sense of a chaotic reality or gives them a small sense of control in a threatening world," said Dr. Ralph Rosnow, a psychologist at Temple University who wrote an article reviewing findings on rumors in the current issue of *The American Psychologist*.

10   From the perspective of the people who hear rumors and pass them on, rumors are news. And while rumors are always about a topic of emotional importance to the teller, gossip need not be. "Gossip is small talk, a kind of intellectual chewing gum, while rumors have the feel of something of great substance," said Dr. Rosnow.

While rumors are naturally elusive, researchers have been resourceful in finding methods to study them. Some studies seize on the opportunity provided by events that spawn rumors, such as wars, murders or other disturbing events. In this approach, researchers survey people to find what rumors they have heard, if they believed them or passed them on and so on.

A similar approach has been used with rumors about companies. When the target is a business, people who hear the rumor frequently call the company to express outrage or to ask if it could be true. Such was the case, for instance, with the rumor in the mid-1980's that Procter & Gamble was somehow involved in Satanism.

Tracking Rumors as They Spread

By interviewing people who hear such a rumor, social scientists can learn what evidence people cite to support it, plan an advertising campaign to combat it and find out if the campaign was effective.

"You can track rumors as they travel across the country," said Dr. Fred Koenig, a social psychologist at Tulane University who advises companies victimized by rumors. "That allows you to target your campaign against it to the locale where it is most active."

15   Researchers sometimes also start rumors in order to study them. For instance, in a study conducted by Dr. Rosnow, confederates started a rumor in college classes that students in another class had been caught smoking marijuana during a final exam. A week later the students were asked if they had passed on the rumor and how sure of its truth they were. Not surprisingly, the more students believed the rumor, the more likely they were to have passed it on.

In some of the most recent experiments researchers carefully manipulate the way rumors are presented to more precisely weigh what makes people believe them or not. Thus in one study at Northwestern University the rumor that McDonald's hamburgers contained worms was accompanied by the information that worms are nutritious and are considered a delicacy in some cultures. "One of the aims of such studies is to see what kind of information will kill a rumor," said Dr. Koenig.

Much of the current rumor research focuses on the role of anxiety. In a direct test of how people's anxieties lead them to pass on rumors, Dr. Rosnow surveyed students several months after the 1986 murder of a student at the University of Pennsylvania.

"Some rumors, such as that the woman was the target of a random attack, increased people's sense of dread, by suggesting that they themselves could have easily been the victim," said Dr. Rosnow. "Other rumors, like one that a former lover had killed her, were more reassuring, suggesting that only she could have been the target of the violence."

Fright Leads to Repetition

The students, on average, had heard three to five rumors about the murder. No matter how many rumors they had heard, Dr. Rosnow found, the students were far more likely to pass on those that made them most anxious.

20   In general, researchers are finding that rumors perpetuate themselves by creating anxiety in the hearer: people who are most distressed by something are more likely to transmit rumors on the topic. For example, in a study of 229 college students, the students most readily passed on the rumors about AIDS that they found most personally relevant and upsetting.

"The more frightened people were by a rumor, the more likely they were to repeat it," said Dr. Kimmel whose study will be published in *The Journal of Applied Social Psychology*.

One motive for people to repeat rumors that frighten them is in the hope of finding that it is wrong. "In repeating something that makes you nervous to someone else, you may learn some contrary fact that will calm you," Dr. Kimmel said. "On the other hand, it can escalate your fears if the person you tell it to believes it."

Those students who already were so anxious about AIDS that they had done something to protect themselves, such as deciding to abstain from sex, were the most likely to repeat the AIDS rumors, Dr. Kimmel found. For these students, the rumors may have served as a justification for their own actions.

The Message from Elvis

The implicit messages of rumors give them their emotional power. Some of the most compelling rumors revolve around basic fears, such as of disease or death. Thus the rumor that Elvis Presley or John F. Kennedy is alive and well has as its subtext the message that it is possible to defeat death.

25   By the same token, those health fears seem to propel rumors such as the story that Mikey, a little boy in commercials for Life cereal, died when he mixed a carbonated beverage with an exploding candy called "pop rocks," Dr. Levin said.

"Such rumors touch on people's basic anxieties: death, disaster, conspiratorial plots, racial tensions," he said.

Of Restaurants and Dogs

The source cited for a rumor is usually specific enough to sound plausible, but distant enough to be unverifiable, such as "a cousin of a friend." But when those trails are actually followed by investigators, they typically find deadends.

One of the most ancient of rumors, still alive and well, has been around for more than a century: that Chinese restaurants serve up the missing dogs of townspeople. In a paper presented in May at the Society for the Study of Contemporary Legend, British researchers traced the rumor in England to the earliest years of the British Empire, and in America to the 1850's.

"The rumor thrives because, in China, they do eat dogs," said Dr. Koenig. "But the same rumor, with a warning to watch your dog, is now going around about Vietnamese immigrants in Texas and elsewhere, about Mexicans in southern California and about Native Americans in Wisconsin."

30   Businesses are among the biggest victims of rumors. Earlier this year Tropical Fantasy, a soft drink marketed to minorities in Northeastern cities, was the target of a rumor, allegedly started by a rival, that the company was controlled by the Ku Klux Klan, and that the drink contained an ingredient that would make black men sterile.

Such rumors, which typically trigger a boycott of the product involved by those who believe them, have been spread about children being kidnapped in K-Mart stores and about Procter & Gamble giving part of its profits to Satanists.

A current rumor is a variation on the Procter & Gamble story: that Liz Claiborne, the clothing company, "is in cahoots with the Church of Satan," said Dr. Koenig.

Satan and a Fading Picture

"The new version holds that Liz Claiborne herself was on the Oprah Winfrey show, and that she said her company gives 30 percent of its profits to the Church of Satan," said Dr. Koenig. "Then the picture faded out, like something was wrong with the transmission, and when the picture came back, she wasn't there." Such specific details are typical of rumors, Dr. Koenig said, lending them the ring of truth.

Dr. Koenig, who has advised several corporations on squelching rumors, said, "If a company is the target of a rumor, it should deny it immediately, as forcefully and publicly as possible showing the evidence that proves it is unfounded."

35   That advice runs contrary to conventional wisdom among public relations firms, which holds that such a public denial only calls more people's attention to what are false allegations.

But Dr. Koenig said: "A public rebuttal takes a rumor and turns it into news. The news shows the rumor to be unsubstantiated. If you try to pass on the rumor after that, you run the risk of being ridiculed."

That tactic was used successfully, for instance, by Entenmann's, a baked goods company in Bay Shore, N.Y. When a rumor spread throughout Boston that the bakery was owned by The Rev. Sun Myung Moon of the Unification Church, the company held a news conference at which Robert Entenmann, the chairman, reviewed the history of his family-owned business and declared that the rumor was untrue. "The rumor stopped within 24 hours," said Dr. Koenig.

● Review Questions   MyWritingLab™

1. Why are people more likely to pass on a rumor they are already anxious about, according to Goleman?

2. In what way does rumor differ from gossip, according to psychologist Ralph Rosnow?

3. How do social scientists such as Rosnow attempt to track rumors and determine which ones are successful at spreading?

4. In what way do people who spread anxiety-causing rumors hope to reassure themselves?

● **Discussion and Writing Suggestions   MyWritingLab™**

1. Recall one of the rumors you have heard, perhaps even helped spread. To what extent were your responses to the rumor driven by anxiety? The responses of other people you know? How did you learn, eventually, whether or not the rumor was true? Did you attempt to investigate the facts yourself, or did you seek verification from friends or relatives? Were you eventually persuaded that the rumor was false because of contrary evidence?

2. As Goleman explains, contemporary psychologists and social psychologists have devoted a good deal of attention to the workings of rumors. What do you think we might learn about individual human motivation and human behavior in groups from the study of rumor?

3. Goleman quotes psychologist Ralph Rosnow: "A rumor is a kind of hypothesis, a speculation that helps people make sense of a chaotic reality or gives them a small sense of control in a threatening world." Explain how this definition applies to a rumor that you have heard or read about.

4. Examine a sensational story in one of the supermarket tabloids that deals in scandal and rumor. What sources or evidence are cited to support the story? To what extent do you believe the story? Does the story provoke anxiety or some other response? Explain.

5. Consider a recent rumor from any realm of public interest (politics, entertainment, business, etc.). How did the target address the rumor? To what extent was the chosen strategy effective? How closely did the subject adhere to Dr. Fred Koenig's advice to "deny it immediately, as forcefully and publicly as possible showing the evidence that proves it is unfounded"?

FIGHTING THAT OLD DEVIL RUMOR

Sandra Salmans

Might buying a can of coffee be a way of supporting "black magic?" Could baking a cake be a form of devil worship? If we are to believe a long-standing rumor about Procter & Gamble, the company behind products such as Folgers coffee and Duncan Hines baking mixes, the answer is yes. Rumors suggesting that the company's distinctive moon and stars logo was a sign of some satanic affiliation became so widespread that the company had to go to court to clear its name. Over the years, P&G sued a number of individuals and other companies it claimed were spreading this devil-worship rumor, including the Amway Corporation. After a court process that dragged on for seventeen years, P&G was awarded over $19 million in damages. By that time, the company had already modified its logo in an attempt to put the rumors to rest. That attempt—a major concession to the rumormongers—helped to quiet the story; it also illustrated that once a rumor takes hold, its grip remains tenacious. In this October 1982 *Saturday Evening Post* article, Sandra Salmans traces the ongoing reverberations of a rumor that grew out of reactions to a simple line drawing. *Note:* To view the logo in question, Google or Bing "procter and gamble logo controversy."

Cathy Gebing's telephone rings every few minutes, and the question is always the same: Is the moon-and-stars design on Procter & Gamble's 70-odd products the mark of the devil?

"No, sir, that's a false rumor," Mrs. Gebing answers patiently. "That's our trademark, we've had it about 100 years."

Normally the consumer services department, this is now the rumor control center for Procter, the consumer goods giant that has lately become the focus of a nationwide rumor campaign.

The rumors, first appearing about two years ago, essentially contend that Procter's 132 year-old trademark, which shows the man in the moon and 13 stars representing the original colonies, is a symbol of Satanism and devil worship. The rumor-mongering also urges a Christian boycott of Procter's products, which include Pampers, Duncan Hines and Folgers, plus dozens of other well-known names.

5   After a great deal of indecision about how to combat the rumors, Procter took formal action in July, filing libel suits against seven individuals for spreading "false and malicious" rumors. The company has said that it may file more suits. "What we have to do is make people realize that we mean business," said Robert Norrish, Procter's public relations director.

It is, in fact, a public relations problem and a difficult one.

"Legal recourse isn't a happy way to go," said Robert Schwartz, president of Manning, Selvage & Lee, a leading New York public relations firm, "but they probably had very few alternatives. The company was diverting resources to deal with this, and at some point, you have to call a halt." However, Mr. Schwartz added, if Procter loses the suits, its image will certainly suffer.

Procter has firmly rejected suggestions that it simply remove the offending symbol from its packages. That, however, increases the suspicions of some consumers.

"If it causes controversy, I don't see why they have to have it," said Faye Dease, a clinic supervisor at Womack Army Hospital in Fort Bragg, North Carolina. Mrs. Dease said that, when a mirror is held up to the logo, the curlicues in the man's beard become 666—the sign of the Antichrist.

10   Procter is not the only company to have fallen siege to rumors. McDonald's has found itself subject to whisper campaigns contending alternately that the restaurant chain was giving to Satan or that it was putting worms in its hamburgers. Entenmann's, the bakery owned by the Warner-Lambert Company, was rumored to be owned by the Rev. Sun Myung Moon's Unification Church.

But the rumors have been more enduring at Procter, and the company's course—to go not only to news organizations and clergy for help, but also the courts—has been more aggressive.

Procter is going after the rumor with all the diligence that it devotes to a new product introduction. A three-inch-thick file documents the company's strategy: a map of the United States, showing the geographical sweep of the rumors; tallies, state by state, of the queries to the consumer services department; tallies, day by day, of the nature of the complaint ("Satanic"; "Mentions lawsuits"; "Has heard/seen media reports"; "Check more than one if appropriate").

At the consumer services department, whose toll-free telephone number is printed on every Procter package, the calls first began trickling in two years ago, the company said.

Individuals in a handful of Middle Western states said they had heard that Procter was owned by the Rev. Sun Myung Moon's followers. In November 1980 Procter felt compelled to answer the charges by writing to news organizations in those states.

15   But in December 1981, there were suddenly 1,152 queries, by the company's tally, mainly from the West Coast, and the focus shifted from the Moon church to the devil. "In the beginning, God made the tree," a 75-year-old woman wrote the company. "Where did Satan get Charmin?"

Many callers reported hearing that Procter's "owner" had appeared on a television talk show where he admitted selling his soul to the devil in order to gain the company's success.

Anonymous fliers, usually misspelling the company's name, began to appear at supermarkets. "Proctor & Gamble," one said, "announced on *The Phil Donahue Show* Friday that they contribute 10 percent of their earnings to the Satanic religion (which is devil worship)."

"Do you realize," another anonymous flier said, "that if all the Christians in the world would stop buying Proctor and Gamble Products this Company would soon be out of business?"

Procter did a second mailing, to news organizations on the West Coast. But this time there was no letup. By last spring, Procter was getting 12,000 queries monthly about its relationship with the devil. There were reports of ministers, mainly in small Fundamentalist churches, attacking Procter from the pulpit and urging their congregations to boycott its products.

20   Given the dubious results of the news media campaign, John Smale, Procter's president, decided on a less public line of attack. The company wrote to local clergy and enclosed testaments of faith from very prominent clerics, including preachers who led an earlier attack on Procter for sponsoring television shows of what they regarded as questionable morality. The Rev. Jerry Falwell, leader of Moral Majority, a church-based conservative political-action group, wrote that he had talked with Procter's chairman, "and I am certain neither he nor his company is associated in any way with Satanism or devil worship."

By June, however, the center was receiving more than 15,000 queries monthly, including a few from Alaska and Hawaii.

Mr. Smale told Procter's public relations department to forget his earlier cautions. On June 10, "We presented our recommendations to Mr. Smale." William Dobson, of the public relations department, recalled. "It was essentially to go on the offensive."

On July 1, Procter announced its first lawsuits. The litigation was "a very hard-nosed way to generate publicity." Mr. Dobson said. "We were working on the traditional Procter concepts: reach and frequency."

The subjects of those lawsuits and a second wave later in the month—Mike Campbell of Atlanta, William and Linda Moore of Pensacola, Florida, Guy Sharpe of Atlanta, Elma and Ed Pruitt of Clovis, New Mexico, and Sherman and Margaret McCord of Tullahoma, Tennessee—were chosen simply because "they just happened to be the first people where we felt we had enough evidence to go to court," Mr. Dobson said.

25   Most of the leads to ministers had evaporated, and in any case, a suit against a member of the clergy, "frankly, wasn't our optimum choice," Mr. Dobson said.

All but one of the defendants sell products of competing consumer-goods companies, according to Procter. The Moores and Mr. Pruitt are distributors for the Amway Corporation, which sells soap and other consumer products door-to-door. The McCords are distributors for Shaklee, which sells vitamins, household cleaners and personal care products. Mr. Campbell works for a grocery brokerage firm that represents manufacturers of household cleaning products.

However, "there is no evidence that companies are pushing this rumor," Mr. Norrish said. Nor is it clear that they were economically inspired. "We didn't try to figure out motives," he added. "We just want to stop them."

Most of the defendants denied the charges or said that they were convinced the rumors were false.

Mrs. McCord said that she had printed the rumor in her newsletter to other Shaklee distributors, but had realized her mistake and apologized in both the newsletter and a letter to Procter. Mrs. Pruitt said she and her husband stopped distributing anti-Procter leaflets after learning that the rumor was false.

30   William Hurst, the lawyer for Mr. Campbell, said that his client did hand an anti-Procter circular to a supermarket clerk when he was stocking the shelves with Clorox, but it was his only copy, and "he did not believe it."

Mr. Sharpe, a well-known weatherman for WXIA-TV in Atlanta and a Methodist lay preacher, issued a denial that he had made defamatory remarks against Procter & Gamble.

The lawsuits provoked the hoped for flurry of publicity, including network television coverage, and the number of queries to the consumer services department has fallen by half, Procter says. But few of the remaining 250 or so callers each day have heard of the lawsuits. "How do you reach them?" Mr. Norrish wonders.

Review Questions

1. What do the images in the Procter & Gamble logo actually represent?

2. Which component of the logo occasioned the "devil worship" rumor?

3. Aside from exercising its legal recourse, what did P&G hope to accomplish with its first lawsuits?

4. Why did Procter president John Smale reach beyond the usual media outlets in an effort to deflate the rumor?

Discussion and Writing Suggestions

1. The logo rumor led many people to boycott Procter & Gamble. Have you ever been asked to boycott a company? Why? In hindsight, to what extent was the boycott based on rumor?

2. Why do you think that the Procter & Gamble rumor was so persuasive and so resistant over the years to the company's attempts at refuting it? In formulating your response, speculate on some of the possible motivations of those who began the rumor and those who spread it; speculate also on the world views of those who were so receptive to its content.

3. P&G took a variety of approaches over the years to handling the charges of Satanism, ultimately filing lawsuits that took years to resolve. In the meantime, the company changed its logo. Assume you worked at Procter & Gamble during the years when the devil-worship rumor took hold. How might you have advised the company to adopt a different rumor-fighting strategy? In developing your answer, draw upon both your business sense and what you understand about human nature. In the final analysis, how well (or badly) do you think the company dealt with this persistent rumor?

4. The Procter & Gamble rumor is intertwined with religious beliefs and fears. History is filled with rumors of this nature—for example, the Salem witch trials of 1692. What other rumors have you personally encountered, or do you know of, that you can attribute to religious belief, fear, or just simple misunderstanding? How did these rumors spread, and what were their outcomes?

5. This particular rumor spread in the early 1980s, before the widespread availability of the Internet. At that time, rumors were not spread with the same instantaneous pace as they are now; similarly, companies could not simply respond within seconds by "tweeting" a response in an effort to deflate the rumor. How might the slower exchange of information during the 1980s have affected both the life of this rumor and the company's attempts at refutation? Had the rumor started today, do you think its life span would have been as long as it turned out to be?

A Psychology of Rumor

Robert H. Knapp

During World War II, psychologist Robert H. Knapp attempted to classify and identify the numerous rumors circulating at the time (rumors being everywhere in time of war). In his classic article "A Psychology of Rumor," Knapp examined some of the rumors currently or recently in circulation and attempted to create a framework for further study. In this selection, he classifies three main types of rumor, each based on the human emotion that drives it: wish, fear, or hostility. At the time he wrote this paper, Knapp headed rumor control for the Massachusetts Committee on Public Safety. Though the paper (excerpted here) was published nearly seventy years ago, Knapp's classification system continues to be influential in the academic study of rumor and remains useful in accounting for the features of the countless rumors we encounter daily.

[W]e shall define rumor as a *proposition for belief of topical reference disseminated without official verification.* So formidably defined, rumor is but a special case of informal social communications, including myth, legend, and current humor. From myth and legend it is distinguished by its emphasis on the topical. Where humor is designed to provoke laughter, rumor begs for belief.

So defined, rumors have three basic characteristics. They have, first, a distinct and characteristic mode of transmission—mostly by word of mouth. Being spread by means of this primitive medium, rumors are more subject than the formal modes of transmission to inaccuracy and capricious distortion.

A second characteristic of rumors is that they provide "information." A rumor is always about some particular person, happening, or condition.

Finally, rumor satisfies. Mythology, folklore, and humor gather impetus from the emotional gratifications which they afford. The same may be said of rumor. Rumors *express* and *gratify* the emotional needs of the community in much the same way as day dreams and fantasy fulfill the needs of the individual. For convenience of notation, this importance aspect of rumors will be called the "expressive" characteristic.

• • •

The Classification of Rumors

5 We present here a three-fold classification, based upon the already observed fact that rumors almost invariably gratify some emotional need. In practice it has been found that the emotional needs most frequently served by rumors are wish, fear, and hostility. Accordingly, three basic types of rumors can be delineated.

The *Pipe-dream or Wish Rumor.* Such rumors express the wishes and hopes of those among they circulate. They can be popularly identified with "wishful thinking." The following, found in circulation in Boston during the winter of

Knapp, Robert H., "A Psychology of Rumor" from *The Public Opinion Quarterly* 8:1 (Spring 1944): pages 22–31, by permission of Oxford University Press.

1942, are typical examples:

> The Japanese do not have enough oil to last six months.
> There will be a revolution in Germany before summer.
> Lloyd's of London Wall Street are betting 10 to 1 that the war will be over by autumn.

The Bogie Rumor. The precise opposite of the pipe-dream rumor is the bogie rumor. Just as the former mirrors the wishes and hopes of the group, so the bogie is essentially derived from fears and anxieties. Bogies range all the way from rumors with a dour and pessimistic quality to the panic rumors so familiar to social psychologists. Typical examples of this type are these:

> The entire Pacific Fleet was destroyed at Pearl Harbor.
> Several thousand bodies of soldiers have washed up off the town of X.
> Crab meat packed by the Japanese contains ground glass.

The Wedge-driving Aggression Rumor. The wedge-driving rumor is so termed because of its effect in dividing groups and destroying loyalties; its essential motivation is aggression or hatred. In practice almost all aggression rumors turn out to be directed against elements of our own population or our allies. The following are typical examples:

> Churchill blackmailed Roosevelt into provoking war with Japan.
> The British are sabotaging their own ships in American ports so that they will not have to put out to sea.
> The Catholics in America are trying to evade the draft.

• • •

What Makes a Good Rumor

10   1. No successful rumor may exceed a length or complexity greater than the memory span of the group through which it passes. Rumor by its very nature must depend upon the memory of its successive tellers. Typically the successful rumor is short, simple and salient....

2. As perception and memory simplify the things we see, so do they simplify the rumors we hear and read. In time, a successful rumor becomes a "good story." This process of heightening some elements, of leveling or deleting others, is accomplished by the following typical distortions:

> addition of a humorous twist
> addition of striking and aesthetic detail
> deletion of qualifications and syntactic complexities
> simplification of plot and circumstances
> assumption of a more familiar form
> exaggeration

Through the operation of these several processes, the successful rumor emerges with the same vigor that characterizes the folk ballad, the popular witticism, and other products of extensive oral transmission.

3. There are conditions which make it easier for rumors to become distorted. The farther a rumor is removed from known or confirmed fact, the more easily does it seem to get twisted when passed on. Distortion appears to take its greatest toll when a rumor is kept entirely on the person-to-person level and does not appear in the press or on the air. Finally, when there is either great unrest (as in panic) or an acute need for information, rumor tends to undergo its most drastic changes.

4. Names, numbers, and places are typically the most unstable components of any rumor. There are abundant examples of rumors circulating in different totalitarian nations, all of identical plot, yet each employing the names and places familiar to the local populations. Similarly with respect to numbers, rumors are notoriously capricious.

5. From whatever humble beginning a rumor may spring, it is soon attributed to a high authoritative source. This gives the rumor both prestige and the appearance of veracity.

6. Rumors become harmonized with the cultural traditions of the group in which they circulate. The rumors of the secret weapon, rife in France during the early days of the present war, were cast in terms of the Big Bertha* of the last war....

7. The successful rumor, to thrive, must always adapt *itself* to the *immediate* as well as to the traditional circumstances of the group; it must ride the tide of current swings in public opinion and interest. Typically, rumors come in clusters dealing with a single subject. Thus in Boston, rumors of anti-semitic character would dominate the grapevine for one month, only to subside and be replaced with anti-British rumors. The primitive grapevine mentality seems almost incapable of sustaining more than three or four basic ideas at a time. Similarly, in respect to expressive character, rumors at a given time tend to follow a single expressive pattern. This was very clearly demonstrated in England during the last war when waves of "bogie" rumors of defeat or of military disaster were dispelled almost over night by waves of "pipe-dream" rumors telling of the arrival of Russian troops in England.

Review Questions   MyWritingLab™

1. Identify the three basic characteristics of rumor as established by Knapp.

2. Describe Knapp's classification system for rumor.

3. How do successful rumors become heightened into "good stories" as time goes on?

4. Which aspects of a rumor tend to be the most unstable?

---

*Big Bertha was a howitzer—a heavy artillery piece with a 16.5-inch diameter barrel—developed by the German armament manufacturer Krupp just before World War I.

● Discussion and Writing Suggestions   MyWritingLab™

1. Use each of Knapp's categories to classify a rumor you've read about in this chapter.

2. Based on your own experience, and using Knapp's categories, classify at least one rumor that you have heard or helped spread. How does this rumor meet the criteria of the particular category?

3. Knapp's examples of rumor are a product of the public anxieties associated with wartime. What recent rumors can you think of that spring from uneasiness about contemporary events?

4. The World War II examples used here are specific to Knapp's time. Since then, the United States has been involved in a number of wars and other conflicts. What role do you think rumor plays in this country's current military engagements? Consider both rumors that develop on the home front and rumors that develop among soldiers, sailors, and airmen.

5. Knapp states that rumor is transmitted "mostly by word of mouth." To what extent have you found this still to be the case? How is information that is spread by various methods of transmission interpreted in different ways?

6. Knapp suggests that all rumors grow out of basic human emotions such as hope or anxiety. In what ways have you found his observation to be true (or false) in your own experience or the experiences of people you know?

"PAUL IS DEAD!" (SAID FRED)

Alan Glenn

In the late 1960s, The Beatles were the most commercially successful rock band in the world, and Paul McCartney perhaps its most well-known and beloved singer. So when a rumor started in 1969 that Paul might have died three years earlier, music fans were jolted. According to the rumor, Paul's death had been hushed up, but (in the spirit of imaginative fun) the band had left "clues" about the truth throughout its albums for their fans to decipher. Of course, this morbid scheme would have been outrageous if true.

But was it? Originating at a college radio station, the rumor, initially intended as a lark for local audiences, spread across the country. In the pre-Internet age, the rumor moved at record speed, inviting audiences to research the "clues" and find their own. Here, in an article from the November 11, 2009, edition of the University of Michigan's *Michigan Today*, Alan Glenn, a columnist for the *Ann Arbor Chronicle*, explores the relatively innocent beginnings of the rock world's most enduring rumor: "Paul is dead." What happened subsequently is a textbook case of how rumor can spread across the pop-culture landscape. *Note:* Additional illustrations to accompany this selection can be found online. Google or Bing "paul is dead said fred."

In the fall of 1969 a strange and mysterious rumor was circulating on the fringes of college campuses in the Midwest: Paul McCartney of the Beatles was dead.

According to the rumor, McCartney had died three years previously in a horrific car crash. His death—so the story went—was covered up, the surviving Beatles found a double to replace him, and ever since had been hiding clues in their songs and album covers that revealed the truth about their ex-bandmate's grisly fate.

No one knows for certain how the rumor started, or where. But in mid-October it exploded on to the national scene, sweeping the ranks of youth from coast to coast in a matter of days. Suddenly it seemed as if everyone under the age of 30 was either debating the possibility of McCartney's demise or poring over their Beatles records, searching for clues.

The power of the rumor was such that, four decades later, plenty of Baby Boomers still vividly recall the tingling sensation they felt when they first heard an eerie backwards voice emanating from their turntables, and began to consider that Paul might actually be dead.

5   What many do not know is that the rumor might not have come to their attention at all except for a mischievous young U-M natural resources student named Fred LaBour. Indeed, if the McCartney death rumor can be called a modern myth, then Beatles expert Devin McKinney may be correct to identify LaBour as its Homer.

Today, Fred LaBour is best known as "Too Slim," bassist-cum-jokester for the country and western act Riders in the Sky. Forty years ago he was an equally jocular staff writer for the *Michigan Daily* who had been assigned to review *Abbey Road*, the Beatles' latest album.

On October 12, 1969, LaBour was tuned in to radio station WKNR from Detroit when disc jockey Russ Gibb took a call from a listener who wanted to talk about a rumor going around that Paul McCartney was dead. Gibb was skeptical at first, but became intrigued when the caller explained that there were clues pointing to McCartney's death hidden in the Beatles' music.

For the next hour thousands of listeners, including LaBour, stayed glued to their radios as Gibb and his callers discussed the supposed evidence and what could be behind it. The following day LaBour got out his Beatles records, lined them up on his desk, and sat down to write one of the oddest and most influential record reviews ever printed.

On the morning of October 14, the university community awoke to the shocking and incredible report that one of the world's most popular and beloved entertainers was no more. The headline blazoned across the second page of the Michigan Daily proclaimed the awful news:

"McCartney dead; new evidence brought to light."
"Paul McCartney was killed in an automobile accident in early November, 1966," began Fred LaBour's accompanying full-page article, "after leaving EMI recording studios tired, sad, and dejected." McCartney was found four hours later, "pinned under his car in a culvert with the top of his head sheared off. He was deader than a doornail."

10   What LaBour had written was less record review than conspiracy-age fable. He related in detail how the accident had been covered up and a look-alike

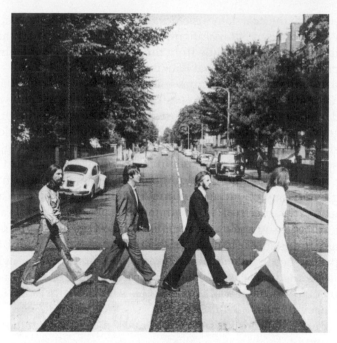

According to rumors, the Beatles left clues to Paul's death. The *Abbey Road* album cover (above) was supposedly flush with such clues, such as Paul's bare feet and a cigarette in his right hand.

found to replace the dead musician—not as a rumor, but as if it were fact. The mysterious clues were held to be part of a strange and disturbing plot orchestrated by John Lennon, who had it in mind to found a new religion with himself as god and the "reborn" McCartney a Christ-like figure at his side.

LaBour's story electrified the campus. The *Daily* sold out its entire run by mid-morning, and a second printing was ordered to meet demand. "I remember walking down Ann Arbor streets hearing Beatles music from every single apartment and house," LaBour says. He also recalls occasionally hearing someone trying to play a record backwards—listening for clues.

Indeed, the enigmatic clues seemed to draw most people into the rumor's web—and LaBour's article contained an abundance of evidence for clue-hungry readers to digest.

For instance, the inside cover of *Sgt. Pepper's Lonely Hearts Club Band* features a photo in which McCartney is wearing an arm patch that seems to read O.P.D.—according to LaBour, an abbreviation for "Officially Pronounced Dead," the British equivalent of DOA. On the album's back cover is a photo in which McCartney is the only one of the Beatles facing away from the camera.

LaBour also pointed out that on the front cover of *Abbey Road* McCartney is barefoot, signifying death because that is how corpses are buried. Furthermore, in the photo Paul holds a cigarette in his right hand, whereas the "real" McCartney is left-handed.

15   Then there were the now-famous clues to be found by playing certain songs backwards. When reversed, "Revolution 9" reveals something that sounds eerily like "Turn me on, dead man," while from the outro of "I Am the Walrus" seems to emerge a creepy chorus of "Ha ha! Paul is dead."

"I cannot tell you how many times I listened to those records backwards," says actress Christine Lahti (*Chicago Hope*), who in the fall of 1969 was a nineteen-year-old U-M theater student. Dubious at first, after many repetitions—and the encouragement of friends—she found herself more willing to believe. "After a point you started to hear it," she explains, "just by the power of suggestion."

Lahti suspects that this Rorschach-like nature of the clues accounts for much of the rumor's appeal. "It might also have had something to do with the mind-altering drugs that many people were involved with," she adds with a laugh.

Filmmaker Ric Burns (*New York: A Documentary Film*), then a teenaged Beatlemaniac attending Ann Arbor's Pioneer High School, remembers spending hours hunting for clues and debating the rumor with friends. Like Lahti, he believes that a major part of the attraction was the ambiguity of the purported evidence.

"It was not some 'x-marks-the-spot' clue," Burns explains. "You could sort of hear it, but you couldn't. It was like you were seeing the tip of the iceberg of a larger reality."

20   But most people did not realize that many of the clues were nothing more than a college prank.

Fred LaBour's article in the *Daily* presented more than two-dozen clues, most of which he originated himself. Of those, many went on to become an integral part of the rumor.

But LaBour admits—and has always admitted—that he made up his clues on the spot, as a joke. A prime example is his assertion that "walrus"—as in the lyric "the walrus was Paul"—is Greek for "corpse." (It isn't.) LaBour also brazenly fabricated many other "facts": identifying, for instance, McCartney's replacement as a Scottish orphan named William Campbell. (He had considered calling the impostor "Glen" Campbell, after the country singer, but decided it would be too obvious.)

LaBour never expected his article to be taken at face value, and was astonished when the national press picked it up as a serious piece of news. "The story was quoted extensively everywhere," he recalls. "First the Detroit papers, then Chicago, then, by the weekend, both coasts."

After this the rumor truly seemed to catch fire. Suddenly LaBour's playful inventions were being soberly, discussed on the evening news of all three major television networks, and in prestigious national magazines such as *Time* and *Life*.

25   Exactly why LaBour's story was so influential is unclear. It was not the only article on the rumor, nor was it the first. The rumor was also being heavily promoted on alternative radio. But many agree with Beatleologist Andru J. Reeve, who opines that LaBour's story was "the single most significant factor in the breadth of the rumor's spread."

LaBour recalls being worried about his unintentional role in sending the rumor spiraling out of control. "But after a few days," he says, "the theatrical aspect became clearer to me, and, shy as I was in the face of all the attention, I began to enjoy the ride."

The culmination of that ride was being invited to Hollywood in early November to participate in an RKO television special that featured celebrity attorney F. Lee Bailey conducting a mock trial in which he examined various expert "witnesses" on the subject of McCartney's alleged death.

"I was a nervous college kid, way out of my league," LaBour recalls. "I told Bailey during our pre-show meeting that I'd made the whole thing up. He sighed, and said, 'Well, we have an hour of television to do. You're going to have to go along with this.' I said okay."

30   By the time the program was scheduled for broadcast, however, public interest in the rumor had cooled. It received only a single airing, on a local television station in New York City on November 30, 1969.

The popular mania surrounding the "Paul is dead" rumor was short-lived—but even today, despite the thorough debunking of nearly all the so-called evidence, it continues to circulate, mainly among conspiracy buffs and inquisitive Beatles fans.

Fred LaBour doesn't think his adoptive brainchild will ever completely disappear. "Like it or not," he says, "the rumor will be with us as long as the Beatles are with us."

Which will be a very long time indeed.

● Review Questions   MyWritingLab™

1. After LaBour published his article, the campus was "electrified" by the story. Given that the McCartney rumor was already in verbal circulation before his piece was published, why did it have such a galvanizing force?

2. What quality of LaBour's "clues" appeared to draw in the most readers, and ultimately spread the rumor further?

3. The speed and popularity of this particular rumor taught LaBour a lesson about being the "source" of a rumor. What did he learn?

4. What did LaBour discover, through his experience on television, about the popular media's attitude toward rumor?

● Discussion and Writing Suggestions   MyWritingLab™

1. This rumor highlights two aspects of human nature: a fascination with celebrity and a morbid curiosity with death. What does this intersection of rumor, fame, and mortality suggest about human nature?

2. How do you account for the remarkable success of the "Paul is dead" rumor in spreading so quickly and persuading so many people of its truth? To what distinctive elements do you attribute its appeal and its power? Compare this rumor—and the evidence offered for its support—to one or more other rumors you have heard or read about concerning particular celebrities today.

3. To what extent is a rumor more or less believable when its details are ambiguous, as compared, say, to the very particular details associated with the missing kidney rumor discussed in Chapter 6 (pp. 192–198)? Based on your own experience, compare and contrast examples of ambiguous rumors and rumors in which details are precise.

4. On its surface, the "Paul is dead" rumor seems worlds away from the political and military nature of Knapp's examples and his theoretical framework for classifying rumors. Still, can you detect ways in which this case falls within Knapp's framework of rumor? Consider his three types of rumor, along with his analyses of what happens to a rumor as it spreads. Consider, too, Knapp's discussion of the factors that create successful rumors.

THE RUNAWAY GRANDMOTHER

Jan Harold Brunvand

"The Runaway Grandmother" is an example of an urban legend. Rumors and urban legends are similar in that both involve statements or claims that circulate among people about topics they consider important. Unlike urban legends, rumors are typically about real people or real companies and may consist of nothing more than an assertion ("I heard that the company is closing next year," "Marla quit her job and is opening up her own store"). Urban legends typically have a more extended narrative component than rumors. As Nicholas DiFonzo, an author represented later in this chapter, asserts, urban legends are "narratives about strange, funny, or horrible events that could have happened, the details of which change to fit particular locales or time periods, and which frequently contain a moral lesson." Finally, while some rumors may be true, virtually all urban legends are—as the word "legend" suggests—false.

Jan Harold Brunvand is an expert on urban legends, having collected thousands of them from all over the world. A professor of English at the University of Utah, Brunvand is a Fellow of the American Folklore Society and served as editor of the *Journal of American Folklore* from 1976 to 1980. Author of the standard introduction to American folklore, *The Study of American Folklore: An Introduction,* Brunvand writes a popular national column, "Urban Legends," syndicated by United Features Syndicate. He has also written five books on urban legends, including *The Choking Doberman* (1984), *Curses: Broiled Again* (1989), and *The Baby Train* (1993). This selection is from his first book, *The Vanishing Hitchhiker: American Urban Legends and Their Meanings* (1981).

"The Runaway Grandmother" is another popular urban legend in which a corpse is unwittingly pilfered from a car. The death-in-the-family theme implicit in "The Dead Cat in the Package" (the pet as a quasi-relative)[1], is made

---

[1]"The Dead Cat in the Package" is the motif of another urban legend discussed by Brunvand. The tale has numerous variants, but the essential story deals with an individual—generally, a woman—who needs to dispose of a dead cat. She wraps up the body of the feline in a package or a bag, stops at a shop on the way to her destination, then picks up her package and continues on her way. Upon reaching her destination, she opens the package to find a ham or some other unexpected object. The narrative then often switches to the person who has unwittingly picked up the package with the dead cat, describing the effect upon that person—often a fainting spell—when he or she opens the parcel.

explicit here: an actual human relation of the family dies. Disposing of her is the problem, not only as a practical and legal matter, but also because death confuses and upsets people. When an unlucky stranger solves the problem, the family feels relief and release from the tension of confronting the graphic reminder of their own mortality.

Both the dead cat and stolen grandmother stories focus on the bereaved and tend to create in their climaxes a feeling of uneasiness tinged with humor. It is this emotional tone, shared by the legend audience, that links the stories, not any necessary historical connection. The legend of "The Runaway Grandmother" has its own characteristic motifs. While the cat legend usually begins with the problem of corpse-disposal, in "The Runaway Grandmother" this problem occurs unexpectedly in the course of the story, and the motivation for hiding the body is entirely different. There is never an exchange of goods motif in the grandmother heist.

An American folklorist, Robert H. Woodward, noted some of the similarities between the two stories in a 1963 news article in the San Jose, California, *Mercury*; he characterized the grandmother's corpse legend as "an addition to the growing store of urban tales," and he paraphrased it as follows:

> A local resident reports as fact an experience of a Washington State family that he knows. After the family had crossed the Mexican border on a vacation trip, one of the children said, "Mama, Grandma won't wake up." Upon discovering that Grandma had died, the family placed her body in a sleeping bag and secured her to the top of their automobile, planning to report her death to the police at the first town. While they were in the station, their car was stolen—with Grandma's body still aboard. No trace has yet been found of either Grandma or the car. Another resident reports the tale as having happened in Italy.

It should also be noted here that, in common with the London version of "The Dead Cat in the Package," this story involves Americans who are abroad when their funerary problem comes up. Part of their distress seems to come from not being on home ground.

5   The first text of "The Runaway Grandmother" legend published in a folklore study was also collected in 1963, from an English woman who heard it told in Canada by her cousin who in turn had heard it in Leeds. (Obviously the story was getting around pretty well by 1963.) The characters in this version—and several of their terms—are definitely English. Parallel to the Americans visiting Mexico, these tourists have their odd experience during a vacation in Spain:

> This story was told me by my cousin, who had heard it from a friend in Leeds, about a couple whom he knew, who went for a camping holiday in Spain with their car. They had taken his stepmother with them. She slept in a different tent to the others. On the morning that they struck [broke camp], they were very busy, and they didn't hear anything of her for a while, and then, when they went to her tent, they found she had died, and rigor had already set in. They were in a great state, and they didn't know what to do, but they decided to roll her up in the tent, and put her on top of the car, and go to the nearest town, and go to the consul and the police. So they did this, and went to the town, and then they felt very cold and miserable, and they hadn't had a proper breakfast. So they thought they'd get a cup of coffee

to revive them, before they went in search of the consul. So they parked the car, and went to a small cafe, and had their cup of coffee, and then came back to look for the car. But it wasn't there. It had gone.

So they went home to England without the car or the stepmother. But the difficulty was, they couldn't prove [i.e., probate] her will.

Since "The Runaway Grandmother" probably entered American folklore from European tradition, it is not surprising that some American versions have their setting in a simple unspecified "Europe." The following well-detailed text was collected in 1966 from an Indiana student who had "heard it from her mother as a true event." Unlike the English tourists in Spain who stop to eat out of sheer hunger, misery, and exhaustion, the Americans in this tale pause more for standard touristic reasons, in order "to…eat their last European meal at a small, quaint restaurant." The loss of their grandmother seems to strike the family as almost comical:

Well, once there was this family and they had been waiting to go abroad for, oh, a number of years, and finally their big chance came. They packed up all of their things—had their car shipped over—and were soon in Europe and ready to go sightseeing. There were five of them and they had a rather small car and it was pretty crowded. There were the two parents and two children and a grandmother.

Well, a trip to Europe can be quite a strain on an old woman. And she hadn't been in too good of health anyway, and that was one of the reasons they took the trip, so she could see all of the "European Wonders" before she died.

Anyway, one day when they woke up they found that the grandmother had died during the night. Well, they didn't know what to do because here they were, 3,000 miles away from home and across an ocean yet, and they were the grandmother's only living relatives so they couldn't just send a body back to the States with no one to receive it. They were going to be starting home soon, anyway, so out of desperation they wrapped the grandmother's body in a piece of canvas and tied it on the top of their small car—which, by the way, made much more room inside the car.

And as they were making their last round across the village where they were staying they decided to stop and eat their last European meal at a small, quaint restaurant.

Well, it happened that while they were in there someone stole the car with the grandmother on top. For some reason they weren't too worried about the whole situation, they just wondered what the looks on the crooks' face would be when they discovered the strange contents of the canvas.

English folklorist Stewart Sanderson found "The Runaway Grandmother" second in popularity in Great Britain among "motor-car stories" only to "The Vanishing Hitchhiker."[2] His collection of versions of the legend extended back to more than twenty years before the earliest American texts. Sanderson wrote:

I first heard it in Leeds in 1960, from the wife of a colleague who told it as having happened to friends of her friends in Brussels, as they escaped through northern

---

[2]"The Vanishing Hitchhiker" legend is treated in Brunvand's book of the same name. The essential story involves one or more travelers who pick up a hitchhiker who asks for a ride to her home. When these travelers arrive at the hitchhiker's requested destination, she has inexplicably disappeared from the car. Mystified, they knock on the door of the house to which the hitchhiker has asked to be taken. The person answering the knock tells the travelers that his daughter, who matches the description of the hitchhiker, disappeared some years ago on that same road—and that today is her birthday.

France during the German invasion of 1940. A few weeks later, believing with my informant that the tale was true, I repeated it to an academic colleague in Edinburgh who also knew her. To our initial surprise he had recently heard much the same story from a colleague in Cambridge, with the difference that it was set in Spain after the war and involved the difficulty of cremating the corpse.... Other variants involve the loss of a body in a caravan [trailer] which slips its tow on a hill; the theft of a body from the luggage compartment of a holiday tour bus; and a variant I collected at the University of Nsukka, Nigeria in 1965. In this, the body of an old woman, being taken back for burial at her native village on the Crow River, is lost by rolling off the roof of a mammy-wagon [local bus] into the bush.

The European versions, then, seem to fall into two distinct subtypes—one, the wartime story involving crossing an international border, usually to escape the Nazis or to leave Eastern Europe; and second, the postwar tale of vacationers abroad. Indiana folklorist Linda Dégh, who assembled more than one hundred versions of "The Runaway Grandmother" and related stories from Europe and the United States, believed that the legend must have acquired its common form during or just after the Second World War. Possibly it evolved from stories known in Europe in the eighteenth and nineteenth centuries dealing with the mistaken theft of a corpse and ending with the thieves' shock as they inspect their booty. In the wartime context, Dégh speculated this story could have lost its last episode, shifting the climax to the risky crossing of an international border. In later years, and especially in American tradition, the focus seems to have shifted again to emphasize the inconvenience and distress of disposing of a corpse while on a vacation in a foreign country. The "message" of the story, Dégh suggested, derives from "the fear of the return of the dead" and expresses the concern that "the corpse has to receive a decent burial." In addition to the United States and England, Dégh encountered "The Runaway Grandmother" both orally and in print in Norway, Sweden, Denmark, Germany, Switzerland, Italy, Poland, Hungary and Yugoslavia. The completion of her comparative study of all texts ought to clarify further the legend's history and development.

Folklorist Charles Clay Doyle was more willing than Dégh to connect "The Runaway Grandmother" to earlier narratives. He pointed to a Renaissance "jest" (a very grim joke, at best) widely known in Europe in which an Italian Jew attempts to send his dead Jewish friend back home to Venice illegally by pickling the dismembered corpse in spices and honey and packing the pieces in a jar. While he is on a boat during the trip home, various parts of the corpse are stolen and eaten by an unwary Florentine. The switching of corpse and food, Doyle suggested, may link this story also to "The Dead Cat in the Package" (cat swapped for meat). The motif of gnawing or nibbling on a corpse is of course also found in a number of other terror stories similar to "The Roommate's Death." If one agrees that all these tale plots *are* linked, then it would seem that the bereaved family is not just ready to abandon Grandmother, they are willing to devour her as well, or at least they toy with the idea.

10   Two details in texts I have collected might lend support to Doyle's analysis. First, Doyle's Renaissance jest is strangely similar in one respect to the

1906 version of "The Dead Cat in the Package" ("The Ham Cat") which took place partly on a ferryboat; and, second, I have heard versions of the dying-grandmother story in which the corpse is cremated abroad and sent home to relatives by mail. The recipients later say "Thanks for the good curry powder; we've been using it on everything."

Whether the American versions sprang directly from postwar European variants of the border-crossing tradition or not, the particular subtypes found here are distinct. Of eighteen American versions which Dégh collected in Indiana, for example, ten fall into the group represented by the first text given above, in which the family is traveling in Mexico when the grandmother dies. The second largest group (five texts), in which the vacation takes place in the Western desert, is evidently influenced by an incident in John Steinbeck's *The Grapes of Wrath* (1939): Granma Joad's corpse being taken through the California agricultural inspection station wrapped in a blanket on the back of a truck. (Of course, it is possible that Steinbeck deliberately introduced legendary material into his plot.) Here is a summarized version of the desert subtype told to a student by a Gary, Indiana, woman who "was almost in a state of shock," believing the story to be true:

> It happened to her friend's family (I don't know their names) as they were traveling across the desert to California. Within this station wagon there was a father, a mother and their children, and the mother-in-law who everybody called "Grandma." And as they were going across the desert Grandma became sick and she died. Now they didn't want to alarm the children and they didn't want to leave Grandma out in the desert so the only place they had room for her where she—her smell wouldn't bother the children—was to strap her on top of the station wagon along with the baggage with a tarp over her, of course. And as they were traveling across the desert they kept looking for a town where they could deposit Grandma. They finally arrived in a small town in Arizona where they stopped at a filling station and they went in to report Grandma's death. And while they were within the filling station somebody stole the station wagon and when they went out—no station wagon and no Grandma! Well, it wasn't very funny even though it sounds like it because they have to wait seven years now to prove that Grandma is dead before they can collect any insurance. And they've never been able to find either the car or Grandma. This actually happened.

In a third American subtype—or it may be just Midwestern—the family is vacationing in the upper Peninsula of Michigan when Grandma dies. In a text quoted by Dégh, the stripped car is found some weeks later, but Grandma's corpse never turns up.

One cannot help being struck by the American versions' casual—almost callous—treatment of the old woman's death. Often the initially crowded condition of the family car is mentioned, and the decision to make more room by putting the corpse on the roof is made by the survivors without hesitation or debate. There is almost always a reference to the practical difficulty of probating the will or supplying proof of death. Yet almost never is any significant mention made of the car, baggage, and other property also lost to the thieves; it is almost as if this was the price the family had to pay for the relief of being rid of Grandma.

Alan Dundes has analyzed various versions of the legend and concluded that its central message is the rejection of old age and dying in our youth-oriented society. It is significant, he felt, that there is "much more room inside the car" when Grandma is gone—the old lady is out of the way at last. But yet "Grandmother is a burden whether alive or dead"—her body is an unwelcome reminder of human mortality and it must be kept away from the children. Furthermore, although the family "took her for a ride" (and Dundes recalled how gangsters use that phrase), an anonymous third party (the thief)—like a mortician in real life—took care of her after death. Finally, Dundes interpreted the details at the end of the legend as suggesting that Americans' principal interest in their aged relatives is the prospect of inheriting their money. Both the frequent news articles and editorials about the treatment of aged Americans and examples of the "Theater of the Absurd" provide validation of this critique of American values. For the latter, compare how the same themes are handled in two of Edward Albee's most gripping plays, *The Sandbox* and *The American Dream*.

15   "The Runaway Grandmother" is a fully-developed modern legend widely circulated today in many different versions across the United States; still, each story, with its often elaborate local details, is told as a "true" account. There are recent examples of each of the subtypes (the wartime and the postwar). The following was told by a Tucson, Arizona, man to my student Ann Clegg in Fall 1969. It was supposed to have happened to a friend of the informant's, "a prominent businessman in Tucson." Here the family travels to Mexico, and the thieves, usually not identified in the story, are said to be native American "foreigners":

> The businessman went on a trip to Mexico with his wife and his grandmother. The grandmother had always wanted to go to Mexico, and as she was quite old, they knew this would probably be her last chance to go. ["Taking her for a ride" again?]
>
> They got somewhere in the remote mountain areas and the grandmother had a heart attack and died. The odor was terrible because of the heat and because the grandmother had a bowel movement as she was dying. (Apparently this is not uncommon when a person has a heart attack. [Student's comment])
>
> They wrapped the grandmother in a piece of canvas they had to cover their suitcases with and put her body on top of the car. They stopped in the first town with a telephone—a town populated mostly by Indians. It took quite a while to contact their relatives in Arizona and when they came out, the body had been stolen! Imagine how frightened those superstitious Indians must have been when they found they had stolen a body!

Ah yes, this is how the superstitious savages will react to a corpse, at least in the American folk stereotype. But why would they steal a car in the first place, and how could they conceal the vehicle? We "real Americans," the story shows, know better how to regard death—rationally and neatly.

A second Utah report of "The Runaway Grandmother" indicates that the earlier form of the story is still circulating. Early in 1979 I found this note on my desk left by my assistant Sharon Decker Pratt who had often heard me discuss this and other urban legends:

> Last night at a dinner party our friends told of a conversation they had just had at a dinner party Friday night with a fascinating woman originally from Latvia who is staying at Snowbird [a ski resort] this week with some mutual friends. (The hostess was also originally from Latvia.) Both women were recounting various experiences they'd had during various political regimes; the horrors, the resistance movement, and even some of the more humorous things.
>
> The guest is around fifty, either a doctor or a dentist (kept referring to her patients) in Boston, and a perfectly reliable, credible-sounding individual. Anyhow, she told of her family's departure during the '40's whereupon her grandmother died just as they were to leave the country. Inasmuch as it was very cold (zero in the middle of winter) the grandmother's body was frozen solid and, since they did not want to leave her body in Latvia but rather bury her elsewhere, they decided to wrap her as a rather long piece of luggage and take her with them out of the country, along with their other belongings.
>
> Well, you guessed it!!! Someone stole the grandmother at the train station.

This is all very well, except that Mrs. Pratt telephoned me on Monday to say that she had spoken to the woman again, and it was the grandmother of *another* Latvian friend whose corpse had been stolen.

● Discussion and Writing Suggestions   MyWritingLab™

1. Brunvand cites examples of "The Runaway Grandmother" story in numerous countries—in Western and Eastern Europe, in the United States, and in Mexico. Which particular elements of this urban legend do you think make it so universal? How does it draw upon our human anxieties, both as members of families and as natives of a particular country?

2. Brunvand notes that "dead cat and stolen grandmother stories focus on the bereaved and tend to create in their climaxes a feeling of uneasiness tinged with humor." Explain how this mix of uneasiness and humor works in "The Runaway Grandmother." Why, exactly, do we feel uneasiness at such tales? Which elements in the stories tend to foster unease? And why is this story humorous? What, exactly, are we laughing at, and why?

3. Urban legends are often cautionary tales—that is, stories that illustrate the potentially bad consequences of certain types of behavior. What are some of the cautionary tales told to you by your parents or your teachers when you were a child? Were such cautionary tales embedded in stories? What do some of the variants of "The Runaway Grandmother" appear to caution us against? (Consider, for example, why the people in some of the variants leave the grandmother's body unattended.) To what extent do these warnings seem legitimate or worth taking seriously?

4. Brunvand explains that European versions of this story typically fall into one of two categories: "one, the wartime story involving crossing an international

border, usually to escape the Nazis or to leave Eastern Europe; and second, the postwar tale of vacationers abroad." From the versions offered here, examine an example of each of these subtypes and explain how they differ in terms of meaning or emotional impact.

5. Brunvand summarizes the view of one analyst of this story, Alan Dundes, as follows: "its central message is the rejection of old age and dying in our youth-oriented society." To what extent do you agree with the propositions that (1) our youth-oriented society rejects old age and dying, and that (2) "The Runaway Grandmother" stories do, in one form or another, incorporate this message? In responding, consider the details that embellish and also serve to authenticate the multiple variants of this story.

HOW AND WHY RUMORS WORK—AND HOW TO STOP THEM

Nicholas DiFonzo

On general principle we may disapprove of rumors, but their pervasiveness throughout history and across cultures suggests that they serve important personal and social purposes. In this selection, Nicholas DiFonzo, Professor of Psychology at Rochester Institute of Technology and the author of numerous books and articles on rumor, discusses why both individuals and groups find it necessary and even desirable to create and spread rumors. DiFonzo's best-known book is *The Watercooler Effect* (2008). In an interview with Susan Gawlowicz, DiFonzo explains how rumors develop on both personal and social levels.

Visit MyWritingLab to listen to the interview, or go to YouTube and search for "difonzo rumor."

● Review Questions   MyWritingLab™

1. What are the main reasons people spread rumors, according to DiFonzo?

2. How does DiFonzo differentiate rumor from gossip?

3. According to DiFonzo, what are the chief factors that determine how readily people accept rumors as true?

4. Summarize the main strategies for managing and fighting rumors, according to DiFonzo.

● Discussion and Review Questions   MyWritingLab™

1. One reason people spread rumors, according to DiFonzo, is to help them understand the world and to "figure out or make sense of an unclear or ambiguous situation." Draw upon one of the rumors you have read about in

this chapter—or a rumor with which you are personally familiar—to explain how this process of sense-making works. How did buying into this rumor help people—or how did it help you—make sense of how the world (or some part of the world) works?

2. DiFonzo draws a distinction between rumor and gossip. Consider Norman Rockwell's painting "The Gossips" as an example of how gossip works. Now, draw upon DiFonzo's explanation to contrast this particular situation with the situation of one of the rumors treated in this chapter—perhaps the "Frankenchicken" rumor, the rumor about Procter & Gamble's logo, the "Paul is Dead" rumor, or the urban legend about the runaway grandmother. To what extent is DiFonzo's distinction useful in clarifying the differences between rumor and gossip?

3. DiFonzo offers several reasons that people often believe that rumors are true, even without sufficient evidence to support the rumor. Again, select one of the rumors covered in this chapter, or one with which you have some experience, and explain how DiFonzo helps account for this particular rumor being so readily accepted as credible.

4. Toward the end of this interview, DiFonzo offers several suggestions for managing rumors to stop them from spreading or to destroy their credibility. To what extent does your own experience support the wisdom of DiFonzo's suggestions? Under what circumstances might such measures be ineffective? In developing your response, draw upon one or more of the rumors treated in this chapter or rumors from your own experience.

HOW TO FIGHT A RUMOR

Jesse Singal

Political candidates such as Barack Obama and John McCain, who are regularly attacked by rumors, are typically advised either to ignore them or not "dignify" them with a response. According to Singal, this is bad advice and shows a basic misunderstanding of how rumors work. "By using the tools of evolutionary theory," he claims, we can better understand that rumors are more than just idle or malicious gossip. This article originally appeared in the *Boston Globe* on October 12, 2008 (shortly before the conclusion of that year's presidential campaign). "How to Fight a Rumor" should serve to further clarify the dynamics behind some of the political rumors discussed in the previous section.

Singal is an associate editor of CampusProgress.org and of pushback.org at the Center for American Progress. He has also written for the *Daily Beast*, the *New Republic Online*, *Politico*, and the *Washington Monthly*.

For anyone who has ever worried about the power of a vicious rumor, Barack Obama's strategy over the summer must have seemed almost bizarre. Buffeted by rumors about his religion, his upbringing, and controversial statements made by his wife, Obama launched Fight the Smears, a website that lists every well-traveled false rumor about the candidate, alongside rebuttals and explanations for how the rumors arose.

Fighting rumors by publicizing them in vivid, high-profile locations is, to say the least, a surprising tactic. It's hard to imagine someone victimized by workplace rumors summarizing them and posting them on the lunchroom wall. The conventional wisdom about rumors is to take the high road and not respond. When John McCain, during the 2000 Republican primaries, was plagued with rumors that he had fathered an illegitimate child, for the most part he opted not to engage with them at all. Why would anyone want to broadcast negative claims about themselves?

And yet new research into the science of rumors suggests Obama's approach may be a sounder strategy—and the reasons why it makes sense suggest that we misunderstand both how rumors work and why they exist.

By using the tools of evolutionary theory and new approaches to mathematical modeling, researchers are drawing a clearer picture of how and why rumors spread. As they do, they are finding that far from being merely idle or malicious gossip, rumor is deeply entwined with our history as a species. It serves some basic social purposes and provides a valuable window on not just what people talk to each other about, but why.

5   Rumors, it turns out, are driven by real curiosity and the desire to know more information. Even negative rumors aren't just scurrilous or prurient—they often serve as glue for people's social networks. And although it seems counterintuitive, these facts about rumor suggest that, often, the best way to help stem a rumor is to spread it. The idea of "not dignifying a rumor with a response" reflects a deep misunderstanding of what rumors are, how they are fueled, and what purposes they serve in society.

McCain's approach in this election seems more in tune with this theory. With rumors circulating in the blogosphere that Sarah Palin's youngest baby might actually have been her daughter's child, the campaign didn't turn the other cheek: It released a statement from the Palin family that Bristol really was pregnant. The strategy worked. The other rumor was squelched.

Rumor has been around as long as human civilization, and for much of that time has been frowned upon. The Bible has some stern words for those who spread rumors: "A man who lacks judgment derides his neighbor," the Book of Proverbs reads, "but a man of understanding holds his tongue." Rumors have long been seen as at best trivial, and at worst vicious and immoral.

Experts began to look at rumors more analytically in the 1940s and 1950s, in a wave of research fueled by concern about how rumors could be managed during wartime. Though interest waned during the following decades, rumor studies have seen a resurgence in the last decade or so—partly because researchers are now more able to tackle complex, dynamic phenomena, and partly because they're newly armed with the biggest ongoing social psychology experiment in human history, the Internet, which provides them with terabytes of recorded rumors and a way to track them.

In 2004, the Rochester Institute of Technology psychologist Nicholas DiFonzo and another rumor researcher, Prashant Bordia, analyzed more than

280 Internet discussion group postings that contained rumors. They found that a good chunk of the discourse consisted of the participants sharing and evaluating information about the rumors and discussing whether they seemed likely. They realized, in other words, that people on the sites weren't swapping rumors just to gossip; they were using rumors as a vehicle to get to the truth, the same way people read news.

10   "Lots of times people will share a rumor not for their benefit or for the other person's benefit, but simply because they're trying to figure out the facts," says DiFonzo, one of the leading figures in the resurgence of rumor research. He published a book on the topic this fall: *The Watercooler Effect: A Psychologist Explores the Extraordinary Power of Rumors*.

Some types of facts seem to be more urgent triggers than others. Rumors that involve negative outcomes tend to start and spread more easily than ones that involve positive outcomes. Researchers sort rumors into "dread rumors," driven by fear ("I heard the company is downsizing"), and "wish rumors," driven by hope ("I heard our Christmas bonus will be bigger this year"). Dread rumors, it turns out, are far more contagious. In a study involving a large public hospital in Australia that was in the midst of a restructuring, Bordia and his colleagues collected 510 rumors that could be classified as dread rumors or wish rumors. Four hundred and seventy-nine of them were dread rumors.

Perhaps even more than negative stories dominate the news, negative rumors dominate the grapevine. In the absence of other sources of information, people turn to rumors to answer their most urgent concerns—suggesting that rumors play a vital role, not a peripheral or idle one, in times of worry, and can have a profound impact on how a town, city, or society reacts to a negative event.

This is a much more neutral view of rumors than the Bible, or traditional etiquette, might take. And indeed, rumor researchers tend to see them nonjudgmentally, as inherent to human nature—naturally occurring, inevitable human social phenomena, rather than pesky distractions from more civilized discourse.

Aside from their use as a news grapevine, rumors serve a second purpose as well, researchers have found: People spread them to shore up their social networks, and boost their own importance within them. To the extent people do have an agenda in spreading rumors, it's directed more at the people they're spreading them to, rather than at the subject of the rumor.

15   People are rather specific about which rumors they share, and with whom, researchers have found: They tend to spread rumors to warn friends of potential trouble, or otherwise help them, while remaining mum if it would be harmful to spread a given rumor in a certain context or to a certain person.

It's not just altruism: Rumors can build status for the person who spreads them. The psychologists John L. Shelton and Raymond S. Sanders, in documenting the impact of a murder of an undergraduate on the Ohio State University campus in 1972 on the student body, found that those with access to "inside information" about the crime and the administration's response were instantly granted higher social status. So simply possessing—or being seen as possessing—potentially useful information can serve in and of itself as a motivation to spread rumors.

When it comes to rumors about people rather than events, psychologists have found that we pay especially close attention to rumors about powerful people and their moral failings. Frank McAndrew, a professor of psychology at Knox College who studies the evolutionary roots of gossip, has found that we're particularly likely to spread negative rumors about "high-status" individuals, whether they're our bosses, professors, or celebrities.

Our behavior, McAndrew suggests, evolved in an environment in which information about others was crucially important. Back when humans lived in small groups, he theorizes, information about those higher than us on the totem pole—especially information about their weaknesses—would have been hugely valuable, and the only source we had for such information was other people. (McAndrew's work, much of which focuses on our obsession with celebrity culture, suggests our brains aren't terribly adept at distinguishing people who are "actually" important from people who simply receive a lot of attention.)

If the fundamental dynamics of rumor have roots that run deep into history, the means of transmission have been changing a great deal recently. Unlike previous forms of media, the Internet has created a two-way street—a way to quickly connect with like-minded people—that greatly multiplies the power of rumors.

20   "In the course of a single day, people across the country might hear the same rumor spoken in almost exactly the same words," says Eric Foster, a psychologist at Temple University who studies gossip and social networks.

Given what we know about which rumors thrive and persist, the particular rumors that have dominated this campaign season seem almost custom-crafted to replicate themselves and spread to a wide audience: They're negative rumors about high-status individuals that hint at moral failings.

Conservatives spreading the Obama rumors worry he may be lying about his faith to further his political career, or that his wife, Michelle, is cloaking radicalism in a moderate veneer.

The same applies to the Palin rumors: For liberals, the people most likely to spread them, they deal with severe moral failings—the hypocrisy of being a "family-values" politician with a pregnant, unwed daughter, or the whiff of authoritarian tendencies seen in her alleged attempts to ban books when she was mayor of Wasilla, Alaska.

So are such rumors impossible to stop? Not at all, says DiFonzo, who has counseled businesses, organizations, and academic institutions on how to fight rumors.

25   The first and perhaps most obvious point is that it's futile to attempt to rebut a rumor that's true, says DiFonzo. Even if it works initially, "people who are interested in ferreting out the facts are really very good at it over time if they have the proper motivation and they work together."

The recent John Edwards scandal is a perfect example: Rumors had swirled about Edwards and a possible extramarital affair for a long time. Edwards quickly and vociferously denied the rumor, but by August of this year—after persistent reporting by the National Enquirer—he was forced to admit to it. There was little Edwards could do to forestall the inevitable.

Other than denying a rumor that's true, perhaps the biggest mistake one can make, DiFonzo and other researchers say, is to adopt a "no comment" policy: Numerous studies have shown that rumors thrive in environments of uncertainty. Considering that rumors often represent a real attempt to get at the truth, the best way to fight them is to address them in as comprehensive a manner as possible.

Anthony Pratkanis, a psychologist at the University of California, Santa Cruz, who studies persuasion and propaganda, says that an effective rebuttal will be more than a denial—it will create a new truth, including an explanation of why the rumor exists and who is benefiting from it.

"The more vivid that replacement is, the better," says Pratkanis. He and other rumor specialists refer to this tactic as "stealing thunder." When done correctly and early enough in a rumor's lifetime, it can shift the subsequent conversation in beneficial ways.

30   So how have the campaigns done so far? Obama gets relatively high marks, says DiFonzo: The candidate's website, fightthesmears.com, succeeds by "denying [the rumors] aggressively" and providing "a context for his denial." Obama could, however, create even more credible rebuttals by having them backed up by trusted third-party sources, such as religious leaders.

Pratkanis says the McCain campaign has handled the Palin rumors well, too. In the wake of the story about Palin's child, "McCain did the stealing thunder," he says. By coming out and immediately laying the facts on the table, he was able to short-circuit the coverup theories, and reroute the conversation to the more easily managed topic of Bristol's pregnancy.

There are dangers in rebutting rumors by recounting them, of course, the foremost being the inevitability that some people will remember the rumor as true. The University of Michigan psychologist Norbert Schwarz and his colleagues found that listing a rumor first and then rebutting it (the format followed by fightthesmears.com) can backfire, causing some people to remember the rumor but forget the rebuttal.

But in the case of a powerful rumor that looks like it will spread widely, DiFonzo and other experts say it makes sense to assume it will get out, and preemptively target those who are likely to hear it. When thousands of years of human experience are driving something forward, it doesn't make much sense to try to push the other way.

● Review Questions   MyWritingLab™

1. According to Singal, rumor "is deeply entwined with our history as a species" and "serves some basic social purposes." In three or four sentences, summarize these basic social purposes.

2. Why has interest in and research on rumors surged in recent decades, according to Singal?

3. From an evolutionary perspective, why are negative rumors about "high-status" individuals more likely to spread than rumors about lower-status individuals?

4. Why is it better to combat a false rumor by responding to it rather than ignoring it, according to Singal?

5. How does Singal assess the success of rumor-fighting campaigns by Barack Obama, John McCain, and John Edwards?

● Discussion and Writing Suggestions   MyWritingLab™

1. Try to find an Internet discussion group thread similar to those discussed by Singal in paragraph 9. A number of these rumor threads concern speculation and rumors about new consumer electronic products in advance of their actual launch. (One such Internet forum is called "Macrumors.") Examine some of the postings. What seems to be their thrust and their purpose?

2. To what extent do your own experiences with rumors support Singal's ideas about the basic purposes of rumor? Drawing upon Singal's approach to the subject, discuss one or more rumors you have heard, started, or helped spread. Who started the rumors? Against whom were they directed? What purposes were served by the rumor? How did the target respond? To what extent was this response effective?

3. Select a rumor covered in some detail elsewhere in this chapter (or select a rumor treated on Snopes.com) and analyze it in terms of the basic social purposes of rumor discussed by Singal. How, for example, does the "Frankenchicken" rumor or the Procter & Gamble rumor work, in terms of the ways people use rumors for particular social purposes?

4. Singal argues that "the best way to fight [rumors] is to address them in as comprehensive a manner as possible." But in "Truth is in the Ear of the Beholder," Gregory Rodriguez summarizes Cass Sunstein's contrary argument: "efforts at correcting rumors can sometimes even hurt the cause of truth." Sunstein had cited a 2004 experiment showing that people will bend evidence to support their positions even when their positions are factually incorrect. That is, those who have accepted a rumor as true may reject all attempts, even factually correct ones, to counter the rumor. Is it possible to reconcile the conflicting positions of Singal and Sunstein? Under what circumstances is it better to fight the rumor than ignore it? Under what circumstances is fighting the rumor likely to be futile?

THE RUMOR

John Updike

We've become familiar with the public face of rumor: the instantaneous surge of an allegation across the Internet and onto YouTube, the press releases on company letterhead, the politician's talk show appearances. But what happens behind closed doors—when, for example, a rumor ricochets inside the home, affecting both a couple and their circle of friends and colleagues? In the following story, John Updike traces the effects of gossip on a marriage. Updike (1932–2009) was a "Renaissance man" among American writers of the second half of the twentieth century: novelist, short-story writer, poet, essayist, literary critic, art critic. A two-time Pulitzer Prize winner, he is best known for his "Rabbit" novels—*Rabbit, Run* (1960), *Rabbit Redux* (1971), *Rabbit is Rich* (1981), and *Rabbit at Rest* (1990)—which trace the life of Harry C. ("Rabbit") Angstrom (former high school basketball star, car salesman, and indifferent husband and father) as he struggles to make sense of, and break free from, his middle class, suburban life. Like Norman Rockwell earlier in this chapter, Updike is best known for his portrayal of "average" Americans and mainstream life. In this story, originally published by *Esquire* in June 1991, he presents a vivid portrait of a marriage. While initially dismissing as falsehood a rumor that comes to engulf their life, the couple is nonetheless quietly enthralled by it.

Go to: Google or Bing

Search terms: *"updike rumor"*

● Discussion and Writing Suggestions   MyWritingLab™

1. Even as she dismisses the rumors, Sharon is surprised by her friends' certainty about its truth. Do you think she has doubts? Why? Is she bothered—or excited—by the rumor?

2. The rumor in this story is "factually untrue." During the course of the story, however, Frank begins to wonder whether it might be at least partially true. He even wonders whether it would be a good thing for the rumor to be *perceived* as true by his wife and his colleagues. Can you think of other rumors, whether from your own life or from the public stage, that may have been false but have been accepted or even embraced by the subjects?

3. How do Frank's feelings toward his mother and father, as well as his feelings about the kind of men he admires, lend support to his feelings about the rumor?

4. Most of the previous selections in this chapter have focused on rumor functioning on a societal scale. This story, however, deals with the personal life of the Whittiers. How do some of the theories explored in the chapter (by Knapp, Goleman, and DiFonzo) apply here? In which of Knapp's categories does the rumor fit (from the perspective of the friends, as well as Frank himself)?

5. Frank entertains the notion that there may be value, or at least allure, in the rumor's spread. Create a rumor about yourself that you would like to see circulate among your friends and community. What is it? Why would you want people to believe this rumor?

6. Do you like Frank and Sharon Whittier? Why or why not? Do their thoughts and actions seem plausible? Explain.

7. This story is centered on married life, not on a larger societal context like most of the other readings in this chapter. That said, the implications of "The Rumor" might also be applied to larger arenas. What other situations come to mind, whether from other chapter selections or from your own experience, where a company, a politician, or a celebrity indulges in or even encourages a rumor instead of correcting it?

SYNTHESIS ACTIVITIES   MyWritingLab™

1. Write a synthesis that explains *why* and *how* rumors spread. In your discussion, refer to the theories of Goleman, Knapp, DiFonzo, and Singal. Use any of the example rumors treated in this chapter (as well as the stolen kidney case in the "Analysis" chapter, pp. 188–194) to support your discussion.

2. Select one of the rumors treated at length in this chapter. Briefly analyze this rumor from the perspective of the theoretical approaches of Knapp (three categories of rumor; qualities of good rumors); Rodriguez ("biased assimilation"); and DiFonzo (dealing with making sense of the world in at atmosphere of ambiguity and threat). Then, in an argument synthesis, explain which theoretical approach most compellingly reveals the whys and wherefores of the rumor you have selected.

3. Some rumors are created in the spirit of fun and are relatively harmless in their effects—for example, those New York alligators at the beginning of this chapter. Other rumors arise from malicious intent and often devastate their targets. In an argument synthesis, rank several types of rumors on a scale of benevolence/malevolence, according to the motives of those who create and spread them. Draw upon some of the case studies treated in this chapter, as well as the "missing kidney" rumor. Don't hesitate to bring into the discussion rumors based on your own personal knowledge and experience. Draw also upon some of the theoretical pieces such as those of Goleman, Rodriguez, Knapp, DiFonzo, and Singal to help account for and justify your rankings.

4. Select any three of the cases of rumor from this chapter or in Chapter 6, "Analysis." Compare and contrast these rumors, taking account of their origins (and the rationales behind their creation), their spread, and their impact. Try to select cases that appear similar on the surface but may have subtle or even major differences below the surface. Alternatively, choose cases that appear quite different but that, according to your analysis, are essentially similar in nature. A key part of your comparison-contrast synthesis will be answering the

so-what question. Having worked the comparison, what observations can you make about the three rumors you have discussed—and provisionally (based on your small sample size) about rumor itself?

5. In his article on McCain's presidential bid of 2000, McCain's campaign manager Richard H. Davis concluded that to respond to a rumor would only give it weight. Considering everything you have read in this chapter—not just that particular piece—to what extent do you agree with this cautious approach? Should a rumor be addressed at its first sign, or should it be allowed to run its course, however long that takes? What factors should bear most on how best to counteract damaging rumors? Use examples from the readings, as well as the ideas of theorists like Goleman, DiFonzo, and Singal, to support your argument.

6. In 2011, President Obama and his aides attempted to quell the long-standing rumor that he was not born in the United States. Attempting to put the claim to rest, he eventually released the full-length version of his birth certificate. Even in the face of this hard evidence, the rumor persisted, and public figures like Donald Trump and Texas governor Rick Perry suggested that the evidence presented by the new document was insufficient or questionable. What does the refusal to accept concrete evidence suggest about human nature and political affiliation? In drafting your response, an argument synthesis, consider the points made by at least two of the following: Goleman, Rodriguez, Knapp, and Singal.

7. Conventional wisdom suggests that our digital lifestyle (think e-mail, Facebook, Twitter, computers, smartphones, and so on) has accelerated the spread of rumor. To what extent do you find this belief true? In the digital age, can attempts to quell rumors move at the same speed as the rumors themselves? Use examples from the selections in this chapter, along with cases of rumor known to you personally, to develop an argument in response to this question. It might be helpful to consider a rumor from the pre-Internet era as well as one from the present day.

8. Goleman, Knapp, DiFonzo, and Singal explain that rumors are often symptoms of our hopes and fears. What hopes and fears are reflected by one of the following rumors: (1) the genetically modified chicken, (2) the "satanic logo," or (3) "Paul is dead"? Model your response on the analysis paper in Chapter 6, which applied Knapp's categories to the "missing kidney" rumor.

9. Imagine that you work for a public relations firm hired by someone targeted by a rumor. This might be a rumor similar to one covered in this chapter or another you have come across outside of class. Create an argument synthesis that takes the form of an action plan for your client.

10. After the "Paul is Dead" rumor spread, as documented by Glenn, the Beatles seemed to have fun playing along with the story. In John Updike's "The Rumor," we see an untrue rumor spark a sense of excitement in its subject and a surprising determination to keep the rumor alive. What is it about a rumor that, occasionally, might be alluring to its subject? Drawing upon some of the particular cases covered in this chapter, or cases known to you personally, develop your response into an argument synthesis.

RESEARCH ACTIVITIES

1. Throughout his discussion, DiFonzo refers to the numerous rumors that grew out of the terrorist attacks of September 11, 2001. As he explains, some of these rumors were developed as a coping mechanism, and some grew out of newly discovered anxieties and fears about the identity and the nature of our enemies. Research another catastrophic event in American history, and identify some of the rumors that were created in its wake. Knapp offers a glimpse into the rumors circulating around World War II. What about the Vietnam War? The Kennedy assassination? The Martin Luther King assassination? Explore some of the rumors associated with these events (or another such national calamity) and the ways in which theories by Knapp, DiFonzo, or Sunstein help account for them.

2. While some rumors eventually go national and even global, others affect a more limited group of people: employees of a particular company, customers of local establishments, soldiers in a particular military unit, students at a particular school. In the fall of 2011, Smith College was overrun with an explosive culinary news item: All campus dining services were going vegan. This announcement sparked Twitter feeds, campus protests, and even coverage from the leading vegan lifestyle magazine. But the news was a hoax, fueled by the power of rumor. Research two or three other hoaxes of limited impact, and discuss their spread and their impact (try searching for "local rumors" on Snopes.com or the archives of local newspapers). How and why did these rumors spread so fast and alarm so many? Draw upon Goleman's and DiFonzo's ideas about how rumors help us make sense of an uncertain world. What does public willingness to accept these hoaxes as true say about human nature?

3. Some rumors, such as "the missing kidney" (see Chapter 6), have entered popular culture as "urban legends." Urban legends (which often have nothing to do with cities) are defined by DiFonzo as "narratives about strange, funny, or horrible events that could have happened, the details of which change to fit particular locales or time periods, and which frequently contain a moral lesson." There's even a horror film named *Urban Legend*. Picture yourself as a film executive or screenwriter looking for an idea to develop into a movie. Research other urban legends (start with Snopes.com), and write a pitch for a movie based on one that appeals to you. Why do you think audiences will connect to this story? What features about it will engage viewers? What does it have in common with other rumors?

4. In an op-ed for the *Washington Post* (November 17, 2011), Paul Farhi asserts that "the e-mail rumor mill is run by conservatives." While he discusses political rumors associated with both Republicans and Democrats, Farhi claims that "when it comes to generating and sustaining specious and shocking stories, there's no contest. The majority of the junk comes from the right, aimed at the

left." Research some of the more notorious rumors that have been a feature of recent politics. Describe and characterize them. To what extent are their agendas and political purposes clear? Based on your research, do you agree with Farhi? Develop your argument using Knapp's scheme. What do your findings suggest about political discourse in both parties?

5. If you were to receive an e-mail sharing a story about a "missing kidney," you might assume that the alleged events in the story represented a new phenomenon. As Robert Dingwall explains, however (see the model analysis in Chapter 6), the kidney rumor stretches back many years, undergoing transformations in different countries and at different periods of its development.

   Research and discuss another fear-driven rumor. (Once again, a good starting point is Snopes.com. Then learn more about your selected rumor from additional sources.) How far back does the rumor go in the public consciousness? How has it changed over the years?

6. Robert H. Knapp's theory of rumor, included in this chapter, was written over half a century ago, a fact that accounts for his choice of examples relating to World War II. Imagine that you work for a publisher looking to release an updated version of his article, with content footnotes providing examples more likely to be familiar to contemporary readers. Locate new examples of rumor (not treated in this chapter) that illustrate each of Knapp's three categories. In your memo to the publisher, identify each rumor, categorize it, and explain how it fulfills the criteria for that type of rumor.

7. Research the new crop of "reputation defender" services available to those who find their online identities under siege. (Start by searching online with terms like "managing rumor.") Based on your findings, discuss these services and explain how they work and why they may or may not be effective.

MyWritingLab™ Visit Ch. 13 Rumor in MyWritingLab to test your understanding of the chapter objectives.

Chapter 14

Happiness and Its Discontents

Enshrined in the Declaration of Independence are the unalienable rights to "Life, Liberty, and the pursuit of Happiness." The founders believed that a nation should guarantee its citizens' physical safety and freedom—preconditions for the right to life and liberty. As for happiness, they understood that while a government can create the necessary conditions—including the right to vote and to worship freely—ultimately it falls to individuals to *be* happy.

Which, of course, begs one of humankind's oldest, most vexing questions: *What is happiness?* Any attempt to define the word draws on the teachings of our major religious and ethical systems. In the Western tradition, the attempt raises familiar questions and points us toward eternal questions such as these:

- Is happiness found in living a virtuous life (Aristotle)?
- Is happiness found in wrestling with life (Marcus Aurelius)?
- Is happiness found not in this world but the next (St. Augustine)?
- Is happiness whatever provides the greatest good for the greatest number of people (Bentham/Mill)?
- Is happiness possible, given the trade-offs we make to enjoy the benefits of civilization (Freud)?
- Can happiness be found by searching for it (Camus)?

Humankind has debated definitions of happiness for thousands of years, and still a single, acceptable definition eludes us. Perhaps, as some philosophers suggest, the question *What is happiness?* is flawed. Perhaps the answer is ultimately trivial, as Samuel Beckett implies in his absurdist masterpiece *Waiting for Godot*:

> VLADIMIR: Say you are [happy], even if it's not true.
>
> ESTRAGON: What am I to say?

VLADIMIR: Say, I am happy.

ESTRAGON: I am happy.

VLADIMIR: So am I.

ESTRAGON: So am I.

VLADIMIR: We are happy.

ESTRAGON: We are happy. (*Silence.*) What do we do now, now that we are happy?[†]

Beckett wrote in the mid-twentieth century. Sixty years later, we still seek answers—no surprise. But what *is* surprising is that today answers are increasingly couched in the language of science. One recent study shows that people who reported being happy throughout the day, over a five-year span, were 35 percent less likely to die over that span than those who reported being unhappy. Multiple studies have reached a similar conclusion: Happiness, which researchers term *subjective well-being*, is a positive, contributing factor to long, healthy lives.

Claims such as this one differ in kind from ones that have occupied history's philosophers, theologians, and artists—for the social scientists study happiness by conducting experiments. Calling themselves *positive psychologists* (and building on the pioneering work of Abraham Maslow [1908–1970] in self-actualization and peak experiences), they hope to complement psychology's traditional focus on mental *dis*order by investigating conditions that "lead to well-being … [and] positive individuals." Their efforts to understand happiness—and some rather heated challenges to their efforts—provide the focus of this chapter.

As data concerning the correlation between happiness and longevity emerged, two lines of criticism followed: the first, a criticism not of positive psychology, per se, but of the get-happy-quick industry that has skimmed off legitimate research findings and promised gullible consumers easy formulas for the Happy Life. These programs inevitably fail, claim the critics; worse, they mislead the vulnerable into thinking that *if* they read self-help books and attend expensive seminars and *if* they still are feeling sad, then they must somehow be defective. Not true—and the psychologists actually conducting the studies make no claims about quickly transforming gloomy faces to smiley ones.

A second line of criticism directed at happiness studies challenges both its methods and assumptions. Among the questions you will find debated in this chapter:

- Can happiness be measured? Are such measurements reliable and replicable—and, if not, how can we call positive psychology a science?

- To what extent does positive psychology assume that emotional states such as sadness and anger are harmful? Might these states, unpleasant though they are, play a beneficial role in human development?

[†]From *Waiting for Godot*, London: Faber and Faber, 1956.

- Given ongoing human suffering, is the desire to be extremely happy defensible?

- In what ways does an emphasis on positive psychology risk turning ordinary sadness into a psychiatric disorder for which pills are the proffered cure?

The literature on happiness is vast, and we have limited the focus of this chapter to three elements: the emerging science of happiness, critiques of this science, and selections on happiness from the humanist (that is, *non*scientific) tradition. The chapter opens with the nonscientific: four readings that suggest just how elusive our attempts to grasp, let alone define, happiness can be. Former New Hampshire poet laureate Jane Kenyon begins by comparing happiness to a visit from an unknown uncle who "finds you asleep midafternoon." Philosopher Lynne McFall's "Pig Happiness?" presents a playful yet serious run of questions on happiness, a teaser to get your mind primed for engagement. In the "Pursuit of Happiness," cultural critic Mark Kingwell (also a philosopher) sets happiness in a broad cultural context and claims that while the question "What is happiness?" never leads to definitive answers, the question remains an important one worth pursuing. The last of the introductory pieces is Douglas Preston's account of what he learned about happiness from a revered religious leader.

Three selections on positive psychology follow. "A Balanced Psychology and a Full Life" by Martin Seligman, one of the founders of the field, sets out an agenda for the new discipline. "Flow"—as in "being in the flow" or "zone" while engaged in an activity—describes the key contribution of Mihaly Csikszentmihalyi, another founder of the discipline. Then a reviewer for the *New Republic* summarizes the research of Elizabeth Dunn and Michael Norton, who, in a recent book, discuss the ways in which money actually *can* buy happiness.

In the final section of the chapter, critics challenge the methods and assumptions of positive psychology. Sharon Begley reports on a growing backlash to happiness studies in "Happiness: Enough Already." In "Happy Like God," philosopher Simon Critchley takes a swipe at the effort to measure happiness scientifically (while meditating on the philosophy of Rousseau). Cliff Oxford rejects the application of happiness studies to the business world. And David Brooks observes how people may "shoot for happiness but feel formed through suffering."

The authors in this chapter are both approachable and provocative. They offer new terms and fresh ideas through which you can reflect on your own happiness—past, present, and future.

HAPPINESS

Jane Kenyon

We open the chapter with reflections on happiness by two literary artists and two philosophers. Later, you will read attempts by social scientists to quantify happiness and name its key elements. Positive psychologists and their critics will define the term, argue the definition, and also argue the very methods of investigation—experiment versus reflection. Writers and philosophers take a less direct, reflective approach. For instance, the poem you will read here achieves its effects not by appeals to logic but by engaging our emotions and memories.

Neither Kenyon nor the three authors that open this chapter, all from the literary or humanist traditions, will offer clear answers concerning happiness. But they will get you thinking about happiness in general and what it means to you personally.

Jane Kenyon wrote four books of poetry: *From Room to Room* (1978), *The Boat of Quiet Hours* (1986), *Let Evening Come* (1990), and *Constance* (1993). The poem "Happiness" first appeared in *Poetry* magazine (February 1995) and is collected in the posthumously published *Otherwise: New and Selected Poems* (1996). When she died of cancer at the age of forty-seven, Kenyon was poet laureate of New Hampshire.

There's just no accounting for happiness,
or the way it turns up like a prodigal[*]
who comes back to the dust at your feet
having squandered a fortune far away.

5   And how can you not forgive?
You make a feast in honor of what
was lost, and take from its place the finest
garment, which you saved for an occasion
you could not imagine, and you weep night and day
10 to know that you were not abandoned,
that happiness saved its most extreme form
for you alone.

No, happiness is the uncle you never
knew about, who flies a single-engine plane
15 onto the grassy landing strip, hitchhikes
into town, and inquires at every door
until he finds you asleep midafternoon
as you so often are during the unmerciful
hours of your despair.

20 It comes to the monk in his cell.
It comes to the woman sweeping the street
with a birch broom, to the child
whose mother has passed out from drink.
It comes to the lover, to the dog chewing
25 a sock, to the pusher, to the basketmaker,

---

*Kenyon refers to the biblical parable of the "Prodigal (or Lost) Son." A man has two sons. One takes his inheritance, goes off, squanders the money, and returns ashamed and defeated, while the other son remains at home, diligently working. When the father celebrates the return of the one son, the other protests that his long-absent brother should not be a cause for joy. See Luke 15:11–32.

and to the clerk stacking cans of carrots
in the night.
      It even comes to the boulder
in the perpetual shade of pine barrens,
30   to rain falling on the open sea,
to the wineglass, weary of holding wine.

● Discussion and Writing Suggestions   MyWritingLab™

1. Read the biblical story of the "prodigal son" (Luke 15:11–32). What do you learn from the story that can help you understand the poem?

2. In her comparison of happiness and the prodigal child, Kenyon adopts the point of view of the father to whom the son returns. That is, she equates happiness with the prodigal son and the recipient of happiness with the father. Why?

3. In lines 13–19, Kenyon shifts the comparison: Happiness is now like a previously unknown uncle come to visit. Consider the details of the uncle's landing and search—for example, the "single-engine plane" and the hitchhiking into town. In what ways does this mini-narrative suggest the approach and arrival of happiness?

4. Review your answers to Discussion and Writing Suggestions #2 and #3, above. Kenyon offers two comparisons. How is happiness like *both* an unknown uncle *and* a prodigal son? Another way of thinking about this: What qualities do the prodigal son and uncle share that suggest an essential feature of happiness?

5. Reread lines 20–31, images of people and places visited by happiness. Does happiness visiting a boulder tell you more about the boulder or about the nature of happiness? Does happiness visiting a person tell you more about the person or about the nature of happiness? What qualities of happiness is Kenyon exploring here?

6. "[H]ow can you not forgive?" In what sense is forgiveness called for when happiness arrives?

7. Reread the last line. What could it mean, in relation to the rest of the poem?

PIG HAPPINESS?

Lynne McFall

Aristotle wrote that happiness follows from living a virtuous life. Two thousand years later, dramatist and storyteller William Saroyan claimed that the "greatest happiness you can have is knowing that you do not necessarily require happiness." What happiness might be, no one can say for certain; but the question has occupied thinkers and writers for millennia. Philosopher Lynne McFall, emerita associate professor of philosophy at Syracuse

University, takes a playful yet serious run at understanding happiness in this introduction to our chapter. Her questions will amuse and confound you. The passage appeared first in *Happiness* (1989), the first volume in *Studies in Moral Philosophy*.

> It is better to be a human being dissatisfied than a pig satisfied; better to be Socrates dissatisfied than a fool satisfied.
>
> John Stuart Mill
> *Utilitarianism*

Is it? And if it is, which is happier?

Let's call a person, P, *pig-happy*, just in case *P* is satisfied as a consequence of the belief that *P*'s life is going the way *P* wants it to go. [But suppose] *P*'s life is one many would judge unfit for persons: *P*'s desires, values, beliefs, capacities, or circumstances are radically defective in some way. The question I want to raise is: Is someone who is pig-happy really happy[? Is] pig-happiness enough for human happiness? More positively, by what standard should we judge that a person is leading or has led a happy life?

Pig-happiness takes different forms. There are many ways in which a person's life might be seen as defective, but the following five examples illustrate different categories of defect which, in conjunction with satisfaction, present us with conflicting intuitions on the question of happiness.

The *"happy" idiot*. Consider the severely retarded person, one who lacks many of the capacities we regard as characteristically human (e.g., the capacity for self-reflection), and assume she is content for the most part. Is this a happy life?

5   *The incompetent bottlecap collector*. Say someone's only end in life is to amass the largest collection of bottlecaps in the world. He's considered the matter thoroughly, looked into other options, and this is the one goal that inspires him. He *thinks* he has an impressive collection of bottlecaps (actually it's pretty paltry), and so is satisfied with his life. Is he happy?

The deluded fool. Suppose a woman's ideal is the love of a good man. If the man she loves despises her and is despicable, is she happy so long as she is deceived? If she dies believing in his undying affection and moral perfection, was hers a happy life? Is the fool's paradise paradise, or at least happiness?

The successful immoralist. Take any conventionally evil person, e.g., Hitler, Mata Hari, or Idi Amin, and suppose he or she found this life rewarding. Is this "true" happiness?

The impossible idealist. Imagine a woman with a noble ideal: she desires universal peace, perfect justice, and happiness for all. Given that this ideal is unrealizable, could her life be a happy one?

Our intuitions in these cases conflict. On the one hand, we may be inclined to say of such persons that they are not (or could not be) *truly* happy. On the other hand, there is a fairly clear sense in which they are ("At least the poor thing is happy"; "He's happy collecting bottlecaps"; "Ignorance is bliss"; "Hitler doesn't deserve to be happy"; "She's happy with her dreams, let her keep them").

10   But this is not the only problem in sorting out the confusions in our talk about happiness: the explanations of our conflicting intuitions may themselves conflict. If we are inclined to call the retarded, the crazy, the deluded, the immoral, and the

too-idealistic happy, to say that they may lead happy lives, is this because no "objective" standard for appraising persons' lives is defensible (Who are we to say?), because happiness is only one good among others, or simply because this is *one* of the ways we use the word—as a report on someone's state of mind? If we refuse to say that such people can lead happy lives, is this because we do not think they will *remain* happy in such circumstances, because happiness is the greatest good and these are clearly defective lives, because they do not meet *our* standards [for happiness], fail [at happiness], even by their own [standards], or have [no standards]?

● Review Questions   MyWritingLab™

1. Briefly summarize the five categories of ways in which a person's life may be viewed as "defective."

2. In ¶ 2, McFall asks if "pig-happiness" is "enough" for human happiness. What does "enough" mean, in the context of the epigraph by John Stuart Mill?

3. In ¶ 10, the most challenging of the selection, McFall lays out key criteria by which we might judge—or refuse to judge—a person's life as happy. Outline the logic of this paragraph. How is it structured?

● Discussion and Writing Suggestions   MyWritingLab™

1. Philosophers pose difficult, sometimes uncomfortable questions. Of the questions that McFall poses about human defects that bear on a discussion of happiness, which unsettles you most—and why?

2. After discussing each of the ways a person's life may be defective, McFall asks: Is this person, P, happy? Choose one of these defects and answer McFall's question. Explain your answer.

3. John Stuart Mill, quoted by McFall, has no qualms in judging the relative value of types of happiness. Do you? Are you comfortable stating unequivocally that one person's happiness is superior to another's? Why? In your answer, discuss the standards you would use to make the judgment—or the reasons why you might distrust such standards.

4. Using McFall's questions on happiness as an example, discuss what it means to be "seriously playful" in the philosophical sense.

5. Philosophical discussion about the world differs from we might call "ordinary" discussion—the kind of talk that might transpire between friends discussing, say, happiness. Assume that you know *nothing* about the discipline of philosophy. Reread this selection and attempt to define the topics philosophers study and the methods they use to investigate these topics.

Mark Kingwell is an award-winning social critic, essayist, and professor of philosophy at the University of Toronto. In the following excerpt from his book *In Pursuit of Happiness: Better Living from Plato to Prozac* (1998), Kingwell calls the quest for a universal definition of happiness "a mug's game"—that is, a game no one can win. Still, he argues, the question of what happiness is remains important; and so the mug's game continues, as vital to us in the twenty-first century as it was to philosophers in the first. Kingwell's essays have appeared in the *New York Times* and *Harper's*. His numerous books include *Rites of Way: The Politics and Poetics of Public Space* (2009), *Nearest Thing to Heaven* (2006), and *The World We Want* (2000).

The desire to understand happiness, to get hold of it, is one that is common in our culture, central to our many daily judgments about life, love, work, politics, and play. We do not always confront happiness head on, as it were, but it is nonetheless implicit in our decisions and undertakings, the ordering principle or end of our human projects. But if the desire to understand happiness is common, there is every kind of disagreement about what constitutes a good answer. Everyone thinks they know something about what happiness is; very few people manage to convince anyone else that they are right. Indeed, happiness seems to be one of those "essentially contestable concepts" that philosophers love to unleash upon an unsuspecting world. You know the sort of thing: justice, goodness, virtue, beauty, love. Thinkers since Plato have thought they could say what those things were, sometimes in great detail, but the fact that we are still asking questions about them demonstrates that no single answer is good enough.

Just so with happiness. Often we are inclined … to *demand a definition* of it. But, paradoxically, all offered definitions are waved aside like so many feeble tennis lobs, reducing the question itself to a mere ploy, a rhetorical device to confound the speaker… . Nor is that sort of thing much improvement on the kinds of uselessly precise definitions you are likely to find in the dictionary. The *New English Dictionary*, for example, offers the famously unhelpful "state of pleasurable content of mind, which results from success of the attainment of what is considered good." Samuel Johnson neatly evaded the notorious problem in his own *Dictionary* by defining "happiness" as felicity and "felicity" as happiness.

The first thing to realize about happiness, I think, is that trying to provide a one-sentence definition of it is always a mug's game. (One critic of such vacuous definitions noted they mostly worked by "in effect defining happiness as wanting what you want and getting what you get and hoping that the two will coincide."[1]) There are many more questions than answers in this particular quarter of the philosophical field, and we must learn to accept that. No sentence beginning "Happiness is …" is likely to do us much good.

There is also a related and larger problem, as many a philosopher of happiness has discovered over the centuries. It is difficult to say anything intelligent about a subject that is at once so apparently clear and yet so resistant to explication. There is something about the implicit profundity of the issue of happiness, in other words, combined with the nearly inevitable banality of most sentiments given to it, that makes of happiness-talk a din of misfiring attempts at eloquence. Getting a grip on happiness is therefore far from easy. Indeed, for many, the concept is the paragon of ineffability, something about which nothing meaningful can be said or written. "Happiness writes white," said Henri de Montherlant of the banality of contentment when it came to literature.

5   John Stuart Mill fingered an even more troubling problem. "Ask yourself whether you are happy," he wrote in his 1873 *Autobiography*, "and you cease to be so." "The search for happiness is one of the chief sources of unhappiness," agreed twentieth-century essayist Eric Hoffer, while novelist Nathaniel Hawthorne famously compared happiness to a butterfly which, if pursued, always eludes your grasp, but which, if you sit quietly, may just land upon you.[2] The contemporary critic John Ralston Saul argues that notions of happiness have suffered such a decline from their ancient philosophical robustness that they now speak of mere material comfort or simply "pursuit of personal pleasure or an obscure sense of inner contentment"; accordingly, he suggests dropping the world from our lexicon altogether. "As economic and social conditions have gradually sunk, happiness, with its twisted meaning at the ethical and legal centre of our society, has seemed increasingly lugubrious and out of place," he writes. "In a more practical world, there would be a formal process for retiring a world from active use until it finds itself again."[3]

On this view, asking about happiness can only result in unhapiness or confusion, and therefore the project must succumb to its own self-contradiction. The question "What is happiness?" is judged by these thinkers to be a bad one, logically ill formed, misleading, or maybe just pointless. Pursuing it can only bring vexation and misery, the opposite of what we desire. (I don't know about Hoffer or Hawthorne, but Mill wasn't a very happy type: a celebrated child prodigy who learned Greek at three and had read all of Plato at seven, he suffered a nervous breakdown at nineteen.)

Those who would turn their backs on the pursuit of a definition for happiness would even seem to have scientific authority on their side. In 1996, several genetic and behavioral studies appeared in scientific journals that offered evidence to support the conclusion that one's achievable degree of happiness is genetically determined. You are either happy or you're not, and there is nothing that talking or writing about it is going to do to change that; indeed, nothing in your own life plans or aspirations and accomplishments will alter a built-in, hard-wired capacity for contentment. Try as you might, you cannot overcome the fact that, when it comes to happiness, biology is destiny.

Edward and Carol Diener, psychologists at the University of Illinois, reported in *Psychological Science* magazine that their study of surveys from more than forty countries demonstrated that money, education, and family background were less important in determining one's level of happiness than was basic genetic predisposition. David Lykken, a behavior geneticist at the University of Minnesota, concurred in his report on a survey of more than 1,300 sets of twins. "People who have to go to work in overalls on the bus can feel as happy as people who wear suits and ties and drive a Mercedes," Lykken said (as if that should be surprising).[4]

The geneticists were far from confident in predicting a solution to the problem of happiness, but they nevertheless demonstrated a high degree of scientific confidence—a confidence shared by those who had reviewed the studies, including Dr. Jerome Kagan, a well-known developmental psychologist at Harvard University. "It's clear that T. S. Eliot was by nature dour, and Jay Leno is congenitally upbeat," Kagan told the *New York Times*. "But we're far from filling in the biological blanks. [Lykken's study] is a brilliant idea—it's well worth pursuing." The studies, and others that demonstrated a correlation between dopamine levels in the brain and expressions of subjective satisfaction, were widely reported in articles in publications as diverse as scientific journals and glossy in-flight magazines, often with jaunty titles like "How Your Genes Put a Smile on Your Face" or (rather illogically, considering the evidence) the old imperative "Get Happy!"[5]

10   Hawthorne's brand of common sense and these new genetic-predisposition theories, both of which seek to ground the happiness inquiry before it is launched, sound good— but only until you recognize their essential conservatism. If followed honestly and to their logical conclusion, such views would mark the end of rational human life, suspending us in intellectual nullity. So, while there is some measure of truth in the observation that questioning happiness will result in a certain kind of unhappiness, Mill, Hawthorne, Hoffer, and the rest of the naysayers are unnecessarily and preemptively pessimistic. So are the geneticists, who condemn us to a prison of biological limitation without ever raising the deeper question of what they, or we, mean by happiness—a failure that says more about the current popularity of this kind of reductive genetic "explanation" of human behavior than it does about the real limits of human life and experience. The happiness question is a good one, indeed a very good one. It is both answerable and important. … We can speak meaningfully about happiness, in short, and we can do so with intelligence and with reasonable prospect of results—not perhaps the kind of results that some happy-merchants promise you, but results nonetheless.

Notes

[1] Howard Mumford Jones, *The Pursuit of Happiness* (Cambridge: Harvard University Press, 1953), p. 6, in a chapter on what he calls "The Glittering Generality," borrowing the phrase from Rufus Choate's wry 1856 comment on the natural law provisions of the U.S. Constitution. Copyright © 1957 by the President and Fellows of Harvard College. Reprinted by permission of Harvard University Press. This and all further quotations used by permission.

[2] Eric Hoffer, *The Passionate State of Mind and Other Aphorisms* (New York: Harper & Row, 1955). See also Paul Nowell Elbin, *The Paradox of Happiness* (New York: Hawthorn Books, 1975).

[3] John Ralston Saul, *The Doubter's Companion: A Dictionary of Aggressive Common Sense* (Toronto: Viking, 1994), pp. 153–54.

[4] Quoted in Sanjida O'Connell, "How Your Genes Put a Smile on Your Face," *Toronto Star* (1 September 1996), pp. Al and A4.

[5] Rae Corelli, "Get Happy!" *Maclean's* (16 September 1996). Also Daniel Goleman, "Forget Money: Nothing Can Buy Happiness," *USAir* (November 1996), pp. 70–90 (inter.); and Goleman, "Happiness Is … Genetic, Researchers Say," *New York Times* (15 July 1996), reprinted in *Globe and Mail* (16 July 1996).

● **Review Questions**   MyWritingLab™

1. In what way is happiness an "essentially contestable concept"?

2. "Happiness writes white," suggests one commentator. What does this mean?

3. Compare and contrast Mill's, Hawthorne's, and Saul's comments on happiness in ¶ 5.

4. What do studies of genetics add to the discussion of happiness?

5. Kingwell disagrees with the findings of geneticists and the opinions of Mill, Hawthorne, and Hoffer. Why?

● **Discussion and Writing Suggestions**   MyWritingLab™

1. If, as Kingwell writes, "no single answer [to the question of happiness] is good enough" and "[n]o sentence beginning 'Happiness is ...' is likely to do us much good," what accounts for humankind's endless attempts to define the term?

2. Reread ¶ 5 and the lines quoted from Hawthorne and Saul. How might the search for happiness be self-defeating? Why would those who search for happiness fail to grasp it or, worse, turn unhappy *because* of the search?

3. Reread ¶ 5. Use Kingwell's references to John Stuart Mill, Nathaniel Hawthorne, or Eric Hoffer as a principle with which to analyze an experience of your own. What do you discover?

4. Consider Kingwell's quotation of John Stuart Mill: "Ask yourself whether you are happy, and you cease to be so." In your experience, is Mill correct?

5. Kingwell rescues the possibility of an inquiry into happiness from the "conservatism" of the geneticists and Hawthorne, concluding that "[w]e can speak meaningfully about happiness." Based on your experience, do you think it useful to discuss happiness? Is it better not to inquire and simply embrace the experience of happiness when it comes? Explain.

THE DALAI LAMA'S SKI TRIP: WHAT I LEARNED IN THE SLUSH WITH HIS HOLINESS

Douglas Preston

Most of us take happiness seriously. We *want* to be happy. Who doesn't! That's not to say, though, that the topic can't be treated, and treated well, with a light, even humorous touch. In this next selection, writer Douglas Preston tells the story of how he helped play host to a famous religious and political figure who was visiting the United States in 1991. The ending will likely bring a smile. The piece first appeared in *Slate* on February 26, 2014.

The Dalai Lama, recipient of the Nobel Peace Prize in 1989, is revered among Tibetan Buddhists as the fourteenth incarnation of a great teacher. When China occupied Tibet in 1959, the Dalai Lama and others fled over the Himalayas and established a Tibetan government-in-exile in Dharamsala, northern India. The author of over sixty books and recipient of more than twenty honorary doctorates and numerous other awards, the Dalai Lama is widely regarded among Buddhists and non-Buddhists alike as an international emissary of compassion and non-violence.

In the mid '80s, I was living in Santa Fe, N.M., making a shabby living writing magazine articles, when a peculiar assignment came my way. I had become friendly with a group of Tibetan exiles who lived in a compound on Canyon Road, where they ran a business selling Tibetan rugs, jewelry, and religious items. The Tibetans had settled in Santa Fe because its mountains, adobe buildings, and high-altitude environment reminded them of home.

The founder of the Tibetan community was a man named Paljor Thondup. Thondup had escaped the Chinese invasion of Tibet as a kid, crossing the Himalayas with his family in an epic, multiyear journey by yak and horseback. Thondup made it to Nepal and from there to India, where he enrolled in a school in the southeastern city of Pondicherry with other Tibetan refugees. One day, the Dalai Lama visited his class. Many years later, in Dharamsala, India, Thondup talked his way into a private audience with the Dalai Lama, who told Thondup that he had never forgotten the bright teenager in the back of the Pondicherry classroom, waving his hand and answering every question, while the other students sat dumbstruck with awe. They established a connection. And Thondup eventually made his way to Santa Fe.

The Dalai Lama received the Nobel Peace Prize in 1989. Thondup, who had heard that he was planning a tour of the United States, invited him to visit Santa Fe. The Dalai Lama accepted and said he would be happy to come for a week. At the time, he wasn't the international celebrity he is today. He traveled with only a half-dozen monks, most of whom spoke no English. He had no handlers, advance men, interpreters, press people, or travel coordinators. Nor did he have any money. As the date of the visit approached, Thondup went into a panic. He had no money to pay for the visit and no idea how to organize it. He called the only person he knew in government, a young man named James Rutherford, who ran the governor's art gallery in the state capitol building. Rutherford was not exactly a power broker in the state of New Mexico, but he had a rare gift for organization. He undertook to arrange the Dalai Lama's visit.

Rutherford began making phone calls. He borrowed a stretch limousine from a wealthy art dealer, and he asked his brother, Rusty, to drive it. He persuaded the proprietors of Rancho Encantado, a luxury resort outside Santa Fe, to provide the Dalai Lama and his monks with free food and lodging. He called the state police and arranged for a security detail.

5   Among the many phone calls Rutherford made, one was to me. He asked me to act as the Dalai Lama's press secretary. I explained to Rutherford that he had the wrong person, that I had no experience in that line, and that it would surely be a disaster. Rutherford said that he didn't have time to argue. The Dalai Lama, he explained, was a person who would stop and talk to anyone who asked him a

question. He treated all people the same, from the president of the United States to a bum on the street, giving every person his full time and attention. Someone had to manage the press and keep the Dalai Lama from being buttonholed. And that person was going to be me.

I desperately needed the money, and so I agreed. As Rutherford was about to ring off, I asked how much I'd be paid. He was incredulous and told me he was saddened by my avarice. How could I even think about being paid for the privilege of spending a week with His Holiness? On the contrary, the volunteers were expected to give, not get. He had the pledge sheet right in front of him; how much could he put me down for?

I pledged $50.

The Dalai Lama arrived in Santa Fe on April 1, 1991. I was by his side every day from 6 a.m. until late in the evening. Traveling with him was an adventure. He was cheerful and full of enthusiasm—making quips, laughing, asking questions, rubbing his shaved head, and joking about his bad English. He did in fact stop and talk to anyone, no matter how many people were trying to rush him to his next appointment. When he spoke to you, it was as if he shut out the rest of the world to focus his entire sympathy, attention, care, and interest on you.

He rose every morning at 3:30 a.m. and meditated for several hours. While he normally went to bed early, in Santa Fe he had to attend dinners most evenings until late. As a result, every day after lunch we took him back to Rancho Encantado for a nap. ...

10   On the penultimate day of his visit, the Dalai Lama had lunch with Jeff Bingaman and Pete Domenici, the senators from New Mexico, and Bruce King, the state's governor. During the luncheon, someone mentioned that Santa Fe had a ski area. The Dalai Lama seized on this news and began asking questions about skiing—how it was done, if it was difficult, who did it, how fast they went, how did they keep from falling down.

[Later that day, the Dalai Lama asked to go to the mountains and see people skiing.]

•   •   •

It was a splendid April day, perfect for spring skiing—the temperature in the upper 50s, the slopes crowded, the snow of the kind skiers call "mashed potatoes." The Dalai Lama and his monks looked around with keen interest at the activity, the humming lifts, the skiers coming and going, and the slopes rising into blue sky.

"Can we go up mountain?" the Dalai Lama asked Rutherford.

Rutherford turned to [Benny] Abruzzo [owner of the ski area]. "The Dalai Lama wants to go up the mountain."

15   "You mean, ride the lift? Dressed like that?"

"Well, can he do it?"

"I suppose so. Just him, or ...?" Abruzzo nodded at the other monks.

"Everyone," Rutherford said. "Let's all go to the top."

Abruzzo spoke to the operator of the quad chair. Then he shooed back the line of skiers to make way for us, and opened the ropes. A hundred skiers stared in disbelief as the four monks, in a tight group, gripping each other's arms and taking tiny steps, came forward. Underneath their maroon and saffron robes the Dalai Lama and his monks all wore the same footwear: Oxford wingtip shoes. Wingtips are terrible in the snow. The monks were slipping and sliding and I was sure that one would fall and bring down the rest.

20   We made it to the lift without spilling, and the operator stopped the machine, one row of chairs at a time, to allow everyone to sit down in groups of four. I ended up sitting next to the Dalai Lama, with Thondup to my left.

The Dalai Lama turned to me. "When I come to your town," he said, "I see big mountains all around. *Beautiful* mountains. And so all week I want to go to mountains." The Dalai Lama had a vigorous way of speaking, in which he emphasized certain words. "And I hear much about this sport, *skiing*. I never see skiing before."

"You'll see skiing right below us as we ride up," I said.

"Good! Good!"

We started up the mountain. The chairlift was old and there were no safety bars that could be lowered for protection, but this didn't seem to bother the Dalai Lama, who spoke animatedly about everything he saw on the slopes. As he pointed and leaned forward into space, Thondup, who was gripping the arm of the chair with whitened knuckles, kept admonishing him in Tibetan. Later he told me that he was begging His Holiness to please sit back, hold the seat, and not lean out so much.

25   "How fast they go!" the Dalai Lama said. "And *children* skiing! Look at little boy!"

We were looking down on the bunny slope and the skiers weren't moving fast at all. Just then, an expert skier entered from a higher slope, whipping along. The Dalai Lama saw him and said, "Look—too fast! He going to hit post!" He cupped his hands, shouting down to the oblivious skier, "Look out for post!" He waved frantically. "*Look out for post!*"

The skier, who had no idea that the 14th incarnation of the Bodhisattva of Compassion was crying out to save his life, made a crisp little check as he approached the pylon, altering his line of descent, and continued expertly down the hill.

With an expostulation of wonder, the Dalai Lama sat back and clasped his hands together. "You see? Ah! Ah! This skiing is *wonderful* sport!"

We approached the top of the mountain. Abruzzo had organized the operation so that each quad chair stopped to unload its occupants. The monks and the Dalai Lama managed to get off the chairlift and make their way across the mushy snow in a group, shuffling cautiously.

30   "Look at view!" the Dalai Lama cried, heading toward the back boundary fence of the ski area, behind the lift, where the mountains dropped off. He halted at the fence and stared southward. The Santa Fe ski basin, situated on the southernmost peak in the Sangre de Cristo mountain range, is one of the highest ski areas in North America. The snow and fir trees and blue ridges fell away to a vast, vermilion desert 5,000 feet below, which stretched to a distant horizon.

As we stood, the Dalai Lama spoke enthusiastically about the view, the mountains, the snow and the desert. After a while he lapsed into silence and then, in a voice tinged with sadness, he said, *"This look like Tibet."*

The monks admired the view a while longer, and then the Dalai Lama pointed to the opposite side of the area, which commanded a view of 12,000-foot peaks. "Come, another view over here!" And they set off, in a compact group, moving swiftly across the snow.

"Wait!" someone shouted. "Don't walk in front of the lift!"

But it was too late. I could see the operator, caught off guard, scrambling to stop the lift, but he didn't get to the button in time. Just then four teenage girls came off the quad chair and were skiing down the ramp straight at the group. A chorus of shrieks went up, of the piercing kind that only teenage girls can produce, and they plowed into the Dalai Lama and his monks, knocking them down like so many red and yellow bowling pins. Girls and monks all collapsed into a tangle of arms, legs, skis, poles, and wingtip shoes.

35   We rushed over, terrified that the Dalai Lama was injured. Our worst fears seemed realized when we saw him sprawled on the snow, his face distorted, his mouth open, producing an alarming sound. Was his back broken? Should we try to move him? And then we realized that he was not injured after all, but was helpless with laughter.

"At ski area, you keep eye open always!" he said.

We untangled the monks and the girls and steered the Dalai Lama away from the ramp, to gaze safely over the snowy mountains of New Mexico.

He turned to me. "You know, in Tibet we have *big* mountains." He paused. "I think, if Tibet be free, we have *good* skiing!"

We rode the lift down and repaired to the lodge for cookies and hot chocolate. The Dalai Lama was exhilarated from his visit to the top of the mountain. He questioned Abruzzo minutely about the sport of skiing and was astonished to hear that even one-legged people could do it.

40   The Dalai Lama turned to Thondup. "Your children, they ski too?"

Thondup assured him that they did.

"Even Tibetan children ski!" he said, clapping his hands together and laughing delightedly. "Yes, this wonderful sport!"

As we finished, a young waitress with tangled, dirty-blond hair and a beaded headband began clearing our table. She stopped to listen to the conversation and finally sat down, abandoning her work. After a while, when there was a pause, she spoke to the Dalai Lama. "You didn't like your cookie?"

"Not hungry, thank you."

45   "Can I, um, ask a question?"

"Please."

She spoke with complete seriousness. "What is the meaning of life?"

In my entire week with the Dalai Lama, every conceivable question had been asked—except this one. People had been afraid to ask the one—the really big—question. There was a brief, stunned silence at the table.

The Dalai Lama answered immediately. "The meaning of life is *happiness*." He raised his finger, leaning forward, focusing on her as if she were the only person in the world. "Hard question is not, 'What is meaning of life?' That is easy question to answer! No, hard question is what *make* happiness. Money? Big house? Accomplishment? Friends? Or …" He paused. "Compassion and good heart? This is question all human beings must try to answer: *What make true happiness?*" He gave this last question a peculiar emphasis and then fell silent, gazing at her with a smile.

50   "Thank you," she said, "thank you." She got up and finished stacking the dirty dishes and cups, and took them away.

● Discussion and Writing Suggestions   MyWritingLab™

1. The Dalai Lama exhibits a kind of child-like wonder, and yet he is no child. Discuss this paradox. What does he say, and what does he do, to suggest the enthusiasms of children? What does he say and do to suggest that his enthusiasm is not childish?

2. At the end of the piece, Preston gives one person at the ski-lodge considerable attention: He describes how "a young waitress with tangled, dirty-blond hair and a beaded headband began clearing our table." She's the one who asks "the really big" question. And she's the one, not the Dalai Lama, who receives Preston's close attention in the selection's closing lines. What is going on here? What's the reason for the shift to the waitress's point of view?

3. What do you think of the Dalai Lama's response to the waitress's question (the one about the meaning of life, not about whether or not he liked his cookie)? What do you think of her response to the Dalai Lama's answer? And why do you think Preston concluded the article with that detail about her clearing away the dirty dishes?

4. Do you agree with the Dalai Lama that "The meaning of life is *happiness*"?

5. There's no bigger question than the meaning of life, and yet, Preston writes, "[p]eople had been afraid to ask" about it for the entire duration of the Dalai Lama's visit. Why might people have been hesitant?

6. Preston is a fine storyteller. What are some of the techniques he uses to keep you reading and interested?

A BALANCED PSYCHOLOGY AND A FULL LIFE

Martin E. P. Seligman, Acacia C. Parks, and Tracy Steen

Philosophers, theologians, and artists have long pondered happiness, unable to agree on what the word might mean. For thousands of years, they have based their observations and arguments on appeals to logic, personal reflection, and speculation. Recently, however, social scientists have entered the discussion with a new investigative tool—experiments designed to clarify behaviors that "help people become lastingly happier." Martin Seligman is one of the founders of this new inquiry, called positive psychology.

Zellerbach Family Professor of Psychology and director of the Positive Psychology Center at the University of Pennsylvania and past president of the American Psychological Association, Seligman has won dozens of awards and is widely credited for his work on positive psychology. Seligman's research on happiness has been supported by numerous foundations and institutions, among them the National Institute of Mental Health, the National Science Foundation, the Department of Education, and the MacArthur Foundation. He has authored and coauthored hundreds of articles, including this introduction to positive psychology in the *Philosophical Transactions of the Royal Society* (London, 2004). His many books, translated into multiple languages, include *Authentic Happiness: Using the New Positive Psychology to Realize Your Potential for Lasting Fulfillment* (2002) and *Flourish: A Visionary New Understanding of Happiness and Well-Being* (2011). Coauthor Acacia C. Parks teaches psychology and conducts research on happiness at Hiram College in Ohio. Tracy Steen grounds her work as a personal coach on the principles of positive psychology.

1. A Balanced Psychology

American psychology before World War II had three objectives: the first was to cure mental illness, the second was to make relatively untroubled people happier, and the third was to study genius and high talent. All but the first fell by the wayside after the war. Researchers turned to the study of mental disorders because that was where the funding was. The biggest grants were coming from the newly founded National Institute of Mental Health, whose purpose was to support research on mental illness, not mental health. At the same time, practitioners suddenly became able to earn a good living treating mental illness as a result of the Veterans Administration Act of 1946. Psychopathology became a primary focus of psychology in America because it made sense at that time. Many very distressed people were left in the wake of World War II, and the high incidence of mental disorders had become a pressing and immediate problem.

A wealth of excellent research resulted from this chain of events. In 1946, there were no effective treatments for any of the psychological disorders, whereas now we can cure two and treat another 12 via psychotherapy and/or pharmacology (Seligman 1993). Furthermore, the intensive study of psychopathology has given rise to methods of classifying the mental disorders (*International classification of diseases*, 9th edition, and *Diagnostic and statistical manual of mental disorders*, 4th edition), and these methods have allowed clinical psychologists to produce diagnoses with acceptable accuracy, and to reliably measure symptoms that were once quite difficult to pinpoint. After 50 years and 30 billion dollars of research, psychologists and psychiatrists can boast that we are now able to make troubled people less miserable, and that is surely a significant scientific accomplishment.

The downside of this accomplishment is that a 50-year focus on disease and pathology has taken its toll on society and on science. In our efforts to fix the worst problems that people face, we have forgotten about the rest of our mission as psychologists. Approximately 30% of people in the USA suffer from a severe mental disorder at one time or another (Kessler *et al.* 1994) and we have done an excellent job of helping that 30%. It is time now to turn to the other 70%. Although these people may not be experiencing severe pathology, there is good evidence to indicate that the absence of maladies does not constitute happiness (Diener & Lucas 2000). Even if we were asymptotically successful at removing depression, anxiety and anger, that would not result in happiness. For we believe 'happiness' is a condition over and above the absence of unhappiness.

That said, we know very little about how to improve the lives of the people whose days are largely free of overt mental dysfunction but are bereft of pleasure, engagement and meaning. We do not know much about what makes a person optimistic, kind, giving, content, engaged, purposive or brilliant. To address this, the first author proposed, during his term as President of the American Psychological Association in 1998, that psychology be just as concerned with what is right with people as it is with what is wrong. As a supplement to the vast research on the disorders and their treatment, we suggest that there should be an equally thorough study of strengths and virtues, and that we should work towards developing interventions that can help people become lastingly happier.

2. What Is Happiness?

5   Towards this goal, our first order of business is to determine what it is we were trying to increase. What is happiness? More words have been written about this great philosophical question than perhaps any other. Science can no more presume to answer this question than other classic philosophical questions, such as 'what is the meaning of life'? But science can illuminate components of happiness and investigate empirically what builds those components. With that said, a review of the literature led us to identify three constituents of happiness: (i) pleasure (or positive emotion); (ii) engagement; and (iii) meaning. We define these three routes to happiness in the paragraphs that follow.

The first route to greater happiness is hedonic, increasing positive emotion. When people refer in casual conversation to being happy, they are often referring to this route. Within limits, we can increase our positive emotion about the past (e.g. by cultivating gratitude and forgiveness), our positive emotion about the present (e.g. by savouring and mindfulness) and our positive emotion about the future (e.g. by building hope and optimism). However, unlike the other two routes to happiness, the route relying on positive emotions has clear limits. Positive affectivity is heritable, and we speculate that, for important evolutionary reasons, our emotions fluctuate within a genetically determined range. It is possible (and worthwhile) to increase the amount of positive emotion in our lives, but we can boost our hedonics only so high. Further, when people fluctuate within a relatively 'down' range of positive emotion, but live in a society like the USA that promotes an upbeat disposition, they can feel discouraged and even defective. Fortunately, positive emotion is not the sole determinant of happiness, and our most liberating goal is to offer a broader conception of happiness than mere hedonics (Seligman 2002).

A second route to happiness involves the pursuit of 'gratification'. The key characteristic of a gratification is that it engages us fully. It absorbs us.

Individuals may find gratification in participating in a great conversation, fixing a bike, reading a good book, teaching a child, playing the guitar or accomplishing a difficult task at work. We can take shortcuts to pleasures (e.g. eating ice cream, masturbating, having a massage or using drugs), but no shortcuts exist to gratification. We must involve ourselves fully, and the pursuit of gratifications requires us to draw on character strengths such as creativity, social intelligence, sense of humour, perseverance, and an appreciation of beauty and excellence.

Although gratifications are activities that may be enjoyable, they are not necessarily accompanied by positive emotions. We may say afterwards that the concert was 'fun', but what we mean is that during it, we were one with music, undistracted by thought or emotion. Indeed, the pursuit of a gratification may be, at times, unpleasant. Consider, for example, the gratification that comes from training for an endurance event such as a marathon. At any given point during the gruelling event, a runner may be discouraged or exhausted or even in physical pain; however, they may describe the overall experience as intensely gratifying.

Finding flow in gratifications need not involve anything larger than the self. Although the pursuit of gratifications involves deploying our strengths, a third route to happiness comes from using these strengths to belong to and in the service of something larger than ourselves; something such as knowledge, goodness, family, community, politics, justice or a higher spiritual power. The third route gives life meaning. It satisfies a longing for purpose in life and is the antidote to a 'fidgeting until we die' syndrome.

10   Peterson *et al.* (2005) develop reliable measures for all three routes to happiness and demonstrate that people differ in their tendency to rely on one rather than another. We call a tendency to pursue happiness by boosting positive emotion, 'the pleasant life'; the tendency to pursue happiness via the gratifications, 'the good life'; and the tendency to pursue happiness via using our strengths towards something larger than ourselves, 'the meaningful life'. A person who uses all three routes to happiness leads the 'full life', and recent empirical evidence suggests that those who lead the full life have much the greater life satisfaction (Peterson *et al.* 2005).

3. Interventions to Nurture Happiness?

We have designed and tested interventions to nurture each of the three routes to happiness (pleasure, gratification and meaning). Positive emotions are increased and the pleasant life is promoted by exercises that increase gratitude, that increase savouring, that build optimism and that challenge discouraging beliefs about the past. Interventions that increase the good life identify participants' signature strengths and use them more often and in creative new ways. Meaningful life interventions aim toward participants' identifying and connecting with something larger than themselves by using their signature strengths. Some of these interventions can be found at www.authentichappiness.org.

We are in the process of testing the efficacy of these interventions by randomly assigning individuals to interventions or to a placebo control, and measuring their level of happiness and depression before the intervention, immediately after it, one week later, one month later, and three months later. Early results demonstrate that (i) it is possible to boost individuals' levels of happiness, and (ii) these effects do not fade immediately after the intervention (as is the case with the placebo). The 'good things in life' exercise provides an example of an efficacious intervention. Designed to increase positive emotion about the past, this exercise requires individuals to record, every day for a week, three good things that happened to them each day and why those good things occurred. After completing this exercise, individuals were happier and less depressed at the three-month follow-up (Seligman & Steen 2005). Note that these research designs are exactly parallel to the random-assignment, placebo-controlled experiments that are the bulwark of the medication and psychotherapy outcome literature, except that the intervention is targeted to increase happiness rather than just to decrease suffering.

Our research places us among a growing number of positive psychologists who are committed to understanding and cultivating those factors that nurture human flourishing, and we are encouraged that the field of positive psychology seems to be thriving as well. Researchers who were studying positive strengths, emotions and institutions long before the term 'positive psychology' was coined are receiving increased recognition and support for their work, while young researchers worldwide can apply for research and intellectual support via positive psychology research awards and conferences.

One reason for optimism that the field of positive psychology may make substantial gains in the next several years is that it does not start from square one. Rather, it draws on the proven methodologies that advanced the understanding and treatment of the mental illnesses. When it is no longer necessary to make distinctions between 'positive psychology' and 'psychology as usual', the field as a whole will be more representative of the human experience. Our goal is an integrated, balanced field that integrates research on positive states and traits with research on suffering and pathology. We are committed to a psychology that concerns itself with repairing weakness as well as nurturing strengths, a psychology that concerns itself with remedying deficits as well as promoting excellence, and a psychology that concerns itself with reducing that which diminishes life as well as building that which makes life worth living. We are committed to a balanced psychology.

References

Diener, E. & Lucas, R. E. 2000 Subjective emotional wellbeing. In *Handbook of emotions* (ed. M. Lewis & J. M. Haviland-Jones), pp. 325–337. New York: Guilford.

Kessler, R. C., McGonagle, K. A., Zhao, S., Nelson, C. B., Hughes, M., Eshelman, S., Wittchen, H. & Kendler, K. S. 1994 Lifetime and 12-month prevalence of DSM-III-R psychiatric disorders in the United States. *Arch. Gen. Psychiatry* 51, 8–19.

Peterson, C., Park, N. & Seligman, M.E.P. 2005 Approaches to happiness: the full life versus the empty life. Unpublished manuscript, University of Michigan. *Am. Psychol.* (Submitted.)

Seligman, M. 1993 *What you can change and what you can't*. New York: Knopf.

Seligman, M. 2002 *Authentic happiness*. New York: Free Press.

Seligman, M. E. P. & Steen, T. 2005 Making people happier: a randomized controlled study of exercises that build positive emotion, engagement, and meaning. *Am. Psychol.* (Submitted.)

● **Review Questions**   MyWritingLab™

1. What is the broadest goal of positive psychology?

2. Instead of defining the word "happiness," which Seligman, Parks, and Steen recognize as a notoriously difficult, if not impossible, task, the authors explore what three "components of happiness"?

3. How do the results of positive psychology differ from the results of meditations on happiness by philosophers, theologians, and artists? (Reread ¶ 5 in developing your response; when writing, be sure you understand and discuss the word *empirical*.)

4. What are the limits of positive emotion, and why are these limits not necessarily an obstacle to a person's overall happiness?

5. How do the authors define the pleasant life? The good life? The meaningful life? The full life?

● **Discussion and Writing Suggestions**   MyWritingLab™

1. Illustrate the authors' three components of happiness with accounts of brief experiences from your life (or the life of someone you know personally). Write one-paragraph narratives focused on each component of happiness.

2. In ¶ 7, the authors write that "no shortcuts exist to gratification." What do the authors mean? Given their definition of gratification, do you find their statement true to your experience?

3. In ¶ 12, the authors report that routes to happiness are teachable; that is, you can learn to be happy by practicing specific activities such as "'the good things in life' exercise." What do you think of this suggestion? Could you learn to be happier? Before answering, consider this: Seligman, Parks, and Steen are not reporting stories when they make their claim about the teachability of happiness. They say they are reporting scientific *evidence*: measurable, objective evidence that could be reproduced in other studies. In their view, this evidence is no less valid or authoritative than evidence from experiments in medicine or physics.

4. "There is good evidence," write the authors, "to indicate that the absence of maladies does not constitute happiness." Reflect on your own experiences or those of others you know well. Use this insight to analyze that experience.

FINDING FLOW

Mihaly Csikszentmihalyi

As a child growing up in an Italian prison camp during the late 1930s and early 1940s, Mihaly Csikszentmihalyi (pronounced as "cheeks sent me high") watched many adults become "empty shells" when the world war upended the comfortable routines of their lives. Yet some people, he observed, maintained their dignity and values in the face of extreme hardship. When the war ended, Csikszentmihalyi immigrated to the United States to learn why. Winner of numerous awards and honorary degrees, he is best known for his theory of "flow," which he explains in the following excerpt from *Flow: The Psychology of Engagement with Everyday Life* (1997). Csikszentmihalyi is C. S. and D. J. Davidson Professor of Psychology and management director of Quality of Life Research Center at the Claremont Graduate University. Along with Martin Seligman, Csikszentmihalyi is credited with founding positive psychology. He has written hundreds of articles and nineteen books, one of which was translated into twenty-five languages.

> If we really want to live, we'd better start at once to try;
> If we don't, it doesn't matter, but we'd better start to die.
>
> W. H. Auden

The lines by Auden reproduced above compress precisely what this book is about. The choice is simple: between now and the inevitable end of our days, we can choose either to live or to die. Biological life is an automatic process, as long as we take care of the needs of the body. But to live in the sense the poet means it is by no means something that will happen by itself. In fact everything conspires against it: if we don't take charge of its direction, our life will be controlled by the outside to serve the purpose of some other agency. Biologically programmed instincts will use it to replicate the genetic material we carry; the culture will make sure that we use it to propagate its values and institutions; and other people will try to take as much of our energy as possible to further their own agenda—all of this without regard to how any of this will affect us. We cannot expect anyone to help us live; we must discover how to do it by ourselves.

So what does "to live" mean in this context? Obviously, it doesn't refer simply to biological survival. It must mean to live in fullness, without waste of time and potential, expressing one's uniqueness, yet participating intimately in the complexity of the cosmos. This book will explore ways of living in this manner, relying as much as possible on findings in contemporary psychology and my own research, as well as on the wisdom of the past, in whatever form it was recorded.

I will reopen the question of "What is a good life?" in a very modest fashion. Instead of dealing in prophecies and mysteries I will try to stay as close to reasonable evidence as possible, focusing on the mundane, the everyday events that we typically encounter throughout a normal day.

A concrete example may illustrate best what I mean by leading a good life. Years ago my students and I studied a factory where railroad cars were assembled. The main workplace was a huge, dirty hangar where one could hardly hear a word because of the constant noise. Most of the welders who worked there hated their jobs, and were constantly watching the clock in anticipation of quitting time. As soon as they were out of the factory they hurried to the neighborhood saloons, or took a drive across the state line for more lively action.

5   Except for one of them. The exception was Joe, a barely literate man in his early sixties, who had trained himself to understand and to fix every piece of equipment in the factory, from cranes to computer monitors. He loved to take on machinery that didn't work, figure out what was wrong with it, and set it right again. At home, he and his wife built a large rock garden on two empty lots next to their house, and in it he built misty fountains that made rainbows—even at night. The hundred or so welders who worked at the same plant respected Joe, even though they couldn't quite make him out. They asked his help whenever there was any problem. Many claimed that without Joe the factory might just as well close.

Throughout the years I have met many CEOs of major companies, powerful politicians, and several dozen Nobel Prize-winners—eminent people who in many ways led excellent lives, but none that was better than Joe's. What makes a life like his serene, useful, and worth living?

•   •   •

In everyday life, it is rare for the different contents of experience to be in synchrony with each other. At work my attention might be focused, because the boss gave me a job to do that requires intense thinking. But this particular job is not one I ordinarily would want to do, so I am not very motivated intrinsically. At the same time, I am distracted by feelings of anxiety about my teenage son's erratic behavior. So while part of my mind is concentrated on the task, I am not completely involved in it. It is not that my mind is in total chaos, but there is quite a bit of entropy in my consciousness—thoughts, emotions, and intentions come into focus and then disappear, producing contrary impulses, and pulling my attention in different directions. Or, to consider another example, I may enjoy a drink with friends after work, but I feel guilty about not going home to the family and mad at myself for wasting time and money.

Neither of these scenarios is particularly unusual. Everyday life is full of them: rarely do we feel the serenity that comes when heart, will, and mind are on the same page. Conflicting desires, intentions, and thoughts jostle each other in consciousness, and we are helpless to keep them in line.

But now let us consider some alternatives. Imagine, for instance, that you are skiing down a slope and your full attention is focused on the movements of the body, the position of the skis, the air whistling past your face, and the snow-shrouded trees running by. There is no room in your awareness for conflicts or contradictions; you know that a distracting thought or emotion might get you buried facedown in the snow. And who wants to get distracted? The run is so perfect that all you want is for it to last forever, to immerse yourself completely in the experience.

10   If skiing does not mean much to you, substitute your favorite activity for this vignette. It could be singing in a choir, programming a computer, dancing,

playing bridge, reading a good book. Or if you love your job, as many people do, it could be when you are getting immersed in a complicated surgical operation or a close business deal. Or this complete immersion in the activity may occur in a social interaction, as when good friends talk with each other, or when a mother plays with her baby. What is common to such moments is that consciousness is full of experiences, and these experiences are in harmony with each other. Contrary to what happens all too often in everyday life, in moments such as these what we feel, what we wish, and what we think are in harmony.

These exceptional moments are what I have called *flow experiences*. The metaphor of "flow" is one that many people have used to describe the sense of effortless action they feel in moments that stand out as the best in their lives. Athletes refer to it as "being in the zone," religious mystics as being in "ecstasy," artists and musicians as aesthetic rapture. Athletes, mystics, and artists do very different things when they reach flow, yet their descriptions of the experience are remarkably similar.

Flow tends to occur when a person faces a clear set of goals that require appropriate responses. It is easy to enter flow in games such as chess, tennis, or poker, because they have goals and rules for action that make it possible for the player to act without questioning what should be done, and how. For the duration of the game the player lives in a self-contained universe where everything is black and white. The same clarity of goals is present if you perform a religious ritual, play a musical piece, weave a rug, write a computer program, climb a mountain, or perform surgery. Activities that induce flow could be called "flow activities" because they make it more likely for the experience to occur. In contrast to normal life, flow activities allow a person to focus on goals that are clear and compatible.

Another characteristic of flow activities is that they provide immediate feedback. They make it clear how well you are doing. After each move of a game you can tell whether you have improved your position or not. With each step, the climber knows that he has inched higher. After each bar of a song you can hear whether the notes you sang matched the score. The weaver can see whether the last row of stitches fits the pattern of the tapestry as it should. The surgeon can see as she cuts whether the knife has avoided cutting any arteries, or whether there is sudden bleeding. On the job or at home we might go for long periods without a clue as to how we stand, while in flow we can usually tell.

Flow tends to occur when a person's skills are fully involved in overcoming a challenge that is just about manageable. Optimal experiences usually involve a fine balance between one's ability to act, and the available opportunities for action (see Figure 1). If challenges are too high one gets frustrated, then worried, and eventually anxious. If challenges are too low relative to one's skills one gets relaxed, then bored. If both challenges and skills are perceived to be low, one gets to feel apathetic. But when high challenges are matched with high skills, then the deep involvement that sets flow apart from ordinary life is likely to occur. The climber will feel it when the mountain demands all his strength, the singer when the song demands the full range of her vocal ability, the weaver

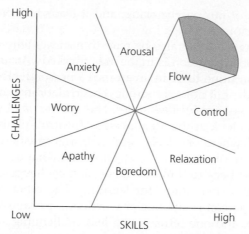

Figure 1   The quality of experience as a function of the relationship between challenges and skills. Optimal experience, or flow, occurs when both variables are high.
Sources: Adapted from Massimini & Carli 1988; Csikszentmihalyi 1990.

when the design of the tapestry is more complex than anything attempted before, and the surgeon when the operation involves new procedures or requires an unexpected variation. A typical day is full of anxiety and boredom. Flow experiences provide the flashes of intense living against this dull background.

15   When goals are clear, feedback relevant, and challenges and skills are in balance, attention becomes ordered and fully invested. Because of the total demand on psychic energy, a person in flow is completely focused. There is no space in consciousness for distracting thoughts, irrelevant feelings. Self-consciousness disappears, yet one feels stronger than usual. The sense of time is distorted: hours seem to pass by in minutes. When a person' entire being is stretched in the full functioning of body and mind, whatever one does becomes worth doing for its own sake; living becomes its own justification. In the harmonious focusing of physical and psychic energy, life finally comes into its own.

        It is the full involvement of flow, rather than happiness, that makes for excellence in life. When we are in flow, we are not happy, because to experience happiness we must focus on our inner states, and that would take away attention from the task at hand. If a rock climber takes time out to feel happy while negotiating a difficult move, he might fall to the bottom of the mountain. The surgeon can't afford to feel happy during a demanding operation, or a musician while playing a challenging score. Only after the task is completed do we have the leisure to look back on what has happened, and then we are flooded with gratitude for the excellence of that experience—then, in retrospect, we are happy. But one can be happy without experiencing flow. We can be happy experiencing the passive pleasure of a rested body, a warm sunshine, the contentment of a serene relationship. These are also moments to treasure, but this kind of happiness is very vulnerable and dependent on favorable external circumstances. The happiness that follows flow is of our own making, and it leads to increasing complexity and growth in consciousness.

The graph in Figure 1 can also be read to indicate why flow leads to personal growth. Suppose a person is in the area marked "Arousal" on the graph. This is not a bad condition to be in; in arousal a person feels mentally focused, active, and involved—but not very strong, cheerful, or in control. How can one return to the more enjoyable flow state? The answer is obvious: by learning new skills. Or let us look at the area labeled "Control." This is also a positive state of experience, where one feels happy, strong, satisfied. But one tends to lack concentration, involvement, and a feeling that what one does is important. So how does one get back to flow? By increasing challenges. Thus arousal and control are very important states for learning. The other conditions are less favorable. When a person is anxious or worried, for example, the step to flow often seems too far, and one retreats to a less challenging situation instead of trying to cope.

Thus the flow experience acts as a magnet for learning—that is, for developing new levels of challenges and skills. In an ideal situation, a person would be constantly growing while enjoying whatever he or she did. Alas, we know this is not the case. Usually we feel too bored and apathetic to move into the flow zone, so we prefer to fill our mind with ready-made, prepackaged stimulation off the video shelf or some other kind of professional entertainment. Or we feel too overwhelmed to imagine we could develop the appropriate skills, so we prefer to descend into the apathy engendered by artificial relaxants like drugs or alcohol. It takes energy to achieve optimal experiences, and all too often we are unable, or unwilling, to put out the initial effort.

How often do people experience flow? That depends on whether we are willing to count even mild approximations of the ideal condition as instances of flow. For example, if one asks a sample of typical Americans: "Do you ever get involved in something so deeply that nothing else seems to matter, and you lose track of time?" roughly one in five will say that yes, this happens to them often, as much as several times a day; whereas about 15 percent will say that no, this never happens to them. These frequencies seem to be quite stable and universal. For instance, in a recent survey of a representative sample of 6,469 Germans the same question was answered in the following way: Often, 23 percent; Sometimes, 40 percent; Rarely, 25 percent; Never or Don't Know, 12 percent. Of course if one were to count only the most intense and exalted flow experiences, then their frequency would be much more rare.

20   Flow is generally reported when a person is doing his or her favorite activity—gardening, listening to music, bowling, cooking a good meal. It also occurs when driving, when talking to friends, and surprisingly often at work. Very rarely do people report flow in passive leisure activities, such as watching television or relaxing. But because almost any activity can produce flow provided the relevant elements are present, it is possible to improve the quality of life by making sure that clear goals, immediate feedback, skills balanced to action opportunities, and the remaining conditions of flow are as much as possible a constant part of everyday life.

Review Questions   MyWritingLab™

1. What is flow? Summarize its main characteristics.

2. Summarize Figure 1, using your own language. Explain in your summary how the figure can be used as a tool for "personal growth."

3. What are the reasons that a person in flow is not happy—though he or she might recall the experience of being in flow as a happy one?

4. Csikszentmihalyi writes that "one can be happy without experiencing flow." What are some other sources of happiness? How do these compare with the happiness that follows from flow experiences?

5. How can the experience of flow be increased, and why might people not seize opportunities to increase flow?

Discussion and Writing Suggestions   MyWritingLab™

1. Use Csikszentmihalyi's concept of flow to analyze an experience in your own life. To what extent does this principle help you to understand your experience?

2. Csikszentmihalyi remarks that of all the CEOs and Nobel laureates he has met, none led a life "that was better than Joe's"—that is, Joe the welder. What does the author mean, "better than"? Do you know any people like Joe? Describe them.

3. Csikszentmihalyi opens with a meditation on living fully, with intention. He claims that if we do not "choose" to live, our biology, our culture, and other people will use us to their own ends. What does Csikszentmihalyi mean by "live"—and what does his definition have to do with the epigraph by W. H. Auden that opens the selection?

4. Csikszentmihalyi writes that "Flow experiences provide the flashes of intense living against a dull background." To what extent would you find it desirable for most if not all of your experiences to be flow experiences—such that there would be no "dull background"? Explain.

YES, MONEY CAN MAKE YOU HAPPY

Cass R. Sunstein

In the two previous selections, Martin Seligman and Mihaly Csikszentmihalyi define principles of an emerging discipline called positive psychology. This next selection illustrates the kinds of studies that follow from their desire to create a social science that is "just as concerned with what is right with people as it is with what is wrong." To that end, social scientists may design experiments to gather data on age-old questions, like: Can money buy happiness? Conventional wisdom says *no*; but conventional wisdom may be wrong, according to Elizabeth Dunn and Michael Norton in *Happy Money: The Science of Happier Spending* (2013). Dunn is an associate professor of psychology at the University of British Columbia. Michael Norton is an associate professor of Business Administration at Harvard Business School. What follows is a summary of their work, the first part of a book review written by Cass Sunstein, a professor at Harvard Law School and former head of the Obama White House Office of Information and Regulatory Affairs. His review of *Happy Money* appeared originally in the *New Republic* on August 2, 2013. Note: Section headings in this article have been added by the present editors.

Suppose that you find yourself with an unexpected windfall of $25,000. You are neither rich nor poor. You are deciding among three options for using the money:

1. Buy a new car
2. Renovate your home
3. Have a dream vacation with your family

You might think that 1 would be best, especially if your current car is not exactly a joy, and if you anticipate that a new one would give you a daily burst of pleasure. Or maybe you are tempted by 2, especially if your house really needs an upgrade. After all, you spend much of your life in it, and it might as well be as nice as possible. You might be inclined to dismiss 3, on the ground that however wonderful, any vacation is likely to be pretty short, and a short vacation cannot possibly compete with a new car or a renovated home.

If that is what you are thinking, think again. If your goal is to use the windfall to promote your own happiness, there is a strong argument for 3, especially if you plan to have the vacation a few months from now. Experiences can have a much bigger impact on people's happiness than things, and a big part of that happiness lies in looking forward to the experience that you are going to have.

This is one of the central arguments made by Elizabeth Dunn and Michael Norton, who have studied happiness for many years. Their book is filled with surprising, counterintuitive findings that also produce a spark of recognition. Don't we all know that anticipating a wonderful experience can be as good as the experience itself, and maybe even better? True, there is something disquieting about the idea that, in deciding how to spend their money, people should focus on a single question, which is what would make them happy. ... But the question is sometimes highly relevant, and for those who ask it, Dunn and Norton have some instructive answers.

1. Choose experience over things

Dunn and Norton offer five general principles. Of these, the preference for experiences over commodities may be the most important. Strikingly, people who move to new homes do not show even small increases in overall happiness. Harvard students care a lot about getting into the most beautiful and well-located of Harvard's houses, but the evidence suggests that the students' happiness is utterly unaffected by where they end up. By contrast, trips, movies, and sporting events can have a real impact on people's subjective experience.

5   One reason for the difference is that people tend to adapt to commodities. After a while, they do not much think about them, treating them instead as part of life's furniture. A nice car or a nice house may be wonderful at first, but after a relatively short period it is simply a background fact. (Consider in this light the striking finding that, while both men and women experience a remarkably large increase in happiness during and immediately after the time of marrying, their happiness returns to its premarital state after a year or two.) Novel experiences, by contrast, provide the basis for valuable memories that endure, and that can help to define the texture of a life. It is tempting to think that a two-week trip to Paris is pretty short, but if the vacation is terrific it will have a lifelong effect. In your mind, you will keep coming back to it.

Dunn and Norton also emphasize that "in general, the more we're exposed to something, the more its impact diminishes." If people get what they want whenever they want it, the relevant "it" stops giving them pleasure. The idea was nicely captured by a memorable episode of "The Twilight Zone," in which the main character, a criminal named Rocky Valentine, is shot and killed by the police, only to end up in a place where he can get immediate access to whatever he likes, with the help of his guide Pip. After a while the absence of any delays or obstacles makes Rocky quite miserable, and he exclaims to Pip, "If I gotta stay here another day, I'm gonna go nuts! I don't belong in Heaven, see? I want to go to the other place." Pip's response: "Heaven? Whatever gave you the idea that you were in Heaven, Mr. Valentine? This is the other place!"

2. "Make it a treat"

The power of adaptation leads Dunn and Norton to their second suggestion, which is to "make it a treat," perhaps by deferring and scheduling gratification. Their central claim, and probably their most important one, is that, for experiences that tend to be uniform, the effect of interruptions is to "help to 're-virginize' us, wiping our pleasure slates clean." Smart businesses exploit this idea, making desirable products available "for a limited time only." (As parents know, the *Star Wars* movies are periodically re-released for limited times.) Surprisingly, commercial interruptions have been found to improve people's enjoyment of television, by disrupting the experience of viewing.

Consider in this regard the fact that people can be cranky and impatient with their own romantic partners, even when they are prepared to be quite friendly and cheerful with strangers. One of Dunn's own studies (based on her own less-than-ideal experience with her longtime boyfriend!) show that when members of a couple try to treat their partners the same way they would a stranger, everyone can end up having a better time. Dunn and Norton contend that, in multiple domains, it is best for people to "re-virginize" themselves by using money to create special times and spaces for desirable activities.

3. "Buy time"

We tend to think that psychological distress is a product of large life events, but research suggests that minor and recurring hassles, such as troublesome neighbors and filling out forms (a true pathology of our era), can have a more serious adverse effect. This finding leads Dunn and Norton to their third suggestion, which is that people should use money to "buy time." Too often we spend our time looking for ways to save money—as, for example, by shopping for cheap gas and special deals—when we would do better to spend our money to find ways to save time. In the same vein, Dunn and Norton suggest that it is a big mistake to commit to do something far in advance, unless you are pretty sure you will not regret it when the time comes around. (A rule of thumb: don't commit to an activity in six months unless you would be willing to do it next week.)

10   A general implication is that in deciding where to live and what to do, the allocation of time is crucially important. Many of us should consider using our money to decrease the time we spend on commuting and to increase the time we spend with friends and family. People tend to hate commuting, and most of us "would be better off sticking with a job close to home, even if it pays less." And if it is necessary to commute, it makes sense to consider paying for the train rather than driving yourself. Socializing, by contrast, has positive effects on well-being, and if people spend money for birthday parties and road trips to visit their friends and family, they are probably spending it well.

4. Delay gratification—anticipate the future

In an especially intriguing discussion, Dunn and Norton contend that it is a large mistake for people to take the increasingly popular path, facilitated by credit cards, of consuming now and paying later. Intuition strongly suggests this path is the right one, because enjoyment is best today and suffering seems less bad next week. On standard economic grounds, that thought makes a lot of sense; but Dunn and Norton argue that it is exactly backward. People often get a lot of pleasure from anticipating the future. The French even have a term for this phenomenon: *se réjouir*.

I have noted that people tend to be especially happy in the period before vacations, but the phenomenon is far more general. Many people think that Sunday is the happiest day of the week (because it is a day off from work), but there is good evidence that Friday is actually happier. On Sunday people are thinking about Monday, but on Friday they are thinking about the weekend. One reason for the immense appeal of the future is its ambiguity. With respect to both goods and services, people tend "to fill in the details as we would like them to be." A coming trip, vacation, book, film, or romance may be especially appealing for that reason. Similarly, newly elected politicians are popular because people can "envision a rosy future absent the buzzkill of reality." Uncertainty allows people to see the future in the most optimistic light, and it also keeps people's attention focused on it, which increases its allure.

For this reason, it makes special sense for people to delay consumption when anticipation itself is fun or exciting, and when the delay gives them a chance to look for "enticing details that will promote positive expectations about the consumption experience." Some people seem to know this, at least with respect to some activities. Given a chance to purchase a kiss from their favorite movie star, people would pay less to have the kiss immediately than to postpone it for three days. These points explain not only the potential advantages of deferred gratification but also the potential disadvantages of paying later, which can be a lot worse than it seems. The central problem is that debts create a psychological burden. That burden is corrosive, and it can have a serious adverse effect on happiness.

5. Spend on others

Dunn and Norton also contend that people benefit from spending on others, not on themselves. When people give money away, they experience a significant hedonic boost. In one study, the best prediction of people's happiness was not how much they devoted to personal spending, but instead how much they gave to others. Even small children have been found to be happiest (as measured by their facial expressions) when they give their treats away. Indeed, giving has been found to be associated with improved health. Dunn and Norton urge that the benefits of giving are highest when givers feel that giving is their own free choice, when they feel personally connected with the recipients, and when they think that the gift will have a real impact. Clever charities are entirely aware of these facts and act accordingly.

15   Most of Dunn's and Norton's disparate claims are unified by two phenomena: attention and adaptation. Our affective states are greatly influenced by what we attend to, and we attend to what is new, not what is familiar (hence the idea of "re-virginizing"). Moreover, human beings have remarkable power to adapt both to bad and to good. After a year, lottery winners are not much happier than they were before they won the lottery, and paraplegics do not appear to be a lot less happy than they were before they lost the use of their legs. Many of the authors' findings reflect a simple claim, which is that people should be spending money on items that will continue to claim their attention, and on goods and services to which they will not quickly adapt.

● **Review Questions**   **My**Writing**Lab**™

1. According to Sunstein, "Experiences can have a much bigger impact on people's happiness than things, and a big part of that happiness lies in looking forward to the experience that you are going to have." How so?

2. How can interrupting routines enhance happiness?

3. What is "buying time," and how can it enhance happiness?

4. Credit card logic ("consume now and pay later") is a mistake, according to Dunn and Norton. Why?

5. What is the effect of spending on others?

6. "Attention" and "adaptation" unify Dunn's and Norton's claims, according to Sunstein. How so?

● Discussion and Writing Suggestions   MyWritingLab™

1. Dunn and Norton emphasize the benefits of anticipating pleasurable events. Describe an experience from your own life that illustrates—or contradicts—their point.

2. Children often demand immediate pleasure: for instance, to eat their ice cream *now*, to buy a new toy *now*. Write a dialogue, or the scene of a movie, between a hypothetical child and you in which you try to teach the value of delayed gratification. (You can assume the child will resist your best efforts.)

3. Which of Dunn's and Norton's five principles surprised you most? Why?

4. Select any of the five principles for spending money in ways that promote happiness; then use that principle to analyze an event in your life. Why were you (or why were you *not*) happy at that time?

HAPPINESS: ENOUGH ALREADY

Sharon Begley

We turn, now, to four critiques of positive psychology. In this first selection, Sharon Begley, an award-winning staff writer at *Newsweek*, surveys critiques of happiness studies from within the profession of psychology. Begley has written scores of articles that decode the complexities of science for lay readers. In a five-year break from *Newsweek*, she wrote the "Science Journal" column for the *Wall Street Journal*. The selection here first appeared on the *Newsweek*-affiliated Web site the *Daily Beast* on February 2, 2008.

[C]onsider these snapshots of the emerging happiness debate. ... Lately, Jerome Wakefield's students have been coming up to him after they break up with a boy-friend or girlfriend, and not because they want him to recommend a therapist. Wakefield, a professor at New York University, coauthored the 2007 book "The Loss of Sadness: How Psychiatry Transformed Normal Sorrow Into Depressive

"Happiness: Enough Already" by Sharon Begley from *The Daily Beast*, February 2, 2008. The Newsweek/Daily Beast Company LLC. All rights reserved. Used by permission and protected by the Copyright Laws of the United States. The printing, copying, redistribution, or retransmission of the Material without express written permission is prohibited.

Disorder," which argues that feeling down after your heart is broken—even so down that you meet the criteria for clinical depression—is normal and even salutary. But students tell him that their parents are pressuring them to seek counseling and other medical intervention—"some Zoloft, dear?"—for their sadness, and the kids want no part of it. "Can you talk to them for me?" they ask Wakefield. Rather than "listening to Prozac," they want to listen to their hearts, not have them chemically silenced.

University of Illinois psychologist Ed Diener, who has studied happiness for a quarter century, was in Scotland recently, explaining to members of Parliament and business leaders the value of augmenting traditional measures of a country's wealth with a national index of happiness. Such an index would measure policies known to increase people's sense of wellbeing, such as democratic freedoms, access to health care and the rule of law. The Scots were all in favor of such things, but not because they make people happier. "They said too much happiness might not be such a good thing," says Diener. "They like being dour, and didn't appreciate being told they should be happier."

Eric Wilson tried to get with the program. Urged on by friends, he bought books on how to become happier. He made every effort to smooth out his habitual scowl and wear a sunny smile, since a happy expression can lead to genuinely happy feelings. Wilson, a professor of English at Wake Forest University, took up jogging, reputed to boost the brain's supply of joyful neurochemicals, watched uplifting Frank Capra and Doris Day flicks and began sprinkling his conversations with "great!" and "wonderful!", the better to exercise his capacity for enthusiasm. When none of these made him happy, Wilson not only jumped off the happiness bandwagon—he also embraced his melancholy side and decided to blast a happiness movement that "leads to halflives, to bland existences," as he argues in *Against Happiness,* a book now reaching stores. Americans' fixation on happiness, he writes, fosters "a craven disregard for the value of sadness" and "its integral place in the great rhythm of the cosmos."

It's always tricky to identify a turning point, at least in real time. Only in retrospect can you accurately pinpoint when a financial market peaked or hit bottom, for instance, or the moment when the craze for pricey coffee drinks crested. But look carefully, and what you are seeing now may be the end of the drive for evergreater heights of happiness. Fed by hundreds of selfhelp books, including the current *The How of Happiness: A Scientific Approach to Getting the Life You Want,* magazine articles and an industry of life coaches and motivational speakers, the happiness movement took off in the 1990s with two legitimate developments: discoveries about the brain activity underlying wellbeing, and the emergence of "positive psychology," whose proponents urged fellow researchers to study happiness as seriously as they did pathological states such as depression. But when the science of happiness collided with pop culture and the marketplace, it morphed into something even its creators hardly recognized. There emerged "a crowd of people out there who want you to be happier," write Ed Diener and his son, Robert Biswas-Diener, in their book, *Rethinking Happiness,* due for publication later this year. Somewhere out there a pharmaceutical company "is working on a new drug to make you happier," they warn. "There are even people who would like to give you special ozone enemas to make you happier." Although some 85 percent of Americans say they're pretty happy, the happiness industry sends the insistent message that moderate levels of wellbeing aren't enough: not only can we all be happier, but we practically have a duty to be so. What was once considered normal sadness is something to be smothered, even shunned.

5   The backlash against the happiness rat race comes just when scientists are releasing the most-extensive-ever study comparing moderate and extreme levels of happiness, and finding that being happier is not always better. In surveys of 118,519 people from 96 countries, scientists examined how various levels of subjective well-being matched up with income, education, political participation, volunteer activities and close relationships. They also analyzed how different levels of happiness, as reported by college students, correlated with various outcomes. Even allowing for imprecision in people's self-reported sense of wellbeing, the results were unambiguous. The highest levels of happiness go along with the most stable, longest and most contented relationships. That is, even a little discontent with your partner can nudge you to look around for someone better, until you are at best a serial monogamist and at worst never in a loving, stable relationship. "But if you have positive illusions about your partner, which goes along with the highest levels of happiness, you're more likely to commit to an intimate relationship," says Diener.

In contrast, "once a moderate level of happiness is achieved, further increases can sometimes be detrimental" to income, career success, education and political participation, Diener and colleagues write in the journal *Perspectives on Psychological Science*. On a scale from 1 to 10, where 10 is extremely happy, 8s were more successful than 9s and 10s, getting more education and earning more. That probably reflects the fact that people who are somewhat discontent, but not so depressed as to be paralyzed, are more motivated to improve both their own lot (thus driving themselves to acquire more education and seek ever-more-challenging jobs) and the lot of their community (causing them to participate more in civic and political life). In contrast, people at the top of the jolliness charts feel no such urgency. "If you're totally satisfied with your life and with how things are going in the world," says Diener, "you don't feel very motivated to work for change. Be wary when people tell you you should be happier."

The drawbacks of constant, extreme happiness should not be surprising, since negative emotions evolved for a reason. Fear tips us off to the presence of danger, for instance. Sadness, too, seems to be part of our biological inheritance: apes, dogs and elephants all display something that looks like sadness, perhaps because it signals to others a need for help. One hint that too much euphoria can be detrimental comes from studies finding that among people with late-stage illnesses, those with the greatest sense of well-being were more likely to die in any given period of time than the mildly content were. Being "up" all the time can cause you to play down very real threats.

Eric Wilson needs no convincing that sadness has a purpose. In his *Against Happiness*, he trots out criticisms of the mindless pursuit of contentment that philosophers and artists have raised throughout history—including that, as Flaubert said, to be chronically happy one must also be stupid. Less snarkily, Wilson argues that only by experiencing sadness can we experience the fullness of the human condition. While careful not to extol depression—which is marked not only by chronic sadness but also by apathy, lethargy and an increased risk of suicide—he praises melancholia for generating "a turbulence of heart that results in an active questioning of the status quo, a perpetual longing to create new ways of being and seeing." This is not romantic claptrap. Studies show that when you are in a negative mood, says Diener, "you become more analytical, more critical and more innovative. You need negative emotions, including sadness, to direct your thinking." Abraham Lincoln was not hobbled by his dark moods bordering on depression, and Beethoven composed his later works in a melancholic funk. Vincent van Gogh, Emily Dickinson and other artistic geniuses saw the world through a glass darkly. The creator of "Peanuts," Charles M. Schulz, was known for his gloom, while Woody Allen plumbs existential melancholia for his films, and Patti Smith and Fiona Apple do so for their music.

Wilson, who asserts that "the happy man is a hollow man," is hardly the first scholar to see melancholia as muse. A classical Greek text, possibly written by Aristotle, asks, "Why is it that all those who have become eminent in philosophy or politics or poetry or the arts are clearly melancholic?" Wilson's answer is that "the blues can be a catalyst for a special kind of genius, a genius for exploring dark boundaries between opposites." The ever-restless, the chronically discontent, are dissatisfied with the status quo, be it in art or literature or politics.

10   For all their familiarity, these arguments are nevertheless being crushed by the happiness movement. Last August, the novelist Mary Gordon lamented to the *New York Times* that "among writers … what is absolutely not allowable is sadness. People will do anything rather than to acknowledge that they are sad." And in a "My Turn" column in *Newsweek* last May, Jess Decourcy Hinds, an English teacher, recounted how, after her father died, friends pressed her to distract herself from her profound sadness and sense of loss. "Why don't people accept that after a parent's death, there will be years of grief?" she wrote. "Everyone wants mourners to 'snap out of it' because observing another's anguish isn't easy."

It's hard to say exactly when ordinary Americans, no less than psychiatrists, began insisting that sadness is pathological. But by the end of the millennium that attitude was well entrenched. In 1999, Arthur Miller's *Death of a Salesman* was revived on Broadway 50 years after its premiere. A reporter asked two psychiatrists to read the script. Their diagnosis: Willy Loman was suffering from clinical depression, a pathological condition that could and should be treated with drugs. Miller was appalled. "Loman is not a depressive," he told the *New York Times*. "He is weighed down by life. There are social reasons for why he is where he is." What society once viewed as an appropriate reaction to failed hopes and dashed dreams, it now regards as a psychiatric illness.

That may be the most damaging legacy of the happiness industry: the message that all sadness is a disease. As NYU's Wakefield and Allan Horwitz of Rutgers University point out in *The Loss of Sadness*, this message has its roots in the bible of mental illness, the *Diagnostic and Statistical Manual of Mental*

Disorders. Its definition of a "major depressive episode" is remarkably broad. You must experience five not-uncommon symptoms, such as insomnia, difficulty concentrating and feeling sad or empty, for two weeks; the symptoms must cause distress or impairment, and they cannot be due to the death of a loved one. Anyone meeting these criteria is supposed to be treated.

Yet by these criteria, any number of reactions to devastating events qualify as pathological. Such as? For three weeks a woman feels sad and empty, unable to generate any interest in her job or usual activities, after her lover of five years breaks off their relationship; she has little appetite, lies awake at night and cannot concentrate during the day. Or a man's only daughter is suffering from a potentially fatal blood disorder; for weeks he is consumed by despair, cannot sleep or concentrate, feels tired and uninterested in his usual activities.

Horwitz and Wakefield do not contend that the spurned lover or the tormented father should be left to suffer. Both deserve, and would likely benefit from, empathic counseling. But their symptoms "are neither abnormal nor inappropriate in light of their" situations, the authors write. The DSM definition of depression "mistakenly encompasses some normal emotional reactions," due to its failure to take into account the context or trigger for sadness.

15   That has consequences. When someone is appropriately sad, friends and colleagues offer support and sympathy. But by labeling appropriate sadness pathological, "we have attached a stigma to being sad," says Wakefield, "with the result that depression tends to elicit hostility and rejection" with an undercurrent of " 'Get over it; take a pill.' The normal range of human emotion is not being tolerated." And insisting that sadness requires treatment may interfere with the natural healing process. "We don't know how drugs react with normal sadness and its functions, such as reconstituting your life out of the pain," says Wakefield.

Even the psychiatrist who oversaw the current DSM expresses doubts about the medicalizing of sadness. "To be human means to naturally react with feelings of sadness to negative events in one's life," writes Robert Spitzer of the New York State Psychiatric Institute in a foreword to *The Loss of Sadness*. That would be unremarkable if it didn't run completely counter to the message of the happiness brigades. It would be foolish to underestimate the power and tenacity of the happiness cheerleaders. But maybe, just maybe, the single-minded pursuit of happiness as an end in itself, rather than as a consequence of a meaningful life, has finally run its course.

● **Review Questions**   MyWritingLab™

1. In what way has happiness become a "rat race," according to Begley?

2. According to research, how might happiness beyond a moderate level have a detrimental effect?

3. In what ways has the definition of normal or appropriate sadness changed over time?

● Discussion and Writing Suggestions   MyWritingLab™

1. Most, if not all, of us have suffered a broken heart at some point with the loss of another's affections. How reasonable and appropriate would you find it to take medication to lessen feelings of sadness in such an unhappy state?

2. Begley quotes Eric Wilson: America's "fixation on happiness fosters 'a craven disregard for the value of sadness and its integral place in the great rhythm of the cosmos.' " What is the value of sadness, in your view? If you care to speculate, what might "the great rhythm of the cosmos" be—and what integral role might sadness play?

3. If you've read or seen a production of *Death of a Salesman*, comment on Arthur Miller's response to the verdict of two psychiatrists who find Willy Loman clinically depressed. *Note:* Two of the most celebrated productions of this play, available on DVD, are those featuring Lee J. Cobb (1966), who appeared as Willy Loman in the original Broadway production (1949), and—and in a considerably different interpretation of the same role—Dustin Hoffman (1986).

4. Begley makes a distinction between "the single-minded pursuit of happiness as an end in itself" and happiness that comes "as a consequence of a meaningful life." Why is this distinction important?

5. Begley writes that we respond differently to those who are sad and those who receive a medical diagnosis of clinical depression. Is this distinction meaningful to you? Explain.

6. Begley quotes Ed Diener, one of the founders of happiness studies: "If you're totally satisfied with your life and with how things are going in the world, ... you don't feel very motivated to work for change. Be wary when people tell you you should be happier." Use Diener's observation as a principle to analyze an experience in your life.

HAPPY LIKE GOD

Simon Critchley

Those committed to the humanist tradition—including the study of philosophy, literature, and religion—have little patience for a science that defines happiness too simply and then attempts to measure it. Simon Critchley's essay and the one that follows offer a sharp critique of happiness studies. Critchley is a British philosopher who teaches at the New School for Social Research. He has written numerous books on philosophy, including *On Humor* (2002), *Things Merely Are: Philosophy in the Poetry of Wallace Stevens* (2005), *and The Book of Dead Philosophers* (2008). This essay first appeared in the *New York Times* on May 25, 2009. You will find in Critchley's humanist reflections on happiness an approach far different from that of positive psychologists. Consider the differences as you read, and consider which perspective on the question of happiness appeals to you more.

What is happiness? How does one get a grip on this most elusive, intractable and perhaps unanswerable of questions?

I teach philosophy for a living, so let me begin with a philosophical answer. For the philosophers of Antiquity, notably Aristotle, it was assumed that the goal of the philosophical life—the good life, moreover—was happiness and that the latter could be defined as the *bios theoretikos*, the solitary life of contemplation. Today, few people would seem to subscribe to this view. Our lives are filled with the endless distractions of cell phones, car alarms, commuter woes and the traffic in Bangalore. The rhythm of modern life is punctuated by beeps, bleeps and a generalized attention deficit disorder.

But is the idea of happiness as an experience of contemplation really so ridiculous? Might there not be something in it? I am reminded of the following extraordinary passage from Rousseau's final book and his third (count them—he still beats Obama 3 to 2) autobiography, "Reveries of a Solitary Walker":

> If there is a state where the soul can find a resting-place secure enough to establish itself and concentrate its entire being there, with no need to remember the past or reach into the future, where *time is nothing to it*, where the present runs on indefinitely but this duration goes unnoticed, with no sign of the passing of time, and no other feeling of deprivation or enjoyment, pleasure or pain, desire or fear than the simple *feeling of existence*, a feeling that fills our soul entirely, as long as this state lasts, we can call ourselves happy, not with a poor, incomplete and relative happiness such as we find in the pleasures of life, but with a sufficient, complete and perfect happiness which leaves no emptiness to be filled in the soul. (emphases mine)

This is as close to a description of happiness as I can imagine. Rousseau is describing the experience of floating in a little rowing boat on the Lake of Bienne close to Neuchâtel in his native Switzerland. He particularly loved visiting the Île Saint Pierre, where he used to enjoy going for exploratory walks when the weather was fine and he could indulge in the great passion of his last years: botany. He would walk with a copy of Linneaus under his arm, happily identifying plants in areas of the deserted island that he had divided for this purpose into small squares.

5   On the way to the island, he would pull in the oars and just let the boat drift where it wished, for hours at a time. Rousseau would lie down in the boat and plunge into a deep reverie. How does one describe the experience of reverie: one is awake, but half asleep, thinking, but not in [a] … calculative or ordered way, simply letting the thoughts happen, as they will.

Happiness is not quantitative or measurable and it is not the object of any science, old or new. It cannot be gleaned from empirical surveys or programmed

---

"Happy Like God" by Simon Critchley, from the *New York Times*, May 25, 2009 © 2009 New York Times. All rights reserved. Used by permission and protected by the Copyright Laws of the United States. The printing, copying, redistribution, or retransmission of this Content without express written permission is prohibited.

into individuals through a combination of behavioral therapy and anti-depressants. If it consists in anything, then I think that happiness is this *feeling of existence*, this sentiment of momentary self-sufficiency that is bound up with the experience of time.

Look at what Rousseau writes above: floating in a boat in fine weather, lying down with one's eyes open to the clouds and birds or closed in reverie, one feels neither the pull of the past nor does one reach into the future. Time is nothing, or rather time is nothing but the experience of the present through which one passes without hurry, but without regret. As Wittgenstein writes in what must be the most intriguing remark in the "Tractatus," "the eternal life is given to those who live in the present." Or, as Whitman writes in "Leaves of Grass": "Happiness is not in another place, but in this place … not for another hour … but this hour."

Rousseau asks, "What is the source of our happiness in such a state?" He answers that it is nothing external to us and nothing apart from our own existence. However frenetic our environment, such a feeling of existence can be achieved. He then goes on, amazingly, to conclude, "as long as this state lasts we are self-sufficient like God."

God-like, then. To which one might reply: Who? Me? Us? Like God? Dare we? But think about it: If anyone is happy, then one imagines that God is pretty happy, and to be happy is to be like God. But consider what this means, for it might not be as ludicrous, hubristic or heretical as one might imagine. To be like God is to be without time, or rather in time with no concern for time, free of the passions and troubles of the soul, experiencing something like calm in the face of things and of oneself.

10   Why should happiness be bound up with the presence and movement of water? This is the case for Rousseau and I must confess that if I think back over those experiences of blissful reverie that are close to what Rousseau is describing then it is often in proximity to water, although usually saltwater rather than fresh. For me, it is not so much the stillness of a lake (I tend to see lakes as decaffeinated seas), but rather the never-ending drone of the surf, sitting by the sea in fair weather or foul and feeling time disappear into tide, into the endless pendulum of the tidal range. At moments like this, one can sink into deep reverie, a motionlessness that is not sleep, but where one is somehow held by the sound of the surf, lulled by the tidal movement.

Is all happiness solitary? Of course not. But one can be happy alone and this might even be the key to being happy with others. Wordsworth wandered lonely as a cloud when walking with his sister. However, I think that one can also experience this feeling of existence in the experience of love, in being intimate with one's lover, feeling the world close around one and time slips away in its passing. Rousseau's rowing boat becomes the lovers' bed and one bids the world farewell as one slides into the shared selfishness of intimacy.

… And then it is over. Time passes, the reverie ends and the feeling for existence fades. The cell phone rings, the e-mail beeps and one is sucked back into the world's relentless hum and our accompanying anxiety.

● **Discussion and Writing Suggestions** MyWritingLab™

1. Describe an experience of reverie in your own life, an experience that calls to mind the state of happiness described by Rousseau. Where were you? (In the presence of water, like Rousseau and Critchley?) How common is this experience of reverie for you? Can you go "there" any time, at will? If not, under what conditions can you achieve this state?

2. In ¶ 8, Critchley writes: "However frenetic our environment, such a feeling of existence can be achieved." How is this possible—to be in a "frenetic" environment, yet to be happy in the sense Rousseau is describing?

3. In ¶ 6, Critchley directly challenges a key premise of positive psychology: that happiness can be quantified and measured. How persuasive do you find Critchley on this point? As you consider this question, make notes and anticipate (if you're interested) a paper-long response. See Synthesis Activity #1.

4. In ¶ 7, Critchley quotes the philosopher Ludwig Wittgenstein and the poet Walt Whitman. Considered together, these quotations suggest that one can live an "eternal life." *Eternal* in what sense?

5. Critchley acknowledges that the claim that we could be "self-sufficient like God" is provocative. Do you find this assertion to be "ludicrous, hubristic or heretical"? Explain.

6. Reflecting on the work of Rousseau, Critchley writes: "[H]appiness is this *feeling of existence*, this sentiment of momentary self-sufficiency that is bound up with the experience of time." Use Critchley's statement as a principle with which to analyze an experience of your own. What do you discover?

HIGH PERFORMANCE HAPPY

Cliff Oxford

In this next selection, entrepreneur Cliff Oxford rejects the application of happiness studies to the workplace and derides employers who pamper workers with birthday cakes and team-building exercises. Calling such "Human Resource" happiness a wasted effort, he prefers a happiness that comes from deep engagement with a demanding job. Oxford has the experience to make a compelling case. He is an entrepreneur who, after leading United Parcel Service in a strategic management position that saved the company hundreds of millions of dollars, founded and sold the international information technology company STI Knowledge. Most recently, he founded the Oxford Center for Entrepreneurs, an education company that helps CEOs and owners of fast-growth companies manage success and plan for the future. Oxford Center members are offered "no-nonsense ... seminars [that] challenge their thinking." In that same spirit, Oxford wrote this piece for the *New York Times* blog "You're the Boss" on May 7, 2013.

"Tell me something I *don't* know," is what I think every time I see another article, blog post or book on the value of happy employees. And here is what I find disturbing about these happy-employee propagandists. They are mostly off about what it takes to motivate employees and keep them happy in a fast-growth culture.

Don't get me wrong—I want happy employees, too. But I think there are two types of happiness in a work culture: Human Resources Happy and High Performance Happy. Fast-growth success has everything to do with the latter and nothing to do with the former. Unfortunately, 99 percent of the discussion and solutions are focused on Human Resources Happy.

Here's how I define H.R. Happy: Bosses are at least superficially nice and periodically pretend to be interested in employees as people. These employees can count on birthday-cake celebrations and shallow conversations about what their hobbies are outside of work. This approach allows H.R. people to do the job they love—compliance and regulations—instead of the job they should be doing—finding and recruiting the best available talent.

And this may work in a call-center environment or in a second-rate corporate culture where people resign themselves to the fact that they will get more if they accept being treated like children. But these H.R. Happy employees can have a rough time at fast-growth companies when they meet people who are High Performance Happy. Think of an Olympic athlete jumping into the pool for those 4:30 a.m. laps. High Performance Happy is an attitude with a skill set that says we are on a mission that is bigger than any one of us. We find our happiness in being on a world class team that is making a difference.

5   H.R. Happy says we should do what pleases us first—bring your dog to work! High Performance Happy says I will fight for every inch. I will be there at 4:30 a.m. no matter what and until the last dog dies. Respect is core to the success of High Performance Happy, and it is based on what you are giving not on what you are taking. For example, if one person has a sick child, we all have a sick child, and we all give more that day. And this is why High Performance Happy builds deeper bonds.

In the movie *American Beauty*, Annette Bening played Carolyn, the personification of Happy H.R. Set aside her bedeviled husband, and no matter what was said to her, she felt compelled to say something positive, even though it was as phony as the eye-lashes she batted. But that is what the H.R. propaganda teaches on how to build a company. Be nice to people and they will work hard for you. But, by the way, that was not the approach at successful companies like UPS and Apple, which magnify the outcomes of the high-performance elite and obliterate the happy talk.

Steve Jobs was well known for his rants about time-clock punching morons, but his high performance elite got better not bitter. Why? Apple's mission—making technology cool—was far more important than a few harsh words or even a little immaturity. And before its founder passed way, UPS was a great example of high performance elite with an almost military culture. At UPS, performance reviews were called "agent orange" because they were orange in color and dreaded if you had not met or exceeded your commitments. Back in the late '80s, UPS was disciplined by the Occupational Safety and Health Administration for being too hard on its management employees at its six-week, basic-training school for supervisors. I attended it, and let's just say it was taxing. The company ended the program shortly thereafter. On the other hand, UPS managers often had to be disciplined for working too many hours, week after week. Why? We truly believed that the American economy depended upon our moving packages from point A to point B.

High Performance Happy means you give employees tremendous responsibility, and they are happy to show that they are the best. You don't have to con them into doing things with a flavor-of-the-month methodology that suggests they will only perform if you make them happy first. H.R. Happy says, I want you to think that I like you. High Performance Happy says, I believe in you. Here are the guideposts for building a High Performance Happy culture.

First, you can't hide the duds the way you can in corporate America. If high performance is level 10, then duds aren't the two and threes who are quickly shown the door. The duds are the fives and sixes who are the happy slackers—the ones who do just enough to get by, but hey, they're happy! They befriend the boss, love meetings and are the first to check the scores and Facebook when they get back from lunch. Their H.R. Happy habits will do one of two things—bring the high performance elite down to the middle or push them out the door. The duds have to go. Today.

10   Here's what you tell the high performers. Come spend time with us if you want to do something special. Don't take it personally if you get yelled at for something you did not do. Get over it, and I am sure we will apologize when we find time. If you ask for help, we will be there. If you do not ask for help, we will assume that you are performing in a blaze of glory so be ready to show it.

Don't tell us later that you were confused or did not agree with what we were doing. You can say whatever you want to whomever you want when the decision is up for discussion—and this will be encouraged in many formats, from quick huddles to day-long strategy sessions. But when the decision is made, you march with the decision and not with what makes you happy.

High Performance Happy does not like a lot of unnecessary processes and rules, which is why entrepreneurs have to let high performance people make decisions. If you trust them with your mission and with hundreds of important daily choices, you can also trust them to handle their vacation schedule, their paid time off, and the tools they need to get the job done.

High performance organizations do not hire family members. That's because it's very hard to fire family, and you have to earn your spot in a high performance lineup every day. Here is the deal: I love your work if you are making the plays. If you are not, I have to find someone who can.

In High Performance Happy, you cannot have people behaving like liberal Democrats or right-wing Republicans. It has nothing to do with politics. In fast-growth organizations, life is not fair every day, and you can't have liberals running around trying to make sure everything is equal and no one is offended. I am sorry but there are going to be days when not all is equal and someone is offended. We always try to go back and make it up, but there are times when you have to take it for the team—and not bring it up three years later at a company meeting.

15   But you also don't want right-wing types who really don't understand how the world works and lack the emotional intelligence to get over anything that bothers them. If they think somebody got more than they did, they stew over it every day until you give them more. Again, I am sorry, but in fast growth there are times when one group gets more than the other. "Get over it" is the natural response in a high performance environment. Of course, that would be considered the height of hypocrisy at an H.R. Happy company.

The toughest part of High Performance Happy is dealing with the exit of a high performance employee. What do you do when one of the chosen chooses to leave? First, you ask if there is an issue that you have not discussed. Then you ask if there is anything you can do. If the answer to both questions is no, and the employee is just leaving to go to another team, the person exits with a thank you. No good-bye parties. No H.R. exit interviews. No farewell dinners. The person is gone, and the quicker the better.

But here's the flip side. When it comes to lay offs of high performance employees during downturns, you simply cannot do it. You have to figure out other ways. In 2001, after the dot-com crash, my information technology company lost about 20 percent of its revenue. I remember the chief financial officer came to see me with what was supposed to be good news. With some belt-tightening measures, he said, we only had to lay off 12 or 13 people. We looked at our list of folks and could find nothing but High Performance Happy.

We had just made the Inc. 500, so they had delivered, and I did not want to break the we-are-in-this-together bond. So I decided the 40 highest paid people would take a 10-percent pay cut, and we would make up the rest in travel reductions. I was not surprised when I did not hear any whining, moaning or groaning from the top 40. I *was* surprised when the person who would have been No. 41 came into my office and said he wanted the same cut. The next day, the H.R. director came to see me and said, "Cliff, I have had a stream of people in my office all day—team leaders, front-line people, just about every role—asking if they can take the 10-percent pay cut, too. I don't even think we need the money."

I think it was that day that I knew for sure we had a great company that was High Performance Happy.

Review Questions   MyWritingLab™

1. What's the difference between Human Resources Happiness and High Performance Happiness?

2. How does High-Performance Happiness build deep bonds?

3. Who are "dud" employees, according to Oxford? What are their fates in Human Resource Happy jobs vs. High Performance Happy jobs?

4. Describe the High Performance Happy workplace culture.

5. What is the High Performance Happy view of layoffs?

● **Discussion and Writing Suggestions**   MyWritingLab™

1. Straight off, beginning in the first paragraph, Oxford goes on the attack against positive psychology, labeling those who write articles, blogs, or books on the value of happy employees "propagandists." Find other examples of this direct, assertive tone. What's effective—or not—about his strategy? What is your response to it?

2. Do you have direct experience working in a company that promoted Human Resource Happiness or High Performance Happiness? Write about that experience and your reactions to it. Based on your experience, do you agree with Oxford's assessment that Human Resource Happiness is inherently flawed and that High Performance Happiness, while sometimes achieved in a harsh work environment, is superior? Perhaps you've had experience with both management approaches. In this case, compare and contrast your experiences.

3. Based on Oxford's description of High Performance Happy and Human Resource Happy workplaces, at which kind of workplace would you prefer to be employed—and why?

4. Oxford finds that "99 percent" of advice on happiness promotes the type of happiness he finds so problematic. Could 99 percent be all wrong, all the time? What are some arguments *for* Human Resource Happiness? For instance, might Human Resource Happiness be appropriate for some types of business more than others?

WHAT SUFFERING DOES

David Brooks

Happiness is but one part of the human drama; suffering is another. In this essay, David Brooks reflects on what we learn, and how we change, from suffering. In so doing he—along with Sharon Begley, Cliff Oxford, and Simon Critchley—offers a counterweight to positive psychologists, who study the ways people can maximize their happiness. Brooks is both a commentator for the PBS *News Hour* and a columnist for the *New York Times*, in which this selection first appeared *on* April 7, 2014. For a fuller biography, see pages 312–313.

Over the past few weeks, I've found myself in a bunch of conversations in which the unspoken assumption was that the main goal of life is to maximize happiness. That's normal. When people plan for the future, they often talk about all the good times and good experiences they hope to have. We live in a culture awash in talk about happiness. In one three-month period last year, more than 1,000 books were released on Amazon on that subject.

But notice this phenomenon. When people remember the past, they don't only talk about happiness. It is often the ordeals that seem most significant. People shoot for happiness but feel formed through suffering.

Now, of course, it should be said that there is nothing intrinsically ennobling about suffering. Just as failure is sometimes just failure (and not your path to becoming the next Steve Jobs) suffering is sometimes just destructive, to be exited as quickly as possible.

But some people are clearly ennobled by it. Think of the way Franklin Roosevelt came back deeper and more empathetic after being struck with polio. Often, physical or social suffering can give people an outsider's perspective, an attuned awareness of what other outsiders are enduring.

5   But the big thing that suffering does is it takes you outside of precisely that logic that the happiness mentality encourages. Happiness wants you to think about maximizing your benefits. Difficulty and suffering sends you on a different course.

First, suffering drags you deeper into yourself. The theologian Paul Tillich wrote that people who endure suffering are taken beneath the routines of life and find they are not who they believed themselves to be. The agony involved in, say, composing a great piece of music or the grief of having lost a loved one smashes through what they thought was the bottom floor of their personality, revealing an area below, and then it smashes through that floor revealing another area.

Then, suffering gives people a more accurate sense of their own limitations, what they can control and cannot control. When people are thrust down into these deeper zones, they are forced to confront the fact they can't determine what goes on there. Try as they might, they just can't tell themselves to stop feeling pain, or to stop missing the one who has died or gone. And even when tranquillity begins to come back, or in those moments when grief eases, it is not clear where the relief comes from. The healing process, too, feels as though it's part of some natural or divine process beyond individual control.

People in this circumstance often have the sense that they are swept up in some larger providence. Abraham Lincoln suffered through the pain of conducting a civil war, and he came out of that with the Second Inaugural. He emerged with this sense that there were deep currents of agony and redemption sweeping not just through him but through the nation as a whole, and that he was just an instrument for transcendent tasks.

It's at this point that people in the midst of difficulty begin to feel a call. They are not masters of the situation, but neither are they helpless. They can't determine the course of their pain, but they can participate in responding to it. They often feel an overwhelming moral responsibility to respond well to it. People who seek this proper rejoinder to ordeal sense that they are at a deeper level than the level of happiness and individual utility. They don't say, "Well, I'm feeling a lot of pain over the loss of my child. I should try to balance my hedonic account by going to a lot of parties and whooping it up."

10   The right response to this sort of pain is not pleasure. It's holiness. I don't even mean that in a purely religious sense. It means seeing life as a moral drama, placing the hard experiences in a moral context and trying to redeem something bad by turning it into something sacred. Parents who've lost a child start foundations. Lincoln sacrificed himself for the Union. Prisoners in the concentration camp with psychologist Viktor Frankl rededicated themselves to living up to the hopes and expectations of their loved ones, even though those loved ones might themselves already be dead.

Recovering from suffering is not like recovering from a disease. Many people don't come out healed; they come out different. They crash through the logic of individual utility and behave paradoxically. Instead of recoiling from the sorts of loving commitments that almost always involve suffering, they throw themselves more deeply into them. Even while experiencing the worst and most lacerating consequences, some people double down on vulnerability. They hurl themselves deeper and gratefully into their art, loved ones and commitments.

The suffering involved in their tasks becomes a fearful gift and very different than that equal and other gift, happiness, conventionally defined.

● Discussion and Writing Suggestions   MyWritingLab™

1. People do not willingly seek out suffering; yet when they encounter suffering they often "feel formed" by it in extraordinary ways. Why? What does "formed" mean in this sense?

2. Brooks observes that people who suffer can respond well: Lincoln wrote the Second Inaugural after the Civil War. Roosevelt gained empathy after being stricken with polio. Brooks admires their "proper rejoinder" to suffering. To what extent do you think ordinary people, not just extraordinary ones like former presidents who faced momentous challenges, can achieve this ennobling response to suffering? Do we all have the capacity? What is it that calls forth from us an ennobled response to suffering?

3. Brooks writes that people who suffer "sense that they are at a deeper level than the level of happiness and individual utility." What does he mean by "a deeper level"?

4. "Holiness" as a response to pain: "trying to redeem something bad by turning it into something sacred." If you have suffered and recognize the "holiness" that Brooks writes of, write about the experience: what you learned, what you felt, how you were "formed."

5. Happiness and suffering are "equal" but very different "gifts," according to Brooks. We learn from each, but we learn differently from each. How so?

SYNTHESIS QUESTIONS   MyWritingLab™

1. What are the guiding principles of positive psychology, and what do critics claim are its greatest weaknesses? In explaining positive psychology, draw on the selections by Seligman, Sunstein, and Csikszentmihalyi. In explaining the criticisms, draw on the work by Critchley, Brooks, Oxford, and Begley. Conclude by commenting on how both camps, despite their differing methods, strive to understand more about happiness.

2. Researchers on happiness have found a strong correlation between a person's happiness and the quality of that person's network of friends and family. At the same time, Critchley, writing on Rousseau's and his own experiences of happiness, extols the virtues of the solitary person's happiness. And Csikszentmihalyi writes of "flow" as a private experience. Allowing that both types of happiness are possible and that one view does not negate the other, with which view of happiness do you identify more strongly: social or solitary? Develop your response into an explanatory synthesis.

3. McFall, Critchley, Preston, and Kenyon write about happiness far differently than do Seligman and Csikszentmihalyi. These two sets of writers—philosophers, a novelist, and a poet on the one hand; social scientists on the other—use different assumptions, logic, and types of evidence to explore the topic of happiness. In an explanatory synthesis, identify these different assumptions, logic, and types of evidence. Conclude with an observation on which approach to studying happiness appeals to you more.

4. The following observation is attributed to psychoanalyst and philosopher Adam Phillips: "[A]nyone who could maintain a state of happiness, given the state of the world, is living in a delusion." Do you agree? Develop your answer into an argument.

5. Lynne McFall does not answer the questions implied by John Stuart Mill's famous statement: "It is better to be a human dissatisfied than a pig satisfied; better to be Socrates dissatisfied than a fool satisfied." Instead, she poses a series of questions herself, none of which she answers. Write an argument responding to any one of McFall's questions. To the extent possible, draw on the selections in this chapter for evidence in your argument.

6. Mark Kingwell paraphrases Nathaniel Hawthorne, who "famously compared happiness to a butterfly which, if pursued, always eludes your grasp, but which, if you sit quietly, may just land upon you." The existential philosopher Albert Camus writes: "You will never be happy if you continue to search for what happiness consists of. You will never live if you are looking for the meaning of life." In her last paragraph, Begley writes: "But maybe, just maybe, the single-minded pursuit of happiness as an end in itself, rather than as a consequence of a meaningful life, has finally run its course." What are the differences between happiness that comes as a consequence of living—which includes, as Cliff Oxford would argue, working—and happiness that comes as the result of an explicit search for happiness? To what extent do you agree with these writers? Develop your response into an argument.

7. Drawing on selections in this chapter, especially on the column by David Brooks, argue for the need to acknowledge and respond thoughtfully to sadness and/or suffering. What do we risk by emphasizing extreme happiness—personally, socially, and culturally? Develop your response into an argument.

8. Three philosophers are represented in this chapter: McFall, Kingwell, and Critchley. What can you infer from these writers about the types of questions philosophers ask? About the logic of their answers? About the types of evidence they use? Develop your responses into an argument synthesis.

9. Reflect on an experience in your life when you were happy. Analyze this experience using two different principles for analysis that you've discovered in this chapter. Note that what you observe about your experience will change as you change analytical tools. Compare and contrast these observations. If you're feeling ambitious, extend your comparative analysis into an argument that answers these questions: Which analytical principle is more powerful? Which helped me understand my experience more deeply? Why?

10. Several writers have reflected on the phenomenon that we cease being happy the instant we realize we're happy. See Csikszentmihalyi, ¶16, and Kingwell, quoting John Stuart Mill in ¶5. (Kingwell also quotes Eric Hoffer, who claims that searching for happiness brings *un*happiness.) Do you agree? Can you be happy and *know* you're happy? Develop your response into an argument, drawing upon the sources in the chapter along with anecdotes from your own experience.

11. Cliff Oxford argues that we achieve happiness by committing ourselves to hard, meaningful work. How would you compare and contrast his approach to High Performance Happiness and what you take to be the Dalai Lama's approach to happiness, as Douglas Preston presents it? In responding, you may want to consider the extent to which Oxford and the Dalai Lama mean the same thing by the word "happiness." Organize your thoughts into a comparison-contrast synthesis.

RESEARCH ACTIVITIES   MyWritingLab™

1. Conduct an Internet search on "happiness." Spend about half an hour reading and browsing through the first two or three pages of results. What will readers discover from conducting this exercise? What definitions of happiness, approaches to the study of happiness, projects on happiness, insights about happiness, and ways of achieving happiness will this brief Internet search reveal?

2. Locate and read any of the sources that the authors of this chapter cite in developing their own selections. Choose a source that you find especially interesting. Locate the source in your library or in an online database and prepare a report for your classmates.

3. Read Darrin McMahon's "The Quest for Happiness," a brief history of humankind's efforts to understand happiness. You will find the article online, in your library's *JStor* database. See *Wilson Quarterly*, Winter 2005 (Vol. 29, No. 1), pp. 62–71. Select one of the figures McMahon discusses and conduct further

research. Prepare a ten-minute talk for your classmates on this person's views of happiness.

4. Investigate the cities and towns in the United States that have begun distributing surveys to their citizens to learn about what makes them happy—with the expectation of incorporating their answers into public policy. (You might begin with Somerville, MA.) How successful has the experiment been?

5. Choose a religious tradition with which you are familiar and investigate its traditional pathways to happiness. Don't rely on your recollected understanding of these pathways, perhaps from early religious study. Research the core texts of this tradition. Report on the essential conditions of what counts as a happy life. Do you encounter individuals who are held out as inspirational examples of people who lived good, happy lives?

6. Research Abraham Maslow's concept of self-actualization and his concept of the peak experience. Compare this latter concept to Csikszentmihalyi's concept of "flow." What is Maslow's "hierarchy of needs"? At what point in this hierarchy is self-actualization possible? What is the relationship between happiness and self-actualization?

7. Research the nation of Bhutan's programs to improve the happiness of its citizens. What prompted the focus on happiness? What assumptions guide the policy? What specific initiatives have been put in place? What are the successes and (thus far) failures of the program?

8. Research the so-called "Easterlin Paradox," the finding that after a certain point, rising national wealth is not matched with rising levels of happiness. The paradox has been recently challenged. Write a synthesis that explains the paradox, the evidence in favor of its existence, and the challenges to its existence.

9. How do *pleasure* and *happiness* differ? What have various commentators written on the distinction over the centuries? What is your view of the distinction?

MyWritingLab™   Visit Ch. 14 Happiness in MyWritingLab to test your understanding of the chapter objectives.

Obedience to Authority

Would you obey an order to inflict pain on another person? Most of us, if confronted with this question, would probably be quick to answer, "Never!" Yet if the conclusions of researchers are to be trusted, it is not psychopaths who kill noncombatant civilians in wartime and torture victims in prisons around the world, but rather ordinary people following orders—or caught up in the singularly *un*ordinary circumstances of the moment. People obey. This is a basic, necessary fact of human society. As psychologist Stanley Milgram has written, "Obedience is as basic an element in the structure of social life as one can point to. Some system of authority is a requirement of all communal living."

The question, then, is not, "Should we obey the orders of an authority figure?" but rather, "To what *extent* should we obey?" Each generation seems to give new meaning to these questions. During the Vietnam War, a number of American soldiers followed a commander's orders and murdered civilians in the hamlet of My Lai. In 1987, former White House military aide Oliver North was prosecuted for illegally diverting money raised by selling arms to Iran— considered by the U.S. government to be a terrorist state—to fund the anticommunist Contra (resistance) fighters in Nicaragua. North's attorneys claimed that he was following the orders of his superiors. And, although North was found guilty,* the judge who sentenced him to perform community service (there was no prison sentence) largely agreed with this defense when he called North a pawn in a larger game played by senior officials in the Reagan administration. In the 1990s, the world was horrified by genocidal violence in Rwanda and in the former nation of Yugoslavia. These were civil wars, in which people who had been living for generations as neighbors suddenly, upon the instigation and orders of their leaders, turned upon and slaughtered one another.

In April 2004, the world (particularly, the Muslim world) was horrified by accounts—and graphic photographs—of the degrading torture and humiliation of Iraqi prisoners at the hands of American soldiers in a Baghdad prison. Among the questions raised by this incident: Were these soldiers obeying orders

---

*In July 1990, North's conviction was overturned on appeal.

to "soften up" the prisoners for interrogation? Were they fulfilling the roles of prison guards they thought were expected of them? Were they abusing others because, given the circumstances, they could? President Bush asserted that this kind of abuse "does not reflect the nature of the American people." Yet, in January 2012, Americans learned of another act presumably not representative of its well-trained soldiers: U.S. Marines were videotaped urinating on the bodies of insurgents in Afghanistan—a desecration that some consider a war crime. And, again, a powerful U.S. official, this time Defense Secretary Leon Panetta, decried the "utterly deplorable" behavior. But as you will read in this chapter, we are likely to be unpleasantly surprised by revelations of what people can do when they find themselves in unfamiliar and dehumanizing circumstances. The chapter takes on a fundamental question: What is our "nature," not only as Americans but, more fundamentally, as human beings?

In less-dramatic ways, conflicts over the extent to which we obey orders surface in everyday life. At one point or another, you may face a moral dilemma at work. Perhaps it will take this form: The boss tells you to overlook file X in preparing a report for a certain client. But you're sure that file X pertains directly to the report and contains information that will alarm the client. What should you do? The dilemmas of obedience also emerge on some campuses with the rite of fraternity or sports-related hazing. Psychologists Janice Gibson and Mika Haritos-Fatouros have made the startling observation that whether the obedience in question involves a pledge's joining a fraternity or a torturer's joining an elite military corps, the *process* by which one acquiesces to a superior's order (and thereby becomes a member of the group) is remarkably the same.

In this chapter, you will explore the dilemmas inherent in obeying the orders of an authority figure. First, psychoanalyst and philosopher Erich Fromm discusses the comforts of obedience in "Disobedience as a Psychological and Moral Problem." Next, in "The Power of Situations," social psychologists Lee Ross and Richard Nisbett provide an overview of the situational forces that can strongly influence behavior. Then, Saul McLeod reports on the landmark Milgram experiments, which revealed the extent to which ordinary individuals will obey the clearly immoral orders of an authority figure. The results were startling, not only to the psychiatrists who predicted that few people would follow such orders, but also to many other social scientists: some applauded Milgram for his fiendishly ingenious design; some bitterly attacked him for unethical procedures. Columnist David Brooks of the *New York Times* then reviews other paradoxes of power—of both leadership, among those exercising authority, and what he calls "followership," among those who willfully obey leaders, or do not.

The chapter concludes with three selections devoted to the special case of obedience in groups. Writer Doris Lessing sets the context by discussing how we are quick to call ourselves individualists without pausing to appreciate the power of situational influences on our behavior. Next, psychologist Solomon Asch describes a classic experiment (involving the apparent length of lines) that demonstrates the influence of group pressure on individual judgment. Finally, you will be directed online for a dramatic account of a mock-prison experiment conducted at Stanford University by psychologist Philip Zimbardo, who found that student volunteers exhibited astonishingly convincing authoritarian and obedient attitudes as they playacted at being prisoners and guards.

DISOBEDIENCE AS A PSYCHOLOGICAL AND MORAL PROBLEM

Erich Fromm

Erich Fromm (1900–1980) was one of the twentieth century's distinguished writers and thinkers. Psychoanalyst and philosopher, historian and sociologist, he ranged widely in his interests and defied easy characterization. Fromm studied the works of Freud and Marx closely, and published on them both, but he was not aligned strictly with either. In much of his voluminous writing, he struggled to articulate a view that could help bridge ideological and personal conflicts and bring dignity to those who struggled with isolation in the industrial world. Author of more than thirty books and contributor to numerous edited collections and journals, Fromm is best known for *Escape from Freedom* (1941), *The Art of Loving* (1956), and *To Have or To Be?* (1976).

In the essay that follows, first published in 1963, Fromm discusses the seductive comforts of obedience, and he makes distinctions among varieties of obedience, some of which he believes are destructive, and others, life affirming. His thoughts on nuclear annihilation may seem dated in these days of post–Cold War cooperation, but it is worth remembering that Fromm wrote his essay just after the Cuban missile crisis, when fears of a third world war ran high. (We might note that today, despite the welcome reductions of nuclear stockpiles, the United States and Russia still possess—and retain battle plans for—thousands of warheads. And, in the wake of the 9/11 attacks, the threat of terrorists acquiring and using nuclear weapons against the United States seems very real.) On the major points of his essay, concerning the psychological and moral problems of obedience, Fromm remains as pertinent today as when he wrote more than forty years ago.

For centuries kings, priests, feudal lords, industrial bosses, and parents have insisted that *obedience is a virtue* and that *disobedience is a vice*. In order to introduce another point of view, let us set against this position the following statement: *human history began with an act of disobedience, and it is not unlikely that it will be terminated by an act of obedience.*

Human history was ushered in by an act of disobedience according to the Hebrew and Greek myths. Adam and Eve, living in the Garden of Eden, were part of nature; they were in harmony with it, yet did not transcend it. They were in nature as the fetus is in the womb of the mother. They were human, and at the same time not yet human. All this changed when they disobeyed an order. By breaking the ties with earth and mother, by cutting the umbilical cord, man emerged from a prehuman harmony and was able to take the first step into independence and freedom. The act of disobedience set Adam and Eve free and opened their eyes. They recognized each other as strangers and the world outside them as strange and even hostile. Their act of disobedience broke the primary bond with nature and made them individuals. "Original sin," far from corrupting man, set him free; it was the beginning of history. Man had to leave the Garden of Eden in order to learn to rely on his own powers and to become fully human.

The prophets, in their messianic concept, confirmed the idea that man had been right in disobeying; that he had not been corrupted by his "sin," but freed from the fetters of prehuman harmony. For the prophets, *history* is the place where man becomes human; during its unfolding he develops his powers of reason and of love until he creates a new harmony between himself, his fellow man, and nature. This new harmony is described as "the end of days," that period of history in which there is peace between man and man, between man and nature. It is a "new" paradise created by man himself, and one which he alone could create because he was forced to leave the "old" paradise as a result of his disobedience.

Just as the Hebrew myth of Adam and Eve, so the Greek myth of Prometheus sees all human civilization based on an act of disobedience. Prometheus, in stealing the fire from the gods, lays the foundation for the evolution of man. There would be no human history were it not for Prometheus' "crime." He, like Adam and Eve, is punished for his disobedience. But he does not repent and ask for forgiveness. On the contrary, he proudly says: "I would rather be chained to this rock than be the obedient servant of the gods."

5   Man has continued to evolve by acts of disobedience. Not only was his spiritual development possible only because there were men who dared to say no to the powers that be in the name of their conscience or their faith, but also his intellectual development was dependent on the capacity for being disobedient—disobedient to authorities who tried to muzzle new thoughts and to the authority of long-established opinions which declared a change to be nonsense.

If the capacity for disobedience constituted the beginning of human history, obedience might very well, as I have said, cause the end of human history. I am not speaking symbolically or poetically. There is the possibility, or even the probability, that the human race will destroy civilization and even all life upon earth within the next five to ten years. There is no rationality or sense in it. But the fact is that, while we are living technically in the Atomic Age, the majority of men—including most of those who are in power—still live emotionally in the Stone Age; that while our mathematics, astronomy, and the natural sciences are of the twentieth century, most of our ideas about politics, the state, and society lag far behind the age of science. If mankind commits suicide it will be because people will obey those who command them to push the deadly buttons; because they will obey the archaic passions of fear, hate, and greed; because they will obey obsolete clichés of State sovereignty and national honor. The Soviet leaders talk much about revolutions, and we in the "free world" talk much about freedom. Yet they and we discourage disobedience—in the Soviet Union explicitly and by force, in the free world implicitly and by the more subtle methods of persuasion.

But I do not mean to say that all disobedience is a virtue and all obedience is a vice. Such a view would ignore the dialectical relationship between obedience and disobedience. Whenever the principles which are obeyed and those which are disobeyed are irreconcilable, an act of obedience to one principle is necessarily an act of disobedience to its counterpart and vice versa. Antigone is the classic example of this dichotomy. By obeying the inhuman laws of the State, Antigone necessarily would disobey the laws of humanity. By obeying the latter, she must disobey the former. All martyrs of religious faiths, of freedom, and of science have had to disobey those who wanted to muzzle them in order to obey their own consciences, the laws of humanity, and of reason. If a man can only obey and not disobey, he is a slave; if he can only disobey and not obey, he is a rebel (not a revolutionary); he acts out of anger, disappointment, resentment, yet not in the name of a conviction or a principle.

However, in order to prevent a confusion of terms an important qualification must be made. Obedience to a person, institution, or power (heteronomous obedience) is submission; it implies the abdication of my autonomy and the acceptance of a foreign will or judgment in place of my own. Obedience to my own reason or conviction (autonomous obedience) is not an act of submission but one of affirmation. My conviction and my judgment, if authentically mine, are part of me. If I follow them rather than the judgment of others, I am being myself; hence the word *obey* can be applied only in a metaphorical sense and with a meaning which is fundamentally different from the one in the case of "heteronomous obedience."

But this distinction still needs two further qualifications, one with regard to the concept of conscience and the other with regard to the concept of authority.

10   The word *conscience* is used to express two phenomena which are quite distinct from each other. One is the "authoritarian conscience" which is the internalized voice of an authority whom we are eager to please and afraid of displeasing. This authoritarian conscience is what most people experience when they obey their conscience. It is also the conscience which Freud speaks of, and which he called "Super-Ego." This Super-Ego represents the internalized commands and prohibitions of father, accepted by the son out of fear. Different from the authoritarian conscience is the "humanistic conscience"; this is the voice present in every human being and independent from external sanctions and rewards. Humanistic conscience is based on the fact that as human beings we have an intuitive knowledge of what is human and inhuman, what is conducive of life and what is destructive of life. This conscience serves our functioning as human beings. It is the voice which calls us back to ourselves, to our humanity.

Authoritarian conscience (Super-Ego) is still obedience to a power outside of myself, even though this power has been internalized. Consciously I believe that I am following *my* conscience; in effect, however, I have swallowed the principles of *power*; just because of the illusion that humanistic conscience and Super-Ego are identical, internalized authority is so much more effective than the authority which is clearly experienced as not being part of me. Obedience to the "authoritarian conscience," like all obedience to outside thoughts and power, tends to debilitate "humanistic conscience," the ability to be and to judge oneself.

The statement, on the other hand, that obedience to another person is *ipso facto* submission needs also to be qualified by distinguishing "irrational" from "rational" authority. An example of rational authority is to be found in the relationship between student and teacher; one of irrational authority in the relationship between slave and master. Both relationships are based on the fact that the authority of the person in command is accepted. Dynamically, however, they are of a different nature. The interests of the teacher and the student, in the ideal case, lie in the same direction. The teacher is satisfied if he succeeds in furthering the student; if he has failed to do so, the failure is his and the student's. The slave owner, on the other hand, wants to exploit the slave as much as possible. The more he gets out of him the more satisfied he is. At the same time, the slave tries to defend as best he can his claims for a minimum of happiness. The interests of slave and master are antagonistic, because what is advantageous to the one is detrimental to the other. The superiority of the one over the other has a different function in each case; in the first it is the condition for the furtherance of the person subjected to the authority, and in the second it is the condition for his exploitation. Another distinction runs parallel to this: rational authority is rational because the authority, whether it is held by a teacher or a captain of a ship giving orders in an emergency, acts in the name of reason which, being universal, I can accept without submitting. Irrational authority has to use force or suggestion, because no one would let himself be exploited if he were free to prevent it.

Why is man so prone to obey and why is it so difficult for him to disobey? As long as I am obedient to the power of the State, the Church, or public opinion, I feel safe and protected. In fact it makes little difference what power it is that I am obedient to. It is always an institution, or men, who use force in one form or another and who fraudulently claim omniscience and omnipotence. My obedience makes me part of the power I worship, and hence I feel strong. I can make no error, since it decides for me; I cannot be alone, because it watches over me; I cannot commit a sin, because it does not let me do so, and even if I do sin, the punishment is only the way of returning to the almighty power.

In order to disobey, one must have the courage to be alone, to err, and to sin. But courage is not enough. The capacity for courage depends on a person's state of development. Only if a person has emerged from mother's lap and father's commands, only if he has emerged as a fully developed individual and thus has acquired the capacity to think and feel for himself, only then can he have the courage to say "no" to power, to disobey.

15   A person can become free through acts of disobedience by learning to say no to power. But not only is the capacity for disobedience the condition for freedom; freedom is also the condition for disobedience. If I am afraid of freedom, I cannot dare to say "no," I cannot have the courage to be disobedient. Indeed, freedom and the capacity for disobedience are inseparable; hence any social, political, and religious system which proclaims freedom, yet stamps out disobedience, cannot speak the truth.

There is another reason why it is so difficult to dare to disobey, to say "no" to power. During most of human history obedience has been identified with virtue and disobedience with sin. The reason is simple: thus far throughout most of history a minority has ruled over the majority. This rule was made necessary by the fact that there was only enough of the good things of life for the few, and only the crumbs remained for the many. If the few wanted to enjoy the good things and, beyond that, to have the many serve them and work for them, one condition was necessary: the many had to learn obedience. To be sure, obedience can be established by sheer force. But this method has many disadvantages. It constitutes a constant threat that one day the many might have the means to overthrow the few by force; furthermore there are many kinds of work which cannot be done properly if nothing but fear is behind the obedience. Hence the obedience which is only rooted in the fear of force must be transformed into one rooted in man's heart. Man must want and even need to obey, instead of only fearing to disobey. If this is to be achieved, power must assume the qualities of the All Good, of the All Wise; it must become All Knowing. If this happens, power can proclaim that disobedience is sin and obedience virtue; and once this has been proclaimed, the many can accept obedience because it is good and detest disobedience because it is bad, rather than to detest themselves for being cowards. From Luther to the nineteenth century one was concerned with overt and explicit authorities. Luther, the pope, the princes, wanted to uphold it; the middle class, the workers, the philosophers, tried to uproot it. The fight against authority in the State as well as in the family was often the very basis for the development of an independent and daring person. The fight against authority was inseparable from the intellectual mood which characterized the philosophers of the enlightenment and the scientists. This "critical mood" was one of faith in reason, and at the same time of doubt in everything which is said or thought, inasmuch as it is based on tradition, superstition, custom, power. The principles *sapere aude* and *de omnibus est dubitandum*—"dare to be wise" and "of all one must doubt"—were characteristic of the attitude which permitted and furthered the capacity to say "no."

The case of Adolf Eichmann [see note, p. 591] is symbolic of our situation and has a significance far beyond the one in which his accusers in the courtroom in Jerusalem were concerned with. Eichmann is a symbol of the organization man, of the alienated bureaucrat for whom men, women and children have become numbers. He is a symbol of all of us. We can see ourselves in Eichmann. But the most frightening thing about him is that after the entire story was told in terms of his own admissions, he was able in perfect good faith to plead his innocence. It is clear that if he were once more in the same situation he would do it again. And so would we—and so do we.

The organization man has lost the capacity to disobey, he is not even aware of the fact that he obeys. At this point in history the capacity to doubt, to criticize, and to disobey may be all that stands between a future for mankind and the end of civilization.

Review Questions   MyWritingLab™

1. What does Fromm mean when he writes that disobedience is "the first step into independence and freedom"?

2. Fromm writes that history began with an act of disobedience and will likely end with an act of obedience. What does he mean?

3. What is the difference between "heteronomous obedience" and "autonomous obedience"?

4. How does Fromm distinguish between "authoritarian conscience" and "humanistic conscience"?

5. When is obedience to another person *not* submission?

6. What are the psychological comforts of obedience, and why would authorities rather have people obey out of love than out of fear?

● Discussion and Writing Suggestions   MyWritingLab™

1. Fromm suggests that scientifically we live in the modern world but that politically and emotionally we live in the Stone Age. As you observe events in the world, both near and far, would you agree? Why?

2. Fromm writes: "If a man can only obey and not disobey, he is a slave; if he can only disobey and not obey, he is a rebel (not a revolutionary)" (¶ 7). Explain Fromm's meaning here. Explain, as well, the implication that to be fully human one must have the freedom to both obey and disobey.

3. Fromm writes that "obedience makes me part of the power I worship, and hence I feel strong" (¶ 13). Does this statement ring true for you? Discuss, in writing, an occasion in which you felt powerful because you obeyed a group norm.

4. In ¶s 15 and 16, Fromm equates obedience with cowardice. Can you identify a situation in which you were obedient but, now that you reflect on it, were also cowardly? That is, can you recall a time when you caved in to a group but now wish you hadn't? Explain.

5. Fromm says that we can see ourselves in Adolf Eichmann—that as an organization man he "has lost the capacity to disobey, he is not even aware of the fact that he obeys." To what extent do you recognize yourself in this portrait?

THE POWER OF SITUATIONS

Lee Ross and Richard E. Nisbett

Erich Fromm conceives of obedience and disobedience as products of one's character or of one's moral choices. In the selection that follows, Lee Ross and Richard E. Nisbett present findings from experiments in social psychology that suggest that situations, rather than some essential personal quality or the dictates of one's conscience, tend to determine behavior. From this vantage point, a "helpful" person may not be consistently helpful nor a "kind" person consistently kind. In each new situation, subtle and profound social cues influence our ultimate behavior—which is why, as we all know, people behave inconsistently. According to philosopher Gilbert Harman, "It seems that ordinary attributions of character traits to people are often deeply misguided, and it may even be the case that there is no such thing as character, no ordinary character traits of the sort people think there are, none of the usual moral virtues and vices." Harmon reached this radical notion after reading accounts of the same experiments in social psychology that you are about to read in this chapter. You may not draw the same conclusions, but Ross and Nisbett, Milgram, Asch, Lessing, and the account of the mock-prison experiment will almost certainly convince you that the situation in which we act can powerfully influence our behavior—including our choice to obey or disobey a questionable order.

Lee Ross is a professor of psychology at Stanford University. Richard E. Nisbett is professor of psychology at the University of Michigan. This selection is excerpted from their text *The Person and the Situation: Perspectives of Social Psychology* (1991).

Undergraduates taking their first course in social psychology generally are in search of an interesting and enjoyable experience, and they rarely are disappointed. They find out many fascinating things about human behavior, some of which validate common sense and some of which contradict it. The inherent interest value of the material, amounting to high-level gossip about people and social situations, usually ensures that the students are satisfied consumers.

The experience of serious graduate students, who, over the course of four or five years, are immersed in the problems and the orientation of the field, is rather different. For them, the experience is an intellectually wrenching one. Their most basic assumptions about the nature and the causes of human behavior, and about the very predictability of the social world, are challenged. At the end of the process, their views of human behavior and society will differ profoundly from the views held by most other people in their culture. Some of their new insights and beliefs will be held rather tentatively and applied inconsistently to the social events that unfold around them. Others will be held with great conviction, and will be applied confidently. But ironically, even the new insights that they are most confident about will tend to have the effect of making them less certain than their peers about predicting social behavior and making inferences about particular individuals or groups. Social psychology rivals philosophy in its ability to teach people that they do not truly understand the nature of the world. This book is about that hard-won ignorance and what it tells us about the human condition.

• • •

Consider the following scenario: While walking briskly to a meeting some distance across a college campus, John comes across a man slumped in a doorway, asking him for help. Will John offer it, or will he continue on his way? Before answering such a question, most people would want to know more about John. Is he someone known to be callous and unfeeling, or is he renowned for his kindness and concern? Is he a stalwart member of the Campus Outreach Organization, or a mainstay of the Conservative Coalition Against Welfare Abuse? In short, what kind of person is John and how has he behaved when his altruism has been tested in the past? Only with such information in hand, most people would agree, could one make a sensible and confident prediction.

In fact, however, nothing one is likely to know or learn about John would be of much use in helping predict John's behavior in the situation we've described. In particular, the type of information about personality that most laypeople would want to have before making a prediction would prove to be of relatively little value. A half century of research has taught us that in this situation, and in most other novel situations, one cannot predict with any accuracy how particular people will respond. At least one cannot do so using information about an individual's personal dispositions or even about that individual's past behavior.

· · ·

5   While knowledge about John is of surprisingly little value in predicting whether he will help the person slumped in the doorway, details concerning the specifics of the situation would be invaluable. For example, what was the appearance of the person in the doorway? Was he clearly ill, or might he have been a drunk or, even worse, a nodding dope addict? Did his clothing make him look respectably middle class or decently working class, or did he look like a homeless derelict?

Such considerations are fairly obvious once they are mentioned, and the layperson, upon reflection, will generally concede their importance. But few laypeople would concede, much less anticipate, the relevance of some other, subtler, contextual details that empirical research has shown to be important factors influencing bystander intervention. Darley and Batson (1973) actually confronted people with a version of the situation we've described and found what some of these factors are. Their subjects were students in a religious seminary who were on their way to deliver a practice sermon. If the subjects were in a hurry (because they thought they were late to give a practice sermon), only about 10 percent helped. By contrast, if they were not in a hurry (because they had plenty of time before giving their sermon), about 63 percent of them helped.

Social psychology has by now amassed a vast store of such empirical parables. The tradition here is simple. Pick a generic situation; then identify and manipulate a situational or contextual variable that intuition or past research leads you to believe will make a difference (ideally, a variable whose impact you think most laypeople, or even most of your peers, somehow fail to appreciate), and see what happens. Sometimes, of course, you will be wrong and your manipulation won't "work." But often the situational variable makes quite a bit of difference. Occasionally, in fact, it makes nearly all the difference, and information about traits and individual differences that other people thought all-important proves all but trivial. If so, you have contributed a situationist classic destined to become part of our field's intellectual legacy. Such empirical parables are important because they illustrate the degree to which ordinary men and women are apt to be mistaken about the power of the situation—the power of particular situational features, and the power of situations in general.

People's inflated belief in the importance of personality traits and dispositions, together with their failure to recognize the importance of situational factors in affecting behavior, has been termed the "fundamental attribution error"

(Ross, 1977; Nisbett & Ross, 1980; see also Jones, 1979; Gilbert & Jones, 1986). Together with many other social psychologists, we have directed our attention to documenting this...error and attempting to track down its origins.

References

Darley, J. M., & Batson, C. D. (1973). From Jerusalem to Jericho: A study of situational and dispositional variables in helping behavior. *Journal of Personality and Social Psychology, 27,* 100–119.

Gilbert, D. T., & Jones, E. E. (1986). Perceiver-induced constraints: Interpretation of self-generated reality. *Journal of Personality and Social Psychology, 50,* 269–280.

Jones, E. E. (1979). The rocky road from acts to dispositions. *American Psychologist, 34,* 107–117.

Nisbett, R. E., & Ross, L. (1980). *Human inference: Strategies and shortcomings of social judgment.* Englewood Cliffs, NJ: Prentice-Hall.

Ross, L. (1977). The intuitive psychologist and his shortcomings. In L. Berkowitz (Ed.), *Advances in experimental social psychology* (Vol. 10). New York: Academic.

● Review Questions   MyWritingLab™

1. In the final sentence of ¶ 2, what is the "hard-won ignorance" made possible by social psychology? Ross and Nisbett offer an example of this "ignorance." Summarize that example.

2. What is the key predictor of John's behavior in the experiment cited by Ross and Nisbett? How does this predictor defy common sense?

3. What is the "fundamental attribution error"?

● Discussion and Writing Suggestions   MyWritingLab™

1. Conceive of another scenario, analogous to John encountering the man slumped in the doorway. What kinds of situational factors might determine how one behaves when faced with this scenario?

2. How did you react to what is known as the "Good Samaritan" experiment (involving John and the person slumped in the doorway)? Most people would like to think they would behave differently, but the experiments suggest otherwise. Your comments? Can you see yourself responding differently in a variety of circumstances?

3. "Social psychology," write Ross and Nisbett, "rivals philosophy in its ability to teach people that they do not truly understand the nature of the world." How solid do you feel your understanding is of "the world"? If you guessed

incorrectly about John and how he would react to the person slumped in the doorway, are you prepared to see your commonsense understanding of how people behave undermined?

4. Reconsider the radical proposition mentioned in the headnote: that based on experiments such as the "Good Samaritan" described in this selection, one might conclude, "It seems that ordinary attributions of character traits to people are often deeply misguided, and it may even be the case that there is no such thing as character, no ordinary character traits of the sort people think there are, none of the usual moral virtues and vices." That is, one might conclude from Asch, Milgram, and the mock-prison experiment at Stanford (which you will view online later in this chapter) that enduring character traits do not determine our behavior; rather, our behavior is determined by situational variables (like whether or not we are late for a meeting). Even assuming you do not accept this extreme view, are you troubled by the assertion that "character" might be a fiction—or, at least, overrated? That people, for example, do not possess some inner quality called "honor" or "loyalty" that is impervious to all situational pressures (such as financial need, health crises, old age, threats to one's family's well-being or safety)? At what point, if any, despite one's misgivings, are situational exigencies likely to overwhelm consistent character?

THE MILGRAM EXPERIMENT

Saul McLeod[1]

In 1963, a Yale psychologist conducted one of the classic studies on obedience. Stanley Milgram designed an experiment that forced participants either to violate their conscience by obeying the immoral demands of an authority figure or to refuse those demands. Surprisingly, Milgram found that few participants could resist the authority figure's orders, even when the participants knew that following these orders would result in another person's pain. Were the participants in these experiments incipient mass murderers? No, said Milgram. They were "ordinary people, simply doing their jobs." The implications of Milgram's conclusions are immense.

Consider these questions: Where does evil reside? What sort of people were responsible for the Holocaust, and for the long list of other atrocities that seem to blight the human record in every generation? Is it a lunatic fringe, a few sick but powerful people who are responsible for atrocities? If so, then we decent folk needn't ever look inside ourselves to understand evil since (by our definition) evil lurks out there, in "those sick ones." Milgram's study suggested otherwise: that under a special set of circumstances the obedience we naturally show authority figures can transform us into agents of terror.

Stanley Milgram (1933–1984) taught and conducted research at Yale and Harvard Universities and at the Graduate Center, City University of New York. He was named Guggenheim Fellow in 1972–1973 and a year later was nominated for the National Book

[1]http://www.simplypsychology.org/milgram.html

Award for *Obedience to Authority*. His other books include *Television and Antisocial Behavior* (1973), *The City and the Self* (1974), *Human Aggression* (1976), and *The Individual in the Social World* (1977).

The article on Milgram's experiments by Saul McLeod was published online in 2007 on the Web site *Simply Psychology*. McLeod works at Wigan and Leigh College and lives in the United Kingdom. Note that the first part of McLeod's article follows the typical organization for reports on science and social science experiments: Aim, Procedures, Results, and Conclusions.

For a vivid illustration of the anxieties Milgram generated among participants in his obedience experiments, see the film clips and listen to the audio clips that accompanied this article in its initial publication on the Web.

Go to: Google or Bing

Search terms: *"milgram experiment simply psychology"*

One of the most famous studies of obedience in psychology was carried out by Stanley Milgram (1963).

Stanley Milgram, a psychologist at Yale University, conducted an experiment focusing on the conflict between obedience to authority and personal conscience.

He examined justifications for acts of genocide offered by those accused at the World War II, Nuremberg War Criminal trials. Their defense often was based on "obedience"—that they were just following orders of their superiors.

The experiments began in July 1961, a year after the trial of Adolf Eichmann in Jerusalem. Milgram devised the experiment to answer the question "Could it be that Eichmann and his million accomplices in the Holocaust were just following orders? Could we call them all accomplices?" (Milgram, 1974).

5   Milgram (1963) wanted to investigate whether Germans were particularly obedient to authority figures as this was a common explanation for the Nazi killings in World War II.

Milgram selected participants for his experiment by newspaper advertising for male participants to take part in a study of learning at Yale University. The procedure was that the participant was paired with another person and they drew lots to find out who would be the 'learner' and who would be the 'teacher.' The draw was fixed so that the participant was always the teacher, and the learner was one of Milgram's confederates (pretending to be a real participant).

The learner (a confederate called Mr. Wallace) was taken into a room and had electrodes attached to his arms, and the teacher and researcher went into a room next door that contained an electric shock generator and a row of switches marked from 15 volts (Slight Shock) to 375 volts (Danger: Severe Shock) to 450 volts (XXX).

Aim

Milgram (1963) was interested in researching how far people would go in obeying an instruction if it involved harming another person. Stanley Milgram was interested in how easily ordinary people could be influenced into committing atrocities, for example, Germans in WWII.

Procedure

Volunteers were recruited for a lab experiment investigating "learning" (re: ethics: deception). Participants were 40 males, aged between 20 and 50, whose jobs ranged from unskilled to professional, from the New Haven area. They were paid $4.50 for just turning up.

10   At the beginning of the experiment they were introduced to another participant, who was actually a confederate of the experimenter (Milgram). They drew straws to determine their roles—learner or teacher—although this was fixed and the confederate always ended [up being] the learner. There was also an "experimenter" dressed in a grey lab coat, played by an actor (not Milgram).

Two rooms in the Yale Interaction Laboratory were used—one for the learner (with an electric chair) and another for the teacher and experimenter with an electric shock generator.

The "learner" (Mr. Wallace) was strapped to a chair with electrodes. After he has learned a list of word pairs given him to learn, the "teacher" tests him by naming a word and asking the learner to recall its partner/pair from a list of four possible choices.

The teacher is told to administer an electric shock every time the learner makes a mistake, increasing the level of shock each time. There were 30 switches on the shock generator marked from 15 volts (slight shock) to 450 (danger—severe shock).

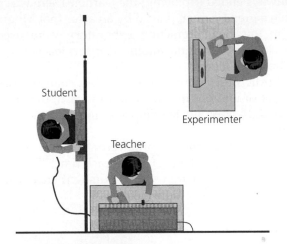

The learner gave mainly wrong answers (on purpose) and for each of these the teacher gave him an electric shock. When the teacher refused to administer a shock and turned to the experimenter for guidance, he was given the standard instruction/order (consisting of 4 prods):

Prod 1: Please continue.

Prod 2: The experiment requires you to continue.

Prod 3: It is absolutely essential that you continue.

Prod 4: You have no other choice but to continue.

Results

15   65% (two-thirds) of participants (i.e. teachers) continued to the highest level of 450 volts. All the participants continued to 300 volts.

Milgram did more than one experiment—he carried out 18 variations of his study. All he did was alter the situation to see how this affected obedience.

Conclusion

Ordinary people are likely to follow orders given by an authority figure, even to the extent of killing an innocent human being. Obedience to authority is ingrained in us all from the way we are brought up.

People tend to obey orders from other people if they recognize their authority as morally right and/or legally based. This response to legitimate authority is learned in a variety of situations, for example in the family, school and workplace.

Milgram summed up in the article "The Perils of Obedience" (Milgram 1974), writing:

> The legal and philosophic aspects of obedience are of enormous import, but they say very little about how most people behave in concrete situations. I set up a simple experiment at Yale University to test how much pain an ordinary citizen would inflict on another person simply because he was ordered to by an experimental scientist. Stark authority was pitted against the subjects' [participants'] strongest moral imperatives against hurting others, and, with the subjects' [participants'] ears ringing with the screams of the victims, authority won more often than not. The extreme willingness of adults to go to almost any lengths on the command of an authority constitutes the chief finding of the study and the fact most urgently demanding explanation.

Milgram's Agency Theory

20 Milgram (1974) explained the behavior of his participants by suggesting that people actually have two states of behavior when they are in a social situation:

- The **autonomous state** – people direct their own actions, and they take responsibility for the results of those actions.
- The **agentic state** – people allow others to direct their actions, and they pass off the responsibility for the consequences to the person giving the orders. In other words, they act as agents for another person's will.

Milgram suggested that two things must be in place in order for a person to enter the agentic state:

1. The person giving the orders is perceived as being qualified to direct other people's behavior. That is, they are seen as legitimate.
2. The person being ordered about is able to believe that the authority will accept responsibility for what happens.

Agency theory says that people will obey an authority when they believe that the authority will take responsibility for the consequences of their actions. This is supported by some aspects of Milgram's evidence. For example, when participants were reminded that they had responsibility for their own actions, almost none of them were prepared to obey. In contrast, many participants who were refusing to go on did so if the experimenter said that he would take responsibility.

Milgram Experiment Variations

The Milgram experiment was carried out many times whereby Milgram varied the basic procedure. By doing this Milgram could identify which factors affected obedience. Obedience was measured by how many participants shocked to the maximum 450 volts (65% in the original study).

In total 636 participants have been tested in 18 different variation studies.

Change of Location Condition

- The experiment was moved to a set of run down offices rather than the impressive Yale University.
- Obedience dropped to 47.5%.
- This suggests that status of location effects obedience.

Two Teacher Condition

- When there is less personal responsibility obedience increases.
- When participants could instruct an assistant (confederate) to press the switches, 92.5% shocked to the maximum 450 volts.
- This relates to Milgram's Agency Theory.

Touch Proximity Condition

- The teacher had to force the learner's hand down onto a shock plate when they refuse to participate after 150 volts.
- Obedience fell to 30%.
- The participant is no longer buffered/protected from seeing the consequences of their actions.

Uniform Condition

- Milgram's experimenter wore a laboratory coat (a symbol of scientific expertise) gave him a high status.
- But when the experimenter dressed in everyday clothes obedience was very low.
- The uniform of the authority figure can give them status.

Social Support Condition

- Two other participants (confederates) were also teachers but refused to obey.
- Confederate 1 stopped at 150 volts and confederate 2 stopped at 210 volts.
- The presence of others who are seen to disobey the authority figure reduces the level of obedience to 10%.

Absent Experimenter Condition

- Authority figure distant.
- It is easier to resist the orders from an authority figure if they are not close by.
- When the experimenter instructed and prompted the teacher by telephone from another room, obedience fell to 20.5%.
- Many participants cheated and missed out shocks or gave less voltage than ordered by the experimenter.
- Proximity of authority figure effects obedience.

Criticisms

25 The Milgram studies were conducted in laboratory type conditions and we must ask if this tells us much about real-life situations. We obey in a variety of real-life situations that are far more subtle than instructions to give people electric shocks, and it would be interesting to see what factors operate in everyday obedience. The sort of situation Milgram investigated would be more suited to a military context.

Orne & Holland (1968) accused Milgram's study of lacking "experimental realism," i.e. participants might not have believed the experimental set-up they found themselves in and knew the learner wasn't really receiving electric shocks.

Milgram's sample was biased:

- The participants in Milgram's study were all male. Do the findings transfer to females?

- Milgram's study cannot be seen as representative of the American population as his sample was self-selected. This is because they became participants only by electing to respond to a newspaper advertisement (selecting themselves). They may also have a typical "volunteer personality"—not all the newspaper readers responded so perhaps it takes this personality type to do so.

    Yet a total of 636 participants were tested in 18 separate experiments across the New Haven area, which was seen as being reasonably representative of a typical American town.

Milgram's findings have been replicated in a variety of cultures and most lead to the same conclusions as Milgram's original study and in some cases see higher obedience rates.

However, Smith & Bond (1998) point out that with the exception of Jordan (Shanab & Yahya, 1978), the majority of these studies have been conducted in industrialized Western cultures and we should be cautious before we conclude that a universal trait of social behavior has been identified.

Ethical Issues

- **Deception** – the participants actually believed they were shocking a real person, and were unaware the learner was a confederate of Milgram's.

    However, Milgram argued that "illusion is used when necessary in order to set the stage for the revelation of certain difficult-to-get-at-truths." Milgram also interviewed participants afterwards to find out the effect of the deception. Apparently 83.7% said that they were "glad to be in the experiment," and 1.3% said that they wished they had not been involved.

- **Protection of participants** – Participants were exposed to extremely stressful situations that may have the potential to cause psychological harm. Many of the participants were visibly distressed.

  Signs of tension included trembling, sweating, stuttering, laughing nervously, biting lips and digging fingernails into palms of hands. Three participants had uncontrollable seizures, and many pleaded to be allowed to stop the experiment.

  Full blown seizures were observed for 3 participants; one so violent that the experiment was stopped.

  In his defense, Milgram argued that these effects were only short term. Once the participants were debriefed (and could see the confederate was OK) their stress levels decreased. Milgram also interviewed the participants one year after the event and concluded that most were happy that they had taken part.

- However, Milgram did debrief the participants fully after the experiment and also followed up after a period of time to ensure that they came to no harm.

References

Milgram, S. (1963). Behavioral study of obedience. *Journal of Abnormal and Social Psychology*, 67, 371–378.

Milgram, S. (1974). *Obedience to authority: An experimental view*. Harpercollins.

Orne, M. T., & Holland, C. H. (1968). On the ecological validity of laboratory deceptions. *International Journal of Psychiatry*, 6(4), 282–293.

Shanab, M. E., & Yahya, K. A. (1978). A cross-cultural study of obedience. *Bulletin of the Psychonomic Society*.

Smith, P. B., & Bond, M. H. (1998). *Social Psychology Across Cultures* (2nd Edition). Prentice Hall.

● Review Questions   MyWritingLab™

1. After WWII, war criminals justified their actions by claiming they had followed orders. What was Milgram's chief question regarding these justifications?

2. Explain the primary aim of Milgram's experiments. What were the main results, and, in Milgram's own words, "the chief finding of the study"?

3. Summarize the difference between what Milgram calls the "autonomous state" and the "agentic state." What is the significance of these states for investigations of obedience to authority?

4. How did variables such as location of the experiment, the perceived legitimacy of the authority figure, and peer support of the authority figure affect the results of Milgram's obedience experiments?

5. Summarize some of the chief criticisms of the Milgram experiments.

● **Discussion and Writing Suggestions   MyWritingLab™**

1. Milgram has written: "Conservative philosophers argue that the very fabric of society is threatened by disobedience, while humanists stress the primacy of the individual conscience." Develop the arguments of both the conservative and the humanist regarding obedience to authority. Be prepared to debate the ethics of obedience by defending one position or the other.

2. Would you have been glad to have participated in the Milgram experiments? Why or why not?

3. McLeod summarizes some of the chief criticisms, both procedural and ethical, of the Milgram experiment. To what extent do you agree with some of these criticisms? How might you counter some of these criticisms?

4. Does the outcome of the experiment upset you in anyway? Do you feel the experiment teaches us anything new about human nature?

5. The wife of one of the experimental subjects said to him after he described what he had done: "You can call yourself Eichmann."[2] Do you agree with her? Explain.

6. View the video clip—or listen to some of the sound clips—revealing that one of the experimental subjects, identified by Milgram as Fred Prozi, continued to shock the learner upon being urged to continue by the experimenter, even after the learner repeatedly screamed out in pain. Appreciating that Prozi was debriefed—that is, was assured that no harm came to the learner—imagine what Prozi might have been thinking as he drove home after the experiment. Develop your thoughts into a monologue, written in the first person, with Prozi at the wheel of his car.

7. Milgram concluded: "ordinary people . . . without any particular hostility on their part, can become agents in a terrible destructive process." What present-day situations occur to you that suggest that Milgram's findings are just as valid as they were in the 1960s when he conducted his experiments? Consider both events of national and international scope that you have read about or seen on television or situations closer to home.

THE FOLLOWER PROBLEM

David Brooks

For many who grew up during the counterculture of the 1960s, authority was in and of itself malign and corrupt. "Never trust anyone over 30" went one of the slogans of the time. The Vietnam War and the Watergate scandal of the early 1970s appeared to confirm the

---

[2]*Adolf Eichmann* (1906–1962), the Nazi official responsible for implementing Hitler's "Final Solution" to exterminate the Jews, escaped to Argentina after World War II. In 1960, Israeli agents captured him and brought him to Israel, where he was tried as a war criminal and sentenced to death. At his trial, Eichmann maintained that he was merely following orders in arranging the murders of his victims.

widespread belief that people in charge would almost always abuse their authority—just like Milgram's white-coated "experimenters." Yet even Milgram acknowledges, "Some system of authority is a requirement of all communal living, and it is only the person dwelling in isolation who is not forced to respond, with defiance or submission, to the commands of others." The British writer and physician Theodore Dalrymple once encountered a fellow airline passenger who maintained, "I've always been against all authority." He asked her, "What about the pilot of this aircraft? I assume you would prefer him to continue to fly it, rather than, say, for me to take over, and that were I to attempt to do so, he would exert his authority over me as captain?" The point is that if we were to routinely defy the authority of parents, teachers, police officers, employers, clients, etc., what we call civilization would cease to function, leaving us to fend for ourselves in a Darwinian world where only the strong would survive. True, in such a world, the law would not impose authority, but neither would it protect the weak. In such a world, might would make right. And so we agree to obey most laws for our own welfare—until, that is, they become unreasonable. Knowing when and why to obey, and to resist, is the subject of this chapter.

In the following op-ed, first published in the *New York Times* on June 12, 2012, columnist David Brooks argues that partly because of a legacy of antiauthoritarianism, America may not have a leadership problem, but "it certainly has a followership problem." In the course of his article, Brooks refers to a number of monuments in and around the National Mall in Washington, D.C. You can readily find images and videos of these monuments online. For additional information on David Brooks, see pp. 312–13, the headnote to "Amy Chua Is a Wimp" in Chapter 10.

If you go to the Lincoln or Jefferson memorials in Washington, you are invited to look up in admiration. Lincoln and Jefferson are presented as the embodiments of just authority. They are strong and powerful but also humanized. Jefferson is a graceful aristocratic democrat. Lincoln is sober and enduring. Both used power in the service of higher ideas, which are engraved nearby on the walls.

The monuments that get built these days are mostly duds. That's because they say nothing about just authority. The World War II memorial is a nullity. It tells you nothing about the war or why American power was mobilized to fight it. The Rev. Dr. Martin Luther King Jr. memorial brutally simplifies its subject's nuanced and biblical understanding of power. It gives him an imperious and self-enclosed character completely out of keeping with his complex nature.

As Michael J. Lewis of Williams College has noted, the Franklin Delano Roosevelt Memorial transforms a jaunty cavalier into a "differently abled and rather prim nonsmoker." Instead of a crafty wielder of supreme power, Roosevelt is a kindly grandpa you would want to put your arm around for a vacation photo.

The proposed Eisenhower memorial shifts attention from his moments of power to his moments of innocent boyhood. The design has been widely criticized, and last week the commission in charge agreed to push back the approval hearing until September.

"The Follower Problem" by David Brooks from the *New York Times*, July 12, 2012 © 2012 New York Times. All rights reserved. Used by permission and protected by the Copyright Laws of the United States. The printing, copying, redistribution, or retransmission of this Content without express written permission is prohibited.

5   Even the more successful recent monuments evade the thorny subjects of strength and power. The Vietnam memorial is about tragedy. The Korean memorial is about vulnerability.

Why can't today's memorial designers think straight about just authority?

Some of the reasons are well-known. We live in a culture that finds it easier to assign moral status to victims of power than to those who wield power. Most of the stories we tell ourselves are about victims who have endured oppression, racism and cruelty.

Then there is our fervent devotion to equality, to the notion that all people are equal and deserve equal recognition and respect. It's hard in this frame of mind to define and celebrate greatness, to hold up others who are immeasurably superior to ourselves.

But the main problem is our inability to think properly about how power should be used to bind and build. Legitimate power is built on a series of paradoxes: that leaders have to wield power while knowing they are corrupted by it; that great leaders are superior to their followers while also being of them; that the higher they rise, the more they feel like instruments in larger designs. The Lincoln and Jefferson memorials are about how to navigate those paradoxes.

10   These days many Americans seem incapable of thinking about these paradoxes. Those "Question Authority" bumper stickers no longer symbolize an attempt to distinguish just and unjust authority. They symbolize an attitude of opposing authority.

The old adversary culture of the intellectuals has turned into a mass adversarial cynicism. The common assumption is that elites are always hiding something. Public servants are in it for themselves. Those people at the top are nowhere near as smart or as wonderful as pure and all-knowing Me.

You end up with movements like Occupy Wall Street and the Tea Parties that try to dispense with authority altogether. They reject hierarchies and leaders because they don't believe in the concepts. The whole world should be like the Internet—a disbursed semianarchy in which authority is suspect and each individual is king.

Maybe before we can build great monuments to leaders we have to relearn the art of following. Democratic followership is also built on a series of paradoxes: that we are all created equal but that we also elevate those who are extraordinary; that we choose our leaders but also have to defer to them and trust their discretion; that we're proud individuals but only really thrive as a group, organized and led by just authority.

I don't know if America has a leadership problem; it certainly has a followership problem. Vast majorities of Americans don't trust their institutions. That's not mostly because our institutions perform much worse than they did in 1925 and 1955, when they were widely trusted. It's mostly because more people are cynical and like to pretend that they are better than everything else around them. Vanity has more to do with rising distrust than anything else.

15   In his memoir, *At Ease*, Eisenhower delivered the following advice: "Always try to associate yourself with and learn as much as you can from those who know more than you do, who do better than you, who see more clearly than you." Ike slowly mastered the art of leadership by becoming a superb apprentice.

To have good leaders you have to have good followers—able to recognize just authority, admire it, be grateful for it and emulate it. Those skills are required for good monument building, too.

● **Discussion and Writing Suggestions**   MyWritingLab™

1. In Brooks's view, what is a "just" authority? What are its key elements? Cite present-day examples of such authority that in your view we should admire, emulate, and be proud to follow.

2. Brooks asserts: "We live in a culture that finds it easier to assign moral status to victims of power than to those who wield power." Comment on this assertion, using examples from your reading and your own observations and experience to support or rebut Brooks's contention.

3. Brooks suggests that "our fervent devotion to equality" undermines respect for just authority. To what extent do you agree? If you believe everyone is, or must be, equal, how then (that is, on what terms) can we have leaders—of a society, community, school, or household? To function well, must a society, community, etc., have leaders? Must leaders have more authority, more power, than followers?

4. How do you think leaders can wield power without being corrupted by it? Is the ability to "navigate those paradoxes" of power a matter of personal character, of education, of growing up in a particular family or community environment, or of something else?

5. Brooks writes that we may need to "relearn the art of following." What does he mean? Why use the word *art?*

6. If you have visited any of the monuments on the National Mall, write about your impressions, then discuss Brooks's insights in light of your own.

7. Brooks writes that there are paradoxes both of leading and following. Review these paradoxes and choose one to explore in a freewheeling journal entry. Don't try to shape your thoughts into an essay. A few hours or a day later, read what you wrote. What statements stand out to you? Why?

GROUP MINDS

Doris Lessing

Doris Lessing sets a context for a discussion of obedience in group settings by illuminating a fundamental conflict: We in the Western world celebrate our individualism, but we're naive in understanding the ways in which groups largely undercut our individuality. "We are group animals still," says Lessing, "and there is nothing wrong with that. But what is dangerous is . . . not understanding the social laws that govern groups and govern us." This chapter is largely devoted to an exploration of these tendencies. As you read selections by Milgram and the other authors here, bear in mind Lessing's troubling question: If we know that individuals will violate their own good common sense and moral codes in order to become accepted members of a group, why then can't we put this knowledge to use and teach people to be wary of group pressures?

Doris Lessing, the daughter of farmers, was born in Persia, now Iran, in 1919. She attended a Roman Catholic convent and a girls' high school in southern Rhodesia (now Zimbabwe). From 1959 through to the present, Lessing has written more than twenty works of fiction and has been called "the best female novelist" of the postwar era. Her work has received a great deal of scholarly attention. She is, perhaps, best known for *The Golden Notebook* (1962), *The Grass is Singing* (1950), and *The Fifth Child* (1988).

People living in the West, in societies that we describe as Western, or as the free world, may be educated in many different ways, but they will all emerge with an idea about themselves that goes something like this: I am a citizen of a free society, and that means I am an individual, making individual choices. My mind is my own, my opinions are chosen by me, I am free to do as I will, and at the worst the pressures on me are economic, that is, I may be too poor to do as I want.

This set of ideas may sound something like a caricature, but it is not so far off how we see ourselves. It is a portrait that may not have been acquired consciously, but is part of a general atmosphere or set of assumptions that influence our ideas about ourselves.

People in the West therefore may go through their entire lives never thinking to analyze this very flattering picture, and as a result are helpless against all kinds of pressures on them to conform in many kinds of ways.

The fact is that we all live our lives in groups—the family, work groups, social, religious and political groups. Very few people indeed are happy as solitaries, and they tend to be seen by their neighbors as peculiar or selfish or worse. Most people cannot stand being alone for long. They are always seeking groups to belong to, and if one group dissolves, they look for another. We are group animals still, and there is nothing wrong with that. But what is dangerous is not the belonging to a group, or groups, but not understanding the social laws that govern groups and govern us.

5   When we're in a group, we tend to think as that group does: we may even have joined the group to find "like-minded" people. But we also find our thinking changing because we belong to a group. It is the hardest thing in the world to maintain an individual dissident opinion, as a member of a group.

It seems to me that this is something we have all experienced—something we take for granted, may never have thought about it. But a great deal of experiment has gone on among psychologists and sociologists on this very theme. If I describe an experiment or two, then anyone listening who may be a sociologist or psychologist will groan, oh God not *again*—for they will have heard of these classic experiments far too often. My guess is that the rest of the people will never have heard of these experiments, never have had these ideas presented to them. If my guess is true, then it aptly illustrates my general thesis, and the general idea behind these talks, that we (the human race) are now in possession of a great deal of hard information about ourselves, but we do not use it to improve our institutions and therefore our lives.

A typical test, or experiment, on this theme goes like this. A group of people are taken into the researcher's confidence. A minority of one or two are left in the dark. Some situation demanding measurement or assessment is chosen. For instance, comparing lengths of wood that differ only a little from each other, but enough to be perceptible, or shapes that are almost the same size. The majority in the group—according to instruction—will assert stubbornly that these two shapes or lengths are the same length, or size, while the solitary individual, or the couple, who have not been so instructed will assert that the pieces of wood or whatever are different. But the majority will continue to insist—speaking metaphorically—that black is white, and after a period of exasperation, irritation, even anger, certainly incomprehension, the minority will fall into line. Not always, but nearly always. There are indeed glorious individuals who stubbornly insist on telling the truth as they see it, but most give in to the majority opinion, obey the atmosphere.

When put as badly, as unflatteringly, as this, reactions tend to be incredulous: "I certainly wouldn't give in, I speak my mind...." But would you?

People who have experienced a lot of groups, who perhaps have observed their own behavior, may agree that the hardest thing in the world is to stand out against one's group, a group of one's peers. Many agree that among our most shameful memories is this, how often we said black was white because other people were saying it.

10   In other words, we know that this is true of human behavior, but how do we know it? It is one thing to admit it, in a vague uncomfortable sort of way (which probably includes the hope that one will never again be in such a testing situation) but quite another to make that cool step into a kind of objectivity, where one may say, "Right, if that's what human beings are like, myself included, then let's admit it, examine and organize our attitudes accordingly."

This mechanism, of obedience to the group, does not only mean obedience or submission to a small group, or one that is sharply determined, like a religion or political party. It means, too, conforming to those large, vague, ill defined collections of people who may never think of themselves as having a collective mind because they are aware of differences of opinion—but which, to people from outside, from another culture, seem very minor. The underlying assumptions and assertions that govern the group are never discussed, never challenged, probably never noticed, the main one being precisely this: that it *is* a group mind, intensely resistant to change, equipped with sacred assumptions about which there can be no discussion.

But suppose this kind of thing were taught in schools?

Let us just suppose it, for a moment.... But at once the nub of the problem is laid bare.

Imagine us saying to children, "In the last fifty or so years, the human race has become aware of a great deal of information about its mechanisms; how it behaves, how it must behave under certain circumstances. If this is to be useful, you must learn to contemplate these rules calmly, dispassionately, disinterestedly, without emotion. It is information that will set people free from blind loyalties, obedience to slogans, rhetoric, leaders, group emotions." Well, there it is.

● Review Questions   MyWritingLab™

1. What is the flattering portrait Lessing paints of people living in the West?

2. Lessing believes that individuals in the West are "helpless against all kinds of pressures on them to conform in many kinds of ways." Why?

3. Lessing refers to a class of experiments on obedience. Summarize the "typical" experiment.

● Discussion and Writing Suggestions   MyWritingLab™

1. Lessing writes that "what is dangerous is not the belonging to a group, or groups, but not understanding the social laws that govern groups and govern us." What is the danger Lessing is speaking of here?

2. Lessing states that the human race is "now in possession of a great deal of hard information about ourselves, but we do not use it to improve our institutions and therefore our lives." First, do you agree with Lessing? Can you cite other examples (aside from information on obedience to authority) in which we do not use our knowledge to better humankind?

3. Explore some of the difficulties in applying this "hard information" about humankind that Lessing speaks of. Assume she's correct in claiming that we don't incorporate our knowledge of human nature into the running of our institutions. Why don't we? What are the difficulties of *acting* on information?

4. Lessing speaks of people's guilt in recalling how they succumbed to group pressures. Can you recall such an event? What feelings do you have about it now?

OPINIONS AND SOCIAL PRESSURE

Solomon E. Asch

In the early 1950s, Solomon Asch (1907–1996), a social psychologist at Rutgers University, conducted a series of simple but ingenious experiments on the influence of group pressure upon the individual. Essentially, he discovered, individuals can be influenced by groups to deny the evidence of their own senses. Together with the Milgram experiments of the next decade (see the selection earlier in the chapter), these studies provide powerful evidence of the degree to which individuals can surrender their own judgment to others, even when those others are clearly in the wrong. The results of these experiments have implications far beyond the laboratory: They can explain a good deal of the normal human behavior we see every day—at school, at work, at home.

In what follows I shall describe some experiments in an investigation of the effects of group pressure which was carried out recently with the help of a number of my associates. The tests not only demonstrate the operations of group pressure upon individuals but also illustrate a new kind of attack on the problem and some of the more subtle questions that it raises.

A group of seven to nine young men, all college students, are assembled in a classroom for a "psychological experiment" in visual judgment. The experimenter informs them that they will be comparing the lengths of lines. He shows two large white cards [see Figure 1]. On one is a single vertical black line—the standard whose length is to be matched. On the other card are three vertical lines of various lengths. The subjects are to choose the one that is of the same length as the line on the other card. One of the three actually is of the same length; the other two are substantially different, the difference ranging from three quarters of an inch to an inch and three quarters.

The experiment opens uneventfully. The subjects announce their answers in the order in which they have been seated in the room, and on the first round every person chooses the same matching line. Then a second set of cards is exposed; again the group is unanimous. The members appear ready to endure politely another boring experiment. On the third trial there is an unexpected disturbance. One person near the end of the group disagrees with all the others in his selection of the matching line. He looks surprised, indeed incredulous, about the disagreement. On the following trial he disagrees again, while the others remain unanimous in their choice. The dissenter becomes more and more worried and hesitant as the disagreement continues in succeeding trials; he may pause before announcing his answer and speak in a low voice, or he may smile in an embarrassed way.

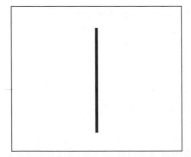 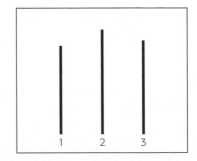

Fig. 1. Subjects were shown two cards. One bore a standard line. The other bore three lines, one of which was the same length as the standard. The subjects were asked to choose this line.

5   What the dissenter does not know is that all the other members of the group were instructed by the experimenter beforehand to give incorrect answers in unanimity at certain points. The single individual who is not a party to this prearrangement is the focal subject of our experiment. He is placed in a position in which, while he is actually giving the correct answers, he finds himself unexpectedly in a minority of one, opposed by a unanimous and arbitrary majority with respect to a clear and simple fact. Upon him we have brought to bear two opposed forces: the evidence of his senses and the unanimous opinion of a group of his peers. Also, he must declare his judgments in public, before a majority which has also stated its position publicly.

The instructed majority occasionally reports correctly in order to reduce the possibility that the naive subject will suspect collusion against him. (In only a few cases did the subject actually show suspicion; when this happened, the experiment was stopped and the results were not counted.) There are 18 trials in each series, and on 12 of these the majority responds erroneously.

How do people respond to group pressure in this situation? I shall report first the statistical results of a series in which a total of 123 subjects from three institutions of higher learning (not including my own Swarthmore College) were placed in the minority situation described above.

Two alternatives were open to the subject: he could act independently, repudiating the majority, or he could go along with the majority, repudiating the evidence of his senses. Of the 123 put to the test, a considerable percentage yielded to the majority. Whereas in ordinary circumstances individuals matching the lines will make mistakes less than 1 per cent of the time, under group pressure the minority subjects swung to acceptance of the misleading majority's wrong judgments in 36.8 per cent of the selections.

Of course individuals differed in response. At one extreme, about one quarter of the subjects were completely independent and never agreed with the erroneous judgments of the majority. At the other extreme, some individuals went with the majority nearly all the time. The performances of individuals in this experiment tend to be highly consistent. Those who strike out on the path of independence do not, as a rule, succumb to the majority even over an extended series of trials, while those who choose the path of compliance are unable to free themselves as the ordeal is prolonged.

10   The reasons for the startling individual differences have not yet been investigated in detail. At this point we can only report some tentative generalizations from talks with the subjects, each of whom was interviewed at the end of the experiment. Among the independent individuals were many who held fast because of staunch confidence in their own judgment. The most significant fact about them was not absence of responsiveness to the majority but a capacity to recover from doubt and to reestablish their equilibrium. Others who acted independently came to believe that the majority was correct in its answers, but they continued their dissent on the simple ground that it was their obligation to call the play as they saw it.

Among the extremely yielding persons we found a group who quickly reached the conclusion: "I am wrong, they are right." Others yielded in order "not to spoil your results." Many of the individuals who went along suspected that the majority were "sheep" following the first responder, or that the majority were victims of an optical illusion; nevertheless, these suspicions failed to free them at the moment of decision. More disquieting were the reactions of subjects who construed their difference from the majority as a sign of some general deficiency in themselves, which at all costs they must hide. On this basis they desperately tried to merge with the majority, not realizing the longer-range consequences to themselves. All the yielding subjects underestimated the frequency with which they conformed.

Which aspect of the influence of a majority is more important—the size of the majority or its unanimity? The experiment was modified to examine this question. In one series the size of the opposition was varied from one to 15 persons. The results showed a clear trend. When a subject was confronted with only a single individual who contradicted his answers, he was swayed little: he continued to answer independently and correctly in nearly all trials. When the opposition was increased to two, the pressure became substantial: minority subjects now accepted the wrong answer 13.6 per cent of the time. Under the pressure of a majority of three, the subjects' errors jumped to 31.8 per cent. But further increases in the size of the majority apparently did not increase the weight of the pressure substantially. Clearly the size of the opposition is important only up to a point.

Disturbance of the majority's unanimity had a striking effect. In this experiment the subject was given the support of a truthful partner—either another individual who did not know of the prearranged agreement among the rest of the group, or a person who was instructed to give correct answers throughout.

The presence of a supporting partner depleted the majority of much of its power. Its pressure on the dissenting individual was reduced to one fourth: that is, subjects answered incorrectly only one fourth as often as under the pressure of a unanimous majority. The weakest persons did not yield as readily. Most interesting were the reactions to the partner. Generally the feeling toward him was one of warmth and closeness; he was credited with inspiring confidence. However, the subjects repudiated the suggestion that the partner decided them to be independent.

15   Was the partner's effect a consequence of his dissent, or was it related to his accuracy? We now introduced into the experimental group a person who was instructed to dissent from the majority but also to disagree with the subject. In some experiments the majority was always to choose the worst of the comparison lines and the instructed dissenter to pick the line that was closer to the length of the standard one; in others the majority was consistently intermediate and the dissenter most in error. In this manner we were able to study the relative influence of "compromising" and "extremist" dissenters.

Again the results are clear. When a moderate dissenter is present the effect of the majority on the subject decreases by approximately one third, and extremes of yielding disappear. Moreover, most of the errors the subjects do make are moderate, rather than flagrant. In short, the dissenter largely controls the choice of errors. To this extent the subjects broke away from the majority even while bending to it.

On the other hand, when the dissenter always chose the line that was more flagrantly different from the standard, the results were of quite a different kind. The extremist dissenter produced a remarkable freeing of the subjects; their errors dropped to only 9 percent. Furthermore, all the errors were of the moderate variety. We were able to conclude that dissents *per se* increased independence and moderated the errors that occurred, and that the direction of dissent exerted consistent effects.

In all the foregoing experiments each subject was observed only in a single setting. We now turned to studying the effects upon a given individual of a change in the situation to which he was exposed. The first experiment examined the consequences of losing or gaining a partner. The instructed partner began by answering correctly on the first six trials. With his support the subject usually resisted pressure from the majority: 18 of 27 subjects were completely independent. But after six trials the partner joined the majority. As soon as he did so, there was an abrupt rise in the subjects' errors. Their submission to the majority was just about as frequent as when the minority subject was opposed by a unanimous majority throughout.

It was surprising to find that the experience of having had a partner and of having braved the majority opposition with him had failed to strengthen the individuals' independence. Questioning at the conclusion of the experiment suggested that we had overlooked an important circumstance; namely, the strong specific effect of "desertion" by the partner to the other side. We therefore changed the conditions so that the partner would simply leave the group at the proper point. (To allay suspicion it was announced in advance that he had an appointment with the dean.) In this form of the experiment, the partner's effect outlasted his presence. The errors increased after his departure, but less markedly than after a partner switched to the majority.

20   In a variant of this procedure the trials began with the majority unanimously giving correct answers. Then they gradually broke away until on the sixth trial the naive subject was alone and the group unanimously against him. As long as the subject had anyone on his side, he was almost invariably independent, but as soon as he found himself alone, the tendency to conform to the majority rose abruptly.

As might be expected, an individual's resistance to group pressure in these experiments depends to a considerable degree on how wrong the majority was. We varied the discrepancy between the standard line and the other lines systematically, with the hope of reaching a point where the error of the majority would be so glaring that every subject would repudiate it and choose independently. In this we regretfully did not succeed. Even when the difference between the lines was seven inches, there were still some who yielded to the error of the majority.

The study provides clear answers to a few relatively simple questions, and it raises many others that await investigation. We would like to know the degree of consistency of persons in situations which differ in content and structure. If consistency of independence or conformity in behavior is shown to be a fact, how is it functionally related to qualities of character and personality? In what ways is independence related to sociological or cultural conditions? Are leaders more independent than other people, or are they adept at following their followers? These and many other questions may perhaps be answerable by investigations of the type described here.

Life in society requires consensus as an indispensable condition. But consensus, to be productive, requires that each individual contribute independently out of his experience and insight. When consensus comes under the dominance of conformity, the social process is polluted and the individual at the same time surrenders the powers on which his functioning as a feeling and thinking being depends. That we have found the tendency to conformity in our society so strong that reasonably intelligent and well-meaning young people are willing to call white black is a matter of concern. It raises questions about our ways of education and about the values that guide our conduct.

Yet anyone inclined to draw too pessimistic conclusions from this report would do well to remind himself that the capacities for independence are not to be underestimated. He may also draw some consolation from a further observation: those who participated in this challenging experiment agreed nearly without exception that independence was preferable to conformity.

● Review Questions   MyWritingLab™

1. What is "suggestibility"? How is this phenomenon related to social pressure?

2. Summarize the procedure and results of the Asch experiment. What conclusions does Asch draw from these results?

3. To what extent did varying the size of the majority and its unanimity affect the experimental results?

4. What distinction does Asch draw between consensus and conformity?

● Discussion and Writing Suggestions   MyWritingLab™

1. Before discussing the experiment, Asch considers how easily people's opinions or attitudes may be shaped by social pressure. To what extent do you agree with this conclusion? Write a short paper on this subject, drawing upon examples from your own experience or observation or from your reading.

2. Do the results of this experiment surprise you? Or do they confirm facts about human behavior that you had already suspected, observed, or experienced? Explain, in two or three paragraphs. Provide examples, relating these examples to features of the Asch experiment.

3. Frequently, the conclusions drawn from a researcher's experimental results are challenged on the basis that laboratory conditions do not accurately reflect the complexity of human behavior. Asch draws certain conclusions about the degree to which individuals are affected by group pressures based on an experiment involving subjects choosing matching line lengths. To what extent, if any, do you believe that these conclusions lack validity because the behavior

at the heart of the experiment is too dissimilar to real-life situations of group pressure on the individual? Support your opinions with examples.

4. We are all familiar with the phenomenon of "peer pressure." To what extent do Asch's experiments demonstrate the power of peer pressure? To what extent do you think other factors may be at work? Explain, providing examples.

5. Asch's experiments, conducted in the early 1950s, involved groups of "seven to nine young men, all college students." To what extent do you believe that the results of a similar experiment would be different today? To what extent might they be different if the subjects had included women as well and subjects of various ages, from children to middle-aged people to older people? To what extent do you believe the social class or culture of the subjects might have an impact upon the experimental results? Support your opinions with examples and logical reasoning. (Beware, however, of overgeneralizing, based upon insufficient evidence.)

PRISONER AND GUARD: THE STANFORD EXPERIMENT

As well known—and as controversial—as the Milgram obedience experiments, the Stanford Prison Experiment (1973) raises troubling questions about the ability of individuals to resist authoritarian or obedient roles, if the social setting requires these roles. Philip G. Zimbardo, professor of psychology at Stanford University, set out to study the process by which prisoners and guards "learn" to become compliant and authoritarian, respectively. To find subjects for the experiment, Zimbardo placed an advertisement in a local newspaper:

> Male college students needed for psychological study of prison life. $15 per day for 1–2 weeks beginning Aug. 14. For further information & applications, come to Room 248, Jordan Hall, Stanford U.

The ad drew 75 responses. From these, Zimbardo and his colleagues selected 21 college-age men, half of whom would become "prisoners" in the experiment, the other half "guards." The elaborate roleplaying scenario, planned for two weeks, had to be cut short due to the intensity of subjects' responses. You will find numerous video accounts of the experiment online. View one or more lasting longer than twenty minutes to gain a clear (and perhaps uncomfortable) sense of how intensely students responded to playacting at being prisoners and guards:

Go to: Google or Bing
Search terms: *"zimbardo prison experiment documentary"*

● Review Questions   MyWritingLab™

1. What was Zimbardo's primary goal in undertaking the prison experiment?
2. Who were the subjects of this experiment? What was their initial psychological state at the beginning of the experiment?

3. Describe the process by which subjects became prisoners or guards.

4. What psychological relationships developed between prisoners and guards?

5. What was the result of the prison "riot"?

6. Why did prisoners have no respect for each other or for themselves?

7. What are some of the lessons learned by participants (including Zimbardo) in this experiment?

● Discussion and Writing Suggestions   MyWritingLab™

1. Write about your visceral, "gut" reaction on watching the video(s). How did what you watch make you feel?

2. You may have thought, before watching the video, that being a prisoner is a physical fact, not a psychological state. What are the differences between these two perspectives?

3. To what extent do you believe that ethical behavior is an internal state, determined by one's upbringing and considered view of the world—and that a truly ethical person's behavior cannot be so readily changed as was the behavior of subjects in the prison experiment?

4. Zimbardo has written (in the *New York Times*, April 8, 1973) that at the beginning of the experiment each of the "prisoner" subjects "was completely confident of his ability to endure whatever the prison had to offer for the full two-week experimental period." Had you been a subject, would you have been so confident, prior to the experiment? Given what you've learned of the experiment, do you think you would have psychologically "become" a prisoner or guard if you had been selected for one of these roles? (And if not, what makes you so sure?)

5. Identify two passages in the video: one that surprised you relating to the prisoners and one that surprised you relating to the guards. Write a paragraph explaining your response to each. Now read the two passages in light of each other. Do you see any patterns underlying your responses?

6. Zimbardo claims that the implications of his research matter deeply. How so? Do you agree?

7. Consider the results of the Zimbardo experiment. The people giving the orders in that experiment did not rise to the top by virtue of their talents or their behavior. Instead, they were randomly selected to be either guards or prisoners. Given this circumstance, to what extent does the Zimbardo experiment still bear out some of the findings about authority figures reported by Lessing?

SYNTHESIS ACTIVITIES   MyWritingLab™

1. To what extent do you believe that ethical behavior is a stable, internal state, determined by one's upbringing and essential moral character—and that a truly ethical person's behavior could not be so readily changed by situations as were the behaviors of subjects in the Milgram and mock-prison experiments? Write a synthesis that explains the power of situations, as distinct from individual conscience, to influence a person's behavior. Use at least one example of a particular situation. Draw on the conclusions of the four experiments reported in this chapter: the Good Samaritan experiment, as related by Ross and Nisbett; the line drawing experiments of Asch; the obedience experiments of Milgram; and the mock-prison experiment at Stanford.

2. The outcomes of the experiments reported on in this chapter—Ross and Nisbett call them "empirical parables"—defy common sense: One would expect passers-by to help a man slumped in a doorway; one would not expect people, ordered by a researcher, to inflict what they thought were painful electric shocks on others. One would expect people to believe the evidence of their eyes and insist that one line was longer than another; one would not expect college students to take on the roles of guard and prisoner so exuberantly that an experiment would need to be canceled for fear of harm to participants. Ross and Nisbett suggest that experiments such as these bring us a "hard-won ignorance." What is so valuable about such "ignorance"? Write a synthesis arguing that, at least with respect to human behavior, "common sense" may not be a dependable guide.

3. Reread Doris Lessing's "Group Minds." In this chapter, you have become familiar with some of the experiments in social psychology that she drew on in making her point that we must use the knowledge of social science to advance as a species. As Lessing suggests, we have gained information from social science, on the one hand; and on the other, we have ample evidence that people continue behaving in ways that prove we have learned little from landmark studies of obedience. Write a critique of Lessing. Is she asking too much—that we can actually progress as a species?

4. Ross and Nisbett observe (¶ 2, p. 580) that the experience of graduate students in social psychology can be "intellectually wrenching." Explain how this might be so, based on the four experiments you have read about in this chapter: (1) the "Good Samaritan" experiment, as reported by Ross and Nisbett; (2) Milgram; (3) Asch; and (4) the mock-prison experiment. How might such experiments upset some people? Consider one potentially upsetting conclusion drawn by philosopher Gilbert Harman from the experiments: "It seems that ordinary attributions of character traits to people are often deeply misguided and it may even be the case that there is no such thing as character, no ordinary character traits of the sort people think there are, none of the usual moral virtues and vices." Why might such a claim prove "emotionally wrenching" to some people? Does it to you?

5. What is a "group mind"? Write an explanatory paper that defines the term. As you develop and discuss elements of your definition, refer to the selections by Lessing and Asch and also to the mock-prison experiment at Stanford.

6. Milgram has written that "perhaps the most fundamental lesson of our study [is that] ordinary people, simply doing their jobs, and without any particular hostility on their part, can become agents in a terrible destructive process." Using this statement as a principle, analyze several situations recounted in this chapter, or perhaps some outside this chapter of which you are aware because of your studies, your reading, and possibly even your own experience. Draw upon not only McLeod's account of the Milgram experiments, but also Asch, the mock-prison experiment, and Fromm.

7. Doris Lessing argues that children need to be taught how to disobey so they can recognize and avoid situations that give rise to harmful obedience. David Brooks argues that we may need to "relearn the art of following." Taken as a pair, Lessing and Brooks present two ends of a continuum upon which civilization is built: that is, upon our following leaders (obeying them and their laws) and resisting leaders (disobeying them). If you were the curriculum coordinator for your local school system, how would you teach children the "art" of responsible obedience and disobedience? What would be your curriculum? What home- work would you assign? What class projects? What field trips? One complicated part of your job would be to train children to understand the difference between *responsible* disobedience and anarchy. What is the difference?

   Take up these questions in a paper that draws on both your experiences as a student and your understanding of the selections in this chapter. Points that you might want to consider in developing the paper: defining overly obedient children; appropriate classroom behavior for responsibly disobedient children, as opposed to inappropriate behavior; reading lists; homework assignments; field trips; class projects.

8. A certain amount of obedience is a given in society. Stanley Milgram and oth- ers observe that social order—civilization itself—would not be possible unless individuals were willing to surrender a portion of their autonomy to the state. David Brooks emphasizes the importance, and the paradoxes, of what he calls "followership." Allowing that we all are obedient (we must be), define the point at which obedience to a figure of authority becomes dangerous.

   As you develop your definition, consider the ways you might use the work of authors in this chapter and their definitions of acceptable and unacceptable levels of obedience. Do you agree with the ways in which others have drawn the line between reasonable and dangerous obedience? What examples from current stories in the news or from your own experience can you draw on to test various definitions?

9. Describe a situation in which you were faced with a moral dilemma of whether or not to obey a figure of authority. After describing the situation and the action you took (or didn't take), analyze your behavior in light of any two read- ings in this chapter. (Take a hard look at the Brooks selection and the principles

implicit in what he calls paradoxes of power and of "followership." Also consider Fromm and Lessing.) You might consider a straightforward, four-part structure for your paper: (1) your description; (2) your discussion, in light of source A; (3) your discussion, in light of source B; and (4) your conclusion, an overall appraisal of your behavior.

10. In response to the question "Why is man so prone to obey and why is it so difficult for him to disobey?" Erich Fromm suggests that obedience lets people identify with the powerful and invites feelings of safety. Disobedience is psychologically more difficult and requires an act of courage (see ¶s 13 and 14). Solomon Asch notes that the tendency to conformity is generally stronger than the tendency to independence. In a synthesis that draws on these two sources, explore the interplay of *fear* and its opposite, *courage*, in relation to obedience. To prevent the paper from becoming too abstract, direct your attention repeatedly to a single case, the details of which will help keep your focus. This case may be based upon a particular event from your own life or the life of someone you know.

RESEARCH ACTIVITIES   MyWritingLab™

1. Milgram's results, published in book form in 1974, generated enormous response (see, for instance, Ian Parker's article on Milgram in the Autumn 2000 issue of *Granta*). Research reactions to the Milgram experiments and discuss your findings. Begin with the reviews listed and excerpted in the *Book Review Digest*; also use the *Social Science Index*, the *Readers' Guide to Periodical Literature*, and newspaper indexes to locate articles, editorials, and letters to the editor on the experiments. (Note that editorials and letters are not always indexed. Letters appear within two to four weeks of the weekly magazine articles to which they refer, and within one to two weeks of newspaper articles.) What were the chief types of reactions? To what extent were the reactions favorable?

2. Milgram begins his book *Obedience to Authority* with a reference to Nazi Germany. The purpose of his experiment, in fact, was to help throw light on how the Nazi atrocities could have happened. Research the Nuremberg war crimes tribunals following World War II. Drawing specifically on the statements of those who testified at Nuremberg, as well as those who have written about it, show how Milgram's experiments do help explain the Holocaust and other Nazi crimes. In addition to relevant articles, see Telford Taylor, *Nuremberg and Vietnam: An American Tragedy* (1970); Hannah Arendt, *Eichmann in Jerusalem: A Report on the Banality of Evil* (1963); Richard A. Falk, Gabriel Kolko, and Robert J. Lifton (Eds.), *Crimes of War* (1971).

3. Obtain a copy of the transcript of the trial of Adolf Eichmann, the Nazi official who carried out Hitler's "final solution" for the extermination of the Jews. Read also Hannah Arendt's *Eichmann in Jerusalem: A Report on the Banality*

of Evil, along with the reviews of this book. Write a critique both of Arendt's book and of the reviews it received.

4. The My Lai massacre in Vietnam in 1969 was a particularly egregious case of overobedience to military authority in wartime. Show the connections between this event and Milgram's experiments. Note that Milgram himself treated the My Lai massacre in the epilogue to his *Obedience to Authority: An Experimental View* (1974).

5. Investigate the court-martial of Lt. William Calley, convicted for his role in the My Lai massacre. Discuss whether President Nixon was justified in commuting his sentence. Examine in detail the dilemmas the jury must have faced when presented with Calley's defense that he was only following orders.

6. Research the Watergate break-in of 1972 and the subsequent cover-up by Richard Nixon and members of his administration, as an example of overobedience to authority. Focus on one particular aspect of Watergate (e.g., the role of the counsel to the president, John Dean, or why the crisis was allowed to proceed to the point where it actually toppled a presidency). In addition to relevant articles, see Robert Woodward and Carl Bernstein, *All the President's Men* (1974); Leon Jaworski, *The Right and the Power: The Prosecution of Watergate* (1976); *RN: The Memoirs of Richard Nixon* (1978); John Dean, *Blind Ambition* (1976); John Sirica, *To Set the Record Straight: The Break-In, the Tapes, the Conspirators, the Pardon* (1979); Sam Ervin, *The Whole Truth: The Watergate Conspiracy* (1980); John Ehrlichman, *Witness to Power: The Nixon Years* (1982).

7. In April 2004, news broke of the systematic abuse, including beatings and sexual humiliation, by American military police of Iraqi "detainees" at Baghdad's Abu Ghraib prison. The scandal was intensified—as was outrage in the Muslim world—by graphic photographs that the soldiers had taken of these activities. A high-level American inquiry uncovered some of the following abuses:

> Punching, slapping, and kicking detainees; jumping on their naked feet . . . positioning a naked detainee on a MRE Box, with a sandbag on his head, and attaching wires to his fingers, toes, and penis to simulate electric torture . . . having sex with a female detainee. . . . Using military working dogs (without muzzles) to intimidate and frighten detainees, and in at least one case biting and severely injuring a detainee. . . . Breaking chemical lights and pouring the phosphoric liquid on detainees. . . . Beating detainees with a broom handle and a chair. . . . Sodomizing a detainee with a chemical light and perhaps a broom stick.

In the days following, many commentators noted the similarities between the Abu Ghraib guards' behavior and the behavior of some of the subjects in the Milgram and prison experiments.

Research the Abu Ghraib scandal; then write a paper comparing and contrasting what happened in the Baghdad prison with what happened in the prison experiment at Stanford—and possibly also in Milgram's electric shock experiments. Focus not only on what happened, but also on *why* it may have happened.

8. Examine conformity as a social phenomenon in some particular area. For example, you may choose to study conformity as it exists among schoolchildren, adolescent peer groups, social clubs or associations, or businesspeople. You may want to draw upon your sociology or social psychology textbooks and such classic studies as William H. Whyte's *The Organization Man* (1956) or David Riesman's *The Lonely Crowd* (1950), or focus upon more recent books and articles, such as Rosabeth Moss Kantor's *A Tale of "O": On Being Different in an Organization* (1980) and John Goldhammer's 1996 book *Under the Influence: The Destructive Effects of Group Dynamics* (1996). You may also find enlightening some fictional treatments of conformity, such as Sinclair Lewis's *Babbitt* (1922), Sloan Wilson's *The Man in the Gray Flannel Suit* (1950), and Herman Wouk's *The Caine Mutiny: A Novel of World War II* (1951). What are the main factors creating the urge to conform among the particular group you are examining? What kinds of forces may be able to counteract conformity?

9. At the outset of his article, Stanley Milgram refers to imaginative works revolving around the issue of obedience to authority: the story of Abraham and Isaac; three of Plato's dialogues, "Apology," "Crito," and "Phaedo"; and the story of Antigone (dramatized by both the fifth-century BC Athenian Sophocles and the twentieth-century Frenchman Jean Anouilh). Many other fictional works deal with obedience to authority—for example, George Orwell's *1984* (1949), Herman Wouk's novel *The Caine Mutiny* (and his subsequent play *The Caine Mutiny Court Martial*), and Shirley Jackson's "The Lottery." Check with your instructor, with a librarian, and with such sources as the *Short Story Index* to locate other imaginative works on this theme. Write a paper discussing the various ways in which the subject has been treated in fiction and drama. To ensure coherence, draw comparisons and contrasts among works, showing the connections and variations on the theme of obedience to authority.

MyWritingLab™   Visit Ch. 15 Obedience in MyWritingLab to test your understanding of the chapter objectives.

Credits

CHAPTER 1

Page 9: *Sticks and Stones*, by Emily Bazelon, Random House, 2013. **Pages 9–15:** Paul Bloom, "The Baby in the Well: The Case Against Empathy." *The New Yorker*, 20 May 2013. Copyright by The New Yorker. Used by permission of The New Yorker. **Page 10:** *Sticks and Stones*, by Emily Bazelon, Random House, 2013. **Page 25:** Excerpt of 338 words by Steven A. Camarota from *Immigrants in the United States: A Profile of America's Foreign-Born Population*. Copyright by Center for Immigration Studies. Used by permission of Center for Immigration Studies. **Page 28:** Survey on Favored Requirements for Illegal Immigrants from "Immigration: Key Data Points from Pew Research." Copyright © 26 June 2013 by Pew Research Center. Used by permission of Pew Research Center. **Page 30:** "Growth of Total U.S. Immigrant Population Compared to Decline in Unauthorized Immigration" from *Pew Research Hispanic Center tabulations of 2011 American Community Survey*. Copyright © 2011 by Pew Research Center. Used by permission of Pew Research Center. **Page 30:** "Percentages of Immigrants With and Without High School Diplomas" from Pew Research Hispanic Center tabulations of 2011 American Community Survey. Copyright © by Pew Research Center. Used by permission of Pew Research Center. **Page 32:** Ruth Ellen Wasem [Specialist in Immigration Policy], "U.S. Immigration Policy: Chart Book of Key Trends," C[ongressional] R[esearch] S[ervice]: *Report for Congress*. www.crs.gov,http://www.fas.org/sgp/crs/homesec/R42988.pdf, p. 5 (second chart—pie). Used by permission. **Page 33:** "The United States Is the World's Leader as Destination for Immigrants" from Pew Research Hispanic Center. Copyright © by Pew Research Center. Used by permission Pew Research Center. **Page 33:** "Visas Issued in 2012." by Jill H. Wilson from "Immigration Facts: Temporary Foreign Workers" 18 June 2013. Copyright © 2013. Used by permission of The Brookings Institution. **Page 37:** Mieth, Dietmar: Excerpt from "In Vitro Fertilization: From Medical Reproduction to Genetic Diagnosis" by Dietmar Mieth. From *Biomedical Ethics: Newsletter of the European Network for Biomedical Ethics 1.1* (1996): 45. Copyright 1996. Used by permission of the author. **Page 41:** Keegan, John. Excerpt from "The First World War." Published by Alfred A. Knopf, Inc. New York, 1998. **Pages 41–42:** From *Biology*, 2/e, by Patricia Curtis. Copyright © 1975 by Worth Publishers. Used with permission of the publisher. **Page 46:** "America's 'Cinderella'" by Jane Yolen taken from *Children's Literature in Education* 8 (1977). Copyright © 1977 by Springer. Used by permission of Springer. **Pages 47–48:** Walter Isaacson. Excerpt from *Eintsein: His Life and Universe*. Simon and Schuster. 2007. **Page 49:** Richard Rovere, "The Most Gifted and Successful Demagogue This Country Has Ever Known," *New York Times Magazine*, 30 Apr. 1967

CHAPTER 2

Pages 55–57: Charles Krauthammer, "The Moon We Left Behind," from *The Washington Post*, July 17, 2009. Copyright © 2009 Washington Post Company. Used by permission and protected by the Copyright Laws of the United States. The printing, copying, redistribution, or retransmission of the Content without express written permission in prohibited. **Page 58:** Charles Murray, "The Coming White Underclass," *Wall Street Journal*, October 20, 1993. **Page 66:** United States Congressional House Committee on Oversight and Government Reform. *The Financial Crisis and the Role of Federal Regulators*. 110th Congress., 2nd session. Washington: GPO, 2008. **Page 70:** John F. Kennedy.

CHAPTER 3

Page 84: Sarah Chayes,"Blinded by the war on terrorism," *Los Angeles Times* July 28, 2013. **Pages 84–85:** Akhil Reed Amar, "Second Chances." © 2013 The Atlantic Media Co., as first published in *The Atlantic Magazine*. All rights reserved. Distributed by Tribune Content Agency, LLC. **Pages 86–87:** James Fallows. "Hacked!" *The Atlantic*, November 2011. **Page 87:** James Parker, "Brideshead Regurgitated: The Ludicrous Charms of Downton Abbey, TV's Reigning Aristo-soap." *The Atlantic* Jan./Feb. 2013, p. 36. **Page 88:** Eugene Robinson, "Japan's Nuclear Crisis Might Not Be the Last." *The Washington Post*, March 15, 2011. **Page 89:** H. Sterling Barnett, "Wind Power Puffery." *Washington Times*, 4 Feb. 2004. **Page 90:** Maria Tatar, "An Introduction to Fairy Tales." *The Annotated Classic Fairy Tales* (2002), ed. and trans. by Maria Tatar. W.W. Norton & Company, Inc. **Page 91:** From "Towards an AIDS Vaccine" by Bruce D. Walker and Dennis R. Burton. *Science* 9 May 2008: 760-764, p. 764. DOI: 10.1126/science.1152622. Reprinted with permission from AAAS. http://www.sciencemag.org /content/320/5877/760.abstract. **Page 92:** Newton S. Minow, "A Vaster Wasteland." *The Atlantic*, Apr 2011, p. 52. **Pages 93–94:** Stephen Baker, "Watson Is Far From Elementary." *Wall Street Journal*, 14 Mar. 2011. Copyright © 2011. Used by permission.

CHAPTER 4

Pages 100–101: Why a GM Freeze? from *The GM Freeze Campaign*, November 11, 2010. Used with permission. **Pages 104–106:** Reproduced with permission from "The Physics of the Space Elevator" by P. K. Aravind in *American Journal of Physics* 75.2 (2007): 125. Copyright 2007, American Association of Physics Teachers. **Pages 106–108:** Edwards, Bradley C. The Space Elevator: National Institute for Advanced Concepts Phase II Report. n.p.: 2003. PDF file. **Pages 108–110:** Lemley, Brad. "Going Up." Discovermagazine.com. From *Discover Magazine*, 25 July 2004. All rights reserved. Used by permission and protected by the Copyright Laws of the United States. The printing, copying, redistribution, or retransmission of this content without express written permission is prohibited. **Page 123:** Kent, Jason R. "Getting into Space on a Thread: Space Elevator as Alternative Access to Space." Maxwell AFB: Air War College, 2007. PDF file. **Page 124:** Reproduced with permission from "The Physics of the Space Elevator" by P. K. Aravind in *American Journal of Physics* 75.2 (2007): 125. Copyright 2007, American Association of Physics Teachers. **Page 124:** Ocean-based platform for a space elevator by Alan Chan of the Space Elevator Visualization Unit. Copyright by Alan Chan. Used with permission. **Page 124:** Space elevator in earth orbit showing tether and laser power beam by Alan Chan of the Space Elevator Visualization Unit. Copyright by Alan Chan. Used by permission.

CHAPTER 5

Page 135: L. A. Kauffman, "Socialism: No," *Progressive*, 1 Apr. 1993. **Page 137:** Susan Jacoby, "Talking to Ourselves: Americans Are Increasingly Close-Minded and Unwilling to Listen to Opposing Views," *Los Angeles Times* 20 Apr. 2008: M10. **Pages 140–141:** GLSEN, Inc., the Gay, Lesbian and Straight Education Network. **Page 141:** "Olweus Bullying Prevention Program: Scope and Sequences" from Hazelden Foundation. Copyright © by Hazelden Foundation. Used by permission of Hazelden Foundation. **Pages 142–143:** Philip Rodkin. "White House Report: Bullying—And the Power of Peers: Promoting Respectful Schools," *Educational Leadership: Promoting Respectful Schools*. September 2011, Volume 69, Number 1, pp. 10-16. Web. Used by permission. **Page 149:** Eva Porter, "Bully Nation," Paragon House Publishers. **Page 150:** Smith, J., David, Barry H. Schneider, Peter K. Smith, and Katerina Ananiadou. "The Effectiveness of Whole-School Antibullying Programs: A Synthesis of Evaluation Research." *School Psychology Review* 33.4 (2004): 547-560. PDF file. **Page 150:** Villarreal, Daniel. "Jamey Rodemeyer's Bullies Are Happy He's Dead, But Is It a Bad Idea to Prosecute Them?" *Queerty*. Queerty, Inc., 27 Sept. 2011. Web. 16 Oct. 2014. Used by permission. **Page 150:** Dan Olweus. *Bullying At School: What We Know and What We Can Do*. Oxford, England: Blackwell, 1993. Print. **Page 150:** Gay-Straight Alliance Project. "Make It Better." *Gay-Straight Alliance Project*. GSA Network, 26 Sept. 2011. Web. 15 Oct. 2014. **Page 150:** Sacco, Dena, Katharine Silbaugh, Felipe Corredor, June Casey, and Davis Doherty. *An Overview of State Anti-Bullying Legislation and Other Related Laws*. Cambridge: Berkman Center for Internet and Society,

2012. **Page 151:** Emily Bazelon. *Sticks and Stones: Defeating the Culture of Bullying and Rediscovering the Power of Character and Empathy.* New York: Random, 2013. Print. **Page 151:** Rodkin, Philip C. "White House Report/Bullying—And the Power of Peers." *Educational Leadership: Promoting Respectful Schools* 69.1 (2011): 10-16. ASCD. Web. 16 Oct. 2014. **Page 151:** Hu, Winnie. "Bullying Law Puts New Jersey Schools on Spot." *New York Times.* New York Times, 20 Aug. 2011. Web. 12 Oct. 2014. **Page 151:** Ferguson, Christopher J., Claudia San Miguel, John C. Kilburn, JR, and Patricia Sanchez. "The Effectiveness of School-Based Anti-Bullying Programs: A Meta-Analytic Review." *Criminal Justice Review* 32.4 (2007): 401-414. Sage Publications. Web. 15 Oct. 2014. **Page 151:** Merrell, Kenneth W, Barbara A. Gueldner, Scott W. Ross, and Duane M. Isava. "How Effective are School Bullying Intervention Programs? A Meta-analysis of Intervention Research." *School Psychology Quarterly* 23.1 (2008): 26-42. **Page 151:** Hazelden Foundation. "Olweus Bullying Prevention Program: Scope and Sequence." *Hazelden.org.* Hazelden, 2007. PDF file. **Page 152:** Fox, James Alan, Delbert S. Elliott, R. Gil Kerlikowske, Sanford A. Newman, and William Christenson. *Bullying Prevention is Crime Prevention. Fightcrime.org.* Fight Crime/Invest in Kids, 2003. PDF file. **Page 152:** Rodkin, Philip C. "White House Report/Bullying—And the Power of Peers." *Educational Leadership: Promoting Respectful Schools* 69.1 (2011): 10-16. ASCD. Web. 16 Oct. 2014. **Pages 152–153:** Flannery, Mary Ellen. "Bullying: Does It Get Better?" *National Education Association.* National Education Association, Jan./Feb. 2011. Web. 16 Oct. 2014. **Page 153:** Sacco, Dena, Katharine Silbaugh, Felipe Corredor, June Casey, Davis Doherty. "An Overview of State Anti-Bullying Legislation and Other Related Laws." Cambridge: Berkman Center for Internet and Societ, 2012.

CHAPTER 6

Page 174: Harvey Greenberg, *The Movies on Your Mind* (New York: Dutton, 1975). **Page 175:** Peter Dreier, "Oz Was Almost Reality," *Cleveland Plain Dealer* 3 Sept. 1989. **Page 176:** Harvey Greenberg, The Movies on Your Mind (New York: Dutton, 1975). **Pages 177–178:** From *The Plug-In Drug, Revised and Updated 25th Anniversary Edition* by Marie Winn, copyright © 1977, 1985, 2002 by Marie Winn Miller. Used by permission of Viking Penguin, a division of Penguin Group (USA) LLC. **Pages 186–187:** "Paradise Lost (Domestic Division)," by Terry Martin Hekker, from "Modern Love," *The New York Times,* January 1, 2006. **Page 187:** "Paradise Lost (Domestic Division)," by Terry Martin Hekker, from "Modern Love," *The New York Times,* January 1, 2006. **Page 189:** Knapp, Robert H. "A Psychology of Rumor." *Public Opinion Quarterly* 8.1 (1944): 22–37. Print. **Pages 189–190:** Dingwall, Robert. "Contemporary Legends, Rumors, and Collective Behavior: Some Neglected Resources for Medical Technology." *Sociology of Health and Illness* 23.2 (2001): 180–202. Print. **Page 190:** "You've Got to Be Kidneying." *Snopes.com.* Snopes, 12 Mar. 2008. Web. 4 Nov. 2014. Used by permission. **Page 192:** Dingwall, Robert. "Contemporary Legends, Rumors, and Collective Behavior: Some Neglected Resources for Medical Technology." *Sociology of Health and Illness* 23.2 (2001): 180–202. Print. **Page 192:** Knapp, Robert H. "A Psychology of Rumor." *Public Opinion Quarterly* 8.1 (1944): 22–37. Print.

CHAPTER 7

Page 202: University of California Santa Barbara (UCSB) Library. The Regents of the University of California, All Rights Reserved. **Page 203:** University of California Santa Barbara (UCSB) Library. The Regents of the University of California, All Rights Reserved. **Page 203:** University of California Santa Barbara (UCSB) Library. The Regents of the University of California, All Rights Reserved. **Page 205:** Wikimedia Foundation. **Page 210:** Reprinted courtesy of JSTOR. JSTOR © 2013. All rights reserved. **Page 211:** A Discovery Service search box. Seton Hall University. Used by permission of Seton Hall University Libraries for Information Technology. **Page 214:** University of California Santa Barbara (UCSB) Library. The Regents of the University of California, All Rights Reserved. **Page 224:** Gorham, Eric B. *National Service, Political Socialization, and Political Education.* Albany: SUNY P, 1992. **Page 224:** Bureau of Labor Statistics. 27 Jan. 2010. Web. 17 Feb. 2011. http://www.bls.gov/news.release/volun. t01.htm. **Page 225:** Gergen, David. "A Time to Heed the Call." *U.S. News & World Report* 24 Dec. 2001: 60-61. **Page 226:** University of California Santa Barbara (UCSB) Library. The Regents of the University of California, All Rights Reserved. **Page 227:** University of California Santa Barbara (UCSB) Library. The Regents of the University of California, All Rights Reserved.

CHAPTER 8

Page 246: Gregory Blair/Pearson Education. **Pages 253–256:** John Turrentine, "Why do Great American Songbook albums by pop artists so often disappoint?" from *Slate.com*, February 28, 2012, The Slate Group. All rights reserved. Used by permission and protected by the Copyright Laws of the United States. The printing, copying, redistribution, or retransmission of this Content without express written permission is prohibited. **Pages 259–261:** "Rolling Stone Readers Pick the Top 10 Greatest Covers," by Andy Greene, *RollingStone.com*, March 2, 2011. Copyright © Rolling Stone LLC 2011. All Rights Reserved. Used by Permission.

CHAPTER 9

Page 264: Stephen J. A. Ward, "Ethics in a Nutshell" from Center for Journalism Ethics at the University of Wisconsin. **Pages 267–270:** Daniel Sokol, "What If ..." *BBC News*. 2 May 2006. Web. http://news.bbc.co.uk/2/hi/uk_news/magazine/4954856.stm. Used by permission of BBC Worldwide America, Inc. **Pages 271–274:** De George, Richard T., *Business Ethics*, 6th Ed., © 2006. Reprinted and Electronically reproduced by permission of Pearson Education, Inc., Upper Saddle River, New Jersey. **Pages 274–279:** Manuel Velasquez et al. "A Framework for Thinking Ethically." May 2009. Web. http://www.scu.edu/ethics/practicing/decision/framework.html. Copyright © 2009. Reprinted with permission of the Markkula Center for Applied Ethics, Santa Clara University (www.scu.edu/ethics). **Pages 279–282:** Ronald F. White. "Moral Inquiry." Excerpts from pp. 3-4, 11-12, 15-16, 23-24. Web. http://inside.msj.edu/academics/faculty/whiter/ethicsbook.pdf. **Pages 282–289:** Crain, William, *Theories of Development: Concepts and Applications*, 6th Ed., © 2011, pp. 159-165. Reprinted and Electronically reproduced by permission of Pearson Education, Inc., Upper Saddle River, New Jersey. **Pages 289–290:** Rosetta Lee, Seattle Girls' School. From teaching packet titled: "The Lifeboat." Used by permission of Rosetta Lee. **Pages 290–291:** Garrett Hardin, "Lifeboat Ethics." Sept. 1974. *Psychology Today*. Reprinted by permission from *Psychology Today Magazine*, (Copyright © 1974 Sussex Publishers, LLC.). www.Psychologytoday.com. **Pages 291–293:** "Should I Protect a Patient at the Expense of an Innocent Stranger?" by Chuck Klosterman. From *The New York Times*, May 10, 2013 © 2013 The New York Times. All rights reserved. Used by permission and protected by the Copyright Laws of the United States. The printing, copying, redistribution, or retransmission of this Content without express written permission is prohibited. **Pages 293–294:** "No Edit" by Randy Cohen. Originally appeared in "The Ethicist" in the *New York Times Magazine*, May 20, 2007. Used by permission. **Page 294:** Kelley L. Ross. "The Tortured Child." From "Some Moral Dilemmas." Scenario 5. As adapted from Moral Reasoning, by Victor Grassian (Prentice Hall, 1981, 1992). **Page 295:** Kelley L. Ross. "A Callous Passerby." From "Some Moral Dilemmas." Scenario 6. As adapted from *Moral Reasoning*, by Victor Grassian (Prentice Hall, 1981, 1992).

CHAPTER 10

Pages 304–309: Adapted from *Battle Hymn of the Tiger Mother* by Amy Chua, copyright © 2011 by Amy Chua. Used by permission of The Penguin Press, a division of Penguin Group (USA) LLC. **Pages 309–312:** "Mother Inferior" by Hanna Rosin from *Wall Street Journal*, Jan. 16, 2011. Reprinted with permission of the *Wall Street Journal*, Copyright © 2011 Dow Jones & Company, Inc. All Rights Reserved Worldwide. **Pages 312–314:** "Amy Chua is a Wimp" from *The New York Times*, January 17, 2011, The New York Times. All rights reserved. Used by permission and protected by the Copyright Laws of the United States. The printing, copying, redistribution, or retransmission of this content without express written permission is prohibited. **Pages 314–316:** "Tiger Mother stirs reflections on parenthood" by Tina Griego from *The Denver Post*, January 20, 2011. Copyright 2011. Used by permission. **Pages 316–318:** "Tiger Mom vs. Tiger Mailroom" by Patrick Goldstein published February 6, 2011 in the *Los Angeles Times*. Copyright 2011. Used by permission. **Pages 318–322:** Elizabeth Kolbert. "America's Top Parent." Originally from *The New Yorker*, Jan. 31, 2011. Copyright © 2011. Used by permission of the author. **Pages 322–325:** "Tiger Moms Don't Raise Superior Kids, Says New Study," From *Forbes.com*, May 8, 2013, Forbes. All rights reserved. Used by permission and protected by the Copyright Laws of the United States. The printing, copying, redistribution, or retransmission of this content without express written permission is prohibited.

CHAPTER 11

Page 333: J. D. Salinger, *The Catcher In The Rye*, Little, Brown and Company, 1951. **Pages 337–342:** "Chapter 1: The Hook" by K.M Weiland from *Structuring Your Novel: Essential Keys for Writing an Outstanding Story*. PenForASwordPublishing, LLC. Copyright 2013. Used by permission. **Pages 343–355:** Chapter 3, "Starting Your Story" from *The Art and Craft of Fiction: A Writer's Guide* by Michael Kardos. Copyright © 2013 by Macmillan Higher Education/Bedford/St. Martin's. Used by permission of the publisher. **Pages 356–360:** *The Magic Show* by Tim O'Brien. Copyright © Tim O'Brien. Used by permission of Tim O'Brien. **Page 408:** Vincent Canby, "Review/Film; Coppola's Dizzying Vision Of Dracula," *The New York Times*, November 13, 1992. **Page 414:** Bosley Crowther, "Shane," Bosley Crowther, *The New York Times*, April 24, 1953. **Page 418:** *Do The Right Thing: A Spike Lee Joint*. Spike Lee with Lisa Jones. New York: Simon and Schuster, 1989, p. 29. **Page 419:** Thomas Schatz, *Hollywood Genres: Formulas, Filmmaking, and the Studio System*, McGraw-Hill, 1981. **Page 423:** A. O. Scott, "Soldiers on a Live Wire Between Peril and Protocol," *The New York Times*, June 25, 2009. **Page 423:** Karen Idelson, "Editors Get in Rhythm," *Variety*, 12 Jan., 2010. **Page 424:** Chang, Justin. *Variety*, August 28, 2013. **Page 424:** Margaret Mitchell, *Gone With the Wind*, MacMillan, 1936. **Page 426:** "12 Years A Slave' Was A Film That 'No One Was Making,'" *NPR.org*, October 24, 2013.

CHAPTER 12

Page 432: Jenna Brager. "Post-College Flow Chart of Misery & Pain." Used by permission. **Pages 433–435:** Job Outlook for 2014 College Grads Puzzling" from *USA Today* May 19, 2014, by Hadley Malcolm. Copyright © by PARS. Used by permission of PARS. **Pages 435–439:** "College as Vocational Training: Wise?" by Peter Cappelli from the *Wall Street Journal*. November 15, 2013. Reprinted with permission of the *Wall Street Journal*, Copyright © 2013 Dow Jones & Company, Inc. All Rights Reserved Worldwide. **Pages 440–445:** "Outsourcing: Bigger Than You Thought" by Alan S. Blinder taken from *The American Prospect*, Volume 17, Number 11. Copyright by The American Prospect. Used by permission of *The American Prospect*. (www.prospect.org). **Pages 446–450:** Peck, Don. "They're Watching You at Work: The Job Interview." Copyright © 2013 The Atlantic Media Co., as first published in *The Atlantic Magazine*, December 2013. All rights reserved. Distributed by Tribune Content Agency. **Page 452:** Graph: "Rising Earnings Disparity Betweenn Young Adults with and Without a College Degree." Copyright © Pew Research Center. Used by permission of Mary Seaborn. **Page 453:** Graph: Disparity among Millennials Ages 25-32 By Education Level in Terms of Annual Earnings…." From "The Rising Cost of Not Going to College." February 10, 2014. Copyright © by PEW Research Center. Used by permission of Mary Seaborn. **Page 453:** Graph: "Education and Views About Work." Copyright © Pew Research Center. Used by permission of Mary Seaborn. **Page 454:** Table: "Percentage of Generation in Poverty, by Educational Attainment. Copyright © Pew Research Center. Used by permission of Mary Seaborn. **Page 454:** Table: "The Generations Defined." Copyright © Pew Research Center. Used by permission of Mary Seaborn. **Page 455:** Graph: "Usefulness of Major, by Field of Study." Copyright © Pew Research Center. Used by permission of Mary Seaborn. **Page 455:** Anthony P. Carnevale and Ban Cheah. "Unemployment and Earnings for College Majors" in *Hard Times: College Majors, Unemployment and Earnings*. Georgetown Public Policy Institute/Center for Education and the Workforce. May 29, 2013. Used by permission. **Pages 463–465:** Jeff Haden. "Do What You Love? @&## That!" Originally from Time, Inc., November 14, 2012. Copyright 2012. Used by permission of the author. **Pages 466–467:** "Dear Grads, Don't 'Do What You Love'" from the *Wall Street Journal*. May 27, 2013. Reprinted with permission of the *Wall Street Journal*, Copyright © 2013 Dow Jones & Company, Inc. All Rights Reserved Worldwide. **Pages 468–472:** "In the Name of Love" from *Jacobin*, by Miya Tokumitsu/*Jacobin*. Copyright © by Bhaskar Sunkara. Used by permission of Bhaskar Sunkara.

CHAPTER 13

Page 481: Norman Rockwell. "The Gossips." Printed by permission of the Norman Rockwell Family Agency. Copyright © 1948 the Norman Rockwell Family Entities. **Pages 484–485:** Gregory Rodriguez. "Truth is in the Ear of the Beholder" originally published in the *Los Angeles Times*, 28 Sept. 2009.

Copyright 2009. Used by permission. Gregory Rodriquez is founding director of the Center for Social Cohesion at Arizona State University. **Pages 486–490:** Daniel Goleman. "Anatomy of a Rumor: It Flies on Fear" from *The New York Times*, June 4, 1991. Copyright © 1991 The New York Times. All rights reserved. Used by permission and protected by the Copyright Laws of the United States. The printing, copying, redistribution, or retransmission of the Content without express written permission in prohibited. **Pages 491–494:** Salmans, Sandra. "Fighting That Old Devil Rumor" article © SEPS licensed by Curtis Licensing Indianapolis, IN. All rights reserved. **Pages 496–498:** Robert H. Knapp, "A Psychology of Rumor" from *Public Opinion Quarterly* 8:1 (Spring 1944): 22-31 ff, by permission of Oxford University Press. **Pages 499–503:** "Paul is Dead" by Alan Glenn from *Michigan Today*, 11 Nov. 2009. Copyright © 2009. Used by permission. **Page 501:** Express Newspapers/AP Images. **Pages 504–510:** From *The Vanishing Hitchhiker: American Urban Legends and Their Meanings* by Jan Brunvand. Copyright 1981. Used by permission of W. W. Norton & Company, Inc. **Pages 512–516:** Jesse Singal. "How to Fight a Rumor: Stopping Rumors Means Understanding Not Why They're Ugly, but Why They're Necessary." Originally appeared in Oct 12, 2008 from *The Boston Globe*. Copyright © 2008. Used by permission.

CHAPTER 14

Pages 523–524: Samuel Beckett/Grove Press. **Pages 525–527:** Jane Kenyon, "Happiness" from *Collected Poems*. Copyright © 2005 by The Estate of Jane Kenyon. Used with the permission of The Permissions Company, Inc. on behalf of Graywolf Press, www.graywolfpress.org. **Pages 527–529:** "Three Conceptions of Happiness" by Lynne McFall taken from *Happiness*, New York: Peter Lang, 1989, pp. 5-6. Copyright by Peter Lang Publishing Inc. Used by permission of Peter Lang Publishing Inc. **Pages 530–532:** *In Pursuit of Happiness: "Better Living from Plato to Prozac"* by Mark Kingwell taken from New York: Crown. Copyright © 1998 by Alison Bond Literary Agency. Used by permissions of Alison Bond Literary Agency. **Pages 533–538:** Preston, Douglas. "The Dalai Lama's Ski Trip: What I learned in the slush with His Holiness." Copyright © 2014 by Douglas Preston, as first published in *Slate™ Magazine* (www.slate.com). **Pages 538–543:** Martin Seligman, *Philosophical Transactions of the Royal Society of London*, pp. 359, 1379-1381. Copyright © 2004. Used by permission. **Pages 544–548:** Mihaly Csikszentmihalyi, "Finding Flow: The Psychology of Engagement with Everyday Life," New York: Basic Books/HarperCollins, 1977, pp. 1-3, 28-34. All rights reserved. Used by permission and protected by the Copyright Laws of the United States. The printing, copying, redistribution, or retransmission of this content without express written permission is prohibited. **Pages 549–553:** Excerpt from "What You Can Learn from the New Science of Smarter Spending: Yes, Money Can Make You Happy" by Cass R. Sunstein from http://www.newrepublic.com/article/114031/money-happiness-and-new-science-smarter-spending. Copyright © 2013 by *The New Republic*. Used by permission of *The New Republic*. **Pages 554–558:** Sharon Begley, "Happiness: Enough Already," from *The Daily Beast*, February 2, 2008. All rights reserved. Used by permission and protected by the Copyright Laws of the United States. The printing, copying, redistribution, or retransmission of this content without express written permission is prohibited. **Pages 559–561:** Simon Critchley, "Happy Like God," from *The New York Times*, May 25, 2009. All rights reserved. Used by permission and protected by the Copyright Laws of the United States. The printing, copying, redistribution, or retransmission of this content without express written permission is prohibited. **Pages 562–565:** Cliff Oxford, "Where Happy Talk About Corporate Culture is Wrong," from *The New York Times*. May 7, 2013. All rights reserved. Used by permission and protected by the Copyright Laws of the United States. The printing, copying, redistribution, or retransmission of this content without express written permission is prohibited. **Pages 566–568:** David Brooks, "What Suffering Does," from *The New York Times*. April 7, 2014. All rights reserved. Used by permission and protected by the Copyright Laws of the United States. The printing, copying, redistribution, or retransmission of this content without express written permission is prohibited.

CHAPTER 15

Pages 574–578: "Disobedience as Psychological and Moral Problem" [pp. 1-12: 2500 words] from *On Disobedience and Other Essays* by Erich Fromm. Copyright © 1981, 2010 by The Estate of Erich Fromm.

Reprinted by permission of HarperCollins Publishers. **Pages 579–582:** Ross, Lee and Richard E. Nisbett. *The Person and the Situation: Perspectives of Social Psychology.* Copyright © 1991 McGraw-Hill Education. Used by permission. **Pages 583–590:** Sam McLeod. "The Milgram Experiment." Copyright © Simple Psychology. Used by permission. www.simplypsychology.org. **Page 585:** From the film "Obedience" © 1968 by Stanley Milgram. **Pages 591–594:** David Brooks, "The Follower Problem," from *The New York Times*, June 12, 2012. All rights reserved. Used by permission and protected by the Copyright Laws of the United States. The printing, copying, redistribution, or retransmission of this content without express written permission is prohibited. **Pages 597–602:** Solomon Asch, "Opinions and Social Pressure." November 1955. Reproduced with permission. Copyright © 1955 Scientific American, Inc. All rights reserved. **Pages 594–597:** Lessing, Doris. Pages 47–50 and p. 60 from "Group Minds" from *Prisons We Choose to Live Inside* by Doris Lessing. Copyright © 1988 by Doris Lessing. Reprinted by permission of HarperCollins Publishers and House of Anansi Press, Inc. All rights reserved.

Index

CHECKLIST FOR WRITING SUMMARIES

- **Read** the passage carefully. Determine its structure. Identify the authors' purpose.
- **Reread.** *Label* each state of thought. *Underline* key ideas and terms.
- **Write one-sentence summaries** of each state of thought.
- **Write a thesis:** a one- or two-sentence summary of the entire passage.
- **Write the first draft of your summary.**
- **Check your summary against the original passage.**
- **Revise and edit your summary.**

CHECKLIST FOR WRITING CRITIQUES

- **Introduce** both the passage being critiqued and the author.
- **Summarize** the author's main points, making sure to state the author's purpose for writing.
- **Evaluate** the validity of the author's presentation.
- **Respond** to the author's presentation.
- **Conclude** by summing up your assessment of the overall validity of the piece.